Mass Communication and Society

Mass Communication and Society

Edited by
James Curran
Michael Gurevitch
Janet Woollacott

Assistant Editors
John Marriott
Carrie Roberts

 Edward Arnold

in association with The Open University Press

Printed in Hong Kong by
Wing King Tong Co Ltd

Contents

*Except where otherwise indicated, all the articles in this volume
are original and have not been previously published.*

List of Contributors

Jay G. Blumler   Director, Centre for Television Research, University of Leeds

Oliver Boyd-Barrett   Lecturer in Educational Studies, Open University

Tom Burns   Professor of Sociology, University of Edinburgh

James Carey   George Gallup Professor of Journalism, School of Journalism, University of Iowa, Iowa City, Iowa

David Chaney   Lecturer in Sociology, University of Durham

James Curran   Senior Lecturer, School of Communication, Polytechnic of Central London

Philip Elliott   Research Fellow, Centre for Mass Communication Research, University of Leicester

Peter Golding   Research Officer, Centre for Mass Communication Research, University of Leicester

Michael Gurevitch   Senior Lecturer, Faculty of Social Science, Open University

Stuart Hall   Director, Centre for Contemporary Cultural Studies, University of Birmingham

Dick Hebdige   Centre for Contemporary Cultural Studies, University of Birmingham

Krishan Kumar   Senior Lecturer in Sociology, University of Kent

Denis McQuail   Professor of Mass Communication, University of Amsterdam

Graham Murdock   Research Fellow, Centre for Mass Communication Research, University of Leicester

Anthony Smith   TV Producer, Writer on Media Affairs, Research Fellow, St Anthony's College, Oxford

Michael Tracey   Research Fellow, Centre for Mass Communication Research, University of Leicester

John Westergaard   Professor of Sociological Studies, University of Sheffield

Theodor Adorno, Walter Benjamin and Max Horkheimer are no longer alive.

Members of the *Mass Communication and Society* Course Team

Authors
Tony Bennett
Jay Blumler
Oliver Boyd-Barrett
Peter Braham
James Curran
Margaret Gallagher
Michael Gurevitch *(Chairman)*
James Halloran
John Hartley
Terence Hawkes
Graham Martin
Graham Murdock
Carrie Roberts *(Course Assistant)*
Susan Triesman
Janet Woollacott

Others
Ben Cosin *(Educational Studies)*
Stuart Hall *(External Assessor)*
Pam Higgins *(Designer)*
Vic Lockwood *(BBC)*
Brian Lund *(IET)*
John Marriott *(Editor)*
John Miller *(BBC)*
Mike Philps *(BBC)*
Gwynn Pritchard *(BBC)*
Viv Ruscoe *(Project Control)*
Nell Smith *(BBC)*
Paul Smith *(Liaison Librarian)*

Acknowledgements

The publishers wish to thank the following for permission to reprint the copyright material listed below:
Sage Publications Inc., Cal. for 'Mass Communication Research and Cultural Studies: an American View' by James W. Carey; Jonathan Cape Ltd for 'The Work of Art in the Age of Mechanical Reproduction' from *Illuminations* by Walter Benjamin, translated by Harry Zohn, ed. Hannah Arendt also Harcourt Brace Jovanovich copyright © 1955 by Suhrkamp Verlag, Frankfurt a. M.; English translation copyright © 1968 by Harcourt Brace Jovanovich, Inc., reprinted with their permission; John Wiley & Sons Inc., N.Y. for 'Linkages between Mass Media and Politics: a model for the analysis of political communications systems, by Dr Michael Gurevitch and Dr Jay G. Blumler from G. Gerbner (ed.) *Mass Communication Policies in Changing Cultures*; The University of Birmingham for 'Reggae, Rastas and Rudies' by Dick Hebdige from *Cultural Studies*, WPCS 7/8; Penguin Books Ltd and The Seabury Press, N.Y. for 'The Culture Industry: enlightenment as mass deception' by Theodor Adorno and Max Horkheimer from *Dialectic of Enlightenment* (Allen Lane, 1973), Translation © 1972 Herder and Herder Inc., N.Y. and Oxford University Press and the author for 'Holding the Middle Ground: the BBC, the Public and the Professional Broadcaster' by Krishan Kumar from *Sociology*, vol. 9 (1975) 67—88.

Editors' Introduction

This collection of readings on the mass media and society has been prepared with two purposes in mind. In the first place, it aims to serve the needs of students taking the Open University Course DE353 *Mass Communication and Society* by providing them with a number of overview articles designed to summarize current discussion and research on some of the central issues in this field. Many Open University students do not have ready access to university libraries and it is, therefore, especially important that the range of readings supplied to them should be as varied as that which is available to students at face-to-face universities. In the second place, the Reader aims to serve a wider audience of students of the media and society — from social science students and teachers in institutions of higher education, those who are professionally engaged in various branches of the 'media industries', to the generally interested reader — by providing a collection of articles which would represent up-to-date intellectual efforts in the analysis of mass communication and would sketch out the frontiers of this area of study.

For these reasons we have based the Reader on a large number of original articles, especially commissioned for publication here. While most of these have been written by authors who are primarily interested in mass communications, we have also deliberately attempted to secure contributions from scholars whose areas of academic concern do not lie mainly, or exclusively, in this field of study. The study of mass communication as an academic enterprise has suffered for a long time from a curious irony: those who are engaged in it have long recognized and proclaimed the inter-disciplinary nature of the field, involving sociologists, political scientists, linguists, psychologists, students of culture and so on, but at the same time, the eclectic nature of the field resulted in an uneasy sense of marginality among mass communication researchers, who sometimes feel that their work exists precariously on the peripheries of these various disciplines, rather than in their mainstream. One response to this sense of marginality has been the constant search for a 'theory of mass communication', which could help to legitimate the field in its own right.

Another has been the attempt, prevalent mainly, but not exclusively, in the United States, to institutionalize the study of mass communication through the establishment of 'journalism schools', with their mixture of academic and vocational training. The editors of this Reader, however, were less concerned with establishing mass communications as an independent and legitimate area of academic study than with locating the central concerns of media studies in terms of theoretical developments in the social sciences.

This Open University Course and Reader in mass communication then constitutes an attempt to focus on mass communication from a specific theoretical perspective which is holistic and which concentrates on the relationship between systems of production, the division of labour and systems of domination and control. This orientation attempts to define and analyse the mass media, their relations of production, their institutions and their specialized occupations, their internal power structure and their ideological and cultural role in relation to the general sectors of production and the class system. This endeavour differs from the empiricist investigation and analysis which typified mass communication as a field for research, in that it attempts to specify and analyse the role of the mass media in society in its own theoretic terms rather than taking for granted common-sense assumptions about individuals, social groups and institutions.

Readers compiled in the fifties and the early sixties traditionally followed the Lasswellian research formula of 'who says what in which channel to whom with what effect'. (Lasswell, 1948 p. 37.) They were modelled on the continuum of the communication process, subdivided into discrete specialist departments: control analysis (who), content analysis (what), audience analysis (whom) and effects analysis (*audience* effects). Although there are, of course, differences between these collections – for instance, Schramm (1960) includes an historical section, while Berelson and Janowitz (1966) contains both a methodological and a comparative section – they are all essentially variations on the same theme.

In the second half of the sixties and the early seventies, two significant developments occurred in mass communications research which were reflected in some contemporary Readers. The production of communications was analysed as an organizational rather than as an intra-individual process: communicators were seen as 'performers' within an organizational setting rather than as individual 'senders' of messages. And renewed interest was shown in audience uses and gratifications derived from mass communications—a subject that had received uneven attention since the short-lived boom of uses and gratifications research in the 1940s. The flow in the traditional communication continuum was reversed; instead of asking how audiences are manipulated by communicators, the question was put the other way round. These developments are echoed in Tunstall

(1970) which contains a large section on communication organizations and in McQuail (1972), Davison and Yu (1974) Emery *et al.* (1973), which contain material on both media organizations and audience gratifications.

Important and valuable developments though these are, they still represent no more than a refinement of the Lasswellian formula. Media organizations in the new approach are analysed, with few exceptions, as bounded organizational systems. Audiences, in the uses and gratifications perspective, are still generally abstracted from the social structure. The traditional demarcation lines separating different stages in the communication continuum have been retained. Little attempt has been made to examine mass communications within the context of society as a whole.

Indeed, these advances represent in one sense a forced retreat after years of inconclusive research. As Jeremy Tunstall writes in his introduction to *Media Sociology*, the new interest in media organizations represents a repudiation of the view that 'the discovery of some kind of measurable "effect" on the audience is the ultimate purpose of research' (Tunstall, 1970 p. 5.) It is no coincidence that many researchers are now examining audience exploitation of communications, after a generation of research testifying to the marginality of the media as an influence upon attitude change, even if the approach is sometimes represented as a new way of plotting the study of media effects. (Katz, Blumler and Gurevitch, 1974.) Nor is it a coincidence that the early preoccupation with the 'who' in the Lasswellian paradigm, often associated with concern about 'responsible' behaviour amongst communicators (Schramm, 1957; 1960), should have dissolved into descriptive sociological studies of organizations and professions. The initial driving force behind the Lasswellian formulation has petered out, as research 'findings' apparently demonstrate the marginal nature of media influence.

This partly accounts for the widespread sense of disillusionment and disaffection expressed by media sociologists (e.g. Gans, 1972; Morley 1974). Most academic students of the media were first attracted to the subject by the belief that the mass media constitute a powerful and important source of influence; they spend most of their working lives apparently discovering that it is not. The classic exposition of 'effects' research by Klapper (1960) represents a landmark in this process of disenchantment. All that is left is a research tradition which has proved relatively barren within its own terms and which has stunted theoretical development in the field. For the Lasswellian formula makes sense only as an instrumentalist empirical model for the analysis of short-term effects. Its very dominance has been a permanent and, despite some tokenism to the contrary, a surprisingly resilient block to theoretical thinking about mass communications.

It is illuminating in this context that the most interesting contemporary research emerged from very different theoretical traditions, hitherto unrepresented in mass communications research — Marxism, cultural studies and the sociological analysis of deviance. *The Manufacture of News* (Cohen and Young, 1973) was an early manifestation of this rapidly developing field. While adhering to the Lasswellian formula (rephrased as 'selection, presentation and effects') as a theoretical framework for the book, it nonetheless included research which departed radically from the traditional conception of the communication process. It represented a bridge between the old and the new in mass communications research, although some theoretical contradictions have emerged from this intermeshing of diverse approaches.

Our own Reader reflects some of the ambiguities and continuing uncertainties of the field as it is developing. Nevertheless, it represents an attempt to engage in a theoretical discourse about the media, and to raise questions which have not merely gone unanswered in traditional mass communication research but which have not even been recognized as questions that need to be asked. The central concern of this Reader is with whole societies, their class structure and forms of class dominance and an exploration of the role of the media as ideological and signifying agencies within that whole. The concept of ideology is, therefore, of central concern. We would argue that dominant ideologies do not necessarily crudely and simply represent the interests of the ruling class but that they always constitute a whole view of the world. As Hall suggests, 'ideologies are one of the principal mechanisms which expand and amplify the dominance of certain class interests into a hegemonic formation.' (Hall, 1974 p. 290.) Most importantly, dominant ideologies are not mere reflections of the social conditions of the dominant class but represent the political relationship between the dominant and subordinated classes in a specific social formation.

The argument that ideological systems are relatively autonomous *vis-à-vis* economic formations, and yet contain within them the same contradictions at the level of ideology, demands a serious examination of media messages and their realization in institutions, rituals and practices.

It is probably clear from the foregoing that the perspective of the Reader and the Course is potentially integrative of the social sciences. Discussion of the relationship between the media and whole societies, emphasizing the economic and political processes in cultural formation, transcends conventional disciplinary boundaries between sociology, political science, history and so forth. This orientation attempts to identify a social scientific definition of reality against which it is possible to compare media-based modes of constructing reality.

References

Berelson, B. and Janowitz, M. (eds.), 1966: *Reader in Mass Communication and Society*, 2nd edition. Free Press.

Cohen, S. and Young, J. (eds.), 1973: *The Manufacture of News: Social Problems, Deviance and the Mass Media*. Constable.

Davison, W. P. and Yu, F. T. C. (eds.), 1974: *Mass Communication Research*. Praeger.

Emery, E., Ault, P. H. and Agee, W. K. (eds.), 1973: *Introduction to Mass Communication*. Dodd, Mead and Co.

Gans, H., 1972: The Famine in Mass Communication Research. *American Journal of Sociology* 78.

Hall, S., 1974: Deviancy, Politics and the Media. In Rock, P. and McIntosh, M. (eds) *Deviance and Social Control*. Tavistock.

Katz, E., Blumler, J. G. and Gurevitch, M., 1974: Utilization of Mass Communication by the Individual. In Blumler, J. and Katz, E. (eds.) *The Uses of Mass Communications*, Sage.

Klapper, J. T., 1960: *The Effects of Mass Communication*. Free Press.

Lasswell, H., 1948: The Structure and Function of Communication in Society. In Lyman, B. (ed.) *The Communication of Ideas*. Harper.

McQuail, D. (ed.), 1972: *Sociology of Mass Communications*. Penguin.

Morley, D., 1974: Reconceptualising the Media Audience: Towards an Ethnography of Audiences. *Occasional paper, Centre for Contemporary Cultural Studies, University of Birmingham*.

Schramm, W., 1957: *Responsibility in Mass Communications*. Harper.
   (ed.) 1960: *Mass Communications*, 2nd edition. University of Illinois Press.

Tunstall, J. (ed.) 1970: *Media Sociology: A Reader*. Constable.

Section I:

Mass Media and Society: general perspectives

Introduction

This introductory section contains articles characteristic of the different ways in which researchers approach the study of the media, rooted in very different ideological perspectives of society. Researchers in the Marxist tradition usually adopt a holistic view of the role of the media, focusing upon the relationship between ownership and control of the media and the power structure in society, the ideological signification of meaning in media messages and its effects in reproducing the class system. The two articles by John Westergaard and by Graham Murdock and Peter Golding take this approach. Researchers in what may be broadly called the liberal democratic tradition tend to adopt a more pragmatic approach, in which media institutions and media professionals are assumed to have a considerable degree of autonomy within a pluralist model of advanced industrial society. This has usually resulted in studies focusing upon particular aspects of the communication process — upon organizational processing of communications, the inter-relationships between communicators and their audiences, audience effects, the place of the media in the political system, the institutional development of the media and so on. The remaining articles in this section are characteristic of this approach in that they concentrate upon a particular aspect of the communication process. They are untypical, however, in that they situate their analysis, to a lesser or greater extent, in the wider context of society as a whole.

In the first article, Peter Golding and Graham Murdock argue that the mass media are one of the means by which class inequalities are maintained and legitimated in society. Explicitly dissociating themselves from some versions of Marxist analysis which treat as self-evident propositions that need to be empirically tested, they document the processes which, they argue, have contributed to the reproduction of class relations in Britain: the shift from concentration to conglomeration of media ownership; the trend towards 'centralization interconnectedness' amongst media controllers indicating that they constitute an identifiable capitalist class with shared interests; the mediation of control through hierarchical institutions, occupational ideologies and media structures subject to external economic constraints; and the systematic exclusion of oppositional media through the operation of the market forces. The article thus challenges not only traditional liberal assumptions about the role of the media in society but also assumptions made by some writers in the same tradition as themselves.

Tom Burns, writing from a very different but no less prescriptive perspective, examines the historical development of the media in relation to the political system in Britain and argues that different media have performed a variety of different roles at different points in time; as compliant agents of government and as aggressive watchdogs against government abuse; as channels of communication between pressure groups, governments and political parties and as the personal platforms of press proprietors; as vehicles of social and political reform and as instruments of power and social control. Currently, he argues, the media have come to reflect a narrow band of consensus as a consequence of the increasing economic pressures on the media, the growing professionalization of communicators and the continued hierarchical control of broadcasting so that the media are no longer an effective channel of communication between government and governed at a time of increasing dissensus.

Denis McQuail devotes most of his attention to providing an overview of audience effects research. But in his critical summary of research into media effects, he emphasizes that the impact of the mass media needs to be examined 'at a level beyond that of the individual audience member and the aggregate of individual behaviours.' His analysis not only reproduces the salient conclusions of empirical effects research — which no serious student of the mass media can afford to ignore — but also identifies its limitations, notably the lack of inquiry into the indirect influence of the media in its role as constructor of social reality. He also argues for a reconceptualization of media effects in terms not merely of audience response, but in terms of its effects on institutions, 'relationships' and the social structure, situated, as his concluding note suggests, in the wider context of power relationships in society. This theme is taken up by John Westergaard who examines in the following article the effect of the media in constructing reality and in imposing a selective framework which effectively excludes oppositional meanings systems. This is done within a wider analysis that situates the control of the media, professional communicator values and the economic determination of media structures and audiences in the wider context of the power structure. His article links up also with the analysis provided by Tom Burns, although John Westergaard reaches rather different conclusions about the place of the media in the political system. This is due not to significantly different empirical perceptions of media institutions — indeed both articles draw upon some of the same empirical evidence — but because of the different models of the power structure that underlie each article.

The academic study of the mass media in Europe and the United States has long suffered from a deeply ingrained ethnocentric bias, and this collection of articles is no exception (out of necessity rather than choice). Yet, the development of the mass media in developing countries has long been dominated by the United States and, to a lesser extent, by the two ex-colonial powers, Britain and France. Oliver Boyd-Barrett proposes, in his article, an analytic framework for describing the processes of 'media imperialism'. He documents the extent of Western, and in particular American, media dominance and examines the factors that underly it, concluding with a discussion of its wider implications.

The general perspectives provided in this section, and the questions that they raise, are explored in greater detail in the two sections that follow, concerned with media production and the mediation of cultural meanings.

1

Capitalism, Communication and Class Relations

Graham Murdock and Peter Golding

The basic argument underlying this paper is that the sociological study
of mass communications should not be seen as a self-contained professional specialism, and still less as one element in a grand multi-disciplinary
approach to 'communications', but as part of the overall study of social
and cultural reproduction which has traditionally occupied the heartland
of sociological analysis. In the case of the advanced capitalist societies of
North America and Western Europe with which we are specifically concerned here, this means that the sociology of mass communications should
derive from, and feed into, the continuing debate on the nature and
persistence of class stratification. More particularly, media sociology should
address itself to the central problem of explaining how radical inequalities
in the distribution of rewards come to be presented as natural and
inevitable and are understood as such by those who benefit least from this
distribution. In short, our argument is that the sociology of mass communications should be incorporated into the wider study of stratification
and legitimation.

At first sight this seems a perfectly straightforward and unexceptionable
position to take up. On the one hand there is an impressive amount of
evidence showing that class inequalities remain the central structural axis
of capitalist societies (see for example Westergaard and Resler, 1975).
And on the other hand, the available evidence indicates that most people
in these societies get most of their information about the social structure
from the mass media, and that by and large control over this crucial flow
of social imagery is concentrated in the hands of groups towards the top
end of the class structure. Given this situation, the relations between mass
communications and class stratification present an obvious and central
topic for investigation. Yet paradoxically neither media sociologists nor
sociologists of stratification have made much headway in this direction.
In fact there is something of a double vacuum in contemporary sociological analysis. Questions of stratification are largely absent from studies
of the mass media, while most analyses of class and legitimation lack any
concrete consideration of the role of mass communications.

Media Sociology and Stratification Theory: the double vacuum

Media sociologists periodically bemoan the fact that empirical studies have run ahead of theory, so that although we now know much more than we used to about the structure, operations and impact of the mass media, we still lack a comprehensive analysis of the ways in which the various levels of the mass communications system are related to each other and to the central dimensions of the wider social structure. However, in searching for a suitable integrating framework, most commentators have studiously avoided the possibilities presented by stratification theory. Indeed, questions of class have either been ignored altogether or denuded of their full potential.

One of the most favoured proposals for overcoming the present fragmentation of the field and developing a more holistic approach to the relations between mass communications and social life, is through the creation of a general theory of communications. As the editor of a new journal of communications recently put it in his introduction to the first issue:

In the past, we have atomized people in the same way that we have atomized knowledge. One way of putting the pieces back together again is through the organizing principle that underlies every human and social whole — through communication .... There is nothing in human or social life which does not involve communication in some way. The ways in which we relate to each other communicatively determine what kind of society we are going to have. (Thayer, 1974.)

Superficially, this promise of interdisciplinary dialogue seems to offer an appealing solution to the problem of fragmentation. But it is an illusory solution. It ignores the fact that disciplinary divisions are the product not simply of organizational convenience or academic empire building but of basic and genuine differences of intellectual approach. Many sociologists, ourselves included, would disagree fundamentally with the proposition that modes of communication 'determine what kind of society we are going to have'. On the contrary, sociological analysis should start from the exactly opposite assertion that modes of communication and cultural expression are determined by the structure of social relations. How this basic proposition is elaborated however, depends primarily on how the social structure is conceived, and at this point sociologists begin to divide into camps.

For some, an adequate sociological analysis of the structures and operations of mass communications entails placing them in their 'total social context' by tracing their connections with social institutions at every level from the family to the economy (Halloran, 1974). Underlying this approach is a conception of the social structure as a series of separate but connected institutional domains, none of which necessarily takes priority over the others. The class system therefore appears not as the fundamental axis of the social structure but as one dimension among a number of others. This kind of pluralistic model of social structure commands a good deal of explicit and implicit support among media sociologists on both sides of the Atlantic. In his introduction to the first major British reader on media sociology, for example, Jeremy Tunstall offered an elegant appraisal of the gaps in the field and outlined some areas for future investigation. They included the 'working class and the media' and 'elite values and the media' (Tunstall, 1970 p. 36). These are presented, however, as intrinsically interesting but discrete topics, and the possibility of integrating them both into a more general theory of stratification and legitimation is consequently ignored. In place of an integrated class analysis of mass communications therefore, we are encouraged to undertake studies of 'the mass media and class' to put alongside the studies of 'the mass media and children' and 'the mass media and women'.

However, if media sociologists have generally failed to relate their work to ongoing debates on stratification, theorists of stratification have equally failed to develop an analysis of mass communications. Indeed, in most recent British discussions of class and legitimation, the role of the mass media is either ignored altogether (e.g. Parkin, 1971; Mann, 1973) or else only mentioned in passing (e.g. Giddens, 1973). Given the central role of mass communications in relaying social knowledge and social imagery, this collective silence on the part of sociologists concerned with stratification 'represents an extra-ordinary omission' (Downing, 1975 p. 18). Not that they have entirely neglected the processes through which social knowledge is distributed through the class structure. On the contrary, the operations of the other main distributive mechanism — the education system — have been quite extensively analysed and investigated. But the relative abundance of studies in this area simply serves to highlight the extraordinary underdevelopment of thought on the role of mass communications in reproducing class relations.

Faced with this vacuum within academic sociology, many of those interested in the relations between communications and class have increasingly turned to the only other system of social analysis in which these relations are systematically addressed — namely, Marxism. But here again there are problems, for Marxism, like sociology, embraces a variety of contending approaches and styles of analysis.

Marxism and Cultural Analysis: the insecure base

In the spring of 1851, after an intensive bout of study in the British Museum, Marx declared that he 'had got so far' with his economic researches that he 'could be finished with the whole economic shit in five weeks' (Blumberg, 1972 p. 104). In the event, it turned out to be a drastic underestimate. The work on economics continued to consume the lion's share of his intellectual energy and was still unfinished at his death, thirty-two years later. As a result, other aspects of his work, including his analysis of culture, remained fragmented and underdeveloped.

Throughout his working life, Marx was active in journalism. In his mid twenties he edited newspapers in Germany, and later, after settling in London, he became a European correspondent of the *New York Tribune* and wrote regularly for radical newspapers in Britain and on the Continent. Despite this close personal involvement, however, he never found the time to develop a comprehensive account of the role of the press in capitalist societies. This gap in turn was simply one aspect of the overall lack of a sustained analysis of the production and distribution of social knowledge. Scattered throughout his work as a whole, however, is a series of programmatic outlines in which he identifies the key areas that such an analysis should tackle, and lays down a general approach. One of the best known of these outlines is the celebrated passage in *The German Ideology* of 1845, an early work written jointly with Engels while Marx was in his late twenties.

> The class which has the means of material production at its disposal has control at the same time over the means of mental production, so that thereby, generally speaking, the ideas of those who lack the means of mental production are subject to it . . . . In so far, therefore, as they rule as a class and determine the extent and compass of an epoch, it is self-evident that they . . . among other things . . . regulate the production and distribution of the ideas of their age: thus their ideas are the ruling ideas of the epoch. (Marx and Engels, 1938, p. 39.)

This passage puts forward three important propositions; that control over 'the production and distribution of ideas' is concentrated in the hands of the capitalist owners of the means of production; that as a result of this control their views and accounts of the world receive insistent publicity and come to dominate the thinking of subordinate groups; and that this ideological domination plays a key role in maintaining class inequalities. Each of these propositions in turn raises a series of key questions for empirical investigation: questions about the relations between communications entrepreneurs and the capitalist class, about the relations between ownership and control within the communications industries, about the processes through which the dominant ideology is translated into cultural commodities; and about the dynamics of reception and the extent to which members of subordinate groups adopt the dominant ideas as their own.

As the work on economics moved to the forefront of Marx's intellectual life, so these questions tended to fade into the background. However, although he did not tackle them specifically, he periodically returned to the general relations between the economy and culture, extending and refining his earlier formulations in line with his developing analysis of the capitalist system. One of the most important of these extensions occurs in the preface to *A Contribution to the Critique of Political Economy*, which he wrote in 1859, as an attack on the prevailing economic theories of the day.

> In the social production of their existence, men inevitably enter into definite relations, which are independent of their will, namely relations of production . . . . The totality of these relations of production constitutes the economic structure of society, the real foundation, on which arises a legal and political superstructure and to which correspond definite forms of social consciousness. The mode of production of material life conditions the general process of social, political and intellectual life. (Marx, 1975 p. 425.)

In this passage, Marx is concerned to emphasize the fact that the system of class control over the production and distribution outlined in *The German Ideology* is itself embedded in and conditioned by the fundamental dynamics underpinning the capitalist economy. Hence, an adequate analysis of cultural production needs to examine not only the class base of control, but also the general economic context within which this control is exercised. Unfortunately, the way this argument is presented in the passage has led to a good deal of confusion and misrepresentation.

The first misunderstanding revolves around Marx's assertion that intellectual and cultural life is 'conditioned' by economic relations. Many commentators, particularly those hostile to Marxism, have taken this as evidence that Marx was an 'economic determinist' who saw people's ideas and actions as totally conditioned by economic forces beyond their control. To interpret it in this way is fundamentally to misunderstand Marx's basic position. A careful reading of the piece as a whole and of Marx's other mature works, reveals that he uses the notion of determination and conditioning not in this narrow sense but in a much looser sense of setting limits, exerting pressures and closing off options (Williams, 1973 p. 4). Hence, although he saw the basic economic relations of capitalism as structuring the overall framework and 'general process' of intellectual life, within these general limits he allowed a good deal of room for intellectual autonomy and innovation. In fact, the relations between creativity and constraint constitute a major theme in his work.

The second mistake concerns his image of economic relations as the 'real foundations' and of cultural and intellectual life as a 'superstructure' built on top. Many commentators have chosen to interpret this metaphor literally, arguing that Marx's comparison of the economic base with the foundations of a building indicates that he saw it as something static and unchanging. Once again this interpretation conveniently ignores the fact that, in the passage immediately following, Marx is at pains to emphasize the fact that capitalism is a dynamic system which is still in the process of development. Consequently, analysis needed to be both concrete and specific. For Marx, then, it was not enough simply to outline the general features of capitalism, it was also necessary to show how they were developing and changing in response to concrete historical circumstances. 'Unless material production is understood in its specific historical form' he argued, 'it is impossible to grasp the characteristics of the intellectual production which corresponds to it.' (Bottomore and Rubel, 1963 pp. 96–7.)

Despite their underdevelopment in Marx's own work (or perhaps because of it), the relations between the economic base and the cultural superstructure have subsequently attracted the attention of many notable Marxist scholars. Paradoxically, however, a great deal of this analysis has revised, and even reversed, the approach recommended by Marx. Instead of starting from a concrete analysis of economic relations and the ways in which they structure both the processes and results of cultural production, they start by analysing the form and content of cultural artifacts and then working backwards to describe their economic base. The characteristic outcome is a top-heavy analysis in which an elaborate anatomy of cultural forms balances insecurely on a schematic account of economic forces shaping their production.

There are powerful historical reasons why Marxist cultural analysis developed in this way. In the first place, Marx's work offers not only a sociological analysis of the underlying dynamics of capitalist society, but also an ethical critique of this society coupled with a call for its over-throw and replacement by communism. As a result, it has given rise 'in one direction, to a broadly positivist sociology, and in another direction to a style of thought which has generally been referred to as "critical philosophy".' (Bottomore, 1975 p. 11.) While both styles can quite legitimately claim to be Marxist, they involve radically different forms of analysis, and in the case of the Marxist analyses of culture which developed in Western Europe after 1918, 'critical philosophy' tended to predominate over more sociological styles. This shift, in turn, can largely be explained as a reaction to the ascendency of the Soviet version of Marxist sociology, which after a brief period of creative innovation in the immediate post revolutionary period, reverted to a crudely deterministic view of base-superstructure relations in which cultural forms were reduced to more or less simple reflections of economic and class relations. In opposition to this, Western Marxists outside the Soviet sphere of influence responded by stressing both the complexity and relative autonomy of cultural forms, and insisting on the centrality and importance of cultural criticism. In rejecting the 'economic determinism' of the Soviet line, however, they tended to evacuate any sustained analysis of the economic base, thereby jettisoning the very elements that give Marxist sociology its distinctiveness and explanatory power.

This tendency to place cultural criticism rather than economic analysis at the centre of Marxist cultural theory has taken a variety of forms, but as an illustration we can briefly look at the work of Theodor Adorno, a Marxist whose work on culture has recently enjoyed a considerable vogue both in Britain and America.

Along with Max Horkheimer and Herbert Marcuse, Adorno was a leading member of the Institute for Social Research which opened in Frankfurt in 1923 as a centre for Marxist scholarship. While most Institute members were concerned to develop a more adequate analysis of culture, Adorno's interest was given an added impetus by his own personal involvement in artistic activity. Before joining the Institute, he had tried his hand as a composer, studying under Alban Berg, one of the leading figures in the Viennese avant-garde. In addition, he had written extensively on music for a variety of avant-garde journals. These formative experiences were instrumental in focusing his intellectual attention on aesthetic forms rather than on cultural production.

This focus emerges particularly clearly in the analysis of American popular music which he developed during his residence in New York, where he had moved after the Nazis closed the Institute in Frankfurt in 1933. Adorno saw popular music in general and jazz in particular as a perfect example of the 'standardization, commercialization and rigidification' which capitalist production imposes on artistic expression:

Competition on the culture market has proved the effectiveness of a number of techniques, including syncopation and semi-opulent instrumentation. These techniques are then sorted out and kaleidoscopically mixed into ever-new combinations . . .. The investments made in 'name bands', the money used to promote musical bestseller programmes make every divergence a risk . . .. And even if there were attempts to introduce anything really different into light music, they would be doomed from the start by virtue of economic concentration. [Further,] this standardization means the strengthening of the lasting domination of the listening public and of their conditioned reflexes. (Adorno, 1967 p. 124.)

Adorno's insistence that the process of cultural domination has its roots in the economic dynamics of the 'culture industry' is an indispensable starting point for any Marxist analysis. But it is only a starting point. It is not sufficient simply to assert that the capitalistic base of the 'culture industry' necessarily results in the production of cultural forms which are consonant with the dominant ideology. It is also necessary to demonstrate how this process of reproduction actually works by showing in detail how economic relations structure both the overall strategies of the cultural entrepreneurs and the concrete activities of the people who actually make the products the 'culture industry' sells — the writers, journalists, actors and musicians. Even when he was appointed to Paul Lazarsfeld's Radio Research project and expressly asked to investigate the structure of the American music industry, he declined to conduct empirical studies of production. Indeed, he saw such work as redundant. Since the basic structures of the industry were reproduced in the cultural commodities it produced, he argued, they could be adequately inferred from a critical analysis of these forms and did not need to be studied independently. In place of the concrete analysis of material production advocated by Marx, therefore, we are offered only a very general and schematic description of the basic features of capitalism. This description is correct as far as it goes but does not go nearly far enough towards explaining how the American 'culture industry' actually works.

A similar imbalance between cultural and economic analysis also characterizes the writing of two most consistently illuminating Marxists working in the field of cultural studies in Britain — Raymond Williams and Stuart Hall. Here again, a detailed and often dazzling dissection of cultural forms sits uneasily on an underdeveloped analysis of the economic bases of their production. Stuart Hall, for example, begins a recent paper on broadcasting by declaring that to him '. . . the role of broadcasting in reproducing the power relations and ideological structure of society appears far more central an issue than its incidental financial kickbacks.' (Hall 1972 p. 8.) He then goes on to offer an impressive analysis of the ways in which the content of political television and the forms within which it is presented serve to relay and reinforce dominant definitions of the situation and to exclude alternatives. So far so good. But we would argue this process of ideological reproduction cannot be fully understood without an analysis of the economic context within which it takes place and of the pressures and determinations which this context exerts. Far from being 'incidental', questions of resources and of loss and profit play a central role in structuring both the processes and products of television production, including the output of news and current affairs. Economics is clearly not the only factor in play, but equally it cannot be ignored.

Marxism's distinctiveness and promise as a framework for the sociological investigation of culture and communication lies precisely in the fact that it focuses on the complex connections *between* economics and intellectual production, between base and superstructure. Once these connections are devalued or left undeveloped, much of Marxism's theoretical power evaporates, as many of its opponents have grasped only too well. Daniel Bell, for example, prefaces his recent anti-Marxist account of culture in advanced capitalist societies by declaring that Marx's insistence on the centrality of property and economic relations is obsolete and that it is now 'more useful to think of contemporary society as three distinct realms' the economic, the political and the cultural, 'each of which is obedient to a different axial principle.' (Bell, 1976 p. 10.)

To summarize the argument so far then: neither Marxism nor academic sociology has progressed very far in producing a detailed analysis of the role of mass communications in the production of class relations. Consequently, as John Goldthorpe has put it, 'The work of showing exactly how socialization "from above" takes place — remains almost all to be done.' (Goldthorpe, 1972 p. 360.) This paper makes a preliminary start on this work, taking Britain as an instance of the current situation in advanced capitalist societies. Elsewhere we hope to deal with the question of audiences within a class perspective, but in the present context we are concentrating on the prior questions of ownership, control and production. To the extent that we take the questions Marx raises in *The German Ideology* as our initial departure point, and to the extent that we begin from a concrete analysis of the economic formations and process that underpin the contemporary communications industry, our approach can be considered as Marxisant (Goldthorpe, 1972).

The Last Instance: the limits of economic determinism

We have said that economics are not the sole determinant of media behaviour, and in this sense we are not arguing a thesis of bald economic determinism. Nevertheless, by concentrating on the economic base, we are suggesting that control over material resources and their changing distribution are *ultimately* the most powerful of the many levers operating in cultural production. But clearly such control is not always exercised directly, nor does the economic state of media organizations always have an immediate impact on their output.

In following through the effect of economics on cultural production, we come to two groups; owners of media corporations, and the creative producers or 'communicators'. The motivations and activities of these groups require concrete analysis for a full understanding of media output. The extent to which the owners of media companies give priority to economics, and the extent to which they are able or willing to influence production to meet such a priority are empirical questions. We discuss below the thesis that a 'managerial revolution' has separated ownership and control in such industries as the media. But it is important to bear in mind the difference between analyses of motivation and of economic logic. Characterization of media corporations and those who manage them derives from their structural location in a capitalist economy, which is unaltered by the mixed ambitions of owners and managers, however 'non-economic' these may be. In discussing the second group, the 'humble workers on the shop floor of the great image factory', as Robin Day describes them, the analytical problem is that of mediation. In other words, however compelling the economic logic, how do we explain the emergence of cultural output without making the mistake of assuming it simple and direct reproduction of the ideological pattern congenial to those groups who own and control the media? We return to this problem below.

Two obvious departures from a strict thesis of economic determinism are immediately apparent. The first are the state-operated media, financed wholly or partly either by public subscription or from taxation, and operating as a 'public service' in the sense that their declared objective is to provide a social utility rather than to maximize private profit. In Britain, of course, this description applies to the BBC.

The concept of public service broadcasting is, however, under permanent attack from those who would apply cost-effective criteria to all publicly operated organizations. They argue that broadcasting must prove its social value by trial in the market place like any other commodity, and that excellence and efficiency can only be guaranteed by severing the umbilical cord of public subsidy and throwing all media into open commercial competition. But beyond this explicit attack there is already a set of economic imperatives which retrieve organizations like the BBC for our argument. Such organizations have to behave according to the dictates of cost-effectiveness and as quasi profit-maximizing for a number of reasons. For example, the BBC has to avoid accumulating a deficit and it has to persuade Parliament that if one is in sight it has earned the right to an increase in its licence fee. Its evidence is in large part the size of the audience, determined by its success in competing with commercial broadcasting companies licenced by the IBA. Thus, as with any public corporation operating in a capitalist economy, the BBC behaves in many ways as though it were itself a commercial undertaking (see Hood, 1972 p. 411). In recent years, with rapid increases in costs, the BBC deficit has risen steadily leading to an intensification of the ratings battle between ITV and BBC 1, and extensions of programme marketing overseas, co-productions, cost consciousness, and more recently discussion about the continued existence of the Corporation in its present form. This is not the whole story, of course, but it is a caveat to be set against any attempt to consider the BBC as beyond the influence of economics.

The second departure arises from the existence of media which, far from providing profits, generate long-term financial losses. There are many incidental examples in the cinema and publishing, but in Britain the most obvious instances are to be found in the national press. The aggregate circulation of the national daily press declined by 10.8% from 1961 to 1975. In 1974 only three dailies and three Sunday papers made profits, in 1975 only four dailies and one Sunday did so (Royal Commission on the Press, *Interim Report* 1976 p. 5). Titles have continued to disappear both in Fleet Street and in the provinces, and now no city other than London is served by more than one evening paper. In 1975 the 'quality' daily and Sunday nationals between them made a loss of £6.8 million (*ibid* p. 99).

media Bias

These facts are stark and dramatic and they prompt the often asked question as to why proprietors should continue to maintain newspapers which are such a drain on their resources. Without an exhaustive analysis here, there are three points which can be made briefly. First, it is economics which have determined which newspapers have survived. However eccentric, public spirited, politically ambitious or vain the proprietor of a loss-making newspaper may be, he is unable to display such traits without command of substantial financial resources from elsewhere. Thus newspapers survive not because of the whims or ambitions of oddly motivated proprietors, but because they are part of profitable conglomerates able and willing to sustain their losses. They are a luxury for profitable enterprise, not a hobby for the financially disinterested. Second, the running of a national newspaper may not be without reward, however indirect. To the extent that national newspapers are part of large industrial enterprises, they can and will act as flagships for those enterprises as a whole, and the values and beliefs they represent. This does not mean newspapers are the passive carriers and promoters of a free enterprise philosophy supported by the firms that own them, but equally it lessens the probability of there being widespread opposition to such philosophies in the pages of the national press. In addition the newspaper may confer prestige and publicity on other group products which make its continued existence valuable. The most obvious example is *The Times*, whose losses were made good by Lord Thomson from his private family company and thus did not hit the value of the Thomson Organization. The magazines produced by the group, however, bearing *The Times* title (the Literary and Educational Supplements) are prestigious and successful, and on occasion provide sufficient profit to balance losses on *The Times.*

Finally, the fact that newspapers may be unsuccessful does not discredit the accuracy of an analysis of their behaviour in profit-maximizing terms. Most national newspapers have spent the last few years desperately juggling with layout, editorial style, marketing and circulation strategies, cover prices and advertising rates, in an attempt to avoid the calamitous situation that prompted the setting up of yet another Royal Commission in 1974. There is also the problem that it may be cheaper to keep a moribund paper alive than to kill it. The distribution of that part of common costs borne by the ailing title to other enterprises in a group might be more harmful than the costs of preservation. Far from casting doubt on the importance of economics as a determinant of press behaviour, their parlous financial state has exacerbated and made even more immediate the responsiveness of newspapers to their economic environment.

In turning to the actual patterns of ownership and control then we are well aware of the limitations to a simple view of economic reductionism. Equally, however, such qualifications should not be taken to reduce the

importance for an understanding of cultural production of its material
base and economic context.

Mapping the Communications Industry: from concentration to conglomeration

While radio, cinema, television, recording, advertising and public relations . . . are
being keenly discussed, each in its own term, the mind industry, taken as a whole, is
disregarded. (Enzensberger, 1974 p. 6.)

The last hundred years have seen an underlying shift in the structure of
advanced capitalist economies in which the ownership of the means of
production has become progressively less dispersed and increasingly concentrated in the hands of a relatively few large corporations (Aaronovitch
and Sawyer, 1975 p. 157). This shift towards concentration has proceeded
in bursts. The first occurred at the turn of the century between 1889 and
1902, the second after the First World War between 1919 and 1921, and
the latest and most significant in the nineteen sixties. There are a variety
of measures of concentration but the one that we are particularly concerned
with here is the Concentration Ratio, which measures the degree of concentration within a particular sector by taking the proportion of the
market controlled by the top five firms in the sector. The higher the
proportion, the greater the degree of concentration.

The ten years between 1958 and 1968 saw significant rises in the
concentration ratios of a number of industrial sectors. On the basis of a
representative sample of manufactured products, for example, Kenneth
George has recently calculated that during this ten year period, the average
concentration ratio for industry as a whole increased from 56.6% to 65.5%
(George, 1975 p. 125). As with all averages, however, these figures conceal
significant variations. A ten per cent rise in the concentration ratio was by
no means characteristic of all the products in the sample. For some, of
course, the increase was greater, for some more modest, and in a
significant minority of cases the concentration ratio actually fell during
this period. Certainly, the various sectors of the communications industry
display considerable variations in their patterns of concentration during
this period, depending on their past history and on the current state of
the market for their products.

In some sectors, such as daily newspapers and cinema exhibition, the
decisive shift towards concentration had already taken place before the
mid-fifties, with the result that there were only small increases during the
period 1957—68. By 1955, for example, the leading five concerns
accounted for 68.6% of the total circulation of all daily newspapers,
provincial as well as national (PEP, 1955 p. 216.) By 1970, this figure
had increased only marginally to 70.9%. (Press Council, 1970 pp. 114—

17.) There were some significant shifts in the structure of ownership during this period but they did not appreciably affect the overall level of concentration.

In 1959, for example, the Canadian newspapers' proprietor, Roy Thomson (later Lord Thomson) bought the Kemsley Group, then the leading publisher of provincial dailies, and later, in 1965, he acquired the country's most prestigious national daily — *The Times*. But in 1970 the rank overall position of the Thomson Organization was the same as Kemsley's had been in 1955 — fourth, while their actual share of the daily newspaper market was slightly less — 8% as against 9.2%. In cinema exhibitions too, concentration was already well advanced by 1957. The domination of the Rank—ABC duopoly dated from the early 1940s, although the steady decline of audiences throughout the fifties certainly consolidated their position still further as small chains were forced either to close or to merge with the majors. Once again, however, the most significant change of the period was a shift in ownership, which occurred in 1969 when the ABC group was acquired by EMI, the country's leading record company. In the record industry itself, however, the level of concentration actually decreased.

Since the early 1930s the record market had been dominated by two firms, EMI and Decca, with EMI the market leader, and this duopolistic dominance continued for the next thirty years. The second half of the sixties, however, saw an unprecedented boom in record sales, sparked off by the rise of the Beatles and the other British beat groups and sustained by the emergence of a lucrative campus market for 'progressive' rock LPs. Encouraged by the prospects of continuing profits from this large and expanding youth market, the leading European record firms like Philips and Polydor and the major American concerns like CBS, RCA and Warner Brothers, made vigorous attempts to increase their share of the British market. Their attempts met with considerable success, with the result that the situation became much more open and the EMI—Decca duopoly was steadily eroded. Between 1965 and 1970 their joint market share fell from 58% to 38% while the concentration ratio for the industry as a whole dropped from 82% to 64.5%. (EIU, 1966 p. 24; 1971 p. 26.)

This pattern was repeated in the case of paperback books. Once again the mid-sixties saw a spectacular expansion in the size of the market. In 1964, there were 12,500 paperback titles in print, two years later the figure had rocketed to 22,000 and by the end of 1969 it stood at 37,351. (EIU, 1970 p. 29.) The sharp upturn in sales which accompanied this 'paperback explosion' again encouraged new entrants, among them the Thomson Organization which established a paperback subsidiary, Sphere books, in 1966. As with the record industry, this increase in competition eroded the market dominance of the established firms, headed by Penguin Books. Hence, whereas in the mid-sixties the top five firms had accounted for over 90% of paperback sales, by the end of the decade their market share had fallen to around 70% (EIU, 1970 p. 26).

Despite these variations, however, the communications industry still exhibited a remarkably high level of concentration in every sector. Certainly, if the mean ratio 65.5% calculated by George is taken as a base, most sectors had concentration ratios well above the average for industry as a whole. By the beginning of the seventies the top five firms in the respective sectors accounted for 71% of daily newspaper circulation, 74% of the homes with commercial television, 78% of the admissions to cinemas, 70% of paper back sales and 65% of record sales. (Press Council, 1970 pp. 114–17; PIB, 1970 p. 5; EIU, 1972; 1970 p. 26; 1971 p. 26.)

Not surprisingly this situation has attracted a good deal of comment and debate. Indeed, the growth of concentration and monopoly has been a persistent and dominant theme in analyses of the communications industries since the end of World War Two. Almost without exception, however, studies have concentrated on the situation in one particular sector. At the time of writing, for example, government commissions are in the process of investigating the two key communications sectors – the press and broadcasting. But these enquiries are entirely self-contained and there is little liaison between them. This separation is more than a convenient division of labour; it is symptomatic of the fragmentation that characterizes contemporary analyses of the communications industry, academic as well as governmental. By focusing on the situation within a particular sector, this piecemeal approach necessarily devalues the centrality and importance of the emerging *relations between* sectors. The recent growth of these interconnections is indicative of a basic shift in the structure of the communications industry, away from the relatively simple situation of sector specific monopolies and towards something altogether more complex and far reaching. It is not simply that a handful of firms predominate in each sector. Increasingly, the largest concerns command leading positions in several sectors simultaneously.

This development is part of a general tendency for the leading firms in the economy to acquire a greater and greater proportion of the overall means of production. Again this movement has accelerated sharply in the last twenty years. Whereas, in 1957, the top hundred corporations controlled just over a half (51%) of the total net assets of British industry, by 1969 this proportion had increased to almost two-thirds (64%) (George and Silbertson, 1975 p. 181). At the heart of this shift lies the trend towards diversification. Diversification occurs whenever a company with interests in one particular sector branches out and acquires interests in another sector. Two examples have already been mentioned – the Thomson Organization's move into paperback books, and EMI's acquisition of the ABC cinema chain. In cases where diversification entails a move into a field more or less unrelated to the company's 'core' interests, as with

EMI's move into catering with the acquisition of the Golden Egg restaurant chain, the resulting amalgam is conventionally referred to as a *conglomerate*.

In a capitalist economy, a corporation's chances of survival and growth depend ultimately on its ability to maintain and increase its profits. From the early sixties onwards, however, there has been a consistent tendency for the rate of profit to decline, giving companies a smaller and smaller rate of return on their investments (see, for example, Burgess and Webb, 1974). Faced with this continuing crisis of profitability, diversification offers one strategy for maintaining profits, or at least of arresting the rate of decline. It is certainly no accident that the trend towards diversification has occurred at the same time as the squeeze on company profits. Diversification is particularly attractive in situations where opportunities for further expansion within a particular market are limited by falling demand.

Faced with the steady decline in cinema going, for example, the Rank Organization attempted to protect its long-term profit prospects by acquiring interests in expanding leisure fields such as hotels, motorway services, and television and hi-fi equipment. Opportunities for internal expansion can also be limited by legal restrictions, as in the case of commercial television programming. Lord Thomson's acquisition of interests in such growth areas of leisure as paperback publishing and package holidays, for example, was in part a response to the fact that he was debarred from increasing his holdings in commercial television under the terms of the Television Act. However, diversification also represents a cushion against downswings in the profitability of particular sectors. It is a practical expression of the old adage that it is best not to put all your eggs in one basket. The wisdom of this strategy is well illustrated in the case of the Associated Television Corporation (ATC).

ATC is a good example of a multi-conglomerate. In addition to controlling the Midlands commercial television station, ATV Network, the Corporation also has extensive interests in feature film production; in records, cassettes and music publishing; in theatres; in telephone answering equipment, and in merchandizing, insurance and property. These diversified interests had already proved their worth in 1969 when their continued profitability had cushioned the worst effects of the squeeze of television profits following the increase in the government levy on the turnover of the programme companies (Murdock and Golding, 1974 pp. 219—20). They were to prove their value again in the early months of 1974 when the three-day-week and the general lack of business confidence led to a withdrawal of advertising and a sharp decline in revenue. As a result, ATV's pre-tax profits for the 1974 financial year were only 3.06 million pounds, a drop of almost a million pounds on the previous year's figure of 4.01 million. Despite this, however, the pre-tax profits for the group as a whole actually increased marginally from 7.25 to 7.26 million pounds, thanks largely to substantial rises in the profitability of the other sectors, most notably the music interests. In the smaller companies like Westward, however, which had by the Chairman's admission 'pursued a conservative policy in the possible fields of diversification', there was nothing to cushion the blow, and consequently between 1973 and 1974 pre-tax profits dropped dramatically from £538,000 to £186,000.

Although ATC and the Thomson Organization are among the leading examples of the emerging British multi-media conglomerates, they are by no means the only ones. Other prominent instances include the Granada Group and EMI. Companies within the Granada Group, for example, feature among the top five companies in three sectors; commercial television programming, paperback publishing and cinema exhibition. Similarly, the EMI group owns not only the country's largest record company but also the second-ranked cinema chain, the controlling interest in one of the leading commercial television contractors (Thames Television), and significant interests in consumer and industrial electronics, and leisure provision. In addition, several prominent communications companies are themselves integrated into more broadly based conglomerates with interests in a wide range of industrial and financial sectors. For example, as well as controlling the country's leading newspaper and magazine publishing companies, Reed International has significant interests in paper and paint manufacture. Similarly, S. Pearson and Son not only controls the leading local newspaper group (The Westminster Press), the leading paperback house (Penguin Books) and a top hardback publishing group (Longman) but also owns Lazards, the merchant bank, and has extensive industrial interests in glass and ceramics.

The emergence of multi-media conglomerates is certainly not unique to Britain. On the contrary, it is a trend which is discernible throughout the advanced capitalist economies. It is furthest advanced in the United States where the relatively stringent anti-trust laws have given an added impetus to diversification by blocking opportunities for expansion within single markets. Two of the most notable US media conglomerates are RCA (Radio Corporation of America) and CBS (Columbia Broadcasting System). In addition to controlling one of the three major television networks, CBS also has significant interests in records, feature films and book publishing. The interests of RCA are even more broadly based and are currently sufficient to make it the thirty-ninth largest company in the United States. The RCA empire includes one of the major television networks, NBC, a sizeable market share of the record industry, the giant Random House book publishing group, substantial subsidiaries engaged in domestic and industrial electronics, plus interests in a variety of consumer goods and services ranging from convenience foods to car rentals. (Network Project,

1973.) This basic pattern is also repeated in varying degrees throughout Western Europe. To take just one example: the West German Bertelsmann group is not only the country's second largest book publisher but also the second largest record company, and in addition has substantial interests in general and specialist magazines and in the film industry. (Diederichs, 1973 p. 189.)

To sum up then; the communications industries of the advanced capitalist countries are currently being shaped by two basic shifts in the corporate structure of capitalism. The first is the long-term trend towards concentration which has led to an increasing number of sectors being dominated by a handful of large companies. The second is the more recent increase in diversification which has produced conglomerates with significant stakes in several sectors of the communications and leisure industries. Although considerably less well publicized than the question of concentration, this second development is in fact much more far-reaching in its implications. By adding not simply to the number, but also to the range of communications facilities that the large corporations own, the conglomeration enables the latter to significantly extend their potential control over 'the production and distribution of the ideas of their age'. How far this potential for control is actually realized in practice, how exactly it operates and in whose ultimate interest, are, however, empirical questions. As an initial step to finding the answers, it is necessary to examine the structure and operations of the large corporations, and more particularly to find out who the owners are and how far they control company policy and company operations. Both these areas raise complex issues of conceptualization and evidence which have not been made any easier by the fact that both have been the subject of continuing controversy and polemics.

The Capitalist Corporation and the Capitalist Class: patterns of ownership — questions of control

As we have already seen, Marx argued that those who owned the means of production also controlled the distribution of economic resources and the uses of the resulting surplus. Hence, while their position as owners made the capitalist class the dominant economic class, their consequent control over the production and distribution of material goods and symbol systems provided the means through which this domination was maintained. For Marx, then, property ownership, economic control and class power were inextricably tied together. Since his death, however, this assertion of interconnectedness has been challenged from a number of directions and one of the strongest lines of attack has focused on the relationship between ownership and control.

The debate started in earnest in 1932 with the publication of an

American book, *The Modern Corporation and Private Property*, in which the authors, Adolf Berle and Gardiner Means, argued that control of the modern corporation was being progressively divorced from ownership. This argument was subsequently taken up and elaborated by many of the most eminent social scientists including not only leading American authorities like Kenneth Galbraith and Talcott Parsons, but also prominent European scholars such as Ralph Dahrendorf. This discussion in turn fed into the wider debates about changes in the overall structure of advanced capitalist societies and became an important plank in the widespread effort to replace Marx's class analysis with more pluralistic conceptions of the stratification system. (Zeitlin, 1974; Stanworth, 1974.) Both the wider ramifications and the more specific details of 'the ownership and control' debate are explored elsewhere (Murdock, forthcoming) but in the present context we want to focus more specifically on the central assertion that control is increasingly separated from ownership.

The basic argument is reasonably straightforward; indeed its simplicity is one of its strongest attractions. As they have grown, so the argument runs, the large corporations have increasingly looked to outside sources for extra finance with the result that ownership as expressed in the legal form of shareholdings has become progressively dispersed. Consequently, the traditional company structure in which the founder and his family held the majority of the shares has been replaced by a corporate structure in which the shares are parcelled out into relatively small holdings, none of which provides a sufficient basis for effective control over the allocation of resources. In addition, the founding families have progressively withdrawn from their traditional entrepreneurial and executive roles with the result that operational control of the large corporations has passed into the hands of the new elite of professional managers who are the only group with the necessary specialized knowledge and expertise to run the increasingly complex operations of the modern business enterprise. Hence, command over the means of administration has decisively replaced ownership of the means of production as the basis for effective control over the contemporary corporation.

At first sight this argument appears eminently plausible. However, the empirical evidence usually cited in its support is by no means clear-cut. On the contrary, questions of conceptualization and interpretation are the subject of continuing argument (see for example Zeitlin, 1976; Allen, 1976). The communications industry has been even less well served for evidence than many other sectors of the economy, and at the moment we lack a comprehensive account either of the structure of ownership or of its relation to levels of control. However, information from work currently in progress suggests that Marx's analysis may not be as irrelevant and passé, as many critics have made out. The full results of this work will be published elsewhere (Murdock and Golding, forthcoming), but for the moment we want to outline some of the preliminary findings which bear directly on the central issue of the ownership and control debate — the question of separation.

In the first place, there are strong indications that the age of the owner-entrepreneur is by no means entirely over, even among the conglomerates where, according to the supporters of Berle and Means, the separation of control from ownership should be at its most advanced. In fact, in a significant number of the leading multi-media conglomerates, the founding family and/or its descendants retain a significant and often controlling share holding, and in a number of instances they also occupy key executive and managerial positions which give them a significant degree of control over the formulation of the companies' general allocation policies, together with a degree of operational control over their day-to-day implementation. Notable examples include S. Pearson and Sons, the Thomson Organization, the Granada Group, and the Associated Television Corporation. The controlling interest in the Granada Group, for example, remains firmly in the hands of the Bernstein family, who occupy three of the eight seats on the board of directors, including the key roles of Chairman and Vice Chairman. Similarly, in addition to holding the crucial positions of Chairman and Chief Executive, the founder of the Associated Television Corporation, Sir Lew Grade, is also the second largest shareholder with 23.7% of the ordinary voting shares, being surpassed only by Reed International's holding of 29.6%. Besides its intrinsic significance, this instance is also indicative of another trend which goes against the Berle and Means thesis — the rise of institutional shareholdings.

The last two decades have seen a decisive shift in corporate share ownership, out of the hands of individuals and into the hands, firstly, of financial institutions and, secondly, of other industrial corporations. In part, this trend can be seen as a further facet of the general growth of diversification. Buying a significant shareholding enables a company to diversify without having to make the more substantial financial commitment involved in outright acquisition. Whereas, in 1957, nearly two-thirds (63.8%) of the ordinary shares quoted on the London Stock Exchange were in the hands of private individuals, by 1975 the proportion had fallen to well under a half (42.1%) representing a corresponding gain in the proportion held by institutions (Moyle, 1971; Royal Commission on the Distribution of Income and Wealth, 1975 p. 13). Far from having become increasingly dispersed among a mass of isolated individuals therefore, shareholdings in the large corporations have become progressively concentrated in the hands of the dominant financial institutions and of other large corporations. Moreover, compared to the general passivity of most private shareholders, institutional investors are likely to pursue a much more 'interventionist' policy with respect to the operations of companies in which they have holdings. Where the holding is of sufficient

size or of particular strategic importance, the investing company will
usually have a representative on the Board of Directors. In addition to
monitoring carefully the company's general progress and prospects, these
representatives are likely to attempt to shape the company's policies
along lines which are consonant with the long-range plans and general
interests of their 'home' institution.

At the strategic level of allocation therefore, control is by no means
as radically divorced from ownership as most critics have argued. Indeed,
it appears that those who own the means of production still exercise a
considerable degree of control over the key processes of production and
distribution. But this still leaves open the question of how far they continue
to constitute a coherent group with significant interests in common.

Again, the available evidence is relatively sparse, but on balance it
tends to suggest that the overall concentration of ownership, coupled with
the expanding network of interlocking corporate shareholdings and reciprocal directorships, has served to sustain a high degree of connectedness
and communality of interests between the various sectors of industrial and
financial capital. Richard Whitley's recent work on Britain, for example,
has demonstrated the extent and the coherence of the connections
between the dominant financial institutions of the City and the leading
industrial corporations. (Whitley, 1974.) As yet, information on the communications industry is somewhat thin on the ground but the evidence
currently emerging suggests that here too the various sectors are increasingly
interconnected, both with each other and with other significant centres of
financial and industrial power.

Besides Reed International, for example, the institutional shareholders
in the Associated Television Corporation also include BPM Holdings, the
Birmingham based newspaper group. Apart from the controlling interests
of the Iliffe family, the other major shareholder in BPM is S. Pearson and
Son Limited, which is linked to Reed International through their joint
ownership of Throgmorton Publications Limited. The result is the pattern
of ordinary share interlocks illustrated in Figure 1.

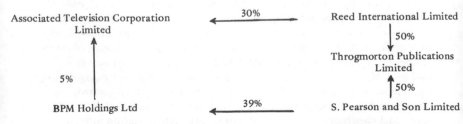

Figure 1 *Interlocking Shareholdings Between Selected British Communications
Companies* (Percentages rounded off to the nearest whole number).

In addition, each of the companies at the corners of the diagram is itself a node in a much more extensive network of interlocking shareholdings and joint enterprises which includes the other four top newspaper publishing groups — Beaverbrook, Associated, News International and the Thomson Organization — and several of the other leading commercial programme contractors including London Weekend Television, The Granada Group and Trident Television. Again, this emerging pattern of inter-media interlocks is not peculiar to Britain but is also characteristic of other advanced capitalist societies. In West Germany, for example, four out of the five leading multi-media conglomerates are linked through cross ownership. (Diederichs, 1973 p. 190.) Not only are the major communications companies increasingly interconnected with each other, however; they are also enmeshed with the dominant financial and industrial concerns.

After examining the shareholders and directors of Britain's first commercial television companies, Clive Jenkins concluded that 'the same banking, insurance and industrial interests that make up the nerve and motor centres of the British economy also control the heartbeats of the commercial television programme contractors.' (Jenkins, 1961 p. 12.) The evidence available on the present situation, although incomplete as yet, suggests that the reallocation of the contracts in 1967 has done little to alter this general assessment. Once again, the British situation is simply an instance of a general pattern which is repeated in varying degrees throughout the advanced capitalist economies. Certainly, the more extensive evidence available on the current situation in the United States, suggests that communications companies are intimately bound up with dominant financial and industrial interests. The Rockefeller controlled Chase Manhattan Bank, for example, has strategic holdings in all three of the major American television networks ranging from 4.2% in RCA to 9.2% in CBS. In the latter case the links are further cemented through interlocking directorships, with no less than seven of the eighteen-man Board having connections with other Rockefeller enterprises. (Network Project, 1973 pp. 27–31.)

Of course, a great deal more detailed work still needs to be done before we have anything like an adequate map of the structure and connections of the communications industries in advanced capitalist societies. Clearly, the various sectors are likely to vary considerably in their degree of interconnectedness, both with each other and with financial and industrial interests. Nor can it be assumed that these interests themselves constitute a coherent block, although Whitley's work goes a long way towards demonstrating this. Certainly the existing studies, sparse as they are, have revealed a consistent tendency towards greater centralization interconnectedness. Taken together, they suggest not only that control over the key processes of resource allocation is still significantly tied to ownership, but that the owning group continue to constitute an identifiable capitalist class with recognizable interests in common. This in turn suggests that Marx's definition of the situation in *The German Ideology* continues not only to pose relevant questions but also to provide a pertinent general framework within which to begin looking for answers. Indeed, far from having been overtaken by history, Marx's propositions have, if anything, been rendered more relevant by recent developments in the structure of capitalism.

Cultural Production: the problem of mediation

In advancing the case for injecting an economic analysis into the sociology of mass communications, we have concentrated on the overall patterns of ownership and control and on the general market situation of the mass media. Too often, however, radical critiques of the communications industries, while accepting such a priority in principle, have failed to follow through by providing detailed accounts of the implications and results of market forces. In particular, two tendencies have appeared.

The first has taken the form of assuming a simple relationship between economic structures and relationships and the nature of the culture produced by the mass media in a capitalist society. Thus, the simple assertion that the media, in Miliband's much quoted phrase, are 'both the expression of a system of domination, and a means of reinforcing it' (Miliband, 1969 p. 221) is given the status of a self-evident truism. Without the context of the sophisticated analysis of the state and of legitimation which Miliband himself offers, this assertion leads to crude and over-simplified accounts of both the mass media and of their legitimizing function. Nedzynski, for example, argues that 'it is evident that those who own and control the mass media are most likely to be the men whose ideological viewpoints are soundly conservative. In the case of newspapers the impact of their views is likely to be immediate and direct . . . .' (Nedzynski, 1973 p. 418.) A similar view has appeared in a recent book on 'the political sociology of the press', in which the author argues that 'the media, together with the state apparatus, act as a kind of secretariat for these common ruling-class interests, and seek to have [them] accepted . . . .' (Hoch, 1974 p. 11.) However, the most influential version of this argument has been developed by a group of French Marxists led by Louis Althusser (Althusser, 1971 pp. 136—7; Poulantzas, 1972 p. 251). They present the mass media, along with the Church, schools, and the family, as 'ideological state apparatuses' whose function is to act as the ideological partners to the repressive apparatuses of the state such as the police and the army.

We are not entirely rejecting these formulations or their conclusions. But there is an important note of caution to be sounded against evacuating history by collating these institutions into a shopping list of undifferentiated state agencies with the same functions and roles whenever and wherever found, and against evacuating sociology by presenting the mass media as a simple relay system for the direct transmission of a ruling ideology to subordinate groups. Such institutions do play important roles in legitimizing an inegalitarian social order, but their relationship to that order is complex and variable and it is necessary to analyse what they do as well as what they are.

The second tendency is to examine critically the output of the mass media, and to infer back to the avowed intentions and deliberations of the producers. Of course, analysis of content is always intended to suggest likely effects on audiences or assumptions by producers; it is its purpose to do so and its limitation that it cannot go beyond hypothesis in either direction. This is a limitation often forgotten, as for example, in much semiotic analysis where a sociological self-sufficiency is seen to lie in the analysis of symbols *per se*. Occasionally, this form of critical analysis is tempted to obliterate entirely any active interpretation or awareness at the level of production. Rock, working entirely from a textual reading of newspapers, infers that there are institutional imperatives that provide the categories comprising 'news sense': 'If journalists themselves are unable to articulate those categories, it is perhaps because they do not fully understand the larger contours of the context in which they work.' (Rock, 1973 p. 75.) As well as being alarmingly arrogant, this conclusion fails to convince because it is quite divorced from any investigation of the actual institutional imperatives, organizational routines, and working exigencies which do indeed explain a great deal of news production.

These two tendencies both underplay the problem of mediation which so preoccupied Sartre in his criticism of 'lazy Marxism' — which tends to make 'real men into the symbols of its myths' instead of erecting a 'hierarchy of mediations which would . . . grasp the process which produces the person and his product . . . .' (Sartre, 1968 pp. 53, 56.)

Most studies of occupational practice in the media, however, have leaned to the purely descriptive and have avoided or neglected any relationship between, on the one hand, the sociological problems of legitimation and social order, and on the other the immediate observation of a work situation. The best of these studies, such as Tunstall's work on specialist correspondents or Cantor's on Hollywood producers, draw on research traditions in occupational sociology whose first priority is the clear analysis of an occupational group, without recourse to theories placing the group in context, as occupying a strategic role in the class structure (see the overview by Elliott, Chapter 6, in Section II of this volume). This is not to devalue such studies, but simply to argue that they do not supply the answer to the problem of mediation left unanswered by the two tendencies described earlier.

The relationships need to be drawn at two levels. The first is situational, linking work situation and market situation. Changing market conditions affect the resources available to a media organization and the extent to which creativity is hedged about by accountancy. The resources available will change styles and ambitions; demand for new technology and techniques will come as response to varying economic pressure. Very often work styles and practices which are especially favoured are virtues made of necessity.

The second level of mediation is normative, linking the general set of values and frame within which culture is set to the particular norms of occupational practice; in a phrase, linking the ruling ideology to occupational ideologies. The link is seldom complete and cannot be analysed solely within the context of the media. Beliefs about the inevitability of a given social order and about the limits to acceptable social practice and values are diffused throughout the social structure. In a sense, what needs explaining is how oppositional values ever emerge. But within the media it is essential to show just how the relationships work. The first task is to spell out the nature of the ruling ideology, and to specify the propositions and assumptions of which it is composed. Secondly, the appearance and entrenchment of such propositions and assumptions in media output needs to be clearly demonstrated. Thirdly, the norms which guide the process of production; standards, expectations, routine evaluations and implicit limitations, have to be made explicit and related again to these more general propositions and assumptions. For example, if news coverage of industrial relations is cumulatively unsympathetic to militancy, radicalism or union activism in general, is it simply because of the hostility of capitalist media entrepreneurs or even anti-socialist sentiment among industrial relations correspondents? A fuller explanation must look for the complex of inter-relationships between pervasive definitions of industry, the Nation, responsibility and the like, with trends in industrial news practice, the conventions of interview, film and narrative, and so on (see Hartmann, forthcoming). We have suggested some relationships of this kind in an earlier article (Murdock and Golding, 1974).

The methods for demonstrating mediation are both historical and sociological. Historically, the evolution of an occupational ideology can be shown to emerge from the changing market and work situation of that occupation. A sociologically informed history of journalism, for example, would focus on the emergence of beliefs about objectivity, impartiality, accuracy, brevity, style and so on in the context of an economic and social history of the press in the nineteenth century. To complement this, we need a sociology of media occupation which looks beyond them to social structural questions of order and change.

Economy and Ideology: market pressure and cultural domination

Our first aim in this chapter has been to outline the main patterns of economic control in the media, and to suggest their centrality in a full sociological analysis of mass communications. In turning briefly now to some of the consequences for cultural production, we wish to stress the sequential logic of examining economic structures prior to their cultural products. It is only by situating cultural products within the nexus of material interests which circumscribe their creation and distribution that their range and content can be fully explained. While there is little space here to follow the argument through in detail, we can briefly suggest the directions it might take. In doing so it is necessary to note how much work remains to be done.

Most studies concerned with media output have not been concerned to discover its ideological underpinning, while those that have, have concentrated almost entirely on news, and have consequently neglected the main dramatic, fictional and entertainment forms which make up the bulk of most people's media fare. As a result, we lack a comprehensive and detailed map of the way in which class stratification is presented and explained in the contemporary mass media. This gap, however, been filled by a good deal of speculation, more often than not, based on rather selective and cursory 'readings' of media imagery. A number of critics, for example, have argued that the prevailing imagery tends to conceal the centrality and pervasiveness of class inequalities by, first, emphasizing other social divisions such as age, sex and ethnicity, and secondly by evoking the communality of interests that supposedly stem from shared citizenship of a single nation state (e.g. Poulantzas, 1973 pp. 214–5). Others have maintained that where images of class do appear, they tend to focus on the sphere of consumption rather than on the sphere of production and to stress the differences of consumer taste and leisure styles rather than structural inequalities in market and work situation in which these differences are rooted. Moreover, these critics argue, by emphasizing people's shared situation as consumers and their nominal access to leisure commodities and life styles, this insistent imagery of consumerism conceals and compensates for the persistence of radical inequalities in the distribution of wealth, work conditions and life chances (see for example: Berger, 1972 p. 149; Barthes, 1973 p. 141). These and similar conjectures offer fruitful starting points for an exploration of the basic ideological categories underlying media imagery, the implicit messages about class and power which Adorno called the 'hidden meaning' of mass communications. (Adorno, 1954.) But they are only a bald beginning. A very great deal more systematic work needs to be done across the whole range of output before we have anything like a full account of how far and how deeply dominant assumptions are embedded in media imagery, of the variety of forms through which they are expressed, and of the extent of counter instances where dissenting or oppositional perspectives are presented. This analysis in turn will need to be backed up by detailed studies of the way in which imagery is actually produced and shaped by economic forces.

In general terms, however, there are two consequences for cultural production of the economic processes we have outlined. First the range of material available will tend to decline as market forces exclude all but the commercially successful. While this trend is not uniform, (for example the number of book titles has until recently continued to increase despite concentration among publishers), it has generally been the case that as concentration and diversification advance, so less and less voices survive in each media sector. The second general consequence is that this evolutionary process is not random, but systematically excludes those voices lacking economic power or resources. This process of deletion is by no means random however. On the contrary, the underlying logic of cost operates systematically, consolidating the position of groups already established in the main mass-media markets and excluding those groups who lack the capital base required for successful entry. Thus the voices which survive will largely belong to those least likely to criticize the prevailing distribution of wealth and power. Conversely, those most likely to challenge these arrangements are unable to publicize their dissent or opposition because they cannot command the resources needed for effective communication to a broad audience.

Of course, this exclusion is not total. Small inroads can be made at the margins. Newspapers based in political organizations for example, are able to survive because they are subsidized on both costs and revenues. Costs are reduced by voluntary help with production, distribution and selling, while revenues may be boosted by direct grants from party funds and by donations from individual members. However, these subsidies are unlikely to be sufficient to enable these publications to reach the threshold of expansion into the mainstream. Hence they are obliged to serve primarily as rallying points for the committed rather than as means of promoting alternative views among a wider audience. In the absence of a coherent organizational base, however, marginal media are unlikely even to survive for very long as the brief life span of non-party papers of the left like Seven Days and Ink illustrates.

Unable to sustain their own channels of effective communication, dissident or alternative views are equally unable to gain a significant foothold in the mainstream commercial media and for sound economic reasons. Given the insistent pressure to maximize audiences and revenues, there is not surprisingly a consistent tendency for the commercial media to avoid the unpopular and tendentious and to draw instead on the values and assumptions which are most familiar and most widely legitimated, which almost inevitably means those which flow authoritatively downwards through the social structure. Hence because dissenting and oppositional views do not fit very easily into the prevailing frameworks of imagery and expression, they tend to be excluded. Once again, however, there are exceptions to this general tendency at the margins. Within broadcasting, for example, recent years have seen a proliferation of participatory programmes such as 'phone-ins', studio shows where the audience joins in the discussion, and programmes produced by non-professional groups. These developments represent an attempt to accommodate the mounting pressure from excluded and under-represented groups for greater access to scarce communications facilities. Although welcome, these sorts of incorporative strategies are subject to several crucial limitations. By and large they are allocated only very limited amounts of time and resources and consequently they are easily swamped by the volume of mainstream output. Moreover, the fact that the presentation of oppositional views is largely confined to these contexts means that they are implicitly labelled as 'minority' enthusiasms, which further reinforces their marginality and hinders them in gaining wider credibility.

In general then, the expression of dissenting or challenging views rooted in interests unable themselves to support media, are also largely absent from the spectrum of legitimated views and ideas provided by the major media.

We can briefly illustrate how these two processes occur. First, pressures of rising costs cause all media to attempt to maximize their audience. This may be achieved by expanding an undifferentiated audience — a film which is a box-office hit remains so no matter who the customers are — or by maximizing a particular target audience. The latter strategy is conducted by advertising-based media who seek the maximum audience in higher spending groups, or among specialist consumer groups who are the targets of manufacturers of particular ranges of products. Media unable to maximize their audiences in either of these ways must decline and eventually disappear, however desired they may be by their remaining audience. Thus newspapers serving a largely working-class readership must achieve much higher sales than those serving groups with greater purchasing power. Consequently they become unviable with circulations several times that of a middle-class paper. Similarly, to be commercially viable, local media have to serve populations larger than any meaningful sociological definition of a community. Thus, smaller poorer communities must remain unserved by local media except as part of larger populations. Small, locality based newspapers are unable to satisfy this unmet need. Unlike the organization-based media referred to earlier, such newspapers have no revenue subsidy and thus have difficulty in competing with larger commercial local papers. While they are able to keep costs down by voluntary labour or cheap production methods, this is at the expense of remaining technically inferior to the papers they seek to challenge or complement and therefore relatively unattractive to potential readers.

In order to maximize audiences, production must minimize risks by concentrating on the familiar and on formulae which are as similar as possible to the tried and tested. Hence innovation is muted since it entails the risk of offending and losing audiences, and curtails opportunities for forward planning. Thus the long-running radio and television soap-opera was evolved to capture a loyal audience, whose size and composition were predictable far enough ahead to facilitate campaign planning by advertisers. Similarly, the two chains which dominate British film exhibitions rely on careful selection of likely audience maximizers. Since the number of cinemas has massively declined, the range of material available to cinema-goers is severely constrained, as anyone comparing the reviews of London film critics with the film column in their local paper could testify.

Audience maximization is the goal of both news and entertainment, indeed the two categories increasingly fuse as the news media adopt audience holding and presentation as criteria in preparing their products. In the case of newspapers this has been exacerbated as the press has faced declining sales and a steady reduction in the number of titles. In the provincial press the move to local monopoly has seen the decline of morning papers from 28 in 1948 to 18 in 1974, and from 1,307 weekly and bi-weekly papers in 1948 to 1,121 in 1974. In this situation, dissenting or oppositional views are eliminated, not merely by the disappearance of organs willing to voice them, but by the economic needs of those that survive. Hirsch and Gordon have described the process thus: 'When a small number of firms compete, there is a tendency for all of them to aim at the centre and for their products to be different only in the incidentals . . . . The increasing conformity of the British quality press, in style and in substance, is an example of this fundamental tendency of oligopolistic competition to serve the centre of the market at the expense of minority tastes.' (Hirsch and Gordon, 1975 p. 45.) We would go further and extend this analysis to the national press as a whole. It is important, too, to realize that rather than 'minority tasks' we are talking of minority political views. What is excluded by the convergence to the centre (itself a dynamic position) is the voice of the politically powerless.

Indeed, looking at the specific area of electoral partisanship, Seymour-Ure has demonstrated a steady decline in overt, strident partisanship in Fleet Street since the war. (Seymour-Ure, 1974 Chapter 8.) Similarly, in the field of industrial news reporting, Hartmann's recent study has shown how the range of images presented by the press on the central institution of industry, and on the nature of 'industrial relations', are contained within a set of consensual assumptions about capital-labour relations.

Sectional interests are disguised by concentration on the national interest rather than the competing claims arising from structured inequality. (Hartmann, 1975/5.) In general, the needs of production, limitations of cost, and concern for audiences, produce news in which the world is portrayed as fragmented and unchanging, and in which dissent and opposition appear as ephemeral, peripheral or irrational. News becomes palliative and comforting, intentionally undisturbing and unthreatening, focusing on institutions of consensus maintenance and the handling of social order (Golding *et al.*, forthcoming.)

Two further strategies for audience maximization entail getting the maximum mileage out of single cultural products. The first strategy is that of multi-marketing or spin-offs, whereby successful products in one medium are converted into a form amenable to marketing in another medium. Thus, successful television series become feature films. Films provide best-selling records, paperbacks become films and television series, and so on. Second, products are recycled and become successful at different points in time. The market for feature films on television, the sustained nostalgia market in records (coupled with the planned regeneration of enthusiasm for more recent successes such as the Beatles) are examples of fruitful expansion of cultural consumption with minimal cost and minimum innovation. A third dimension is added to these two audience-maximizing strategies by the development of international markets, elevating even higher the scale of operations required for cultural production while lowering the possibility for diversity because of the need for a product which can satisfy several markets.

In general, then, the determining context for production is always that of their market. In seeking to maximize this market, products must draw on the most widely legitimated central core values while rejecting the dissenting voice or the incompatiable objection to a ruling myth. The need for easily understood, popular, formulated, undisturbing, assimilable fictional material is at once a commercial imperative and an aesthetic recipe.

Conclusion

In this chapter we have suggested that major lacunae exist in both the sociology of mass communications and of stratification. In particular, we have drawn attention to the need for an analysis of patterns of ownership and control of media industries and the implications of such an analysis for discussion of the form and stability of a ruling class. We have only been able here to suggest the directions this work might take. However, we would argue that such an approach is vital for a fuller understanding of the dynamics of class relations in a capitalist society, and to restore the sociology of mass communications to a more relevant, and indeed central, position in sociological inquiry.

References

Aaronovitch, Sam, and Sawyer, Malcolm, 1975: *Big Business: Theoretical and Empirical Aspects of Concentration and Mergers in the United Kingdom*, London: Macmillan.

Adorno, Theodore W., 1954: 'Television and the Patterns of Mass Culture', *The Quarterly of Film, Radio and Television* 8. Reprinted in W. Schramm (Ed.), *Mass Communications*. University of Illinois Press, 1960. 1967: *Prisms*. London. Neville Spearman.

Allen, Michael, 1976: 'Management Control in the Large Corporation: Comment on Zeitlin'. *American Journal of Sociology*. 81 (4), pp. 885—94.

Althusser, L., 1971: *Lenin and Philosophy and Other Essays*. London: New Left Books.

Barthes, Roland, 1973: *Mythologies*. London: Paladin.

Bell, Daniel, 1976: *The Cultural Contradictions of Capitalism*. London: Heinemann

Berger, John, 1972: *Ways of Seeing*. Harmondsworth: Penguin.

Blumberg, Werner, 1972: *Karl Marx: An Illustrated Biography*. London: New Left Books.

Bottomore, Tom, 1975: *Marxist Sociology*. London: Macmillan

Bottomore, T. B. and Rubel, Maximilien, 1963: *Karl Marx: Selected Writings in Sociology and Social Philosophy*. Harmondsworth: Penguin.

Burgess, G. J. and Webb, A. J., 1974: 'The Profits of British Industry'. *Lloyds Bank Review* 112 (April), pp. 1—18.

Diederichs, Helmut H., 1973: *Konzentration in den Massenmedien: Systematischer Überblick zur Situation in der BRD*. Munich: Carl Hanser Verlag.

Downing, John, 1975: *Grave-Diggers' Difficulties: Ideology and Working Class Opposition in Advanced Capitalist Societies*. Paper presented to the Annual Conference of the British Sociological Association. University of Kent at Canterbury, Spring 1975.

EIU (Economist Intelligence Unit) 1966: 'Special Report No. 2: Gramophone Records', *Retail Business* 98 (April), pp. 20—32. 1970: 'Special Report No. 1: Books Part 1', *Retail Business* 149 (July), pp. 13—32. 1971: 'Special Report: Gramophone Records', *Retail Business* 159 (May), pp. 18—34. 1972: 'Special Report: Cinemas', *Retail Business* 177 (November).

Enzensberger, Hans Magnus, 1974: *The Consciousness Industry: On Literature, Politics and the Media*. New York: The Seabury Press.

George, Kenneth D., 1975: 'A Note on Changes in Industrial Concentration in the United Kingdom'. *The Economic Journal* 85, March, pp. 124—8.

George, Kenneth D. and Silbertson, Audbrey, 1975: 'The Causes and Effects of Mergers', *Scottish Journal of Political Economy* Vol. XXII (2) June, pp. 179—93.

Giddens, Anthony, 1973: *The Class Structure of the Advanced Societies.* London: Hutchinson.

Golding, P., Elliott, P. *et al.* (forthcoming): *Making the News.* University of Leicester, 1976.

Goldthorpe, John H., 1972: 'Class, Status and Party in Modern Britain: Some Recent Interpretations, Marxist and Marxisant'. *European Journal of Sociology* XIII (2) pp. 342—72.

Hall, Stuart, 1972: *The External—Internal Dialectic in Broadcasting: Television's Double Bind.* Paper delivered to the Manchester Broadcasting Seminar, February 1972.

Halloran, James D., 1974: *Mass Media and Society: The Challenge of Research.* Leicester University Press.

Hartmann, P., 1975/6: 'Industrial Relations in the News Media'. *Journal of Industrial Relations* 6(4) (Winter) pp. 4—18.

(forthcoming). *The News Media and Industrial Relations.* University of Leicester: Centre for Mass Communications Research.

Hirsch, F. and Gordon, D., 1975: *Newspaper Money.* London: Hutchinson.

Hoch, Paul, 1974: *The Newspaper Game.* London: Calder and Boyars.

Hood, Stuart, 1972: 'The Politics of Television'. In D. McQuail (Ed.), *Sociology of Mass Communications.* Harmondsworth: Penguin.

Jenkins, Clive, 1961: *Power Behind the Screen: Ownership, Control and Motivation in British Commercial Television.* London: Macgibbon and Kee.

Mann, Michael, 1973: *Consciousness and Action Among the Western Working Class.* London: Macmillan.

Marx, Karl, 1975: *Early Writings* (Ed. L. Colletti). Harmondsworth: Penguin.

Marx, Karl and Engels, Frederick, 1938: *The German Ideology* (trans. R. Pascal). London: Lawrence and Wishart.

Moyle, John, 1971: *The Pattern of Ordinary Share Ownership 1957—1970.* Cambridge University Press.

Murdock, Graham (forthcoming): Course Unit 10. Patterns of Ownership: Questions of Control. Open University. Course DE353, *Mass Communication and Society.*

Murdock, Graham and Golding, Peter, 1974: 'For a Political Economy of Mass Communications'. In Ralph Miliband and John Saville (Eds.), *The Socialist Register 1973.* London: Merlin Press, pp. 205—234.

Murdock, Graham and Golding, Peter (forthcoming): *Cultural Capitalism: The Political Economy of Mass Communications.* London: Routledge and Kegan Paul.

Nedzynski, S., 1973: 'Inequalities in Access to Communication Facilities for Working Class Organizations'. In Gerbner, G. *et al.* (Eds.), *Communications Technology and Social Policy.* New York: John Wiley and Sons, pp. 413—23.

Network Project 1973: *Notebook Number Two: Directory of the Networks.* New York: The Network Project.

Parkin, Frank, 1972: *Class Inequality and Political Order.* London: Paladin.

PEP (Political and Economic Planning), 1955: 'Ownership of the Press'. *Planning* XXI (338), November, pp. 209—224.

PIB (National Board for Prices and Income), 1970: *Report No. 156: Costs and Revenues of Independent Television Companies.* London: HMSO Cmnd 4524.

Poulantzas, Nicos, 1972: 'The Problem of the Capitalist State'. In R. Blackburn (Ed.), *Ideology in Social Science.* London: Fontana.

1973: *Political Power and Social Classes.* London: New Left Books.

Press Council, 1970: *The Press and the People: 17th Annual Report of The Press Council.* London: The Press Council.

Rock, Paul, 1973: 'News as Eternal Recurrence'. In S. Cohen and J. Young (Eds.), *The Manufacture of News.* London: Constable, pp. 73—80.

Royal Commission on the Press, 1976: *Interim Report: The National Newspaper Industry.* London: HMSO, Cmnd. 6433.

Royal Commission on the Distribution of Income and Wealth, 1975: *Report No. 2: Income from Companies and its Distribution.* London: HMSO, Cmnd 6172.

Sartre, Jean-Paul, 1968: *Search for a Method.* New York: Vintage Books (original French edition 1960).

Seymour-Ure, C., 1974: *The Political Impact of Mass Media.* London: Constable.

Stanworth, Philip H., 1974: 'Property, Class and the Corporate Elite'. In Ivor Crew (Ed.), *British Political Sociology Yearbook, Volume 1: Elites in Western Democracy.* London: Croom Helm, pp. 243—63.

Thayer, Lee (Ed.), 1974: 'Editor's Introduction', *Communication* 1 (1), pp. 1—4.

Tunstall, Jeremy, 1970: Introduction in Jeremy Tunstall (Ed.), *Media Sociology: A Reader.* London: Constable, pp. 1—38.

Westergaard, John and Resler, Henrietta, 1975: *Class in a Capitalist Society: A Study of Contemporary Britain.* London: Heinemann.

Whitley, Richard, 1974: 'The City and Industry: The Directors of Large Companies, Their Characteristics and Connections'. In Stanworth, Philip and Giddens, Anthony (Eds.), *Elites and Power in British Society.* Cambridge University Press, pp. 65—80.

Williams, Raymond, 1973: 'Base and Superstructure in Marxist Cultural Theory'. *New Left Review* 82, November—December, pp. 3—16.

Zeitlin, Maurice, 1974: 'Corporate Ownership and Control: The Large Corporation and the Capitalist Class'. *American Journal of Sociology* 79 (5), pp. 1073—1119.

1976: 'On Class Theory of the Large Corporation: Response to Allen', *American Journal of Sociology*, 81 (4), pp. 894—903.

2

The Organization of Public Opinion

Tom Burns

One principal component of virtually all interpretations of the role of press and broadcasting in politics concerns the ambiguity of that role; it acts either as the voice, reflector, or the organ of 'public opinion' or it is the controller, regulator or even creator of public opinion. Some writers, indeed, treat it — in different places — as both. This essay is an attempt to fathom this ambiguity by treating the role in historical perspective. The British experience is used for this purpose, partly because the historical context is more familiar; but principally because it serves in many ways either as a paradigm or as a compendium of the ways in which the role has been played out in western societies. (Aspinall, 1949 p. 1.)

From the very beginning, controversy about broadcasting has been dominated by strong and almost universally held beliefs about its immense potentialities as a means of influencing, and possibly even controlling or directing, public opinion. This belief rests on a single and manifest truth: broadcasting makes it possible for one man to address an audience of millions, indeed, nowadays, of hundreds of millions. For the first two or three decades the power of broadcasting was seen as vested in its possibilities as an instrument of propaganda. Indeed, the very first use of broadcasting made in Britain was the foreign broadcasts operated directly by the Foreign Office immediately after the end of the 1914—18 war. Twenty years later, the BBC's European services were begun to counter the foreign broadcasting services mounted by Germany, Italy and Russia. After the Second World War, claims about the propaganda power of broadcasting, both political and commercial, tended to become more modest. Even so, the fact of the sheer pervasiveness of broadcasting still carried with it the belief that it is powerful *because* it is pervasive, and a corresponding fear of the ways in which, and of the groups by whom, that power might be exercised.

More recently, fear of the persuasive power of broadcasting over 'the masses' has tended to slacken, much in the way that fear of broadcasting as propaganda faded earlier on. Neither fear, though, has entirely disappeared. It is revived from time to time by claims still being made by interested parties about the effects of propaganda and persuasion through broadcasting. Social scientists and specialist writers on mass communications find it equally difficult to surrender the belief altogether, despite the accumulation of almost entirely negative findings from research over thirty-five years into the extent to which broadcasting actually influences political opinion and voting behaviour. In retrospect, concludes Denis McQuail, 'the expectation of great persuasive power from the new media has been largely misplaced' (McQuail, 1969), and many others have reached much the same conclusion. Yet McQuail, two or three pages away from that statement, asserts that the media 'are largely responsible for the creation of public opinion' The Langs, equally short of supporting evidence for the political persuasiveness of television, nevertheless conclude that 'The media also structure a very real political environment which people can know about only through the media. Information about this environment is hard to escape. It filters through and affects even persons who are not directly exposed to the news.' (Lang and Lang, 1968 p. 305.)

I

We are dealing, in fact, with a set of beliefs much older than broadcasting. During its own formative years (which extended from the beginning of the eighteenth century until well into the nineteenth), the press was regarded with even greater alarm and suspicion. Windham, says Aspinall, laid most of the blame for the mutinies at Spithead and the Nore at the doors of the press, and Burke saw in it 'the grand instrument of the subversion of order, morals, religion, and human society itself'. (Aspinall, 1949 p.1.)

To draw on Aspinall's opening pages again, he quotes Sir James Macintosh remarking in 1803 on the great change which had taken place in the discussion of public affairs: 'The multiplication of newspapers has produced a gradual revolution in our government by increasing the number of those who exercise some sort of judgment on public affairs' (Aspinall, 1949, p. 1) and cites Brougham's considered assessment in 1831 of the importance of the press in the pre-Reform era: 'it alone rivalled the House of Commons, in that it was the only organ of public opinion capable of dictating to the Government, since nothing else could speak the sense of the people.' (Aspinall, 1949, p. 3.) This is the press in the full panoply of its classic Fourth Estate role, and it is no historical accident that this particular term was coined to designate the political role of the press towards the end of the eighteenth century.

It was probably Burke who first used the term to signify the political power (a usurped and malignant power) of the press, and certainly Burke would have relished and exploited the full historical irony only partially evoked by the words, 'the fourth estate', when they first gained currency. For, during the fifty years (1780—1830) when the unreformed Parliament assumed the political stance, the attitudes, the strategy and the legislative and administrative tactics of the absolutist *anciens régimes*, it was the press which took up the original role from which the third estate proper, the Commons, had apparently abdicated.

Herein lies the key to the perpetual ambivalence which dogs the political role of the press and, later, of broadcasting. For the Commons itself had begun life as the spokesman — and merely spokesman — of public opinion. The primary purpose of including representatives of the *bourgeois* and of propertied countrymen (the burgesses and knights of the shire) in the Model Parliament of 1295 and in subsequent Parliaments was 'to inform the crown about local conditions and help it to influence public opinion'. (Lapsley, 1936.) They discharged this function, moreover, by acting as the bearers, intermediaries, or discussants of the large number of petitions for relief or remedy presented to the king in Parliament — petitions of a kind that, 'whatever their origin, were held to be of interest to the community at large'. (Lapsley, 1936, p. 5.) This particular function, what is more, seems to have been anterior certainly to any legislative powers and probably to any contributory legislative function which the Commons later, along with barons, churchmen and the king's counsellors, ministers and servants were called upon to discharge. In fact, the earliest discernible functions of Parliament are much more those of what might be called a national jury of public opinion than of the supreme body of legislative, executive and judicial power which Parliament became five centuries later. For Edward I, summoning representatives of the Commons to a parliament provided an effective instrument for consulting — and for influencing — public opinion. It was only when the voices of that public opinion became organized themselves, during the following century, that the Commons began to encroach on the legislative powers of the king and his council. But such power as the Commons acquired then and later rested on the validity of its claim to speak for the people — to be, in fact, public opinion made articulate. By the eighteenth century, the Commons was not only the voice of the people; constitutionally, it was the people:

The British Parliament had always been, was then (1789) and remains now, a sovereign and constituent assembly. It can make and unmake any and every law, change the form of government or the succession to the crown, interfere with the course of justice, extinguish the most sacred private rights of the citizen. Between it and the people at large there is no legal distinction, because the whole plenitude of the people's rights and powers resides in it, just as if the whole nation were present within the chamber where it sits. In point of legal theory it is the nation. (Bryce, 1914 pp. 35—6.)

Applied to an age which extended from the Black Act of 1723 to the Combination Acts of 1799 and 1800 and beyond to Peterloo and the Six Acts, such a statement stands condemned as the most cynical of paradoxes.

So it is. But it is a paradox which actions and events within the framework of the British political system worked, ultimately, towards accommodating rather than emphasizing, in much the same way as they did in the parallel case of the law. (Thompson, 1975 p. 269.) The political role of the press evolved as it did during the eighteenth century largely *because* the practice of Parliament and the relationship of Parliament to the commons departed so grossly from the constitutional principles on which the authority and powers of Parliament were claimed to rest.

The first politically flavoured journals, towards the beginning of the century: Defoe's *Review*, Tutchin's *Observator*, Swift's *Examiner* and, later, Bolingbroke's *Craftsman*, were merely indicators of the emergence of parliamentary parties (not the critical organs of a politically-minded public that Habermas saw in them (Habermas, 1965 p. 72)). Such journals did undoubtedly play a part in the articulation of distinctive principles and policies for the parties of Government and of Opposition, but it was not until the 1760s that the extra-parliamentary political role of the press becomes visible. Until that time, as Blackstone's *Commentaries*, written in that same decade of the 1760s, indicate, freedom of the press meant no more — and no less — than freedom of speech, one of the three basic constitutional rights secured by the 'Glorious Revolution' of 1689 (the other two being the right of public meeting and the right to petition Parliament). In formal, constitutional, terms, freedom of the press had been established in 1695 with the expiration — at the express instance of the House of Commons — of the Printing Act, by which press censorship had been maintained. Anyone was free, thereafter, to publish anything he liked, but it was in law as well as in practice a heavily qualified freedom, as Blackstone made clear:

The liberty of the press is indeed essential to the nature of a free state; but this consists in laying no *previous* restraints on publication, and not in freedom from censure of a criminal matter when published. Every freeman has an undoubted right to lay what sentiments he pleases before the public: to forbid this, is to destroy the freedom of the press: but if he published what is improper, mischievous, or illegal, he must take the consequence of his own temerity . . . . Thus the will of individuals is left free; the abuse only of that free will is the object of legal punishment. Neither is any restraint hereby laid upon freedom of thought or inquiry: liberty of private sentiment is still left; the disseminating, the making public, of bad sentiment, destructive to the ends of society, is the crime which society corrects. (Blackstone, 1857 pp. 161—2.)

Of course, the decision as to what was 'improper, mischievous, or illegal', or which sentiments were 'bad' or 'destructive to the ends of society' rested with Parliament and the court — as John Wilkes was discovering at the very time that Blackstone was writing. The significance of Wilkes's eventual victory in 1771, when the House of Commons tacitly abandoned its right to forbid reporting and even prevent publication of its proceedings, does not lie in any shift of the boundary between legitimate freedom and illegitimate abuse of freedom to which Blackstone's words refer; it lies in the acknowledgment of the existence of extra-parliamentary political interests and processes. In a way, 1771 is as crucial a date as 1295. Then, the king in Council — the supreme executive, judicial and legislative authority — sought to inform himself about the condition, needs, opinions and desires of his subjects by summoning representatives of the Commons to his Parliament. In 1771, Parliament, now itself the supreme executive, judicial and legislative authority, acknowledged the right of the common people at large to be informed about the needs, opinions and desires expressed in Parliament.

But the confinement of the role of the press to serving as a 'medium' for purveying information about Parliament to the people was even more short-lived than had been the role of the Commons in merely purveying information about the people to the king in Council. Moreover, significant as the date, 1771, became for later developments, the impact of the change it represented was hardly noticeable at the time. After all, there were only nine daily newspapers published in great Britain in the early 1780s; no less than five of these were advertising journals; in the other four, news filled less than half their rather scanty column space. Yet there was a change, and a change of decisive importance in the development of the political role of the press. Parliamentary reports and political information formed an integral part of the staple of such news as was purveyed. Second, and more important still, in acting as 'media' for the dissemination of this kind of news, newspapers tended to assume the stance of independence of political parties.

Thus, albeit tacitly, two fundamental principles were established before, to quote Aspinall, 'the progress of revolutionary doctrines in France, the outbreak of hostilities on the Continent, the threat of war between Great Britain and France, and the existence of much popular discontent at home, made the *regulation* [my emphasis] of public opinion a matter of prime importance to Pitt's Government in 1792'. (Aspinall, 1949.) First, the very existence of newspapers, and the nature of their contents, presumed the existence of a public, political, opinion external to the small and enclosed world of parliamentary politics. Second, their role was assumed to be that not merely of purveying information but of articulating and expressing public opinion; in so far as they were successful — i.e., in so far as their sales grew, and their views were taken seriously by government ministers — they were not only the 'independent and responsible organs of public opinion' they claimed to be, but *organizers* of public opinion. That they were taken to be no less than this is plain from the quantity of money spent by the Government in buying editors and journalists,[1] founding new newspapers

1 cf. Aspinall. No less than nine of Aspinall's sixteen chapters are filled with his account of the extent to which Government was involved in subsidies and bribery,

and subsidizing others, and harrassing its critics. Money was not the only weapon. The Attorney-General could take proceedings against anyone on the grounds of information laid before the Crown ('*ex officiis*'); the 1799 Act required every printing press to be registered and the names and addresses of the printer and publisher of every book, pamphlet, poster and newspaper to be recorded. Superimposed on the libel laws alone, the 1799 Act put a powerful instrument into the hands of government for suppressing news or views which it chose to regard as contrary to the 'national interest'; but, beyond this, an act passed the year before, in 1798, had provided more ample grounds for proceedings: persons printing or publishing any 'matters tending to excite hatred and contempt for the person of His Majesty and of the Constitution and Government established in these Kingdoms' were liable to a year's imprisonment.

As in other cases, the rapid accumulation of suppressive measures is an index of the strength, frequency and variety of the activities they are designed to suppress as much as of the anxiety and determination of the government. There was plenty to be anxious about. In 1793,

A convention met in Edinburgh where delegates from popular societies made preparations for secret meetings of delegates to deal with a foreign landing or resist government interference. For this three of the leaders . . . were transported. The response of the radicals was to issue appeals in 1794 for a further national convention. In doing so they obviously challenged the authority of parliament. However moderate their proposals for reform, they were, in proposing to meet on a national scale, claiming to be a rival body expressing the will of the people better than the House of Commons. (Watson, 1960 p. 359.)

Such conventions were difficult and expensive to organize, and rare even before they became illegal. Hence the importance of the radical press — pamphlets as well as newspapers — which not only were easier and less dangerous instruments for articulating and promoting opposition and protest than were meetings, but could themselves provide the occasion for regular, semi-clandestine, meetings, it being common practice for them to be read aloud in public houses and coffee houses throughout the country. 'The "Jacobinical" Societies of United Irishmen, United Scotsmen, United Englishmen, United Britons and the London Corresponding Society had been publishing and circulating large quantities of "irreligious, treasonable and seditious" literature among the "lower classes of the community, either gratis or at very low prices, and with an activity and

---

in discriminatory taxation, and in legislation and court proceedings in its endeavours to suppress or control the dissident press. The titles of the chapters themselves are illuminating. Government Subsidies (England); Government subsidies (Ireland); Indirect Subsidies (Advertisements); Newspapers and Pamphlets Circulated Gratis; Treasury 'Hirelings'; Assistance from the Post Office; Official Intelligence for Friendly Newspapers; The Government 'Instructs' the Press.

profusion beyond all former example".' (Aspinall, 1949.) As early as
1793, a minister claimed that almost all newspapers 'were in the pay of
the Jacobins'. Even when the threat, real or imagined, of Jacobin
revolution had passed, *Black Dwarf*, Cobbett's *Political Register* and
other journals kept alive the movement for radical reform which the
Opposition tacitly disowned for a whole generation after 1797, when
the Whigs, having 'nailed their colours to the mast', in Trevelyan's phrase,
with the forlorn gesture of a parliamentary motion for reform, 'proceeded
to desert the ship'.

II

The ambivalence which besets the political role of the press is integral
to it and therefore inescapable. But at least around 1800 the line which
could be drawn between the press which the opposition, both Parliamentary and radical, regarded as a medium for the 'expression' of public
opinion, and the press which the government saw as a means of 'regulating'
it was clear, and individual newspapers could be identified as lying on one
side of the line or the other. Later in the century, while Lord Grey could
write that, 'newspapers could be divided into two classes: those which
sought to mould public opinion, and those which took their tone from
it', in either case, as he had good cause to know, newspapers chose which
political side they pleased to support; in 1830 there was scarcely one
newspaper which found a good word to say for the Tories, and ten years
later most of them were against the Whigs. (Aspinall, 1949.)

There are other ambivalences. Those newspapers which became profitable became, eventually, financially independent of Treasury subsidies
and party payments and shed their party ties; the people's press, which
had flourished when it had been bullied in the courts and persecuted by
high taxation, dwindled into extinction in the very years, from 1825 to
1861, when restrictions in size were removed, tax on pamphlets repealed,
advertisement duty reduced and stamp duty and paper duty finally abolished.

So the axis, along which the antithetical positions visible in the role
of the press are drawn, itself changes. In the twentieth century this applies
with equal force, though in different ways, to broadcasting as well as to
the press. In the 1920s, mass circulation 'popular' newspapers had long
filled the vacuum left by the demise of the people's press. Along with
popular weeklies, pulp fiction and children's comics, they had subverted
the role of the printed word as an instrument of religious, cultural, social
and political enlightenment; in a later view, indeed, they had become
elements in, and supporters of, the institutional structure of established
authority and of economic and political power which it had once been
the primary task of the press, and its chief boast, to expose, discuss and
criticize. Geoffrey Crowther, in his history of *The Economist*, was able
to say with some justice that, 'The printed word has always been the

organization operating, as previously, very much as an ordinary private firm under the provision of the Companies' Act, but consisting of a number of Commissioners, 'persons of judgment and independence, free of commitments, with business acumen and experience in affairs', who would act corporately as Trustees for the national interest. An alternative arrangement, also canvassed by the Crawford Committee, was that the 'British Broadcasting Commission' should be set up by act of parliament. Mitchell-Thomson rejected both these proposals, the first because 'it would lack a certain amount of status and dignity' and the second because the Corporation might be invested 'in the mind of the public with the idea that in some way it is a creature of Parliament and connected with political activity'. (Mitchell-Thomson, 1926 pp. 4466—8.)

Having argued the case for giving the new Corporation a privileged position, and at least the appearance, in the mind of the public, of *not* being a creature of Parliament, the Postmaster-General provided himself with overriding rights over transmission (including the wavelengths to be used, the location and the power of transmitters) and powers over the content of broadcasting; indeed, even before the corporation came into being on the last day of 1926, the Postmaster-General had instructed it not to broadcast on matters of political, industrial or religious controversy; nor was it to broadcast any opinion of its own on matters of public policy.

These instructions, which rejected the Crawford Committee's recommendations, were a belated affirmation, in explicit terms, of the control exercised over the British Broadcasting Company by the government a few months previously at the time of the General Strike. In fact, they were no more than an insurance — a stick held well behind the back of the government — and used very rarely. A broadcast by Ramsay Macdonald during the General Strike had been forbidden, even though his general line fully supported the government's stand; five years later, with a labour government in power, Winston Churchill was denied the right to broadcast his own views of the Conservative Party line on India, his violent opposition to which had led to his resigning from the shadow cabinet. (It was the Secretary of State for India, and not the PMG who applied the veto — which it was, although Reith's own words for it was 'a request emphatically made by the Minister responsible'.)

'Control', then, becomes an inapposite word. The powers assumed by the Postmaster-General have never been exercised publicly and officially. It was, in fact, hardly necessary to do so. The kind of arrangement arrived at between the Government and the BBC at the time of the General Strike provided the mould for the kind of compromise solution and understanding which has prevailed since then.

In 1926, Reith made it quite clear, in a memorandum to Baldwin, that the BBC could be relied on to support the Government:

Assuming the BBC is for the people and that the Government is for the people, it follows that the BBC must be for the Government in this crisis too. (Reith, 1949 p. 108.)

An *obiter dictum* inserted by a High Court judge on a case which came before him towards the very end of the General Strike, to the effect that the 'so-called General Strike was illegal', gave Reith an opportunity to assert to his senior staff that 'we were unable to permit anything which was contrary to the spirit of that judgment, which might have prolonged or sought to justify the Strike.' But on their side, the Trade Unions saw the picture differently, and, according to their lights, much more clearly; at the start of the General Strike, the TUC warned its members against believing the BBC, 'because radio would be just another tool in the hands of the Government', and Beatrice Webb noted that 'directly the news began, it was clear that the BBC had been commandeered by the Government and the main purpose was to recruit blacklegs for the closed services'. (Cole, 1956 pp. 91–2.)

It took seven years, which included two years of a Labour Government, for the situation to ease sufficiently for the Parliamentary Opposition to be given the chance to respond to 'political' (as against 'ministerial') broadcasts by the Government. Almost certainly, it was the exaggerated fears of the 'power of broadcasting' which prevailed at the time which led to this development, since every time the Government used it for blatantly political purposes (as for example Churchill did in his broadcast on his 1928 Budget) there were counterblasts from the Opposition in Parliament and in the Press; the BBC felt able 'not to invite' Churchill to repeat the performance in 1929. At times of crisis, of course, the BBC could prove as reliable as it had in 1926; during the critical months of 1931, after the National Coalition Government had been formed in August, but before the election campaign opened in October, no Labour speaker broadcast, (although in the three weeks of the election campaign itself, time was doled out between the contending parties, fractured as they were). After the election, Attlee raised the first demand for 'equal time', a demand which was laughed out then, but eventually became the principle which governed 'access' by major political parties to broadcast time.

On the other hand, political altercation about 'fair play' between Government and Opposition seems, if anything, to have strengthened Government control, both direct — and, more effectively — indirect, over the broadcasting of anything controversial. Throughout the 1930s, the BBC was ridden with a tight rein. Mild as the incursions by commentators into foreign politics and genteel as discussions between political figures were, there were frequent occasions on which objections were raised in the House and in the Press to what were labelled errors in editorial judgment or lapses in taste. Such occasions reinforced the propensity of the chief officials of the BBC to prove themselves even more 'reliable'; and, as ever, self-censorship proved to be the most effective form of censorship. As

Andrew Boyle remarks, 'BBC controllers and producers were not encouraged to flaunt their consciences or to demonstrate their powers of initiative. The most sensible course, especially for newcomers in the early 30s, was to dispense outright with such luxuries.'

The formal terms of the relationship between the BBC and Government were laid down explicitly by the Ullswater Committee, and have never been challenged or amended. Paragraphs 51 and 52 of the Report read:

51. The position of the Corporation is thus one of independence in the day-to-day management of its business, and of ultimate control by His Majesty's Government. We find that this line of demarcation has been observed in practice, and we are convinced that no better can be found. We agree with those who in recent years have examined the question that the constitutional independence of the BBC brings advantages to the general public and to listeners which could not otherwise be secured. Our proposals under this heading are designed to make both sides of this two-fold position simpler and more evident.

52. It is inevitable that the State, in establishing a sole broadcasting authority, should reserve to itself those powers of ultimate control; but we have no reason to suppose that, in practice, divergent views of the lines of public interest have been held by the Corporation and by Government departments, or that the Corporation has suffered under any sense of constraint or undue interference. Where the interests of the State appear to be at all closely involved, it is open to the Corporation to consult a Minister or Department informally and of its own accord. This method leaves decision and discretion in the hands of the Corporation and is consistent with the independent status which was formulated ten years ago as the desirable objective. (Ullswater Committee Report, 1936.)

Nevertheless, the BBC's relationships with Government, Parliament and political parties, and its handling of current political affairs have confronted it with a perpetual and unresolvable dilemma. From time to time, the terms in which the dilemma manifests itself have changed. In its contemporary form the BBC has come to be regarded as occupying a position of political power, while it sees itself as the custodian of the nation's interests in the uses to which an instrument for the exercise of political power may be put. In short, the BBC's position may be construed as having responsibility without power — the privilege of the intellectual and the artist throughout the ages.

The contemporary dilemma is revealed fairly clearly in two quotations, one from the report of the Select Committee on Nationalised Industries (Sub-Committee B) published in 1972:

There has been a shift of emphasis from considering the broadcasting media solely in terms of the programmes they produce to one in which the BBC and the Authority are seen as powerful institutions in their own right, whose whole style of decision making and action profoundly affects the community.

The other is taken from an article in *The Listener* (6 June 1974) by Oliver Whitley, formerly Assistant to the Director General of the BBC:

Neither the broadcasting organizations nor the public in this country really know what the objectives of the broadcasting organizations are supposed to be, because these objectives have never been properly and officially defined. . . . If you reflect that broadcasting is the medium which everyone nowadays seems to regard as chief public-impression former, is it not very strange, indeed rather alarming, that Parliament, which decides who should provide these uniquely influential services, apparently has nothing of practical significance to say about their main purposes?

Parliament, he went on to say, was 'particularly inept in its handling of broadcasting'. A reading of parliamentary debates over the years since the early twenties suggests that, while this is not an altogether fair judgment, it is true that, for the most part, leading politicians have treated broadcasting very much as the Post Office did at the outset — as a nuisance. On the other hand, the kind of interest which leading politicians like Churchill in the 1920s, Kingsley Wood in the 1930s, Wedgwood Benn in the 1960s have occasionally taken in broadcasting, has not been altogether welcome to the BBC.

Not surprisingly, therefore, the BBC's relationships with national politics, political parties and politicians, uneasy at the beginning, have been more and more difficult and troubled. Throughout, BBC programmes have become at times increasingly circumspect, at other times increasingly adventurous, its pronouncements increasingly simple-minded and increasingly devious, and its handling of individual politicians and groups increasingly clumsy and increasingly finicky.

There is a world of difference between the picture of Reith editing and polishing the script of Baldwin's *Message to the Nation* during the General Strike, broadcast from Reith's home, or 'titivating' Baldwin's election broadcast in 1929 (Adam, 1972 p. 208) and that of the anxious trimming of the course of balance and impartiality by constant consultation with Party Whips. On the other hand, the decision to risk presenting programmes like *The Question of Ulster* and *Yesterday's Men* is even farther removed from the time, in 1930, when Wedgwood Benn *père*, as Secretary of State for India in a Labour Government, could deny Churchill the opportunity of airing his views on the Conservative Party's India policy, over which he had just resigned from the Shadow Cabinet, or when Chamberlain, as Chancellor of the Exchequer, could forbid any Opposition reply to his broadcast talk on the 1933 Budget.

In the 1950s, the 'fourteen day rule' forbade any broadcast discussion of matters which were to be the subject of Parliamentary debate at any time within the next two weeks, an embargo which seems improbably crude and arbitrary compared with the gentlemanly provision recommended by the Crawford Committee in 1926, which was that 'a moderate amount of controversial matter should be broadcast, provided that the material is of high quality and distributed with scrupulous fairness, and that the discretion of the Commissioners [i.e. Governors of the BBC] in this connection should be upheld.'

Yet again, the crude stopwatch conception of 'scrupulous fairness' that operates nowadays is accompanied by a quite extraordinary acceptance of the notion that 'when politicians or any public figures have access to the powerful platform of television, they should be open to questioning of a critical and challenging nature'[2] — by 'television journalists' or by 'invited audiences', themselves selected, and their interventions stage-managed, by broadcasting producers or by the television journalists themselves.

Every year seems to reveal more depths and more versions of the basic dilemma. Reporting on the television coverage of the February 1974 Election, Blumler wrote that much of the effort 'was channelled into the main evening TV news programmes. Fully merging its news and current affairs staffs, the BBC devoted a further half hour of each edition of the *Nine O'Clock News* to the Election, and often presented campaign items in the more topical first half as well . . . . But the disturbing consequence of the campaign role of television news was a tendency for news events to dictate much of the flow of the subsequent argument'. He goes on to detect an even more indefinable and unmanageable source of bias: 'The British communication media are apparently so organized that the Conservatives may count on the entirety of their message, whatever it may be, receiving a thorough airing. In so far as Labour is a Party for egalitarian redistribution and radical social change, it cannot rely on the same treatment . . . . The bulk of the mass media tended to present the Election issues in middle-class terms.'

It is variously argued that this fundamental dilemma is inescapable, given the nature of broadcasting itself, given the fact that broadcasting was a monopoly, or alternatively, that it is now dominated by competition between the BBC and Independent Television for numbers of viewers; that, being so powerful a means of influencing opinion, it must be subject to governmental control, or, that being so important to the functioning of a democracy, it should be free from government control;

2 Robin Day 'Troubled Reflections of a TV Journalist' *Encounter*, May 1970 p. 88. Mr Day took what might be thought a more reasonable line — and what was in the circumstances assuredly a more accommodating one — in his evidence to the Select Committee on Broadcasting of Proceedings in the House of Commons in 1966, when he said, as his second argument for televising Parliament, 'In particular, television viewers would be able to see parliamentary leaders being questioned and challenged by those elected to do so on the floor of the House and not *merely* [my emphasis] by television journalists in studio interviews'. (*First Report from the Select Committee on Broadcasting, etc., of Proceedings in the House of Commons*, 1966, Minutes, Evidence, p. 62.)

that being so expensive, its programmes must be such as to appeal to the
majority most of the time, or, at the very least, not offend the majority,
or, being so important a medium of communication, it must make room
for the expression of minority views and dissenting opinion. (Blumler,
1974 p. 572.)

In considering the political role of broadcasting in particular, in the
contemporary situation, it is as well to remember two things. First, despite
the intentions of the people who founded public service broadcasting, and
the constitutional machinery which applied to see their intentions were
carried out, machinery which applied as much to Independent Television
as to the BBC, they could not alter the fact that in the beginning, broadcasting existed to provide entertainment, free entertainment. Later on,
broadcasting entertainment served as a carrier for advertising in the United
States and elsewhere, and for cultural improvement in Britain. But even
now the primary function of broadcasting, so far as its audiences are concerned, is to provide entertainment, and whatever else it provides depends
very largely on its capacity to deliver enough, good enough, and varied
enough entertainment.

The second point is that the political role of broadcasting was thrust
on it by politicians — by Baldwin in this country, and by Roosevelt, with
his fireside chats, in America. The use of the press in this way (conceivable
as it may have been in the eighteenth century) is inconceivable in the
twentieth century. Chief executives in every country have the right to
claim the use of broadcasting services for the purposes of government.
R. S. Lambert, in writing of his experiences of the Reith era, said as much:
'Today, the BBC holds — in the field of art, intellect and politics — the
power once exercised by the Court. It has become the main indirect
organ of government, all the more potent because its influence *is* indirect.'
(Lambert, 1940 p. 317.)

Such freedoms as broadcasting authorities in this country and elsewhere have in the publication of news and the discussion of public issues
are probably due more to the gradual takeover of the constitutional
doctrine of 'the freedom of the press' as they are to any strenuous assertion
on their own part of political independence. The assimilation of broadcasting into the fourth estate role has been furthered, especially in the last two
decades, by the increasing tendency of journalists, political and other, to
pursue their personal careers in both newspapers and broadcasting.
Nevertheless, broadcasting in all countries is controlled by government
licence in a way that the press is not, and in most European countries is
further subject to direct financial control by the government, in the way
that the press, at least in Western democracies, is not.

From one point of view, therefore, the degree of political independence
achieved by broadcasting systems is remarkable. American broadcasting
can exercise far more licence in its treatment of politics and political

issues than it can in the treatment of sex or the use of obscene language —
a licence, moreover, which it owes as much to the decision of Congress
to allow live television broadcasts of committee and other proceedings,
and the desire of politicians to make their own use of broadcasting
facilities, as it does to the public-spirited endeavours of broadcasting
organizations and journalists.

This, I believe, explains to some extent the extraordinary sense of
shock with which Vice-President Agnew's Iowa speech was received.

The purpose of my remarks tonight, is to focus your attention on this little group of
men who not only enjoy right of instant rebuttal to every Presidential address, but,
more importantly, wield a free hand in selecting, presenting and interpreting the
great issues of our nation. . . . They decide what forty-fifty million Americans will
learn of the day's events in the nation and the world. We can't measure this power
and influence by the traditional democratic standards, for these men can create
national issues overnight. They can make or break by their coverage or their commentary, a Moratorium on the war. They can elevate men from obscurity to national
prominence within a week. They can reward some politicians with national exposure
and ignore others. The American people would rightly not tolerate this concentration of power in government. Is it not fair and relevant to question its concentration
in the hands of a tiny, enclosed fraternity of privileged men elected by no one and
enjoying a monopoly sanctioned and licensed by the Government. (Barrett, Ed.,
1969—70.)

Three years later, Clay Whitehead, the Director of the Office of Telecommunications Policy appointed by the President urged on the
managements of local stations their duty, in buying network news and
other programmes:

The station owners and managers cannot abdicate responsibility for news judgment.
When a reporter or disc jockey slips in or passes over information in order to line his
pockets, that's plugola, and management will take quick corrective action. But men
also stress or suppress information in accordance with their beliefs. Will station
licensees or network executives also take action against this ideological plugola?
(Barrett, Ed., 1971—2.)

One can match these statements by one made by Norman Angell
forty years earlier, about the popular press:

A few newspaper proprietors — Northcliffe's, Hulton's, Beaverbrook's, Bottomley's —
come nearer, at just those junctures which are crucial, really to governing England
and 'making it what it is' than Commons, or Cabinet, Church or Trade Union . . . .
One used to hear many an English householder talk most contemptuously of 'those
Harmsworth fellows and their ha'penny sensations' and become indignant at the
notion that he could be influenced in his opinions thereby . . . . 'But I don't take
my opinion from the papers; I never read their leading articles'. If one led him on

to expressions of opinion concerning the government of the day, its merits and de-
merits; his estimate of the persons that composed it; his ideas of the character of
other nations; his notions of fiscal policy, and national education, of the country's
past and future foreign policy, and so on, one would discover that every single
opinion he expressed responded accurately to just that distribution of emphasis in
the news of our time which marks the Northcliffe press. Given the facts as this
householder conceived them, he could conjure no other opinion; and those facts —
one group of them stressed day after day, and another group, intrinsically as
important, hidden away in corners, were presented as Lord Northcliffe had decreed
they should be presented. (Angell, 1933 pp. 10—11.)

Power has many forms. The critics of newspapers and broadcasting see
their power as lying in controlling the agenda, in their ability to select
certain issues for discussion and decision and to ignore others, or to treat
them as non-existent; and in the ability to treat certain conflicts of interest
as manifestly proper material and others as too complex, or marginal, or
unmanageable. Perhaps the greatest constraint of all lies in the conventions
of what is called 'news tasting' — the job of the aide to the chief sub-editor
who has to decide, almost instantly, which messages coming through to
the office are to count as news, and which aren't. This constraint is even
stricter on broadcasting than on newspapers. Writing of the 1968 Democratic Convention at Chicago, Whale saw this innate handicap as more
serious than any other of the many constraints, technical and visual, on
the presentation of television news and current affairs. 'Television viewers
were never given more than a cursory explanation of why the mayor
[Mayor Daly of Chicago] of a provincial city was able to rule not only
his own region but a national political convention with an iron fist. They
could not have been: the juncture of patronage was too complex, too
abstract, too private to be set out on television. There was nothing to
photograph.'

Nevertheless, five years later, there was Watergate — far more complex,
more abstract, and much more private, but which was nevertheless set out
in extraordinary detail in all its complexity — and on television.

The response of the controllers of the press and broadcasting has
always been that the media serves as a mirror to society. R. D. Kasmire,
giving evidence to the US National Commission on the Causes and
Prevention of Violence, said, 'There is no doubt that television is, to a
large degree, a mirror of society. It is also a mirror of public attitudes and
preferences'. The President of NBC, Julian Goodman, claimed that the
medium was being blamed for the message, while the President of CBS,
Frank Stanton, claimed that, 'what the media do is to hold up a mirror to
society and to try and report it as faithfully as possible'. Closely allied is
the view of the news as essentially a random process. 'Newspapers and
news programmes could almost be said to be random reactions to random
events. Again and again the main reason they turn out as they do is

accident: accidents of a kind which recurs so haphazardly as to defeat
statistical examination.'[3]

David Brinkley, in an NBC news special, remarked, 'What television
did in the sixties was to show the American people to the American
people . . . it did show the people places and things they had not seen
before. Some they liked, and some they didn't. It was not that television
produced or created any of it'. (Epstein, 1973 p. 10.)

Perhaps the biggest change over the past ten years has been the
enormous increase in the criticism of the claim by newspapers and,
especially, broadcasting, that it served as a mirror, whose due task was 'to
reflect society as it is'. This was certainly the dominant view of television's
role in the early sixties, when Hugh Greene's 'Young Lions' were winning
back audiences from ITV with their new-style magazine programmes. The
claim that the media serve as a kind of inertial guidance system for the

nation, casting a neutral, impartial, balanced, but observant eye on the
life of the nation and the world at large, and giving an inevitably selected,
but honest, account of what is there, has been challenged by the conception of newspapers and broadcasting as instruments of power.

While this radical view is articulated and backed by minority groups
of the political left and right, it has some support from large sections of
the population, some of them organized (e.g. trade unionists). It is also
an occasional presence in the minds of an increasing proportion of people
as one moves farther from London and Washington.

In published writings, this interpretation manifests itself under a
number of different titles. To a large extent, however, (much larger, I
should make it clear, than the proponents of any one of them would
admit) all of them are variants on one theme. Shifts from one form of
expression to another, therefore, represent not so much increased insight
and knowledge, as varieties of the same basic belief which becomes
dominant at different levels of political or social or economic stress.

This is most obviously the case with the first two: conspiracy theory
and the 'power élite' notion. In the earlier part of the century, conspiracy
theory was much favoured by left wing critics, but was successfully taken
over by the right wing (notably, of course, by the Nazis). After this
happened, the Left seems to have developed the notion of 'power élite',
fully articulated by C. Wright Mills in his book of that title, which was
published twenty years ago.

Since the War, the most striking exploitation of conspiracy theory was
undoubtedly Senator McCarthy's, who very successfully married it to

3 John Whale quoted by Charles Curran in 'Researcher/Broadcaster Co-operation:
Problems and Possibilities', in J. D. Halloran and M. Gurevitch, *Broadcaster/
Researcher Co-operation in Mass Communication Research*, Centre for Mass Com-
munication Research, 1971. p. 43.

traditional populist hostility towards the traditional elite — the east coast establishment of bankers, government officials and intellectuals.

Conspiracy theory has almost as long a history as journalism itself. It is the inevitable consequence of assumptions about the power and pervasiveness of the 'media'. Spiro Agnew spoke for more than himself when he claimed that a few journalists held 'a concentration of power over American public opinion unknown in history'.

The attack on the power élite, the core of which is what C. Wright Mills (and President Eisenhower) called the 'military-industrial complex' has remained much the same since 1950; broadcasting, in this case, features as an instrument — if not *the* instrument — by which the power élite maintains itself. The general position, which may be regarded as common to the militant left in Britain, as in the United States, has been most clearly stated by Ralph Miliband in *The State in Capitalist Society* (1969), in which he writes of the 'ownership and control of the means of mental production'.

Among the New Left, however, in broadcasting and outside it, the tendency is to plump for the third variant form: ideological hegemony. Miliband himself occasionally makes the slight shift necessary to assume this more general, and much more powerful, critique:

The agencies of communication and noticeably the mass media are in reality, and the expression of dissident views notwithstanding, a crucial element in the legitimation of capitalist society.

The mass media in advanced capitalist societies are mainly *intended* [my emphasis] to perform highly 'functional' roles; they too are both the expression of a system of domination, and the means of reinforcing it. (Miliband, 1969 pp. 197, 198.)

Hegemony, a term adopted at two or three or even more removes from Gramsci's writings, represents a social order held in equilibrium by a consensus, which is both moral and intellectual and is diffused throughout the whole of the population and informs their daily lives. As applied to broadcasting, it has some long standing in Britain. During the 'Golden Days of Wireless', right through to the fifties, it was seen in very explicit terms as identified with 'BBC culture', 'BBC types', and indeed, 'BBC English'. The Ullswater Committee, in 1935, was at one point driven to defend the BBC against the 'suspicion that in appointments an undue preference was given to candidates with Oxford or Cambridge degrees'. They regarded this contention as disproved by quoting figures that, out of all monthly-paid non-engineering staff who were graduates, only 60 per cent were from Oxford and Cambridge!

It is not that broadcasting organizations, among others, are instruments of a power elite, of the establishment, or of an existing social order whose rulers are determined to maintain the status quo — if necessary, by making marginal concessions. The picture is much more of a recruitment and promotion *process*. The hierarchy of a broadcasting organization appears not so much a hierarchy of power as a hierarchy of models, power consisting not so much in the issue of directives, instructions, or even policy documents, but in the laying down of a set of tacit principles by which individuals can gain membership, in the first place, of the organization, and thereafter, by a sedulously monitored appointment system, the rewards of 'interesting' jobs and promotion.

Of course, the small population from which recruits are selected, itself changes; so does the cultural and social and political ambience within which broadcasting organizations exist. Thus, in 1972, in his *Sunday Times* article ('What's to become of the BBC?') Jay could write:

There is [in the BBC] a kind of consensus, a pool of shared social and political assumptions, which on many subjects — abortion, divorce, censorship, drugs, emigration, promiscuity, capital punishment, penal policy, education and so on, are at the best partisan opinions and at the worst the opinion of a small educated middle class and left-wing minority.

It is into this area that the main debate over the political role of broadcasting and the press has shifted in recent years. In this regard, as in others, both the area of debate and the national circumstances in which debate occurs have changed.

Before the war, Reith saw his public service broadcasting system acting as 'a dependable keeper of the nation's conscience', standing as 'an arbiter above the clamour of all political and social factions' and regarded as 'the paragon of impartiality, honesty and respectability'. He pursued his objectives with missionary zeal, and quite openly. He did this by bringing to bear what he called 'the brute force of monopoly' as his instrument. In fact, although his motives and his aims were utterly different, his view of broadcasting as an instrument was much the same as Rothermere's or Beaverbrook's. Government and influential public opinion supported his objectives, seeing them, as he did, as a means of promoting at least an appearance of national social and cultural integration in a country deeply divided but fearful of the destructive forces present and gaining strength in Britain and abroad. The forties and fifties did bring integration, but of a totally unprecedented kind. They seem now to have been a curious historical interlude, a social interregnum in which fundamental political differences and the whole structure of social and economic inequality seemed to be made either irrelevant because of the war, or obsolescent through the magic of technological progress.

The imposed consensus of the thirties, the consciousness of national unity of the wartime years and the surface appearance of inevitable progress towards improved economic welfare and social equality had all dissipated by the mid-sixties. Conceivably, the country by then had recovered sufficient assurance and essential unity for people to acknowledge once again the existence of the divisions which had always been a familiar part of everyone's common experience and awareness as a citizen, and which had, moreover, though latent, persisted since the twenties. But, so far as broadcasting, broadcasting authorities, and broadcasters were concerned, dissensus of the kind which then revealed itself and has remained with us since was a shatteringly novel experience.

It seems to be common ground that 'a dangerous gulf' has opened between leaders (i.e. politicians) and led (i.e. voters); that the consensus which has prevailed in Britain (seemingly from time immemorial) has broken up, and divisions which previously did not exist, or at least were unrevealed, had become obtrusively apparent; that trades unions, and trade unionism, have become much more militant, both industrially and politically; that Scottish and Welsh nationalism, as well as Irish, within the United Kingdom, has gained enormously in strength; that re-politicization, especially among the young, has led to extremism, both of the Left and the Right, with a consequent increase in the use of the vocabularly of Marxism and Fascism; that a new wave of feminism has emerged with much broader claims to equal rights; and, finally, all these manifestations of 're-politicization' are, for the most part, particularistic and have been quick to adopt the organizational structure, the tactics, and the armoury of pressure groups within the Parliamentary system, and of dissident factions outside it.

There are striking resemblances between what has been happening in Britain during the past ten years and the period between 1830 and 1870, so comprehensively and admirably documented in the collections of writings edited by Patricia Hollis: *Pressure from Without* (1974).

Changes in the power structure (or, more precisely, the distribution of rights and privileges within society) are brought about in ways which can be broadly classified into two: Parliamentary and extra-Parliamentary political processes.

By itself, Parliamentary process is lengthy, arduous, and tedious. Institutionalized as it now is, and mediated, as it now is, by the institutionalized processes of party politics, Parliament, if left to itself (i.e. shielded or safe from outside pressure, as it was for the most part during the inter-war years), follows a single principle: intertia. But, though Parliament is not in any statistical (i.e. J. S. Mill) sense representative of the people, it 'represents' the people.

However, changes in the structure of society are implemented through the Parliamentary process. It does so by responding to 'pressures from without', although the response is not necessarily adequate, direct, correct, or even positive. It does so most obviously and formally at election times, but this response, is again, mediated by the machinery of party politics. At election times, and at all times, it can be made aware of 'pressure from without' by four main means:

1. Public opinion as manifested in public meetings and demonstrations.
2. Public opinion as manifested in public utterances, spoken or written.
3. Action which focuses attention on grievances or demands through attacks on property, through riots, through assassination.
4. Action designed to enforce change either through the organized disruption of civil life or by revolution.

Extra-Parliamentary political action has taken all four forms in this country, as in others. Historically, the English and Irish, and to a lesser extent, Scots and Welsh, have been no more docile politically than the people of any other country. The major difference, in the past, has been the greater responsiveness of the Parliamentary process to pressure from without. Even during the nineteenth century, it was the first two forms of pressure which gained the real successes, but how far this was so because these two forms had gained a legitimacy which they did not have elsewhere, or because they were recognized for what they were: the milder manifestations of pressure which could easily range into the more violent forms; how far the breadth and intensity of the first two kinds of manifestations allowed Parliamentary politicians to assess the strength of the pressure; or how far these modes of manifestation of pressure ('public opinion') have become recognized and institutionalized as modes of political action, it is impossible to say.

But during the past decade or so, things have changed, and the reason for this rather lengthy excursus is that what seems to have changed is that the first two modes of expression of 'pressure from without' have become ineffective.

There are three reasons for this:

1) Increasingly, from the 1930s on, the 'pressures from without', political, economic and social, have come from outside the country, so that the Parliamentary system has had to respond to them, as well as to pressures from within society. (Before a generation or so ago, these pressures were largely political — i.e., concerned diplomacy or war; over the last generation they have become increasingly manifold, complex, and unmanageable, so far as Parliament itself is concerned.)

2) The diminution of British power and prestige, which has been concomitant with, and the consequence of, the increase in extra-national pressure, has diminished the supreme sovereignty of Parliament.

Both factors have combined to reduce both the effective and the apparent force of the first two modes of exerting pressure on Parliament from without.

3) There has been a very great reduction in the number of different means by which public opinion can be made manifest, together with — an almost inevitable consequence — firmer and more comprehensive control by professionals: professional politicians, professional journalists, professional broadcasters, professional publicists.

It is this situation, I believe, which lies behind (and is largely concealed by) Mr Wedgwood Benn's by now familiar pronouncement on the matter:

> The whole political process in a democracy rests on the maintenance of a delicate fabric of communication within society which reveals the common 'nterest that exists, identifies conflict where it arises and painfully builds the consent which leads people to accept the policies that emerge as these conflicts are resolved by upholding the ground rules of the system. . . .

> The media are engaged in the same process and are so much more effective in disseminating information simultaneously to large groups of people that they not only supplement the political and educational systems but in some respects supplant them, because of their enormous power.[4]

The power of the press barons, claimed with such assurance during the 1920s and acknowledged by Baldwin even as he challenged it, has gone, to be replaced by the power of the balance sheet, which drives newspapers to compete not for numbers of readers, but for the numbers of pounds their readers have for spending on consumer goods. It is this which has driven the national press into the narrowly confined consensus not of opinion but of the agenda for discussion which they now display, and which, as Hirsch and Gordon so clearly document, is based on a minority of the well-heeled professional and managerial middle classes. 'The consensus is a broad band, not a party line — not even a Fleet line. The picture that we suggest of the quality press is of a band of opinion and approaches occupying the broad centre of British politics from about half-way into the moderate Left through to the edges of the extreme right; with individual papers occupying different and sometimes shifting positions within the band, and the band itself moving over time in response to events and political changes. But the most important characteristic of the consensus band lies not in the nuances of the attitude taken on different items on the political agenda, but rather in the common agreement on that agenda itself — on the issues for discussion and the way in which they should be approached.'

4 A. W. Benn in F. S. Badley (Ed.) *Fourth Symposium on Broadcasting Policy* (mimeo) University of Manchester 1972, p. 37.

The consequence of all this is that, so far as the representation of opinion among the public is concerned, 'minorities with high spending power find themselves excellently catered for. Minorities who have less pull on advertisers find themselves neglected. There is no newspaper their money can buy.'

Of course, the remedies are there, and are found: the creation of new publications which do cater for minorities. And it is significant that the last twelve or thirteen years have seen the appearance of a number: *New Society*, *Private Eye*, *Socialist Worker*, *Black Dwarf*, which added themselves to *Tribune* and the *Morning Star* to preserve a modicum of unestablished political opposition, informed criticism, and to serve, in Geoffrey Crowther's words, as 'the chief lieutenant of discontent'. The response to the claim for 'access' is always to hand.

But the press, nowadays, is only half the matter — perhaps less than half. The increasing concern about the press which has expressed itself in the institution of three Royal Commissions since the War is centrally concerned with the shrinking of the number of national newspapers and the consequent shrinkage of the 'band of consensus' within which they operate. The quality newspapers may have survived, at a cost, but the mass circulation newspaper has certainly suffered, and this directly as a consequence of television, especially commercial television, because commercial television lives off the advertising money which would otherwise go to the mass circulation newspaper and *not* the quality newspaper. Since 1960, the *Daily Mirror*, the *Daily Express*, the *Daily Mail* have all lost a substantial proportion of their average daily circulation; the *Daily Sketch* died in 1970; the exception, the *Sun*, has almost four times the circulation of the *Herald* which it replaced in 1962, but has forfeited any pretence of representing opinion.

Broadcasting, then, has cut the readership of the mass circulation newspaper. More to the point, it has replaced it almost completely as a source of news and information about current affairs. Yet there is every indication that BBC news and current affairs, ITN, and current affairs programmes of ITA companies all operate within the same 'consensus-band' as the quality newspapers. The range of opinion available to newspaper readers, radio listeners, and television viewers, all, has narrowed much more over the past twenty years than is indicated by the decline in the range and number of national newspapers.

Moreover, this narrowing of range has not necessarily been towards any particular political, social or cultural mean (whatever this might signify in any of those three respects). The limits for broadcasting are roughly those within which the quality press operates.

The conclusion is, then, that although it has been manifest to every-body that political, social, economic and cultural interests, values and opinions have appeared to become more and more disparate, and this disparity more and more organized, the kind of opinions and attitudes and values and, above all, information, conveyed by broadcasting and the press has tended to become more constrained and more internally consistent.

References

Adam, K., 1972: 'Fifty Years of Fireside Elections'. *The Listener* 91 (14 February).

Angell, Norman, 1933: *The Press and the organization of society.* Gordon Fraser, 1933.

Aspinall, A., 1949: *Politics and the Press, 1780–1850.* Home and Van Thal.

Barrett, Marvin (Ed.), The Alfred I. Dupont – Columbia University Survey of Broadcast Journalism 1969–70, Appendix A.
    The Alfred I. Dupont – Columbia University Survey of Broadcast Journalism 1971–2, Appendix 4

Blackstone, *Commentaries* (ed. R. M. Kerr) Murray, 1857, Vol. 4.

Blumler, J., 1974: 'The Media and the Election'. *New Society* 27 (7 March).

Bryce, James, 1914: *The American Commonwealth*, 3rd edn. Macmillan.

Cole, Margaret (Ed.), 1956: *Beatrice Webb's Diaries, 1924–1932*, Longman.

Crowther, Geoffrey, 1943: *The Economist, 1843–1943*, Oxford University Press.

Ensor, R. C. K., 1936: *England, 1870–1914*, Oxford University Press.

Epstein, Edward J., 1973: *News from Nowhere.* Random House.

Habermas, J., 1962: *Strukturwandel der Offentlichkeit.* Luchterhand, 2nd revised edn. 1965.

Hirsch, F., and Gordon, D., 1975: *Newspaper Money: Fleet Street and the search for the Affluent Reader.* Hutchinson.

Hollis, Patricia, 1974: *Pressure from Without in Early Victorian England.* Arnold.

Lambert, R. S., 1940: *Ariel and all his equality – an impression of the BBC from within.* Gollancz, quoted Anthony Smith, *The Shadow in the Cave*, Allen and Unwin, 1973.

Lang, Kurt and Lang, G. E., 1968: *Politics and Television.* Quadrangle Books.

Lapsley, G., 1936: (ed.), Editorial Note to F. W. Maitland, *Selected Essays*, Cambridge University Press.

McQuail, D., 1969: *Towards a Sociology of Mass Communications.* Collier-Macmillan.

Miliband, R., 1969: *The State in Capitalist Society.* Weidenfeld and Nicolson.

Mitchell-Thomson (Postmaster-General) in *Hansard* 14 July 1926, Vol. 198.

Reith, J. C. W., 1949: *Into the Wind.* Hodder and Stoughton.

Taylor, A. J. P., 1965: *English History, 1914—1945.* Oxford University Press.
Thompson, E. P., 1975: *Whigs and Hunters.* Allen Lane.
Watson, Steven, 1960: *The Reign of George III, 1760—1830.* Oxford
    University Press.

3

The Influence and Effects of Mass Media

Denis McQuail

Introduction

The questions most insistently asked of social research on mass communication, and perhaps least clearly answered, have to do with the effects and social influence of the different mass media. The reasons for asking are understandable enough, given the amount of time spent attending to the mass media in many countries and the amount of resources invested in mass media production and distribution./Although much has been written by way of answer and a good deal of research carried out, it has to be admitted that the issue remains a disputed one — both in general about the significance of mass media and in particular about the likely effect of given instances of mass communication. Inevitably, this discussion has to begin with some clarification of terms, since one of the perennial difficulties in the case has been the lack of communication between those who have investigated the question of media influence on the one hand and, on the other, the public, media producers and those concerned with public policy for the media.

Perhaps it should first be claimed that the question of effects is a somewhat unfair one, one rarely asked of comparable institutions like religion, education or the law which all in their way communicate to the public or to particular publics and where questions about effects as well as aims could well be asked. The mass media are highly diverse in content and in forms of organization and include a very wide range of activities which could have effects on society. To make the question not only more fair, but also more meaningful, we need to introduce a number of qualifications and specifications. First, we can distinguish between effects and effectiveness, the former referring to any of the consequences of mass media operation, whether intended or not, the latter to the capacity to achieve given objectives, whether this be attracting large audiences or influencing opinions and behaviour. Both matters are important, but a different set of considerations relates to each. A second, though perhaps minor, point on which to be clear concerns the reference in time. Are we concerned with the past, or with predictions about the future? If the former, we need to be precise. If the latter, and often it is a prediction about what is going on now and its results which is a main concern, then some uncertainty is inevitable.

Third, we need to be clear about the level on which effects occur, whether this is at the level of the individual, the group, the institution, the whole society or the culture. Each or all may be affected in some way by mass communication. To specify the level meaningfully also requires us to name the kinds of phenomena on which influence may be exerted. We can investigate some phenomena at several levels — especially opinion and belief which can be a matter of individual opinion as well as the collective expression of institutions and societies. On the other hand, to study the effect of the media on the way institutions operate requires us to look at the relationships between people occupying different roles and at the structure and content of these roles. Politics provides a good example, where the mass media have probably affected not only individual political opinions but also the way politics is conducted and its main activities organized. Political roles may have been changed, as well as our expectations of politicians, the relationships of followers to leaders, and even perhaps some of the values of political life. All this is a matter of historical change, much slower and less reversible than any influence on opinion, attitude or voting behaviour. Again it is clear that difference of level of effect is also related to different time spans. Changes in culture and in society are slowest to occur, least easy to know of with certainty, least easy to trace to their origins, most likely to persist. Changes affecting individuals are quick to occur, relatively easy to demonstrate and to attribute to a source, less easy to assess in terms of significance and performance. Hence we tend to find a situation in which the larger and more significant questions of media effect are most subject to conflicting interpretation and the most certain knowledge we have is most open to the charge of triviality and least useful as a basis for generalization. Perhaps one could usefully add a further set of distinctions which have to be made early on, whatever the level of analysis. This relates to the direction of effect. Are the media changing something, preventing something, facilitating something or reinforcing and reaffirming something? The importance of the question is obvious, but it is worth stressing early in the discussion that a 'no change' effect can be as significant as its reverse and there is little doubt that in some respects the media do inhibit as well as promote change.

The History of Research into the Effects of Mass Communication

Research into mass communication has its own 'natural history' and the study of media effects is of so much interest to the public and the phenomenon of mass media so 'visible' that it has been strongly influenced by currents which have little to do with scientific criteria of relevance. On the one hand there are staple matters of anxiety like crime, or violence, the state of culture and morals or the power of the media to brainwash or educate. Each of these is subject to historical influences of increasing or decreasing importance. On the other hand, there are the facts of changing technology and social behaviour which introduce changes of media provision and use. The popular newspaper or comic, the cinema, radio and television have been successively objects of research interest, as they have attracted public attention. Of course what we know of the effects of mass media is not only the result of research oriented to social science or public concern. It also stems from the needs of the media industry and, especially, a concern with the effectiveness of advertising. Scientific investigations have thus been carried out typically in a context shaped by the practical interests of media producers to achieve their specific aims or by the concern in society to prevent 'harmful' effects. The 'effects' of the media which relate to neither of these have not always been examined with the same zeal. When we come to assess the state of knowledge about the question as a whole we will have to acknowledge a rather large gap on matters which may be most central to understanding the contribution of mass media in modern society.

There has, nevertheless, been some progress and we can characterize the 50 years or more of interest in media effects in terms of three main stages. In the first phase, which lasts from the turn of the century to the late nineteen thirties the media, where they were developed in Europe and North America, were attributed considerable power to shape opinion and belief, change habits of life, actively mould behaviour and impose political systems even against resistance. Such views were not based on scientific investigation but were based on empirical observation of the sudden extension of the audience to large majorities and on the great attraction of the popular press, cinema and radio. The assumption of media power was also acted upon, as it were, by advertisers, government propagandists in the First World War, newspaper proprietors, the rulers of totalitarian states, and accepted defensively by nearly all as the best guess in the circumstances. It is not irrelevant that this stage of thinking coincided with a very early stage of social science when the methods and concepts for investigating these phenomena were only developing. The second stage extends from about 1940 to the early 1960s and it is strongly shaped by growth of mass communication research in the United States and the application of empirical method to specific questions about the effects and effectiveness of mass communication. The influence of this phase of research is surprisingly great, given the rather narrow range of the questions tackled and relatively small quantity of substantial studies. Most influential, perhaps, were the studies of Presidential elections in 1940 and 1948 by Lazarsfeld (1944), Berelson and others (1954) and the programme of research into the use of films for training and indoctrination of American servicemen undertaken by Hovland *et al.* (1950). An earlier and longer tradition of social-psychological inquiry into the effects of film and other media on crime, aggression and racial and other attitudes should also be mentioned (e.g. Blumer, 1933). In practice, a small number of much cited studies provided the substance for the general view of media effects and effectiveness which was generally being disseminated in social and political science by the end of the 1960s. Where there was research outside the United States (e.g. Trenaman and McQuail, 1961), it was in the same mould and tended to confirm rather than challenge the agreed version of media effects. Basically, this version affirmed the ineffectiveness and impotency of mass media and their subservience to other more fundamental components in any potential situation of influence. The mass media — primarily radio, film or print at the time most research was conducted — emerged as unlikely to be major contributors to direct change of individual opinions, attitudes or behaviour or to be a direct cause of crime, aggression or other disapproved social phenomena. Too many separate investigations reached similar negative conclusions for this to be doubted. The comment by Klapper (1960) in an influential review of research, that 'mass communication does not ordinarily serve as a necessary and sufficient cause of audience effects, but rather functions through a nexus of mediating factors' well sums up the outcome of the second phase. Of course, research had not shown the different media to be without effects, but it had established the primacy of other social facts and showed the power of the media to be located within the existing structures of social relationships and systems of culture and belief. The reversal of a prior assumption by scientific investigation was striking and seemed the more complete because the myth of media power was so strong and occasionally uncritical and naive. At the same time, it should be admitted that neither public anxiety about the new medium of television nor professional opinion in the field of advertising and mass communication was much changed by the verdict of science. In fact, hardly had the 'no effect' conclusion become generally accepted than it became subject to re-examination by social scientists who doubted that the whole story had yet been written. The third phase, which still persists, is one where new thinking and new evidence is accumulating on the influence of mass communication, especially television, and the long neglected newspaper press. As early signs of doubts we could cite Lang and Lang (1959) or Key (1961) or Blumler (1964) or Halloran (1964). The case for re-opening the question of mass media effects rests on several bases. First of all, the lesson of 'no-effects' has been learned and accepted and more modest expectations have taken the place of early belief. Where small effects are expected, methods have to be more precise. In addition, the intervening variables of social position and prior audience disposition, once identified as important, could now be more adequately measured. A second basis for revision however, rested on a critique of the methods and research models which had been used. These were mainly experiments or surveys designed to measure short-term changes occurring in individuals, and concentrating especially on the key concept of attitude. Alternative research approaches might take a longer time span, pay more attention to people in their social context, look at what people know (in the widest sense) rather than at their attitudes and opinions, take account of the uses and motives of the audience member as mediating any effect, look at structures of belief and opinion and social behaviour rather than individual cases, take more notice of the *content* whose effects are being studied. In brief, it can be argued that we are only at the start of the task and have as yet examined very few of the questions about the effects of mass media, especially those which reveal themselves in *collective* phenomena. Some of these matters are returned to later, and at this point it is sufficient to conclude that we are now in a phase where the social power of the media is once more at the centre of attention for some social scientists, a circumstance which is not the result of a mere change of fashion but of a genuine advance of knowledge based on secure founda- tions. This advance has been uneven and buffeted by external pressure, but it is real enough.

Processes and Models of Mass Media Effects

One of the spheres in which some progress has been made is in our understanding of how and why effects do or do not take place as expected. One of the reasons why questions about the influence of mass com- munication are so difficult to answer lies in the uncertainty about the 'mechanisms' by which effects are produced. This uncertainty applies even to the relatively simple case of effects at the level of individuals and in practice, both empirical research and speculative comment have tended to be imprecise about the question of *why* any demonstrated or postulated effect should occur at all. Obviously, there is much diversity of explana- tions, but without some attempt to order the possibilities, the study of media 'effects' is likely to be incomplete and possibly sterile.

Some guidance is available from early social psychological investigations of influence, but the lessons have not been generally applied to mass com- munication research. For instance, Janis and Hovland (1959) discussed various factors associated with 'persuasibility' and suggested that 'persuasive' effects might depend, amongst other things, on the prestige of the source, or on the significance of the message for the receiver, or on the attitudes of the receiver to the source. Implicitly, such work offers the framework for a more general account of models of the influence process, but no general framework emerges. Kelman (1961) comes closer to this in his analysis of social influence, suggesting that three main processes might be involved in opinion change. One of these, 'compliance', refers to the acceptance of influence in the expectations of some reward or to avoid punishment. Another, 'identification', occurs when an individual wishes to be more like the source and hence imitates or adopts behaviour accordingly. A third, 'internalization', is intended to describe influence guided by the receiver's own pre-existing needs and values. This latter process may be described as a 'functional' explanation of influence (or effects), since change is mainly explicable in terms of the receiver's own motives, needs and wishes. Katz (1960) recommends this approach to explaining the influence of mass communication in preference to what he considers to have been the two dominant modes of explanation in the past. One of those he describes as based on an 'irrational model of man' which represents people as a prey to any form of powerful suggestion. Another is based on a 'rational' model in which people are viewed as using a calculative and logical approach to new information. Both he regards as unrealistic and less likely to account for any change of attitude than his suggested functional approach.

A further example of social-psychological thinking deserves mention, since it does offer a fairly comprehensive framework for studying social influence and social power, even if it is not directly concerned with mass communication. This is the work of French and Raven (1953) which offers five main possibilities of a communicative relationship in which social power may be exercised and influence accepted. Power based on 'reward' or on 'coercion' are the first two categories and largely self-explanatory, although we need to translate them into concepts appropriate to mass communication. Both imply some interaction between the intentions of the sender and the needs of the receiver. 'Referent' power is similar to Kelman's 'identification'. Fourth, 'legitimate' power is based on the assumption of a *right* to expect compliance — present only where such a relationship is institutionally defined, as it may be in a number of different circumstances. Finally, there is 'expert' power, based on the attribution of superior knowledge of the sender. While the conceptual framework needs careful adaption to the circumstances of mass communication, it does at least help to supply the missing element in the discussion of effects. (McQuail, 1975.) An analysis which is more specifically concerned with mass communication and which tells us succinctly how thinking has tended to develop is offered by De Fleur (1970). He outlines five types of theory or models of the effects process which have been developed successively as knowledge has advanced. First, there is the model of simple conditioning, stimulus — response, a model which fits with the early views about the power of the media as direct, and dependent on the source rather than the recipient. An early refinement was the 'individual differences of theory' of mass communication which sought to take account of the diversity of the audience, acknowledging that the media message contains 'particular stimulus attributes that have differential interactions with personality characteristics of members of the audience'. In brief, different people are likely to respond differently to what must be complex stimuli. The third phase of thinking is referred to as a 'social categories' theory, since it takes account of the fact that the audience is stratified according to such variables of social position as life-cycle, occupation or class, region, sex and so on. De Fleur notes that 'members of a particular category will select more or less the same content and will respond to it in roughly equal ways.' Here we have the notion of selective exposure and response according to broad social position. A fourth refinement of theory builds in the findings of social group and personal influence studies of the 1940s and 1950s (e.g. Katz and Lazarsfeld, 1956) and is labelled a 'social relationships' theory. The basic thought is that inter-relationships between people as well as their individual attributes have to be taken into account, perhaps even more so: 'informal social relationships play a significant role in modifying the manner in which a given individual will act upon a message which comes to his attention via the mass media.' Finally, De Fleur describes the cultural norms theory which 'postulates that the mass media, through selective presentations and the emphasis of certain themes, create impressions among their audiences that common cultural norms concerning the emphasized topics are structured and defined in some specific ways. Since individual behaviour is usually guided by cultural norms or the actors' impressions of what the norms are with respect to a given topic or situation, the media would then serve indirectly to influence conduct.' This is an important statement of one of the basic processes which helps to keep alive a concern with the effects and power of the mass media, since it contains the thought that the media work most directly on consciousness, by providing the constructed images of the world and of social life and the definitions of social reality. In effect, the audience member learns about his or her social world and about himself from the media presentation of society (given that most of the time, most of this is not directly accessible). The media provide the materials for responding to experience and these accumulate over time in a long-term process of socialization. The effects of the media on the individual are not only indirect, they may have happened long ago, certainly in the past. The difficulty of investigating such a process need hardly be emphasized, but our attention is at least directed to the content of the media and its consistency or otherwise over time and across different media sources.

These attempts to clarify the effects process in the main deal only with the level of individual effect. In addition, De Fleur's analysis is oriented very much to the persuasion process and to understanding how the media might be used for persuasive objectives. In this, it still deploys a limited version of the general part played by mass media in society. A framework which helps to escape from this early tradition, formulated specifically for the study of politics but generalizable to other cases, is suggested by Seymour-Ure (1974). He asks about the effects of mass media on 'political relationships' rather than on individuals. Thus the relationship is not simply an intervening variable in this question, but becomes the dependent variable. The first sort of relationship which he discusses is that between individual and political system. The mass media will affect the individual's knowledge about, and attachment to, the political system as a whole and this can happen over a long period of time as the structure of the media change (for instance, the emergence of a mass press) or it can happen more quickly by coverage of particular issues and people (for instance, immigration and Enoch Powell). Second, the relationship between the political system as a whole and its constituent institutions may be affected. The instances cited include: the institution of the British Monarchy, which receives so much support from the mass media; Parliament itself, whose place in the system could be affected by broadcasting of its proceedings; or the political parties, whose role is open to modification. A third level of media effect is in the relationship between institutions, for instance the relative strength of different political parties or the relationship between the American President and Congress. Fourth, we can look at relations between individuals and institutions, as in the case of support for a particular party or the attraction of individuals to leaders. Finally, the relationship between one individual and another, especially prominent political actors, can be affected by mass media and the case of the Kennedy/Nixon debates comes to mind as well as those other occasions where internal leadership contests are conducted on the public stage of the media.

The particular examples are less important than the general lesson to be learnt from this framework, that in many areas of social life the content and structure of mass media and the lines of activity which are chosen can have profound effects, not through the scale of effects on mass audiences, but through their consequences for particular individuals especially those with power, or the adaptive responses of other institutions when the media provide new ways of meeting old needs or begin to encroach on the territory of other institutions. Some specific cases of institutional effects are mentioned below. Here it should be emphasized that the media are themselves separate institutions with their own place in society, their own objectives to pursue, their own power and institutional dynamics. They are not merely neutral 'message-carrying' networks nor is the only or most fundamental relationship involved that between the 'mass communicator' and the audience. Our questions about the effects of mass media have to include those which concern the effects of the media *institution* as well as the effect of the media *message*. This matter has been neglected, in part because it requires the skills of rather different sorts of people — historians and political scientists especially. Gradually, the two kinds of knowledge of effects are being brought together, but we are in a phase of speculation rather than demonstrated fact. The connection that needs to be established is between (1) the political, social and economic forces which shape media institutions, (2) the effect of media institutions on other institutions, (3) the effect of media institutions on messages they disseminate, (4) the effect of these messages on people and on institutions.

The Evidence of Effects

In order to discuss the results of research into mass media effects in a meaningful way, it may be helpful to divide up the problem under a set of headings which in a composite way reflects the various distinctions which have already been mentioned: of level; of kind of effect and of process; of research strategy and method. Although the headings which follow do not divide up the field in a mutually exclusive way, they do separate out the main topics which have been discussed and provide a basis for evaluating research evidence. Basically what is being indicated is a set of media situations or processes which have distinctive features and require separate evaluation. The most important media situations are: (1) the campaign; (2) the definition of social reality and social norms; (3) the immediate response or reaction; (4) institutional change; (5) changes in culture and society.

The campaign

Much of what has been written about the effects or effectiveness of the media either derives from research on campaigns or involves predictions about hypothetical campaign situations. In fact, the campaign is not the most common form of media provision nor its reception the most usual audience experience. Nevertheless, because the campaign is often treated as the paradigm case it is useful to pick it out, try and define what it means and what kinds of media experience are illustrated by campaign-based evidence. The kinds of media provision which might fall under this heading include: political and election campaigns, attempts at public information; commercial and public service advertising, some forms of education; the use of mass media in developing countries or generally for the diffusion of innovations. We recognize the similarity of these different activities. The campaign shows, in varying degrees, the following characteristics: it has specific aims and is planned to achieve these; it has a definite time-span, usually short; it is intensive and aims at wide coverage; it's effectiveness is, in principle, open to assessment; it usually has authoritative sponsorship; it is not necessarily popular with its audience and has to be 'sold' to them; it is usually based on a framework of shared values. The campaign generally works to achieve objectives which in themselves are not controversial — voting, giving to charity, buying goods, education, health, safety, and so on. We can recall many variants and daily examples and readily see the distinctive features of this form of media content. There are fringe areas where the relevance of the campaign concept is unclear, for instance the case of news which has presumably an informative intention and may be given the features of a campaign by a particular newspaper or regarded in this light by part of an audience.

The main aim in singling out this special kind of media situation is to bring together, in summary form, the accumulated evidence bearing on campaign effects and in doing so to reduce the risk of transferring these conclusions to situations where they may not be appropriate. We can also say more with certainty about the conditions affecting the success of campaigns than about any other kind of media situation. Rather than discuss evidence in detail, which space would not allow, a brief assertion of a general condition of effect is made, with some reference to a source or summarizing work which justifies the assertion. One set of relevant factors has to do with the audience, another with the message and a third with the source or the system of distribution. Amongst audience factors, an obvious primary condition is that a large audience should be reached. Second, the appropriate members of the audience should be reached, since size alone does not guarantee the inclusion of those for whom the campaign is relevant. The classic example of an information and orientation campaign reaching an already informed and well oriented public is described by Star and Hughes (1951). Third, the dispositions of the audience should at least be not antipathetic or resistant. Political campaigning is most subject to this constraint and there is evidence that the lack of strong disposition either way and a condition of casual attention may be most favourable to the success of mass propaganda. (Blumler and McQuail, 1968.) A part of this condition relates to the need for consistency with the norms of locality and sub-culture as well as the presence of broad societal consensus. Fourth, success is likely to be greater when, within the audience, the flow of personal communication and structure of relevant interpersonal status is supportive of the mass media campaign and its aims. (Lazarsfeld, 1944; Katz and Lazarsfeld, 1956; Rogers and Shoemaker, 1971.) Fifth, it is important that the audience understands or perceives the message as intended by its originators (Cooper and Jahoda, 1947; Belson, 1967) and does not selectively distort it.

Factors to do with the message or content are also important. First, the message should be unambiguous and relevant to its audience. The factor of relevance and a parallel self-selection by the audience makes it likely that campaigns are most successful at reinforcing existing tendencies or channelling them into only slightly different pathways. Second, the informative campaign seems more likely to be successful than the campaign to change attitudes or opinions. (Hovland et al., 1951; Trenaman and McQuail, 1961.) Third, in general, subject matter which is more distant and more novel, least subject to prior definitions and outside immediate experience responds best to treatment by the campaign. The essential point is that the receiver has no competing sources of information and no personal stake in resisting an appeal or disbelieving information. It is easier to form opinions and attitudes about events abroad than events at home, about unfamiliar than about familiar matters. Fourth, the campaign which allows some immediate response in action is most likely to be effective, since behaviour generally confirms intention and attitude, whether in voting or buying, or donating to a charity. Fifth, repetition can be mentioned as a probable contributor to effect, although this is a common-sense assumption rather than well demonstrated. As far as the source is concerned, we should mention first the condition of monopoly. The more channels carrying the same campaign messages, the greater the probability of acceptance. This is not easy to demonstrate and there are circumstances where an imposed monopoly invites distrust and disbelief. (e.g. Inkeles and Bauer, 1959.) But, in general, this condition is pre-supposed in several of the conditions already stated. Second, there is evidence that the status or authority of the source contributes to successful campaigning and the principle is applied in most campaigns whether com-mercial or not. The source of attributed status can of course vary, including the strongly institutionalized prestige of the political or legal system or the personal attractiveness of a star or other 'hero' of society or the claim to expert knowledge. Endorsement by an individual or institution embodying strong claims to trust and attachment can be crucial in a campaign. Third, there is a variable condition of affective attachment to a media source. There is evidence that loyalty and affective ties exist in relation to some media rather than others which may affect their ability to influence. (Butler and Stokes, 1969; Blumler *et al.*, 1975.)

These factors are all important in the process of intentional influence. While our knowledge of them is variable and incomplete they provide, even in this summarily listed form, some guide to the complex matter of determining or predicting the short-term effects of the media. We need to be careful in translating their lessons to other non-campaign circumstances, but, as we will see, they often do have a wide range of application even in adapted forms. If we accept the validity of these points we are already very far from thinking the mass media to be ineffective, or can it be said that we have no certain knowledge of the effects of mass media.

The definition of social reality and the formation of social norms
The topics we should look at under this heading are diverse and the processes involved equally so. Here we mainly consider the process of learning through the media, a process which is often incidental, un-planned and unconscious for the receiver and almost always unintentional on the part of the sender. Hence the concept of 'effectiveness' is usually

inappropriate, except in societies where the media take a planned and deliberate role in social development. This may be true of some aspects of socialist media (see Hopkins, 1970) or of some media in applications in developing countries. (Pye, 1963; Frey, 1973.) There are two main aspects to what occurs. On the one hand, there is the provision of a consistent picture of the social world which may lead the audience to adopt this version of reality, a reality of 'facts' and of norms, values and expectations. On the other hand, there is a continuing and selective interaction between self and the media which plays a part in shaping the individual's own behaviour and self-concept. We learn what our social environment is and respond to the knowledge that we acquire. In more detail, we can expect the mass media to tell us about different kinds of social role and the accompanying expectations, in the sphere of work, family life, political behaviour and so on. We can expect certain values to be selectively reinforced in these and other areas of social experience. We can expect a form of dialogue between persons and fictional characters or real media personalities and also in some cases an identification with the values and perspectives of these 'significant others'. We can also expect the mass media to give an order of importance and structure to the world they portray, whether fictionally or as actuality. There are several reasons for these expectations. One is the fact that there is a good deal of patterning and consistency in the media version of the world. Another is the wide range of experience which is open to view and to vicarious involvement compared to the narrow range of real experience available to most people at most points in their lives. Third there is the trust with which media are often held as a source of impressions about the world outside direct experience. Inevitably, the evidence for this process of learning from the media is thin and what there is does little more than reaffirm the plausibility of these theoretical propositions. The shortage of evidence stems in part from a failure to look for it, until quite recently, and in part from the long-term nature of the processes which make them less amenable to investigations by conventional techniques of social research than are the effects of campaigns. That the media tend to be both consistent amongst themselves over time and also rather given to patterning and sterotyping has been demonstrated often enough in studies of content. We can cite Galtung and Ruge (1965) on foreign countries, Berelson and Steiner (1950) on American ethnic minorities, Baker and Ball (1969) on the portrayal of violence, De Fleur (1964) on occupations, Franzwa (1974) on the representation of women's roles, Hartmann and Husband (1974) on immigrants in Britain, Halloran et al. (1970) on the newspaper portrayal of a militant demonstration, Hartmann (1976) on reporting of industrial relations. A long list of studies can be cited showing the media to have certain inbuilt tendencies to present a limited and recurring range of images and ideas which form rather special versions of reality. In some areas, as with news reporting, the pattern is fairly inescapable, in others the diversity of media allows some choice and some healthy contradiction. What we lack is much evidence of the impact of these selective versions of the world. In many cases discount by the audience or the availability of alternative information must make acceptance of media portrayals at face value extremely unlikely or unusual. We should certainly not take evidence of content as evidence of effect. There is no close correspondence between the two and some studies show this. For example Roshier (1973) found public views about crime to be closer to the 'true' statistical picture than the somewhat distorted version one might extract from the content of local newspapers. Similarly Halloran's study of audience reaction to television reports of the 1968 demonstration shows this to have been rather little affected by the 'one-sided' version presented on the screen. Even so, there is enough evidence as well as good theory for taking the proposition as a whole quite seriously. The case of the portrayal of an immigrant, especially coloured, minority provides a good test, since we may expect the media to be a prominent source of impressions for those in Britain who have little or very limited personal contact with 'immigrants'. Hartmann and Husband (1974), in an investigation of school children, show that, while degree of media exposure and degree of 'prejudice' are not directly correlated, the media are a more important source of knowledge and ideas than are personal contacts in areas where immigrant populations are small. They also show that the media are associated with a view of immigrants as likely to be a cause of trouble or be associated with conflict. It also seems that impressions attributed to the media as source show a rather higher degree of internal similarity and to be in general less evaluative than those derived from personal contact. The main contribution of the mass media is not, according to this study, to encourage prejudice (often the reverse) but in defining the presence of immigrants as an 'objective' problem for the society.

Another case of a somewhat different kind can be found in the portrayal of certain out-groups and in defining the degree and nature of their deviance. Again the media stand in for experience. Cohen's (1973) study of the media portrayal of Mods and Rockers has no evidence of effect, but here the direction of public response, guided by a near-fictional media presentation of events seems predictable. The view taken by Cohen is that 'the mass media provide a major source of knowledge in a segregated society of what the consensus actually is and what the nature of deviation is.' In his view the media are responsible for promoting 'moral panics', identifying scapegoats, and acting as a guide to social control. The terms 'amplification' and 'sensitization' and 'polarization' have been used to describe the tendency of the media to exaggerate the incidence of a phenomenon, to increase the likelihood of it being noticed and to mobilize society against a supposed threat. In recent times, it has been argued that this treatment has been allotted to drug-taking (by Young, 1973), to mugging and to left-wing militants. It is notable that the groups receiving this form of polarizing treatment tend to be small, rather powerless and already subject to broad social disapproval. They are relatively 'safe' targets, but the process of hitting them tends to reaffirm the boundaries around what is acceptable in a free society.

When the question of media effects on violence is discussed, a rather opposite conclusion is often drawn. It seems as if general public opinion still holds the media responsible for a good deal of the increasing lawlessness in society (Halloran, 1970), a view based probably on the frequency with which crime and violence is portrayed, even if it rarely seems to be 'rewarded'. It is relevant to this section of the discussion to explore this view. American evidence obtained for the Kerner Commission on Violence and reported by Baker and Ball (1969) shows there certainly to be much violence portrayed on the most used medium, television. It also shows that most people have rather little contact with real violence in personal experience. The authors chart the public expression of norms in relation to violence and also television norms as they appear in content and find a gap between the two. Thus, while public norms cannot yet have been much affected directly, the gap suggests that the direction of effects is to extend the boundaries of acceptable violence beyond current norms. In brief then, the authors of this study lend support to one of the more plausible hypotheses connecting crime and violence with the media — that the tolerance of aggression is increased by its frequent portrayal and it becomes a more acceptable means of solving problems whether for the 'goodies' or the criminals. It should not be lost sight of, even so, that most dependable research so far available has not supported the thesis of a general association between any form of media use and crime, delinquency or violence. (Halloran, 1970.) The discussion linking social norms with violence takes place on the level of belief systems, opinions, social myths. It would require a long-term historical and cultural analysis to establish the propositions which are involved. Nor should we forget that there are counter-propositions, pointing for instance to the selectivity of public norms about violence and aggression. It is not disapproved of in general in many societies, only in its uncontrolled and non-institutionalized forms. Violence, aggression and competition are often held up for admiration when used with 'correct' aims. Whatever the strength and direction of effects, it seems justifiable to conclude that the mass media remain, for most of us, our most persuasive source of representations of violence, crime and socially disapproved behaviour and provide the materials for shaping personal and collective impressions. There is also a strong pattern in the representations put before us, shaped in the one hand by the 'demands' of the audience, and on the other by forces of social control seeking to make rules and draw boundaries. (Gerbner and Gross, 1976.)

Under this heading we can shift ground somewhat to return to a clearer and perhaps better established example of the process of defining reality and influencing norms. It has already been suggested that the media help to establish an order of priorities in a society about its problems and objectives. They do this, not by initiating or determining, but by publicizing according to an agreed scale of values what is determined elsewhere, usually in the political system. Political scientists have been most alert to the process and the term 'agenda-setting' has been given to it by McCombs and Shaw (1972). They found the mass media to present a very uniform set of issues before the American public in the 1968 Presidential election and found public opinion to accord in content and order rather closely to this pattern. The phenomenon had been noted earlier in election campaign studies, where order of space given to issues in media content was found to be predictive of changes in order of importance attributed to issues over the course of the campaign. (Trenaman and McQuail, 1961; Blumler and McQuail, 1968.) In one sense the media only record the past and reflect a version of the present but, in doing so, they can affect the future, hence the significance of the 'agenda' analogy. A rather more specific case of this kind of influence from the media is indicated by Seymour-Ure (1974) who correlates exceptional publicity given to Enoch Powell in the media with a marked increase in public importance attaching to the issue of immigration and a polarization of views on the question. The likelihood of this occuring is accentuated by the tendency for agreement on news values between different newspapers and different mass media. (Halloran, 1970.)

Given the sparseness of evidence, it is not surprising that we cannot so adequately state the conditions for the occurrence or otherwise of effects from the media in the sphere of forming impressions of reality and defining social norms. In particular, we are dealing with society-wide and historically located phenomena which are subject to forces not captured by normal data-collecting techniques in the social sciences. However, if we re-inspect the list of conditions associated with media campaign success or failure, a number will again seem relevant. In particular, we should look first at the monopoly condition. Here what matters is less the monopoly of owner-ship and control than the monopoly of attention and the homogeneity of content. Uniformity and repetition establish the important result of monopoly without the necessity for the structural causes to be present. The more consistent the picture presented and the more exclusively this picture gains wide attention then the more likely is the predicted effect to occur. (cf. Noelle-Newmann, 1972.) We can suppose, too, that matters out-side immediate experience and on which there are not strongly formed alternative views will also be most susceptible to the level of influence spoken of. Further, we can think that here, as with media campaigns, a trust in the source and an attribution of authority will be an important

factor in the greater extension of media-derived opinions and values.
Other conditions of social organization must also be taken into account.
It is arguable, but untestable, that circumstances of greater individuation
and lower ties of attachment to intermediary groups and associations will
favour an influence from the media. Finally, we might hypothesize that
conditions of social crisis or danger might also be associated with strong
short-term effects from the media on the definition of problems and
solutions.

Immediate response and reaction effects
To discuss this, we return to questions relating largely to individuals and
to direct and immediate effects. We are concerned exclusively with un-
intended, generally 'undesirable', effects which fall into two main
categories. One relates again to the problem of crime and violence, another
to cases of panic response to news or information, where collective
responses develop out of individual reception of the media. Basically, this
field of effects derives from the circumstances of immediacy of reception
and from the speed (approximating sometimes to simultaneity) with
which information can be transmitted by electronic means. A related factor
is the possibility (often realized) of unmediated contact between source
and recipient and the relative absence of institutional control over response.
It is the possibility enshrined in the ideal type of mass communication
proposed by theorists of mass society and students of collective behaviour.
While sociologists have generally stressed the dominance of normative
controls by the society and group, it is certainly possible for direct uncontrolled responses to take place. There are numerous individual cases of
imitation of acts of suicide or crime which have in themselves fed the
belief that the media in general must contribute to lawlessness or disorder.

A considerable amount of research attention has been paid to direct
response to the media since at least the time of the Payne Fund studies
(Peterson, 1933), mainly by social and clinical psychologists, normally
using experimental methods. The results remain confusing and contradictory. One school of thought is now convinced that media portrayals of
aggression can provoke aggression in child audiences. (e.g. Berkovitz, 1964.)
Another favours the view that the effect of fictional evidence is more
likely to be a cathartic or aggression-releasing tendency. (Feshbach, 1971.)
Many experiments have been inconclusive and majority opinion seems
inclined to the cautious conclusion that direct effects involving disapproved behaviour are rare or likely to occur only where there is a strong
disposition in that direction amongst a small minority of the already
disturbed. The problem of interpretation and prediction is exacerbated
by the familiar vice of experimentation that its findings cannot easily be
transferred to a real-life situation and it can rarely do more than simulate
both the stimulus and the response. (Noble, 1975.) Since the evidence in

these matters is so inconclusive, the conditions favouring direct responses in behaviour of a criminal or aggressive kind cannot be stated. At best we can say that solitary use of the media and other conditions of conflict and maladjustment are likely to increase the tendency for the media to stimulate or create fear and anxiety.

There is no shortage of evidence that mass media of all kinds do frequently invoke immediate responses of an affective kind, if any evidence were needed. The responses include fear, excitement, identification. laughter, tears and theses are, of course, often the intended and appropriate results of many 'performances', to use Chaney's (1972) term. The concern of many investigators has been to trace the longer-term behavioural consequences of these immediate responses and it is this which has presented most difficulties. It might also be suggested that this search has been misconceived, however justifiable the aim. Too little research has been directed at understanding the nature of the immediate response in a real-life setting. To pursue the question of long term consequences without a basis in knowledge of the experience itself is unlikely to succeed.

The possibility that information received from the mass media will 'trigger' widespread and collective panic responses has often been canvassed, but rarely demonstrated. The 1938 radio broadcast of Wells' *War of the Worlds* which involved simulated news bulletins reporting an invasion from Mars is the case most often cited in this connection mainly because of Cantril's (1940) research after the event. An event with some similarities in Sweden in 1973 was investigated by Rosengren *et al.* (1975) and the results cast doubt on the thesis as a whole. It seems that in neither case was there much behavioural response, and what there was was later exaggerated by other media. Investigations of news transmission in times of crisis, for instance the studies by Greenberg of the dissemination of news of the assassination of Kennedy (Greenberg, 1965) tells us a good deal more of the processes which begin to operate in such circumstances. Essentially, what happens is that people take over as transmitters of information and those who receive news seek independent confirmation from other media or trusted personal sources. The circumstance of solitary, unmediated, reception and response is unusual and short-lived. Shibutani (1966) reminds us that rumour and panic response are the outcome of situations of ambiguity and lack of information and, on the whole the mass media operate to modify rather than magnify these conditions.

In dealing with this aspect of potential media effects, more attention should perhaps be paid to various kinds of 'contagion' or spontaneous diffusion of activities. The situations most often mentioned relate to the spreading of unrest or violence. For instance at times during the late 1960s when urban violence and rioting was not uncommon in American cities it was suggested that television coverage of one event might lead to occurrences elsewhere. Research into the possibility (e.g. Palatz and Dunn, 1967) does not settle the matter and it remains a reasonable expectation that given the right preconditions, media coverage could spread collective disturbance by publicity alone. Political authorities which have the power to do so certainly act on the supposition that unrest can be transmitted in this way and seek to delay or conceal news which might encourage imitators. The imitation of acts of terrorism or criminality, such as hijacking, seems also likely to have occurred, although the proof is lacking and the phenomenon is different because of its individual rather than collective character. In many areas where there is no institutionalized prohibition there is little doubt that spontaneous imitation and transmission do occur on a large scale by way of the mass media. In the sphere of music, dress, and other stylistic forms, the phenomenon is occurring all the time. It is this which has led to the expectation that the media on their own are a powerful force for change in developing countries (Lerner, 1958), through their stimulation of the desire first to consume and then to change the ways of life which stand in the way of earning and buying. Research evidence (e.g. Rogers and Shoemaker, 1971) and more considered thought (e.g. Golding, 1974) have led to the realization, however, that facts of social structure and of social institutions intervene powerfully in the process of imitation and diffusion. Even so, we should beware of dismissing the process as a misconception or, where it occurs, always as trivial. It is at least plausible that the movement for greater female emancipation owes a good deal to widely disseminated publicity by way of mass media.

Consequences for other social institutions

It was emphasized at the outset that the 'effects' of mass media have to be considered at a level beyond that of the individual audience member and the aggregate of individual behaviours. The path by which collective effects are produced is, in general, simple enough to grasp, but the extent to which effects have occurred resists simple or certain assessment and has rarely been the subject of sustained investigation or thought. As the mass media have developed they have, incontrovertibly, achieved two things. They have, between them, diverted time and attention from other activities and they have become a channel for reaching more people with more information than was available under 'pre-mass media' conditions. These facts have implications for any other institution which requires allocation of time, attention and the communication of information, especially to large numbers and in large quantities. The media compete with other institutions and they offer ways of reaching continuing institutional objectives. It is this which underlies the process of institutional effect. Other social institutions are under pressure to adapt or respond in some way, or to make their own use of the mass media. In doing so, they are likely to alter. Because this is a slow process, occurring along with other kinds of social change, the specific contribution of the media cannot be accounted for with any certainty.

If this argument is accepted, it seems unlikely that any institution will be unaffected, but most open to change will be those concerned with 'knowledge' in the broadest sense and which are most universal and unselective in their reach. In most societies, this will suggest politics and education as the most likely candidates, religion in some cases and to a lesser degree, legal institution. In general we would expect work, social services, science, the military to be only tangentially affected by the availability of mass media. Insofar as we can regard leisure and sport as an institution in modern society this should perhaps be added to politics and education as the most directly interrelated with the mass media. The case of education is an interesting one where we can see at first sight a set of circumstances favourable to the application of mass media, or the technologies of mass media, to existing purposes, yet in practice rather little use made of them. Developed educational institutions have resisted any extensive change of customary ways or adaptation of content to take advantage of new ways of communicating to large numbers. (McQuail, 1970.) The mass media have often been regarded as a threat to the values of the institution, but also accepted in those spheres where innovation is taking place, for instance for the extension of education to adults or for more general educational purposes in developing countries. This conflict and correlated resistance is partly a consequence of the early definition of mass media as belonging to the sphere of entertainment and leisure and partly due to normal institutional conservatism.

The case of politics, as conducted in those societies with a broadly liberal-democratic basis, provides more evidence of adaptation and change to the circumstances of a society where the mass media are the main source of public information. In this case, the modern mass media inherited from the press, and retained, an established political function as the voice of the public and of interest groups and as the source of information on which choices and decisions could be made by a mass electorate and by politicians. The case presented for analysis involves an interaction between a profound change in the media institution as a result of broadcasting and a response by political systems which were not generally subject to profound changes. In these circumstances, it is easier to trace a plausible line of connection, although even here the process is interactive. The challenge to politics from media institutions has taken several forms, but has been particularly strong just because the press was already involved in political processes and because the introduction of broadcasting was a political act. The diversion of time from political activity was less important than the diversion of attention from partisan sources of information and ideology to sources which were more accessible and efficient, often more attractive as well as authoritative, and which embodied the rather novel political values of objectivity and independent 'expert' adjudication. As we have seen, it has increasingly seemed as if it is the mass media which set the 'agenda' and define the problems on a continuous, day to day, basis while political parties and politicians increasingly respond to a consensus view of what should be done. The communication network controlled by the modern mass party cannot easily compete with the mass media network and access to the national platform has to be competed for on terms which are partly determined by the media institutions themselves. In Britain, for instance, the last twenty-five years have seen several tendencies which seem related to these circumstances, with particular reference to television: relaxation of controls on coverage of parliament and political events; the use of advertising for political ends; a decline in importance of the face-to-face political campaign; more attention to the personality of the leader; a de-localizing of politics; a form of competition between parties which stresses performance rather than ideology; a convergence of policy aims; some de-politicizing of local government; a greater attention to opinion polls. The connection with television can only be an assertion, but the fact of some important institutional adaptation is unlikely to be denied and recognition of the mass media by politicians as a highly significant factor is easy to demonstrate. Some parts of the story are well-told by Seymour-Ure (1974) or Blumler (1970).

Changes of culture and society
If we follow a similar line of analysis for other institutions, it is not difficult to appreciate that we can arrive at one or more versions of ways in which culture and social structure can be influenced by the path of development of media institutions. If the content of what we know, our way of doing things and spending time and the organization of central activities for the society are in part dependent on the media, then the fact of interdependence is evident. Again, the problem is to prove connections and quantify the links. The 'facts' are so scarce, open to dispute and often puny in stature that the question is often answered by reference to alternative theories. For some, the answer may still be provided by a theory of mass society of the kind advanced by Mills (1956) or Kornhauser (1959) and criticized by Shils (1975). Such a theory suggests that the mass media encourage and make viable a rootless, alienated, form of social organization in which we are increasingly within the control of powerful and distant institutions. For others, a Marxist account of the mass media as a powerful ideological weapon for holding the mass of people in voluntary submission to capitalism (Marcuse, 1964; Miliband, 1969) provides the answer to the most important effects of the rise of the mass media. A more complex answer is offered by Carey (1969), in his suggestion that the mass media are both a force for integration and for dispersion and individuation in society. Gerbner (1967) sees the key to

the effects of mass media in their capacity to take over the 'cultivation' of images ideas and consciousness in an industrial society. He refers to the main process of mass media as that of 'publication' in the literal sense of making public: 'The truly revolutionary significance of modern mass communication is . . . the ability to form historically new bases for collective thought and action quickly, continuously and pervasively across the previous boundaries of time, space and status.' The ideas of McLuhan (1962 and 1964), despite a loss of vogue, remain plausible for some (e.g. Noble, 1975), especially in their particular reference to the establishment of a 'global village' which will be established through direct and common experience from television. The various theories are not all so far apart. A common theme is the observation that experience, or what we take for experience, is increasingly indirect and 'mediated' and that, whether by chance or design, more people receive a similar 'version' of the world. The consequences for culture and society depend, however, on factors about which the theories are not agreed, especially on the character and likely tendency of this version of reality. Similarly, the available theories are not agreed on the basis of the extraordinary appeal of the mass media, taken in general. Do they meet some underlying human needs? If so, what is the nature of these needs? Alternatively, is the apparent 'necessity' of the media merely the result of some imposed and artificial want? Certainly, the question of what most wide-ranging consequences follow from the media must also raise the question of motivation and use.

The Social Power of Mass Media — A Concluding Note

It has been the intention of this whole discussion to make very clear that the mass media do have important consequences for individuals, for institutions and for society and culture. That we cannot trace very precise causal connections or make reliable predictions about the future does not nullify this conclusion. The question of the power of the mass media is a different one. In essence, it involves asking how effectively the mass media can and do achieve objectives over others at the will of those who direct, own or control them or who use them as channels for messages. The history of mass media shows clearly enough that such control is regarded as a valued form of property for those seeking political or economic power. The basis for such a view has already been made clear in the evidence which has been discussed. Control over the mass media offers several important possibilities. First, the media can attract and direct attention to problems, solutions or people in ways which can favour those with power and correlatively divert attention from rival individuals or groups. Second, the mass media can confer status and confirm legitimacy. Third, in some circumstances, the media can be a channel for persuasion and mobilization. Fourth, the mass media can help to bring certain kinds of public into being and maintain them. Fifth, the media are a vehicle for offering psychic rewards and gratifications. They can divert and amuse and they can flatter. In general, mass media are very cost-effective as a means of communication in society; they are also fast, flexible and relatively easy to plan and control. If we accept Etzioni's (1967) view that 'to some degree power and communication may be substituted for each other', then mass communication is particularly well-suited to the 'stretching' of power in a society.

The general case which can be made out along these lines for treating the mass media as an instrument of social power is sufficiently strong for many commentators to regard it as settled. In this view, all that remains is to discover not *whether* the media have power and how it works, but *who* has access to the use of this power. Generally this means asking questions about ownership and other forms of control, whether political, legal or economic. It is arguable, however, that we need to take the case somewhat further and to probe rather more carefully the initial general assumption. That is, we cannot assume that ownership and control of the means of mass communication does necessarily confer power over others in any straightforward or predictable way. The question of how power works may be the critical one. There are likely to be important structural variations in the power relationship established between 'sender' and 'receiver' in mass communication, which need also to be clarified. Compared to other forms of compliance, the case of mass communication is somewhat unusual, since it is generally entered into voluntarily and on paparently equal terms. Given such a situation, it is not so obvious how a position of dominance can usefully be attained by the 'communicators'. To analyse the process of influence in either structural or social-psychological terms is beyond the scope of this paper, but it is important to place the matter on the agenda for further study. In particular, more attention should be given to the various structures of legitimation which attract and retain audiences and which also govern their attitudes to different media sources. There are critical differences between alternative forms of control from above and between alternative types of orientation to the media, both within and between societies. This is, as yet, a relatively unexplored area but meanwhile we should be as wary of trying to answer questions of power solely in terms of ownership or control as we should be of doing so in terms of 'effects'.

References

Baker, R. K. and Ball, S. J., 1969: *Mass Media and Violence.* Report to the National Commission on the Causes and Prevention of Violence.

Belson, W., 1967: *The Impact of Television.* Crosby Lockwood.

Berelson, B., Lazarsfeld, P. F. and McPhee, W., 1954: *Voting.* University of Chicago Press.

92 DENIS McQUAIL

Berelson, B. and Steiner, G., 1963: *Human Behaviour*. Harcourt Brace.
Berkovitz, 1964: 'The effects of observing violence'. *Scientific American* vol. 210.
Blumler, H., 1933: *Movies and Conduct*. Macmillan.
Blumler, J. G., 1964: British Television: the Outlines of a Research Strategy, *British Journal of Sociology* 15(3).
Blumler, J. G. 1970: 'Television and Politics'. In Halloran, J. D. (Ed.) *The Effects of Television*, Paladin.
Blumler, J. G. and McQuail, D., 1968: *Television in Politics: its uses and influence*. Faber.
Blumler, J. G., Nossiter, T. and McQuail, D., 1975: *Political Communication and Young Voters*. Report to SSRC.
Blumler, J. G. and Katz, E. (Eds.), 1975: 'The Uses and Gratifications approach to Communications Research'. *Sage Annual Review of Communication*, vol. 3.
Butler, D. and Stokes, D., 1969: *Political Change in Britain*. Macmillan.
Cantril, H., Gaudet, H. and Herzog, H., 1940: *The Invasion from Mars*. Princeton University Press.
Carey, J. W., 1969: 'The Communications Revolution and the Professional Communicator'. In Halmos, P., (Ed.), *The Sociology of Mass Media Communicators*. Sociological Review Monograph 13. University of Keele.
Chaney, D. C., 1972: *Processes of Mass Communication*. Macmillan.
Cohen, S., 1973: *Folk Devils and Moral Panics*. Paladin.
Cooper, E. and Jahoda, M., 1947: 'The evasion of propaganda'. *Journal of Psychology* 15, pp. 25–25.
Defleur, M., 1964: 'Occupational roles as portrayed on television'. *Public Opinion Quarterly* 28, pp. 57–74.
    1970: *Theories of Mass Communication*. McKay.
Etzioni, A., 1967: *The Active Society*. Free Press.
Feshbach, S. and Singer, R., 1971: *Television Aggression*. Jossey-Bass.
Franzwa, H., 1974: 'Working women in fact and fiction'. *Journal of Communication*, 24 (2), pp. 104–9.
French, J. R. P. and Raven, B. H., 1953: 'The bases of social power'. In Cartwright, D. and Zander, A. (Eds.) *Group Dynamics*, Free Press.
Frey, F. W., 1973: 'Communication and Development'. In de Sola Pool, I. and Schram, W. (Eds.) *Handbook of Communication*, Rand McNally.
Galtung, J., and Ruge, M., 1965: 'The structure of foreign news'. *Journal of Peace Research* vol. 1.
Gerbner, G. and Gross, L., 1976: 'The scary world of TV's heavy viewer'. *Psychology Today*, April.
Golding, P., 1974: 'Mass communication and theories of development'. *Journal of Communication*, Summer.
Greenberg, B. and Parker, E. B. (Eds.), 1965: *The Kennedy Assassination and the American Public*. Stanford University Press.
Halloran, J. D., 1964: *The Effects of Mass Communication*. Leicester University Press.
Halloran, J. D., Brown R. and Chaney, D. C., 1970: *Television and*

Delinquency. Leicester University Press.
Halloran, J. D., Elliott, P. and Murdock, G., 1970: *Demonstrations and Communication*. Penguin.
Hartmann, P., 1976: 'Industrial relations in the news media'. *Journal of Industrial Relations*. 6(4) pp. 4—18.
Hartmann, P. and Husband, C., 1974: *Racism and the Mass Media*. Davis-Poynter.
Hopkins, M. W., 1970: *Mass Media in the Soviet Union*. Pegasus.
Hovland, C. I., Lumsdaine, A. and Sheffield, F., 1950: *Experiments in Mass Communication*. Princeton University Press.
Inkeles, A. and Bauer, R., 1959: *The Soviet Citizen*. Harvard University Press.
Janis, I. and Hovland, C., 1959: 'An overview of persuability research'. In *Personality and Persuability*, Yale University Press.
Katz, D., 1960: 'The functional approach to the study of attitudes'. *Public Opinion Quarterly* 24, pp. 163—204.
Katz, E. and Lazarsfeld, P. F., 1956: *Personal Influence*. Free Press.
Kelman, H., 1961: 'Processes of opinion change'. *Public Opinion Quarterly* 25, pp. 57—78.
Key, V. O., 1961: *Public Opinion and American Democracy*. Knopf.
Kornhauser, F. W., 1959: *The Politics of Mass Society*. Routledge.
Lang, K. and Lang, G., 1959: 'The Mass Media and Voting'. In Burdick, E. J. and Brodbeck, A. J., (Eds.), *American Voting Behaviour*, Free Press.
Lazarsfeld, P. F., Berelson, B. and Gaudet, H., 1944: *The People's Choice*. Columbia University Press.
Lerner, D., 1958: *The Passing of Traditional Society*. Free Press.
McCombs, M. and Shaw, D. L., 1972: 'The agenda-setting function of mass media'. *Public Opinion Quarterly* 36.
McLuhan, M., 1962: *The Gutenberg Galaxy*. Routledge.
   1964: *Understanding Media*. Routledge.
McQuail, D., 1975: *Communication*. Longman.
   1970: 'Television and Education'. In Halloran, J. D. (Ed.) *The Effects of Television*, Panther.
Marcuse, H., 1964: *One Dimensional Man*. Routledge.
Mills, C. W., 1956: *The Power Elite*. Free Press.
Miliband, R., 1969: *The State in Capitalist Society*. Weidenfeld and Nicolson.
Noelle-Neumann, E., 1974: 'The spiral of silence'. *Journal of Communication*, Spring.
Noble, G., 1975: *Children in Front of the Small Screen*. Constable.
Paletz, D. H. and Dunn, R., 1967: 'Press coverage of civil disorders'. *Public Opinion Quarterly* 33, pp. 328—45.
Peterson, R. C. and Thurstone, L. L., 1933: *Motion Pictures and Social Attitudes*. Macmillan.
Roberts, D. F., 1971: 'The nature of communication effects'. In Schramm W. and Roberts, D. F., *Process and Effects of Mass Communication*, University of Illinois Press, pp. 347—87.
Rogers, E. and Shoemaker, F., 1971: *Communication and Innovations*. Free Press.

Rosengren, K. E., et al, 1976: *The Barsebäck "Panic"*, Lund University.

Roshier, B., 1973: 'The selection of crime news by the press'. In Cohen, S. and Young, J. (Eds.), *The Manufacture of News.* Constable.

Seymour-Ure, C., 1973: *The Political Impact of Mass Media.* Constable.

Shibutani, T., 1966: *Improvised News.* Bobbs-Merril.

Shils, E., 1975: 'The Theory of Mass Society'. In *Centre and Periphery*, Chicago University Press

Star, S. A. and Hughes, H. M., 1951: 'Report on an educational campaign. *American Journal of Sociology* 55 (4), pp. 389—400.

Trenaman, J. and McQuail, D., 1961: *Television and the Political Image.* Methuen.

Weiss, W., 1969: 'Effects of the Mass Media of Communication'. In Lindzey, G. and Aronson, E. (Eds.) *Handbook of Social Psychology*, 2nd edn. vol. v.

Young, J., 1973: 'The amplification of drug use'. In Cohen, S. and Young, J. (Eds.) *The Manufacture of News*, Constable.

4

Power, Class and the Media

John Westergaard

I

The media may or may not 'mirror society'. Whether they do turns in
part on the meaning given to that phrase. But there is no such ambiguity
of metaphor to the point that contemporary debate about the media —
about their social role and character — mirrors contemporary debate about
the condition of society. Socio-political commentary of right-wing, centre
and left-wing inspiration casts the media in correspondingly different
parts; and all diagnoses of the nature and impact of media production
carry with them at least hints of some conception of the general drift of
social existence. The very word 'mass' usually attached to 'media' suggests
reference, of course, to one version or another of a characterization of
society today as a 'mass society'. Even those diagnoses of the press and
broadcasting which couple emphasis on a relative professional immunity
of media producers from outside influences with scepticism about the
capacity of the product in turn to influence the audience imply, if they
do not always directly express, a view of society at large. Their effect is
to assign little social significance to the media, except as sources of
entertainment and of images, comment and information selectively
absorbed by audiences to fit in with pre-existing views and orientations;
thus to dismiss much of the debate about the media as beside the point.
But that dismissal assumes a particular state of society — a state conducive
to some sort of mutual autonomy of different groups and institutions,
where professionals are able to resist pressures from the markets, organizations and ideological climates in which they work; where groups and sub-
groups in the audience of the media can maintain their own 'constructions
of social reality' with little reference to the constructions on tap from the
media; where multiple social interaction takes place, in short, accompanied
by only limited mutual influence.

Defence of the media against critics sometimes takes just that form.
But the combination of arguments is difficult for those engaged in media
production themselves to sustain. It serves their image. to themselves and
others, well enough to argue that journalists and broadcasters can and do

assert professional independence in their work; but it serves their self-confidence and their presentation of a *raison d'être* poorly to accept an argument that what they produce carries little weight in affairs, events and ideas. Professional integrity is then left with no very substantial professional service to perform. Understandably, media spokesmen therefore usually assign more influence to their product. However much the press, radio and television are there to entertain, we are commonly told, they are also there to do more: perhaps, as in the paternalistic specification once set for the BBC by Lord Reith, to educate and elevate public taste; always, in some manner or another, to contribute an essential element of enlightenment to democracy.

There are different recipes for that task of public enlightenment. One, associated not least with the American press and in tune with demands for 'open government', ascribes to journalists a prime role as active keepers of the public conscience: watchdogs on behalf of some silent majority, bloodhounds for ever on the scent of corruption and abuse of power, pretence and incompetence. 'Muck-raking' is then central to the business of the profession. In glorifications of the American version of this formula, the press acquires the character of an independent fourth arm of the constitution; journalists that of unofficial Ombudsmen with a roving commission of enquiry. Other prescriptions stress vigilance in critical investigation less, sensitivity of media antennae more. Their emphasis is on the service of the media as sounding boards for comment on public affairs, as platforms from which a diversity of voices may be heard. There are variations of model here too. The diversity of comment allowed voice may, as a matter of express policy, be confined within limits that take consonance with orthodoxy and 'established' opinion as the touchstone of legitimacy; or the constraints may be relaxed in conscious recognition of heterodoxy — if still within the bounds of some so-called 'consensus', then a consensus acknowledged to be hard to identify and susceptible to change. Broadcasting in France and Italy, under direct government control at least until recently, have followed something like the first variant of the model. So, by its own task-prescription, in a different style and despite constitutional separation from government, did the BBC when it set out to speak 'for the nation' under the guidance of Lord Reith. But from the 1950s and 60s, broadcasting in Britain — commercial as well as state-financed — has shifted more to the second conception of its function as a forum for socio-political comment. There is no clear line between the two in any case; and what they have in common overrides their differences: the assertion of an important role for the media in the political processes of liberal democracy, through their transmission — reflection, magnification, exploration — of relevant opinion on public affairs, proposals and counter-proposals for policy, to the electorate. Spokesmen for the press claim the same role for their sector of the industry. In both sectors, it is argued, the professional integrity and independence of journalists and broadcasters help to ensure a representative variety of significant voices on the platforms provided by the media. If that guarantee is backed in the case of broadcasting by formal requirements of 'balance', 'impartiality', 'fairness' and so on — as ostensibly it is in Britain and the United States, by different devices — so in the case of the press it is said to be backed by the range of newspapers and magazines of different stances on offer. Even if editorial control exercised by professional criteria were not enough to give a fair hearing to all views with a fair claim to be heard, the span from *The Times* to the *Sun* (or the equivalent) should do the job.

Add to these functions ascribed to the media — whatever the emphases in the particular recipe — that also of transmission of information about public affairs: of news as well as views; and of news, in the professional conventions of journalism, quite distinct from views by its objective, factual character. The role in the polity cast for press and broadcasting services is then substantial. It may not be to persuade. Indeed, those models of the social functions of the media which stress their independence rule out any collective role of persuasion. Taken together, as an institutional sector of society, press and broadcasting services then have no joint view, no common ideology, no corporate set of policy prescriptions of their own to propagate; and their capacity to do their job depends upon just that collective neutrality. They make up, to put this conception of their task at its grandest, a 'free-floating intelligentsia' serving the general public; an academy for the masses; a prime source of such popular enlightenment as popular participation in the common business of society requires. Journalists and broadcasters are critics perhaps, if so with disparate commitments; communicators of criticism certainly, of alternative perspectives and interpretations of affairs, of facts against which opinion is to be weighed; open-minded sceptics too, by the demands of that business of communication. Fourth arm of the constitution, fourth estate, muckrakers, gadflies, cross-examiners of the great on behalf of the common people, convenors of public debate and conveyors of hard fact — taking on all or some of these parts, in one mixture or another, they help to keep liberal democracy alive in societies too populous and too complex for face-to-face exchange to suffice.

II

Practitioners of media communication may not usually put their claims to perform a public service in quite such strident terms. Professional characterization of the business of the media — even of their business in news reportage and socio-political commentary — for the most part gives much weight to other objectives: entertainment, for example, and stimulation of interest, as ends more or less in themselves. Criticisms from

right and left that the media corrupt their publics — debase taste, pander
to preoccupations with trivia, undermine established morality or conversely propagate acceptance of the status quo — are likely to provoke
disclaimers of influence: arguments, first, that journalists and especially
broadcasters are tightly bound by technical constraints on what they can
put over; second, that in any case they go, and have to go, where demand
leads them — they are prisoners, not producers, of popular tastes, interests
and orientations. But disclaiming influence, to repeat a point made earlier,
verges on a confession of professional bankruptcy. So it is commonly,
though paradoxically, coupled with claims that the media have a positive
'social responsibility'.[1] Explicit or implicit in this is an assertion of a
significant share in responsibility for public enlightenment.

If such claims were no more than an example of tactics familiar in
attempts by occupational groups to secure themselves by establishing
professional legitimacy, their interest would be quite limited. Their
significance is a good deal larger, however, because these are claims for
the media which are widely echoed — indeed amplified — in conventional
political wisdom. Liberal democratic theory has seen the press historically,
and the various forms of mass communication now, in just that socially
responsible role ascribed to it by media spokesmen in their positive mood.
That view is embodied, expressly or by clear implication, also in the most
influential contemporary version of liberal democratic theory: the postulate that power in western societies of the mid- and late-twentieth century
is 'pluralistically' diffused among a diversity of separate, competing groups
and interests of which none is dominant. The media are parts of the
machinery by which, in this description, rival pressures and policy
proposals are expressed, made known, brought to arbitration, in a
multiple contest that makes for shifting equilibria of influence.

Two prime features of this pluralistic model of power need to be noted.
First, with regard to its substance, it runs counter to those interpretations
which assign continuing dominant influence to a single set of interests in
contemporary western societies, despite the ostensibly indeterminate
push and pull of contending forces in the democratic market place. It runs
counter especially, of course, to Marxist interpretations; and it has, in
many of its versions, been deliberately aimed at these. Second, with
regard to its methodology and underlying conception of the phenomenon
of power, the pluralistic model takes a resolutely 'behaviourist' approach.
Power, so it is asserted, is manifest in the outcome of active conflict and
competition among contending groups and individuals. The locus of power
at any given time can, and can only, be established by reference to the
visible results of visible contests for influence over 'decision making'. It is
incumbent on theorists who attribute dominance in affairs to a particular

1 See for example, Brown (1969); and on different views of the tasks of broadcasting
   held within the BBC, Burns (1970).

interest — to private business, for example — to show that policies eventually adopted come substantially closer to those advocated by identifiable representatives of that interest than to those advocated by any or all of their rivals. The allegation of dominance otherwise falls to the ground — as does, so pluralists argue, the Marxist ascription of dominance to private business, when it is put to this hard test by scrutiny of decision-making processes.[2]

There is strength to this position at first glance. It pins down power — so slippery a concept in much debate — as an observable phenomenon: it defines power by reference to activities which can be systematically watched. But there is the crucial flaw to it — as I am among many critics to suggest — that only a fraction of the reality of power in fact is so observable. Excluded from such a conception of power is power that is effective without any active exercise of pressure — covert as well as overt — because it is not actively opposed. To take a limited example, used as one test case in research directed to pluralist conclusions, the outcome of the diverse pushes and pulls which shaped 'urban renewal' schemes in American cities in the 1950s and 60s could, demonstrably, be described as a complex compromise between proposals and counter-proposals pressed by a multiplicity of contending interests. But no less demonstrably, the outcome gave short shrift to low-income residents of the areas 'renewed'. Represented though these people were among the contending interests, urban renewal well merited its nickname of 'negro removal'. The explanation of the apparent paradox is obvious. The dice were loaded against the low-income groups well before the contest to hammer out the renewal schemes began. The point is not just that 'real estate' interests, associated business groups and their backers were able to 'manipulate the agenda' for decision-making in advance, as some formulations of the argument against pluralist conceptions have it. Manipulation of the agenda would still be an activity, in principle observable. The point is that the dice were loaded by implicit assumptions, binding in hard practical terms on all contestants for influence, about the limits of policy: by the sheer inertia of the way 'things are done', and the restraints imposed by such inertia on the policy alternatives which contestants could realistically propose. Representatives of the hard-hit residents could not to any effect have pressed, for example, for universal public housing at low rents, because prevailing conceptions of social policy ruled this well out of the range of practical politics. As it was pointless for them to voice the idea, moreover, they would be unlikely for the most part even to think it. In short, the measure of the small rations of power in their hands, and the

2 The most explicit formulations of a pluralist conception of power are American: see, for instance, Dahl (1961, 1967) and Polsby (1963). Similar assumptions underlie much British political analysis but are usually not fully spelled out; see, however, McKenzie (1958) for one example.

large rations in the hands of business, was the implicit, pre-set terms of
the contest for influence; not, significantly or necessarily, their respective
parts in the contest itself or in prior jockeying to manipulate its agenda.[3]

So, by larger application of the same argument, private capital retains
dominant power throughout western liberal democracy: not because
business and its identifiable representatives continuously predominate in
active decision making, or because specific measures advocated by them
inevitably prevail; not to the effect that unions and shopfloor workers
always draw the shortest straws in bargaining and conflict with employers
or government, by the terms in which those disputes are cast; not in the
sense that the state is best described as a 'committee for managing the
common affairs of the whole bourgeoisie', metaphorical point though there
still is to that description; but because the everyday working assumptions
of economy and polity, above all the routine criteria of resource
allocation — the continuing terms, therefore, by which conditions of life
are framed and, significantly, within which jockeying for influence by
rival groups takes place — are still terms set to the maintenance of private
capital and geared to its interests. The practice of common affairs in
western liberal democracies — even in the vastly expanded public
sector — takes the economic logic of property, profit and markets as
a natural and given premise.

Of course the point is not proven by mere assertion. It needs demonstration; but this is not the place for that. The outcome of this enduring
power of private capital is relevant here, however, and itself points to that
power. Inequalities of material circumstances, security and opportunity
remain marked, mutually coincident, and in their relative range little
affected either by public welfare provisions or by overall increments in
production and leisure. Private ownership of the means of production and
exchange is still intensely concentrated, makes a prime direct contribution
to financial inequality, and continues to hold its beneficiaries immune
from the imperative that governs the livelihood, life chances and life styles
of the majority: dependence on the sale of labour power in markets which
work to profit criteria; or alternatively, now, reliance on public provision
set at levels generally below those of labour market earnings and in effect
financed principally from the wage packets of ordinary earners. The
enduring power of private capital, in summary, is reflected in the persistent
configuration of class inequality.[4]

It is in this context that the role of the media in societies like ours

3 Among criticisms of pluralism in which these or related points are made, see
   Bachrach and Baratz (1970), Lukes (1974), Miliband (1969, including Chapter 8
   on the media), Westergaard and Resler (1975, Part 3).

4 See especially Westergaard and Resler (Parts 2 and 4) and for slightly more recent
   evidence that economic inequality in Britain remains much as described there,
   Royal Commission on the Distribution of Income and Wealth (1975).

must be considered. If the media contribute to social critique and democratic public enlightenment, then the independence ascribed to them as
essential to that task must be one which, in some effective way, sets them
apart from the power of capital over the routine of common affairs. Left-
wing critics, of course, deny the media any such capacity for independence.
My argument, from the left too, will be to the same conclusion. But my
particular concern will be with the character of media 'dependence on
capital' — which, I want to suggest, involves everyday acceptance of the
inertia of 'things as they are' more, and far more significantly, than it does
subjection to active pressure. To put the point as I see it briefly, liberal
democratic theory of a pluralist form suffers from the same fundamental
weakness in its ascription of critical 'responsibility' to the media as it does
in its larger denial of any durable concentration of power in western
societies. It focuses on diversity of debate, critique and contest within set
parameters, but is indifferent to the existence and social shape of those
parameters. I shall not be much concerned, as a separate matter, with
attacks directed at the media from the political and cultural right wing —
arguments that the media corrupt traditional morality and subvert public
order by giving sustained voice to liberal scepticism — because such
attacks, in effect, accept the claims made on behalf of the media that
they stand apart from the established mode of affairs; only to put a
negative instead of a positive evaluation on much the same conclusion
as is drawn in conventional democratic wisdom.

III
While the independence prescribed for the media as essential to their
postulated task of enlightenment has been commonly defined as
independence from government, it is precisely that sector of the mass communications industry ostensibly most free of state control — the commercial
press — to which the ascription of independence in any effective social
sense is most evidently invalid. The signs of that are so plain that they do
not need to be spelt out in great detail. Throughout the western world,
the great majority of newspapers and commercial journals of opinion
speak with editorial voices of conservative tone and — despite common
disclaimers of party affiliation — lend their normal support to bourgeois
parties where these are opposed by parties of labour; in the United States
to the Republican in preference to the Democratic Party. True enough,
the aggregate circulations of newspapers editorially inclined towards the
leftward half of the conventional political spectrum may — as in Britain —
roughly equal the circulations of those inclined to the right; especially if,
in this sort of ascription of 'balance' to the press, liberal orientations are
assigned to 'the left' no less than labour orientations. But to see 'balance'
in this — socio-political independence through diversity within the
collectivity of the press — is to ignore two fundamental matters. First,

the number of separate newspapers and journals — thus the range of choice and disparity of editorial voices — is far more limited to the left than to the right; in the press designed with a labour appeal than in the press designed with a bourgeois appeal. Second, the commercial formula for mass circulation newspapers with a labour appeal is one — and as a matter of market necessity one — which both reduces any function of socio-political 'enlightenment' to a small place among editorial aims, and takes a 'radical' editorial orientation no further than to a blend of vacuous populism with support for political moderation and social compromise within the current order. The causes and implications of both points need some elaboration; and they provide one illustration of the character of media 'dependence on capital' as more a matter of the logic of inertia than of subjection to active manipulation.

The press, of course, is now big business: characterized by increasing concentration of production and, in recent years especially, by the growth of a network of financial links between newspaper and magazine publishing on the one hand, other branches of the communication and entertainment industry on the other.[5] Because they themselves are engaged in big business, press controllers — proprietors, board members, chief editors, commercial managers — are likely enough to be sympathetic to the interests of private enterprise. But to attribute the socio-political orientations of the press primarily to the natural ideological leanings of its controllers would be to miss the significance of another corollary of the fact that newspaper and magazine production is business: the dependence on market sales. Even newspapers directed by controllers personally inclined to radicalism of one variety or another — ideological mavericks in the world of press control — cannot escape the commercial logic of the market. That logic is two-fold: newspaper companies must sell copies to readers, of course; but they must also sell space to advertisers, to keep the retail price of copies at a level sufficiently low for survival in the competition for circulation.

There is a special social twist to the fact that advertising provides a substantial part of newspaper revenue. The significance of that fact does not lie, typically, in any major exercise of pressure by advertisers to shape editorial content; nor does it turn just on the proportion of revenue which comes from the sale of space to advertisers — a proportion which, in Britain today, is much higher for the 'quality' than for the 'popular' press, though sizeable even for the latter.[6] What is important is the simple point that wealthy readers — especially if they control corporate wealth as well as private wealth for their own use — count for more in the calculations

5 See especially Murdock and Golding (1973) and their contribution to the present volume.

6 The average proportions in 1975 were 58 per cent for 'quality' dailies, 27 per cent for 'popular' dailies: see Royal Commission on the Press (1976).

of advertisers than do readers on ordinary and low incomes: understandably enough, because they command more purchasing power. So advertisers will pay more to reach a body of wealthy readers than to reach the same number of poorer readers; so in turn newspapers aimed at the top levels of the newspaper-reading public can, and usually do, charge higher advertising rates per head of their readership than newspapers addressed to less prosperous readers; and so a paper for 'top people' can survive with a smaller circulation than a paper for solid citizens of suburbia, while a paper directed principally to wage earners and the poor needs very large sales if advertisers are to be persuaded to buy space on a sufficient scale to keep revenue in line with costs.[7] It is this hierarchial twist to the market logic of newspaper publication which, above all else, explains the twin features that so distinctively disqualify the press from the role of 'fourth estate' claimed for it: the diminution in the number and diversity of newspapers on offer, head for head of population, on the steps down from establishment and bourgeois public to wage-earning public; and the shallow character of such 'radicalism' as newspapers specifically addressed to the latter kind of public mix into their recipe for sales.

Radicalism of a sort is now part of that normal recipe. Commercial newspapers consciously and in their own terms successfully put together to appeal to a manual working-class readership — of British national dailies today only the *Daily Mirror* and the *Sun* — blow a carefully tuned populist trumpet. Their tone is 'matey' and aspires to plain speaking; they pride themselves on talking for, as well as to, ordinary men and women; their editorial slant normally favours Labour at elections. But that, roughly, is the limit of their market-calculated leftward inclination. When they attack and 'expose', their targets are not the routine power of capital, property and profit in common affairs: occasionally, of course, business malpractice — the 'unacceptable face of capitalism', as if the normal face shorn of malpractice were self-evidently acceptable — but far more regularly officialdom — bumbledom, the 'big battalions' of government, of unions rather than business, of militant trade unions and shop-floor organization not least. Their Labour loyalties are firmly behind 'moderation', their acceptance of conventional political wisdom — the need for wage restraint today, for 'partnership' of labour with capital always — unquestioning and loud. Politics and societal affairs, moreover, are a sideline in the make-up of these newspapers. Personalia, sport, sex, snippets of this and that — with much space devoted to pictures and, of course, to advertisements — loom far larger, in a package designed to appeal to what are taken to be the common denominators of casual interest among a 'mass' wage-earning public.

7 For an analysis of advertising charges in relation to circulation and social composition of readership of daily newspapers in 1970/71, see Westergaard and Resler (1975, p. 265).

It is not my point that these are 'low' common denominators of popular interest, in any sense justifying condemnation in themselves. My point is that the image of the 'mass' reader to which the popular newspapers work is a drastically selective one. The press addressed to a working class public does not give its readers 'what they want'. It gives them part of what they want — what is safely enough within the range of most readers' interests to maintain the mass circulations necessary for survival. But it dare not indulge 'minority interests' — even if the minorities might run into many hundreds of thousands — or pursue unorthodox lines beyond a spasmodic display of gimmickry, for fear of losing readers at the margin of circulation. The fate of newspapers which have died with seven-figure yet still not sufficiently massive sales — on the 'labour-appeal' side in Britain notably the *Daily Herald* — is constantly in the minds of editors and commercial managers. Sustained critique of the social order as it is, and information to back it, would find a substantial public in the wage-earning population: popular ideology, as I shall argue later, is an ambivalent mixture of quiescence and dissent. But that public would not secure sales in the millions, to use the market scales relevant in Britain; the current of dissent in popular ideology is too diffuse for that; and so sustained critique goes by the board in the formula for mass-circulation papers addressed to ordinary wage earners. The logic of the market allows no safe alternative: no scope therefore for a commercial popular press to contribute to critical enlightenment in any sense that matters.

IV

Subsidization to keep market pressures at bay may, of course, modify the picture and allow some leeway for survival of a left wing within the popular press. But provision of public funds for the purpose — for example, as has been suggested, from a general levy on advertising revenue — makes little sense: it is highly implausible that any government-sponsored subsidy would be directed mainly and durably where it is needed, to foster radical journalism. Organizations of the left, on the other hand, are by their nature ill-equipped to spare the money for the large and sustained payments needed to overcome the logic of the market. The British labour movement, in the main, has refused to finance a voice of its own in the popular press; and even if this had not been so, its voice — like that of the leadership of the movement and like those of party-and-union-subsidized Social Democratic papers in some other countries — would no doubt have spoken for 'moderation'. All else apart, the need to keep the drain on movement funds in check would dictate commercial, and so also socio-political, prudence.

Broadcasting services can, ostensibly, keep market pressures more at arms-length than the press; and the argument that television and radio allow a real voice for dissent carries some conviction at first sight. True, broadcasting financed from advertising revenue is plainly liable to trim its sails to the commercial wind. Audiences with modest per capita incomes must be kept large to keep advertisers advertising; programmes of safe 'mass' appeal are the means to that; and there is no obvious reason why a prohibition — as in Britain — of direct advertiser-sponsorship of programmes should do much by itself to defeat this logic. Advertisers do not, after all, sponsor particular features and columns in the newspapers; and commercial broadcasting companies that failed to maintain mass audiences at peak hours would soon find their income dwindling. Yet several factors combine, on the face of things, to give a wider margin for diversity and heterodoxy even in commercial broadcasting than in the popular press. With public allocation of channels and wavelengths — in effect, significantly, a restriction of competition at the hands of government — even limited audiences fairly readily go to numbers big enough, in conjunction with mass audiences for popular programmes, to keep advertising revenue rolling. Direct market pressures may be held at a distance to that extent. In Britain, moreover, public supervision of commercial broadcasting by a statutory authority — in much the same way as the supervision exercised by the BBC's governing body over the nationalized sector of the industry — finds expression in rules, guidelines or conventions which, in their prescription of 'balance', 'objectivity' and so on, could provide part of an institutional frame to encourage explorations of dissent and unorthodoxy on the part of broadcasters.

Such prescription, however, cuts two ways. It enjoins impartiality and tolerance; but it sets also a limit to both. These virtues are to be practised with due respect for established morality and conventional orientations to the world: in the words of a 1971 set of BBC guidelines, without offence to 'good taste or decency . . . to public feeling'; within, not only 'the Constitution', but also 'the consensus about basic moral values'.[8] If there is no surprise to the fact that support for Republican 'extremism' in Northern Ireland at present is taken to fall well outside the range of views which merit impartial treatment, it throws perhaps more light on the conception of 'consensus' involved that the same guidelines refer to the BBC's decision under Lord Reith, in 1926, to give 'authentic impartial news' of the General Strike while broadcasting nothing to prolong or justify it, as illustrating a principle still relevant, though capable of application with more 'latitude' today.

It is tempting to see in such formal prescriptions both one source and one proof of major inhibitions on the capacity of television and radio to work as free-wheeling vehicles of critique and dissent. But if there are inhibitions to that effect — as I shall argue that indeed there are — their nature and causes probably cannot be read off from the wording of guide-

8 The words quoted come from an internal BBC circular on 'Principles and practices in news and current affairs', June 1971.

lines to producers or, for that matter, from the establishment cast of the
personnel of the supervisory authorities from which such guidelines
emanate.[9] The formal prescriptions are vague; potentially open to diverse
interpretations; of interest only because they give authoritative force to
the principle that broadcast dissent must stay within the limits of the
'legitimate', not because they fix those limits. Whatever influence
supervisory authorities may have over broadcast output — unobtrusively
and by retrospective comment far more than by active intervention — the
test of tolerance in broadcasting, in the end, is the content of output
itself; and the limits to tolerance are likely to be set, in practical terms,
mainly by broadcasters' own conceptions of how the world ticks and,
especially, of what they themselves are about.

The world which broadcasters see it as their task to reflect is, I suggest,
very much the world 'as it is': as it appears in the eyes of conventional
wisdom, to which conflict, competition, rivalry and disagreement are
certainly visible — and provide a mainstay of news, commentary and
debate — but to which the routine assumptions that both govern everyday
affairs, and also confine the range of contest, are invisible. Political
dispute is described and interpreted in the terms which those actively
engaged — politicians, party and pressure-group spokesmen — themselves
implicitly set to their disputes. Industrial bargaining and unrest are
reported and discussed — at best — in the terms of the immediate points
at issue and their bearing on other issues with which practical politics
associates them. This is to state the obvious. Broadcasters and journalists
will no doubt retort: 'What else?' But the obvious here has a significance
which, by the nature of that retort, is easily missed. For the terms within
which contests in the everyday world of affairs are cast take a lot for
granted. In western liberal societies they take, above all, the principles and
mechanisms of private property, profit and markets for granted; consequently
too, the nature and prime sources of persistent inequality. Practising
politicians do not, for the most part, engage in controversy about the
very existence and operative modes of those institutions. They dispute
about the means to keep inflation in check, hold the pound sterling steady,
set production growing; about whether and how to shift taxation, public
expenditure, income — or more often wage and state benefit — distribution
a fraction this way or that; about whether and how to contain the current
influence of trade unions, or perhaps to give workers a little more semblance
of say in their jobs; and so on: not about the framework of resource
allocation upon which all such policies and counter-policies are only

9 On the backgrounds and connections of BBC governors and other members of the
'cultural directorate' in the 1950s, see Guttsman (1963, Chapter XI); and on the
qualities looked for in selection, see Normanbrook (1965): 'persons . . . with
knowledge and experience of public affairs . . . people of equable temper and cool
judgement, neither hopefully "with it" nor hopelessly past it. . . . '

variations of theme. So, too, union officials and shop stewards do not attempt to bargain with employers' representatives to eliminate private property and profit. They do — some of them, sometimes, like some politicians sometimes — assert an idea of an alternative society without private property and profit; but not when they bargain, or usually even when they call industrial action. They, like the politicians, are practical men and women with their feet on the ground, out for what can be achieved more or less 'as things are'. It is that world of things as they are, and of the pulls and pushes of rival attempts to exercise influence within the frame of things as they are, which broadcasters present to their audiences.

There are technical and practical factors, forces of institutional gravitation, no doubt also prior socio-ideological biases additional to these pressures, which both reinforce the boundaries thus set to broadcasters' conception of public affairs and, within those boundaries, incline broadcasters to give greater weight to the voices of well-established opinion than to those even of 'legitimate' opposition. The journalistic intuition which defines the 'newsworthy'; the assumption that news must be 'hot'; television's concern with visual presentation; the conventions that require variety of content and set tight limits to the time allowed for any one item of news, more flexible but still narrow constraints on time for comment — all these combine to make broadcast news, very largely, an inevitably selective transmission of information about events and incidents accompanied only by interpretations consonant with conventional wisdom; or, with equal significance, by no interpretation, so that conventional interpretation stands by sheer default of any alternative. Definitions of the newsworthy are derived from, views on the news and some of the news itself are sought from, people and organizations at the top: from those who themselves run the machinery of public affairs. The good broadcasting journalist, like the good pressman and the good political scientist of pluralist persuasion, is an 'inside dopester' who knows his way around the corridors of practical power and uses the eyes and ears of the people who move in those corridors. Moreover, just as government draws its royal commission and committee members from limited lists of the great and the good, so broadcasters — the more so because their time is always short — draw their 'representative' spokesmen of interests, their debaters and commentators, from small circles of established men and women with established broadcasting reputations; and they rely on advice from these, and incestuously from each other, for new recruits to the circles.[10]

But above all else, perhaps, broadcasters work to a highly nonvariegated

10 For evidence and impressions to support some of these points, see, for example, Elliott (1972), Halloran et al. (1970), Hood (1972), Murdock (1973), Smith (1973), Winston et al. (1975).

image of their audience: to a conception of their viewers and listeners as a mass of ordinary people of 'ordinary common sense', men and women with their feet on the ground who take the world as it is and for whom the natural interpretation of affairs involves asking, in simplified form, much the same sorts of question which those actively involved in matters of state put to each other's activity. My point is not that this image of 'the public' is totally false; but that it is a caricature which sacrifices the diverse and ambiguous reality of popular outlooks on the world — a contradictory mixture of dissent, disgruntlement, resentment and suspicion with conformity and acquiescent 'common sense' — for a picture of 'mass' opinion and taste which singles out only the safe 'common denominators' of orientation that square with the practical order of things as they are. In this respect, broadcasters' images of their audience are much the same as newspaper producers' images of their readers; and to much the same effect. They are not derived from studies of public opinion — even from studies of the common kind which, by posing questions in conventional terms, are liable to elicit conventional answers. Broadcasters in fact rarely make use of audience research. But they are — of professional necessity, in public sector as well as commercial services — sensitive to fluctuations in demand for their programmes; and at the margins audience demand, like newspaper circulation, is likely to reflect precisely the safe 'common denominators' of popular outlook.[11] The outcome is a down-to-earth, everyday interpretation of the world to a collective 'man in the street', who has a uniform common sense attributed to him consonant with the conventional wisdom on public affairs. That sort of interpretation must, of course, come into any function of 'enlightenment' performed by the media. But it is not enough — irrespective, for that matter, of the make-up of popular opinion at any given time — if enlightenment is to be critical.

The 1960s and early 70s provide a crucial test of my argument. For internal conflict in western countries not only accelerated then, but also took forms which suggested a spread of dissent from the operational routines of the established order. In industrial relations in Britain, for example, shop-floor militancy grew to pose a challenge to conventionally recognized patterns of collective bargaining; unions themselves turned to militant action in response both to that and, particularly, to increased government activity to enforce labour discipline; wage demands for a period were pitched to levels which, if sustained, plainly threatened the viability of profit; industrial disputes inexorably acquired an overt political character and, on more than one occasion, came near to

11   On broadcasters' limited use of audience research and their sensitivity to fluctuations in programme audiences, see Burns (1970). Burns' paper and Kumar (1975) are also relevant, *inter alia*, on the shift in the climate of BBC production referred to earlier and again a little further on.

triggering a general strike. 'Direct action' of a variety of kinds — rent strikes, squatting by homeless people, as well as industrial sit-ins — implied practical rejection of some rights of property, though not full-scale ideological dissent from the institution of private property. In these new circumstances, even if not earlier, it became patently nonsensical to argue that the media could and should apply only conventional wisdom to their interpretation of affairs because there were no alternative interpretations with a reasonable claim to be heard. If the media were vehicles of independent and critical 'constructions of reality', they would have been in the vanguard to search out, explore and give voice to the murmur of non-conformity.

They were not: not, of course, the press; but, beyond a shift of quite limited significance, not the broadcasting services either. In Britain, the socio-political turbulence of the 1960s probably played a part in widening the implicit conceptions of the 'legitimate consensus' to which the BBC had worked earlier; in inclining BBC and commercial broadcasters alike to distance themselves more from authority and adopt a stance of ostensible identification with the 'man in the street', a little sceptical and blunt towards government, officials, parties and large organizations; in broadening the canons of taste and codes of morality observed in television and radio on matters of sex, family relations and personal conduct; in adding provincial and working-class milieux to the staple settings of plays and serials, fragments of labour history — the romantic past rather than the controversial present — to the repertoire of documentary themes. There was liberalization and diversification in all this — much to the chagrin of right-wing opinion. But the widening of broadcasting tolerance hardly at any point extended to a recognition of perspectives on the ends of public policy distinct from those brought to the business of practical politics by its established practitioners: to a recognition that the routine assumptions of resource allocation — and all that hangs on those assumptions — are themselves always contestable and were now, in effect, more the subject of direct and indirect popular questioning than they had been for long.

Strikes — in any case selectively reported or ignored in a manner to suggest their concentration in maverick industries — were and are still presented as irrational and irresponsible; the work of small, unrepresentative knots of militants or of larger groups swayed by shortsighted crowd emotion; almost invariably contrary to the public interest.[12]   It is standard, barely-reflected practice for broadcasters — like other journalists, politicians and accredited public commentators — to describe the labour right as 'moderate'; for news of new industrial action to be referred to as 'bad news tonight', news of the end of industrial action — unless the terms of settlement significantly favour those who took it — as 'good news'.

12 See especially Winston *et al.* (1975).

Widespread unrest, in which it is plausible to see symptoms of dissent from things as they are, may go totally unreported — as did a series of local rent strikes in 1972/73 against the Housing Finance Act of that period; or it may be handled as the manifestation of a popular or sectional 'ungovernability', mindless, aimless and without substantial cause. The presumption in news reporting and commentary remains consistently on the side of order against disorder; and, with only rare aberrations, in line with ruling conceptions of priorities in 'crisis diagnosis' and policy prescription. The possibility, for example, that large wage claims, strikes and go-slows, direct action of other kinds, may reflect popular clamour for equity in a society where inequality is entrenched — at least a partial assertion of priorities different from Westminster and City prescriptions of priority for checking inflation, correcting the balance of payments, expanding business profitability — such a possibility is not so much rejected as, simply, never more than momentarily entertained. When the media publicise dissent, in short, the effect of their interpretation is to minimize its sources and objects, to magnify its fragmentation and incoherence. That effect comes about far less by positive act of will on the part of media producers, or in response to active establishment pressure upon them, than by the sheer inertia of understandings of the world of affairs circumscribed by the horizons of those who run affairs.

V

This may seem a rather sweeping characterization of media orientations. Certainly it needs more sustained substantiation than I have been able to give it here: study directed not least to the circumstances which may produce shifts, and resistance to shifts, in the boundaries of those implicit understandings that inform broadcast presentations of the world; cumulative observations of the production of news and comment, systematic content analyses of output — and there are now examples of both in recent research — which are sensitive to the nuances of emphasis, context and technique underlining, or qualifying, the overt thrust, of what is put before audiences. It is not in any case, however, my argument that the media lend uniform and inflexible support to the status quo; but, to repeat, that such critique of the status quo as finds more than spasmodic and quixotic expression in the media takes as given those constraints on definitions of issues in dispute which are also taken as given by the practitioners of public affairs: by people who are locked into the practical, hurly-burly logic of everyday pressure and bargaining. It is just that point which is made by the demonstrable insensitivity, or indifference, of broadcasting in the 1960s and 70s to incipiently dissident definitions of the issues of 'crisis' in industrial relations and related economic affairs. Even when dissidence has been allowed representation in media debate, it has been to answer questions firmly anchored in established formulations of public problems. So the voice of dissent, when it is heard as more than an indecipherable crackle of background noise, is still heard on the defensive: trapped in a pre-set frame of discourse, with little or no opportunity to substitute another of its own.

This is not a new argument.[13] But it needs reiteration for several reasons: partly, of course, because the contrary conception of the media as effectively 'independent' remains influential; partly because left-wing criticism which, in denying such independence, describes the media as 'agencies' of capital thus resorts to a simplified model of power little less questionable than the pluralist model which goes with the postulate of media autonomy; not least because, if it is inertia far more than manipulation that ties the media to routine interpretations of the world, the implications for the popular impact of media output take on a special character.

The impact of the media certainly cannot be read straight-off from the content of output. People read, hear and see selectively. They pick out, adapt and translate from what is before them, to fit in with orientations set in their minds beforehand; they 'decode' the messages of television, radio and press by codes which will differ in some respects, and may well differ in many, from those used by the broadcasters and journalists who first 'encode' the messages.[14] So there can be, and is, resistance to media 'persuasion'. Yet the truth of that in no way rules out media influence. For one thing, the 'frameworks of perception' which people bring to their viewing, listening and reading — the codes with which they decode media messages — come from somewhere, are formed at some time and liable to be re-formed over time. The problem defies solution by empirical measurement. But it is hardly conceivable that long-term exposure to the media themselves has no significant part to play among the sources for those predispositions by which people make sense both of the world and, in turn, of the particular interpretations of the world on offer from the media. For another, those predispositions do not typically take the shape of neat patterns of coherent and mutually consistent ideas in individual minds: they are often internally contradictory, ambivalent, comprised of elements which point that way as well as this. It is that above all, I suggest, on which the social significance of the slant of press and broadcasting presentation hangs.

It has been common in recent characterizations of British manual working class culture and consciousness to highlight features whose effect is to encourage socio-political accommodation, popular acquiescence in

13 Stuart Hall in several papers (e.g., 1972; 1973) has thus argued vigorously to a similar effect; see also Murdock (1973).
14 Klapper (1960) reviewed much evidence pointing to the limited impact of short-term exposure to media communication. The concepts of 'encoding' and 'decoding' are Stuart Hall's (e.g., 1973).

the present structure of class relations. Radical critique is then, explicitly or by implication, denied significant indigenous roots in the *Weltanschauung* of wage earners. 'Traditional' working-class solidarity, for example, is described as essentially defensive; newly emergent working-class orientations and life styles are sketched as centred upon acquisition of money, on private consumption and domesticity. Old collective loyalties of the kind familiar in labour life are taken to be parochial in source and thrust: commitments restricted for most practical purposes to kin, neighbours and workmates; to local, occupational and workplace communities; to maintenance and protection of the familiar, rather than creation of a different future. New discontent engendered by rising aspirations is seen to be translated into militancy directed to short-term market gains, at most, or to be dissipated in private grumbling as even the solidarity of the past wears away. Popular conceptions of inequality are moving, it is said, to a diagnosis of class divisions as a matter merely of differences in income and individual opportunity: towards an image of society in which power figures little, and clashes of class interest concern no more than limited adjustments of the apportionment of resources for consumption. So, by these accounts, wage earners' horizons — in the past and present alike, though in changing ways — are tied to the here and now. Working-class culture retains distinctive elements of its own; but — pragmatic, earthbound, uncongenial to abstraction and detachment — it is unable to sustain frontal opposition to the current social order.[15]

Such characterizations are, in effect, elaborate versions of the picture of the 'mass public' to which the media address themselves. They are not so much wrong as lop-sided. They present one face — a readily discernible one — of a reality which, even at its simplest, is two-faced. The other face of wage-earner consciousness looks beyong the here and now — mostly just a little beyond; sometimes a good deal further, to a dim vision of a social order substantially more equal and less arbitrary than the familiar world. Workers express their acceptance of conventional wisdom when they agree with pollsters' suggestions that workers — other workers, no doubt — are 'far too ready to go on strike'. But they scorn conventional wisdom — and neatly demonstrate the insensitivity of opinion polling whose questions formulations merely mirror public orthodoxy in the definition of social problems — when they also defend strikes as the only means for workers to 'make themselves heard'. Every strike, moreover, means some sacrifice of comfort today for uncertain gain tomorrow; often a commitment to fellow-strikers unseen and unknown; commonly in the 1960s and 70s a challenge to governmental — even legal — as well

15 This is a crude conglomerate summary of interpretations different elements of which are expressed in, for example, Bernstein (1971), Goldthorpe *et al.* (1968–9), Parkin (1971), Runciman (1966).

as managerial authority: in each respect a step, small or large, outside the
confines of the day-to-day. Workers again may at one moment describe
power as diffusely divided among a multiplicity of different groups, unions
even well to the fore among them; yet the next moment abandon such
subscription to a pluralist picture, by acknowledging that there is 'one
law for the rich and another for the poor'. They are likely to shrug their
shoulders in resigned, if not enthusiastic, acceptance of the way and the
luck of the world when asked about the privileges and power of property
in general terms. But many will also repudiate — in words, sometimes in
action — concrete instances of the exercise of property rights: the right of
employers to dismiss employees rather than lose profit; the rights of land-
lords and house-owners when housing is short; rights of inheritance when
they make for inequality of opportunity or of basic livelihood and
security.[16] In short, acquiescence and pragmatic enmeshment in things
as they are intertwine with dissent — dissent which, in small ways most
of the time, in larger ways sometimes, sets question marks against the
routine assumptions that govern public affairs and set the normal limits of
practical controversy.

It is beside the point in this context whether such dissent carries any
explosive political charge for the future. It may; or it may well not. What
is very much to the point here is that the eddies and currents of dissent
in popular consciousness find little representation in media interpretations of the world — certainly not the kind of crystallization in explicit
confrontation with conventional wisdom which the role of critical
exploration ascribed to the media would require. Television and radio,
little less than the press — the popular press, most notably, because its
style brings it within reach of ordinary people — amplify the practical,
nose-to-ground constructions of reality which the practitioners of public
affairs bring to their business; and which, with variations, also make up a
large part of the social understandings which the wage-earning majority
bring to theirs. But the sensitivity of newspaper and broadcasting antennae
does not reach further. The doubts, suspicions, resentments, partial and
occasionally much fuller-blown challenges to the operational principles of
the current order, which also form part of popular social understandings,
go largely without echo in the media. Those strains of latent subversion
depend for their survival, for transmission and magnification when it
occurs, on their own resources: on the circumstances of wage-earning life
and livelihood which give rise to them; on the formal and informal networks of dissident communication within labour; on resources which,
resilient as they are, cannot normally draw on the financial and technical
means of the media. It is that point, the outcome of an inertia that takes

16 For evidence and arguments in support of these points see, for example, Moor-
    house *et al.* (1972), Moorhouse and Chamberlain (1974), Westergaard (1970;
    1975), Westergaard and Resler (1975, Part 5, Chapter 2).

controversy essentially as institutionalized contest defines it, against which designation of the media as a fourth estate founders.

References

Bachrach, P. and Baratz, M. S., 1970: *Power and Poverty.* New York: Oxford University Press.

Bernstein, B., 1971: *Class, codes and control*, vol. 1. London: Routledge and Kegan Paul.

Brown, R. L., 1969: 'Some aspects of mass media ideologies'. In *The sociology of mass media communicators, Sociological Review Monograph* no. 13.

Burns, T., 1970: 'Public service and private world'. In Tunstall, J. (Ed.) *Media sociology*, London: Constable.

Dahl, R. A., 1961: *Who governs?* New Haven: Yale University Press.
    1967: *Pluralist democracy in the United States.* New York: Rand McNally.

Elliott, P., 1972: *The making of a television series.* London: Constable.

Goldthorpe, J. H., Lockwood, D., Bechhofer, F. and Platt, J., 1968–9: *The affluent worker*, 3 volumes. Cambridge: Cambridge University Press.

Guttsman, W. L., 1963: *The British political elite.* London: MacGibbon and Kee.

Hall, S., 1972: 'External influences on broadcasting'. In Bradley, F. S. (Ed.) *Fourth symposium on broadcasting policy,* University of Manchester, Dept. of Extra-Mural Studies (mimeo).
    1973: 'The "structured communication" of events' for *Obstacles to communication symposium,* UNESCO Division of Philosophy (mimeo).

Halloran, J. D., Elliott, P. and Murdock, G., 1970: *Demonstrations and communication.* Harmondsworth: Penguin Books.

Hood, S., 1972: 'The politics of television'. In McQuail, D. (Ed.) *Sociology of mass communications*, Harmondsworth: Penguin Books.

Klapper, J. T., 1960: *The effects of mass communication.* Glencoe: Free Press.

Kumar, K., 1975: 'Holding the middle ground: the BBC, the public and the professional broadcaster'. *Sociology* (1). 9(3).

Lukes, S., 1974: *Power: a radical view.* London: Macmillan.

McKenzie, R. T., 1958: 'Parties, pressure groups and the British political process'. *Political Quarterly*, January–March.

Miliband, R., 1969: *The state in capitalist society.* London: Weidenfeld & Nicolson.

Moorhouse, H. F., Wilson, M. and Chamberlain, C., 1972: 'Rent strikes – direct action and the working class'. In Miliband, R. and Saville, J. (Eds.) *The Socialist Register 1972,* London: Merlin Press.

Moorhouse, H. F. and Chamberlain, C., 1974: 'Lower class attitudes to property'. *Sociology*, 8 (3).

Murdock, G., 1973: 'Political deviance: the press presentation of a militant mass demonstration'. In Cohen, S. and Young, J. (eds.) *The manufacture of news*, London: Constable.

Murdock, G. and Golding, P., 1973: 'For a political economy of mass communications'. In Miliband, R. and Saville, J. (Eds.) *The Socialist Register 1973*, London: Merlin Press.

Normanbrook, Lord, 1965: 'The functions of the BBC's governors'. *BBC Lunchtime Lectures*, 4th series, no. 3, London: British Broadcasting Corporation.

Parkin, F., 1971: *Class inequality and political order*. London: McGibbon and Kee.

Polsby, N. W., 1963: *Community power and political theory*. New Haven: Yale University Press.

Royal Commission on the Distribution of Income and Wealth, 1975: *Report no. 1: initial report on the standing reference*, Cmnd 6171, London: HMSO.

Royal Commission on the Press, 1976: *Interim report*, Cmnd 6433, London: HMSO.

Runciman, W. G., 1966: *Relative deprivation and social justice*. London: Routledge & Kegan Paul.

Smith, A., 1973: *The shadow in the cave*. London: Allen & Unwin.

Westergaard, J. H., 1970: 'The rediscovery of the cash nexus'. In Miliband, R. and Saville, J. (Eds.) *The Socialist Register 1970*, London: Merlin Press.

      1975: 'The power of property'. *New Society*, 11 September.

Westergaard, J. H. and Resler, H., 1975: *Class in a capitalist society*. London: Heinemann Educational Books.

Winston, B. *et al.*, 1975: *Television coverage of industrial relations* (evidence to the Committee on the Future of Broadcasting). Glasgow University, SSRC Media Project (mimeo).

Acknowledgement: I am grateful to the Open University course team, especially Caroline Roberts, for guiding me to some of the recent work on the media with which I was not fully familiar, and for making available copies particularly of some papers unpublished or of difficult access, including work not referred to above.

5

Media Imperialism: towards an international framework for the analysis of media systems

Oliver Boyd-Barrett

Studies of media development and processes of mass communication in the developed or advanced industrial countries of the world have typically adopted a *national* framework of reference. Everyday experience of the media on the other hand reveals a highly visible *international* dimension. Of 92 distinct feature films on exhibition in London's West End in one week of May 1976, for example, 73 were of overseas origin. The average British television viewer's picture of the United States in the period 1975—6 was as likely to be fashioned by routine US exports such as *Kojak*, *Cannon*, *Policewoman*, *The Streets of San Francisco*, *McLeod*, *Colombo* and *Marcus Welby* as by the BBC's historical *America* (actually a co-production with the American Time Life Inc.), or its *Spirit of '76*. Yet most countries have a far *higher* proportion of imported television fare than Britain.

The international dimension does not go entirely unremarked. Western pop music in the Soviet Union or formula-made Hammer horror-movies in Asia may excite an occasional sense of political or cultural incongruity. Devotees of cinema as high art look reverentially to pace-setter trends from abroad — the post-war French and Italian 'new wave' for example — and their critical appraisal extends sympathetically even to the 'spaghetti' western or oriental 'Kung Fu'.

Regularities of international media activity are less often observed, close to the surface though they may be. Almost nightly there is reference to North America in broadcast news programmes, for example, while one account of political developments in Bangladesh or the Philippines in the space of a month would pass as generous coverage, despite their especially volatile and internationally significant character. A plethora of action series from the US on British television is made all the more conspicuous by the almost complete absence of alternative offerings from other parts of the English-speaking world, let alone dubbed versions of programmes from non-English speaking countries. A season of foreign films on Britain's minority channel, BBC 2, and the more occasional use of non-American foreign documenatry, are noted exceptions. American show-business personalities are as common on British television 'chat' shows as their colleague 'artists' from Britain. The acceptability of American cultural influence through the media is indeed phenomenal by comparison with the apparent non-acceptability of alternative influence.

The academic analysis of international media activities has revealed two outstanding features of the influence process. The first of these is the *uni-directional* nature of international media flow. While there is a heavy flow of exported media products from the US to, say, Asian countries, there is only a very slight trickle of Asian media products to the US. Even where there may appear to be a substantial return flow, as is sometimes the case in news, the apparent reciprocity merely disguises the fact that those who *handle* or manage this return flow are primarily the agents of major western media systems, whose criteria of choice are determined above all by their domestic market needs. The second outstanding feature, therefore, of the influence process is the very small number of *source* countries accounting for a very substantial share of all international media influences around the world. These countries are primarily America, then Britain, France, West Germany, Russia, followed a long way behind by relatively minor centres of international media influence including Italy and Japan. If sources are identified only by *country* of origin, however, this obscures the fact that the real sources are even more limited, located as they are in a handful of giant media conglomerates, mostly American.

The term 'media imperialism' is here adopted in reference to forms of international media activity which exemplify these two outstanding features, and while the authors might not themselves use the term, the processes to which it refers have received recent attention in the works of such academics as Dizard (on television, 1966), Guback (on films, 1969); Katz and Wedell (on broadcasting);[1] Schiller (general, including satellites, 1969 and 1973); Tunstall (general, including advertising and press);[2] and Varis (on television, 1973), amongst others, and in the author's own study of the international news agencies.[3] Broadly speaking, the term refers to the process whereby the ownership, structure, distribution or content of the media in any one country are singly or together subject to substantial external pressures from the media interests of any other country or countries without proportionate reciprocation of influence by the country so affected. The term 'substantial' is necessarily indefinite, and it allows for both objective measurements of influence and the subjective perceptions of influence. Under certain conditions for example, it is possible that while the extent of external media influence appears low in overall quantitative terms, it may still be sufficient to generate considerable con-

1 Tunstall, J., *The Media are American*, Constable, 1977.
2 Katz, E. and Wedell, E. G., *Broadcasting in the Third World*, Macmillan, 1978.
3 Boyd-Barrett, J. O., *The World Wide News Agencies*, Ph.D thesis, Open University, 1976.

cern and national resentment, perhaps because the influence is
concentrated in one particular sphere of media activity. Alternatively,
very high objective levels of external influence in all or most spheres may
occasion relatively little concern at the level of national decision-making,
perhaps because the influence is especially concentrated in the less visible
spheres of media activity (advertising, ownership and control of media
systems) or because a high degree of cultural identification exists, at least
at the elite level, with the country which originates the media influence.

The absence of reciprocation of media influence by the affected
country combines both the element of cultural invasion by another power
and the element of imbalance of power resources between the countries
concerned. These two elements of invasion and imbalance of power
resources justify the use of the term 'imperialism'. The study of
imperialism as a general political and economic phenomenon typically
relates it to the structural and economic requirements of the imperial
powers, and as such provides a framework for the understanding of *all*
international relationships in which those powers engage. Similarly the
study of media imperialism is concerned with all aspects of relationship
between media systems, not simply between those of the developed and
of the developing countries.

The approach of 'media imperialism' therefore represents a new and
much-needed framework for systematic analysis of international media
activities, one which promises to identify relationships between different
national media systems, and to locate these relationships within the
historical context of international political and economic developments
of the late nineteenth and twentieth centuries. It raises questions and
generates hypotheses in a number of important areas, including the role
of international media influences in terms of socialization and ideological
control, the scope for media contribution to modes of national development, and the interaction of foreign media influences and local cultures.

As these considerations imply, the issue of media imperialism ultimately
belongs to a broader sphere of investigation altogether, namely that of
imperialism itself as a process of dominance and dependency between
nations. Mediating the notions of imperialism and media imperialism, as
Peter Golding argues in this volume, is that of cultural imperialism. Studies
of international media activities have not so far generally adopted the
framework either of imperialism or of cultural imperialism. Nor have the
studies of those who are interested in explaining the dynamics of
imperialism had much to offer on the role of the media. But for those
who do see the concept of imperialism as central to the understanding of
international relations, their point of view can only be strengthened by
the fact that international media studies have identified relationships
between media systems that would conform in many respects to what
would be expected from an imperialism analysis, even though few such

studies have been directly inspired by such analysis. Be that as it may, the scope of this paper is mainly confined to the range of relationships that have been identified *so far*, but it is also argued in a later section that future studies will need to adopt a broader level of analysis to allow for the identification of the role of the media in contemporary processes of dominance and dependence. In the meantime it can be said that the term 'media imperialism' continues to have considerable value as a distinct analytical tool. It refers to a much more specific range of phenomena than the term 'cultural imperialism' and lends itself much more easily to rigorous study. It is also possibly the single most important component of cultural imperialism outside formal educational institutions, from the view-point of those who are actively engaged in extending or containing given cultural influences.

Four Modes of Media Imperialism

Studies of international media activity have often left it unclear whether the influences they describe have been the product of deliberate commercial or political strategy, the haphazard result of cultural contact, or the inevitable outcome of a given imbalance of power in international relationships which does not require intentionality at any specific level. This paper proposes to consider all the major forms of media imperialism as the inevitable or highly probable outcomes of an imbalance of power resources. Within this context it is also useful to distinguish between different modes of influence by the degree of intentionality which preceded them or with which they were accepted. We can say therefore that the country which originates an international media influence either *exports* this influence as a deliberate commercial or political strategy, or simply *disseminates* this influence unintentionally or without deliberation in a more general process of political, social or economic influence. The country which is affected by a media influence either *adopts* this influence as a deliberate commercial or political strategy, or simply *absorbs* this influence un-reflectively as the result of contact. The overall context of power imbalance within which media activities occur and are transmitted indicates that far greater freedom of choice or option accompanies the processes of export and dissemination than the processes of adoption and absorption. But because the term media imperialism refers to the transmission of media influence both to relatively developed as well as to so-called 'Third World' countries, and because there are important differences in gross wealth even between countries of the latter category, it would be mistaken to exclude the factor of political discretion at the receiving end of media influence. Even poorer countries can and sometimes do take measures to reduce the impact of foreign media influences. The term 'country', finally, should be taken as shorthand reference to the dominant interests *within* a nation state, those interests which generally have the most to gain from the pattern of media imperialism. But it serves to remind us that power in the world is concentrated in a very small number of countries.

The question of what international media activities actually consist of may be thought of as referring to four major components of the communication process, which we will label in terms of their essential features. We may employ the term 'media-formation model' as a generic concept which refers to a given conception of what constitutes a typical media form. It involves four major components and these relate to (i) *the shape of the communication vehicle*, involving a specific technology at the consumer end, and a typical range and balance of communication contents; (ii) *a set of industrial arrangements* for the continuation of media production, involving given structural relationships and financial facilities; (iii) *a body of values* about ideal practice; and (iv) *specific media contents*.

These categories are not of course mutually exclusive; but it is useful to consider them separately because export or dissemination activity in relation to media-formation models is often heavily concentrated in just one or two of these particular spheres. The dissemination of the idea that a particular communication vehicle is most suited for a given content *range* (category i) may occur even without actual export of given media contents (category iv); dissemination of values (category iii) can occur without the export of finance or other industrial arrangements (category ii) although the reverse would be more difficult to conceive. It is rare for an entire media-formation model to be exported or disseminated because the model in its entirety will be the product of very specific political and economic conditions. There are however certain countries where resistance to imported media models is so low that one may say that their media systems are simply extensions of the media system of another country, that both belong or are part of the same media model.

The Shape of the Communication Vehicle

By virtue of their early advance in industrialization and the development of sophisticated modes of communication which served to link together geographically separate populations for the expedition of business and the development of national consciousness, Britain, France, Germany and above all the United States were responsible for what we may call crucial 'strategic choice' decisions in the formulation of media systems. These decisions have to do in the first place with the shape taken by each successive vehicle for mass communication.

Each shape is the result of certain commercial choices in the light of perceived general market conditions; we deliberately evade the notion of 'determination' which implies a lack of choice and an absence of genuine entrepreneurship. The shape taken by each successive vehicle was not entirely *necessary* therefore. The duplication of these original vehicles in other countries has to be explained in terms of export and dissemination activity from the economically strong nations to the weaker nations which lagged behind in the development of media systems and which preferred or were forced to adopt or absorb existing models rather than engage in their own developmental activities. They were therefore saddled with the results of choices made in alien conditions in response to alien market demands. Thus the *range* of content typically provided by the first news agencies of the strong powers, which represented a specific choice to give primacy to the communication demands of *daily* news media, became the dominant model for most other agencies established throughout the world. The development of a mass press which took the form of a news-entertainment-advertising amalgam with 'middle-market' orientation was a specific Anglo-American invention still in the process of establishing its dominance in most parts of Europe and South America and to a lesser extent in Asia and Africa. The earlier model of a press based on direct or hidden political patronage and serving highly differentiated markets is correspondingly on the decline. Radio and television were mainly developed in the United States as specifically *one-way* communication media for *domestic* distribution, yet neither of these features was absolutely necessary in technological or market terms. Until very recently they have been by far the dominant models for the rest of the world; only now, and then only with great perseverence, are alternative models tested, suited to specific conditions. The concept of 'radio forum' for instance, in some Third World countries drops the insistence on the one-way character of broadcast media, and also adopts an original content *range* allegedly appropriate for goals of national development. The shape of the communication vehicles, however, is in general highly standardized across the world, and in particular within the non-communist world. This standardization is sustained by a technological infrastructure developed largely in America and which benefits enormously from economies of scale and which provides much of the important technological equipment for other countries, creating a situation of technological dependency. This situation is especially crucial for the developing countries. Although some of these have begun to manufacture their own broadcast receiver sets for example, all are dependent on imports for the expensive production and distribution technology. Major suppliers are RCA, Schulberger, EMI, Philips, Telefunken, Siemens, Thompson CSF, Fernsehen, and more recently, Shibadan and Nippon Electric.

The Set of Industrial Arrangements

Behind the shape of a communication vehicle lies a structure of organization and of finance. These too are subject to activities of export and dissemination. The early structure of the Hollywood film industry is a particularly important example. Hollywood innovated a number of structural arrangements which have come to seem entirely natural, which in many ways inspired the shape taken by other film industries across the world and are contributory factors to Hollywood's early dominance of overseas export markets. Central organizational features of Hollywood included: —

1   A vertically-integrated structure that initially reached from studio through to production, distribution and exhibition.

2   A vast public-relations and sales machinery which helped generate the so-called 'star system' for the promotion of movies and a unique pattern of distribution of new films from 'showcase' cinemas to metropolitan houses down to suburban and non-metropolitan outlets.

3   A high degree of specialization and rationalization, involving a relatively well-defined division of labour which allowed for made-to-formula movies, and created a degree of employment security and profitability unknown to the early European industry.[4]

So successful were these organizational arrangements that by the 1920s Hollywood accounted for some 80% of all film screenings throughout the world. These structural features were associated with a particular *kind* of film, the feature film, oriented to the tastes of the immigrant working classes of America, often reflecting the violent conditions in which they lived. The American feature film contrasted successfully with both the theatrically-associated and 'high art' conceptions of cinema in Europe.

The set of industrial arrangements involves two elements: the character of industrial structure which we have just illustrated and which we can say is usually *disseminated* and also the nature of finance for that structure, which is usually *exported*. The British film industry is a good example of the role of finance exports from America. In 1971, as in 1925, Britain was the most important foreign market for US film companies, and US features accounted for 39% of all films registered by the Board of Trade in 1971, while British features accounted for only 23%. But many of these British films were produced or at least partially financed by UK subsidiaries of US movie companies or by other American investors. In 1968, 88% of all British first features or co-features exhibited on two main circuits were wholly or partially financed by US investors. This situation is repeated in other European markets. US subsidiaries, for example, contribute about half the annual budget of ANICA, the Italian motion-picture trade association.[5] The power of US finance overcomes even government action designed to protect these affected markets. Early

4   I have identified these features from the discussion on Hollywood in Tunstall, *op. cit.*
5   The figures on US financing of foreign films is taken from Phillips, J. D. (1975).

attempts at market protection were greatly resisted by exhibitors who valued the reliable box office income of American films. And although in more recent times governments have offered subsidies in order to encourage competition with US filmmakers, many of these subsidies actually go to subsidiaries of US film companies. And as the concept 'media imperialism' implies, there is no evidence that foreign film companies play a significant and reciprocal role in the production, financing or distribution of films in the US.

The multi-national media organization therefore represents an important channel for the export of media finance, one which often involves the simultaneous export or dissemination of other aspects of industrial arrangement, of values and of content. In this way British and French interests penetrated many parts of Africa and Asia in the colonial period or immediately after the granting of political independence; American interests are well represented in Latin America. It has been argued that the cultural impact of foreign media ownership and control is strongest where there has been little opportunity for the development of local cultural autonomy. In the Caribbean for example, all television stations were developed with extensive British and American financial support. Foreign media interests own four of the 13 island daily newspapers, controlling 41% of the total daily circulation, while papers controlled by local political parties command only 2% of the total daily circulation. Roy Thomson controls two dailies, the *Barbados Advocate-News* and the *Trinidad Guardian*, which serve the region, and the *Evening News*. These three alone represent 39% of the total daily circulation in the islands. Thomson also owns part of *Capital Broadcasting* in Bermuda. Another London-based organization, *Rediffusion*, also has extensive interests in the Caribbean, and owns radio stations on Jamaica, Barbados, Trinidad and Tobago, St Lucia and Tortola.[6]

Another form of the export or dissemination of industrial models involves the structural control of new media systems without entailing ownership. One means whereby this occurs is through the offer of initial capital aid and advice in the establishment of new systems. The BBC and ORTF were extremely influential in the setting up of broadcast systems in the ex-colonial territories, and these new systems naturally resembled and incorporated many of features of the 'parent' organizations which need not necessarily have been appropriate to new conditions. Reuters has been actively involved in initial financial, organizational, and staffing support of many national news agencies in the Middle East, Africa, South America and the Caribbean. This kind of aid serves the interests of the adviser power in a number of ways. The new media system which is thus

6 The Caribbean details are taken from Lent, J. A. (1975). For a general discussion on the role of the multi-national corporation in relation to broadcasting, see Rita Cruise O'Brien (1974).

established often becomes an important client for the exports of media products; also for the necessary technology to maintain the system; and in the case of news agencies may also become an important but cheap source of 'raw material' since it will supply the news for the adviser agency at a favourable rate in part exchange for international news.

No less important than these other forms of ownership and control in the export of finance is the role of advertising. Advertising as a major source of media revenue itself derives from Anglo-American experience. In many countries it has served to substitute for political funding as a base of support for media systems, instead fostering so-called 'neutrality' or at least 'centrality' of approach to political issues, with the aim of maximization of audiences (or of those audiences of particular interest to advertisers). Ironically, some of the countries possibly least affected by this strategy are the very poorest countries, which cannot serve up sufficiently wealthy audiences to attract advertising revenue, and this is one reason why domination of the media by the party in power is especially prevalent in these countries. Here, political funds remain an important source of support. Elsewhere, advertising ranks very high among the factors that must be considered as falling within the sphere of 'media imperialism'.

The influence of advertising reflects media imperialism first, by virtue of the fact that by far the largest advertising agencies in the global market are American agencies; and second, because a considerable share of advertising demand comes from the giant multi-national conglomerates, which are mostly American. Their advertising revenue operates in much the same way as it does in the US. It is attracted to those media which can promise to reach the audiences most likely to buy the products which the conglomerates have to sell. And these media tend to be ones which can deliver the same kind of consumerist programming to be found in the US since in the US programming is designed primarily with a view to attracting advertising revenue. It is not surprising therefore to find that much of the most successful programming outside America in the non-communist block is nevertheless American imported from America at rates far below the costs for producing equivalent domestic programming. Even local programming is often financed with the help of American capital, sometimes in the form of 'co-productions' suited also for the domestic US market.

In the early 1970s domestic American advertising expenditure accounted for around 60% of the world's total; of all advertising outside the US, about a third was placed by Anglo-American agencies. At least half the top 20 agencies in West Germany, France, Canada, Australia and Britain were American; three of the five largest agencies were American in Argentina, Belgium, India, Italy, Mexico, Netherlands, New Zealand, Norway, Spain and Venezuela; and in at least another twenty countries the largest single advertising agency was American.[7]In Canada most of the revenue of commercial radio and television broadcasting comes from the giant American companies operating across the border. In 1969 the top ten broadcasting advertisers were General Motors of Canada, Procter Imperial Tobacco of Canada, Colgate-Palmolive, Ford Motor Company of Canada, Lever Brothers, Government of Canada and Bristol-Myers of Canada.[8] And to the south of the US two thirds of the largest advertising investors in Colombian television in 1974 were multinational corporations and these included Colgate-Palmolive, Lever Brothers, Bayer Laboratories, Johnson and Johnson, and Quaker Inc.[9] In 1970, the top 25 American advertising agencies placed advertising worth around $1,800 million abroad, and this represented an increase over the previous decade of no less than 385%.[10]

Values of Practice

The term 'values of practice' refers both to highly explicit and visible cannons or rules about appropriate task behaviour in media organizations, and also to less explicit but effective attitudes and assumptions about what is appropriate or what is the 'usual way of going about things', which may not normally be subject to reflective consideration. Examples of values of practice include the idealized notion of 'objectivity' in news reporting; assumptions about the most appropriate forms of technology for specific media tasks; assumptions about what constitutes a 'good' television series.

A typical case of the _export_ of such values is the formal training provided by western media organizations for non-western journalists and broadcasters; a typical case of _dissemination_ is the exposure of non-western journalists and broadcasters to the products and practices of western media organizations — for example, exposure to western values of 'objectivity' through the handling of wire copy from the international News agencies. (For an extended discussion of these forms of media imperialism see the article by Peter Golding in this volume).

The incorporation and reinforcement of the principles of 'objectivity', 'impartiality' or 'balanced reporting' as dominant components in the professional ethics of news-gathering was greatly influenced by the development of news agencies in France, Britain, and US, accompanied by the simultaneous development of what Tunstall[11] has called the middle-market newspaper. The news agencies of the leading powers had a very special role in the export and dissemination of this ethic overseas. Their

7 Tunstall, _op. cit._
8 Schiller (1973, p. 131)
9 Cardona (1975)
10 Annual Advertising Agency Issue of Advertising Age
11 Tunstall, _op. cit._

mode of news reporting was adopted by the BBC in its first decade of existence when all news read over the air-waves was taken from the wire services. Wire-service news was an important ingredient in the BBC's external services established in the Second World War. The news agencies' adoption of 'objectivity' occurred in response to two main factors. First of all the earliest clients for the services of Reuter in Britain and many of the clients for Havas in France were bankers and financiers. Reuter took great care to ensure that none had privileged access to his information, which was distributed simultaneously. If one client had privileged access, the information would lose its value to the others, and credibility would be threatened. *Similarity* of his clients' interests as a determining factor gave way to *diversity* of interests with respect to the newspaper market into which Reuter later moved. Newspapers belonged to different political factions and short of wanting a service which supplied news of their own political persuasion they wanted a service of no apparent persuasion. But the very provision of such a service, as D. L. Shaw (1967) demonstrated in his study of the influence of the American agencies, actually influenced the way in which newspapers themselves began to report the news. In being influenced they were also no doubt responding to the growing pull of advertising as a major revenue consideration, away from concerns of political factionalism. The 'objectivity' of the news agencies and of their newspaper clients of course merely represented a mode of centrality within a context whose boundaries were circumscribed by the existing values of the daily newspaper press.

The agencies eschewed factionalism and yet in their selection of certain issues for news coverage and not others (and the selection was at first exceedingly limited) they did truly reflect the social character of the market they served, and the prejudices and values of that market. These original markets (the US, France and Britain) have remained the most important markets for the major agencies in revenue terms, and still greatly restrict their capacity for response to more specific needs and values of media systems in other parts of the world. They remain however the single most important source of world news for all countries outside the communist block.

Arguably one example of the export or dissemination of values concerning appropriate technology is the role of western interests in encouraging the adoption of educational television by developing countries. Although superficially an attractive means of boosting educational resources, it is also extremely expensive, its advantages tend to be confined to more affluent urban areas, and may not be so effective in some instances as radio or even non-media techniques for the improvement of education.[12] Radio is very cheap, and is sometimes much more flexible: portable radio

12 An excellent analysis of the limitations of educational television can be found in Carnoy (1975).

transmitters, for example, may allow for convenient two-way communication and field interviews that are difficult for television in developing countries.

Values concerning the appropriate style and content of given kinds of media programming are inevitably bound up with economic and organizational constraints. But here again we should be aware of these constraints not as absolute determinants but as factors impinging on what is essentially a matter of *choice*. It is not absolutely necessary to regard the ratings as the single most important precedent to bear in mind when considering future programme possibilities, if only because the ratings are often unreliable even as valid means of providing the information they are meant to provide. And although they give some indications of relative popularity, this in itself does not justify the dominant concern for maximizing audiences at the expense of the alternative strategy of differentiating the audience and seeking to meet the requirements of each specific segment. But of course following-the-ratings is dominant orthodoxy in America. It was exported to Britain through commercial television, which was itself pushed into existence with considerable help from American advertising interests. The consequences of the ratings system have been well documented. The television 'series' may also be interpreted as a response to the ratings game, since it offers a formula for securing maximum audiences over a period of time on the strength of a single major dramatic idea. A one-off production requires great originality in terms of character and situation; each one-off production represents a high degree of risk with regard to the ratings it is likely to achieve because it is relatively *unknown*. The television series on the other hand is based on the idea of finding a *proven* situation and repeating it for as long as the audience can stand it. It solves the problem of shortage of original writing talent, and provides some short-term security to production companies, actors and crews, while allowing advertising agencies to buy time before specific programmes have even been produced. The Latin American 'telenovela' corresponds in many ways to the western 'series'.

Media Content and Market Penetration

 The actual export of media *contents* is probably the most visible form of media imperialism. We have left it till last not because it is least important but simply to highlight the less visible but equally significant modes of influence. The market penetration of many countries by a few is especially evident in films, television programmes, records, news (and through its heavy consumption of records and news, radio), books, and periodicals. Even newspapers must be included; the English-language press of Asia for instance, which has high elite status in many Asian countries, is often partly controlled by Anglo-American media interests and receives a

disproportionate share of all Anglo-American media advertising. In this
section we will look at two aspects of market penetration: the export of
television programmes and the export of news.[13]

In a study unique to the field for its range and specificity of information, Nordenstreng and Varis (1974) were able to document the actual
extent to which television companies around the world were dependent
on imported programming. The amount of imported programme material
in various Latin American countries for example ranged from 10% to
84%, and roughly one half of television programming in Latin America
was of foreign origin. Most of these programmes came from the United
States, and on average nearly one-third of the total programming in Latin
American countries studied consisted of imported US material. In some
cases this dependence had increased over time. A later study by Katz and
Wedell[14] has shown that even where there exists an official determination
to reduce dependence on American and other imports, this may be
extremely difficult to achieve in practice. The actual extent of dependence
was actually higher than the formal figures indicated in many countries,
because imported fare was generally shown in peak viewing time. In
other words the share of the audience captured by imported programmes
was higher than their share of total programming.

In news provision the extent of dependence is even more marked.
Outside a handful of western countries there are hardly any countries with
media systems that can support foreign correspondents in even the most
powerful capitals of the world. In 1975, for instance, there was not one
full-time correspondent in America from a black African country. The vast
majority of foreign correspondents in any country of the world are
American, British, French, Japanese, West German or Russian. The biggest
single category of employer in this field is the news agency, and in a substantial number of all Third World countries it is only the agency
correspondents or their stringers who feed news and information of these
countries to the media systems of the great powers. Thus many media
systems outside the major powers are dependent on two major sources for
their general international news: the news agencies and some of the most
active international broadcasters. Of the latter, many in fact take the bulk
of *their* news from the leading agencies, and only a few (the BBC and the

13 Lack of space compels selection but this should not be read to imply that other
media exports are less important. Of considerable importance to both processes
of media and cultural imperialism is the role of publishing exports. Of more than
500,000 titles issued every year, 80% are from Europe, Japan, USSR and the USA.
In 1970, Africa, Latin America and Asia (except Japan) produced only 19% of
all titles, although they accounted for 50% of the world's literate adults and 63%
of all children in school. 72% of all translations are of texts originally published
in English, French, German, and Russian, whereas only 3% were from the
languages of developing countries. See Barker and Escarpit (1973).
14 Katz and Wedell, *op. cit.*

American networks) have strong independent resources of foreign newsgathering. The major agencies, those which gather news from most
countries and sell or distribute it to most countries are AP and UPI (based
in New York), Reuters in London, Agence France Presse in Paris and Tass
in Moscow. Through Reuters Economic Services and AP-Dow Jones the
agencies also control the world supply of business news; and through
Visnews (owned mainly by Reuters and the BBC) and UPITN (owned
mainly by UPI, ITN and the Sacramento Union Corporation) they control
the world supply of television news-film. The agencies derive most of their
revenues from western markets, and they therefore attend more to the
news interests of these markets than those of other countries. This is
reflected in the heavily disproportionate share of their organizational
resources which are concentrated in the western markets, in their patterns
of executive recruitment, and not least by the general composition of the
news services which they feed both to western and non-western markets.

The Antecedent Conditions of Media Imperialism

We have so far attempted a descriptive categorization of the many forms
typically taken by the phenomenon of media imperialism. Those who have
studied this phenomenon have generally sought to identify at least the
immediate factors which brought it about; but it is also fair to say that a
great deal of work has yet to be done before the full pattern of contributory factors and their relationship with general economic and political
developments finally emerges.

Evidently the work must begin with an examination of the role of
the mass media in the general process of industrialization which gave to
certain West European powers and to North America a clear political and
economic advantage in the struggle for security and power in international relationships. The imperialism of late nineteenth-century Europe
is especially important in understanding the distribution of media
influence from Britain and France to many parts of Africa, Asia and
South America. Economic explanations for this general development have
been for long debated and often focus on the presumed needs of
industrial societies for cheap raw materials, for additional markets to
consume rising levels of production and for investment outlets to
absorb accumulating capital. Whether these requirements logically
necessitated the acquisition of colonies however, or whether this particular
form of imperialism was motivated more by the need to preserve the
'balance of power' between the great European nations than by strictly
economic considerations, is still open to question. Once imperialism is
seen as something much broader than territorial acquisition it becomes
possible to consider both West European and North American overseas
strategies in the light of similar factors, not only in the late nineteenth

century but also in the second half of the twentieth century. In this light as some have argued, *territorial* imperialism may simply represent a particularly expensive and possibly ineffective means of achieving the same ends as general economic imperialism.[15]

At the same time moreover, study of the role of the media in the process of general economic imperialism must take into account attempts to identify *changes* in the relationship between capitalism and imperialism in accord with the changing circumstances of capitalism itself. Baran and Sweezy (1968), for example, took one step in this direction when they proposed the concept of 'economic surplus' or the 'tendency of economic surplus to rise' to explain the continued necessity of economic imperialism. Surplus tended to rise, they maintained, because under monopoly or oligopoly conditions the giant conglomerates could set their *own* prices rather than be subject to general price levels established under conditions of competition. This in turn generated a surplus which could not be absorbed at home and which could not maintain full employment, despite surplus-assimilating activities such as advertising or defence. Studies of media imperialism might therefore need to consider the role of media conglomerates in relation to the general role of multi-nationals in the development of capitalism; these media organizations play a much more important role in this context than their mere size might suggest. It would also be useful to consider the extent to which foreign media exports are structurally and economically *necessary* for their respective industries. In the case of films for instance, the high proportion of total North American revenues obtained from export markets might seem to justify the idea of media imperialism as *necessary* in this sense; whereas the same probably would *not* be true of television film exports, unless one were to consider these perhaps as only part of a total conglomerate package, to be thought of alongside the total exports of parent organizations.

At a level of greater specificity the conditions that surrounded the emergence of Hollywood are of considerable strategic importance, since Hollywood created an industrial infrastructure on which radio, television and the record industry were later established. We identified some of the basic structural features of Hollywood in an earlier section. We should also mention two further factors at this point since they are general to American media systems. The first is *economies of scale.* This was particularly important in cinema, because once a film had been made it was extremely cheap to distribute prints at high profit, and much the same is true of television. But because television itself is so expensive many newer countries cannot afford to pay high prices for programme imports. The second important feature is *market size.* The sheer size of the

---

15 But see the critical review of theories of classical imperialism and contemporary dominance-dependence in Cohen (1974).

American market not only brought about economies of scale made possible by high profits, but it allowed for the combination of giant enterprise on the one hand, and competition on the other. The market was big enough to generate huge profits for more than one enterprise. Competition *between* enterprises, sustained by anti-trust legislations, generated or accelerated the penetration of foreign markets, often aided by the extreme receptivity of those markets to the products on offer. Intensive competition also brought about originality and invention in the development of technology, products and business practice on a scale probably unequalled in any other part of the globe.

So large was the American market, so early was it cultivated, that it led to a degree of concentration and economy of scale which made it very difficult for any non-American media system to compete in the global market, and in many cases even to hold its own domestic market. Entry into the American market by foreign media systems has always required an investment far beyond the capacity of most potential candidates to raise, and even if raised would not necessarily secure a place against the entrenched competition. Once secure in their position of market hegemony, the large American media corporations were in a position to incur luxury costs, costs that arose from their very size and power, and to do this because they were increasingly able to set their own prices without fear of real competition from new market entrants. Despite the economies of scale it affords, therefore, market size may tend to bring about higher prices in the long run.

The Consequences and Implications of Media Imperialism

In focusing on the need for further work in the area of general relationships between media and broader economic and political systems, we did not intend to imply that even at the descriptive level the work is complete. A great deal more research needs to be done, for example, on the exact degree of penetration of different media systems and different forms of media activity in each country; also on the extent to which these activities vary or under which conditions one is substitute for another. All this will call for much more detailed analysis of national media systems and their potential for growth in the face of international media activities. In particular more attention should be focused on the relatively under-developed study of the processes of *adoption* and *absorption* of media influences by affected countries. Such work has clearly begun in the recent work of Tunstall[16] and Katz and Wedell.[17]

The required shift of emphasis to the processes of adoption and absorption is all the more imperative for the development of our knowledge of the actual, as opposed to postulated, consequences of media imperialism.

16 Tunstall, *op. cit.*
17 Katz and Wedell, *op cit.*

Some of these consequences emerge from the study of the general development of media imperialism. Indigenous media systems of new countries, for instance, cannot compete with the media fare of more affluent powers, and come to rely on it as much and often more than on their own material to fill in the programme slots. These and similar consequences are sometimes thought to represent a state of overall cultural dependency of many nations on a few. But if we wish to argue that cultural dependency is the general effect of media imperialism there are two difficult questions that must be answered. If the *volume* of western media export dissemination activity is greatest in the *developed* world, then is it not precisely in the developed world that the resources exist for the generation of autonomous and counter influences? Second, if these western media influences have greater cultural *impact* in the less developed countries which lack the resources for the generation of counter influences how can this be reconciled with the relatively low rate of exposure to mass media products in such countries? Culture is a notoriously elusive concept; we cannot hope to trace a precise causal link between mass media exposure and cultural change. In the case of the developing countries for instance, by far the most important cultural changes occurred before the coming of the mass media, in the days of colonialism, or as a result of neocolonial influences of trade and investment.

A particular sub-species of the cultural dependence argument, however, sees media imperialism as a process which serves to reinforce existing economic and political relations between nations. The media in other words perform an *ideological* role. This occurs overtly in the form of explicit propaganda channels; covertly through the expression of certain values in what otherwise appears to be neutral entertainment and informational fare.

A great many nations in fact engage in international propaganda; but only a few have the resources for *sustained* international broadcasting (the most important form of media propaganda) backed with powerful transmitters and with the kind of technical and professional expertise necessary to capture sizable audiences. The Soviet Union currently ranks second largest international broadcaster and between 1969 and 1972 put out more programme hours than the United States (1,950 hours a week in 1973, in 84 languages).[18] But a commercial study of radio listening in Kenya, Tanzania, Uganda and Ghana in 1970 suggested that at least in this region the BBC was the only foreign station apart from those in neighbouring countries ever likely to be tuned into by more than 50% of the listeners, and that such stations as Radio Moscow, Radio Peking, Radio Cairo, Deutsche Welle and Radio Berlin International were listened to by no more than 10% (and usually far less) of the radio listening

18   Hale (1975, pp. 17—18).

population even on an occasional basis.[19]

Even if it could be assumed that the major western countries and the communist block had equal influence in the overt propaganda activity of international broadcasting, the covert influence of western values through the export and dissemination of (especially American) commercial programming material and of general western media models would tip the balance of influence well in the direction of the west. This of course can be demonstrated descriptively by identifying the scope and penetration of such export and dissemination. Future studies will need to consider the actual content of exported programming for their covert philosophies and assumptions about how life really is or should be. Dorfman and Matterlat's (1975) analysis of the much-syndicated Donald Duck cartoons shows there a particular view of underdeveloped peoples which reflects dominant American stereotypes of foreign nationals and expresses a morality that is wholly supportive of American foreign policy objectives. But if we need to know whether that kind of interpretation is the interpretation shared in common by the audience for such exported media material in affected countries we face an even thornier methodological problem, which is none the less necessary for that. Even supposing, however, that confirming evidence of the ideological role of international media influences was not forthcoming from studies of their impact on given audiences, it would still be necessary to consider the 'opportunity cost', of such imported programming, namely, the cost of foregoing *other* uses of a national resource. Instead therefore of developing a national television system heavily dependent on imported programming, a country might have benefited from expansion of its radio system for the promotion of particular national economic or developmental goals.

It has been argued that the export of media influences from the industrialized countries actually helps to promote economic development or 'modernization', and acceptance of this point of view by many developing countries has accelerated the process of adoption. The term 'modernization', however, has been criticized for its ideological content and for implying the existence of differences between developed and developing countries which do not necessarily exist.[20] And although the development of new media systems in developing countries through western aid or based on western models may create a potential means of promoting developmental goals, the overall economic relations of the developing and developed countries tend to inhibit such use in practice. The export of media contents from the developed countries is on the face of it unlikely to promote national goals of economic development. Wells (1972), for instance, has argued that in Latin America the influence of

19 Quoted in Browne, D. R. in Head (1974, p. 183).
20 See Peter Golding (1974).

American media contents and of American advertising money generates public identification with *consumption* values, whereas economic development requires an emphasis on *production* values. Production values are similar to those incorporated by the concept 'protestant ethic' and include a high propensity to invest accumulated gains and a corresponding antagonism to immediate gratification for its own sake.

Some countries have attempted to resist the dangers of cultural dependence and ideological control which they see in the heavy export and disseminåtion of media contents and media models from a few powerful nations. Future study of media imperialism will need to focus much more on what happens when countries begin to substitute for the products of other countries, and whether their substitutions do deviate appreciably from the patterns initially established by foreign media systems. A particularly important mode of resistance in the direction of greater self-sufficiency is the pooling of resources in regional cooperatives, in the form, for instance, of regional broadcasting unions and news agency exchanges. Do these effectively reduce dependence or do they simply rationalize it? The significance also of minor centres of media activity needs to be better understood — the export of film and news from Cairo for instance to other African countries, or the export of film, music and periodicals from Mexico or Argentina to other South American countries. Is it possible that the consolidation of a more affluent core of countries within what has traditionally been described as the 'Third World', based on oil revenue, will make such centres more important and more influential? Finally we need to know a great deal more about media system relations in the communist block, whether and to what extent these are similar to relations in the western sphere of influence, and also whether western media influence can be said to have penetrated communist systems and with what consequences. These considerations require us to determine whether the phenomenon of media imperialism is a relatively short-term development or whether the economic conditions which brought it about are such that it is likely to be a feature of international relations for the indefinite future.

References

Baran, P. A. and Sweezy, Paul M., 1968: *Monopoly Capital.* Harmondsworth: Pelican.
Barker, R. and Escarpit, R., 1973: *The Book Hunger.* London: Harrap.
Boyd-Barrett, J. O., *The World-Wide News Agencies.* Ph.D thesis, Open University, 1976.
de Cardona, E., 1975: 'Multinational Television'. *Journal of Communication* 25 (2), pp. 122—7.

Carnoy, M., 1975. 'The Economic Costs and Returns to Educational Television'. *Economic Development and Cultural Change*, 23, (2), pp. 207—48.

Cohen, B. J., 1974: *The Question of Imperialism*. London: Macmillan.

Cruise O'Brien, R., 1975: 'Domination and Dependence in Mass Communication'. *Institute of Development Studies Bulletin*, 6 (4), pp. 85—99.

Dizard, W. P., 1966: *Television: A World View*. Syracuse, New York: Syracuse University Press.

Dorfman, A. and Mattelart, A., 1975: *How to Read Donald Duck: imperialist ideology in the Disney comic*, International General.

Golding, P., 1974: 'Media Role in National Development'. *Journal of Communication*, 24 (3), pp. 39—53.

Guback, T. H., 1969: *The International Film Industry*. Bloomington: Indiana University Press.

1974: 'Film as International Business'. *Journal of Communication*, 24 (1), pp. 90—101.

Hale, J., 1975: *Radio Power*. London: Paul Elek Ltd.

Head, S. W., 1974: *Broadcasting in Africa*. Philadelphia: Temple University Press.

Katz, E. and Wedell, E. G. *Broadcasting in the Third World*, London: Macmillan, 1978.

Lent, J. A., 1975: 'The Price of Modernity'. *Journal of Communication*, 25 (2), pp. 128—35.

Nordenstreng, K. and Varis, T., 1974: *Television Traffic: A One-Way Street?* Paris: Unesco.

Phillips, J. D., 1975: 'Film Conglomerate "Blockbusters"', *Journal of Communication*, 25 (2), pp. 171—82.

Schiller, H. I., 1969: *Mass Communication and American Empire*. New York: Augustus M. Kelly.

1973: *The Mind Managers*. Boston: Beacon Press.

Shaw, D. L., 1967: 'News Bias and the Telegraph: A Study of Historical Change'. *Journalism Quarterly*, Spring 1967, vol. 44, pp. 3—12.

Tunstall, J., 1977: *The Media are American*. London: Constable.

Varis, T., 1973: *International Inventory of Television Programme Structure and the Flow of Programmes Between Nations*. Finland, University of Tampere.

Wells, A., 1972: *Picture-Tube Imperialism?* New York: Orbis Books.

Section II

Media Organizations and Occupations

Introduction

The different theoretical perspectives which have been discussed in the preceding section have all focused, in various ways, upon issues arising from the control which media organizations and professionals have over the processes of communication in society. Questions have been raised concerning the relationship between ownership and control in the media, and the consequences of these for the production process in media organizations. These questions, in turn, raise another set of problems, which have to do with the relationship between media organizations and the structure of power in society. Indeed, if the function of the media, as is implied by that term, is one of mediation, then the media ought to be conceived as interposed between those groups or classes which constitute the audience for the media, and those whose definitions of social reality and of the issues facing society are being communicated. Where, then, do these definitions of social reality originate? Are they to be seen as part of the ideology of a 'ruling class?' Are they generated by media professionals? Or are they the product of the interaction between the professional ideologies which have developed within media organizations and the dominant, or prevailing, ideology in society? and if so, what is the nature of that interaction? The articles which follow in this section explore some of these questions.

The opening article, by Philip Elliott, provides an overview of the literature on professionalism in the media, and interprets it within a specifically British context. The author's interpretation is designed to show the complex, and often ambivalent relationship between cultural production, commercialism and the values and attitudes of the elite in this country. This relationship is expressed in the various types of social control exercised over the organizations and the professionals engaged in media production in Britain, and in some characteristic variations in media culture which embody and express a mix of commercialism and elitism.

The following two articles by Anthony Smith and James Curran take an historical look at the evolution and development of the media. Although the literature on this subject is voluminous, these articles attempt novel, or dissenting approaches.

Smith focuses on the evolution of the role of the journalist and attempts, through some selected historical examples, to illustrate the ways in which the interaction between various structural dimensions of the Press — such as available technologies, techniques of journalists' work, audience groupings and structures of editorial control — have shaped the changes in the journalist's role. He argues that technological innovations in the media ought to be seen as opening up new ranges of possibilities for the direction in which the journalist's role may be performed. The specific evolutionary paths which are then followed are determined by the interaction between these new technological possibilities and other societal factors — be they economic, cultural or political — which impinge upon the options for change provided by the new technologies. Curran's article, on the other hand, deploys a historical perspective in an examination of the economic relations that have shaped the ownership, professional values, structures and audiences of the British press since 1800. Challenging orthodox interpretations of that period he argues that the free play of market forces succeeded, where legal censorship and repression failed, in narrowing the range of diversity of opinions available in the press by eliminating from the scene oppositional voices, thus rendering the press a more powerful instrument of social control. This he contends had important and lasting consequences for the development of British society.

Present-day examples of the interrelationship between media profes-sionals and the institutional frameworks within which they function are provided in the articles by Kumar and Tracey. Kumar focuses on the roles of the producer and the presenter in the BBC and demonstrates the manner in which the professional presenter is utilized by his broadcasting organization as an essential element in the organization's survival strategy. Given the strains and pressures of a changing social and political climate in Britain, the professionalism of the presenter in the BBC 'compounded equally of aggresiveness, scepticism, irony and detachment' is seen as a device which facilitates the BBC's hold on 'the middle ground'. Broadcaster professionalism, however, is not always a safe haven and may occasionally rock the Corporation's 'Survival' boat, as is demonstrated in Tracey's case-study of the controversial *Yesterday's Men* programme, which was broadcast by the BBC in 1971. In this case the 'professionalism' of the broadcasters clashed sharply with the sensitivities of powerful politicians, and although the BBC insisted on maintaining its autonomy and decided to broadcast the contentious programme, the incident led, in Tracey's view, to a considerable reduction in the scope for innovation allowed to the broadcasters, and to a tightening of the editorial reins in political communication. The two articles thus illustrate the variety of intra- and extra-organizational constraints which define and shape the roles of professional mass media communicators.

A more generalized view of the process of political communication is presented in the chapter by Gurevitch and Blumler. Adopting a systemic perspective, the authors offer a framework for the analysis of the relationship between politicians and broadcasters which emphasizes the structural and goal differences between political institutions and broadcasting organizations and regards the tensions between the two as inherent in these discrepancies. Since the precise nature of the relationship between these two sets of institutions may vary in accordance with variations in the political culture of different societies, the validity of such an analytical framework rests on its ability to illuminate the nature of the political communication process in different socio-political contexts. Like any other theoretical framework, it is subject to empirical validation.

The section closes with Peter Golding's discussion of the issue of media professionalism in the Third World. This is but one aspect of the wider debate on 'cultural imperialism' — the dominance of the cultural models and the institutional patterns of the developed countries in the lesser developed countries of the world. Although the article deals with one specific issue within the larger problem area it adds a cross-cultural dimension to the somewhat more parochial settings within which the problems of media organizations and occupations have been dealt with in the earlier parts of the section.

6

Media Organizations and Occupations: an overview

Philip Elliott

Introduction

The title of this paper may come as a surprise to those used to the familiar complaint that media sociologists have neglected the study of mass communicators. Only a few years ago there was not so much a field of work to survey as an area of ground to clear. (Elliott and Chaney, 1969.) Nearly a decade later there are still vast gaps in our descriptive knowledge of the way particular media and types of cultural production are organized and of the roles and functions of those who work within them. This ignorance is reflected in the simple conspiracy theories which still survive in much public debate about the power and influence of the media. This is encouraged by the mystique and secrecy with which many media organizations surround themselves. There are still peculiar problems involved in gaining access for research into media production. (Halloran and Gurevitch, 1971.)

Nevertheless the past decade has seen a considerable increase in activity in the area, so much so that mass communicators have begun to identify media sociologists as a new bogeyman, another ill-defined threat to their own autonomy and status.[1] A number of different studies have been or are about to be published covering the range of organizations and activities involved in the production of cultural artefacts. There is still a heavy bias towards the study of journalism, news and factual programming. Research in this area, however, has taken up topics beyond the scope of the gatekeeper model of news flow which for so long dominated journalism research in the United States.[2] A number of recurrent styles of research can be identified in recent work. For example the influence of the new

1 This can be seen in much of the review comment, particularly that by broadcasters and ex-broadcasters, on many of the studies referred to in this paper.
2 The classic gatekeeper study is White (1950). For a recent review of gatekeeper research and contemporary use of the concept see Donohue (1972). For more critical comments and studies which have specifically renounced it in favour of a less mechanistic approach see Halloran, Elliott and Murdock (1970), Chibnall (1975), Tracey (1978), Schlesinger (1978), Golding and Elliott (1979).

Chicago school of occupational sociology and more recently of ethno-
metholology has been particularly apparent in America (Cantor, 1971;
Faulkner, 1971; Tuchman, 1973; Moloch and Lester, 1974). Taken
together with the more pragmatic and exploratory approaches adopted in
Britain, these provide more than a descriptive understanding of work in the
communication media, looked at in isolation as a peculiar set of occupations or form of work organization. They provide the basis for an
analysis of the production of media culture under the conditions of
democratic capitalism.

The aim of this paper is to pursue such an analysis within the specific
context of contemporary Britain. The argument will be that Britain is a
case of more than parochial interest because of the peculiar mix of elite
and commercial values which find expression in the culture. These are
built at different points into the organization of cultural production and
into the careers and work situations of cultural producers. A similar mix
is to be found in other sectors of British life reflecting the interpenetration
of the aristocracy and the commercial bourgeoisie in positions of power
and status in British society. The analysis presented in this paper,
particularly the account of variations in media culture with which it ends,
is little more than a prolegomenon to a study of cultural production in
Britain. Not only does the study of cultural production for the mass
media need to be extended but comparisons need to be drawn with the
products and processes of other intellectual and artistic fields, as for
example in Anderson's account of the components of national culture,
and extended to other countries whose cultural institutions and
experiences have been different. The account which follows draws on the
experience of other countries for confirmation or contrast but the main
theme will be to show that the peculiarities of media organizations and
occupations set in the context of British history and social structure have
real consequences for the production of media culture.

Status Ambiguity and Occupational Uncertainties

One continuing gap in our knowledge of media communicators is the lack
of systematic data on recruitment and social background. Such recruitment studies have predominated in research on other social elites in Britain
(Stanworth and Giddens, 1974) but the media communicators' claim to
be numbered among such elites is highly ambiguous. Looked at in terms
of recruitment, only those media communicators in the most prestigious
positions in the most prestigious organizations share the same background
characteristics as the other British social elites. The distinction Tunstall
(1971) draws in journalism between an elite career path straight into the
national press from the prestigious sectors of the educational system and a
provincial career path for the majority of entrants may well be of more

general application in the study of the recruitment of creative personnel in all types of cultural production. In most sections of the industry there are groups like the foreign correspondents in the quality press identified by Tunstall, who come from upper middle-class homes and were educated at independent schools and the older universities, the background which characterizes such other social elites as the officer corps, the episcopacy, the liberal professions and the higher echelons of the civil service. (Stanworth and Giddens, 1974; Urry and Wakeford, 1973.) This elite is most evident in those sectors most insulated from the pressures of populism and commercialism — the BBC, the quality press, traditional publishing houses and creative rather than commercial writing.[3]

By contrast the majority of cultural producers are drawn more widely from the whole spectrum of the middle class. (Boyd-Barrett, 1970.) For the elite, educational background provides a claim to status but it has little vocational significance for either group.[4] Educational qualifications either provide a minimum entry requirement for the occupation, as in journalism, or an optional extra which may or may not assist in the process of building a career, as in acting. (Peters, 1971.) No occupation in cultural production has been professionalized to the extent that a prior period of education and training provides the first situation for career competition. Instead, many careers involve extensive periods of learning by doing in the less prestigious and rewarding sectors of the industry, for example the provincial press, repertory theatre or the various entertainment circuits. Workers in these sectors provide an available pool of competence and talent which can be drawn upon for more prestigious positions in the industry. In many of the occupations there are recognized career paths in the *ad hoc* sense that the successful are known to have worked in similar situations in the past. Burns' (1972) identification of four age grades in the BBC is a particularly interesting example of the way groups recruited at different periods shared similar backgrounds though different from each other.

In no case, however, is there a routinized and organized career route. This is true in the sense that a variety of career goals are possible. Not only do media men tread the path common in other middle-class occupations from performer or producer to executive or administrator. They also quite regularly change back. Many never make the transition at all. For some there are opportunities to develop a public persona, to become a 'personality' or a 'star', for others similar opportunities to build a personal reputation, though within the occupation rather than with the public at large. Further, it may be possible to use the reputation,

3 The evidence for this is more suggestive than systematic but see Jay (1972), Kumar (1975), Lane (1970), Laurenson (1969), Altick (1962).
4 For a discussion of the distinction between vocational and status education see Elliott (1972a).

experience and contacts gained in the media as a 'bridge' into some other field of employment such as public relations or politics. (Tunstall, 1971, p. 65; Golding, 1974, p. 59.)

There are also no career routes in the media in the sense that rarely is advancement predicated on universalistic criteria. Instead personal, particularistic criteria apply. Information about employment opportunities circulates by word of mouth. Even after formal training in journalism securing a position depends on pressing a personal case. (Boyd-Barrett, 1970.) The reputations of individual producers and performers are assessed in the same gossip networks. Hirers may seek personnel with 'a proven track record' (Blum, 1970) but the ephemeral nature of most media output introduces an element of topicality. In television there is a saying, 'You're only as good as your last show.'

Media gossip is particularly rich in such aphorisms, summing up various aspects of the job market and the working environment. Career uncertainty is underlined by the different mythologies of selection and rejection to be found in these settings. The television production team I studied joked about coming in one morning and finding their office taken over — a joke with a long pedigree in the Hollywood studios. (Elliott, 1972b.) Tunstall (1971, pp. 63—4) notes a similar belief among specialist correspondents that journalists were particularly liable to capricious dismissal. This belief apparently had little basis in their own work experience. The myth of rejection seems to be less characteristic of the performing occupations than the myth of discovery, perhaps because rejection is the more usual experience. (Peters, 1971.) In such fields there are many more aspirants than can be supported by the job opportunities regularly available. The myth of discovery is functional at a personal level both for the unsuccessful by attributing their failure to chance and for the hirers in allowing them to claim an ability to pick winners and a cultural sense in recognizing creative talent. Nevertheless such occupations have their 'inner circles' — people with the reputation and contacts to keep them regularly in work, people whom the producers think of first when setting up a new production. (Faulkner, 1971.) The opportunity to pick and choose parts is one of the rewards for discovery in acting.

For many involved in performing or cultural production, their work in this field may not be their only or even their main occupation. Peters (1971) reported that a large proportion of her sample of aspiring actresses depended on parental subsidies or other employment to keep them while they waited for the break. Creative work may become regularly associated with other types of occupation. These provide both a regular income and the opportunity to carry on writing or performing on the side. For example, Malcolm Bradbury (1971) has pointed to the development of a 'literary salariat' of writers holding posts in the educational system, the modern equivalent of patronage. In his study of the BBC Burns noted how even those with relatively permanent and secure jobs in a media organization more bureaucratic than most, used their rest days to moonlight or take freelance employment. From the performer's or producer's point of view freelancing is a source of income, an opportunity to make contacts throughout the industry, to keep in touch with developments and, perhaps most important, to build the public persona or the industry-wide reputation which will ensure membership of the 'inner circle'. From the point of view of the industry, freelancing and other systems involving short-term hire rather than long-term commitment reduce overhead costs and allow for changes in the labour force in line with changes in fashion and taste.

Media occupations like others in the cultural and creative field are also morally ambiguous. Baldwin attacked the British press lords for exercising the prerogative of the harlot. Performers and producers as well as owners and executives have often been associated with immorality in a less allegoric way. Star publicity in the days of the major studios in Hollywood trod the narrow line between titillating public interest and arousing moral obloquy. Peters (1971) mentions that most outside interest in her study of aspiring actresses centred on what happened on the casting couch.

As well as being associated with sexual deviancy or licence, cultural producers are also regarded as deviants from the work ethic. (Becker, 1963.) Tunstall reports the self-mocking judgement of newsmen on journalism that 'It's better than working' (Tunstall, 1971, p. 61), a judgement which draws attention to the lack of routine and fringe benefits in the working day, the satisfactions to be had from intellectually challenging work associated with the great and famous, the bizarre and interesting, but also carries an undertone of the notion that journalism is parasitic on such people and their activities. Popular ambivalence is also apparent in attitudes to the rewards earned by successful performers and entertainers. Indeed, success in the industry, surrounded as it is by a mythology of chance and discovery, can be seen as analogous to success in a lottery or in the football pools, a mechanism by which anyone may be catapulted from obscurity to stardom without reference to the bourgeois values of hard work and forward planning. Mason Griff (1962), in his study of artists, noted how this ambivalence was expressed in parental support for artistic flair in children. Parents tended to encourage this while the children were young but to be much less enthusiastic when the child reached the point of entering the labour market.

Some of these ambiguities of morality and status and the uncertainties of employment and career are more obvious in the case of performers than others involved in media occupations. There are cases where working for one of the prestigious British organizations — the BBC, *The Times*, the older university publishing houses — carries with it notions of appropriate style and behaviour which are met by reciprocal public respect. In such cases working for the particular organization may provide an employee with his key occupational identity and career focus.[5] Nevertheless, one theme which runs through all these ambiguities and uncertainties in Britain is whether work in broadcasting, the press and other types of cultural production is properly regarded as a high or low cultural activity, as a contribution to the cultural heritage by a social elite intimately associated with other centres of power and prestige in the nation or simply as a mechanism for filling the leisure time of the mass audience. Grace Wyndham Goldie's (1972) account of her reception at a social engagement at Oxford University when she was urged not to reveal she worked for television, not only shows the ambivalence with which one social elite – established academics – regarded the new potential elite of mass communicators, but also underlines the insecurity and irritation which this ambivalent reception produced in the communicators.

Role Conflict and Professionalism

Another version of this cultural dilemma is to be seen in the suggestion that media communicators and others involved in cultural production experience role conflict between the demands of art and the demands of commerce. The dilemma may be expressed in various ways – as a conflict between different ideals or goals, as a conflict between the demands of different audiences, constituents or reference groups or as a conflict over control and autonomy in the work situation. The demands of commerce, the despised polar position in the dilemma, have come to invoke most types of control over the creative process. These range from true commercialism – turning culture into a marketable commodity – to the controls involved in organizing production for administrative convenience, political expediency or the whims of the ultimate audience. On the other side the valued polar position of the autonomous creative artist is grounded more firmly in the ideas of romanticism and bohemianism than in historical fact about the work situation of the artist in any particular period.

One suggestion that the dilemma is nonetheless a real one comes from the prevalence of high cultural heroes and unrealistic cultural ideals among producers and performers. The popular entertainer's ambition to be a classical actor has become a cliché, ridiculed for example by Peter Sellers with his creation, Twit Conway, the aspiring pop star who wanted to play Hamlet. But equivalent ideals are to be found in all types of media performance and production from the journalists who want to be novelists (Boyd-Barrett, 1970), popular musicians who want to play jazz (Becker, 1963), advertising designers who want to be fine artists (Griff, 1964) to

5 See Burns' study of the BBC (1977) and in particular his paper on 'Commitment and Career in the BBC' in McQuail (1972).

the television producers who want to make films. (Cantor, 1971.) Such a disjunction between the heroes and ideals of an occupation and the reality of the work situation is not uncommon in such established professions as medicine and law. (Elliott, 1972a.) They are usually apparent, however, in the initial period of education and training, and are gradually 'cooled out' as part of the process whereby the acolyte is socialized into the reality of his occupation. Such mechanisms are apparent in creative and performing occupations. Faulkner (1971) reports how studio musicians, for example, come to value the variety and special skills characteristic of their work, in place of their earlier ambition to become concert soloists. Nevertheless, because of the fragmented nature of work opportunities in different sectors of cultural production and the opportunities available to move across on a temporary basis, it is possible for people in these occupations to keep alive their ideals by taking on freelance work or working in their leisure time. Lane (1970b) borrowed Goffman's concept of 'special self' to describe one technique which publishers used to resolve the conflict between cultural and commercial goals. In many such occupations the 'special self' is not just a state of mind but something which finds expression in fringe activities and blurred distinctions between work and leisure.

Another possibility, beyond the control of any individual, is that the relative status of different occupations and different ideals may change. Tom Wolfe (1975) for example has claimed that whereas all journalists used to want to write novels, now novelists have begun to write journalism. Journalism has become the pre-eminent form, both as a means of reaching an audience and as a means of expression. Novelists such as Norman Mailer and Truman Capote have recognized this and begun writing extended journalism instead of old-style creative novels.

Sufficient examples have been quoted to show that the simple art — commerce dichotomy conflates a number of different ideals — autonomy, creativity, working in the most prosperous, culturally prestigious sector of the industry or even reaching the largest audience. The dilemma may involve a distinction between high and low culture, between professional or craft standards and commercial judgement, between self-regulation and close bureaucratic control of the work situation, between self-motivation and financial inducement, between self-monitoring and serving an audience, between using one's talents for a purpose and having them used for none except the survival or commercial success of the organization for which the work is done.

Just as the dilemma is more complex than a simple dichotomy, so studies have suggested there are more complex adaptations to it than the polar opposites of alienation or acceptance more clearly expressed in the fictional accounts of writers' experiences in the Hollywood studios. One type of communicator who emerges from various studies of journalists as well as from Cantor's (1971a) study of television producers is the one for whom the last version of the dilemma is particularly acute, who are concerned about the social relevance, the meaning or purpose of their work. To say purpose is not to suggest that such communicators want to be propagandists for a particular cause. Their aim is to stimulate and explain things to the audience in a more active way than is allowed for by the established professional orthodoxy of their particular occupation. Cantor (1971a), for example, identified three types of television producers, two of whom put a premium on the craft skills and established routines of the occupation. These were the 'film-makers' who looked on television production as an opportunity to acquire the craft skills necessary for future work on films and 'old-line producers' proud of their ability to turn in entertaining commercial hits as a matter of routine. The third group 'writer-producers' tried to make 'meaningful series', series which had some relevance to life in contemporary society.[6] As suggested by their label most of these producers were also writers and authors and most had chaotic work histories, having moved from one medium to a another in search of an expressive vehicle.

In journalism a similar orientation, though differently labelled, has appeared in a number of studies. (Cohen, 1963; Johnstone *et al.*, 1976; Argyris, 1974; Janowitz, 1975.) In these cases the contrast is between straight reporters, content to collect the facts through recognized channels and to leave to the reader the task of interpreting and evaluating them, and participant or committed journalists who believe more attention should be paid to newsgathering, investigation, to providing background and analysis, even to making judgements on behalf of the reader about the relative worth of different accounts or the implications of particular statements and events.

Straight reporters positively value the craft skills associated with their style of news production. Claims to professionalism in journalism are based on such routine competences as factual accuracy, speed at meeting deadlines, style in presentation and a shared sense of news values. Such claims are echoed in other media occupations where professionalism again means skill and competence in the performance of routine work tasks. Burns (1972), for example, notes that the word 'professional' had an extraordinarily wide currency in the BBC, being used most commonly to mean the opposite of amateur, to denote 'good of its kind, expert, finished'. Reference has already been made to the studio musicians studied by Faulkner (1971) for whom professionalism meant skill and competence at coping with the varying work and restrictions involved in playing music in recording studios. Similarly, Peters (1971) reports that

6 Various accounts are available of the problems involved in launching such series, or even single episodes, as for example Gerrold (1973), Whitfield and Roddenberry (1968), Miller and Rhodes (1964).

for aspiring actresses professionalism involved the ability to keep appointments punctually, to handle a variety of roles and to avoid histrionics on
the set.

Professionalism in media occupations therefore is an adapting to the
dilemmas of role conflict by which skill and competence in the performance of routine tasks becomes elevated to the occupational ideal. The
competence involved is that which suits the organizational structure of
the medium at the particular time, so professional excellence is valued as
much by executives and administrators as by the craft group. At a simple
level some of the competence involved such as punctuality and the ability
to meet deadlines are of particular concern to the administrator. At a
more complex level the techniques devised to observe impartiality and
objectivity (Tuchman, 1972) or skill in presenting a broadcast discussion —
at the same time controlling the participants while drawing them out by
using such techniques as taking the role of the common man (Kumar,
1975; Elliott, 1972b) — can be seen as strategies which are not only
means of achieving professional status for the individual but means by
which the organization may hold its ground in the wider society.

Active participants or 'meaningful communicators' not only challenge
the standards of professionalism used by their peers but are also likely to
come into conflict with their employers. The conflict may be expressed
simply as a failure of professionalism (Kumar, 1975) but, because of the
significance of professionalism as a strategy, it is likely to involve different
interpretations of audience needs and tastes, the application of different
judgements of worth to output and different assessments of the strategies
necessary for the survival and growth of the organization. The American
studies suggest that, given the structure of press and television in the
United States, the participant approach is unlikely to have much effect
on output; indeed it might be best characterized as a stance rather than a
variation in practice. Johnstone, for example, concluded that those
journalists whom he had identified as 'participants' were inspired by an
ideal which was 'incompatible with organizational realities' and so could
not be realized by them. Similarly, Cantor (1971b) pointed out that in
spite of the different orientations she had identified there was only one
option in the end: 'It is impossible for anyone who does not give in to
continuous network pressure to stay on the job'. In other words, no
matter how complex the adaptations which communicators make to the
dilemma, the end result in terms of output will vary only if the adaptation
is supported by the organizational system in which the communicator is
working.

The point is graphically illustrated by considering the case of the BBC.
Burns (1969) found one group among the staff of that organization who
believed the corporation should have a normative relationship with its
audience: that while it should not prescribe a particular moral, political

or cultural code, it should observe the standards of the best of the British people, the professional middle class. Burns (1972, p. 136) christened the holders of this view 'platonists'. These 'platonists' shared with the participant journalists and socially conscious television producers mentioned above the view that communication output should be subjected to normative judgement. The actual norms involved were different — in one case broadly conservative, in the other loosely progressive. So too was the support available for each judgement from the employing organization.

While the 'monolithic structure of the Reithian ethos' survived, 'platonism' was largely an expression of the corporation's avowed philosophy and practice. By the time Burns conducted his study in 1963, 'liberal dissolution' had set in. The 'platonists' were flanked by two groups, the 'pragmatists' who believed there were distinct public demands for information, education and entertainment, the three types of output formally enshrined in the corporation's charter, and another group who held that 'broadcasting should be a mirror of contemporary life'. Kumar (1975) has pointed to similar differences in outlook reflected in the different metaphors used by successive director-generals and senior administrators in the BBC. 'Current BBC metaphors show a dramatic shift from those of leading and directing', for example the nautical metaphor beloved of Reith, 'to those involving far more neutral concepts: essentially the BBC is seen as the "register" of the many different "voices" in society, as the "great stage" on which all the actors, great and small, parade and say their piece'. (Kumar, 1975 p. 84.) Normative judgements are not entirely missing from the exercise of such a function. In the example of the new metaphor which Kumar quotes from David Attenborough, then Director of Television Programmes, BBC, the voices are to be selected according to a string of superlatives — 'the most prophetic, the most significant, the most amusing, the most dramatic, the most typical'. But these verge upon judgements about presentation and form rather than content. Indeed, the continuation of the above quotation highlights the way in which professional broadcasters may distance themselves from the content and disclaim responsibility for the message. The aim of the professional broadcaster is to pass on technical and professional skills to the various voices so that people will know 'how best the case may be presented, how best [they] may appear on the stage and get their message across' (ibid.) A similar distance from the content is built into the valued competence of the professional journalist, the professional broadcaster's contemporary whose aim is the impartial reporting of objective facts. The professionalism of the communicator is itself one example of the way in which mass media are likely to become pre-occupied with the form rather than the content of the message — a conclusion which I encapsulate elsewhere in the paradox 'mass communication — a contradiction in terms?' (Elliott, 1972b, Chapter 8.)

Organizations: constituents and strategies

The elaboration of professional competence is a tactic by which operative staff within the organization can pre-empt executive control. It can also be used by the organization to pre-empt other types of external regulation with the claim that professionalism is the most appropriate mechanism of social control. (Johnson, 1972.) The tactic has two apparent advantages. First, the ideology of professionalism, that it is a guarantee of autonomy rather than a mechanism of control, is particularly significant when liberal democratic theory stresses the need for independence between the media and the state. Second, the claim to professionalism is a claim to the status associated with the social elite of the liberal professions. There is some basis for this claim in Britain in terms of recruitment, aspirations and mechanisms of hierarchic control in some organizations. Nevertheless, however much of a mystique broadcasters or newsmen try to make of their craft, there are severe limitations to the analogy with the traditional professions. Communicators are peculiarly open to attacks such as that lauched by Tony Benn with the phrase 'broadcasting is too important to be left to the broadcasters'.[7] It was, after all, left to them in the first place less because of the special knowledge and skills involved than because they guaranteed to get the balance right between their various political and cultural constituents. (Fairlie, 1959.) The recent renunciation of claims to cultural and moral leadership in favour of analogies with brokerage or mirroring society has happened at a time when cracks have appeared in the moral-political consensus in society. (Hall, 1972.) It has become less clear in which direction society wishes to be led, or indeed whether as a whole it will stand for being led in any one direction.

Professionalism, however, does suggest a claim to leadership, a claim to know better than the client what his needs are. The effectiveness of professionalism as a mechanism of social control over aspects of social life involving conflict and change rests primarily on such a claim. Burns (1969) noted this as the third sense in which the word 'professional' was commonly used in the BBC. He also pointed out that while this apparently involved a reference to the needs of the ultimate client, the audience, in practice most discussion related to 'one's own sense of successful accomplishment, possibly unreliable, and to the regard of the head of one's department, one's fellows and, most constantly and evidently, the studio staff with whom one works'. Other commentators have pointed to similar processes whereby superiors, peers or available members of the public — the studio liftman is a popular example — become the surrogate audience (Hood, 1967; McQuail, 1969; Cantor, 1971.) Another possibility

7 The phrase was used in a speech by Mr Benn on 18 October 1968. For a discussion of the issue with specific reference to the events of the time see Halloran, Elliott and Murdock (1970, Chapter 1).

is reference to more traditional centres of creative activity outside the media, as expressed for example in such phrases as 'the legitimate theatre'. In the course of production itself the audience can be coopted by those involved as an ally for their side of any argument. (Elliott, 1972b.) The form of words, however, rarely conceals the way power is distributed among those involved. (Miller and Rhodes, 1964.)

Professionalism both justifies the weight given to the judgement of the colleague group and provides a reason for rejecting the twin goals of audience satisfaction and commercial success. Both of these come under the commercial pole of the dichotomy discussed above. Professionalism, however, has links with high culture, especially in senses such as a mastery of technique, a style and cultivation, a hierarchy of taste, which have been most acceptable in British culture. In British broadcasting this link with a broad concept of cultural excellence was most apparent under Reith. It was one tactic by which the BBC was able to win its place as a central institution in the national culture and a particularly important one when the organization's main constitutents were the people and institutions of the 'establishment', the British status elite. It is a tactic which BBC spokesmen still employ and the deliberations of the Pilkington Committee (1962) revolved around it. The 1976 Dimbleby lecture given by Huw Wheldon, ex-managing director BBC TV, provides a recent example of a similar ploy. The cultural excellence missing from American broadcasting is present in Britain and so, by implication, all is well with the British organizations. One novelty in Huw Wheldon's presentation of this case was that it embraced the IBA as well as the BBC. Many of his examples of 'excellent' programmes were produced by the commercial television companies.

Smith (1973) has pointed to the way in which periodic reviews by committee serve to remind broadcasters of the power of another of British broadcasting's constituents: the state. The process of periodic review has been one mechanism by which governments have induced a mood of permanent crisis among broadcasters. Another is the way in which threats to the security of the state — the General Strike, the Second World War, Suez, Ulster — immediately become occasions for reviewing the relationship between broadcasting and government.[8] The implication is that in a mood of crisis broadcasters will be specially wary of contravening the letter of the regulations governing their activities and the spirit of the conventions which have built up about the way these obligations are to be interpreted. In Britain the conventions are maintained through such public mechanisms as questions in parliament and occasional consultations by the Home Secretary, but also more covertly through contact between the ministers, press officers or party whips and senior broadcasting executives.

8 On the General Strike see Tracey (1978), on Ulster, Smith (1972) and Schlesinger (1978).

The relationship between recent Labour governments and the BBC tends to belie the claim that such conventions and contacts are sufficiently well established to cope with partisan political conflict within the British parliamentary system. (Tracey, forthcoming.) They work well enough in the field of news where the conventions of impartiality and objectivity are most firmly established (Schlesinger, forthcoming.) The use of such conventions may produce unwitting bias but the victims of this bias are generally the deviant or disadvantaged with little power in society. (Halloran, Elliott and Murdock, 1970; Cohen and Young, 1973.) The conventions are less successful in the general field of current affairs programming.

In spite of brokerage metaphors, more is involved in broadcasting professionalism in current affairs than simply providing a stage on which others can walk. One way in which the broadcaster can make sure the others observe the rules as well as giving himself the opportunity to walk there too is by taking the role of the audience. There are various examples of this, from making independent judgements about what are the 'interesting' issues in an election (Blumler, 1969), through persistent devil's advocacy such as is associated with the interviewer and presenter, Robin Day, to adopting a populist stance and style as the representative of the common man, the moderate, the man in the middle of the pressures and constraints of modern life. (Kumar, 1975.) As this last example makes clear, the tendency in adopting such a role is to define all the others on the stage as sectional interests, a consequence which contrasts oddly with Reith's famous dictum at the time of the General Strike — 'Assuming the BBC is for the people and the government is for the people, it follows that the BBC must be for the government in this crisis too'. (Reith, 1949.) The difference in broadcasting presentation in 1976 is not that the TUC has been admitted as another representative of the people, but that the government has come to be another sectional interest. Of course there is now a Labour government in power. As Anderson (1966) reminds us, the role of the government in the power system of British society is analytically distinct according to which party is in power. A Conservative government 'is an integral part of a continuous landscape which extends in a smooth, unbroken space around it. When a Labour government is in power, it is an isolated, spot-lit enclave, sur-rounded on almost every side by hostile territory, unceasingly shelled by industry, press and orchestrated public opinion' (p. 46). The only qualification that needs to be added to this analysis is that the tensions inherent within the Conservative party between its aristocratic legacy and the demands of the industrial bourgeoisie have become more apparent in recent years, with the result that the Conservative party has lost some of its claim to general national leadership.

Change in society is one of the factors to which Burns points to explain the demise of the Reithian ethos, but one to which he pays little attention beside the advent of television and then the introduction of commercial television. It could be argued however that the major social change has itself taken an ideological form. There has been a change in the characteristics and validity of the hegemonic ideology of the British ruling class as Britain's continuing economic and imperial decline have made the tensions within that class more apparent. There has been a move away from those elements which drew on the aristocratic legacy, such as traditionalism, respect for constitutional forms and the hierarchies of the social order, patriotism and the values of leadership associated with Britain's imperial role towards more ubiquitous values of commercial populism and efficiency.

Both developments in television can be seen as themselves contributing to this process. First television and then commercial television tipped the balance in British broadcasting away from 'cultural excellence' towards popular entertainment. The ultimate audience took on a new importance, if only in terms of a viewing statistic. Brown (1969) pointed out that media men challenge elitist criticism of declining cultural standards by reference to both popular and commercial values, claiming that there is no point in a mass medium without a mass audience, and that entertainment is itself a criterion of excellence. The point of the present analysis is not to enter into such a discussion in terms of critical standards, but to analyse the change in the mechanisms of social control applied to broadcasting. In general, economic survival is a more serious problem for commercial media systems than meeting or playing off the demands of organizational constituents discussed in this section. These constituents ensure other elite values are represented in the system of control as well as commercialism.

In Britain, for example, the elements of the constituent system which are built into the structure of commercial broadcasting take the form of an over-arching authority with a membership similar to that of the BBC board and provision for periodic re-allocation of contracts. As the London Weekend Television submission for the television franchise in the London area showed, these may have a considerable effect on the cultural and political pretentions of the commercial broadcaster if not on his programme policy.[9] On occasions commercial companies may be prepared to trade off cultural prestige against a commercial loss. Such prestige may be the important currency when contracts are reallocated or a new channel awarded.

So far as political constituents are concerned, however, a better strategy may be to ignore them. (Tracey, 1978.) In recent years current affairs output on British television has been cut back to a few

9 Published in the first number of *The Open Secret*, the Journal of the Free Communications Group and discussed in subsequent issues.

recognized slots; in spite of their regional base the commercial companies make relatively limited provision for local news and there has, in Tracey's phrase, been a tendency to 'miscellanize' the content so that a large number of subjects fill a small space of time with plenty of provision for light relief. Against this, the *News at Ten* has been a popular success on ITV and the three regular current affairs programmes are notably adventurous. The reasons for this are to be found partly in particular circumstances, the personnel and organization that produce the programmes, and partly in the way the mix of constituent and economic demands are experienced in the British system of commercial television.

The situation in the United States is less complicated in that there is no socio-cultural elite of sufficient size or power to act as a constituent and the interests of politicians are largely taken care of through the mechanism of commercial control. Vice-President Agnew's speech at Des Moines in 1969 was a comparatively rare example of a political constituent pressing a demand in public with the implicit threat that if the broadcasters took no action, the government might. Hall's description of the 'polarization of the moral-political consensus' (1972) is even more applicable to events in the United States at that time. Nevertheless, one reason why the speech received so much attention was its unique character as a political threat to American broadcasters and journalists. Prior to that, political control had been exercised as a by-product of commercial control, with apparent success so far as broadcasting's powerful political constituents were concerned. One consequence of commercial control has been a lack of news and current affairs programming much more marked than in Britain. (Wolf, 1972.) Wolf's study also exposes a case in which attempts to mitigate economic control by constituent control through the regulatory commission, the FCC, might only make the effects of economic control — less news and current affairs programming — more apparent. Wolf suggests this would follow from any attempt to break up network ownership and control of broadcasting stations. Network stations carry little enough of this programming but independent stations can't afford to allocate it any resources or transmission time.

Organizations: means and goals

The previous section examined media organizations in terms of strategies developed to meet the demands of significant constituents in their environment. This method of analysis is particularly appropriate to the study of public service media organizations whose activities are hedged about with regulations and reviews. To deal with other media, this analysis needs to be complemented by one which starts from the organization itself and examines its goals and the means available to meet them. Such an analysis is particularly appropriate to commercial media. Both types of analysis are important in the British case. The mechanisms of social control over the media are mixed, reflecting the variety of elites and values to be found intermeshed in the British ruling class.

Commercial media organizations which are not exposed to the demands of different constituents through any formal channels may nevertheless pursue a variety of goals. Lane (1970) and Tunstall (1971) have pointed to the way in which publishing houses and newspapers pursue non-economic as well as economic goals. There is a formal difference between these two types of goal: 'Where economic goals are sought there may be conflict over the means to achieve them, but there will be a high degree of unanimity over both the definition of the end and the operationalization of that definition' whereas 'acute cognitive disagreements arise over both ends and means if the sought goals are cultural' (Lane 1970b, p. 372). Non-revenue goals are as vague and various in newspapers as in publishing. In both cases considerable emphasis is placed on historical precedent, on continuing to publish the sort of material that made publishers' or journalists' reputations in the past. Tunstall (1971) shows how this is more apparent in some types of journalism, for example foreign and political reporting, than in others which more clearly have audience-revenue or advertising-revenue goals. Revenue and non-revenue goals are mixed throughout the organization and provide bargaining currencies between such groups as news gatherers and news processors differently involved in successive stages of news production.

The two sources of revenue make up a different proportion of total revenue in different types of newspapers. Generally advertising revenue provides the largest proportion in the quality national press; more than a half of the revenue of quality dailies and two-thirds that of quality Sundays coming from this source in 1975. (Royal Commission on the Press, 1976.) This compares with about a quarter of the revenue of the popular dailies and nearly a third of that of the popular Sundays. In all cases the proportion of newspaper revenue coming from advertising has declined in the past decade as continuing economic crisis has kept total advertising expenditure depressed and as the cover prices of newspapers have risen. But though the proportion has declined, the fact that advertising is the most immediately flexible source of revenue means its importance in newspaper finance has not decreased. Hirsch and Gordon (1975) note how different papers tend to pursue slightly different groups in the audience but that because the main value of such groups is their worth to advertisers, there tends to be a persistent 'up-market' bias throughout the press. They go on to argue that this is one reason why there is a tendency to conformity in national journalism, with all papers expressing the same opinion over issues like Britain's entry to the Common Market and, more obviously, all agreeing that they should discuss and report basically the same agenda of public affairs.[10] The national news media in Britain provide a neat illustration of the old saw that competition produces similarity not difference. Much of the variation in content which does exist is the result of cross-subsidies which keep papers like the *Guardian* and *The Times* alive. One reason why owners persevere with cross-subsidization is the value they place on non-economic goals.

The pursuit of policy is one of the non-economic goals to which Tunstall refers and one which has been regarded as the prerogative of the owner by which he may seek to further some general or specific political objective. Financial loss through cross-subsidy may be exchanged for political influence or simply the social prestige of running an historic newspaper. In general, however, the growth of the commercial national press has led to a decline in partisanship in the British press. (Seymour-Ure, 1974.)

In other countries overtly partisan papers still exist, though in decline. In these the policy goal is a positive aim, not a residual category, and so poses particular problems of enforcement within the organization. (Gerbner, 1964; and 1969.) Stark (1962) studied a metropolitan newspaper in the United States in which the proprietors subscribed to a clear policy line. Their conservative policy was at variance with the liberal inclinations of many journalists on the staff and its implementation also violated their ideas of professional practice in journalism. These 'pro' journalists, whose main orientation was to the occupation of journalism, made up one group in the newspaper's staff. There was another group, 'locals', who accepted the proprietors' policy and who were oriented towards the employing organization rather than journalism as an occupation. Editors were appointed from this group and it was on them that the main task of implementing proprietorial policy fell. The 'pros' did not conceal their objections to this policy and, in so far as they could, sought to subvert it. The main consequence of the conflict, however, was that there was a very quick turnover of pros, who left the paper for more congenial organizations in which they could practice professional journalism. But the paper needed their skills to hold its audience and so had to keep on hiring new 'pro' journalists.

Stark's study is unusual in that it reveals overt conflict within a media organization rather than a process of adaptation whereby employees come to assimilate organizational goals and adjust their work accordingly. Brown (1969, p. 155) remarks that 'anyone who has had the chance of an extended conversation with members of the editorial staff of one of Britain's tabloid dailies or sensational Sundays may well have been struck by the firmness and determination with which the more senior members

10 For a case study of a news story making the same points, see Halloran, Elliott and Murdock (1970).

of the organization have defended the editorial policies and practice of
their newspaper . . . a cynical division of mind between what is stated in
public and believed in private turns out to be the exception rather than
the rule'. One difference seems to be that, in the British press as in the
newspaper studied by Breed (1955), policy is less distinctively partisan
than the relatively covert consequence of following what appear to be
organizational and economic imperatives. In such cases there is not a
conflict between policy and professional practice because, as we have
seen, professionalism is itself defined in terms of the skills necessary to
meet the organization's goals.

Even in such cases, however, there may still be a disjunction between
professional belief and professional practice at the more descriptive level
of what makes up the routine tasks of the occupation. Media production
is necessarily a non-routine activity in so far as each unit of output is
different. There are degrees of difference between, say, drama serials and
one-shot plays. Nevertheless, those working in media production tend to
experience their work as non-routine and to emphasize non-routine aspects
in their accounts of it. Epstein (1973), for example, found that none of
the three central journalistic norms held by the television newsmen he
studied — that news should be immediate, unexpected and original — were
reflected in the news produced; immediate, unexpected and original news
could not be produced within the structural and organizational constraints
of television. Such beliefs survive partly because other aspects of the work
situation of journalists and other mass communicators, for example irregular
hours, changing places of work and contacts with different sources, are
experienced as non-routine and partly because there are occasionally
programmes or stories in which one or more of the professional norms are
realized. Swedish journalists were in the habit of carrying live VTR coverage
of football and ice hockey games in the main television news bulletin, a
practice fully justified one evening by a goal scored in the brief moment
when the game was on the air.[11] Just as unusual individuals provide an
occupation with its heroes, so unusual cases provide it with its ideals of
practice.

Nevertheless, by examining routine procedures, it is possible to
develop an account of the material and sources used regularly in media
production. Such an account is necessary to any sociological analysis of
the type of knowledge and culture the media purvey. In my study of the
production of a documentary series for television (Elliott, 1972b) I
identified three mechanisms whereby the production team contacted
material; through its use in other media, principally the national press;
through organizations and associations, mainly pressure groups with an

11   This illustration is taken from a comparative study of television news-making in
     three countries — Sweden, Nigeria and the Republic of Ireland, to be reported in
     Golding and Elliott (1979).

appropriate interest, and through personal contacts. Many of the latter involved people who had been contacted before by a member of the production team when he or she had been working on another television programme. The result was that a relatively fortuitous sample of the 'conventional wisdom' already available in the media culture appeared on the screen.

Similar continuity is built into the work of journalists whose routine search and checking procedures are likely to be applied with particular vigour to any story which is unexpected in the sense that it challenges conventional beliefs. Schlesinger (1978) provides an account of BBC newsmen's suspicious reactions to a story of a massacre in Wiriyamu, a village in Mozambique, by the Portuguese. They doubted the source, a Roman Catholic priest, and the film he produced as evidence and set out to secure more film, eye-witness accounts and to balance the story with a statement on behalf of the Portuguese Government.

Accepting some sources as official and reliable while questioning or ignoring others is an important part of journalistic routine. Several journalists have commented on the special difficulties of reporting in Ulster where they or their colleagues have been misled by sources they had previously been prepared to trust. (Winchester, 1975; Stephens, 1976.) There is more to journalist-source relationships than simply accepting or rejecting the material offered. Both have rather different interests in the account that will finally be produced and different means of influencing that outcome. (Chibnall, 1975.) Nevertheless, the result, as Sigelman (1973) has put it, is that 'newsmen are in an important sense hypothesis testers, whose newsgathering procedures consist of checking the empirical validity of their preconceptions'. Sigelman, like Breed, goes on to show that previous experience of the policy and practices of the news organization provide an important source for these preconceptions. In the papers he studied, 'bias' was again a product of the organization and system of reporting rather than directed and controlled policy bias.

So far the process of routinization has been discussed mainly with reference to the work procedures of production staff. A similar analysis, however, can be applied to the procedures organizations adopt to achieve their objectives. Hirsch (1972) has provided an account of the techniques used by different organizations engaged in the production and mass distribution of cultural items to cope with 'highly uncertain environments at their input and output boundaries'. Uncertainty is particularly characteristic of cultural production because there is no way of knowing which creative items will appeal to the audience, which, if selected for production and distribution, will be the greatest economic success. Instead, one possibility, as in record production or book publishing, in which the unit cost of each item of output is relatively low, is to over-produce, writing off failures against successes, while ensuring there are enough of the latter by employing 'contact' men to keep watch on relevant creative activity outside the organization and recruit likely talent. For over-production to be successful, potential buyers must be made aware of what is being offered, but this cannot be done through the individual promotion of each item. Instead, products are promoted by use in the mass media, either directly as in the case of record plays or by serializing, adapting or excerpting from books or indirectly through interviews and news items about the artists or authors involved. In Hirsch's terms, the mass media become 'gatekeepers' or 'strategic checkpoints' regulating innovation. The result is that the media culture is the product of a continual interchange of people and products between the various cultural production and media systems.

Unit costs are too high in other types of cultural production to allow for over-production. This applies to the making of feature films and television programmes. In the latter case there is the further consideration that distribution is limited and highly competitive – there are only so many hours in peak time and the audience for one channel is the potential audience of another. In consequence, attention is paid to techniques which will reduce the uncertainty surrounding the production and distribution of each item as well as techniques which will promote the whole service. The star system in film production was a means of achieving both objectives. Before anti-trust suits challenged studio control over film distribution in the United States and before competition developed with television, the stable of stars maintained by the studio was one way of spreading audience appeal across the whole range of its output. Star names on the billing for a particular picture also provide a specific inducement for the audience to see that film. Schary (1950, p. 40) recounts that casting stars might add 25% to the cost of making an individual film, but was generally worth doing as 'a very practical form of insurance, they protect our investment. . . .' Other means of protecting the investment included picking a story which was 'a pre-sold property – one which had already proved its success in another medium' (Griffiths, 1959, p. 11; Fadiman, 1973); hiring a production team of 'professionals with a proven track record' (Blum, 1970) or who 'know the score' (Kael, 1970) – a recurring theme in Kael's film criticism is the aesthetic consequences of the fact that most feature film directors now prove themselves on television, a medium with more limited resources, more emphasis on keeping within budget limits and production deadlines, and so placing more value on professional competence than artistic flair; casting roles with actors who, if not stars, have some individual characteristic which could be exploited in the promotion of the film – Griffiths (1959) recounts how one of the reasons for casting Joseph N. Welch, an attorney from the Army-McCarthy hearings as the judge in the film *Anatomy of a Murder* was the novel possibilities this opened up for publicity; relating the story or the style of production to some previous success — the development and appraisal of production ideas tends to be carried on in a shorthand code whereby new ideas are labelled in terms of their nearest precedent.

More than that, successful films and programmes become models whose influence extends beyond the organization or country in which they were first produced. The BBC television programme *Tonight*, for example, has been an influential model throughout Europe as well as in Britain. In this country its influence can be linked to the spread of the 'Tonight' generation of programme makers working on BBC television current affairs programmes at the time, to posts in production and administration throughout British broadcasting. An example of the model's dispersion through Europe turned up recently in Sweden, with the introduction of a miscellany programme modelled on *Tonight* but called *Halv-Sju* (Half Past Six) on SR channel I. The subsequent controversy echoed many of the issues that had originally been raised about *Tonight*. As well as the question of whether it was more properly considered entertainment than current affairs, there was also the point that it took viewers away from the main current affairs programme on the second channel, *Rapport*. In spite of its popular success *Halv-Sju* was dropped and provisions made to regulate competition between the two channels to protect news and current affairs programmes. The continuing power of constituent control in Sweden overruled the requirement that the two channels should compete. That requirement was based on constituent (government) planning, not on the need to secure commercial finance. In Britain *Tonight* was one of the programmes which the BBC itself used to win an audience back from ITV. In that case BBC finances were not directly threatened by the loss of its audience though BBC management felt they were indirectly. They feared the organization's constituents, again principally government, might withdraw support unless the BBC's share of the audience was about equal to that of ITV. (Greene, 1969, Goldie, 1977.)

Two other techniques used by organizations engaged in cultural production to reduce uncertainty or simply increase revenue are to licence or develop ancillary products related to the original film or programme and to make the film or programme itself with an eye to overseas markets. The Hollywood studios employed distribution executives, one of whose functions was to ensure films did not include anything offensive to important ethnic or religious audiences in the home or overseas market (Lewis 1933.) More recently, series have appeared on British television made in a 'mid-Atlantic' style in the hope of securing American sales. In a time of increasing financial stringency, the BBC and the commercial television companies have begun to look to other companies and organizations abroad for financial help in setting up co-productions as well as for markets for finished programmes. At home they have begun to exploit the potential of ancillary marketing in such fields as records, books, clothing and toys, spreading the compass of media culture further and elaborating the links involved in its production.

More and more, this media culture has come to be produced by a few large scale conglomerates diversified across the whole field of what their directors now call the 'leisure industry'. Murdock and Golding (1974) have argued that a similar cycle can be discerned in every field of cultural production from books in the middle of the last century to television in this. A period of growth based on the development and exploitation of new production and distribution technologies comes to an end when the market for that cultural product is saturated. Because of market saturation, rising costs cannot be met out of revenue, a situation which may be further exacerbated by the development of competitive media based on new technologies. Throughout the cycle there is a tendency for control to become concentrated in fewer hands because of the need to secure financial capital to exploit the technology and the economies of scale which accrue from large-scale production. Murdock and Golding show that this has led to a situation in Britain where the major companies in each field of cultural production control the bulk of the market. The companies are themselves interrelated, sharing the same directors, holding each other's shares and investing in the same subsidiaries. Through diversification, amalgamation and take over, their interests spread throughout the leisure industry until media production is no longer their main activity or their central concern.

In the course of this cycle, it becomes more difficult to secure the necessary financial backing for production in any particular cultural field and more apparent that that is where control ultimately lies. The various means by which production organizations try to reduce uncertainty can also be seen as a means of insuring the investment. So far as the output is concerned, it makes little difference whether the investment is formally their own or provided by a parent company or a financial backer. It is a common theme in histories of each type of media production that each successive generation in control of the industry is more distanced from the product, more obviously motivated only by financial interests. Looked at in this perspective, even movie moguls and press barons acquire a nostalgic glow. (Fadiman, 1973.)

Hirsch's analysis suggests that different means of reducing uncertainty are available to different sectors of the industry according to the unit cost of the output, but within each sector there is a remarkable similarity in the means used at different times, regardless of the form of organization current in the industry. In 1933 Lewis listed the ways in which the major Hollywood studios set about predicting a successful film. It is unlikely that any but a large organization, engaged in continuous production, would employ a psychologist to predict trends in human taste, as Lewis reported the Universal Picture Corporation did in 1929. Apart from such minor differences, however, there is little difference between the ways then available to the Hollywood studios and those used now by independent production companies to convince first a distributor and then a backer that their plan will be a success. The independent company may have more difficulty because of market changes. The audience which remains for the cinema is both smaller and less predictable than the mass, family audience. Given this, any contemporary proposal to produce a film is, in the words of Pauline Kael, 'a fantastic long-shot gamble against public apathy'.

Just as the ways of predicting success are similar, so too are the results. Opening the door 'to independent production provided, in theory, opportunities for risk and adventure, and proved, when it came to the point, that producers, directors and actors, left to themselves, would make much the same kind of films they had been working on for their studio overlords' (Houston, 1963). Production personnel had exchanged control by studio contract for control by insecurity.

Generalizations and Variations in Media Culture

Throughout this paper the concept of media culture has been used to draw attention to the similarity and interpenetration between the output of different media and types of cultural production. The paradigm case of cultural production under the conditions of democratic capitalism current in the twentieth century is not developing a commodity for a particular market, such as the 'reading public' of the eighteenth and nineteenth centuries (Watt, 1963), so much as producing artefacts which will appeal to the mass market or which can be developed in different forms to incorporate different publics. While production for a specific public depended on the separation and development of distribution as a specific function, so that novelists, for example, could sell their books through booksellers, production for a mass market involves the further separation of promotion from distribution. The promotion function is performed primarily by the most recent media, radio, television and the popular press — whose financial survival is most dependent on reaching the mass audience.

Murdock and Golding (1974) suggest two consequences following from their analysis of the political economy of mass communications — constriction of choice in leisure and entertainment and the consolidation of the consensus through information control. To these might be added a third — the neutering of cultural content. This charge has been associated with such elitist critics of mass society as T. S. Eliot and Ortega Y. Gasset, concerned that the debasement of high culture in popular culture was another reflection of the rising power of the masses. Again, such elitist critics can be seen as representatives of aristocratic paternalism in a debate within the ruling class between traditionalism and commercialism. The fact that a concept like 'Kitsch' has been used by these social critics is no reason to avoid it completely in social analysis, particularly as those critics were concerned about what they identified as the mainstream of social change towards populist commercialism. Dwight Macdonald (1957, p. 72) has described Kitsch as 'a debased, trivial culture that avoids both the deep realities (sex, death, failure, tragedy) and also the simple, spontaneous pleasures, since realities would be too real and the pleasures too lively to induce what Mr Seldes calls "the mood of consent", i.e. a narcotized acceptance of mass culture and of the commodities it sells as a substitute for the unsettling and unpredictable (hence unsaleable) joy, tragedy, wit, change, originality and beauty of real life'. Kitsch is a type of culture in which form predominates over content, which exploits not just high culture but folk-cultures and avante garde culture, all types of culture which express the life experience of particular groups within the society. In the transformation of content into form such expressive contact is lost.[12]

Rather than cite examples of this restricted, consensual and anodyne culture, I shall explore the sources of variation revealed in the preceding analysis of organization and employment in cultural production. Such variations provide the contrary cases which can be used to question generalizations about media culture, with the implication that if a few exceptions are to be found things can't be quite so bad after all. By examining the source of such variations, however, it is possible to show that they are relatively rare, unstable and grounded in the margins of the cultural production process in democratic, capitalist society. In Britain, too, several of these sources reflect the continuing conflict between bourgeois commercialism and an older aristocratic form of social order. (Rex, 1974.) The variations made possible by this conflict are as broadly supportive of the political and economic system as Kitsch itself, though they put more faith in the authority of social elites than in unbridled economic logic. British society is founded on a coalition between these two forces. Generally they work together but occasionally, when one throws up a cultural form with radical potential, there are mechanisms associated with the other available to incorporate or control it:

12 In the production of drama series for British television, considerable attention is paid to 'authenticity' — getting the period and setting right. The way 'authenticity' functions as a professional value, similar to others discussed in this paper, seems to be most apparent in those historical series where it provides a cover for making points, for example about the radicalism of the working class, which would not be allowed in any contemporary context. The recent BBC TV series, *Days of Hope*, for instance, seems to have broken television's equivalent of the fifty year rule by dealing with too recent a period so that the cover of 'authenticity' was not sufficient to disguise its radical content.

1 The main source of variation in media culture in the direction of socio-cultural elites is the system of constituent control discussed extensively above. It is this which provides the main justification for treating the mass media in Britain as a social institution with some autonomy, not simply as an arm of the state or the capitalist class. In a debate with Poulantzas, Miliband (1972) has argued that such institutions as the church, the schools, the political parties, the family and the mass media in Britain are formally separate from the state and 'never cease to insist on their "unideological", "unpolitical" and "neutral" character'. To follow Althusser (1971) and lump them all together as ideological state apparatuses because in the last analysis they are supported by the state power embodied in the repressive state apparatuses (Poulantzas, 1972) obscures rather than clarifies the way in which they perform an autonomous ideological function.

2 A second source of variation is in the structure of competition to be found in some sectors of cultural production. The prime example here is the British national press in which small circulation, quality newspapers can survive alongside mass circulation popular papers because of their ability to charge higher rates to advertisers who wish to reach an elite audience and a higher cover price to the elite audience itself. Other examples in the magazine field show how this source of variation only works to the advantage of wealthy groups with consumptive power or groups whose interests are open to exploitation as a separate market for trade or leisure products. Those groups which constitute a special market may find material produced for them, but those which simply have special interests based on such common experiences as unemployment, poverty and old age have no vehicles in which to share such experience or develop a common consciousness.

3 A third source of variation results from the phenomenon of over-production which Hirsch identified in those sectors of the industry with low unit costs. In such cases provision for minorities may itself be profitable as well as being an inevitable consequence of the technique of covering all possible sources of cultural innovation so that no potential winner is missed. This, taken together with the process of surveying the environment embodied in objective news reporting, seem to provide the main sources of change in the content and perspectives of media culture. But there are no autonomous folk cultures. All cultural innovation will take place in an environment set by media culture, a fact of especial importance given the tendency to turn leisure activities, including cultural performances, into markets for expensive technologies. Further, economic logic requires that cultural innovations in a minority field should be adapted and promoted for mass consumption.

4 A fourth source, allowing variations in media culture of a more limited extent, is the presence of economic slack in the system allowing organizations to be less rigorous in judgements about the cost effectiveness of particular items of output. There is greater scope for such variation in times of economic prosperity, and most of the variations allowed tend to be towards traditional, elite, cultural values as, for example, in the publishing field where criteria of rational, commercial efficiency still do not hold complete sway in spite of gloomy prophecies for nearly two centuries.

Both audience and advertising revenue seem particularly sensitive to general economic conditions as each is a relatively marginal type of expenditure in the overall budget of the individual consumer or producing organization. Financial stringency in British television, for example, has progressively reduced the proportion of new and expensive types of programme in favour of repeats and cheaper productions. In the press the survival of several national newspapers depends on cross-subsidization from the other interests of its parent company or from a profitable paper in a different market, but one which may itself be vulnerable in periods of slump, as for example in the relationship between the *Guardian* and and the *Manchester Evening News.*

5 A fifth source of variation which also tends to be squeezed out by the economic logic of production for the market is the exercise of the prerogatives of ownership. British press barons such as Rothermere or Beaverbrook played a particularly important part in putting their own individual stamp on the hegemonic ideology of the British ruling class. Moreover, owners may take the opportunity their media give them to pursue arguments within that class as to the relative merits of traditional as against commercial values. There are qualitative differences in style in the contemporary output of the British commercial television companies, differences which are often related to the different origins and personalities of their chairmen and managing directors. This explanation could be extended from a personal account to a more structural analysis of the particular social elites, and the financial and industrial backgrounds from which these leaders are drawn.

Sources of variation are also located in the work force engaged in cultural production though throughout this paper stress has been laid on the way work routines adapt to structural conditions. In a sense variations at the production level are made possible by sources of variation in the structure of the industry already listed.

6 The source of variation at the production level which has received most attention in this paper is the development of professionalism. While the predominant form of professionalism is simply routine competence in the skills necessary to produce media culture, there remains a sense in which

it is both a claim to autonomy and to a link with high culture and the activities of status elites, and so it becomes an independent source of pressure moving cultural production in that direction.

7 Another source of variation among performing and producing personnel is the phenomenon of subsidy and patronage. In some areas of cultural production it is common for individuals to depend more on external sources of support than on the financial rewards of the activity itself. Again, this is most common through mechanisms which encourage activities in the high cultural field, but they also provide support for the avant-garde and bohemian fringe which adopt a more radical stance towards the social order.

8 So far as production personnel are concerned, there is one value, novelty, which is supported by features of their occupational situation. The individualism associated with making a name or a career in most fields of cultural production ensures that producers try to mark off their work from that of others in the field. The scope they have to do so is necessarily limited. Novel innovations themselves tend to become repetitive as, for example, in attempts to present political television by probing the personalities and personal circumstances of politicians rather than simply repeating their publicly known positions and statements.[13] The emphasis on novelty also tends to be most apparent at the start of the production cycle when production personnel have most opportunity to formulate their plans in creative terms. This may be particularly necessary to recruit some of the talent or material necessary for the final product. Eric Ambler (1949), for example, has provided an archetypal account of the process of filming a novel. At the start the producer wins the novelist's co-operation with money and by defining his responsibility in creative terms — 'to create the enthusiasm within the small creative group which really makes the picture, to give that group a dynamic of its own' (p. 23). As the production develops, however, the producer moves in to reorganize character and plot in line with the organization of the production process, possible 'censorship' problems and perceived audience demand. Thus, though the drive towards novelty would seem to provide a source of cultural innovation and change, it is one which is progressively ironed out by the structural constraints which operate throughout the course of production.

9 Finally, reference must be made to the audience. It would be incorrect to argue that media culture is simply imposed on the public without reference to its wishes when much of the basis for the production of that culture is founded on those wishes, at least in the negative sense of avoiding

13 For a case in point see Tracey's account of 'The *Yesterday's Men* Affair' in this volume.

disturbance and offence. It would also be naive to suggest that the producers of media culture have simply underestimated the potential of their audience. Instead, I wish to draw attention to the process whereby sections of the audience may coopt particular items of media culture as symbols 'for a loosely defined social position, marking out social boundaries and the lines of potential social conflict'. (Elliott, 1974, p. 264.) It still seems to be the case that while some fads and fashions are 'hypes' founded on extensive commercial development and promotion, others are founded on active audience reaction. These are less predictable or explicable except with the benefit of hindsight to explain how the content could be used by the group to promote its own social identity.

This account of the sources of variation in British media culture has shown both that most exist in the margins of contemporary cultural production and that most give expression to differences of emphasis and tradition within the British social elite, or rest simply on the problems and potential of following commercial logic in the cultural field. Generalizations, such as that advanced earlier, that the basic tendency in contemporary society is towards a culture which is restricted, consensual and anodyne, cannot be knocked down simply by reference to exceptional cases. Analysis of such cases shows that they are not simply exceptional, but related to the balance of power within the social structure, and especially within the ruling class. To predict trends in the culture it then becomes necessary to predict trends in this balance of power, particularly in the relative weight which is likely to be placed in the future on the aristocratic legacy of elitism, traditionalism and imperialism as against bourgeois commercial values. Such predictions are beyond the scope of this paper, though it is worth noting in passing that Britain has lost the imperial role which provided much of the recent support for the aristocratic legacy and that her economy has become increasingly submerged within international corporate capitalism, both processes conveniently illustrated by Britain's final entry into the European Economic Community. The argument of this paper has been to show that in so far as Britain has a unique media culture, this is because the mixture of elites which dominate British society make possible some variation in the organizations and occupations through which it is produced. Such variation, however, takes place against a ground base provided by the commercial logic necessary for the economic survival of these organizations of cultural production.

References

Althusser, L., 1971: 'Ideology and ideological state apparatuses'. In *Lenin and philosophy and other essays*, London: New Left Books.

Altick, R. D., 1962: 'The sociology of authorship'. *New York Public Library Bulletin 66*, No. 6 (June) pp. 389–404.

Ambler, E., 1949: 'The Film of the Book'. In *Penguin Film Review* vol. 9.

Anderson, P., 1966: 'Origins of the Present Crisis' and 'Problems of Socialist Strategy'. In P. Anderson and R. Blackburn (Eds.) *Towards Socialism*, New York: Cornell University Press.

1969: 'Components of the National Culture'. In A. Cockburn and R. Blackburn (Eds.) *Student Power*, Harmondsworth: Penguin.

Argyris, C., 1974: *Behind the front page*. London: Jossey-Bass.

Becker, Howard S., 1963: 'The dance musicians: the culture of a deviant group and careers in a deviant occupational group'. In *Outsiders*, London: Free Press.

Blum, S., 1970: 'Who decides what gets on TV and why?'. In New York Times Staff, *Social Profiles: US Today*, London: Van Nostrand.

Boyd-Barrett, O., 1970: 'Journalism recruitment and training: problems in professionalization'. In J. Tunstall, (Ed.)

Bradbury, M., 1971: *The social context of modern English literature*. Oxford: Blackwell.

Breed, W., 1955: 'Social control in the newsroom'. *Social Forces*, May.

Brown, R. L., 1969: 'Some aspects of mass media ideologies'. *Sociological Review Monograph*, vol. 13 pp. 155–68.

Burns, T., 1972: *Commitment and career in the BBC*. In D. McQuail, (Ed.)

Cantor, Muriel G., 1971a: *The Hollywood TV Producer*. New York: Basic Books.

1971b: 'Producing TV for children'. Paper read to American Sociological Association Conference.

Chibnall, S., 1975: 'The crime reporter: a study in the production of commercial knowledge'. *Sociology* 9 (1), pp. 49–66.

Cohen, B. C., 1963: *The press and foreign policy*. Princeton University Press.

Cohen, S. and Young, J., 1973: *The manufacture of news*. London: Constable.

Donohue, G. *et al.*, 1972: 'Gatekeeping: mass media systems and information control'. In Kline, F. G. and Tichenor, P. J. (Eds.) *Current perspectives in mass communication research*, Sage.

Elliott, P. and Chaney, D., 1969: 'A sociological framework for the study of television production'. *Sociological Review* 17 (3).

Elliott, P., 1972a: *The sociology of the professions*. London: Macmillan.

1972b: *The making of a television series: a case study in the sociology of culture*. London: Constable.

1974: 'Uses and gratification research: a critique and a sociological alternative'. In Blumler, J. G. and Katz, E. (Eds.) *The uses of mass communications*, Sage. *Annual Review of Communications Research*, vol. III, London.

Epstein, E. J., 1973: *News from nowhere*. New York: Random House.

Fadiman, W., 1973: *Hollywood now*. London: Thames and Hudson.

Fairlie, H., 1959: 'The BBC'. In Thomas, H. (Ed.) *The establishment*, London: Blond.

Faulkner, R., 1971: *The Hollywood studio musicians*. Chicago: Aldine.

Gerbner, G., 1964: 'Ideological perspectives and political tendencies in news reporting'. *Journalism Quarterly*, Autumn, pp. 494–508.

1969: 'Institutional pressures on mass communicators'. *Sociological Review Monograph*, vol. 13, pp. 205—48.

Gerrold, D., 1973: *The trouble with Tribbles: the birth, sale and final production of one episode.* New York: Ballantine.

Goldie, Grace Wyndham, 1972: 'The sociology of television'. *Listener* 19 October.

Golding, P., 1974: *The mass media.* London: Longman.

Golding, P. and Elliott, P., 1979: *Making the News.* London: Longman.

Greene, H. C., 1969: *The third floor front.* London: Bodley Head.

Griff, 1962: 'The commercial artist: a study in changing and inconsistent indentities'. In Stein, M. R. *et al.* (Eds.) *Identity and anxiety*, New York: Free Press.

Griffiths, R., 1959: *Anatomy of a motion picture.* New York: St Martin's Press.

Hall, S., 1972: 'The limitations of broadcasting'. *Listener* 16 March.

Halloran, J. D., Elliott, P. and Murdock, G., 1970: *Demonstrations and communication.* Harmondsworth: Penguin.

Halloran, J. D. and Gurevitch, M. (Eds.), 1971: *Broadcaster/researcher co-operation in mass communication research.* Centre for Mass Communication Research, University of Leicester.

Hirsch, F. and Gordon, D., 1975: *Newspaper money.* London: Hutchinson.

Hirsch, P. M., 1972: 'Processing fads and fashions: an organization — set analysis of cultural industry systems'. *American Journal of Sociology*, 77.

Hood, S., 1967: *A survey of television.* London: Heinemann.

Houston, Penelope, 1963: *Contemporary cinema.* Baltimore: Penguin.

Janowitz, M., 1975: 'Professional models in jouralism: the gatekeeper and the advocate'. *Journalism Quarterly*, Winter, pp. 618—26.

Jay, A., 1972: *Public words and private words.* The Society of Film and Television Arts.

Johnson, T. J., 1972: *Professions and power.* London: Macmillan.

Johnstone, J. W. C., Slawski, E. J., Bowman, W. W., 1976: *The News People*, London: University of Illinois Press.

Kael, P., 1970: *Kiss Kiss, Bang Bang.* London: Calder and Boyars.

Kumar, K., 1975: 'Holding the middle ground: the BBC, the public and the professional'. *Sociology* 9 (1), pp. 67—88.

Lane, M., 1970a: Books and their publishers, in Tunstall, J. (Ed.) 1970b: 'Publishing managers, publishing house organization and role conflict'. *Sociology* 4 (3).

Laurenson, D. F., 1969: 'A sociological study of authorship'. *British Journal of Sociology* 20 (3), pp. 311—25.

Lewis, H. T., 1933: *The motion picture industry.* New York: Van Norstrand.

Macdonald, D., 1957: 'A theory of mass culture'. In Rosenberg, B. and White, D. M. (Eds.) *Mass culture*, London: Free Press.

McQuail, D. 1969: 'Uncertainty about the audience and the organization of mass communications'. *Sociological Review Monograph*, vol. 13, pp. 75—84.

(Ed.), 1972: *Sociology of mass communications.* Harmondsworth: Penguin.

Miller, M. and Rhodes, E., 1964: *Only you Dick Daring.* New York: Sloan.

Moloch, H. and Lester, M., 1964: 'News as purposive behaviour: on the strategic use of routine events, scandals and rumours'. *American Sociological Review* 39 pp. 101–12.

Murdock, G. and Golding, P., 1974: 'For a political economy of mass communications'. In *The Socialist Register 1973*, London: Merlin Press, pp. 205–34.

Peters, Anne, 1971: 'Acting and aspiring actresses in Hollywood: a sociological analysis'. Ph.D. Dissertation, University of California, Los Angeles.

Pilkington Committee, 1962: *Report of the Committee on Broadcasting 1960*, London: HMSO.

Poulantzas, N. and Miliband, R., 1972: 'The problem of the capitalist state'. In Blackburn, R., *Ideology in social science*, London: Fontana.

Reith, J., 1949: *Into the wind.* London: Hodder and Stoughton.

Rex, J., 1974: 'Capitalism, elites and the ruling class'. In Stanworth, P. and Giddens, H. (Eds.)

Royal Commission on the Press, 1976: *Interim Report: The National Newspaper Industry.* London: HMSO, Cmnd. 6433.

Schary, D., 1950: *Case history of a movie.* New York: Random House.

Schlessinger, P., 1978: *Putting 'reality' together: BBC News.* London: Constable.

Seymour-Ure, C., 1974: *The political impact of mass media.* London: Constable.

Sigelman, L., 1973: 'Reporting the news: an organizational analysis'. *American Journal of Sociology*, vol. 79 (July).

Smith, A., 1972: 'TV coverage of Northern Ireland', *Index*, Summer.
1973: *The shadow in the cave.* London: Allen and Unwin.

Stanworth, P. and Giddens, A., 1974: *Elites and power in British society.* Cambridge University Press.

Stark, R. W., 1962: 'Policy and the pros: an organizational analysis of a metropolitan newspaper'. *Berkeley Journal of Sociology* 7.

Stephens, A., 1976: 'Reporting in Ulster'. *The Observer*, 29 February.

Tracey, M., 1978: *The production of political television.* London: Routledge and Kegan Paul.

Tuchman, Gaye, 1972: 'Objectivity as strategic ritual: an examination of newsmen's notions of objectivity'. *American Journal of Sociology* 77 (4), pp. 660–79.
1973: 'Making news by doing work: routinizing the unexpected'. *American Journal of Sociology* 79 pp. 110–31.

Tunstall, J. (Ed.), 1970: *Media sociology.* London: Constable.
1971: *Journalists and work.* London: Constable.

Urry, J. and Wakeford, J. (Eds.), 1973: *Power in Britain.* London: Heinemann.

Watt, I., 1963: *The rise of the novel.* Harmondsworth: Penguin.

Wheldon, H., 1976: 'The British experience in television'. Richard
    Dimbleby Lecture, *Listener* 4 March.
Whitfield, A. E. and Roddenberry, G., 1968: *The making of Star Trek.*
    New York: Ballantine.
Winchester, S., 1975: *In holy terror.* London: Faber.
Wolf, F., 1972: *Television programming for news and current affairs.*
    London: Praeger.
Wolfe, T., 1975: *The new journalism.* London: Picador.

7

Technology and Control: the interactive dimensions of journalism

Anthony Smith

The newspaper and the novel were the first cultural forms to emerge directly from printing; they were both essentially publishing phenomena and developed in England in the aftermath of the expiration in 1695 of the Licensing Act when printers, no longer limited in numbers by statute, were free to flourish — or perish — according to the behaviour of the market.[1] Journalism has thus a similar relationship to printing as pop music to the phonograph or the film to photography: it depends upon an industrial activity, it involves the creative individual as a worker within a fairly complex process of manufacturing and distribution. The journalism is, as it were, the 'software' supplied to fill the 'hardware' of the newspaper system, and it thus serves as a pioneer example of the working of modern mechanical media. Unfortunately the newspaper is only now beginning to be studied historically as a *media* system;[2] most of those interested in the history of the press have been hitherto concerned with the newspaper either as a component of 'Whig' history, concentrating on those elements which illustrate the great tide of public freedom swelling from the eighteenth century onwards,[3] or else as a component of a kind of 'Whiggism-in-reverse', bringing out those elements which illustrate the increasing amiseration or exploitation of the new mass readership.[4]

Part of the interest in journalism in Britain lies in the sheer unbroken continuity of its tradition. From the 1620s onwards one may be certain that each generation of journalists has consciously acquired its professional

1 Watt, I. *The Rise of the Novel*, p. 214, Chatto and Windus (1957).
2 McLuhan, M. *The Gutenberg Galaxy: the making of typographic man*, Routledge (1962).
3 Typical are Alexander Andrewes: *History of British Journalism* (1859) F. Knight Hunt: *The Fourth Estate* (1850) Fox Bourne: *English Newspapers* (1887), T. H. S. Escott: *Masters of English Journalism* (1911) and, more recently, Harold Herd: *The March of Journalism*, Allen & Unwin, (1952) and Francis Williams: *Dangerous Estate*, Longmans (1958).
4 Webb, R. K. *The British Working Class Reader 1790—1848*, Allen and Unwin (1955); Williams, R. *The Long Revolution*, Chatto and Windus (1961).

skills from the previous one; the tradition can be traced even beyond Archer, Bourne and Butter who were the first to assemble items of European news into a single periodical publication in running form in the English language; they borrowed this clever publishing idea from the printers of Amsterdam.[5] Their typographical devices, journalistic expedients and tone of voice, even, can be traced through the vigorous partisan journalism of the English Civil War and even into the period after the Restoration when the newspaper was placed under the most stringent monarchical scrutiny. Until then the publication of all news was considered to be part of the royal prerogative, an unimpeachable aspect of the Divine Right of the King, but this doctrine began to fade when William III, no longer a biological heir, ascended the throne.[6] With the ending of the traditional system of licensing which limited the legal number of working master printers — as a means of controlling the whole medium of print — the publishing industry began to develop very rapidly; nonetheless, the actual techniques of printing remained relatively static, and Caxton would have recognized his converted wine press in any newspaper office until the end of the eighteenth century.

The government developed a method of controlling news despite the ending of licensing by placing an ever-growing series of taxes on the press; there were taxes on the paper used in publishing news, on each advertisement, on every newspaper copy. Many forms of journalism developed out of attempts to evade the taxes (like the essay form of the *Tatler* and the *Spectator*, which, by being regular publications but *not* containing hard news, could avoid paying the tax) and all news publications altered in format as a result of the tax. The newspaper still developed rapidly in the era of Queen Anne and her successors because of the growth of mercantile and trading life, because small towns all over the country were developing complex local economies of their own which depended on advertisement, and because of the growth of a political class profoundly involved in the activities of Parliament and government. The government used the revenue from taxation as a slush fund to bribe newspapers and journalists to work in the official interest. Power in Britain, in the aftermath of the Glorious Revolution, rested upon *opinion* not upon Divine Right, and the newspaper, corrupt, vindictive, biased but in essence uncontrollable by the Crown, was the vehicle for creating and reflecting opinion, and sustaining the wide spectrum of factions into which the political class was subdivided. The battle for the freedom of the press which was fought out during the century was a battle for the right to report the affairs of Parliament, and

5 Frank, J. *The Beginnings of the English Newspaper 1621—1660*, University of Harvard Press (1971); Williams, J. B. *History of English Journalism to the Foundations of the Gazette*, (1908).
6 Plumb, J. H. *The Growth of Political Stability in England 1675—1725*, Macmillan (1969).

to mitigate the battery of legal constraints and inhibitions to which the press was shackled.

Throughout this period the number and diversity of social groups with physical, financial and educational access to the press was growing. The arrival of Frederick Koenig in London during the Napoleonic War led to the first of a series of revolutionary developments in printing and newspaper production which were to continue throughout the nineteenth century. The advanced stage coach, improved roads and the train helped to expand the lines of distribution of the press and release it from the dependence on the coffee-house which had been the chief means of circulation since Cromwellian days (and highly consistent with the role of the newspaper as a facilitator of factional rather than *party* politics). The nineteenth century saw at first a major bifurcation within the readership of newspapers between, on one hand, a middle-class press, fully taxed, expensive and legal, which concentrated on developing contact with major demographic groups which were nationally spread and were developing an increasing political consciousness, and on the other, a cheaper working-class press which secured extremely large circulations but little advertising and worked under the particularly irksome constraint of being illegal because unstamped and untaxed. With the ending of the stamp tax, however, in 1855, it was the middle-class newspapers (the *Daily Telegraph* in particular) which were the first to grasp the opportunity of circulating among the growing group of newspaper-reading skilled workers. Thereafter, every major development in the formation of press publics involved the amalgamation of groups previously differentiated according to class or political predilection, into broader, more heterogeneous audiences. The newspaper sought out more variegated material. The newspaper enterprise changed from the joint stock system of the late eighteenth century, in which the shareholders included the printer and the principal advertisers, into the large family firm of the nineteenth century with access to larger blocks of capital to buy equipment for printing and reproducing illustrations, to pay the high costs of the telegraph, transport and squads of reporters and correspondents.

The end of the nineteenth century saw the perfection of technical and distribution methods to the point at which a truly mass newspaper could develop, encompassing a wide enough range of content, styles and audience-attracting material to hold together the first regular national audiences of a million at a cover cost of $\frac{1}{2}$d (the *Daily Mail* by 1912). Until then only the Sunday newspapers, traditionally concentrating more on scandal and crime than the daily papers, had reached out into that vast hardly tapped waiting audience. There had been several 'New Journalisms' in the later nineteenth century, clustered around the styles pioneered by the *Daily News* (1846), the *Daily Telegraph* (1855) and especially the *Pall Mall Gazette* 1865) and they had been concerned with puncturing the hidebound traditionalism of the longer established papers such as *The Times* and the *Morning Post*. Each thrust forwards had involved devising ways of making the content more palatable to an additional group of the population.[7]

The enormous leaps in circulation which took place between the World Wars turned the daily newspaper into a universal medium which henceforth was concerned with penetrating not a non-newspaper public but the public of rival papers. Newspapers devised forms and political positions which would help them each make inroads into the readership of other papers. The family firm gave way to multi-ownership in large corporations, although many papers continued to have single owners; with the demise of the *News Chronicle* and *Daily Herald* in the 1960s no newspaper remained which avowedly belonged to a single class. Sometimes the traditional tones of radicalism remained but only transmitted by the homogenizing voice of modern circulation management. The twentieth century has seen the solidification of a dichotomy between the 'quality' and the 'popular' in journalism, competition taking place mainly, though by no means entirely, between newspapers within one group rather than between the two.

I have merely hinted at some of the major 'formations' through which the newspaper and journalism has passed, although a comprehensive list would be extremely long. Each new system involves a shift in one or more of five partly separable dimensions. First of all, each of them has been characterized by a different grouping of the audience and a different way of grouping towards a larger or different intended audience. Then, in each, the journalist has been coping with different levels and arrangements of material which has necessitated his developing lines of contact with different kinds of news sources. Third, the journalist has been obliged to devise or acquire new techniques for actually performing his work (such as shorthand, typing, translating). Fourth, the state of the available printing technology has itself developed in ways which have helped to change the fundamental stance of journalists towards their readers. Finally, perhaps most importantly, each new formation of the newspaper as a media system has brought about a new structure of editorial control, leaving the journalist, in his various forms, working within a line of management stretching up towards a board of shareholders or perhaps an eccentric single owner or (in earlier days) the king himself. These five dimensions are *in part* determinants of the nature of journalism as the 'software' to their 'hardware'; but they are themselves, of course, the results of many other strands of social, technological and political history, and have developed along lines of mutual interaction as well as being influenced by

---

7 Morrison, S. *The English Newspaper*, Cambridge University Press (1932) Chapters 13 and 14; Greenwood, F. The Newspaper Press, *Nineteenth Century*, May 1890.

the journalism which they encase. Examination of each of these five dimensions throws a certain light on the ways in which the profession of journalism has developed through its three and a half century tradition and might, as we shall see, help to show how journalism is evolving in the period immediately ahead.

Even in the earliest versions or predecessors of the newspaper one can discern these five elements. The *Mercurius Gallo-Belgicus* was a Latin news periodical which started in 1594 and circulated throughout the Holy Roman Empire.[8] The printers of Cologne, always a prudent and far-sighted body of men, had perceived a method for distributing information concerning military, political and other events via the six-monthly trade fairs at which merchants and other groups of influential people would gather. The fact of *regularity* of publication was the prerequisite for creating a constant public whose needs and interests the publishers would then attempt to satisfy. The *Gallo-Belgicus* was the first publication in history to have a regular title and consistency of printing, which meant that its audience would learn to *expect* it. The sources of the *Gallo-Belgicus*'s information lay in the network of postmasters which existed throughout the Empire, efficiently passing along their routes all important news about the movements of armies and important personalities. The available technology for producing *Gallo-Belgicus* was a press essentially constructed for the making of books and so this earliest news publication appeared as a book and its writers thought of themselves as book-writers specializing in the compiling in a single publication of a quantity of news stories which might otherwise have been published as a series of separate broadsheets. Their professional techniques consisted in recognizing news of importance when it arrived and translating it into Latin. Although we know little about the week to week workings of these early newsmen we do know that their work was publicly supervised and criticized; their operation grew within a craft hierarchy which sprang from the traditions of printing, with political pressures feeding back and tending towards a form of control. The *Mercurius Gallo-Belgicus* was well known in England and John Donne took it to task in an epigram:

> . . . . change thy name: thou art like
> Mercury in stealing, but lyest like a Greeke.[9]

Our five dimensions are thus delineable in this very ancient though sophisticated news service and between them they constitute a set of determining constraints which provided the journalists (if we may call them that) with the basis of their professional and trade outlook. The

8 Shaaber, M. A. *Some Forerunners of the Newspaper in England*, 1476–1622, University of Pennsylvania Press (1929).

9 Crierson, Sir Herbert (Ed.) *The Poems of John Donne*, Oxford University Press, (1933) p. 69.

picture of the world which the compilers of the *Gallo-Belgicus* serviced
and sustained passed through the mesh of conceptual and physical equipment which constituted its media system. I shall try to provide an
historical sketch of each of the five dimensions, taking a specific, almost
random, case study as demonstration of each of them.

I

One is easily sometimes tempted to assume that the audience for newspapers has simply expanded generation by generation until reaching total
social saturation in the present century. Statistically that is perhaps true,
although not all new newspapers have tried merely to maximize their sales;
there have often been specialist papers which increase their profits by concentrating on a single wealthy market, narrowing their editorial focus to
exploit a smaller market more expertly both for sales and advertising. The
journalist on a given publication rapidly learns to recognize, conceptualize
and internalize the supposed needs of the particular target audience of his
paper. He speaks as if through a proscenium arch of his newspaper office
to a public which has been gathered through the tradition and the promotion system of the newspaper concerned. It is the distribution system and
the advertising sales system which feed back into a media institution and
its employees the picture of the audience for which they are writing.

There are, and have often been, papers which are purely ideologically
motivated — journals of opinion — and with these the audience is more
tightly delineated from the start; the provincial papers of the late
nineteenth century, for example, struggled to acquire and maintain special
local audiences sharing a liberal, radical or conservative outlook, which
their journalists recognized and indeed identified with. W. T. Stead,
Wickham Steed, Alfred Spender all learned the business of journalism as
young men on provincial Liberal papers, where their experience as communicators within a particular political constituency provided them with
the qualifications necessary for their first London posts. Spender spent
some years at his uncle's paper the *Eastern Morning News* before
proceeding, in the early nineties, to work on the *Pall Mall Gazette* and
then transferring when the former was sold into the hands of a Tory, to a
new Liberal paper the *Westminster Gazette*.[10] The reader's loyalty was
acquired through political identification; the journalist's credentials, which
remained with him throughout his career, were founded on his ability to
grasp and internalize the outlook of a single political community. Yet, the
development of newspaper readerships as confessional communities was
possible only when methods of distribution and sales had developed in a
manner conducive to the paper reaching its target community on the right
day and at the right price.

10 Harris, W. *J. A. Spender*, Cassell (1946).

Until well into the last century it was impossible to separate postal systems from newspaper delivery systems. The Post Office undertook both tasks. The character of most newspapers emanating from London was designed for the London audience, since only a small proportion of total sales could reach the non-metropolitan public despite the steady improvement of postal services ever since the 1620s. Provincial papers, which started up in the first decade of the eighteenth century, tended to cover very wide areas geographically around their city of origination, too wide in fact to make the papers themselves at all reflective of the interests and problems of any single community. The particular case study I shall use in considering the impact of audience identification upon the styles of journalism consists in an account of how that necessary transition took place within the provincial press between a generation of papers which were non-London but not rooted in a particular locality to a new generation which were non-metropolitan and profoundly rooted in the affairs of a neighbourhood.

The London papers of the eighteenth century were mainly distributed through the hundreds of coffee houses which had first been established during the political terror of the late 1650s as safe locations for political discussion. By the time of Queen Anne, London also had a highly organized distribution system through its many booksellers, street hawkers, coachmen, carriers and watermen. Wealthier readers outside London could have their papers sent by post, which would cost an extra 2d on the cover price, in addition to a $\frac{1}{2}$d surcharge if the paper were brought from the posthouse to a private residence. Simultaneously, however, printers were moving out of London and setting up in rapidly expanding country towns. In fact in the early eighteenth century newspapers began to spread throughout the English provinces; their content consisted mainly of summaries of the London papers which were delivered twice weekly by stagecoach and private transport — 'a faithfull abstract of all the Newspapers of Note' was how one provincial paper advertised itself and another used to refer proudly to its success in providing 'the quintessence of every Print'.[11] What hampered for some decades the development of a real provincial journalism based on events occurring within each town of publication was the small size of the available readership. In order to maintain sufficient readers to cover his production costs a printer would sometimes employ a roundsman who would walk through the countryside delivering the paper to known subscribers within a very wide radius. The *Northampton Mercury* said its 'newsmen' would cover 40 miles on foot once a week. The *Manchester Magazine* said that one of its roundsmen walked 100 miles

11 Cranfield, G. A. *The Development of the Provincial Newspaper, 1700–1760*, Clarendon Press (1962); Belcher, W. F. 'The Sale and Distribution of the British Apollo', in Bond, R. P. *Studies in the Early English Periodical*, University of North Carolina Press (1957) pp. 73–101.

every week on a circuit which took three days to complete. If the weather was bad and the men were unable to set out, publication would occasionally be delayed. There were also street hawkers and specialized delivery systems in the larger towns, but so long as a given edition had to be sold in towns as far apart as Oxford, Northampton and Lincoln, there was little chance of a vigorous local journalism developing. By the 1750s, however, it was becoming possible for printers to engage in intensive distribution within a single town; population had increased and with it the kinds of business activity which depends on advertising. Shops would consider it worth advertising in a paper which could be guaranteed to reach a significant proportion of the buying population in its catchment area, and the growth of advertising made it possible for the printer to concentrate his efforts more within a given area.

With the growth of distribution it was difficult for the printer to add the cost of delivery to the cost of the paper, as had always been the practice with newspapers in London and the provinces. In the 1740s, for example, the newsmen employed by the *Birmingham Gazette* started to be paid a proportion of the cover price of copies sold and this increased the pressures on the printer to provide the kind of material which the newsmen could easily sell. If the paper had little to appeal to readers the newsmen would threaten resignation because this endangered their livelihood. The distribution system acted thus as a constraining pressure on the editor and his tiny staff. The provincial press accordingly began to recognize its target audience more clearly as these and similar pressures accumulated. From the mid-eighteenth century onwards the content of English provincial papers begins to reveal a certain liveliness and originality: the occasional cartoon appears and there is a vigorous growth of political comment when the great Parliamentary schisms of the mid-century began to work up partisan loyalties among the emerging country readership. Above all, however, the provincial press found itself training editors who saw *news* in the affairs of a small town, which until then had appeared merely irrelevant to the concerns of a newspaper. The first indigenous country journalism sprang from the conceptualization of the new urban audiences of the north and west and midlands from the 1760s onwards.

II

It might seem merely obvious to say that journalism depends upon the available sources of news. Much of the literature of the press, however, takes it for granted that to journalists within the English tradition, the same range of matters have always been of equal relevance. In fact, journalism in any given period has functioned mainly as the processor of certain available kinds of material. The demand for a particular kind of information (say, news of the Thirty Year War) is generated through a society which has a particular interest in the events concerned. (In this case, Londoners disapproving of their king's failure to support King Ferdinand.) The flow of information from event to news medium becomes organized when a suitable medium is set up to circulate it (in our example, the printers of Amsterdam and their counterparts in London creating the first weekly books of news). At the newsroom or printing shop end of the process the journalist seeks out the flow of information from ambassadors, spies, mercenaries, imperial postmasters, merchants and continental news-sheets. The journalist had never merely stared out of his window at a total reality; he is only given his desk and chair when an input system already exists. The newspaper is not a mirror of reality, but the realization of the potential of its sources. It may build great influence out of its eloquent advocacy of a cause; it may stimulate new interests and realizations within its audience; it may cause new kinds of information to reach its audience and new sources of information to be organized; but its chief characteristic lies in the selection, arrangement and reformulation of information passing to it through regular channels.

The wire services of the nineteenth century emerged as collectors and pre-processors of information; their customers were newspapers and editors of vastly differing political persuasions and they therefore helped to generate the idea that at the root of all news there lay 'hard facts' which could be discovered and disseminated in a value-free manner.[12] A successful newspaper like *The Times* rejected Paul Julius Reuter's service as long as it could: it seemed that to rely on people outside immediate editorial control to supply news would endanger the intellectual and ideological integrity of the paper; the growth of a fiercer competition between London papers and the enormous expense involved in maintaining coverage of all the events on which British readers now wanted to be informed, brought about after a time the capitulation of *The Times*. The paper agreed to print the news offered by Reuters and later of other agencies.[13] The wire service and the agency were of course indispensable to the provincial press in its competition with London-based papers which were constantly trying to take over the lucrative newspaper market in the growing Victorian cities. By means of the telegraph a provincial paper could receive a complete flow of foreign news and also publish in full the speeches of local politicians in Parliament, two elements with which they were able to hold their own against metropolitan newspapers. The telegraph, there-fore, both threatened the security of the provincial press and gave it the opportunity of developing its own special services.

One episode which aptly illustrates the way in which an alignment of news services helps to determine the character of a particular form of

12 Kieve, J. L. *A History of the Electric Telegraph*, David and Charles (1974).
13 *History of the Times* Vol. 2 p. 272–3.

journalism is that of the London press of the early Restoration when, for about a decade, the figure of Henry Muddiman, the 'King's Journalist', dominated the world of London journalism.[14] His career and the special system of news flow which he perfected and partly devised aptly illustrates the way in which the character of journalism is heavily influenced by the nature of its sources.

If you look at a typical English or continental newspaper of the late seventeenth century you cannot fail to be struck by the enormous geographical scope of the news. The paper covers but a single sheet but it contains carefully filed material from a score of European cities, arranged in brief, bleak paragraphs each with its clearly marked provenance, the city of origin and the date on which the information was first sent out. Domestic news leads the paper but is very scanty; it consists of news from Court, royal proclamations and other official material, plus a good deal of shipping and commercial news. The flow of material around England was clearly (or apparently) inferior to the network which produced up-to-date intelligence on places as far afield as Muscovy and Naples, Istanbul and Berlin.

The dominant news publication in England in the 1660s and 1670s was the *London Gazette* and its methods of operation had been developed from the papers of the late Commonwealth and the immediate Restoration period.[15] Under Cromwell, Secretary Thurloe had built up a system of European intelligence which had kept the English government among the best informed in Europe ('Cromwell kept the secrets of all the princes of Europe at his girdle'), and Charles II was determined to maintain the system, though with different men. In addition Charles and his Court brought back with them from Breda an acquaintance with the new generation of European Gazettes: Paris had its *Gazette* and the *Nouvelles Ordinaires*, Brussels the *Relations Veritables*, and Amsterdam, for decades the central entrepot of European news, produced the *Gazette D'Amsterdam* and the *Oprechte Haerlemse Dinqsdaege Courant*. They were stylish publications, bearing with them a sense of modernity and efficiency. When the Court retired briefly to Oxford to avoid the plague raging in London in 1665, Charles seized the opportunity to start an *Oxford Gazette* which later became the *London Gazette*; in charge of it was the most experienced news collector and editor of the day, Henry Muddiman. What concerns us here, however, is simply the means by which Muddiman and his rivals and immediate successors procured their information.

The prerogative of the king over the publication of news applied only to printed material. The Stationers' Company was obliged by law to

14 Lane, J. *J. G. Muddiman: The Kings' Journalist 1659–1689*, Bodley Head (1923); Fraser, P. *The Intelligence of the Secretaries of State and their monopoly of Printed News 1660–1688*, Cambridge University Press (1956).
15 Handover, P. M. *A History of the London Gazette 1665–1965*, HMSO (1965).

supervise the whole trade of printing and publishing and ensure that only
duly licensed material was handled by the booksellers (who were also
members of the Company). The Stationers, however, could not be trusted
to perform this task wholeheartedly since it tended to restrict their own
trade and therefore, in 1663, a special Surveyor of the Press was appointed,
the notorious Sir Roger L'Estrange, an old Cavalier who had served the
king faithfully throughout his period of exile. L'Estrange's men guaranteed
that the illegal rivals to the official news publications were rooted out.
L'Estrange's reward for his labours was an exclusive privilege to publish
news, 'All Narratives of relacons not exceeding two sheets of paper and all
advertisements, Mercuries, Diurnals and Books of Publick Intelligence', as
the official proclamation put it. L'Estrange was an odd choice for
exercising this privilege since he was a strong opponent of general publication of political news, thinking that it gave the people 'not only an itch
but a colourable right and licence to be meddling with the Government'.
He proved, however, to be most efficient in destroying the network of
anti-Caroline propaganda, but was confronted with the more long-term
problem of how to set about the dissemination of necessary intelligence
around the governing groups in society.

There was at that period a secondary system by which news travelled
around the country, a system of written newsletters, copied out by a small
army of scriveners and composed by a single man who enjoyed access to
the full flow of political information entering and leaving Whitehall.[16]
Henry Muddiman, originally chosen to take charge of publishing news by
General Monck in the months between the death of Richard Cromwell
and the return of Charles, sat at the centre of a web of contacts throughout England and Europe. At the heart of the Restoration system of
government there were the offices of the two Secretaries of State, one of
whom handled relations with the Northern (i.e. Protestant) countries, the
other with the Southern (i.e. Catholic) countries. Muddiman worked for
the Under-Secretary at the Southern Department and his job was to
monitor the governmental intelligence network, making certain that the
agents were kept working efficiently. He enjoyed a privilege of free
postage in order to perform his task and the Letter Office was at certain
periods kept under the general supervision of one of the Secretaries of
State; Muddiman was allowed to exploit the free postage privilege to send
out his own handwritten newsletters to a string of correspondents
throughout the country, who paid £5 a year directly to Muddiman as a
subscription: the newsletter could be supplied free to members of the
intelligence network, so that a kind of collective European news agency
existed, creating an international côterie of well-informed men.

The printed *Gazette* and the handwritten newsletters developed a
symbiotic relationship. Muddiman would send out newsletters of domestic

16 Fraser *op. cit.*

news to subscribers in Britain and receive from his counterparts on the continent their domestic newsletters which provided material for his printed *London Gazette*. The continental editors in their turn incorporated the material from the English written newsletters in their printed news publications. There were therefore two kinds of audience, one which paid for a relatively inexpensive but authoritative printed medium of international news and another, wealthier or more privileged, group who received the handwritten news on affairs at home, some of whom helped to supply that news as well. At the centre of this apparatus sat Muddiman, his wealth growing with the years, as trade in and with Europe increased and created an expanding demand for both of his news services. He was not left to enjoy his position unhampered for long, however. There were constant rivalries between the two Secretaries of State, their subordinates and the men at the Letter Office upon whose good (and free) postal services the whole machinery of intelligence depended. At one point Muddiman was forced to resign his office and transfer himself to the department of the other Secretary starting a rival paper to the *London Gazette*; the people at the Southern Department, anxious to steal Muddiman's remunerative list of correspondents, had started opening his mail in order to filch the addresses. The 'mercury' women who hawked the printed papers around the streets had to be bribed and fed in order to keep the paper before the public. It was not a stable system but it was a very effective one in collecting and disseminating news; it made a small supplementary income by providing space for half a dozen or so advertisements in each weekly or bi-weekly edition; tea, coffee, books, lost servants and stray animals were the mainstays of the advertising section, although they also played a part in the business of maintaining law and order by helping the tracing of criminals, pickpockets and stolen goods.

Muddiman's professionalism and political position arose from his particular technique for organizing his sources. His outlook was as international as that of the European news agencies of the last century. The typographical layout in which he published his material was the archetypical *Gazette* which acquired an aura of authority and reliability which other news publications had never achieved, whether emanating from a government department or not. Muddiman's predecessors had operated in the greyer area between pamphleteering and intelligence. He made a profession of unadorned intelligence, as pure and devoid of comment as the politics and standards of the time allowed. The journalistic revolution over which he presided consisted in the novel organization of an input system of information.

III

The profession of journalism has been marked by a seemingly endless process of re-demarcation of specialisms and sub-professions. Every new mechanical device (telegraph, typewriter, wireless) has tended to summon into existence a new schism within the business of journalism, or rather, act as the defining catalyst for the emergence of a new brand of journalism. But the devices need not be mechanical, they can relate to a special skill not directly related to a piece of machinery.

One important qualification of a journalist in the early seventeenth century, for instance, was an ability to understand Dutch, because that was the language in which most of the information arrived, via the weekly pack-boat from the Hague. Several of the writers of the newsbooks of the period (until the *Gazette* news was published in the form of a book) were referred to as 'Dutch captains' because the main source of Dutch-speaking Englishmen were soldiers who had enlisted as mercenaries in Holland and been invalided out. Leader writers of a much later date would be more likely to have to understand ancient Greek than Dutch! The growth of reporters as the most important sub-division within journalism in the nineteenth century demanded a whole range of new skills, involving powers of observation, of validation of statements and of rapid accurate recording of information acquired — which had come to be desired.

One of these was shorthand, which did more than any other single phenomenon to establish the stereotype of the journalist as provider of hard facts. With the help of a training in this new skill a reporter in the nineteenth century could at last hold a mirror up to nature, and provide not merely an elegant paraphrase of a speech but also the *ipsissima verba* of a politician or agitator, a judge, prisoner in court or minister of the Crown. Shorthand created an aura of high prestige around the journalist. In the last decades of the eighteenth century, Parliament had been reported by great feats of memory. William Woodfall of the *Morning Chronicle* and William Radcliffe of the *Morning Herald* could carry the substance of an important debate direct from Parliament to the printing room, dictating copy to two compositors at once.[17] When James Perry took over the editorship of the former paper he transformed Parliamentary reporting by employing a team of young barristers, who would attend the House in relays, returning to the printing house in time to produce their report in sections for the morning edition. In the days of 'memory' Woodfall, the reports would have to await his convenience and would continue for some weeks after the end of the Parliamentary session, so that readers would have to wait for the final votes and debates of the Parliament until long after it had finished sitting.[18]

Several journalists had perfected forms of shorthand of their own invention. John Tyas, for instance, the great reporter of *The Times*, who was present at the Peterloo massacre, acquired a form of contracted long-hand which enabled him to produce paraphrase of a high order. In the

17 MacDonagh, M. *The Reporters' Gallery*, Hodder and Stoughton (1912) p. 269.
18 Andrews *op. cit.* vol. 1 p. 196.

1820s a new system was brought out, known as brachygraphy, and popularized by William Brodie Gurney;[19] it was Gurney's system of dots and dashes which Dickens satirizes in David Copperfield. 'I have tamed the savage stenographic mystery', exclaims Copperfield. Parliamentary reporters who learned the Gurney system, however, were able to acquire for themselves an aura of a kind of infallibility, which became important in the development of the profession. In the 1830s O'Connell charged some of the reporters in the Parliamentary Gallery with deliberate mis-representation of his speeches; they responded by announcing a boycott of O'Connell, collectively refusing to publicize him until he had apologized, which he duly did, to the proprietors of The Times.[20] 'There is scarcely a gentleman on our establishment who is not by education and habits the equal of any Member whose opinions he is engaged to record', replied The Times in its editorial columns.[21] The fight between O'Connell and the reporters broke out again the following year but skirmishes of this kind only served to emphasize the growing status of the journalist, which had been considerably aided by the acquisition of the shorthand skill.

With the coming of Pitman and the first easily acquired and transferable shorthand system, a new era in reporting was brought about. The free-lance journalist was conjured into being, who could ply his trade from home without belonging to the staff of a particular paper; the demand for the reports of public speeches and lectures was insatiable among Victorian newspaper readers or, at least, among newspaper editors. A journalist would find out where interesting speeches were being made, and armed with a shorthand notebook, make his report and walk late at night through the newspaper offices of Fleet Street until he found an editor interested in buying the article. Shorthand was the *lingua franca* of the freelance, it democratized the profession, in a sense. It provided it with a 'mystery'.

IV

As far as the production of newspapers is concerned the nineteenth century was the era of great advance between the start of the news-paper as a form and the present day, when we are on the brink of another series of major changes in the method of production. Between the *Gallo-Belgicus* and *The Times* of Thomas Barnes, nothing fundamental changed in the method of producing news periodicals. It was extremely heavy work and each sheet of paper required an immense muscular effort on the part of several men; the formes had to be inked with messy inking balls; circulations were limited by the sheer limitations of human physique. The Victorians saw a dramatic switch to mechanical systems of production,

19 MacDonagh *op. cit.* p. 348.
20 *History of the Times* vol. 1 (1935) p. 311—15.
21 23 June 1832.

the rotary press arrived and multiplied production per hour tenfold; steam engines were attached to printing presses and brought about a further exponential increase in the productivity of printing labour. Every few years fresh development enabled circulations to grow faster, definition of print to improve, and illustrations to become easier to reproduce. But each major improvement helped wholly new forms of publication to be brought into being, and with them new branches of the profession of journalism. *Punch* (1841) and the *Illustrated London News* (1842) were the first successful and lasting pioneers of illustrated journalism, the former bringing the draughtsman-journalist into being and the latter the artist-reporter. A new method of production often dovetailed into a newly emerging audience or a new grouping of existing audiences and the fusion could result in a publication proclaiming yet another 'New Journalism'.

The technical advances of the last century seldom resulted from a random serendipity on the part of the inventors. On the contrary, each development tended to occur after a long period of thwarted endeavour to bring about the required change. In the years of the Napoleonic Wars, for example, the presses could not cope with the increasing demand for copies. *The Times*, already the largest circulating paper of London, had been looking for a mechanical improvement in the existing Stanhope press which would enable it to increase its daily edition without having to bring an extra machine into use. In the first decade of the century it had sometimes had to place three machines together producing the same material from three separate settings of the copy. Frederick Koenig arrived in London from a printing office in Leipzig in 1808 and within three years brought about the most important revolution in the industry since Caxton. He had already wasted several years trying in vain to persuade printers in Germany and Russia to adopt his scheme for power printing before he met Thomas Rewsley, a London printer who commissioned him to build a machine, which was perfected in 1811. The proprietors of the *Morning Chronicle* examined the contraption and rejected it; John Walter II of *The Times* saw it and ordered two more to be made. In November 1814 he succeeded in producing an edition of *The Times* with the Koenig machine and his paper rapidly thereafter climbed to a position pre-eminent in the newspaper world of London, its circulation unbeaten until after the mid-century. It reached production figures of 8,000 copies per hour and was able to build up a circulation equal to that of all other London papers combined.[22] It was this pre-eminence which, anchored to the aspirations of the burgeoning middle class, made the term 'public opinion' almost synonymous with Liberalism for half a century. Charles Pebody, writing of the press in 1882, says 'public opinion, during the past forty or fifty years has been in the main what the Newspaper Press

22 Pebody, C. *English Journalism and the Men who have made it*, Cassell, Petter, Galpin and Co. (1882) p. 107.

has made it, and the Press has been so overwhelmingly Liberal that, until a few years ago when all the press suddenly turned Tory, a Tory Government has been practically impossible.'[23] Pebody was exaggerating, but without doubt the basic values of journalism between the Napoleonic Wars and the Crimean were heavily influenced by the fact of *The Times*'s unassailable supremacy in circulation. The journalist found himself with a dominant professional doctrine of confrontation with government rather than subservience or cooperation with it; the journalist increasingly spoke of himself as part of a 'Fourth Estate' which exercised social power as a legitimate by-product of the circulating of information.

Journalism had most conspicuously acted out this role during the battle for the Reform Bill, in the course of which the London press emerged as an independent political power. Until that moment newspapers had tended to hitch themselves to one politician or faction or another but in the struggle of 1831 the press in general, led by *The Times*, set up shop for itself, joining forces with Grey, Brougham and Russell. The press moved in again during the Corn Law Repeal agitation to enable Peel successfully to defy his own party. Pebody later concluded: 'Parliamentary minority plus the press is more powerful than Parliamentary majority without the press'. For the rest of the century the press behaved as if it shared power with the Government during the Parliamentary sessions, but exercised the prerogative of Parliament during the recess.

There were many social and political trends which reflect themselves in the 'Fourth Estate' self-image of the press; indeed it was an exaggerated notion which totally failed to take account of the enormous readership of the unstamped working-class press circulating among a larger social group which was, however, unenfranchised and played no part in the formal activities of the Parliamentary system. All the same, it is apt to point out the relationship between such evolutions in the ideology of the press and the development of appropriate production technologies. The arrival of the steam press released a series of social forces and made possible a newspaper public which could aspire to a political power synchronous with the broader lines along which political information was enabled to circulate.

Another example of the sudden impact of a long retarded technological development upon journalism is the appearance of the first cheap wood-pulp paper in the 1880s. There had been a frantic search for new ways of making paper since the peace of 1815, a search which became ever more intense in the 1850s when the newspaper started to become a major world industry. France, Prussia and Rome actually prohibited the export of rags in 1857 when American provincial newspapers started to generate so great a demand for paper that the price on the world market rocketed upwards. America was obliged to obtain rags from India, China

23 *Ibid* p. 91.

and Japan and even then, during the Civil War, American newspapers were obliged to more than double their prices. There were periods when the London press thought it would be impossible to hold their prices (even after the abolition of the newspaper tax in 1855) and maintain the existing circulation structure of the newspaper. The newspaper as a commodity is extremely sensitive to minor fluctuations in price and operated on extremely small profit margins per copy. In 1867 the first plant making paper from wood pulp was installed and within four years the price began to fall again, from 30 cents per pound in 1865 to 3 cents in 1870 to one cent in 1880.[24] It was the abolition of the newspaper tax, added to the extremely low price of paper which enabled Newnes in the 1880s and Northcliffe in the 1890s to work towards the modern mass newspaper. In reading the new popular journalism of the *Daily Telegraph*, then the *Pall Mall* and *Westminster Gazettes*, then the new evening papers of the end of the century (the *Echo*, the *Star*, and the *Evening News*), then hard upon their trail, the *Daily Mail* the *Daily Express* of Northcliffe, one can feel the hot breath of owners and editors scrambling after readers as they had never done before. Throughout the provinces little chains of half-penny daily newspapers had sprung up, forerunners of the *Mail*'s first effort as a *national* halfpenny daily. The whole accent of journalism had changed from that of the schoolmaster to that of the huckster. Decreasing costs of production as a result of a series of technological breakthroughs, long awaited, turned the newspaper into a source of enormous profit; the journalist became entertainer first and teacher second. He had to grab his reader before he could address him, because his typical purchaser was no longer a man who had leisure to wait. The subject matter of news was transformed, not merely because the market had changed and enlarged to include social groups interested only in trivia, but because the nature of the newspaper as a marketed industrial commodity had altered. Henceforth the newspaper was sold as it was written; its copy was its packaging. It would be bought for its front page layout, or for its publicity stunts, or its free offers or competitions. Gradually over the century to come the whole output of the newspaper press was to be brought within this system, including the provincial and 'quality' dailies which sought to survive by joining in the fray, the skills of journalism at all levels changing to encompass the new task.

V

The fifth and last of my five 'dimensions' emphasizes the importance of the lines of management within a newspaper enterprise and between a

24 Coleman, D. C. *The British Paper Industry 1494–1860: A study in industrial growth*, Oxford University Press (1958); Smith, D. C. 'Wood pulp and News-papers, 1867–1900' in *The Business History Review* 38 No. 3, 1964 pp. 328–45.

newspaper enterprise and the society it serves. In the seventeenth century the central tension lay between the royal prerogative and the Stationers' Company whose members, controlled, checked, searched, limited in numbers, were the only people allowed to indulge in the business of news publication. In the next century the government exercised its controls through the taxation system and through the highly restrictive libel laws; the 'editor' emerged as the responsible official of a newspaper, a duty previously pertaining to the figure of the printer.[25] The Editor was a new demarcation within the printing fraternity but made increasingly powerful within his particular enterprise because of his responsibilities in law. The owner at that time was a shadowy figure, anxious to shift the risks of the libel system to other shoulders, normally consisting of a cooperative of small businesses.[26] The nineteenth century saw the editor rise to a peak of importance in Barnes and Delane of *The Times*, where a financially successful owner was willing to place his publication virtually at the mercy of a skilled and experienced though still anonymous employee.[27]

As newspapers became more profitable but also more prone to risk as enterprises, an important set of tensions began to develop between owners and editors especially during the last three decades of the century. The notion of press 'freedom' centred around the freedom of the editor whose personal idcology had to be identified with that of his paper. The freedom of the editor from all but the most long-term of proprietorial instructions seemed to be the prerequisite of journalistic independence. The working journalist remained anonymous and utterly dependent on his editor. It is worth taking up the classic example of a nineteenth-century editorial career, that of Sir Edward Cook,[28] and examining his role within the spectrum of the press of the time. The editorial figure was the point at which the whole ideological integrity of a newspaper rested. The area in which newspapers competed was that of politics. It was the political persuasion of a newspaper which anchored it to its regular audience and every political grouping took pains to see that it had a newspaper owned and possibly subsidized by one of its leading adherents. If you look at the spectrum of the daily press of late Victorian times, it is clear how the pattern had emerged. First came *The Times*, read by the whole of the governing class, rather dull at this period and not as wealthy as in the past, but solid and reliable, expressing always a national standpoint. The

25 Siebert, F. S. 'Taxes on Publications in England in the 18th Century' in *Journalism Quarterly* Vol. 21, 1944 pp. 12—24; Hanson, L. *Government and the Press*, Oxford University Press (1936); Stephen, L. *The Evolution of the Editor.*

26 Haig, R. L. *The Gazetteer, 1735—1797: A study in the 18th Century English Newspaper*, University of Southern Illinois Press (1960).

27 Dasent, A. I. *John Thaddeus Delane: Editor of the Times*, John Murray (1908); *History of the Times*, Vol. 2.

28 Mills, J. S. *Sir Edward Cook, K.B.E.*, Constable (1921).

Morning Post was the organ of the aristocracy: it favoured a populist Toryism at home and pure jingoism abroad. The *Standard* was the organ of the business-minded Tories; it spoke for the City rather than the counties. The *Daily Telegraph* was well established, the first of the penny dailies: it supported the Liberals but in foreign affairs clearly preferred the imperialist wing of that party; its readership had been built up partly as a result of its well written articles, relatively popular in tone and covering a wide area of subject matter. The *Daily Chronicle* was read by the educated working class; it was firmly radical in tone with a touch of jingoism in its treatment of foreign affairs. The *Daily News*, founded originally by Charles Dickens, was a paper of traditional liberalism and was slowly slipping in reader support. Two new papers had come onto the scene, the *Pall Mall Gazette* and the *Star*, exponents of a New Journalism (as Matthew Arnold had chosen to label it), each of them selling in the evenings at a halfpenny; they had hit the newspaper scene of the 1880s with a loud trumpet blast, and they were out to abolish the terrible dullness of the press and give their readers what they wanted to read. These papers had pioneered the interview, their columns contained cross-heads, their machinery was the new improved Hoe and Walter Presses, they employed the latest devices for printing illustrations and they eagerly accepted the new cheaper woodpulp paper which suited their printing machinery. The *Star* in fact was printed very elegantly on green paper. They pioneered sensationalism in news coverage, but both realized that their audience was interested mainly in politics. The *Pall Mall Gazette* was independent in politics, under its Liberal editor W. T. Stead, but the *Star* was more avowedly Radical.[29]

Now the total circulation of all eight of these papers was under half a million a day, though all of them ran at a profit or existed on a small political subsidy. They all reported Parliament in some detail and were clearly divisible into two sections, one in which carefully written neutral news was provided to feed their readers' judgments and a second which was devoted unashamedly to partisan editorializing. Their whole existence depended upon their ideological function within the national political spectrum. The editors lived by their public political identity. Yet the papers were run as business enterprises: problems would arise when the ownership of a paper switched from one political persuasion to another or if, in the course of time, issues arose on which editor and owner could not agree. The editor owned no capital; he existed as an experienced newspaper man of a given politics and if he was sacked he could be employed only in a paper of similar scope.

The *Pall Mall Gazette* had been originally founded by George Smith,

29 Scalk, H. G. 'Fleet Street in the 1880's: the Old Journalism and the New', in *Journalism Quarterly*, Summer 1964 pp. 421–6; Stead, W. T. 'A Journalist on Journalism', in Stout, E. H. (Ed.), John Haddon and Co. (1892).

the publisher, and the first editor had been Frederick Greenwood, both of them unswervingly Conservative in politics. In 1880 Smith suddenly lost interest in the paper and sold it to a keen Liberal, Henry Yates Thompson, who fired Greenwood and hired W. T. Stead (a young successful journalist from the *Northern Echo*) and John Morley, both of them equally staunch Liberals. Stead eventually became sole editor and made the paper the primal force in the New Journalism, but later handed over the editorial chair to E. T. Cook, who had no sooner settled into this now most influential position, than its owner announced the sale of the paper to a Conservative, W. W. Astor, for £50,000. Cook and most other members of the staff walked out in a body and were invited by Sir George Newnes within a brief period to start a new rival Liberal evening paper, *The Westminster Gazette*, to be printed on sea-green paper. In 1895 Cook went on to edit the *Daily News*, but within a few years a new set of tensions broke out within Liberal ranks; Cook was an Imperialist Liberal and supported the Boer War; the *Daily News* changed hands and passed into the possession of a pro-Boer (i.e. anti-Imperialist) Liberal; once again Cook had to pack his bags and find employment elsewhere. The years of his maturity had been spent playing a kind of ideological musical chairs with a series of proprietors. There are similar career patterns to be detected among leading Conservative journalists of the period. The whole stance of a paper circulating among a mainly politically-minded class depended upon the political identity of its leading contributors. Only with the coming of a much broader readership did this phenomenon begin to recede.[30] Only in the present century have people seriously argued that a paper has a social duty to provide for the whole spectrum of available political views; the main popular daily of the 1950s to 1970s has operated in the knowledge that its readers vote in different ways. The political views of editors are far less important than they were even fifty years ago. The *professional* code of the editor, and journalists as a whole, has thus been profoundly influenced by the evolution of the distribution methods of newspapers and their successive delineations of appropriate markets.

A medium of communication is a set of technical possibilities, the physical manifestation of which involves the convergence of a series of trends and impulses in society. The various parts of a medium are sustained through mutual and societal pressures. The journalists, like the other parts of the machine, are constantly re-professionalized, as it were, to new tasks, as each formulation of a medium succeeds its predecessor. We do not live at the end of that great evolution. Indeed we can see in the 1970s another 'new' journalist coming into being, a professional trained to supply material to the new electronic apparatus which is already taking over the

30 Mills, J. S. (*op. cit.*) pp. 192—205; Scott, J. W. R. *The Story of the Pall Mall Gazette*, Oxford University Press (1950); Harris, W. *J. A. Spender*, Cassell (1946), pp. 22—7.

production of many newspapers and will spread rapidly between now and the end of the centruy. A journalist who sends his copy into the central newspaper computer through a video display unit will inevitably be quite different from a shorthand reporter whose material was typed, dubbed set and printed. The journalist of the 1980s might want more *control* over his material; for one thing he might prefer to work at home, his VDU attached to his telephone; for another, he might wish to control the fate of his copy more completely than was formerly possible. There is also the possibility that the new electronic processes will enable newspapers to come into being with less founding capital in future than has been necessary for the last forty years, and this could bring new titles into existence and turn back the tide of amalgamation. Of course, the opposite could equally well happen. We might be left with one or two enormous and prosperous newspapers, each much larger and covering a vaster territory of information and ideologies. The kind of analysis offered here is not a basis for prediction, but simply a method for helping to recognize some of the basic processes which lie behind the evolution of media and the professions which service them.

8

Capitalism and Control of the Press, 1800-1975

James Curran*

Introduction

The orthodox interpretation of the formative development of the British press has remained unchanged and virtually unchallenged for over a century. 'The British press,' writes David Chaney, 'is generally agreed to have attained its freedom around the middle of the nineteenth century'. (Chaney, 1972 p. 71.) This view, first advanced in the pioneering Victorian histories of journalism,[1] has been uncritically reiterated in histories of modern Britain and historical studies of the British press ever since.[2]

This watershed in British history allegedly came about partly as a consequence of the heroic struggle against state control of the press. The first major breakthrough is usually said to have occurred during the Interregnum with the abolition of the Court of the Star Chamber. It was followed by the abandonment of press licensing in 1695 and the introduction of a new and less repressive control system, based primarily on press taxes, in 1712. Further concessions were secured in the reign of George III, notably the relaxation of restrictions on the reporting of Parliament in the 1770s and Fox's Libel Act of 1792, which made juries the judges of seditious libel suits. But it was only in the Victorian era, according to the conventional wisdom, that the forces of progress finally triumphed with the reform of libel law in 1843 and the repeal of 'the taxes on knowledge' in the period 1853—61. An independent press emerged free of the legal and fiscal controls by which governments had sought to control it.[3]

* My thanks to the Royal Commission on the Press for permission to reproduce parts of a research paper commissioned by them and to John Dennington for his assistance.
1 See Hunt (1850), Andrews (1859), Grant (1871), Fox, Bourne (1887).
2 The following are merely selected examples, published since 1945; Aspinall (1949), Siebert (1952), Altick (1957), Woodward (1962), Roach (1965), Crawley (1965), Williams, R. (1965), Webb (1969), Christie (1970), Asquith (1975).
3 The best modern general accounts in the Whig tradition are Hanson (1936), Aspinall (1949), Siebert (1952), Altick (1957), Frank (1961), Cranfield (1962), Wiles (1965) and Christie (1970), each containing valuable information not available in the others.

This constitutional struggle was accompanied by a development which is generally held to be of even greater significance for the emergence of a free press — the *economic* emancipation of the press from state control. For 'the true censorship,' John Roach writes of the late Georgian press, 'lay in the fact that the newspaper had not yet reached financial independence'. (Roach, 1965 p. 181.) It was only with the growth of newspaper profits, largely from advertising, that newspapers were supposedly able to free themselves from state and party subsidies and develop an independent organization for gathering news. This conventional wisdom, embedded in all the standard academic histories of the press,[4] has been succinctly restated by Dr Ivon Asquith in a recent study of the early nineteenth century press: 'Since sales were inadequate to cover the costs of producing a paper, it was the growing income from advertising which provided the material base for the change of attitude from subservience to independence. The chief methods by which governments could influence the press — a direct subsidy, official advertisements, and priority of intelligence — were rendered less effective because proprietors could afford to do without them . . . . The growth of advertising revenue was the most important single factor in enabling the press to emerge as the Fourth Estate of the realm'. (*Historical Journal* 1975 p. 721.)

A number of important studies documenting the rise of the early radical press provide evidence which, by implication at least, cast doubt on this conventional wisdom.[5] Unfortunately, in one sense, these studies are primarily concerned with the development of the British working class rather than with the history of British journalism. And, insofar as they are explicitly situated in the context of the historical development of the British press, they accept the Whig framework of a triumphant struggle to establish an independent press [6] (Wickwar, 1929 p. 310; Thompson, 1963 p. 772; Williams, 1965 p. 209; Wiener, 1969a p. xi; Hollis, 1970 p. 10.) In effect, they substitute for traditional Whig heroes new working-class ones. The only two historians in this tradition who pay any serious attention to the middle-class press also subscribe to the legend of advertising as the midwife of press freedom. (Williams, 1965 p. 209 *et passim*; Hollis, 1970 p. 27—8.)

This historical legend is not of merely academic interest. It is a

4 See references in Note 3.
5 This is true even of Wiener (1969a) who more than any other historian provides evidence denting the traditional Whig thesis of a struggle for press freedom. Yet he writes 'Their [press taxes] removal in 1861 has been correctly regarded as a landmark in the history of journalism, comparable in its effects to the termination of press censorship in 1695 and to the modification of libel laws in 1843'. (Wiener, 1969 p. x.
6 The examination of the early development of the radical press, in this article, draws very extensively on these studies — notably Thompson (1963), Wiener (1969a), Hollis (1970) and Epstein (1976).

persuasive interpretation of press history which legitimates the market-based system. It is explicitly invoked, for instance, by popular historians of the press to justify the role of advertising in the press. 'The dangerous dependence of newspapers on advertising,' writes Francis Williams, 'has often been the theme of newspaper reformers — usually from outside its ranks. But the daily press would never have come into existence as a force in public and social life if it had not been for the need of men of commerce to advertise. Only through the growth of advertising did the press achieve independence.' (Williams, 1957 p. 50; *cf.* Herd, 1952 p. 65.) The same historical theme was skilfully deployed by the Advertising Association in its evidence to the last two Royal Commissions on the Press, apparently with remarkable effect. (Advertising Association, 1949; 1961.) It partly explains the innocent view of the first Royal Commission that the receipt of advertising 'creates a relationship both remote and impersonal', a belief largely endorsed by its successor. (Report 1947–9, p. 143 and Report 1960–1, p. 87.)

The portrayal of the mid-nineteenth-century British press that accompanies this historical legend serves a similar mythological purpose. According to the New Cambridge Modern History, for instance, financially independent newspapers became 'great organs of the public mind', amplifying the voice of the people rather than of governments and politicians. (NCMH vol. 9, p. 180.) The rise of an independent press, argues Professor Christie (1970), democratized British political institutions by exposing them to the full blast of public opinion. At the same time, the emergence of an independent press led to an increasingly non-partisan news coverage, enabling people to form balanced political judgements and to participate in a more mature political democracy. 'The period from 1855', writes Raymond Williams, 'is in one sense the development of a new and better journalism, with a much greater emphasis on news than in the faction-ridden first half of the century . . . most newspapers were able to drop their frantic pamphleteering.' (Williams, 1965 p. 218.) Historical convention has thus encouraged a limited model of the role of the press as an independent mediator between government and governed, and as an independent channel of communication. This model has dominated public inquiries into the press in Britain, effectively excluding serious consideration of structural reform.[7]

This article is a long overdue attempt to reappraise the standard interpretation of press history during the formative phase of its development. It indicates the need not only to re-examine critically the accepted view

7 Both Royal Commission Reports subscribed to the view of the press as an independent mediator and channel of communication. (Report 1947–9, pp. 100–6 *et passim*; Report 1960–1, pp. 19–20 *et passim*.) This model inevitably generated its prescriptive set of reforms — greater efficiency, higher professional standards and ineffectual anti-monopoly measures. (Report 1947–9, Ch. 17 and Report 1960–1, pp. 112–18.)

of the historical emergence of a 'free' press but to stand it on its head. The period around the middle of the nineteenth century, it will be argued, did not inaugurate a new era of press freedom and liberty: it introduced a new system of press censorship more effective than anything that had gone before. Market forces succeeded where legal repression had failed in establishing the press as an instrument of social control, with lasting consequences for the development of modern British society.

Breakdown of the Control System

Direct state censorship of the printed word in Britain was never fully effective. Even during the period of the most systematic repression under the early Stuart monarchy when offending authors could be publicly whipped, their faces branded, their nostrils slit, and their ears chopped off (on alternate weeks, allowing for recuperation), the absence of modern law enforcement agencies prevented the effective control of print. As a number of specialist studies demonstrate, the state lacked the sophisticated apparatus necessary to control production, monitor output, regulate distribution, stop the import of prohibited printed material and neutralize or destroy dissident elements in society — essential if coercive censorship were to be effective (Siebert, 1952; Frank, 1961; Rostenburg, 1971.) The celebrated termination of press licensing in 1695, as Hanson (1936) has shown, was prompted not so much by libertarian sentiment as by a realistic recognition that the licensing system was unenforceable. Even the less ambitious control system introduced under Queen Anne was only partly effective. (Cranfield, 1962; Wiles, 1965; Haigh, 1968; Harris, 1974.) By the nineteenth century it had become increasingly inadequate, even when strengthened by the notorious Six Acts of 1819.

The front line in the struggle for an independent press was occupied not by leading respectable publishers and editors, whose famous and much quoted proclamations of independence were belied by their covert attempts to secure illicit subsidies from government in the form of official advertising and by their willingness to cooperate in the system of exclusive intelligence by which successive governments managed the flow of news. (See for instance *History of* The Times, vol. 1–2, 1936–9; and Hindle, 1937.) Ownership and control of the respectable press continued, in any case, to be inextricably linked to government through partisan political involvement in parliamentary politics well into the twentieth century.[8] And

8 Even within its own terms of reference, the traditional thesis of the emergence of an independent Fourth Estate in the nineteenth century, standing above party, is highly debatable. The 1906 Parliament contained, for instance, thirty newspaper proprietors. (Thomas, 1958.) The nature of continuing editorial and proprietorial involvement in partisan politics in the twentieth century is illustrated by numerous biographies, diaries and memoirs (for instance, Spender, 1927; Wrench, 1955; Wilson (Ed.). 1970; King 1972). And if the press is to be conceived of as a

while respectable newspapers increasingly voiced criticism of government policy, this criticism was pragmatic rather than fundamental. Independent criticism was kept well within the confines of the moral framework legitimating the capitalist system.

The principal challenge to hegemonic control came from an increasingly radical press appealing by the 1830s to a predominantly working-class audience. It was confronted not by the subtle systems of control based on exclusive information, official advertising and Treasury subsidies but by the direct force of legal repression.

The first legal sanction available for controlling the press was the law of seditious and blasphemous libel, defined in such all embracing terms that it provided an infinitely flexible instrument of prosecution[9]. Its effectiveness was seriously reduced, however, by Fox's Libel Act of 1792, since successive governments found it increasingly difficult to get juries to convict. It also became increasingly apparent that libel prosecutions, even when upheld, were often counter-productive. The circulation of the *Republican*, for instance, increased by over 50% in 1819 when its editor was prosecuted. (Wickwar, 1929 p. 94.) Seditious libel prosecutions became a valuable source of promotion for the radical press. 'A libeller,' concluded the disillusioned Attorney General in 1832, 'thirsted for nothing more than the valuable advertisement of a public trial in a Court of Justice.' (*cit.* Wiener 1969a p. 196.) For these reasons, the number of libel prosecutions fell sharply. Whereas there were 167 prosecutions for seditious and blasphemous libel in the period 1817–24, there were only 16 in the subsequent period 1825–34. (Wickwar, Appendix B, p. 315.) Libel law was no longer an effective instrument for gagging the press, and was substantially modified by Lord Campbell's Act of 1843.

The government relied increasingly, instead, upon the so called 'taxes on knowledge' — a stamp duty on each copy of a press publication sold to the public, a duty on each advertisement placed in the press, and a tax on paper. The system of control based on press taxes had two objectives: to restrict readership of the press to the respectable members of society by forcing up the price of press publications; and to restrict ownership of newspapers to people who, in the words of Cresset Pelham, 'would conduct them in a more respectable manner than was likely to be the result of pauper management' by increasing the costs of publishing. (*cit.* Hollis, 1970, p. vi.) The last objective was further served by a state security system (£300 for London papers and £200 for provincial papers) ostensibly

---

Fourth Estate, many papers were clearly rotten boroughs — like the *Daily Express*, bought by Beaverbrook to facilitate his entry into politics. (Taylor, 1972.)

9 It was supplemented by '*ex officio* informations' which was used principally as a method of harrassing publishers and journalists and forcing them to incur legal expenses. '*Ex officio*' siuts had to be prosecuted with in 12 months after 1819, and the number of *ex officio* suits declined in common with seditious libel suits.

designed to provide guarantees for the payment of fines but, in reality, aimed to exclude 'pauper' management of newspapers.

Yet, even press taxes, which had been sharply increased in the period 1780–1815, proved increasingly ineffectual as an instrument of censorship. Ever since their introduction in 1712, individual publishers had evaded payment of press taxes and it had been necessary periodically to close loopholes in the law and strengthen law enforcement. By the 1830s, however, the ruling class was faced with a relatively new phenomenon – the systematic evasion of the stamp duty by a highly organized radical press with well developed distribution networks and relatively well endowed 'victim funds' to help the families of people imprisoned by the authorities. The government organized a relentless campaign of suppression, prosecuting publishers and printers, seizing supplies and smashing, wherever possible, networks of distributors. (At least 1,130 cases of selling unstamped newspapers were prosecuted in London alone during the period 1830–36.) By the summer of 1836, the government was forced to concede defeat. The Chancellor of the Exchequer informed the Commons on 20 June that the government 'had resorted to all means afforded by the existing law for preventing the publication of unstamped newspapers. The law officers of the Crown at the same time stated that the existing law was altogether ineffectual to the purpose of putting an end to the unstamped papers'. (*Hansard*, vol. 34, 1836, col. 627–8.)

A crisis had been reached. By the summer of 1836, the gross readership of the radical unstamped press published in London exceeded two million.[10] Its circulation exceeded even that of the respectable newspaper press. (Hollis, 1970.) Ironically the government's own actions had contributed to the very thing it wanted to prevent – the growth of a radical press with a mass audience – since its policy of systematic but ineffectual prosecution of tax evasion had materially assisted its expansion.[11]

The Whig government responded to the crisis with a well-prepared counter-offensive against the radical press. New measures were passed

10 This estimate is derived from the combined total circulation of six leading unstamped papers in 1836 of 200,000 (Hollis, 1970 p. 124) which, on the basis of 10 readers per copy, amounts to 2 million. The total unstamped readership was certainly larger, given the number of unstamped publications in 1836. (Wiener, 1969b.)

11 The rise of the radical press cannot be attributed, however, solely to an artificial price differential and state prosecution. While radical unstamped papers undercut the prices of the established press because they paid no tax, it is extremely doubtful whether they took away readers from the established press since they were not competing for the same audiences. (Nor is the supposition supported by circulation trends.) Furthermore, radical unstamped papers very successfully competed against moderate unstamped papers *selling at the same price*. They did so with one hand tied behind their backs since the authorities seldom interfered with the distribution of moderate unstamped papers. And while state repression boosted sales, it also seriously disrupted both supplies and distribution.

which strengthened the search and confiscation powers of the government; increased the penalties of being found in possession of an unstamped newspaper; and reduced the stamp duty by 75% in order to reduce the advantages of 'smuggling'. What has been widely hailed as a liberalizing measure, a landmark in the advance to press freedom, was manifestly repressive both in intention and effect. As Spring Rice, the Chancellor of the Exchequer, explained to the Commons, a strategic concession, combined with increased coercive powers, was necessary in order to enforce a system that had broken down. (*Hansard*, vol. 34, 20 June, 1836 col. 627–631.) The aim of these new measures, he stated candidly, was 'to protect the capitalist' and 'put down the unstamped papers'. (*Hansard*, vol. 37, 13 April, 1837, col. 1165.)

In the face of this fresh onslaught, the underground press capitulated. 'No unstamped paper can be attempted with success,' declared Hetherington, a leading radical publisher, shortly after being released from prison, unless 'some means can be devised either to print the newspaper without types and presses, or render the premises . . . inaccessable to armed force.' (*London Dispatch*, 17 September 1836.) All the principal radical publishers felt unable to continue resisting the stamp duty. By 1837, the clandestine radical press had disappeared and with it cheap journalism.

Compliance with the stamp duty, even though it was much reduced, forced radical newspapers to increase their prices sharply. Whereas most unstamped papers had sold at 1d in the early 1830s, their successors in the 1840s sold at 4d to 5d — a price that was well beyond the means of individual working-class consumers. Yet, despite the seemingly insuperable obstacle that effective enforcement of the stamp duty created for the continuance of radical working-class newspapers, the Whig Government's counter-offensive failed to destroy the radical press. The working class organized and combined in the purchase of newspapers which the authorities sought to exclude from them. Informal groups of working men pooled their resources to buy every week a radical paper. Work people organized through the branches of their unions, clubs and political associations, the purchase of newspapers. Pressure was also successfully exerted on taverns to purchase radical papers through the threat of withdrawing custom. Despite the stamp duty, new radical papers emerged which attained even larger sales than the leading unstamped papers had achieved. The largest selling unstamped paper, the radical *Weekly Police Gazette,* had a circulation of 40,000.[12] In 1839, the *Northern Star* reached over 50,000

12 Both Wiener (1969 p. 184) and Hollis (1970 p. 124) estimate the circulation of the *Weekly Police Gazette* as 40,000. It may have been more, however, since Spring Rice told the Commons that 40,000 copies of an unstamped paper had been seized on a Thursday two days before it was due to be distributed (*Hansard*, vol. 34, 20 June 1836, col. 627). More copies would certainly have been produced in the extra two days.

circulation (Read, 1961, p. 101) setting a new record for the radical press which was surpassed by its successor, the Chartist *Reynolds' News*, in the 1850s. (Berridge, 1975.)

These circulations seem very small by modern standards. But then circulation provides a highly anachronistic guide to readership in the first half of the nineteenth century. The modal number of readers per copy of national newspapers in the first half of the 1970s has been 2 to 3 (JICNARS, 1970–75): the modal number of readers per copy of cheap unstamped papers in the 1830s was certainly not less than 10 and was probably even higher in the case of its high-priced successors like the *Northern Star*.[13] The *Northern Star* and *Reynolds' News* each reached, at their meridian, at least half a million readers before the repeal of the stamp duty.[14]

Furthermore, radical newspapers were the pace-setters in terms of circulation during the first half of the nineteenth century. *Twopenny Trash*, in 1816–17, gained several times a circulation that of most respectable papers.[15] The radical *Weekly Police Gazette* gained a still bigger circulation which in 1836 was over three times that of *The Times*. The *Northern Star* set yet another record, gaining the largest circulation of any paper published in the provinces. (Select Committee of Newspaper Stamps, 1851, pp. 524–57.)[16] And the Chartist *Reynolds' News*, only a little behind the radical liberal *Lloyds Weekly*, the circulation leader of the early 1850s, also had a leading position in contemporary journalism. (Berridge, 1965.) The extent of the dominance of radical newspapers in the first half of the nineteenth century is, moreover, understated by these comparative circulation figures since radical papers had a very much larger number of readers per sale than the respectable press.[17]

The control system administered through the state had failed. Neither libel law nor press taxes had been able to prevent the rise of a radical popular press in the first half of the nineteenth century representing the interests and aspirations of the working class.

13   Other estimates of readers per copy of papers in the first half of the nineteenth century are as high as 50–80. (Read, 1961 p. 202 and Webb, 1955 pp. 31–4.)

14   Estimated at a ratio of 20 readers per copy.

15   Cole (1947 p. 207) estimates 40,000–50,000, although Hollis (1970 p. 95) estimates 20,000–30,000, probably the more reliable figure.

16   Read's estimate of 50,000 is based on a short term peak. (Read, 1961 p. 101.) The annual average circulation of the *Northern Star* in 1839 was fractionally less than three times more than that of *The Times*. (House of Commons Accounts and Papers 1840.)

17   While individual radical papers set new circulation records, the radical newspaper press as a whole probably never attained before 1855 the gross circulation it had attained in 1836. Nor did radical publishers make substantial inroads into family magazine journalism.

The Impact of the Radical Press

One of the most important, and least commented upon, aspects of the development of the radical press in the first half of the nineteenth century was that its leading publications rapidly developed a country wide circulation. Even as early as the second decade, leading radical papers like the *Twopenny Trash*, *Political Register* and *Republican* were read as far afield as Yorkshire, Lancashire, the Midlands and East Anglia, as well as in the South of England. By the early 1830s, the principal circulation newspapers like the *Weekly Police Gazette*, *Poor Man's Guardian* and *Dispatch* had a distribution network extending on a North-South axis from Glasgow to Land's End and on an East-West axis from Carmarthen to Norwich. This distribution network was further developed by radical papers, notably the *Northern Star* and *Reynolds' News*, in the subsequent decades. Part of the impact of the radical press stemmed from this central fact — the extent of its geographical distribution.

The radical press was important in reinforcing a growing consciousness of class and in unifying disparate elements of the working community partly because its leading publications were national media, providing national coverage and reaching a national working-class audience. It helped to extend the often highly exclusive occupational solidarity of 'the new unionism' to all other sectors of the labour community by showing the common predicament of unionists in different occupations and in different trades throughout the country. Workers struggling to establish an extra-legal union in their locality read in the radical press in 1833–4, for instance, of similar struggles by glove workers in Yeovil, cabinet makers and joiners in Carlisle and Glasgow, shoemakers and smiths in Northampton, brick-layers and masons in London (to mention only some) as well as the struggles of workers in Belgium and Germany. Similarly, the radical press helped to reduce the geographical isolation of local labour communities by showing that localized agitation — whether against local Poor Law Commissioners, new machinery, long working hours or wage cutting — conformed to a common pattern throughout the country. The radical press carried news that none of the respectable papers carried; it focused attention on the common problems and identity of interest of working people as a social grouping; and it coalesced disparate groups fragmented by primitive communications and sectional affiliations into mass working-class audiences. It was, in the words of the Chartist leader, Feargus O'Connor, 'the link that binds the industrious classes together'. (*Northern Star*, 16 January 1841.)

Radical newspapers also profoundly influenced the institutional development of the working class because of their national circulation. They helped to transform local community action into nationally organized campaigns. The *Poor Man's Guardian*, for instance, provided a vital institutional link between the different branches of the National Union of the Working Classes during the early 1830s just as the *Northern Star* was to perform a similar function for the Chartist movement in the late thirties and forties. Both papers acted as important mediators between the leadership and the rank and file. They helped to create a common platform on which to unite; to give a national direction to local activities; and to make local activists conscious of their place in a wider national movement. The radical press helped, in short, to integrate powerful agencies for the development of working-class consciousness.

The radical press also played an important part in promoting both directly and indirectly the growth of working-class political and industrial organizations. It provided material assistance in publicizing in advance notices of meetings and sometimes in raising funds. It brought into national prominence and conferred a new status on the vanguard of the working-class movement. (The publicity given by the radical press to unionists in the remote village of Tolpuddle, for instance, helped to transform them into national working-class martyrs.) Radical press publicity attracted new recruits into the ranks of the activist working-class movement; it stimulated people into spontaneously setting up local branches; and, no less important, it fortified the commitment of working-class activists and sustained through publicity the belief that they were succeeding in the face of seemingly impossible odds. Without the *Northern Star*, declared one speaker at a local Chartist meeting, 'their own sounds might echo through the wilderness'. (*Northern Star*, 18 August 1833.)

Above all, radical newspapers contributed to a major cultural reorganization of the working class. We have become so accustomed to the privatized pattern of newspaper consumption amidst a steady flow of information from a variety of institutionally mediated sources that it requires an effort of historical adjustment to understand the cultural meaning and importance of the newspaper in early nineteenth-century England. The arrival of a newspaper was often an eagerly awaited event. 'On the day', recalls Fielden, 'the newspaper, the *Northern Star*, O'Connor's paper, was due, the people used to line the roadside waiting for its arrival, which was paramount to everything else for the time being.' (*cit.* Epstein, 1976 p. 71.) Newspaper reading was essentially a social activity: newspapers were usually read in a social setting outside the home or shared between friends. Above all, radical newspapers were often read out aloud (and indeed were written to be read aloud), providing a focal point of inter-action. The messages transmitted by the radical press were mediated far beyond the immediate audiences of newspapers on a scale unknown to the twentieth century, although even today they significantly influence the content of personal interaction. (Curran and Tunstall, 1973.)

The radical press, reflecting in the main the perspectives of the vanguard of the working-class movement, profoundly influenced the attitudes and beliefs of large numbers of working people. It eroded passive adherence to the social order, based on cognitive acceptance of the world as natural and inevitable, by defining reality not as a series of more or less discrete events but as a process of exploitation. The early radical papers advanced a simplistic conspiracy definition of reality in which a corrupt and parasitic 'crew' of placemen and pensioners, royalty and priests, lawyers, monopolists and aristocrats, were portrayed as 'feeding upon' the productive class. This became fused with a more sophisticated proto-Marxist analysis in the 1830s, focusing on the ownership of capital as the means by which the capitalist class appropriated the wealth of the community. Reality was defined not as given — 'the way things are' — but as a system of oppression that could be replaced by a new social order organized on different principles. This was in itself an important catalyst to working-class resistance, eroding the legacy of fatalism that had inhibited organized action in the past.

The radical press also helped to undermine normative support for the social order by challenging the legitimacy of the political and economic institutions on which it was based. The sanctity of property ownership was denied on the grounds that all land was the 'natural heritage' of the people stolen from them in a former age and on the grounds that capital accumulation was the product of the labour of working people, appropriated in profits. The law came to be portrayed as the means by which capitalists legitimated this 'fraud'. The 'property people', declared the *Poor Man's Guardian*, 'having all the law making to themselves, make and maintain fraudulent institutions, by which they continue (under false pretences) to transfer the wealth of producers to themselves.' (*Poor Man's Guardian* 26 July 1834.) Parliament was merely an instrument of oppression, controlled by people who had annexed the wealth created by working people. 'A million of individuals,' declared the *Reynolds' News*, 'qualified by the possession of a certain amount of that property which is either produced by the working classes or due to their natural heritage, will be called upon to elect law-makers and tax-imposers for twenty six millions at home and a hundred million abroad.' (*Reynolds' News* 5 January 1851.)

Finally, the radical press helped to activate the working class by fostering a sense of corporate class consciousness and the belief that society could be changed through the force of combination. The way ahead, argued most of the leading radical papers by the early 1830s, lay in confrontation rather than in partnership. 'Don't believe those', declared the *Poor Man's Guardian*, 'who tell you that the middle and working classes have one and the same interest . . . their respective interests (are) as directly opposed to each other as two fighting bulls.' The solution to poverty and oppression lay in the fundamental reconstruction of society based, as *Reynolds' News* was arguing in the early 1850s, on the capture of state power through universal suffrage and even the public ownership of land and 'machinery'.

The radical press never achieved a consistently oppositional perspective of society: its oppositional stance on a number of issues was contained within a 'negotiated' framework. Its analysis was often confused and contradictory, reflecting the ideological confusion of the emerging working-class movement. Yet, it provided vital institutional support for the *development* of political consciousness amongst the working class that gave rise to the organized political and industrial action of the second quarter of the nineteenth century.[18] The change was symbolized by the General Strike of 1842 called to secure universal suffrage through the force of industrial action. As John Foster (1974) has shown, it was not a momentary eruption of frustration but a carefully prepared bid for state power involving discussion and argument on a mass scale and receiving mass support, covering all of industrial Lancashire, much of Yorkshire and parts of the Midlands. While the strike was crushed, and fifteen hundred labour leaders imprisoned, it was a sign of an increasingly unstable society in which the popular press had become a powerfully disruptive force.

Economic Structure of the Radical Press 1815–1855

While the growth of radical journalism reflected the growth of working class agitation, the rise of the radical press can be understood only in the context of the prevailing economic structure of the press industry that *permitted the rise of a radical press.* Since this is an important aspect of the central argument that follows, it is worth examining in some detail the finances of the early radical press.

The initial capital required to set up a radical paper in the early part of the nineteenth century was extremely small. Most of the radical unstamped papers were printed not on a steam press but on hand presses, costing anything from £10 to acquire. Metal type was often hired by the hour and print workers paid on a piece-work basis.

The leading stamped radical papers after 1836 were printed on more sophisticated machinery and were forced to comply with the security system established by law. The *London Dispatch*, for instance, was printed on a Napier machine, bought with the help of a wealthy well-wisher and the retained profits from Hetherington's other publications. The *Northern Star* had a press especially constructed for it in London. Even so, launch costs were extremely small by comparison with the subsequent period. The *Northern Star*, for instance, was launched with a

18 The trend towards radicalization of the popular press was not continuous and uninterupted. The decline of the *Northern Star* in the 1840s and the rise of *Lloyd's Weekly* edited initially by two moral force Chartists, represented a setback. But the *Northern Star* was replaced by *Reynolds' News*, which achieved a meteoric rise of circulation in the early 1850s and once again laid the basis for repudiation of middle-class reform leadership.

total capital of £690 raised by public subscription mostly in northern towns. (Glasgow, 1954.)

The establishment costs of the radical press were also extremely small. Radical unstamped papers paid no tax; they relied heavily upon news reports filed by their readers on a voluntary basis; they recruited street sellers mainly from the army of unemployed; and they had a small newsprint bill due to their high readership per copy. Hollis estimates, for instance, that the *Poor Man's Guardian*, a leading newspaper of the early 1830s, broke even with a sale as small as 2,500. (Hollis, 1972 p. 132.)

Compliance with the law after 1836 substantially increased the establishment costs of the radical press since a penny stamp duty had to be paid on each copy sold. Even so, the running costs of a newspaper, relying on the network of unemployed labourers as street sellers and a large team of worker-correspondents who normally gave their services free, were still very small by later standards. The influential *London Dispatch* reported, for instance, that 'the whole expense allowed for editing, reporting, reviewing, literary contributions, etc., in fact, the entire cost of what is technically called 'making up' the paper is only six pounds per week'. (*London Dispatch*, 17 September 1836.) In the same issue, it reported that, at its selling price of $3\frac{1}{2}$d, it could break even with a circulation of 16,000. Similarly, the *Northern Star*, which developed, unlike its predecessors, a substantial network of paid correspondents, claimed to be spending just over £9.10s a week on its reporting establishment in 1841. Selling at $4\frac{1}{2}$d, Read (1966) reports that it was able to break even with a sale of about 6,200 copies a week. The limited money required to cover running costs before it broke even (which it did almost immediately) was probably met by its controller, Feargus O'Connor. (Epstein, 1976.)

The low launch and establishment costs of newspaper publishing in the first half of the nineteenth century fundamentally affected the character of the British popular press. It was still possible for newspapers to be financed from within the working class, and consequently for the ownership and control of newspapers to be in the hands of people committed, in the words of Joshua Hobson, an ex-handloom weaver and publisher of the *Voice of West Riding*, 'to support the rights and interests of the order and class to which it is my pride to belong'. (Hollis, 1970 p. 94.) Some newspapers like the *Voice of the People*, the *Northern Star*, the *Liberator* and *Trades Newspaper* were owned principally by working men and trade union organizations. Other leading papers were owned by individual proprietors like Cleave, Watson and Hetherington, people mostly of humble origins who had risen to prominence through the working-class movement. While not lacking in ruthlessness or business acumen, the people they entrusted to edit their newspaper were all former manual workers like William Hill and Joshua Hobson or middle class activists like O'Brien and Lorymer whose experience had been shaped by long involvement in working class politics. Indeed, full-time correspondents of both the *Northern Star* and *Reynolds' News* sometimes acted in a double capacity as Chartist organizers.

These men had very different conceptions of their role as journalists from those of the institutionalized journalists of the popular press in the subsequent period. They saw themselves as representatives of a class rather than as professional gatekeepers; they sought to provide a total critique of society rather than act as neutral brokers and intermediaries; they spoke to rather than at their readers (something made possible only by the highly differentiated nature of their audiences and extensive inter-action between journalists and readers); they involved their readers, as we have seen, as reporters; and they saw their function as that of ventriloquist rather than as mediator. As the editor wrote in the *Northern Star* on its fifth anniversary, 'I have ever sought to make it [the *Northern Star*] rather a reflex of your minds than a medium through which to exhibit any supposed talent or intelligence of my own. This is precisely my conception of what a people's organ should be'. (*cit.* Epstein, 1976 p. 85.)

The second important feature of the economic structure of the radical press in the first half of the nineteenth century was that it was self-sufficient on the proceeds of sales alone. The radical unstamped press carried very little commercial advertising and the stamped radical press fared little better. The *London Dispatch* complained bitterly, for instance, of the 'prosecutions, fines and the like *et ceteras* with which a paper of our principles is sure to be more largely honoured than by the lucrative patronage of advertisers'. (17 September 1836.)

The grudge held by the *London Dispatch* and other radical newspapers against advertisers was more than justified. An examination of the official advertisement duty returns reveals a marked difference in the amount of advertising support received by the radical press compared with its more respectable rivals. Set out in Table 1, for instance, are the official returns for advertisement duties paid per 1,000 copies by the *Northern Star* and its principal rivals — Liberal and Tory weeklies in Leeds, where the *Northern Star* was published — and London dailies which, like the *Northern Star*, had a countrywide circulation. While the advertisement duty per 1,000 copies provides a useful index of comparison since it takes into account differences of circulation, it does not take into account the much lower advertising rates (and therefore revenue) of the *Northern Star* compared with its rivals and the much larger market it provided access to due to its more favourable readership per 1,000 copy ratio.[19] Yet even though these figures underestimate the true extent of the differences, they reveal a disparity of massive proportions. In 1840, for instance, the leading

---

19 Even at this early point, many contemporary advertisers were aware of the significance of readership per copy, and newspapers made claims about their readership as part of their sales pitch.

	1838		1840		1842†	
	Advertisement Duty £	Advertisement Duty per 1,000 circulation £	Advertisement Duty £	Advertisement Duty per 1,000 circulation £	Advertisement Duty £	Advertisement Duty per 1,000 circulation £
Leeds Mercury (Whig)	943	2.05	1,042	2.11	948	1.97
Leeds Times (Liberal Reform)	193	1.46	157	0.93	178	1.55
Leeds Intelligence (Tory)	518	2.99	568	2.66	567	1.97
Northern Star (Chartist)	115	0.20	45	0.04	57	0.08
Times (Tory Independent)	11,238	2.63	13,887	2.74	15,223	2.41
Morning Post (Tory)	3,191	3.64	3,468	3.64	3,622	3.08
Morning Chronicle (Whig)	4,796	2.23	4,415	2.22	4,313	2.25
Morning Advertiser (Liberal Free Trade)	3,849	2.46	3,822	2.24	3,068	2.17

*Derived from Stamp and Advertisement Duty Returns, recorded in House of Commons Accounts and Papers.

†Estimated from half-yearly returns.

country paper and the two middle-class papers, published in Leeds, each paid an advertisement duty per 1,000 circulation more than fifty times that of the *Northern Star*. Perhaps of even greater significance for the future development of the press, the Liberal reform *Leeds Times*, edited by Samuel Smiles, with a predominantly lower middle-class audience, but including also a working-class readership, paid twenty-three times more advertisement duty per 1,000 circulation in 1840 than the *Northern Star*.

A similar pattern emerges in the case of other leading radical papers for which returns are available. In 1817, for instance, Cobbett's *Political Register* received only three advertisements: its advertisement duty per 1,000 copies was less than a hundredth of rival periodicals like the *Examiner*, *Age*, *National Register* and *Duckett's Weekly Dispatch*, although this disparity was somewhat reduced by the 1830s. The *London Dispatch* in 1837 was only marginally better off: it paid per 1,000 copies less than one twenty-fifth of the advertisement duty paid by daily papers in London, also with a country circulation; and less than one twenty-fifth of the duty per 1,000 copies paid by leading middle-class weeklies in Manchester, Liverpool, Leeds and York.

This lack of support placed radical stamped newspapers at a serious disadvantage. They were deprived of the patronage which financed increased editorial and promotional expenditure by their competitors. They were forced to close down with circulations which enabled other papers, buoyed up with advertising, to make a profit. This last factor severely inhibited the growth of a radical stamped press at a time when the price of contemporary newspapers, inflated by the stamp duty, was a major deterrent against buying papers amongst the working class.

Yet, despite these very substantial disadvantages, the absence of advertising did not force closure. While fortunes were not easily made from radical newspaper publishing, radical newspapers — both stamped and unstamped — could be profitable. Without significant advertising patronage in 1837, Hetherington, the publisher of the stamped *London Dispatch*, was reported to be making £1,000 a year from his business. (Hollis, 1970 p. 135.) Similarly, the stamped *Northern Star* was estimated to have produced a phenomenal profit of £13,000 in 1839 and £6,500 in 1840 (Schoyen, 1958 p. 133) which, as we have seen, was generated from sales rather than advertising revenue.

This absence of dependence on advertising profoundly influenced the character and development of the radical press. Newspapers could attack industrial and commercial capitalism without the need to pander to the political prejudices of advertisers. They were able consistently to attack 'buy cheap and sell dear shopocrats', 'millocrats' and 'capitalists', yet still flourish and prosper without advertising patronage. Perhaps even more important, they could address themselves directly to the working class without the need to appeal to people who constituted a more valuable advertising market. The development of the early radical press was characterized by larger but more differentiated audiences. Whereas radical newspapers appealed to both middle and working-class readers in the early period, their more radical successors appealed primarily to working-class audiences.[20] These papers were able to project a polarized model of conflict, and substitute for the traditional rhetoric of populism the language of class, without fear of the consequences. They could afford to alienate potential middle-class readers which advertisers wanted to reach. For they depended upon their readers' pennies not the largesse of advertisers for their survival.

The Ugly Face of Reform

The middle-class campaign against 'the taxes on knowledge' was informed by a variety of special interests, not the least the concern of campaigners like Milner Gibson and Cobden in the 1850s to extend the influence of the liberal, free trade press. The central issue that divided middle-class supporters and opponents of press taxes, however, was how best to establish the press as an instrument of social control.

Traditionalists argued that press taxes were the last line of defence holding back a flood of radical publications. The reduction of newspaper prices, following repeal, would result in the general dissemination of 'doctrines injurious to the middle and upper classes, and damaging to the real and lasting interests of the public . . . their malignant influence will be immeasurably increased by the Repeal of the Stamp Duty'. (*cit.* Westmacott, 1836.) It would also facilitate the establishment of many more radical papers by reducing publishing costs. As Morris told the Select Committee on Newspaper Stamps, it is in 'the interest of the public that any branch of industry such as that of producing newspapers should be limited to a few hands, and be in the hands of parties who are great capitalists'. (*cit. History of The Times* vol. 2, 1939 p. 205.)

Middle-class opponents of press taxes argued that, on the contrary, press taxes prevented the dissemination of sound principles since it restricted the development of the press. Repeal of the advertisement duty would release and also redirect a flow of advertising patronage for the establishment of new newspapers. The repeal of the stamp and paper duties would increase access to 'sound doctrines' by reducing newspaper prices. It would dispel 'ignorance', argued the *Spectator*, and put an end to trade unions, rick-burning and machine-breaking. (*Spectator*, 1 August

20 For an assessment of the class composition of readers of unstamped papers, see Hollis (1970); and of readers of the *Northern Star*, see Epstein (1976). At least two-thirds of the urban working class were literate (though not necessarily possessing developed reading skills) during this period. See Webb (1950; 1955) and the more cautious estimates of Stone (1968) and Sanderson (1972).

1835.) 'Readers are not rioters: readers are not rick-burners,' Hickson told the Select Committee on Newspaper Stamps. (1851 p. 479.) The diffusion of sound principles, through the repeal, would prove a more effective instrument of social control than state coercion. 'Is it not time to consider,' declared Bulwer Lytton in a famous speech against the stamp duty, 'whether the printer and his types may not provide better for the peace and honour of a free state than the gaoler and the hangman?' (*cit.* Wiener, 1969 p. 68.)

The confidence placed by opponents of press taxes in the 'free' market place of opinion was more than justified. In the second half of the nineteenth century, following the repeal of the advertisement duty in 1853 and the stamp duty in 1855, the radical popular press was nearly eliminated. Why this happened has never been adequately explained.

Market Forces as a Control System 1855—1920

The decline of radicalism in the popular press in the immediate post-stamp era can be attributed partly to the decline of working-class radicalism with the restabilization of the social order. Yet, as we shall see, the decline of the radical press was part of this process of restabilization. And 'the *zeitgeist*' theory does not explain why the revival of working-class radicalism after 1875 did not lead to a similar revival of radical journalism. Indeed, the national press was very much more radical in 1860, a period of relative tranquility, than it was fifty years later at a time of militant working-class agitation. There was manifestly no close correlation between the climate of opinion in the country and changes in the ideological perspectives mediated by the press in Victorian and Edwardian Britain.

Virginia Berridge (1965) has recently advanced a plausible explanation for the change in popular journalism in a pioneering study of the popular Victorian press. The decline of radicalism, she argues, was due to the 'commercialization' of the popular press. Newspapers concentrated upon the easy arousal of sensationalism rather than taxing political analysis in order to maximize sales: reports of crime, scandal and sport displaced attacks on capitalism as more saleable commodities.

This analysis implies a bigger departure from the tradition of radical journalism of the 1830s and 1840s than is justified. The growth of the radical press in this period had been based partly upon the skill with which some radical publishers exploited the street literature tradition of radical sensationalism and scandal. The shift from a periodical quarto to newspaper broadsheet format amongst unstamped papers in the early 1830s was accompanied by a marked trend towards 'general' and sensational news coverage. Hetherington, publisher of the *Poor Man's Guardian*, *Destructive* and *London Dispatch*, announced the change with characteristic aplomb, promising his readers 'all the gems and treasures, and fun and frolic and news and occurrences of the week . . .. Police Intelligence, Murders, Rapes, Suicides, Burnings, Maimings, Theatricals, Races, Pugilism, and all manner of moving accidents by flood and field. In short, it will be stuffed with every sort of devilment that will make it sell . . . . Our object is not to make money, but to beat the Government.' (*cit.* Hollis, 1970 p. 122.) While the great commercial entrepreneurs of the subsequent period carried this trend towards commercialization a stage further and included a higher proportion of general features and sensational material in their papers, this hardly constitutes an adequate explanation of an extraordinary phenomenon – the complete transformation of the popular press. For not only was the radical press progressively absorbed or eliminated, a whole new generation of national popular newspapers emerged which were predominantly on the right or the extreme right of the political spectrum.

The commercialization thesis is, in effect, an historical version of one variant of the mass culture critique based on the assumption that material processed for a mass audience is inevitably trivialized and sensationalized in order to cater for the common denominator of mass taste (e.g. Wilensky 1964). Not only is this assumption sometimes a dubious one, and the cultural judgements that underly it open to question, as I have argued elsewhere (Curran, 1977), it obscures under the general heading of 'commercialization' the complex system of controls institutionalized by the consolidation of the capitalist press in mid-Victorian Britain.

The Freedom of Capital

One of the central objectives of press taxes – to exclude pauper management of the press – was attained only by their repeal.

The enormous expansion of demand, following the abandonment of newspaper taxation, resulted in what A. E. Musson calls an 'industrial revolution' in the press. (Musson, 1954 p. 214.) Hoe printing presses were introduced in the 1860s and 1870s and were gradually replaced by rotary machines of increasing size and sophistication in late Victorian and Edwardian England. 'Craft' composing was revolutionized by Hattersley's composing machine in the 1860s, and this in turn was replaced by the linotype machine in the 1880s and 1890s. Numerous innovations were also made in graphic reproduction during the Victorian period. These developments led to a sharp rise in fixed capital costs. Northcliffe estimated half a million pounds as 'the initial cost of machinery, buildings, ink factories and the like, and this was altogether apart from the capital required for daily working expenses' in setting up the *Daily Mail*, although this figure almost certainly includes the cost of the establishing the paper as a property around which other publications were grouped. (Pound and Harmsworth, 1959 p. 206.) The enormous increase in capital investment conferred considerable scale advantages on entrepreneurs who established multiple newspapers and jobbing companies making maximum use of shared plant and facilities. The profits from the economic integration of publishing — Edward Lloyd led the way in the 1870s and 1880s by establishing paper mills and growing esparto grass on 100,000 acres of plantation for the production of paper — were also reinvested in the development of newspaper enterprises. But the rising capital costs of newspaper publishing did not constitute an insuperable obstacle to the launch of new publications with limited capital resources even in the national market. Newspapers, like the *Daily Herald* in 1912, could be launched with only limited capital by being printed on a contract basis by an independent printer.

Much more important was the effect of growing demand, released by the repeal of press taxes, on the running costs and cash flow requirements of newspaper publishing. Circulation levels in the mass market soared, enormously increasing the scale of production. *Lloyd's Weekly* had a circulation in 1896 about 15 times that of leading circulation papers fifty years before (although its audience was not proportionately larger due to the sharp reduction in the ratio of readers per copy). The increasing scale of production led to a sharp increase in newsprint and production costs. At the same time, there was a progressive rise of paging levels (and therefore newsprint costs), a steady increase in expenditure on newsgathering and processing, and an increase in promotion costs (not only for advertising and publicity but also for sale-or-return agreements to distributors). This rise in costs led in turn to a steady rise in the circulation levels which were necessary in order to break-even. The breakeven point was further raised by a progressive reduction in newspaper prices. New newspapers could be launched with limited funds and derelict newspapers could be bought relatively cheaply. It was the *establishment* of newspapers that required large capital resources.

This important change can be illustrated by the history of individual newspapers in the period. In 1855, it required a capital investment of £4,000 to relaunch the then liberal *Daily Telegraph* and establish it as the circulation leader in the national daily press. (Burnham, 1955 p. 2.) By the 1870s, Edward Lloyd needed to spend £150,000 to re-establish the *Daily Chronicle* (Herd, 1952 p. 185). During the period 1906–8, Thomasson spent about double that amount attempting to establish the liberal daily, *Tribune*. (Gibbs, 1946 p. 59.) In 1919–22, Beaverbrook invested £200,000 on the development of the *Daily Express* and took nothing out (Taylor, 1972 p. 171); and he invested a further £2 millions in the *Sunday Express* (even though it was able to take advantage of the plant facilities established for the *Daily Express*) before it broke even. (Taylor, 1972 p. 175.) Similarly, Lord Cowdray invested perhaps

£750,000 attempting to convert the *Westminster Gazette* into a morning paper. (Seymour-Ure, 1975 p. 242.)

These statistics illustrate the freedom of capital in the creation of the modern press. Even when the capital costs of launch and establishment were relatively low in the 1850s and 1860s, they still exceeded the resources available to the working class. The *Bee-Hive*, for instance, was launched in 1862 with a capital of less than £250 raised by trade union organizations and a well-to-do sympathizer. Its under-capitalization put it at a serious disadvantage; it sold at a price twice that of its leading competitors; and it lacked the resources necessary to maintain its original commitment to providing general news coverage despite the small amount of additional capital put up by unions and other contributors. In effect, its lack of capital support condemned it to the margins of national publishing as a specialist if influential weekly paper.[21] (Coltham, 1960.)

As the resources of organized labour increased, so did the costs of establishing a national paper. It was not until 1912 that papers controlled by activists in the working-class movement, and financed from within the working class, made their first appearance in national daily journalism, and then their belated appearance occurred long after most national daily papers had become well established. The brief career of the *Daily Citizen*, and the chequered early history of the *Daily Herald*, illustrate the economic obstacles to establishing papers under working-class control. The *Daily Citizen*, launched in 1912 with a capital of only £30,000 sub-scribed mainly by trade unions reached a circulation of 250,000 at its peak within two years and was only 50,000 short of overhauling the *Daily Express* established in 1900. Although it almost certainly had more working-class readers than any other daily in the country, subsequent capital support was insufficient to prevent its closure three years after its launch. (Holton, 1974.) The more left wing *Daily Herald*, launched with a capital of only £300 and sustained by public donations (notably from two wealthy socialists, the Countess de la Warr and R. D. Harben, the son of the chairman of Prudential Insurance) lurched from one crisis to another despite also reaching a circulation of 250,000 at its meridian before 1914. On one occasion, it came out in pages of different sizes and shapes because someone 'found' old discarded paper supplies when the *Daily Herald* could no longer afford to pay for paper. On other occasions, it bought small quantities of paper under fictitious names from suppliers all over the country; the directors of the *Daily Herald* even threatened organized industrial action against paper manufacturers, a stratagem that secured paper supplies without a guarantee. (Lansbury, 1925.) While the *Daily Citizen* closed, the *Daily Herald* survived by switching from being a daily

---

21 Coltham (1960) suggests, however that a different approach might have secured more trade union funds for the *Bee-Hive*.

to becoming a weekly during the period 1914 to 1919. From these humble beginnings emerged a paper that became, for a time, the biggest circulation daily paper in the world.

The rise in publishing costs helps to explain why the genuinely radical press in the late nineteenth century survived only in etiolated form as low-budget, high-price specialist weeklies like the *Clarion* and *Labour Leader* (both of which attained surprisingly large circulations)[22] and in local community papers, an important but as yet undocumented aspect of the residual survival of the radical press.[23] The rise in costs of publishing in the mass market, during its formative period of growth, ensured that ownership and control of the popular press passed progressively into the hands of capitalist entrepreneurs with access to, or control over, large capital resources.

This said, it provides only a partial explanation of the decline of the radical press. It does not explain the ideological absorption or elimination of radical newspapers already in existence before the repeal of press taxes. Nor does it adequately explain why small circulation radical newspapers did not evolve over time into mass circulation media and generate capital through retained profits for the launch of new radical publications. For an answer to these problems we need to look elsewhere.

The New Licensing System

The crucial element of the new control system was the role occupied by advertising in the development of the press after the repeal of the advertisement duty. The reduction of the advertisement duty from 3s to 1s 6d in 1833 led to a 35% growth of London press advertising and a 27% growth of provincial press advertising in the space of one year. (Aspinall, 1950.) This increase, moreover, was sustained. Between 1836 and 1848, the total volume of press advertising in Britain, as measured by the number of advertisements, increased by 36%. (British Parliamentary Papers 1836—50.) Examination of the distribution of this increase shows, however, that a disproportionate amount went to established middle-class newspapers and to the London newspaper press rather than to the regional press in England and Wales. It did not transform popular newspaper publishing.

It was not until the repeal of the duty in 1853 that a radically different situation emerged. The advertisement duty, even in modified form, had influenced the structure of advertising expenditure. As John Cassell, the publisher of useful-knowledge publications complained to the Select Committee on Stamps 'It [the advertisement duty] entirely prevents a

22 *Clarion* had a circulation of 70,000 at its peak in 1906 and *Labour Leader* had a circulation of 40,000—50,000 by 1911. (Holton, 1974.)

23 One of the few studies touching on this subject is Lee (1974).

certain class of advertisements from appearing; it is only such as costly
books and by property sales by auction that really afford an opportunity
of advertising and for paying the duty' (Select Committee on Stamps,
1851 p. 236). Milner Gibson, chairman of the Select Committee, succintly
summarized the point: 'the advertisement duty must really destroy all the
advertisements that are not worth the duty' (Select Committee, 1851
p. 440). The end of the advertisement tax brought into being cheap press
advertising.

This led to an entirely new situation. Popular newspapers attracted an
increasing amount of advertising. In the four years between 1854 and
1858, *Reynolds' News*, for instance, increased its volume of advertising
by over 50%. (Berridge, 1975.) This growth of advertising, in conjunction
with the repeal of the stamp and paper duty, resulted in the modal price
of popular newspapers being halved in the 50s and halved again in the early
60s. This transformed the economic structure of popular publishing. It
had still been possible, as we have seen, for working-class newspapers in
the 1840s to be profitable, with only marginal advertising support,
because of their high retail price. With these massive reductions in price,
all national newspapers in the mass market cost more to produce and
distribute than the price at which they were sold.[24] Advertisers acquired
a *de facto* licensing authority since, without their support, newspapers
ceased to be economically viable. The old licensing system introduced by
Henry VIII, and abandoned in 1695 as unenforceable, was restored in a
new form.

The falling price of newsprint and increasing scale economies offered
no relief from dependence on advertising. There was a rapid growth of
advertising in the period after 1860 as a result of the growth in domestic
consumption and structural changes in the economy. By 1907, Critchley
estimates that total advertising expenditure in the United Kingdom — most
of which was spent on the press — had reached £20 million. (Critchley,
1974.) This flow of advertising to the press exerted an upwards pressure
on costs: it led to a steady increase in editorial outlay and paging levels
noted earlier. More important, it also contributed to a further halving of
the price of most popular papers to $\frac{1}{2}$d in the late Victorian period.
National newspapers continued to depend upon advertising in order to
be profitable.

How advertising patronage was distributed consequently largely determined the structure of the press. There is some evidence that advertisers
withheld their support from papers on political grounds. Certainly, succes-

24 There was nothing new, of course, about newspaper dependence on advertising.
   Even in the late eighteenth century the majority of newspapers depended on
   advertising for their profits. (See Cranfield, 1962; Haigh, 1965; Wiles, 1965;
   Christie, 1970; Asquith, 1972.) What was new was about the post-stamp press
   was that all national newspapers in the mass market depended on advertising.

sive governments normally boycotted opposition papers when placing official advertisements and announcements throughout most of the nineteenth century. In the 1850s, a leading press proprietor like Lord Glenersk of the *Morning Post* expected as a matter of course to receive official advertising from a Tory Government in preference to liberal papers. (Hindle, 1937.) Even as late as the 1880s, government advertisements were usually sent only to pro-government papers and, while the Liberals were in power, the *Morning Post* was not on the list. (Lucas, 1911 p. 113.) Some independent advertisers may also have discriminated against radical publications. Lord Crowther, for instance, urged his friends in 1832 to advertise in the Tory local press. (Aspinall, 1949, p. 367.) Charles Mitchell, the head of probably the largest advertising agency in the country in mid-Victorian Britain, clearly thought it relevant to document the political orientation of every newspaper in the country. As he explained in the introduction of his *Directory* in 1856 (5th edition), 'Till this *Directory* was published, the advertiser had no means of accurately determining which journal might be best adopted to his views, and most likely to forward his interests'. Even as late as 1925, Norman Hunter in *Advertising Through the Press*, one of Pitman's practical handbooks, advised the advertiser to 'pick out those [publications] which by the *soundness of their policy*, the extent of their circulation and the price of their advertisements, appear most likely to be beneficial for his purpose' (Hunter, 1925 p. 50 – my italics). Norman Hunter was the exception rather than the rule; by then it had become common for advertising texts to remonstrate against mixing politics with business. The trouble in practice was that it was very difficult to separate politics from commercial judgement since, in the absence of survey evidence about the social composition of a paper's readership, a paper's politics afforded one of the few guides there were to the purchasing power and class of its readers. This led to the stereotyping of 'socialist' papers as appealing to the working class rather than to a cross-sectional mass market.[25]

While the extent of political discrimination (both conscious and unconscious) by advertisers in the Victorian and Edwardian era can never be clearly established, it is clear that working-class media were consistently discriminated against on the grounds that their audiences did not constitute valuable markets to reach. As Mitchell declared in 1856, 'Some of the most widely circulated journals in the Empire are the worst possible to advertise in. Their readers are not purchasers; and any money thrown upon them is so much thrown away' (Mitchells, 1856 p. 7). The thinking underlying such judgements was simple. As one anonymous expert put it, 'Character is of more importance than number. A journal that circulates

25 The generally low opinion held of down-market media tended also to be confirmed by the analysis of coupon returns and keyed advertisements, developed in the late Victorian era, which put working-class media in an unfavourable light.

a thousand among the upper or middle classes is a better medium than would be one circulating a hundred thousand among the lower classes' (*Guide to Advertisers* (anon.) 1851). The explicit preference expressed for middle-class media in advertising texts of the mid-Victorian period was modified in the latter part of the century with the development of mass marketing. But the stress on the disparity of income persisted in guides to media evaluation. This led to a crucial distinction being made between middle-market and down-market media, between papers which appealed to all classes alike and papers which appealed to the poor. Thus, as Cyril Fox, a lecturer in advertising at the Regent Street Polytechnic wrote in the classic advertising text of the early 1920s, 'for an average proposition, not a Rolls Royce motor car or a three-a-penny fire-lighter, you cannot afford to place your advertisements in a paper which is read by the down-at-heels who buy it to scan the Situations Vacant column . . . . The paper which appeals to the bulk of the buyers is best for you' (Freer, 1921 p. 203).

The strategic control acquired by advertisers over the press profoundly shaped and influenced its development. In the first place, it exerted a powerful pressure on the radical press to move up market as an essential strategy for survival. It forced radical newspapers to redefine their target audience, and this in turn forced them to moderate their radicalism in order to attract readers that advertisers wanted to reach. This process is well illustrated by the career of *Reynolds' News.*

It was founded in 1850 by George Reynolds, who was not only a member of the Chartist National Executive but also a member of its left-wing faction. Reynolds had urged a 'physical force' strategy in 1848 and consistently opposed middle-class collaboration in the early 1850s. His paper was in the *Northern Star* tradition of class-conscious radicalism, attacking industrial capitalism and the exploitation of labour. Like the *Northern Star*, it had close institutional links with the working-class movement, raising money for working-class causes and publishing reports sent in by readers.

Yet, despite its radical origins, *Reynolds' News* progressively changed under the impact of the new economic imperatives of newspaper publishing. The fact that it never provided, even at the outset, a homogeneous theoretical and ideological perspective doubtless made it vulnerable to ideological incorporation. It inevitably responded to the decline of radicalism in the country during the 50s and early 60s. But an important factor in its absorption was the need to attract advertising revenue. The change was symbolized by the inclusion of a regular investment column on friendly societies in the year after the repeal of the advertisement duty as a ploy to attract advertising. A commercial enterprise that had been regularly attacked in radical newspapers as 'a hoax' to persuade working class people to identify with capitalism became a

valuable and much needed source of revenue for the *Reynolds' News*.
While *Reynolds' News* continued for a long time to take a radical stand
on most major events of the day, it came increasingly to express the
individualistic middle-class values of the readers it needed to attract. It
adopted many of the tenets of political economy that it had so
virulently attacked during the 1850s, even to the extent of accepting the
palliatives of 'prudent marriage' (i.e. sexual restraint) and emigration. It
reverted to those common denominators of radicalism that united the
lower middle and working classes — attacks on 'the vices' of the aristocracy,
privilege, corruption in high places, the monarchy, placemen, and the
Church. Attacks on industrial capital were modulated to attacks on
monopoly and speculators: criticism of shopkeepers as the exploitive
agents of capital were displaced by new consumer features. *Reynolds'
News* became a populist paper catering for a coalition of middle-class and
working-class readers necessary for its survival. Under new ownership, it
finally evolved without difficulty into becoming a liberal paper in the late
nineteenth century. Reynolds was accused of commercial opportunism by
his contemporaries, yet it is difficult to see what else he could have
done — if the *Reynolds' News* was to survive the transition to an
advertising-based system intact. Even the Chartist *People's Paper* stressed
in an advertisement placed in Mitchell's *Directory* (1857—8) that it
circulated not only among 'the working class generally' but also 'among
high paid trades and shopkeepers'. Despite the fact that its circulation far
exceeded that of most of its rivals selling at the same price, it was forced
to close down.[26]

Radical newspapers could survive in the new economic environment
only if they moved up market to attract an audience desired by advertisers
or remained in a small working-class ghetto, with manageable losses that
could be met from donations. Once they moved out of that ghetto and
attracted a growing working-class audience, they courted disaster. Each
paper cost more to produce than the price at which it was sold, so that
any increase in circulation meant increased losses unless supported by
increased advertising.

This fate befell the radical *Evening Echo* which was taken over by
wealthy radicals in 1901 and given a further push to the left under its
new editor in 1902. A special number was issued setting out the aims
and policy of the paper under new management, firmly committing it to
'the interests of Labour as against the tyranny of organized capital'. In
the period 1902—4, its circulation rose by a phenomenal 60%, leading to
its abrupt closure in 1905. The growth of advertising had failed to keep
pace with the growth of circulation, making the continuance of the paper

26 Its circulation exceeded that of the *Leader*, *John Bull*, *Britannia*, *Empire*, *Atlas*,
    Illustrated Times and the *Spectator* amongst others. (*Mitchell's Newspaper Press
    Directory 1857—8*.)

impossible. (Pethick-Lawrence, 1943 p. 65.)

The same thing almost happened to the *Daily Herald*, when it was re-launched as a daily in 1919 with substantial capital support enabling it to spend £10,000 on promotion — a small amount by comparison with its rivals (the *Daily Mail* spent over £1 million alone on free gifts and other forms of below-the-line promotion during the 1920s) but sufficient to ensure that a paper like the *Daily Herald* with a naturally large potential readership sharply increased its circulation. 'Our success in circulation,' recalled George Lansbury, 'was our undoing. The more copies we sold, the more money we lost.' (Lansbury, 1925 p. 160.) The situation became increasingly desperate when, partly aided by the unexpected publicity of attacks on the *Daily Herald* by leading member of the government alleging that it was financed with 'red gold', the *Daily Herald*'s circulation continued to rise in 1920. 'Every copy we sold was sold at a loss,' mourned Lansbury. 'The rise in circulation, following the government's attacks, bought us nearer and nearer to disaster.' (Lansbury, p. 161.) The money raised from whist drives, dances, draws and the like was not enough to offset the short-fall of advertising. Even the strategem of increasing the paper's price by 100% did not compensate for lack of advertising, despite the fact that it meant charging twice the price of its rivals for a paper that was very much smaller. Money from the miners and the railwaymen stopped the paper from closing. But the only way the paper survived was by being taken over as the official organ of the Labour Party and TUC in 1922. A paper that had been a free-wheeling vehicle of the left, an important vehicle for the dissemination of syndicalist ideas in the early part of the twentieth century, became the official mouthpiece of the moderate leadership of the Labour movement. Lack of advertising forced it to become subservient to a new form of control.

In short, one of four things happened to national radical papers that failed to meet the requirements of advertisers. They either closed down; accommodated to advertising pressure by moving up market; stayed in a small audience ghetto with manageable losses; or accepted an alternative source of institutional patronage.

The obverse to this is that the section of the press which did prosper and expand consisted of publications which conformed to the requirements of advertisers — professional, trade and technical journals providing a valuable segmentation of the market; middle-class newspapers reaching the quality market; and, in popular journalism, middle-market newspapers straddling the social classes and subject to all the cultural and political constraints of catering for heterogeneous audiences. The rapid growth of advertising created the market opportunities for the launch of these categories of publication; it subsidized their costs, financed their development, and created their profits. Its impact can be observed in the phenomenal growth of magazines in the Victorian era (many of them, trade, technical, professional and 'class' publications) from 557 magazines in 1866 to 2,097 in 1896; in the creation of a regional daily press which did not exist in England before the repeal of the advertisement duty but which numbered 196 regional dailies in 1900; in the rapid expansion of middle-class and middle-market community papers (there were 868 newspapers in 1860, compared with 2,355 in 1896) and, above all, in the development of a middle-market popular national press.[27] The basis was laid for the expansion of a powerful institution of social control reaching wide and deep into society.[28]

Characteristics of the Post-Stamp Press 1855—1920

The development of the post-stamp press helped to divide and fragment the working-class movement and facilitate its incorporation into the Liberal and Tory parties. Most radical papers during the first half of the nineteenth century consistently denounced the parliamentary parties and sometimes adopted a highly relativistic approach to the parliamentary system itself. In contrast, the majority of newspapers that sprung up after the repeal of the press taxes were closely affiliated to one or other of the political parties and almost unanimously portrayed parliament as the means of resolving conflict and effecting social change. Thus, ten of the new regional dailies that emerged between 1855 to 1860 were affiliated to the Liberal party; eighteen of the new regional dailies created between 1860 and 1870 were affiliated to the Tory or Liberal parties; and forty-one of the regional dailies created in the following decade were similarly linked to the two great parties. (Mitchells 1860—1880.) They played an important part in mobilizing working-class support for what had been essentially aristocratic factions in Parliament, converting them into mass political organizations. No less important, the popular press played a significant role, as John Vincent (1966) has shown in his study of the Liberal party, in invigorating the parliamentary parties themselves, by providing a vitalizing channel of communication with their rank and file.

The new popular national press that developed notably during the period 1880 to 1920 was also a powerful source of social cohesion. The values and perspectives that it mediated were at total variance with those

27 The figures for regional dailies relate to Britain and for other categories of publication to the United Kingdom, as reported in *Mitchell's Newspaper Press Directory*.

28 No reference has been made to the strategic control that W. H. Smith acquired over the distribution of newspapers in mid-Victorian Britain. The extent of its market ascendancy is indicated by Chilston (1965) and its role in the censorship of books is suggested by Altick (1957) and Mumby and Norris (1974). Smith's may well have performed a similar role in relation to newspapers. This is an aspect of the development of the press which should be investigated and which can be readily researched in view of the very extensive historical archives retained by the company.

mediated by early radical newspapers. A construction of reality as a system of exploitation gave way to a new definition of society in which even the existence of class conflict was denied (a position resolutely maintained even in relation to the General Strike of 1926).[29] The portrayal of labour as the source of wealth was replaced by the portrayal of 'profits' as the source of wealth and the entrepreneur as the essential midwife of Britain's prosperity. The stress on collective action gave way to a stress on individual self-improvement and the myth that anyone through his own efforts could become successful. The political orientation of the national press can best be indicated by the support given to the different political parties in the 1922 General Election. The national government obtaining 50% of the vote received the endorsement of 96% of national daily papers and 86% of national Sunday papers sold in Britain. The Labour party obtaining 29.5% of the vote received support from 4% of national daily papers sold in Britain and no support from the national Sunday press.[30]

The extent to which the press of Victorian Britain mediated the dominant ideology of society is illustrated by its portrayal of Britain's imperial role. Britain's imperial involvements were portrayed as great adventures, opening up new lands of opportunity in which ordinary people could become rich, and (in some sectors of the press) as evangelical missions for spreading civilization, Christianity and prosperity. The following excerpt from a report of the 1898 Sudan expedition in the *Westminster Gazette* conveys the ethos of the late Victorian press:

A large number of the Tommies had never been under fire before . . . and there was a curious look of suppressed excitement in some of the faces . . . . Now and then I caught in a man's eye the curious gleam which comes from the joy of shedding blood — that mysterious impulse which, despite all the veneer of civilization, still

29 Press coverage in relation to the General Strike described the conflict largely in terms of 'a minority' against 'the majority'. For instance, *The Observer* declared 'Trade unionists in this country . . . are and always will be a minority, and if they seriously try to break the majority, they make it quite certain that the majority, if further provoked, will break them'. (*The Observer*, 16 May 1926.) The minority-majority paradigm contained an implicit explanation of why the conflict had arisen: it was the work of an extremist minority and their defeat was a victory not for the mine owners but for the majority. 'The defeat of the General Strike,' declared the *Daily Mail*, '. . . will end the danger of communist tyranny in Europe.' (*Daily Mail*, 14 May 1926.) Explicit in this formulation was an appeal to the moderate majority to protect themselves against the minority. 'Our people have shown during this crisis an immense courage, and undaunted spirit. They have come forward in their hundreds of thousands to resist the attack upon their hard-won freedom.' (*Daily Mail*, 14 May 1926.) The same labelling device was used in an even more extreme form by the press to delegitimate the National Union of Unemployed Workers during the 1930s, and extensively employed in media coverage of conflict in the 1960s. See the insightful study by Hall (1973).

30 Derived from a content analysis of the press coverage of the 1922 General Election tabulated in terms of circulation.

holds its own in man's nature, whether he is killing rats with a terrier, rejoicing in a prize fight, playing a salmon or potting Dervishes. It was a fine day and we were out to kill something. Call it what you like, the experience is a big factor in the joy of living. (*cit.* Knightly, 1976 p. 41.)

The paper which celebrated 'potting Dervishes' was, in terms of the political spectrum represented by the national press, on 'the left' (i.e. Liberal) and one of the few papers not to join in the hysterical campaign of hatred against the Boers one year later. (Spender, 1927; Price, 1972.)

The Modern Press 1920—76

Space does not permit a detailed examination of the press in the post First World War period, which in any case I have sought to provide else-where. (Curran, 1976.)[31] All that will be attempted is a brief outline of the salient developments of the last half-century.

The structure of the British national newspaper was determined by the interplay of market forces *before* 1920. The rise of publishing costs became so prohibitive, and the market position of leading publications so well entrenched that only two new national papers, both with small circulations, have been successfully established in the last fifty years — the Communist *Sunday Worker,* launched in 1925 and converted into the *Daily Worker* and subsequently *Morning Star,* and the *Sunday Telegraph.*

The structure of the newspaper press has shrunk, however, ensuring that papers established before the First World War, and the multi-media con-glomerates that now own most of them, dominate newspaper publishing in Britain. The three biggest newspaper enterprises before 1890 accounted for only a small fraction of newspaper sales; yet in 1973, the three biggest conglomerates controlled 81% of national Sunday sales and 72% of national daily sales. Underlying this trend towards concentration of owner-ship in the national press are a number of interacting factors of which the effect of scale economies and advertising finance in reducing the number of papers (by enabling market leaders to spend more to enhance their market appeal, thereby, forcing up the costs of their rivals) is perhaps the most important.

The advertising licensing system has remained unchanged. Without exception, every single national paper in the period since 1920 has made a loss on its sales alone (except during the period of stringent newsprint rationing during and immediately after the Second World War). There have been, however, important changes in advertising media planning which have affected the character of the British press. The growth of domestic consumption during the inter-war period enhanced the value of working-class media; the growth of market research, pioneered by the leading advertising agencies in the twenties and thirties, encouraged greater

31 A valuable examination of some of these themes in the post-war period is provided by Hirsch and Gordon (1975).

awareness of the potential advertising value of papers like the *Daily Herald*; and the development of readership research and formalized criteria of media evaluation reduced subjective media judgements that tended to discriminate against radical publications. The change was symbolized by the relaunch of the *Daily Mirror* in 1934–6 as a radical paper, aimed deliberately 'down market'. Nonetheless, the shift was a gradual one. In 1936, for instance, the *Daily Mail* received nearly twice as much display-advertising revenue per copy as the *Daily Herald*. And despite the mythology surrounding the re-launch of the *Daily Mirror*, its conversion to social democracy was tempered by sound commercial judgement and its move down market was a hesitant and cautious one. In 1937, the *Daily Mirror* devoted precisely 8% of its total *news* space to coverage of political, social and economic issues in Britain, less than half of what it had done ten years before. Far from becoming a working-class paper, its readers more closely resembled a cross-section of the population than any other national daily in 1939: it was the perfect middle-market paper.

The post war period witnessed further developments in advertising-media planning, which benefited working class media, notably the development of a new classification system, based on product categories, for analysing newspaper readership that emphasized the increasing purchasing power of working-class readerships. Its effects, as far as the national popular press were concerned, were neutralized by the impact of television, the growth of classified advertising (which mainly benefited the quality press) and the sharp rise in publishing costs encouraged by the non-price competitive strategies of market leaders with large advertising receipts. Myths die hard and it is a recurrent theme of journalists that, in the words of Sir Denis Hamilton (Chairman of Times Newspaper Ltd) 'the *Herald* was beset by the problem which has dogged nearly every newspaper vowed to a political idea: not enough people wanted to read it' (Hamilton, 1976). In fact, the *Daily Herald*, on its death-bed, was read by 4.7 million people — nearly twice as many as the readership of *The Times, Financial Times* and *Guardian* added together. Its readers, as survey research shows, constituted the most committed and the most intensive readers, with the most favourable image of their paper, of any popular national paper in the country. (Curran 1970.) The *Daily Herald*, the lone consistent voice of social democracy in the national daily press, died because its readers were disproportionately poor working class and consequently did not constitute a valuable advertising market to reach.

The effect of the economic structuring of the press is illustrated by the response of the press to the two events in the inter-war period that polarized opinion between social democrats and conservatives — the General Strike of 1926 and the General Election of 1931. Only one national daily paper (*Daily Herald*) out of eleven supported the General Strike (or the 'Strike Evil' as the *Daily Mirror* called it). Only two national daily papers (the

Daily Herald and the newly created *Daily Worker*) supported the Labour Party in the 1931 General Election. Since then, the 'centrality' of the press has become more marked. Every single national daily and national Sunday paper in the country which expressed a preference in the Callaghan—Foot selection for the leadership of the Labour Party (and premiership) supported the right-wing candidate.[32]

Conclusion

The traditional system of control of the press administered through the state broke down in the early nineteenth century in the face of determined opposition from radical journalists sustained by an increasingly politically conscious working class. The ruling class was forced sharply to reduce the stamp duty in 1836 in order to re-establish the stamp as a contol. This arrested but did not prevent the continued development of the radical press which constituted an increasingly disruptive force in society.

In the middle of the nineteenth century, the traditional control system over the press was replaced by a new and more effective control system based on remorseless economic forces which, unlike the law, could be neither evaded nor defied. The capitalist development of the press, with its accompanying rise in publishing costs, led to a progressive transfer of ownership and control of the popular press from the working class to capitalist entrepreneurs, while the advertising licensing system encouraged the absorption or elimination of the early radical press and effectively stifled its re-emergence. Although the character of the modern press has been significantly modified by changes in the operation of market forces since 1920, the press remains a powerful integrative force in society. It has contributed materially to the remarkable stability and high degree of allegiance to British political institutions that has persisted in Britain despite her loss of empire and continuing economic crisis.[33]

References

Advertising Association, 1949: Evidence to the Royal Commission on the Press 1947—1949, *Royal Commission on the Press 1947—9* vol. 5. London: HMSO.

32 Derived from a content analysis of editorials in all national daily and Sunday newspapers. The text relates to the last round of the leadership contest.

33 Despite illusions to the contrary a wealth of empirical evidence documents the high degree of alligiance to British political institutions and the continuing stability of modern British society. See, for example, Almond and Verba (1963), Butler and Stokes (1969), Blumler *et al.* (1971), Rose (1970) and Rose (1974).

1962: Evidence to the Royal Commission on the Press 1961–2, *Royal Commission on the Press 1961–2* vol. 3. London: HMSO.

Almond, Gabrial and Verba, Sidney, 1963: *The Civic Culture.* Princeton: University Press.

Altick, R. D., 1957: *The English Common Reader: a Social History of the Mass Reading Public, 1800–1900.* University of Chicago Press.

Andrews, Alexander, 1859: *The History of British Journalism*, 2 vols. London: Richard Bentley.

Anon, 1935: *History of the Times: 'The Thunder' in the Making 1785– 1841* vol. 1. London: Times.

1939: *History of the Times: The Tradition Established* vol. 2. London: Times.

1851: *Guide to Advertisers.* London.

Aspinall, Arthur, 1949: *Politics and the Press, c1780–1850.* London: Home and Van Thal. (Republished 1973 Harvester Press.)

1950: 'Statistical Accounts of London Newspapers 1800–1836'. *English Historical Review*, LXV.

Asquith, Ivon, 1975: 'Advertising and the press in the late eighteenth and early nineteenth centuries: James Perry and the *Morning Chronicle* 1790–1821'. *Historical Journal*, XVIII (4).

Berridge, Virginia, 1975: 'Political Attitudes and the popular Sunday press in mid-Victorian England'. *Acton Society Paper.*

Blumler, J. G. *et al.*, 1971: 'Attitudes to the Monarchy'. *Political Studies.* XIX (2).

Burnham, Lord, 1955: *Peterborough Court: The Story of the Daily Telegraph.* London: Cassell.

Butler, David and Stokes, Donald, 1969: *Political Change in Britain.* London: Macmillan.

Chaney, David, 1972: *Processes of Mass Communication.* London: Macmillan.

Chilston, Viscount, 1965: *W. H. Smith.* London: Routledge and Kegan Paul.

Christie, Ian R., 1970: *Myth and Reality in Late Eighteenth-Century British Politics and other papers.* London: Macmillan.

Cole, G. D. H., 1947: *The Life of William Cobbett*, 3rd ed. London: Home and Van Thal.

Coltham, Stephen, 1960: 'The *Bee-Hive* Newspaper: Its origins and early development'. In Briggs, Asa, and Saville, John (Eds.), *Essays in Labour History.* London: Macmillan.

Crawley, C. W. (Ed.), 1965: *War and Peace in an Age of Upheaval 1793– 1830.* New Cambridge Modern History vol. 9. London: Cambridge University Press.

Cranfield, George, 1962: *Development of the Provincial Newspaper Press 1700–1760.* Oxford: Oxford University Press.

Curran, James, and Tunstall, Jeremy, 1973: 'Mass Media and Leisure'. In Smith, M., Parker, S. and Smith, C. (Eds.) *Leisure and Society in Britain.* London. Allen Lane.

Curran, James, 1970: 'The Impact of Television on the Audience for National Newspapers 1945–68.' In Tunstall, Jeremy (Ed.), *Media Sociology*, London: Constable.

1976: 'The Impact of Advertising on the Structure of the Modern British Press'. *Royal Commission on the Press Research Paper.*

1977: *Mass Communication as a Social Force in History.* Mass Comcomunication and Society, Course DE353, The Open University Press.

Epstein, J. A., 1976: 'Feargus O'Connor and the *Northern Star*', *International Review of Social History* vol. 22. Part 1.

Foster, John, 1974: *Class Struggle and the Industrial Revolution: Early Industrial Capitalism in Three English Towns.* London: Weidenfeld and Nicolson.

Fox, Bourne, H. R., 1887: *English Newspapers: Chapters in the History of the Press* 2 vols. London: Chatto and Windus.

Frank, Joseph, 1961: *The Beginnings of the English Newspaper 1620– 1660.* Cambridge, Mass.: Harvard University Press.

Freer, Cryil, 1921: *The Inner Side of Advertising: A Practical Handbook for Advertisers.* London: Library Press.

Glasgow, Eric, 1954: 'The Establishment of the *Northern Star* Newspaper'. *History,* XXXIX.

Grant, James, 1871: *The Newspaper Press: Its Origins, Progress and Present Position* 2 vols. London: Tinsley Bros.

Gibbs, Philip, 1923: *Adventure in Journalism.* New York: Harper.

Haigh, R. L., 1968: *The Gazeteer 1735–97.* Illinois: South Illinois University Press.

Hall, Stuart, 1973: 'Deviancy, Politics and the Media'. In McIntosh, M. and Rock, P. (Eds.), *Deviancy and Social Control,* London: Tavistock.

Hamilton, Sir Dennis, 1976: *Who is to own the British Press?* London: Birkbeck College.

Hanson, 1936: *Government and the Press, 1695–1763.* London: Cambridge University Press.

Harris, Michael, 1974: *London Newspaper Press 1700–1750.* Unpub. Ph.D. thesis, University of London.

Herd, Harold, 1952: *The March of Journalism.* London: George Allen and Unwin.

Hindle, W., 1937: *The Morning Post.* London.

Hirsch, Fred and Gordon, David, 1975: *Newspaper Money: Fleet Street and the Search for the Affluent Reader.* London: Hutchinson.

Hollis, Patricia, 1970: *The Pauper Press: A Study in Working-Class Radicalism of the 1830s.* London: Oxford University Press.

Holton, R. J., 1974: '*Daily Herald* v. *Daily Citizen* 1912–15'. *International Review of Social History, XIX.*

Hunt, Frederick Knight, 1850: *The Fourth Estate: Contributions towards a History of Newspapers and of the Liberty of the Press,* 2 vols. London: David Bogue.

Hunter, Norman, 1925: *Advertising Through the Press: A Guide to Press Publicity.* London: Pitman.

JICNARS (Joint Industry Committee for National Readership Surveys), *National Readership 1970–76.* London: Institute of the Practitioners in Advertising.

King, Cecil, 1972: *Diary, 1965—7*. London: Jonathan Cape.
Knightley, Philip, 1975: *The First Casualty: The War Correspondent as Hero, Propagandist, and Myth Maker from the Crimea to Vietnam*. London: Andre Deutsch.
Lansbury, George, 1925: *The Miracle of Fleet Street*. London: Victoria House.
Lee, Alan J., 1974: 'The Radical Press'. In Morris A. J. (ed.) *Edwardian Radicalism 1900—14*. London: Routledge and Kegan Paul.
Lucas, Reginald, 1910: *Lord Glenesk and the Morning Post*. London.
Mumby, F., and Norrie, L., 1974: *Publishing and Bookselling*. London: Methuen.
Musson, A. E., 1954: *The Typographical Association: Origins and History up to 1949*. London: Oxford University Press.
Mitchell's Newspaper Press Directory. London: Mitchell.
Pound, Reginald and Harmsworth, Geoffrey, 1959: *Northcliffe*. London: Cassell.
Pethick-Lawrence, F. W., 1943: *Fate Has Been Kind*. London: Hutchinson.
Price, Richard, 1972: *An Imperial War and the British Working Class: Working Class Attitudes and Reactions to the Boer War 1899—1902*. London: Routledge and Kegan Paul.
Read, Donald, 1961: *Press and People, 1790—1850: Opinion in Three English Cities*. London: Edward Arnold.
Roach, John, 1965: 'Education and Public opinion'. In Crawley, C. W. (Ed.), *War and Peace in an Age of Upheaval (1793—1830)*. London: Cambridge University Press.
Rose, Richard, 1970: *People in Politics: Observations Across the Atlantic*. London: Faber and Faber.
    1974: *Politics in England*. London: Faber and Faber.
Rostenburg, Leona, 1971: *The Minority Press and the English Crown: A Study in Repression 1558—1625*. Nieuwkoop: De Graaf.
Royal Commission on the Press 1947—9 Report. London: HMSO, 1949.
Royal Commission on the Press 1961—2 Report. London: HMSO, 1962.
Sanderson, M., 1972: 'Literacy and Social Mobility in the Industrial Revolution'. *Past and Present* 56.
Schoyen, A. R., 1956: *The Chartist Challenge: A Portrait of George Julian Harney*. London: Heinemann.
Select Committee on Newspaper Stamps, 1851: Report, Together with the Proceedings of the Committee, Minutes of Evidence, Appendix and Index. *Parliamentary Papers*. XVII.
Seymour-Ure, Colin, 1975: 'The Press and the Party System Between the Wars'. In Peele, Gillan, and Cook, Chris (Eds.), *The Politics of Reappraisal 1918—39*. London: Macmillan.
Siebert, Frederick S., 1952: *Freedom of the Press in England 1479—1776: The Rise and Decline of Government Control*. Urbana, Ill.: University of Illinois Press.
Spender, J. A., 1927: *Life, Journalism and Politics* 2 vols. London: Cassell.
Stone, Lawrence, 1969: 'Literacy and Education in England 1640—1900'. *Past and Present* 42.

Taylor, A. J. P., 1972: *Beaverbrook*. London: Hamish Hamilton.

Thomas, J. A., 1958: *The House of Commons 1906—11*. Cardiff.

Thompson, E. P., 1963: *The Making of the English Working Class*. London: Victor Gollancz.

Vincent, John, 1972: *The Formation of the British Liberal Party 1857— 68*. London: Pelican.

Webb, R. K., 1955: *The British Working Class Reader, 1790—1848: Literacy and Social Tension*. London: Allen and Unwin.

Webb, R. K., 1950: 'Working Class Readers in Victorian England'. *English Historical Review* LXV.

Westmacott, C. M., 1936: *The Stamp Duties*. London.

Wickwar, William H., 1928: *The Struggle for the Freedom of the Press 1819—32*. London: Allen and Unwin.

Wiener, Joel H., 1969a: *The War of the Unstamped: The Movement to Repeal the British Newspaper Tax 1830—36*. Ithaca: Cornell University Press.

Wiener, Joel H., 1969b: *A Descriptive Findings List of Unstamped Periodicals 1830—36*. London: Bibliographical Society.

Wilensky, Harold L., 1964: 'Mass Society and Mass Culture', *American Sociological Review*, XXIX.

Wiles, R. M., 1965: *Freshest Advices: Early Provincial Newspapers in England*. Ohio: Ohio State University Press.

Williams, Francis, 1957: *Dangerous Estate: The Anatomy of Newspapers*. London: Longmans, Green.

Williams, Raymond, 1965: *The Long Revolution*. London: Pelican.

Wilson, Trevor (Ed.), 1970: *The Political Diaries of C. P. Scott 1911—28*. London: Collins.

Woodward, L., 1962: *The Age of Reform 1815—70*, Rev. edn. Oxford: University Press.

Wrench, John Evelyn, 1955: *Geoffrey Dawson and our Times*. London: Hutchinson.

9

Holding the Middle Ground: The BBC, the public and the professional broadcaster

Krishan Kumar

Of an Autobiographical Kind

Every new BBC producer finds himself, very early on in his working life, in a certain paradoxical and deeply frustrating situation. It has to do with the selection of broadcasters. At the regular departmental meeting chaired by the Head of Department (or those chaired by the Controller of a channel), concern is voiced at the persistent domination of the programme schedules by the same voices and faces — the 'stage army' of broadcasters. Producers are urged to seek out fresh voices, put fresh views on the air. Everyone at the programme meetings nods agreement, and confirms that they are constantly on the look-out for new people. The newer arrivals among the producers respond with special feeling, having noted this as a point of major criticism of the mass media, from the outside. Now with their newly-acquired power of selection they are anxious to help remedy this situation.

At some subsequent meeting the new producer eagerly offers a set of programme ideas, attached to which are the names of individuals who, he is convinced, are men of knowledge, talent, or wit, but many of whom perhaps are new to broadcasting. After a certain amount of general discussion, the response comes something as follows. Head of department (or Controller):

Yes, I'm sure these are all very good chaps, experts in their field, and all that — but are you sure we can rely upon them as broadcasters? I mean, it looks as if very few of these people have broadcast before, and, you know, it's not all the same thing to write interestingly about a thing and talk about it . . . . Why don't you use them as programme consultants — perhaps even interview one or two of them? But make sure the thing is handled by a professional — get an experienced broadcaster to put the questions, and to present the programme, to give it a shape . . . . We really can't take the risk.

The astounded producer looks around for the expected support of his case from his longer-established colleagues, in the face of this clear volte-face — and reads in their unresponsive faces the equally clear evidence of his naivety.

As a new producer[1] I had to undergo repeated experiences of this kind at programme meetings before finally tumbling to the secret, one which my colleagues had obviously learned and absorbed a long way back in their careers. From then on life became very much easier. My programme ideas slipped through, often on the nod, because I had taken the care to figure in them the names of established and approved broadcasters: as mainline contributors, chairman, or presenters. Conversations with other producers in a wide range of departments revealed innumerable instances of the same thing. But it was only gradually that I realized that my day-to-day frustrations, when I had worried over mainly practical terms, were in fact offering me a way of seeing some fundamental points about the institutional structure, and the political context of action of the BBC.

Of course my seniors were probably often right, in a purely professional sense, in preventing some people from getting on the air who would have made poor broadcasters. And of course they justified their action in strictly professional terms: their job was to put out lively, attractive broadcasting. But this very notion of 'lively broadcasting' expresses a particular stance towards the audience, a judgement of what the audience can and cannot take, which reflects a particular conception of the purposes of broadcasting. But there is more than this. The elevation of professionalism as the prime virtue of the communicator — both as producer and as presenter — itself reflects a particular moment in the evolution of the broadcasting organization. At other times other qualities would have seemed more important. In the time of Reith at the BBC, for instance, professional skills would have been assumed and cultivated. But there would never have been any question but these technical skills should be quite subordinate to the overriding goals of the BBC as Reith had conceived them: the goals of lifting the British nation to new moral and cultural heights. Moreover, it would have been assumed that this was a feasible aim, in the sense that the social and political constraints permitted and indeed encouraged it. To make professional presentation the goal of broadcasting, to elevate, so to speak, the means to the ends, is to indicate a very different reading both of the possibilities of broadcasting and of the social environment in which it operates.[2]

I was confronted, then, with an ideology of professionalism which set

1 I was a producer in the BBC's Talks and Documentaries department during the year 1972—3.
2 Tom Burns, in his study of BBC staff conducted in 1963—4, observes that 'the word "professional" has an extraordinarily wide currency in the Corporation', but notes, interestingly, that of the many different connotations of the term the meaning most frequently alluded to was the simplest one 'merely the opposite of "amateur" — good of its kind, expert, finished' (instead, for example, of emphasizing the service ideal, the duty to clients — in this case, the audience). Burns, 'Public Service and Private World', in J. Tunstall (Ed.), *Media Sociology*, Constable, 1970, p. 153.

severe limitations on my power of selection of people, and which again
and again directed me back to the tried and trusted names of broadcasting.
The reflections which follow, on the current role and functions of the
professional broadcaster, were provoked by that situation. I cannot claim
to be offering more than a general picture. But studies, such as there are,[3]
of professional communicators, have tended to concentrate overwhelmingly
on the newspaper journalist. There is almost nothing on the professional
broadcaster.[4] This fact in itself might serve partly to excuse the unfinished
nature of these thoughts. But there is also the additional possibility of
casting some light on the present situation of the BBC which, because it
comes from an unfamiliar source, might be the more revealing.

The Tightrope

A good deal of assertion, not anything like as much detailed illustration,
exists on the theme of the mass media as constituents of the ideological
structures of the dominant groups and institutions of British society.[5] We
know a certain amount about the 'mobilization of bias' in the media's
handling of news and day-to-day issues of politics, and even more about
it in their conceptions and treatment of political and social deviance.[6] I
don't in general want to disagree with this view. But it can have unfortunate
consequences. It leads often to the scanning of media messages for the
rather too easily readable evidence of the assumptions of the ruling culture.
There is a tendency then, once an exercise of this kind has been done,
either to repeat it because it is easy (black for queers, women for proles),
or simply to write off the media as negligible social factors, the mere
servants of power.

Whether this is a true verdict on the other media I don't know. But I

3 For some lively general observations, mainly to do with the newspaperman, see
James W. Carey, 'The Communications Revolution and the Professional Com-
municator', in P. Halmos (Ed.), *The Sociology of Mass Media Communicators:
Sociological Review Monograph*, No. 13, University of Keele, 1969, pp. 23–8.
4 Although there are a few useful reflections by the professionals themselves – e.g.,
John Whale, *The Half-Shut Eye: Television and Politics in Britain and America*,
London: Macmillan, 1969; Robin Day, *T.V.: A Personal Report*, London:
Hutchinson, 1961.
5 For a clear statement of this view see the Free Communications Groups pamphlet,
Television and the State, Bristol, 1971. See also Stuart Hall, 'The Limitations of
Broadcasting', *The Listener*, 16 March 1972; Stuart Hood, 'The Politics of Tele-
vision', in D. McQuail (Ed.), *Sociology of Mass Communications*, London: Penguin
Books, 1972, pp. 406–34; G. Murdock and P. Golding, 'For a Political Economy
of Mass Communications', *The Socialist Register 1973*, London: The Merlin Press,
1973, pp. 205–34.
6 See for example the collection of essays in S. Cohen and J. Young (Eds.), *The
Manufacture of News: Deviance, Social Problems, and the Mass Media*, London:
Constable, 1973.

think it is likely to be misleading with regard to the BBC, and particularly so at the present time. It ignores certain features of the BBC as an institution which, for reasons of accident or structure, have given it at different times a considerable degree of autonomy *vis-à-vis* other national institutions. And it ignores the fact that the BBC cannot rest content with mere institutional survival, as the cat's-paw of the ruling groups: that in order to survive in something like the terms in which it has marked out its identity, it has been forced to adopt various strategies of survival which again and again put it at risk, and bring it into conflict with the powerful groups outside it. It is in fact a particular strategy of this sort, in the changed conditions of the last twenty years, that has made so prominent the issue of the selection, retention, and fostering of particular broadcasters.

To understand this present strategy we need to take particular note of two considerations, of a historical and cultural kind.

The first is that of the quite unusual cultural importance that attaches to the BBC in Britain. People here who do not know much about the broadcasting systems of other countries are apt to assume that there are equivalents (more or less) of the BBC in many places. And so there are, in a strictly constitutional sense. But the striking thing is the singularity of the BBC's position, as a major component of the national culture, when compared with broadcasting organizations in other countries. In the United States, for instance, it is true that, as elsewhere, most people watch television for a good part of their waking lives (if that is the right term). But very few people think of the broadcasting institutions as of central significance, as genuine contributors to the national culture (although they might think of the film or popular musical industries in that way). It is assumed, rightly, that television and radio are dominated by commercial interests and considerations. The cultural products of broadcasting are regarded as so much moving wall-paper, along with advertising and other expressions of commercial art by which American senses are first assaulted and then made indifferent. No intellectual worth his salt thinks of broadcasting as a worthwhile and intrinsically satisfying career — although it may be followed as a lucrative pursuit.[7]

At the other extreme there is the situation like the French one where, for entirely different reasons, the broadcasting institutions are similarly disregarded by serious intellectuals: because they are assumed, rightly, to be dominated by the interests of the state which directly controls them.

State and commerce: around one or another of these poles are gathered the vast majority of the broadcasting systems of the world.

The BBC has, in certain important ways, been able to resist these two forms of identification. As a non-profitmaking corporate body, set up by

7 Which is not to deny the system threw up some notable talents — outstanding among whom were Ed Murrow and Fred Friendly.

Royal Charter supplemented by a Licence granted by the Minister of Posts and Telecommunications, who also controls the amount, and supervises the collection of the licence fees, its natural pole of gravitation is the state. This pull is strengthened by the absolute veto which the Minister of Posts holds over any matter to be broadcast. As Professor Robson noted in an early (1935) analysis, 'the Government possesses enormous contingent power over the BBC'.[8] And of course the state can and has put a great deal of pressure on the BBC, as was amply shown at the time of the General Strike of 1926.[9]

But the identification with the state, on the French model, did not take place. This fact had a great deal to do with the interpretation put upon his functions — one is tempted in his case to say, his 'calling' — by the first Director-General of the BBC, John Reith. From the earliest days Reith steered clear of direct political confrontations. He gave way at the time of the General Strike; in 1934 Vernon Bartlet, BBC commentator on foreign affairs, was sacked following strong Parliamentary criticism of some of his broadcasts; throughout the 1930s Reith allowed the party whips to dictate which politicians should broadcast — which meant, for instance, refusing the microphone to Winston Churchill.[10] At the same time the BBC made little attempt to extend the scope of news programmes, the other area where political controversy was most likely to flare. Under pressure from the newspaper proprietors the BBC made no efforts to gather news for itself; its news bulletins mainly transmitted items taken from the regular news agencies. Reith's strategy seemed fully to endorse the view of the Sykes Committee of 1923: 'The public is well served by the Press in the matter of news, and we consider that any extension of the broadcasting of news should be carried out gradually, the effect of each extension being carefully watched . . .'.[11]

8 W. A. Robson, 'The BBC as an Institution', *The Political Quaterly*, 6, 1935, p. 470.

9 In 1926 the BBC quite clearly accepted dictation from the government over who should broadcast — and in particular accepted the government's view that, since the courts had declared the General Strike illegal, there should be no speaker from the Labour Party or the trade unions. This was the price paid, as Reith admitted in a confidential memorandum to his senior staff, for keeping the BBC from being commandeered. For the details, including Reith's memorandum, see A. Briggs, *The Birth of Broadcasting* (Vol. 1, *The History of Broadcasting in the United Kingdom*), London: Oxford University Press, 1961, pp. 360—84.

10 See Briggs, *The Golden Age of Wireless* (Vol. II, *The History of Broadcasting in the United Kingdom*), London: Oxford University Press, 1965, pp. 145—6. Briggs comments: 'The mood of the 1930s was not cogenial to the forthright communication of Churchillian themes, and the BBC did not seek to dispel it'. *Ibid.*, p. 146.

11 Quoted A. Smith, *The Shadow in the Cave: The Broadcaster, The Audience, and The State*, London: Allen and Unwin, 1973a, p. 43.

Following this assessment of the position of broadcasting, the early BBC gave political discussion and analysis a low priority in its main concerns. And correspondingly the politicians left it alone in the other areas where it rapidly built up a national reputation and standing quite independently of the other national institutions. In this the politicians showed themselves the prisoners of narrow and outmoded conceptions of politics. They wished to keep the BBC out of politics, and they were satisfied in gaining control over such matters as the appearance of politicians on the air, and the output of matter of an overtly political kind. They could not see, or perhaps they could do nothing about, the shaping influences that operated below the level of political institutions, in the ordinary day-to-day thoughts and activities of the mass of the population. A social revolution had been brewing over the past century in England, and Reith was there to inherit it. Despite the associations of the BBC with 'the Establishment', Reith belongs more with Northcliffe and Henry Ford than (say) with Geoffrey Dawson, editor of *The Times*. His style and purpose were vastly different from those purveyors of mass culture. But he exploited the same social currents and forces. There was the fact of massive urbanization; the rise in working-class incomes; the decline in hours of work; the development of a system of mass education. These developments opened up a vast new cultural terrain into whose features the BBC insinuated itself, at all levels. While the politicians were guarding the entry to the tent, Reith sneaked in under the skirting at the side.

The BBC did not, of course, unlike its American counterparts, seek to rival the other media of mass culture. Reith interpreted the injunction of the BBC's Charter, to inform, educate, and entertain, fully in the spirit of Mathew Arnold. It was through its classical music, plays, poetry, talks discussions — as well as its comedies, reviews, and dance music — that the BBC established itself as a distinctive and finally authoritive national cultural institution. Its claim to have created a 'common culture' can certainly be disputed; what cannot be disputed is that all groups rapidly came to acknowledge that it had asserted for itself an identity that was separate from but equal to that of national institutions of much longer standing. In a sense it could hardly fail to do this. There was the unique mass immediacy of the new medium. There was the BBC's privileged monopoly position. There was its status as a non-profitmaking, non-governmental organization. All these features meant that over the years it was bound to acquire a unique cultural significance. It is generally agreed that it was during the Second World War that the BBC set the seal on its development as a distinctive national institution. What is less clear is whether this was due to the authority conferred on it by its partnership with the National Government, or whether to the authority it conferred on that Government. Certainly it is some

testimony to its continuing importance — at least as perceived — that a
recent poll conducted by *The Times* showed that the BBC was thought
by a cross-section of men and women in *Who's Who* to be more influential
than either Parliament or the Church.[12]

The BBC has become a national institution, a focus of national interest
and concern, in a manner very different from almost all other broadcasting
institutions in other countries. It is thought of — and the commonness of
this view makes it no longer even seem surprising — in the terms usually
reserved for the venerable institutions of British society — Parliament, the
Civil Service, the Law Courts, the colleges of Cambridge and Oxford. As a
result a career within the BBC has come to seem as attractive and worthwhile as a career in any of these other institutions — again, a situation that
has seemed remarkable in the eyes of foreign broadcasters. A General
Traineeship at the BBC was — until its recent suppression — one of the
most prized graduate appointments, more even, for instance, than entrance
for the Foreign Office.[13] Anthony Jay, who sat on the BBC appointments
boards in the 1960s says that 'for years BBC television has been first
choice of a quite disproportionate number of the nation's best qualified
graduates. The number and quality of the BBC's unsolicited applications
still astonishes recruitment officers from other corporations'.[14]

There is this first consideration, then, of the centrality of the BBC[15]
in the national culture. It is a centrality which the BBC itself is acutely
aware of, which it prizes, and which has set the terms in which it has
constructed its identity. It acts as a powerful constraint upon its
behaviour, the source at once of its proverbial caution and conservatism,
as well as of its need and ability to fend off identification with the other
national institutions that press in on it. To this must be added the second
principal consideration which has shaped the BBC's conception of its
position over the long term. It is one which, on the whole, points the
BBC in almost exactly the opposite direction. As Anthony Smith has
pointed out, for most of its fifty-year life the BBC has lived under a more
or less constant threat to its security and perhaps even its sheer survival.[16]
It has lived on the brink of one crisis or another, under the scrutiny of
one commission or another, at the centre of one or another public row,
at regular intervals throughout its life.

Partly this has been due to the obligation to submit its charter for

12 See 'Taste and Standards in BBC Programmes' (London: BBC 1973, p. 4).
13 See A. Smith, in *Daily Telegraph Magazine*, 7 November 1973b.
14 A. Jay, *Public Words and Private Words*, London: Society of Film and Television
    Arts, November 1972, p. 6.
15 And, by extension, of the other British broadcasting institutions that were set
    up — although the fact that they are commercially based has affected not just
    their own standing, but, through their effect on BBC strategy, British broad-
    casting as a whole.
16 Smith 1973a, pp. 88 ff.

renewal every ten years, an occasion which has always given rise to a large-scale public inquiry. Early on there was the Sykes Committee of 1923 and the Crawford Committee of 1926; then the Ullswater Committee of 1936, the Beveridge Committee of 1951, and the Pilkington Committee of 1962; soon the Annan Committee will report. In addition there have been a large number of special government broadcasting memoranda dealing with such matters as the organization of wartime censorship, and the introduction of a television service. Then there have been the major controversies over specific programmes such as *That Was the Week That Was, The Question of Ulster, Yesterday's Men.*

All of these affairs have entailed periods of special tension inside Broadcasting House; every moment of BBC history has been dominated by the shadow or aftermath of one of them . . . and every stretch of time in broadcasting history has been distinguished by some important impending decision which could foster or threaten the vital interests of the entire enterprise.[17]

It is these two considerations, taken together, which have made it difficult for the BBC to act as a simple channel of the attitudes and values of the dominant groups. On the one hand, its national standing has turned essentially on its ability to remain clear of political affiliation or involvement: to be seen or thought to be too friendly to the state would have been the kiss of death, the reduction to a position of Gallic dependence. On the other hand, it has been reminded at every turn of its history of its ultimate reliance on the state (over matters such as the allocation of wavelengths, the renewal of the charter, the increase of the licence fee). This latter factor does of course claim priority. It is about survival in its most basic sense, and must and does figure predominantly in the calculations of the higher management of the BBC. But there is also survival in the only sense valued by most people who work in the BBC, in the terms in which it acquired its cultural significance, especially in the Reithian era, and in which it marked out its role as an independent and equal estate of the realm. Its entire credibility as an institution depends upon its maintaining some sort of existence in these terms. This has meant the adoption of particular strategies which at different times and at various points have jarred against the ruling institutional complexes and assumptions. Generally this has been done in such a way as not seriously to incur the threat of political *Gleichschaltung* — although it has for instance sometimes entailed the appointment of highly unpopular government 'placemen' in the key position of chairman of the BBC's Board of Governors. But it has also meant that the medium of broadcasting retains the capacity for opening up issues in some surprizing and unexpected ways; the mask occasionally slips, and we are given a glimpse of a range of options and possibilities normally closed off.

17   A. Smith, 'Internal Pressures in Broadcasting', *New Outlook*, 4, 1972, p. 4.

Walking the Tightrope: The Role of the Professional Broadcaster

It is in the context of considerations such as these that the position of the professional broadcaster has its special significance. Especially in recent years, it is through the recruitment and deployment of a remarkably small body of professional communicators that the BBC has sought to walk the kind of tightrope that it has to between the drop on the one side into utter governmental dependence and that on the other into suicidal opposition to it.

I am not referring here to the particular individuals who from time to time get established as the ripe 'personalities' of the air, and who develop national reputations on the basis of broadcasting appearances: the Gilbert Hardings, Robert Boothbys, 'Farmer' Ted Moults, and so on. Their importance has in any case declined in recent years. Nor am I referring to the producers, the staff employees of the Corporation. The 'professional broadcasters' that matter in this context are the 'front men' who actually appear on the air: the regular reporters, presenters, interviewers, chairmen – the Robin Days, Kenneth Allsops, Ludovic Kennedys. It is these men, the 'anchor-men' or 'link-men' of the regular programmes who map out for the public – as the BBC management is well aware – the points of identification with the BBC, and who have become increasingly prominent in the broadcasting organization's strategy.

The importance of the professional broadcaster has grown steadily during the course of the BBC's history, to the point where in recent years he has come to rival the earlier-established 'amateur' broadcasting personality. In any case, so far as the matter of identification with the BBC is concerned, he was bound to be in a stronger position since his 'official' status was never in question. This was so right from the early years, when the band of professional broadcasters was very small and consisted mainly of announcers and continuity men, most of whom were anonymous. It is striking that from the very start Reith and his senior staff adopted a deliberate policy of using the announcers to create 'the public image' of the BBC. The very decision to make announcers anonymous followed from this policy, as did the sedulous cultivation of their formality. Both were intended to create a particular style by which the BBC could be identified in the public mind, and which more than any other device was to be used to establish its claim to a special moral and cultural authoritativeness.

There was nothing 'natural' or inevitable about this direction. Other broadcasting styles, emphasizing informality and personality, were current at the time, especially in the United States. But 'highly individualized announcing in the American style' was explicitly rejected. By contrast it was argued that announcers were better placed than any other BBC employees 'to build up in the public mind a sense of the BBC's collective personality'. Reith always put stress on the 'moral' qualities of his staff, as much as on their professional or artistic ones. In 1924 he was urging station directors to think of announcers as 'men of culture, experience and knowledge'. In 1925 Walter Fuller wrote in an official memorandum on programme presentation, that 'the training and equipment of an efficient body of announcers' was a means of presenting to the general public 'not only the daily programmes in an attractive way' but 'the BBC itself, its policy and ideals, as a great public service institution for entertainment, education and inspiration'.[18] By 1936 the language had become positively Hegelian. In a memorandum of that year the Announcement Editor was writing:

The BBC is one Corporation, and can only be thought of by the listener as individual. It has many voices but one mouth. It can speak in many styles, but the variety is due to the difference of subject matter and must not betray any inconsistency of treatment. It is a commonplace that 'announcers sound all alike'. That is a tribute to their training . . . .

The corollary followed that 'it is essential that the announcer should announce two concert parties in the same *style* — *that* is what the BBC thinks of concert parties — but not, however, necessarily in the same words'.[19]

What went for announcers has gone for the later groups of professional broadcasters. They, too, are expected to represent the BBC's 'collective personality'. In the earlier years the announcers acted as both continuity men, and often, newsreaders. When the decision was made, during the Second World War, to identify the newsreaders by name,[20] the personalization of the announcers furthered the process by which the public came to see in them the visible hall-marks of the Corporation. To earlier household names among the announcers, Peter Eckersley, Stuart Hibberd — were added newer ones, associated particularly with the *News,* such as Alvar Lidell, Frank Phillips, John Snagge, later Robin Holmes. And while the distinction between the announcers and the newsreaders has never been made absolute, the enormous extension in news and current affairs coverage since the late 1950s has inevitably brought about something of a specialization. The announcers have the important function of providing continuity on any of the main networks and channels. They carry the listener or the viewer throughout the day — or a substantial part of it —

18 All these statements are quoted in Briggs, *The Birth of Broadcasting*, pp. 292–4.
19 Briggs *ibid.*, p. 123.
20 The anonymity rule was ended in 1940 through the fear that the Germans might try to put out fake bulletins. As Briggs says, the move — which was an immensely popular one — was 'a recognition that the source was more important than the medium or the message'. Briggs, *The War of Words* (Vol. III, *The History of Broadcasting in the United Kingdom*). Oxford University Press, 1970, p. 202. p. 202.

linking the different times, shaping the day's presentations, explicitly or implicitly urging an identification between the audience and the particular network through the person of the announcer. The announcers and continuity men are known by name; they announce themselves at various intervals throughout the day, on both radio and television (in the latter case they are not only seen but have their names printed). The importance of the regular announcers in providing a 'spine' to the day's programmes is perhaps most clearly seen on BBC's Radio One, with its domination by a few strongly-marked personalities, the regular 'disc jockeys', acting as presenters and continuity men; but the phenomenon can also readily be observed on the other networks.[21]

The announcers and continuity men constitute the earliest stratum in a roughly three-layered system of professional presentation. Historically the next layer has been formed by the newsreaders. These have benefitted particularly from wartime associations, when, as one contemporary put it, 'the *News* became in most households an institution almost as sacrosanct as family prayers had once been'.[22] But traditional Reithian attitudes continued at Broadcasting House to inhibit the development of radio news, and it was left to the new medium of television to carry through that revolution in news gathering and news broadcasting that has made the news and current affairs output of almost all contemporary broadcasting organizations the most central and sensitive aspect of their activities.[23]

For our purposes the most important aspect of this revolution was the transformation of the routine news bulletin — for many years on BBC television simply the earlier radio bulletins read over a still picture of Big Ben or Tower Bridge — into the news magazine. Characteristically the breakthrough in the BBC came not from the conservative news division but from the new 'Current Affairs' complex, with the launching in 1957 of *Tonight*, a topical daily programme with a magazine format that won great popularity, and whose form was instrumental in shaping a whole new range of news and current affairs programmes. With the new magazine format the news programmes grew in size and significance, regularly attracting huge audiences and becoming the centres of major controversies. The form was fed back into radio. A whole national network, Radio 4, was constructed around news output, with over a third

21 Sarah Stoddart of the BBC writes in *The Times Special Report on the BBC, On the Air*, 2 November 1972: 'Today there are no prizes for guessing which radio channel you are tuned to. The presenters (i.e. Announcers) set the mood: the erudite formal style of Radio 3 including Cormac Rigby, Tom Crowe and Patricia Hughes; on Radio 1 and 2, the familiar relaxed style of Jimmy Klingsbury's team . . . : on Radio 4, Jim Black, Michael de Morgan, Martin Muncaster and others with the journalistic approach'.

22 P. Fleming, quoted Briggs, *The War of Words*, p. 202.

23 For the details of this process, see Smith, 1973a, pp. 73 ff.

of its daily transmission time taken up with news and current affairs sequences (*Today*, *The World at One*, *PM*, *Newsdesk*, *The World Tonight*, etc).

An inevitable consequence of this heightened importance of the news programmes has been the added prominence given to the newsreaders. To the established radio newsreaders have been added a host of new television personalities, the regular television newsreaders — such as Kenneth Kendall, Richard Baker, Robert Dougall. These men do more than simply read the news bulletins; they are managers, link-men, and presenters of some of the most popular programmes transmitted at peak times: which on the evidence of audience reactions is the way in which we must see that regular television programme, the *News*. As with the old radio announcers, but in a new context of importance and with the added dimension of vision, the newsreaders establish by the style and tone of their presentations not only a particular image of the BBC ('*that's* what the BBC thinks of student demonstrations . . . ' etc.), but by the same token a special reputation and standing as individuals in their own right, as broadcasting personalities. The evidence of this is clear enough across all networks. The newsreaders appear as guests and celebrities on other people's programmes; they compere their own non-news programmes (Richard Baker has at least two popular radio shows, *Start The Week With Richard Baker* and *These You Have Loved*, both classic expressions of the BBC's collective persona); their autobiographies are sought by publishers;[24] they sponsor charity appeals both on the BBC and in the press. In short they, the newsreaders, are news.

To the layer of newsreaders must be added the third layer of professional broadcaster: the presenters, 'link-men', chairmen, 'anchor-men' of the regular programmes. They are a more diffuse group than the other two and, once more, the line separating them from the others is not always firmly drawn. Moreover the most important section of this group are the product of the same 'news and current affairs revolution' that pushed the newsreaders into such prominence: that is, they are mainly presenters of current affairs programmes. Nevertheless there are good grounds for giving them separate treatment, for they perform basically different roles from the others and, while the most recent group, in many ways they are becoming the most important. Of all the professional broadcasters they are probably the best known, as a simple recital of the names of some recent and current presenters should make clear to a contemporary British audience: Robin Day, Kenneth Allsop, Richard Dimbleby (and son David), Ludovic Kennedy, Alastair Burnett, Michael Barratt, Jack de Manio, Robert Robinson, William Hardcastle, Gerald Priestland, Cliff

---

24 E.g., Richard Baker's *Here is The News*, London: 1966. Peter Eckersley. Stuart Hibberd, Freddie Grisewood and Robert Dougall have all published broadcasting autobiographies — in fact if not in form.

Michelmore, David Jacobs . . . and one could no doubt add a good number more, perhaps not so widely known.

To trace the broadcasting biographies of this group of presenters is beyond the scope of this paper. But a reasonably good idea of their importance, as expressed by frequency and ubiquity, can be got from any current issue of the *Radio Times*. There in a given week we can see, for instance, Robin Day presenting the BBC's principal current affairs programme, *Panorama*, on the Monday evening, on television; on Tuesday evening, on Radio Four he is in his regular position as chairman of the phone-in programme, *It's Your Line* (if it happens to be election time he will be chairing an election special phone-in every morning of the week); on Thursday evening on Radio 3 he is chairing a discussion between two speakers on political censorship of the media; on Friday he is chairman — for the occasion — of the regular Radio Four current affairs programme, *Analysis*; on Sunday evening he is back on television chairing the first of a three-part debate on contempory morality in *The Sunday Debate*. And in other weeks there will be additional, or alternative *ad hoc* appearances.

This range of activities is to some extent exceptional in degree, but not in kind. On any given day the programme schedules for all the networks are dotted at regular intervals, almost as fixed markers, with the names of a remarkably small number of regular presenters — small considering the vast total output of all the networks of BBC radio and television. They tend to be presenters who to a disproportionate extent have first made their names in current affairs programmes, thereby reflecting the central place that current affairs has come to occupy in the broadcasting organization. But, once thus established, they do not by any means restrict their activities to this area. So, for instance, we have Robert Robinson presenting *Today*, the news and current affairs sequence, in the morning and, on the evening of the same day, chairing the quiz programme, *Brain of Britain*; then there is Michael Barratt presenting the television current affairs magazine, *Nationwide*, every evening of the week, and appearing on radio on the weekends to chair *Gardeners' Question Time*.

It is this very flexibility and versatility that in one way marks off the presenter's role from that of the newsreader and announcer. His professional skills — as interviewer, or chairman, or whatever — are in demand across a whole variety of programmes. For basically what is required, whether it is for chairing a quiz show or a discussion between senior party politicians, is a reliable, familiar broadcasting personality with whom the audience can identify, and whose authority, derived from his professional skills, enables him to direct and control anyone from an aggressive and aggrieved trade unionist to an eccentric lighthouse keeper from the Scilly Isles on a bad telephone.[25] Such a requirement follows

25 Cf. Michael Barratt's remark concerning his chairmanship of *Gardeners' Question*

both from the producer's considerations and from the general needs of
the broadcasting organization. The organization has to keep up an un-
remitting flow of utterly heterogenous programmes across a large number
of networks. The possibilities for error, embarrassment, or outrage are
tremendous. Given the precarious stability of the organization in relation
to powerful outside groups, mechanisms of control have to be built into
programme-making at every level. The system of 'upward referral' to
which producers are subject is one such important mechanism. But this
of course can only apply up to the point where programmes go out on
the air. In live programmes the presenter becomes a crucial agent of
control; in others, as the carrier of a particular style and particular skills
of communication, his incorporation becomes more or less indispensable
as some sort of assurance of success. His very presence assures a certain
audience, one that has already responded to his identification with other
esteemed or popular programmes.

The BBC exists in an environment which for most of its history has
had a tendency to fluctuate and convulse. Increasingly it has had to seek
out points of stability and rest, if it were going to develop any sort of
autonomy and momentum of its own. The professional broadcasters —
announcers, newsreaders, presenters and others — have become the
agents of a certain kind of adaptive response. Their professional skills,
their cultivation of a particular style, their public standing and reputation,
establish for the BBC a necessary, even though limited, insulation from
its environment. On the one hand they can hold their own with
politicians and other public figures. They hold off the absorption of the
BBC by the state. On the other hand they are strategically deployed in
the system of control of both contributors and producers. In this way,
they prevent potentially dangerous embarrassment to the organization, by
inhibiting the expression of attitudes that openly flout the codes, political
and moral, of the powers-that-be.

New Tensions: the BBC as honest broker

One final observation on the role of the professional broadcaster. I said
at the opening of this paper that in recent years the importance of the
professional broadcaster to the institution had increased; and I want now
to say a little more about this.

In the early Reithian days, and in the war and immediate post-war
period, the problem of the stance and style of the professional broadcaster
was not a difficult one. Reith had refused to confront the government

---

Time — and the fact that he admittedly knows little about gardening: 'I like to
think my ignorance is an advantage, because I see myself representing the listener
who wants to learn very basic things'. *Radio Times*, 2—8 March 1974.

directly on overt political matters; attention was then concentrated, in a missionary, Arnoldian way, on building up a specifically cultural institution. There was never any real question of whose culture it was that was to be diffused throughout the population by the new medium of broadcasting. It was the culture of the upper and upper-middle English classes. Reith believed firmly in 'high culture' (and 'high morality', although this did not square so easily with the behaviour of the upper classes). His professional staff, therefore, whether or not they actually derived from the upper-middle class, were expected to embody and to convey the best of the culture of that class. Their accent, their style at the microphone, the attitudes they conveyed, while in one sense being distinctively 'BBC', in another sense did not clash with the general cultural assumption of the English ruling classes. There was a congruence between the broadcaster's role as Reith had moulded it, and the expectations of the groups and institutions that the BBC had most to worry about — the Church, Parliament, the Oxbridge academic establishment.[26]

Since the mid-1950s the situation had become far less stable for the BBC. The coming of commercial television was a decisive event, breaking the BBC's monopoly not only in the economic sense but perhaps even more importantly in the cultural sense. Reith had always insisted that 'the brute force of monopoly' was basic to the performance of the BBC's task as he had conceived it; and he seemed to be proved right. The BBC now had to fight for its audience, and it was not content simply to steal its opponent's clothes. One consequence of competition was a radical shake-up of personnel within the organization itself. By the mid-60s its new-found persona was threatening to bring about a more dangerous collision with external power groups than ever before in its history.

The BBC's response was not only to the fact of competition. Politicians, moralists, and sociologists on all sides were talking about the break-up of 'the consensus' that had been the underlying force in the stability of the political and social system — and so of the BBC — up to the end of the 1950s. Whether or not such a consensus existed and if so, whether or not it has broken up, does not matter here. The point is that the BBC believed it, along with many others. This meant that it could no longer speak to the one great national audience in the same firm and rather aloof manner that it had adopted for so long. Itself now reduced to 'something sectional and questionable',[27] it felt that it was now addressing

26   And cf. Burns' comment on this era: 'Sports, music, and entertainments which appealed to the lower classes were, of course, included in large measure in programmes, but the manner in which they were purveyed — the context of presentation — remained indomitably upper middle class; and there was, too, the point that they were only on the menu as ground bait'. 'Public Service and Private World', pp. 138—9.

27   Burns, *ibid.*, p. 139.

an audience that was itself sectionalized, fragmented, making contradictory demands, and less willing to be submissive if these demands were not satisfied. The controversies in which it was embroiled during the 1960s seemed to confirm this reading. Not only could it not keep a firm footing in 'the middle ground', it could scarcely find it. Every area it touched, of politics, culture, morality, reacted with extreme sensitivity. It could not find a central point of identification with its audience. It was attacked from Left and from Right, by 'progressives' and 'reactionaries', by those outraged at its boldness as much as by those contemptuous of its caution.

The BBC has been forced to revise the Reithian-Arnoldian conception of its role. One interesting way of seeing the change is by considering the different 'images' and 'pictures' of the broadcasting organization, and its relation to the community, as held by various senior administrators at different times. Reith and his staff were particularly enamoured of the nautical metaphor, with the BBC as the ship and Reith its chief pilot.[28] Reith's successor after the war, Sir William Haley, preferred the image of British society as 'a cultural pyramid slowly aspiring upwards', with the BBC acting as the lever that activated the progressive upward movement in hand.[29] Both conceptions shared the view that broadcasting's essential task was to provide moral and cultural landmarks for the society as a whole.

Current BBC metaphors show a dramatic shift from those involving notions of leading and directing, to those involving far more neutral concepts: essentially, the BBC is seen as the 'register' of the many different 'voices' in society, as the 'great stage' on which all the actors, great and small, parade and say their piece. A typical and influential metaphor of this kind is provided by David Attenborough, until recently the BBC's Director of Television Programmes:

> The model that I find most valuable, is that a public service broadcasting organization ought to be like a theatre in the middle of a town, and the broadcasters — that is to say people like myself and producers and directors — are part of the theatre staff. And it's the job of that staff to find from society, from the town in which they are placed, a whole selection of voices — the most prophetic, the most significant the most amusing, the most dramatic, the most typical — and to enable those voices to be heard in that theatre.

The function of the broadcaster beyond this is mainly technical and professional: it is 'to give those voices the knowledge and grasp that you have as a theatre man, of how best the case may be presented, how best those people may appear on the stage and get their message across'.[30]

28 See especially Reith's autobiography, *Into the Wind*, Hodder & Stoughton (London: 1949).
29 Sir William Haley, 'The Responsibilities of Broadcasting', BBC 1948, in A. Smith (Ed.) *British Broadcasting*, Newton Abbot: David and Charles, 1974, p. 83.
30 David Attenborough, interviewed in 'The Communicators', broadcast on BBC Radio 3, 25 January 1973.

This is a new conception of broadcasting for the BBC: the BBC as middleman, as honest broker, as manager and impresario. And one of its most important consequences has been a heightening of the significance of the professional broadcaster. More than ever before the BBC cannot afford to be identified with any sectional interest in the society — even something as indefinite as 'high culture'. It must, to some extent, go as the wind blows it. But a rudderless ship soon ends on the rocks. What keeps it on an even keel, increasingly, is the 'management' function performed by the professional broadcasters. It is in their stance, through their style and presentation, that the BBC tries to keep its autonomy and ward off the clutching embraces from all around it. It exploits the well-founded fact that audiences tend to identify with the presenter as against contending parties, to let the controversies of society express themselves within the materials of broadcasting; indeed it encourages this controversy through its contribution, since its survival is now better secured by multiplying the areas and groups in contention. If the BBC can no longer rely on the benign patronage of the established groups, and has no prospect of being supported by the dis-established, its future in the short term seems more promising if it goes to some extent on the offensive, playing the role of *tertium gaudens* to the conflicting groups whose differences it fuels.

The professional broadcaster, for his part, has to intensify and extend his role. He has, to a degree, to modify the aloof, well-bred style of the earlier announcers. It becomes a crucial matter to underline his professionalism, his non-partisanship. He must not stand, certainly must not seem to stand, for Left or Right, organized capital or organized labour, the professional 'moralist' or the professional 'libertarian'. One marked expression of this position in recent years has been the way in which the professional broadcaster has taken to 'identifying' with 'us' — that is, 'taking the role' of 'us' as 'the unrepresented', 'the consumers', 'the suffering public', the victims of planners and public servants of all kinds, as well as of large industrialists, selfish trade unions, property speculators and the like.[31] This involves taking something of a 'populist' stance as well as style. Ministers are questioned as aggressively as trade unionists, environmentalist pressure groups as much as planning agencies, along the lines of, 'what are the gains and losses in all this for us, the public?'. More generally there is displayed an attitude of faint cynicism and sceptism towards almost all, 'official' sources, whether in governmental or private organizations.

Much of this style derives from the seminal *Tonight* current affairs programme, which perhaps unwittingly offered the model for the BBC's broadcasting strategy of the 1960s. As the BBC Handbook 1973 observes, its style, 'quizzical, amused, slightly sceptical', caught the spirit of the

31 This point is suggested by D. Morley, University of Kent, in his paper 'Industrial Conflict and the Mass media', forthcoming in *Sociological Review*.

times. Given the domination that news and current affairs came to assume in the organization it was not long before this style, modified in various directions, appeared almost the hallmark of the professional broadcaster on all networks and in all sorts of programmes. Perhaps it can be seen at its clearest in the styles of the presenters of a number of Radio 4 current affairs sequences: in the approaches of Robert Robinson and John Timpson (as well as predecessor Jack de Manio and particular successors) on the *Today* programme, William Hardcastle on *The World At One*, Gerald Priestland on *Newsdesk*. It is in their style of presentation, compounded equally of aggressiveness, scepticism, irony, and detatchment, that we can most easily observe the role played by the professional broadcaster in the BBC's strategy of survival.

I need hardly add that this strategy does not, and is not designed to, make the BBC an 'oppositional' force in society. To go so far would again push the organization in a suicidal direction, outside the confines historically and pragmatically laid down for it. But the strategy does pose great problems of control. The BBC is trying to hold 'the middle ground' on a terrain that is treacherous and unstable. It cannot afford identification with any organized section of the community, however large. It can no longer ignore political issues, since 'politics' has penetrated so many areas areas — the family, school, even entertainment and sport — hitherto regarded and treated as non-political. Its solution has been to choose a certain kind of broadcaster, promote and diffuse him throughout the medium, so that broadcasting can give the appearance of allowing expression to every tendency, every movement, in British society — while at the same time ensuring that basic control is still in trained and trusted hands. But it is a precarious balancing act. Contentious issues, however expertly 'orchestrated' and controlled, have a tendency of sometimes breaking through the medium.[32] Even so safe a programme as *Any Questions*, for long a by-word for the complacency of the 'middle mass', occasionally comes apart in the middle, with contributors fiercely divided, suggesting values and directions that go well outside the conventions of the cosy, agreeable panel show that the programme essentially is. It is an apt illustration of the current dilemma of the BBC. In order to survive in its traditionally-defined form it has to keep moving — and in doing so it may willy-nilly move things with it.

32 Cf. Stuart Hall: 'Some factors, indeed, appear to drive the media right against the steady, uninterrupted reflection of the interests of the state. Oriented to the news in a competitive market, anxious to spot representative trends before they surface, the media seem to be driven at one level, precisely to the danger-zones — to worrying away at movements, people, events and issues which disrupt the even tenor of social life, and which governments and the state would prefer to keep off the screen'. 'The Limitations of Broadcasting', *The Listener*, 16 March 1972.

10

Yesterday's Men—a case study in political communication

Michael Tracey

The only occasion when Harold was extremely angry was after the 1970 election. It was the now famous David Dimbleby interview for a programme called Yesterday's Men *which sparked it off.*

(Marcia Williams, 1972, 234—5.)

The events surrounding the programme *Yesterday's Men* — broadcast on 17 June 1971 — are difficult to disentangle, but once unravelled they throw into sharp relief the intentions of programme makers and the considerations of programme making, the effect of political pressure on programming, and the curiously ambivalent attitude of the Labour Party to the media in general and to the BBC in particular. In short the controversy provides a fascinating insight into the most prominent form of political communication within the political culture, television.

A Narrative

On the day of Harold Wilson's defeat, 19 June 1970, David Dimbleby did an interview at 10 Downing Street with the deposed and surprised Prime Minister. It was at this time that the idea for *Yesterday's Men* began to crystallize in the mind of Dimbleby: 'the loss of power, what does it actually mean?' He describes how he was 'struck by the general air of dismay and by the speed of dismissal', and how he couldn't quite see 'how people could readjust. I assumed there would be a very painful period of readjustment, which indeed there was, Mrs Healey for instance saying that Denis Healey was like having a sportscar in the garage and no petrol.'[1]

The idea for the programme occurred to Dimbleby in June 1970, but he did not prepare a programme synopsis until October. The original idea had been that they 'quite simply make a film by following the Opposition around for a few weeks and see how they were getting on and

1 Unless otherwise stated, all quotes are from interviews with the author. I would like to thank Angela Pope for her comments on the various drafts of this paper.

settling down.' By the time Dimbleby's proposal had been presented to
Paul Fox (Controller BBC 1) and John Grist (Head of Current Affairs
Group (CAG)), several months had elapsed since the election and so the
original intent of looking at the immediate impact of the loss of power
was no longer attainable. No work could begin on making the programme
until the idea had been accepted, a budget allocated and a producer
(Angela Pope) appointed, by which time it was Christmas 1970, six
months after the election and the loss of power.

Dimbleby's synopsis of the programme — incidentally presented under
the title of *Yesterday's Men* — indicated that the film would describe the
impact of defeat on the senior members of the Labour Government; would
consider the role of the Opposition as seen by the ex-Ministers; would
'cover inquiries as to what it was like to lose high office with its rewards
suddenly and unexpectedly, and would include their comments on the
"secrets" that were being made public in memoirs' (Governors, 1971).
The appeal of such a programme, the synopsis argued, would be in showing
the response of former public figures to a period of enforced relative
anonymity. Having been granted permission to go ahead on this basis,
letters were sent by Dimbleby and Pope to the various members of
Wilson's Shadow Cabinet explaining that they were 'preparing a documentary film for the BBC on the Opposition. It would be about the
political and personal nature of the job of Opposition.'[2]

An important consideration is that over the period of months which
had elapsed since the idea was first broached the to and fro of party
politics had been firmly re-established, and in particular the producers
perceived two significant developments in the affairs of the Labour Party:
the appearance of a schism over the Common Market, and a possible
challenge to Harold Wilson as leader of the party. So, gradually, the
passage of time and the movement of events implied a constant flux in
the perspectives of what would be discussed. Work on the programme
did not begin until March 1971, during which time there was a vital
development which throws considerable light on the later events.
Dimbleby's original idea had been that the programme would fill a
Tuesday Documentary slot but he could not be given permission to

---

2 Pope was to note at the time of the controversy: 'It is claimed that the participants
   are being misled as to the context of the programme, that they expected that the
   film would only be about the role of the Opposition and about its policies. At no
   time did I discuss a programme of this kind verbally or in my correspondence with
   the interviewees. Indeed, whilst I see this as an interesting area of British politics,
   it was not one which I felt I could project on television.' She refers specifically to
   the content of the letters which were sent to the participants to support this
   argument.

explore the possibilities for such a programme until the whole idea had been ratified by his superiors in CAG. Having been given permission and having talked to the intended participants he and Pope 'decided we didn't want to do it, too dull, too difficult, too boring.' Pope argued that there was simply insufficient interesting material to sustain fifty minutes since the Labour leaders were felt to have had insufficient time to develop any real impressions of Opposition life. She did feel, however, that there was a possibility of producing a shorter item for inclusion within another programme. Informing the BBC of this, they were told in return that 'you can't not do it, because now you've been and talked to them they'll think it's the BBC being hostile to the Labour Party if we don't put it out. So you've got to do it, no question of dropping it.' Eventually, late in the programme's development, a compromise solution was arrived at. It would no longer be a distinct documentary but would be broadcast under the aegis of *24 Hours*. Dimbleby and Pope had then been effectively locked into a process from which a programme had to emerge and, a supreme irony, the final turning of the key in the lock had been the conceptions held by senior BBC personnel of the sensitivity of the Labour leaders.

Dimbleby and Pope, on resuming work on the programme in March 1971 paid particular attention to the interviews with Wilson and the other Labour leaders which they regarded as the 'absolute core of the film' and on which they worked 'absolutely together'. The organization and shooting of additional film was done principally under the direction of Angela Pope in her role as producer. The circumstances dictated by the passage of time were indicated in a letter to Wilson from Dimbleby written in April, in which he said that the film was 'still conceived as it was when we talked about it in your office earlier this year. It will be both about the defeat and its impact in political and personal terms and about the problems Opposition poses . . . . Obviously the Opposition's handling of events in recent months now plays a bigger part than if the film had been made at the turn of the year.' The particular formulation of this letter and of earlier ones is important in the light of the later accusations about 'deception'. In April 1971 Dimbleby and Pope decided that the original synopsis title, *Yesterday's Men*, would be used and also contacted 'The Scaffold', with a view to their writing and singing a song for the film sound-track. A contract was negotiated with them during May. The Governor's Report states that the title 'was known and accepted by their superiors', but was never, in subsequent correspondence, communicated to the participants.

In the process of making this programme, as with any other programme, editorial control could have been exercised at two points: during the making of the programme, and after the film had been completed but prior to transmission. Two possible levels of editorial control were immediately relevant: the assistant to the head

of CAG, the head of CAG. In April 1971 Pope submitted to the assistant
head of CAG a draft of a detailed account of the topics which they were
going to discuss with the politicians, and details of the song which the
Scaffold were being commissioned to do. To those who wished to know,
it was clear that a 'satirical, funny' song had been commissioned for the
programme by May 1971. This much the Governor's Report acknowledged;
what it did not acknowledge was the question of editorial control once
the programme was being cut and put together in its final form. Three
internal views of this predominate: one view is that those in editorial
control knew about the content of the programme, but failed to take
into account, indeed could not have known, the reactions of the Labour
leaders over the period 16—18 June. A second version has it that the
editorial control was lax because of a broader departmental commitment to other concerns during this period which effectively meant
that they weren't familiar with what was happening until it was
too late. A third version is that they knew what was happening
but refused to take responsibility for it. This latter is rather difficult to
accept if only because they would clearly realize that any serious consequences would be bound to reflect back on to them. The role they
adopted is much more understandable if the premise is that they did not
perceive the serious consequences of the programme, since all that is
called into question then is their judgement, and not their integrity. There
is an important divergence of opinion here between Dimbleby and Pope.
The former argues that there was in fact very little editorial control,
whereas the latter argues that there was much more control than usual
with constant office discussions between herself and either the head of
CAG, Grist, or his assistant, Tisdall, about ideas and content, vetting of
correspondence, viewing of the rough-cut and so on. There is a possible
explanation for this in that Pope seemed to be more permanently located
within the walls of Lime Grove than did Dimbleby, so that any control
which took place would be more likely to happen through her than
through Dimbleby. Whatever the truth about the control, it is almost
certain that no-one foresaw the reactions of the Labour Party.

Arrangements were made to film an interview between Wilson and
Dimbleby at 6 p.m. on May 11 in the rooms of the Leader of the
Opposition at the Commons. The interview covered numerous areas
but when Dimbleby referred to the amount of money which Wilson
received for his memoirs, the Labour leader became rather agitated, and
then extremely angry, demanding that all references to the memoirs be
cut from the recording (the full text of the row is available in Hill (1974).
On the following day, May 12, a telephone conversation took place
between Joe Haines, Wilson's press secretary, and John Crawley, ENCA,[3]

---

3 Editor, News and Current Affairs: in overall charge of output from the news and
   current affairs departments of the BBC and one of the Corporation's most senior
   and prestigious posts.

which covered, as Lord Hill describes it and as is confirmed by a member of other sources, 'the extent of the deletion promised to Mr Wilson by David Dimbleby and Angela Pope' (Hill, 1974 p. 181). In fact the promise of a deletion seems to have been made by Pope (though she denies this), and Dimbleby promises that he will not leak the details of the extractions to the press. The central bone of contention is whether Crawley promised Haines that he would cut out the whole of the reference to the memoirs or whether he only promised to delete part of it. The Governor's Report states (para 7): 'Following a disagreement on the appropriateness of certain questions, an undertaking was given to Mr Wilson on behalf of the BBC that a part of the film would be destroyed and all that was possible to be done to see that the story of the disagreement did not leak. There was a lack of agreement between the parties to this undertaking about the extent of the film which it covered.' Lord Hill claims that 'John Crawley . . . had no doubt that the assurance related only to the third question' (Hill, 1974 p. 181). Dimbleby and Pope are unclear as to the precise implication of the statement in the transcript that an extraction would be made, though they do admit to fighting very hard to keep in what they felt to be the legitimate question of the earnings from the memoirs and to keep in Wilson saying that 'I'm not going to answer that' because they 'thought it was revealing and quite important that it should be seen.' Haines in a piece in the *Guardian* (15 January 1971) wrote that 'On May 12, Mr John Crawley, special assistant to Mr Charles Curran, the Director General, telephoned me to say that he had "no hesitation in saying that the whole of that section will be destroyed formally, lost sight of and forgotten". I still possess my original shorthand notes of that conversation.' Reading this extract from Haines's article, it would be possible to argue that the reference was to the second part of the conversation. When interviewed, Haines declared:

There is no doubt in my mind, there is no doubt I am sure in John Crawley's mind, there was no doubt in Angela Pope's mind, there was no doubt in David Dimbleby's mind, what the objection was. You have to keep coming back to the point that this was a programme, a serious Tuesday Documentary about the workings of Her Majesty's loyal Opposition, and the whole of that section (in the *Guardian*) means simply that. He (Dimbleby) had gone from discussing visits to America, relations with the Common Market, Africa and all that suddenly to the question of Mr Wilson's money. There can be no doubt what we are objecting to. The conversations that I had with Curran, with John Grist subsequently, with Crawley, with Dimbleby, with Pope, they had no doubt, none of them. If they try afterwards to justify a bad programme, that I understand. They may feel compelled to do so because the alternative is to admit that they were wholly in the wrong and I wouldn't expect them to do that. But there's no ambiguity, there was no doubt, none at all. In all the conversations we had with them I don't think there was ever any real possibility of doubt. They knew what I meant and I knew what John Crawley meant.

For a month then, from May 12 to June 16, there is an apparent understanding between Wilson (via Haines) and the BBC (via Crawley).

Even this, however, is not totally clear since Lord Hill, quoting from his diary of 17 June, declares: 'When the incident in the programme, *Yesterday's Men*, concerning Harold Wilson's income from his memoirs was reported to me by the Director General two or three weeks ago, he told me that the questions on this subject were to come out, Wilson having been so assured. Today he said that the assurance given to Wilson . . . was that it was only the third question that should come out, and that the television people proposed to include the first two questions and the answers' (Hill, 1974 p. 181). What seems to have happened is that a precise interpretation of the Crawley-Haines conversation was established at this high administrative level, was in line with Haines's understanding as to the nature of the agreement, but that this was never transmitted to the 'television people'. When these latter were preparing a rough-cut of the film they decided to leave the question in — 'We decided to put in this much of the question, "Mr Wilson, it has been said that you earned several figures (sic) from your book, is that true?" and he answered, "I don't know why that should be of any interest to the BBC", and then he went on. We realised obviously that the row could not be in, so we cut on "It's no interest to the BBC".' One source argues that everyone in the hierarchy, effectively meaning the troika previously described, knew that the question and answer were left in and thought nothing of it, 'None of us knew that it was going to blow like that', and they could not have known because the behaviour of the Labour people was 'totally irrational and unpredictable'. Thus not only was no clear picture of the 'pledge' transmitted to Pope and Dimbleby, but also those in direct editorial control did not have a clear understanding of the extent of deletion promised to Wilson. It does seem that Curran and his assistant were aware that the understanding referred to all the questions relating to the memoir money.

What is crucial is that until Wednesday, 16 June, Wilson and Haines believed that the whole of the extract would be erased. On 10 June, news of the 11 May row was made public for the first time in the 'Londoners Diary' of the *Evening Standard*, and was repeated over the next three days in the rest of the press. By 16 June, Wilson, and particularly Haines, became aware that all was not as they thought it would be. Haines states:

The first thing that alerted us was when we discovered that the programme was called *Yesterday's Men*, and we discovered that by looking in the *Radio Times*. I protested about this . . . . I had spoken to John Grist about this and almost in passing I said 'I take it that these other points, the house and more particularly this conversation, would not be in' and to my astonishment John Grist, who I knew very well, said that he could not help me on that, he would have to refer me to higher authority, and just went all stiff and formal, and when I questioned him he kept repeating that he couldn't help me. By this time we were getting alert. I think that what then happened was that I did refer it to Curran and then Curran told me, or told Wilson, that this part of the conversation was still in.

This was then the making of the second major row, which did not just revolve around the questions having been kept in, but also involved the fact that photographs had been included of Wilson's Buckinghamshire farm and a dislike of the tone of the title, *Yesterday's Men*. The history of the photographs was basically that Pope had wished to include film of the new farm but this had been rejected on the grounds of security. Instead of film, a number of photographs had been included, which was felt by Haines to have been another broken 'promise'. By the night of 16 June the question of the programme had been taken out of the hands of Dimbleby and Pope, and was being dealt with at the very highest levels of the BBC. The central question was what assurance had been made to Wilson about the deletions from the programme. Hill's diary for 17 June notes: 'Last evening there were further talks between the Director General, Huw Wheldon and Wilson's advisers, including Lord Goodman.' The meeting had taken place at Lord Goodman's flat. A particular point of contention was to be that in late May Charles Curran had sent Wilson what he described as the only copy of the tape in existence, along with a memo from Angela Pope to John Grist stating that this was indeed the contentious part of the conversation. On the 16th Wilson and Haines discovered that not only was it not the sole record but that part of it was to be broadcast nationally the following evening. The point was compounded on 18 June when the whole of the conversation was leaked to the press.

By the night of 16–17 June the demands of the Wilson camp had crystallized into three: the title should be changed; the photographs of Grange Farm should be removed; the question and answer about the memoirs should be excluded. A press showing of the programme had been scheduled for 11 a.m. on the 17th, but since the Governors were to see the film this was delayed until noon. The Governors' meeting concentrated on two issues; the legitimacy of Dimbleby's question about the memoirs; the nature of the pledge made to Haines about the extent of the deletion. The question of the Grange Farm photograph and the title were also raised. The decision was made to delete all of the references to the memoirs but to retain the title and the still photographs of Grange Farm.

Haines had initially intended to boycott the press showing on the grounds that they had been promised a separate showing of the film so that they could comment on it but had then had their request for the separate showing turned down. Following the revelations of the night of the 16th, their discovery of the title and a telephone call to Transport House from someone within the BBC 'warning how bad this was', Haines decided to attend. The press reaction was to be mixed but Haines's immediate reaction was that the whole programme was a send-up and that given the fact that they had been assured that it would be a 'serious documentary' there had been a 'carefully calculated, deliberate, continuous deceit over a period of months'. This then brings us to the third and perhaps most significant controversy, the question of the programme's intent — which was rapidly followed by two further points of contention: a statement in the film about Wilson having 'privileged access' to government papers for writing his memoirs (which brought an immediate threat of libel): and then the leaking of the deletions by an anonymous caller to a number of newspapers. The press on 18 June was full of the substance of the deletions. The Labour people were further annoyed when on the night of 18 June, the same spot in *24 Hours* carried a rather celebratory review of Heath's first year in office. Entitled *The Quiet Revolution* it was described by Greene, among others, as a 'programme of a very different character' from *Yesterday's Men* (Greene, 1972). Following the Governor's decision about the content of the programme, the final decision about its actual transmission at 10 p.m. that night seems to have been made by Grist, Head of CAG. He had another production team preparing an alternative programme in case the decision was not to broadcast *Yesterday's Men*, and it was only a very short time before the programme that the decision was finally made to go ahead.

Press comment on the programme dealt with both the details of the row and the critical appraisal of the programme. The accounts of the row were as one might expect, shallow and unclear. Having gone through all the press copy which sought to assess the merits of the programme I estimate that there was a 3:2 favourable comment ratio. The programme was variously described as 'fascinating television' and 'one of the most interesting [programmes on politics] ever shown on British television' (*Daily Telegraph*). It was lauded for turning 'yesterday's people of power into real people' (*Daily Express*) and for refusing to 'look on the touchy untouchables as stuffed penguins . . . . It was human, lively and interesting . . . an entertaining and professional job' (*Daily Mirror*). But it was also criticized for being '45 minutes of television gossip column' (*Guardian*). *The Times* editorial (19 June 1971) attacked the programme for trivialization, the *Daily Telegraph* editorial felt that both sides had cause for complaint and the *Guardian* thought it was a 'night worth forgetting'.

Following the transmission of the programme, the controversy revolved around four main questions: had the Labour leaders been deceived; had the film been cut in such a way as to present a distorted view of the lives of the Labour leaders; had there been a breach of faith by the BBC; who had leaked the extracts to the press? (Hill, 1974 p. 185). These were to provide the central focus of the inquiry which was instituted by Lord Hill on 21 June, and conducted by Maurice Tinniswood, the Director of Personnel, and Desmond Taylor, ENCA. The investigators' Report was delivered to a special meeting of the Governors on 7 July, along with a draft of a possible Governor's statement prepared by Hill. Published in *The Listener* on 15 July, the Governor's Report consisted of an amalgam of the investigators' Report and the Hill draft.

The anger of the Labour leadership culminated in a speech by a senior Labour Party man, Bob Mellish, in which he stated that there was a 'limit to how much democracy can abuse, insult, sneer and jeer . . . . If the BBC go on with this type of campaign, we must counter it by whatever activities we have at our disposal within the party publicity machine.' It was in the context of this furore, particularly over the question of deceit, that the inquiry was instituted. It was amplified when Crossman in his other role as editor of the *New Statesman* made a scathing attack (25 June 1971) on the programme makers, sparking off a further wave of press comment and publicity.

The Governors' Report (1971) was a detailed refutation of the principal charges. It poured forth facts and in doing so sought to swamp the Labour arguments. It showed that the ratio of transcript available to transcript used was for each of the participants on average 12:1. It provided details of the time (minutes and seconds) spent on the different areas, 'Defeat and adapting to the idea of being an Opposition: 4 minutes 48 seconds, Financial consequences: 4 minutes . . . ' etc. It argues that of the seven main areas of questioning 'all the participants were questioned on nearly all of these matters.' The Report then proceeds to 'comment' on the programme and on this factual analysis. It argued that the question about the memoirs and the money were permissible, but that given the misunderstanding on the scope of the deletion it was only right to delete that area. The Report argued that on the whole the area of questioning 'conformed to the description that the programme would be about the "political and personal nature of the job of Opposition" and that no major area of interviewing was omitted.' In any journalistic exercise, it argues there is a need to edit and cut material down to a manageable size and that given their analysis (paras 5 and 6) 'the material finally selected from the interviews for use in the transmitted programme was on the whole representative and fair', and 'there was no improper or inadequate inter-cutting.' The title should have been transmitted to the participants, and the programme makers should have realized that the song used 'represented a substantial change in the atmosphere in which the film would be interpreted by the participants from that which they might have expected from earlier descriptions of the programme.' Certain aspects of the treatment were 'too frivolous'. The leaks are condemned but, the Report adds, there was no conclusive evidence as to where in the BBC they originated, but that there was some evidence that the BBC was not the only source of the leaks. The nature of the placing of *Yesterday's Men* and the Heath programme on the following night was an error. The report ended on a flourish of principles about the fair and impartial nature of BBC news and current affairs coverage, embodied in a 'case law' of 'principles and practices'.

The Report was seen by the press as a defence by the Governors of their own staff, with only a mild rebuke for one or two misdemeanours, and there were such headlines as 'BBC defends Dimbleby', 'BBC Rejects Charges', 'New Labour Fury', 'Carry On Dimbleby'. There is little doubt that in many ways the whole Report was a defensive exercise. Dimbleby thought it a 'very shrewdly devised political exercise by Lord Hill to recover from a disastrous position.' What is also very clear is that the firmness of the support for the programme makers in the Report was based on the fact that (a) the Governors had cleared the film for transmission on 17 June and therefore could not, without severe loss of face, condemn the programme; (b) to have condemned the programme would have been to imply that Pope and Dimbleby were without adequate supervision; but that (c) to have argued that there was full editorial control would have made it even more difficult to take the programme to task since the whole editorial structure of the BBC current affairs would have been implicated.

In mid-July Hill was sent a letter from Wilson's solicitors 'demanding an abject apology, trailed on the air and in the *Radio Times*, plus the payment of his costs and a contribution to a charity named by him. In short we were asked to grovel . . . .' (Hill, 1974 p. 190). The legal question was still over the use of the phrase 'access to privileged documents'. The BBC publicly apologised on Friday, 6 August, for the use of 'certain words [which] might suggest that he had made advantageous use of privileged or secret documents in an unjustifiable fashion.' The controversy of *Yesterday's Men* was ostensibly at an end.

A number of questions need to be considered, not the least of which is the possible light which the controversy throws on the nature and consequences of the relationships between broadcasters and politicians. We need to consider this in terms of the overall consequences of *Yesterday's Men* for programme making since 1971. There is, however, a third point which needs to be considered, and that is, on reflection, perhaps the most profound and significant of the three. This is the insight that the making of the programme provides into the situation and intentions of the programme maker, and the way in which this is generated, not by political malice or bias but by a competitive institutional structure and a limited technology.

There were a number of themes in the public discourse over the programme. The lack of editorial control; the impropriety of the questions; the trivialization of the subject matter; the bias of the BBC against the Labour Party; the contradictions in the position occupied by the Governors.[4] The central theme of the attack by the Labour Party on the

4 It is perhaps not insignificant that in his article in the *New Statesman*, Crossman states of Broadcasting House, 'It is here that the Director General and the Chairman, presumably following the Reithian tradition of not recognizing television, have their headquarters connected only by the Westway and the Central Line to that glass doughnut which is TV Centre and that dank tenement building which is Lime Grove. . . ' (*New Statesman* 25 June 1972). Clearly with ENCA's increased presence in Lime Grove, Broadcasting House would have a more 'significant' presence.

programme was that they had been misled into expecting a serious programme and been served with a send-up. The most forthright presentation of the Labour Party case came from one of the participants, Crossman. Arguing that they had been invited to do a serious programme, the participants, Crossman states, were interviewed at length on a number of issues, and no one doubted for 'a moment that while the programme in which he was due to participate would provide lively television entertainment, its main concern would be to present a fair and objective picture of how the Labour Party . . . had settled down to its role as Her Majesty's Opposition' (Crossman, 1971). The actual programme 'was grotesquely and indecently different' from the programme the ex-Ministers expected. The interview material was chopped away to leave only the 'spicy trimmings', 'distorted' impressions were created of what had been said, and apparently contradictory extracts were juxtaposed:

the effect was achieved first through the deliberate fraud by which the politicians were persuaded to take part and, secondly, by the even greater fraud by which fragments were snipped out of the interviews they gave and juxtaposed in order to convey a false impression of what they had meant and even of what they had actually said.

The whole programme, Crossman states, was 'shallow and trivial', a 'fraud' perpetrated by individuals with inadequate editorial supervision. Broadcasting House, through its negligence, effectively granted them 'a licence to distort and misrepresent'. Haines described the programme as disgraceful. 'It was never any attempt to be a serious film about the Opposition. It was a send up. I remember that Denis Healey's contribution was cut in such a way as to make it appear as though he was bemoaning his loss of income; he said that his income had dropped from whatever it was, £10,000 to £9,000 p.a., to £3,000, and there is stopped, whereas what Denis had in fact gone on to say was 'but I am not complaining — most of my constituents in Leeds are far worse off.' It was that sort of cutting . . . the thing was generally a send-up . . . the intention all along was a send-up. This was really our principal complaint — it was not the question that was asked but the deceit. . . . '

These various charges appear to be refuted by the Governors' Report. The 'facts' however do not speak as loudly as they were made to seem since 'tone' does not lend itself to the type of quantification carried out in the Report: one can produce details of the distribution of question areas etc. but that tells one nothing about the overall character of the programme. The principal view which emerges from press comment on the programme is that it was a send-up, though there was disagreement over the suitability of such a send-up. Difficulty, of course, lies in assessing the impressions created in the minds of the participants by the programme makers, and in assessing the particular motives of the programme makers.

Two questions linger: did Dimbleby and Pope create the impression that it would be a 'serious documentary' as would be understood by seasoned politicians raised amid the conventional forms of *Panorama et al*; did they *intend* to create that impression or indeed to make such a programme? All the evidence points to 'yes' for the first question; a qualified 'no' to the second question. *Yesterday's Men* employed a number of unusual techniques which created the adverse reaction of the participants, but their employment did not flow from any commitment to an anti-Labour line. Indeed, it is possible to argue that the problem lay in a profound disinterest in the more traditional forms of politics and political television which led the programme makers to develop new ideas of presentation, and *this* was to be the spring for the controversy.

A major feature of *Yesterday's Men* was the ambiguous and ultimately contradictory position adopted by the Governors of the BBC. To whom do the Governors owe their loyalty and responsibility, to the public interest or to the programme makers? The problem arose from the Governors not only vetting the programme, and therefore acting in an editorial role (the 17 June role), but also sitting in judgement on that editorial decision (the 15 July role). Hill is aware of the problems involved: 'Reflecting on the sequence of events, a nagging question kept recurring in my mind. Whose role was it to protect those who believe they have been unfairly treated by the BBC? Strictly speaking, the answer is the Governors, for they represent the public. But, as in this case, it is often necessary and right for the Governors to defend the staff of the BBC when they have been unfairly attacked. The more we were seen in this defensive role, the more difficult it was to be seen to be, if not actually to be, the trustees for the public' (Hill, 1974 pp. 189—90). Smith (1972) puts the point succinctly: 'What right had the Governors of the BBC to sit in judgement on a matter of editorial content which they had themselves viewed and sanctioned on the day of the transmission?' In short, for the Chairman and Governors to occupy twin roles of senior executive and public guardian placed them in an impossible position. The supreme irony in this debacle is that the initial step towards the establishment of an executive Board was made first of all by Wilson who, through the appointment of Lord Hill, sought to supplant the authority of Greene. On this most important executive action by a non-executive Board the result was not to Wilson's liking.

An Analysis: the aftermath of controversy

The point about considering *Yesterday's Men* is that because it involved such an extraordinary set of intentions and responses it taps the whole web of relationships and dependencies which together constitute the fabric of political broadcasting and the political process. The numerous personal and institutional relationships encased within it can be seen at a number of levels: personal, intra and inter-institutional, social and so on. It is to a discussion of the wider meaning and significance of the controversy that these conclusions are addressed. Given the fact that this has principally been a study of the making of the programme, attempting to delineate the concerns and motivations of those responsible for its production, the main conclusions are concerned with what one might call the making of political messages. There are however a number of more speculative conclusions that one would wish to at least draw attention to if only for the purpose of indicating future lines of thought.

Politics and programme practices; innovation and inhibition
To understand why *Yesterday's Men* turned out as it did, and to see the interaction between the political sphere and the act of making programmes, one has to consider very carefully the particular conceptions of current affairs television possessed by the programme makers. As described in the preceding narrative, Dimbleby and Pope, following their initial research for the programme, had doubts about the possibilities of the programme but, having informed the Labour people of their intentions, were forced to go ahead and produce a programme. Both wished to avoid what they regarded as the more boring aspects of current affairs television, and the producer declared, 'I certainly wasn't going to make a film about the constitutional position of the Opposition.' From the early stages of the programme the producer had in fact felt that the views of the Labour leaders on their political role, as the official Opposition, would not provide fifty minutes of television, and this in itself led to a focus on the more personal realm of individual adjustments to a new role:

When you go and talk to someone about a programme, ideally it's a two-way thing. I mean, you have a general idea and you go and see whether what they say bears it out or is interesting and whether they have got anything to say. It was perfectly clear that at this early point after the loss of power they had got nothing to say about how the Labour Party was going to function over the whole five years of Opposition. So that area that we had thought out, i.e. 'What are you going to do in Opposition?' in a very general sense wasn't worth including in the film.

In other words, she is arguing that because of the difficulties of discussing the more overtly political questions, they were thrown back on to discussing the more personal questions of the adjustment to the loss of power and status. It is, however, possible to argue that this developing perspective was never transmitted to the participants and, for example, the letter from Dimbleby to Wilson could be interpreted as meaning that there would be more, not less, attention paid to political questions. What must be added though, in fairness to the producer, is that from the inception of the programme the interviewees had been informed that there would be at least some discussion of the more personal aspects of Opposition life.

At the time of *Yesterday's Men* Pope had a clear conception of herself as a producer who, though interested in the machinations of political life, was more concerned with the problems of translating politics into televisually appealing programme content. This was initially based on her critique of existing political television, whose conventions and forms seemed inadequate for dealing with the idea of *Yesterday's Men*. She notes:

I remember that when I was first asked to make *Yesterday's Men* I felt rather daunted and wondered how I would make people watch. I didn't think that seven long interviews would work. There were certain things that David Dimbleby and I wanted to say about the nature of political life — its motives, prizes, privations and so on — as seen through the eyes of seven prominent politicians at a certain traumatic point in their political lives. We decided to use a variety of television techniques to say those things. I was very interested in learning the techniques of film and TV and in mastering them sufficiently to be able to say what I want to say as engagingly as possible.

The task as seen by Pope was then to deal with a serious subject in an entertaining way:

I wanted to ask some serious questions and I hope that I was asking them engagingly. I knew that the programme was sometimes edgy and biting; and also that it was both entertaining and informative.

Within political television different definitions of programming and stylistic criteria derive from different departmental structures. The whole experience of *Yesterday's Men* was based on the exclusivity of form within CAG and therefore on the presuppositions of politicians about the nature of programmes emerging from the Group. Anomaly was the keynote of *Yesterday's Men*, embedded in differential expectations of what the programme would look like — the result was controversy.

The conceptions of the producer were allied to the very similar views held by Dimbleby. Discussing the way that *Panorama* tends to focus on subjects such as Willy Brandt's policy of *Ostpolitik*, he observed:

... Now, *Ostpolitik* is (a) extremely important, (b) very complicated, (c) not very televisual in the sense that there is nothing to look at very much except the faces of German politicians rabbiting on, (d) is therefore pretty dull on the screen. But some people believe that television has a duty to do these dull things because that is what life is like and all the rest of it.

I find that admirable but I'm not sure myself that it is a sensible view. I don't take the view that it's all got to be froth, at all, but I do think that one of the merits of the machine [TV] is that it can make subjects, which people otherwise would not be interested in, interesting and worth watching. You are involved with a constant, almost paternalistic, activity of coaxing people to come and see, come and find out, come and watch.

The challenge in Dimbleby's mind is to take a subject which, though serious, has been done many times previously in a rather boring manner and to make that subject televisually appealing. He chose the example of trade unions to illuminate the point.

To most people in the audience trade unionism is something they've heard so much about, and they are so used to the same old union leaders rabbiting on, that if you are coming to make a film about how trade unionism works, one's first thing is to say 'Well, look, we all know what those people are going to say and the audience know, let's not do that again, let's try and find some way, for instance of explaining the grass roots strength, explaining the role of the shop steward. Now one way of doing it is we can do a sort of university of the air type programme about it, where you interview some shop stewards in a fairly solemn way and explain where they stand on the shop floor. That's one way.

The other thing you can try to do is to make a film which was about them as individuals as well as about them in their political role and which would become something which at an individual level was interesting. People you see work very well on television. Institutions, abstract concepts, don't work so well. And what people like about television — and in a way they are sensible because the abstract concepts come across better in print — what they like is this feeling that you are actually being shown the man who's in this situation. Take the trade unionists; of course you can spend time explaining what the shop steward's role is, of course you can talk to the union or the management about the shop stewards and all that sort of thing. But in a funny way, unless you can also make the shop steward come alive as a person, it won't amount to much more than an awful lot of stuff that's been done already.

Dimbleby's proposition is that by focusing on the more personal aspects of a man's life you can in a sense 'make him come alive' and, in doing so, throw light on the motivations of his political self as opposed to his private self. A key factor in this view of broadcasting and a key to the nature of *Yesterday's Men* was Dimbleby's belief that 'television is not the same kind of medium as books or newspapers, and it's not at heart an intellectual medium, though the process demands intellect of course, but it's not at heart something that appeals to the intellect. It's something that works on all sorts of different levels, much more emotional than intellectual.' The premise is that the political broadcaster is 'an entertainer as well as a political journalist. And people who aren't become very quickly not watched.' And, of the relevance of all this to the programme: 'the idea of the song and the idea of the music and the idea of the cartoon weren't in our minds in the beginning. Those things gradually came in as you try to make a potentially very boring film into something that's watchable.'

The most significant feature in all this and the most relevant to the accusations of the Labour Party was that in making the film the programme makers adopted and developed techniques which were incompatible with the more traditional political formulae of *24 Hours* and *Panorama* which at the time of *Yesterday's Men* were the centrepieces of CAG output. This clearly did not fit with the expectations of the Labour politicians taking part, who were used to the more ritualized aspects of the Robin Day-type interview. Whether they were deceived is difficult to say. The problem was described in the following way: 'They may in a sense have felt that their expectations weren't fulfilled. Certainly their expectations weren't fulfilled but those expectations were based on their own assumptions and not on anything that we had told them.' The fact also remains that at least two of the participants sent friendly, but secret, notes saying that they weren't particularly bothered about the programme.

Much acrimony was caused by the fact that the Labour leaders were not told of the programme title. Part of the problem was that they did not care to ask the title since in the normal course of events a title like *Yesterday's Men* would not have been used. The programme makers argue that at no point were the participants led to believe that the programme would be called 'Her Majesty's Opposition' or the 'Loyal Opposition' or the 'Labour Opposition'. The Labour leaders argue that the term 'Her Majesty's Opposition' was used in their correspondence and that they quite naturally assumed that this would be the title of the programme. However, the two programme makers were clearly aware of the possible difficulties which such a title might engender. They argue that it is not *journalistic* practice to disclose 'headlines', 'we treated the title as a headline in a sense and had we communicated the title they wouldn't have accepted it.' Pope's notes from the time state: 'The second point raised in arguments about the title is that even if the participants did not raise the question of the title, I should have done. I have never been required to do this in the past, nor have I ever heard of any producer being required to do so. As I understand it, it is standard and accepted practice for a producer to choose his title.' There is then another ambiguity or twist in that the programme makers, having moved from the world of 'straight' broadcast journalism, on this point are firmly employing the principles and practices as laid down, albeit informally, within that world. They are commuting between two different explanations of current affairs television in accordance with particular circumstances and it is therefore not too surprising that problems would be induced by such an ambivalent position.

One might expect a clash between broadcasters and politicians of the scale of *Yesterday's Men* to have enormous consequences, at least at the level of the careers of those involved. The two directly involved, Pope and Dimbleby, are both still functioning, and Dimbleby has become the presenter of the programme which epitomized the formal, boring current affairs television that he opposed, *Panorama*. Angela Pope has faced no real consequences though it seems unlikely that she would be allowed near Wilson again. The principal casualty was undoubtedly John Grist, the head of CAG, who was transferred to Controller English Regions. In his book, Hill described a meeting of the Governors on 14 July 1971 at which

Curran proposed 'a change in the headship of current affairs in television. He had had this in mind for some time in order to give John Grist a new area of activity after a long spell in current affairs. He also proposed to strengthen the control exercised by the editor of news and current affairs and to add to the team someone with recent knowledge and experience in the parliamentary field' (Hill, 1974 p. 190). In September Curran informed another Board meeting of the 'fruits' of the changes, with Desmond Taylor, ENCA, 'having a closer and fuller responsibility for all current affairs programmes, *spending more of his time at Lime Grove.*' [5] (my emphasis). Curran 'thought that the new appointments and the redrawing of the lines of responsibility would have a visible and significant effect on *24 Hours*' (Hill, 1974 p. 190).

A clearer statement of the tightening of organizational and editorial control would be difficult to imagine. In fact the civil tones of this piece hide a considerable furore over these events. Contrasted with the placid description by Hill, I was told that at a meeting between Curran and Wilson in May 1971, 'Curran said to Mr Wilson when we met him at a party, "Heads will roll for this", and I guess the heads that rolled was just John Grist's head.' Curran denies emphatically ever having said this. 'Who then did say it, Hill?' I asked him. Curran replied: 'Maybe, I don't know.' I then asked if Curran would have liked to have said it: 'No, and even if I had privately, to have done so would have been political nonsense and a sign of great weakness.'

To understand the meaning of *Yesterday's Men* for our understanding of political communication in Britain and the means by which it is 'structured', it is necessary to consider the range of possibilities which exist for relations between the broadcaster and the state: from the incorporation of the broadcasting institutions within the state structure to the existence of autonomous broadcasting institutions beyond the control of the state. The former 'type' was approximated to during the period of the General Strike in 1926, whereas the latter has historically never been approximated since from their very inception there has always been an at least theoretical domination of the broadcasting institutions by the state. There has never been a time when the broadcasters existed in freedom though there have certainly been occasions when the sense of freedom prevailed. It is against this 'ideal' background that one has to judge the relationships between broadcasting and the state at the present time.

It is quite clear from other studies[6] that the makers of political television are left with a degree of 'autonomy' or 'freedom', that these concepts applied to broadcasting are not meaningless abstractions. Not-

5 Particularly interesting pieces can be found in Hardcastle (1971), Kee (1971), Dimbleby (1972), Jenkins (1971).
6 On this see Tracey, 1975.

withstanding the clear prescriptions on impartiality, the government's holding the institutional licence and the capacity of the government of the day to appoint the 'Controllers', producers do not work solely or mainly in response to directives from above or outside. Nevertheless the State does retain a residual power. In office Wilson sought to influence coverage of politics through the appointment of Lord Hill and out of power he remained a central and powerful figure, evidence of the state's capacity to influence the production of programmes. This situation reflects the real complexity and subtlety of the existing state of broadcasting: that is the organizations are still 'institutions within the constitution' (that after all is what their founding documents are all about) and also institutions that aspire to a level of independent political and social observation. One can readily see the likely difficulties that follow from an attachment to a 'national interest' which ultimately is defined by the state (not the individual government, but the totality of Parliamentary, administrative and judicial institutions) and also an attachment to a defence of their employees against the potentially oppressive effects of the 'national interest'. Thus most broadcasters would see themselves as journalists for whom there is not a national interest but merely a set of competing interests in society about whom they must provide information and description and between whom they must not choose. The problem is, of course, that the luxuries of detached comment and free provision of information are not so readily doled out to the practitioners of *broadcast* journalism.

This does, then, pose the vital, though difficult, question of the extent to which the broadcasting institutions constitute a significant part of the workings of liberal democracy. That they were felt to play a crucial part clearly underlay the reactions of the politicians involved, and it is widely recognized that politicians throughout the West are highly concerned about the possible damage which the ubiquitous box can do to their fragile reputations. The contrary findings of social scientists on these matters, the very real levels of party allegiance which do exist, have done nothing to allay those fears.

Part and parcel of this concern with broadcasting's role within liberal democracy is the increasingly important view that it can and must be made to function as a meaningful part of the machinery of parliamentary democracy, a view which is a constituent of a wider theoretical frame-work in which the Press (and the term is used generically) constitute a 'Fourth Estate', an autonomous part of the 'body politic' providing the flow of information which is considered to be that system's life-blood. Having studied *Yesterday's Men* one begins to see the very real difficulties that would have to be faced in seeking to incorporate broadcasting within such a scheme. We know that television has the potential to become the prime source of political information upon which political man must feed. In such a context, however, the determination of the diet becomes crucial, and one would wish to argue that the ultimate message of this study is that unless broadcasting can extricate itself from the subservient position it has *vis-a-vis* the political system, the likely menu it can offer will remain limited.

One would wish to suggest, then, that the experience of *Yesterday's Men* illuminates something of the way in which the audience's pictures of the political world are structured, and in effect limited. In short, the programme served to confirm the televisual convention that political imagery will be about the presentation of elite figures who will be seen and dealt with in a familiar context which, no matter how harrowing the interviews with professional broadcasters, they fundamentally define. As such it illuminated important features of the total mosaic of those political and cultural structures which define the political tunnel vision of television.

Yesterday's Men, however, remains an interesting example of the limitations which exist on the capacity of one part of the state structure to intervene and influence (the Governors did not after all accept all of Wilson's demands) but at the same time to have certain small but significant, long term but not readily detectable, influences. Examples are changes in personnel, the structural changes — the implications behind the observation that ENCA was to spend more time at Lime Grove — the effective ban on producers from producing in certain areas where they have previously trodden with unfortunate circumstances, etc. This is the stuff of influence but it is the marginality of the influence which is fascinating and it reflects the full complexity and subtlety of these relationships, the difficulties of their analysis, definition and apprehension in the present political context, which contrasts sharply with the real clarity and ready apprehension of the relationships in for example the General Strike.

If the broad meaning of *Yesterday's Men* was the complex interaction of prescription and practice, the illumination of the present limits on political intervention, what then were the detectable consequences of the visible ire of leading State figures on programming? When Wilson had previously sought to influence broadcasting the political motivation was obvious, the method oblique. When he attacked what he thought was an unjust programme the political element was oblique, the method direct — phone calls, writs, press coverage, etc. The visible consequences of power, the manifest relationship between the broadcasters and a key political figure such as Wilson, is not always the most significant area for analysis since it misses the less obvious and tangible aspects of power. In effect it is inadequate always to look for or only to consider the conspicuous manifestations of the impact of the political associations and personalities within the state.

Thus the potential impact of the state as exemplified by *Yesterday's*

Men did not just involve structural change but also an ill-defined feeling among programme makers themselves that such programmes should not be repeated, thus fashioning an image of what in future would be the most appropriate form of programme when dealing with politics. One has therefore to consider the way in which outside pressure was able to influence the largely unspoken assumptions about programme making.

The conception of the producer and the reporter on *Yesterday's Men* echoed a persistent discussion in broadcasting of how one produces programmes in a competitive environment with its emphasis on entertainment and audience size using a medium which only with difficulty is able to treat and discuss the political process. The initial problem with which the programme maker wrestles is not political pressure but the whole meaning of the medium for political communication. It was the attempt by Dimbleby and Pope to solve the problem by breaking out of traditional formulae that led to the political controversy. What one can say, then, is that programmes which stray from forms and practices that normally govern the television coverage of politicians — that is, the formal interviews, studio discussions, reportage of speeches, information about parliamentary affairs, etc. — is likely to provoke a sharp reaction. Wilson's success was to define the 'appearance of things', to ensure that these forms would remain intact, that there would be no repetition of the *Yesterday's Men* programme. It remains the case also that this controversy did not happen in isolation. It has to be seen in the context of a general mood of inhibition which arose within broadcasting in the late 1960s and the first years of this decade. These years were marked not only by Hill's appointment, but also by the 'threat' of an enquiry into the future of broadcasting,[7] mouthings from Benn and from parts of the Labour party that broadcasting was altogether 'too important to be left to the broadcasters' and calls from various sides for the establishment of a Broadcasting Council, a kind of Press Council with teeth.

Let the last word on the significance of the controversy however, lie with Dimbleby and Pope. Dimbleby is perfectly clear in his own mind on the nature of Wilson's impact:

Under Hugh Greene we were still in a stage of trying to discover what television can do. Now I think we are on the retreat in that I don't think you can expect any fireworks for some time. I think everybody is too much aware now of the kind of trouble like this that you get into to allow it to happen. But I think that is allied in many people's minds to a genuine doubt about what the role of television is, and a genuine feeling that perhaps all that was perhaps the wrong way to use it and that you shouldn't be challenging, investigating in quite that way. I don't myself subscribe to this. I think that it is the right way of using it and I think it's a great pity that it hasn't really had a chance. But these new audience-participation programmes

7 For a detailed discussion of how the periodic enquiries into broadcasting have engendered a cycle of crises for the institutions see Prith (1973).

for instance. In theory they are an attempt at enlarging the access to the BBC, in practice they are as disciplined as any other sort of programme . . . . So I detect a rather hideous softening. It's not got very bad yet it's true and you can still see fairly straightforward reports on *Panorama* and *Midweek*. You still have very hard interviews with politicians, but somehow the feeling that it was a medium with which one could experiment has gone. The feeling for instance we had with *Yesterday's Men*, there was a chance to really try and do something different with a political film, try and make it different so that it explained things in an entertaining way. All that's gone.

Perhaps the most interesting and pertinent perception of the impact of the *Yesterday's Men* affair lies in Pope's own conception of the new parameters of the permissible, of how her own programming will be affected. *Yesterday's Men*, she states, was 'sharp and entertaining'

. . . and the kind of telly that politicians have never been part of. In retrospect I can see this much more strongly than I could then. I think that to an extent I have learned an awful lot about that from the whole episode and one of the worst things is that I would never try to do it again. I have had my fingers burnt. I wouldn't try it, and no-one else would try it for a very long time. . . . Nobody must do *Yesterday's Men* again. You mustn't. Better be safe than be imaginative.

References

Crossman, R. H. S., 1971: 'The BBC, labour and the public'. *New Statesman* 16 July.

Dimbleby, D., 1972: 'A broadcaster's hopes'. *The Listener*, 88 16 November.

Governors, 1971: 'Yesterday's Men' A statement by the Board of Governors of the BBC. *The Listener*, 15 July.

Greene, H., 1972: 'The Future of Broadcasting in Britain'. *New Statesman*, 20 October.

Hardcastle, W., 1971: 'The BBC's backbone'. *The Listener*, 15 July.

Hill, C., 1974: *Behind the Screen: The Broadcasting Memoirs of Lord Hill*. Sedgwick and Jackson.

Jenkins, P., 1971: 'Sound and Fury'. *The Guardian*, 21 June.

Kee, R., 1971: 'BBC Errors', *The Listener*, 22 July.

Smith, A., 1972: 'The *Yesterday's Men* Affair'. *New Statesman*, 16 June. 1973: *The Shadow in the Cave*. Allen & Unwin.

Tracey, M., 1975: *The Production of Political Television in Britain*. Ph.D. thesis, University of Leicester.

Williams, M., 1972: *Inside No. 10*. Weidenfeld and Nicolson.

11

Linkages between the Mass Media and Politics: a model for the analysis of political communications systems

Michael Gurevitch and Jay G. Blumler

Introduction

Assumptions about the political impact of the mass media have played a formative part in guiding the direction of mass communication research ever since its inception. Insofar as the pioneer investigators accepted popular impressions of the media as omnipotent and capable of being employed for manipulative purposes, it was natural that much research attention should have been paid to communication influences on people's political opinions and attitudes. It is equally obvious why such a pre-occupation with persuasive effects should have resulted in an imbalance of activity favouring studies of the audience at the expense of other elements in the communication process. Dramatic examples of seemingly successful uses of the mass media to propagate political beliefs and ideologies in World War I and the 1930s, plus the growth of political science interest in empirical analysis of voting behaviour, gave rise to and reinforced the conviction that the prime target for research should be processes of opinion and attitude change among individual receivers of mass communicated messages.

The subsequent erosion of the myth of the media's irresistible powers of persuasion through the publication of contrary evidence had two related repercussions for the study of political communication. First, there was a marked broadening and diversification of the problems regarded as open to enquiry. Consequently, political communication provides a fertile field of study nowadays for researchers steeped in a wide range of disciplines and methodologies: historians may compare the technologies, rhetorics and publics for political communication prevalent at different periods of time; mass media operations may be described through concepts borrowed from pressure-group analysis; the relations of

Authors' note: An earlier version of this paper was presented to the Workshop on 'The Political Role of the Mass Media', at a meeting of the European Consortium of Political Research, Strasbourg, March 1974. We are indebted to the participants at the Workshop for their comments.

media institutions to political parties may be examined; the influence of internal constraints on the political output of the media may be observed; and audience members may be studied from perspectives other than that of effects (as in the so-called 'uses and gratifications' approach). (Blumler and McQuail, 1968; Elliott, 1972; Galnoor, 1973; Hadenius, Hoyer and Weibull, 1973; Halloran *et al.*, 1970; Halmos, 1969; Mendelsohn and Crespi, 1970; Seymour-Ure, 1974; Tunstall, 1971.) Second, in some cases those shifts of focus resulted in a virtual rejection of the audience as an object of research interest. This stemmed mainly from the assumption that the original seekers after persuasion effects had not only exhausted that particular seam of enquiry but had returned from their endeavours with precious little gold to show for their trouble.

The position taken in this paper is that the study of political communication could be enriched by adoption of a systems outlook. As conceived here, this is regarded not as competitive with other research approaches but as capable of incorporating them. It is appreciated that limitations of evidence make the elaboration of such an outlook problematic at this stage and that different analysts attracted to this kind of approach would probably propound different versions of the notion of a political communication system. (For other examples, see Deutsch, 1963 and Tichenor *et al.*, 1974.) Nevertheless, three benefits could ensue from attempts to place political communication phenomena in a systems framework. First, pressure would be generated to link diverse bodies of evidence in broader analytical perspectives. Second, there would be an antidote against the tendency to under- or over-emphasize any single element of the political communication system (e.g. the audience). Third, by drawing attention to system factors which, in varying across countries, might have macro-level consequences that could be measured and compared, cross-national investigation would be facilitated.

An underlying assumption of such an approach, of course, is that the main features of the political communication process may be regarded as if they formed a system, such that variation in one of its components would be associated with variation in the behaviour of its other components. Before developing the implications of this assumption positively, however, it may be useful to see how certain existing tendencies in political communication research could be subsumed under a systems perspective.

Recent Research Directions

1 *Effects research.* A distinct shift of interest can be discerned here, involving a diminished concern to measure the *persuasive* impact of political messages and a heightened interest in charting their likely *cognitive* effects. This is not just a matter of recording simple information gains but one of investigating the ability of the mass media 'to create

images of social reality by which the public may structure their views of the world' (Wade, 1973). Moreover, the influence of the propagation of such images is unlikely in the longer run to be confined only to the cognitive realm. Dissonance theory would predict, for example, that when an individual's attitudinal orientation conflicts with a view of the world that is consistently being projected by a trusted communication source, the former will eventually be modified to fit the latter (Wamsley and Pride, 1972). This feature of the 'new look' in political communication research (Blumler and McLeod, 1973) could be furthered by a systems approach, should there be reason to suppose that the perspectives on social and political reality offered to audience members in communications content depend in turn on other aspects of the organization of the media. Such an assumption would be especially relevant to the many studies now being undertaken of the 'agenda-setting function' of the media. This stipulates that the relative frequency of references to given political issues in media content will be reflected in a corresponding set of issue priorities in the minds of readers, viewers and listeners (McCombs and Shaw, 1972; McLeod et al., 1973). A systems perspective would attempt to link such questions to media and political structural conditions that might determine the kinds of issue agenda that mass media outlets present to their audience members.

2 *Exposure behaviour.* Recent studies of the communication behaviour of audience members have tended to conclude that selective exposure should no longer be taken for granted as the 'natural' mechanism that guides much consumption of media material about political affairs. Reanalysis of past survey evidence has shown that the extent of such selectivity was much less than had hitherto been supposed, while a review of experimental evidence has failed to uncover the existence of a 'general psychological preference for supportive information' (Sears and Freedman, 1967). The implication is that selective exposure has been downgraded to the status of a *variable* from its previous elevation into the dignity of a supposed law. A systems approach, however, would entertain the possibility that variation in rates of audience selectivity could depend on variation in other components of the political communication system, such as those involving differing relationships between media institutions and political institutions.

3 *Audience roles.* In addition to studying the effects of political messages *on* the audience, some investigators have been exploring the 'uses and gratifications' involved in audience members' orientations to political communication. This approach examines what people seek to get out of the political messages they monitor, and some of its results have recently been translated into notions of a number of alternative 'roles' that audience members may adopt when following civic affairs through the media (Blumler, 1973). This concept of 'audience roles' not

only provides a way of structuring the audience that differs from the conventional unidimensional continuum of degree of political interest. It also implies the presence, at the receiving end, of expectations about communication which may be systematically connected to corresponding role orientations among those individuals who originate and transmit political messages, such as media personnel and political spokesmen.

4 *Institutional analysis.* Increasing attention, both theoretical and empirical, has recently been paid to the processes by which recurrent content patterns, especially those embedded in news output, are produced. Much of this work has emphasized the operation of mechanisms that strain toward consonance and tend to yield consensus treatments of political topics (Cohen and Young, 1973). There have also been penetrating theoretical explorations of relationships between political and media institutions at this level. Seymour-Ure (1974) has considered many sources of variation (as in the features of party systems and the values endorsed by political cultures) in press-party parallelism, or the degree to which individual newspapers are identified with specific political parties. Hadenius, Hoyer and Weibull (1973) have examined the evolution of similar relationships over time and identified some of the correlates and consequences of trends away from press-party affiliation and identification. Specifically, they have postulated 'conflict-provoking' consequences for systems in which press-party linkages are close and 'consensus building' ones for systems in which such associations are relatively loose or nonexistent. This line of analysis is especially conducive to a systems approach, since it suggests that variations in the closeness of relationship between media institutions and certain political institutions may have consequences at other levels, including media contents, audience orientations and ultimately the degree of consensus or dissensus prevalent in a given society.

These are some illustrations, then, of the potential of a systems approach to subsume and integrate different strands of current research into a wider conceptual framework. The rest of this paper aims to identify the main components of a political communication system and to show how, when each component is utilized as an 'entry-point' for analysis, critical linkages between the mass media and politics can be identified and hypotheses can be generated about the triggering of variations in one part of the system by variations in one or more of its other parts.

The Elements of a Political Communication System

In very broad terms, the main components of a political communication system may be located in:

    1 Political institutions in their communication aspects.[1]

1 Boundary problems arise in defining what counts as the 'communication aspects' of the activity of political institutions and as the 'political aspects' of mass media

2 Media institutions in their political aspects.[1]
3 Audience orientations to political communication.
4 Communication-relevant aspects of political culture.

Expressed somewhat differently, if we look at a political communication system, what we see is two sets of institutions, political and media organizations, which are involved in the course of message preparation in much 'horizontal' interaction with each other, while, on a 'vertical' axis, they are separately and jointly engaged in disseminating and processing information and ideas to and from the mass citizenry.

The interactions of the two kinds of institutions are to some extent conditioned by mutual power relationships. This pre-supposes that both have an independent power base in society, one source of which arises from their respective relations with the audience. The power of political institutions is inherent in their functions as articulators of interest and mobilizers of social power for purposes of political action. The independent power base of media institutions is perhaps less obvious and may even be denied by those who perceive them as essentially secondary bodies, entirely dependent on others for the news and opinions they pass on, and highly constrained in their operation by a number of political, economic, cultural and technological factors. Nevertheless, at least three sources of media power can be identified. These are structural, psychological and normative in origin.

The *structural* root of the power of the mass media springs from their unique capacity to deliver to the politician an audience which, in size and composition, is unavailable to him by any other means. Indeed, the historical significance of the growing role of mass communication in politics lies, among other things, in the resulting enlargement of the receiver base to such an extent that previous barriers to audience involvement (e.g. low level of education and weak political interest) have been

---

performance. For one thing, it is possible to argue that *all* actions of political institutions have some communication relevance, that is that all the relationships central to political organization — power, authority, obedience, interest aggregation, etc. — imply the existence of a communication function. Similarly, political aspects are so intricately interwoven with all other aspects of the performance of media institutions as to preclude the possibility either of isolating them empirically or even of analytically denoting some part of media content as entirely 'non-political'. Clearly, our definition should not be taken to imply that the communication aspects of the actions of political institutions are separable from other aspects of their behaviour or that the political aspects of mass communication are limited solely to the processes involved in the production of manifestly political content. It depends, rather, on 'the consequences, actual and potential, that communicatory activity has for the functioning of the political system' (Fagen, 1966). Thus, all aspects of the performance of political institutions and of media institutions that are seen or perceived to have such consequences are included in our definition.

largely overcome and the audience for political communication has become virtually co-terminous with membership of society itself.

The *psychological* root of media power stems from the relations of credibility and trust that different media organizations have succeeded in developing (albeit to different degrees) with members of their audiences. This bond is based on the fulfilment of audience expectations and the validation of past trust relationships, which in turn are dependent on legitimized and institutionalized routines of information presentation evolved over time by the media.

It is the combined influence of these structural and psychological sources of strength that enable the media to interpose themselves between politicians and the audience and to 'intervene' in other political processes as well. This is expressed in the way in which they are capable of re-structuring the timing and character of political events (conventions, demonstrations, leader appearances, etc.), defining crisis situations to which politicians are obliged to react, requiring comment on issues that media personnel have emphasized as important, injecting new personalities into the political dialogue (such as television interviewers) and stimulating the growth of new communication agencies (such as public relations firms, opinion poll agencies, and political advertising and campaign management specialists).

Since such forms of intervention may be unwelcome to many politicians, the *normative* root of media power can be crucial at times of conflict. This springs from the respect that is accorded in competitive democracies to such tenets of liberal philosophy as freedom of expression and the need for specialized organs to safeguard citizens against possible abuses of political authority. This tends to legitimate the independent role of media organizations in the political field and to shelter them from overt attempts blatantly to bring them under political control.

It is not the argument of this section that political communication flows are merely the product of a naked power struggle waged between two sets of would-be communicators. On the contrary, the notion that such power-holders are bound together in political communication *system* alerts us to the influence of other forces as well. One such influence arises from audience expectations, which it is the concern of both sorts of communicators to address effectively. In addition, a systems outlook implies that the interactions of the various actors occurs within an over-arching framework of organizing principles that are designed to regularize the relationships of media institutions to political institutions. The implications of those considerations are discussed more fully below.

Entry Points into the System

Any analysis of a system comprising a number of components linked by a network of mutual dependencies is faced with the need to identify a set of relevant conceptual perspectives and to select optimal entry points into the system. The following discussion proposes to proceed by selecting as points of departure those elements in each of the components of the political communication system which are most conducive to generating propositions offering a basis for both theoretical advance and empirical research. We will attempt to present suggestions for analysis of this kind, looking first at the audience, then at certain organizational characteristics of political and media institutions and finally at the political culture, as it is reflected in the principles which organize normative relationships between political and media institutions, which in turn have some consequences for relationships between these institutions and the audience.

Audience Roles

The concept of audience roles has arisen from attempts to apply the 'uses and gratifications' approach to the study of voters' orientations to the political contents of the mass media. Evidence collected from this stand-point supports the implication that different receivers of political information are motivated by different expectations of it, develop different orientations toward it and may therefore be perceived as playing different roles in the political communication system. Investigating such orientations to political communications in Britain, Blumler (1973) has provisionally identified four such audience roles that might be applicable to the political communication systems of other competitive democracies. They include: the *partisan*, seeking a reinforcement of his existing beliefs; the *liberal citizen*, seeking guidance in deciding how to vote; the *monitor*, seeking information about features of the political environment (such as party policies, current issues and the qualities of political leaders); and the *spectator*, seeking excitement and other affective satisfactions.

The notion of audience roles undoubtedly requires further development and refinement.[2] Nevertheless, it offers a point of departure for analysis of political communication systems in two respects. One use of the concept would enquire into the processes that lead people in different societies to take up one or more of the roles available to them. Supposing that the validity of a common repertoire of alternative role possibilities could be established for audience members in a designated set of competitive democracies, it would then be possible to identify some of the sociological and psychological correlates associated with the particular political communication roles that different people adopt and to compare their influence cross-nationally. Sociologically, such an analysis might

2 For example, we still need to test the comprehensiveness of the typology outlined above, to examine the stability of audience role expectations over time, and to explore the interaction of gratifications sought and communication effects.

focus, for example, on age (expected to differentiate partisans from liberal citizens), educational background (expected to differentiate monitors from spectators) and early patterns of socialization to politics in the family and elsewhere. Psychologically, it might examine such variables as strength of partisan identity (expected to pinpoint the partisans at one pole and spectators at the other) and political cynicism (as a possible discriminant of spectators from the rest). The results of such a study might help to show how in the countries studied political culture impinges on political communication expectations at the audience level.[3]

A second line of analysis would pursue the possibility that audience roles are matched by similar orientations among political and professional communicators. The underlying assumption here is that audience members and communicators are linked in a network of mutually shared expectancies (Tan, 1973). It does not follow that such a correspondence of roles will always be perfect. On the contrary, imperfections of feedback, differences of purpose, and especially constraints arising from the disparities of political stratification may all be productive of discrepancies between the orientations of the different participants in the political communication process. Nevertheless, the concept of a 'communication role' is at least as applicable to political communicators and to media personnel as it is to audience members, Moreover, the very notion of communication presupposes some degree of compatibility between the orientations of the originators and the receivers of messages. Figure 1 presents a set of parallels that may be drawn between them.

Figure 1 *The Complementarity of Roles in a Political Communication System*

Audience	Media Personnel[4]	Party Spokesmen
Partisan	Editorial guide	Gladiator
Liberal citizen	Moderator	Rational Persuader
Monitor	Watchdog	Information Provider
Spectator	Entertainer	Actor/Performer

The utility of such a paradigm depends on its ability to stimulate speculation about the structure of a political communication system and to suggest hypotheses about linkages between the components of such a system. Attention to the role relationship indicated in Figure 1 would open up at least three areas of exploration:

3 The approach proposed here is to some extent modelled along lines recently followed by Verba *et al.* (1971) in an attempt to examine the dimensionality of several modes of democratic participation in politics and the correlates thereof in five different countries.

4 For another, partly similar, attempt to identify the primary functions of the media in relation to government see: William L. Rivers and Michael J. Nyhan, (Eds.) *Aspen Notebook on Government and the Media*, New York, Praeger, 1973, pp. 27–8.

1 *System integration.* The degree of integration of a political communication system might be conceived in terms of the degree of
correspondence between its constitutent parts. Thus, a highly integrated
system would be one with high inter-correlations between role orientations across levels, i.e. where all the participants in the communication
process share equivalent orientations and consequently speak on, or are
'tuned in' to, similar wave-lengths. Conversely, a system with a low
level of integration would be one with low inter-correlations between
parallel roles, reflecting a situation where the leading elements are at
cross-purposes with each other, and in which a high degree of communication conflict across levels prevails.

The measurement of system integration by communication role
parallelism should not be taken to imply some utopian touchstone of
complete complementarity. One-to-one correspondence across levels is
likely to be impeded not only by the discrepancies and conflicts that stem
from political stratification but also *via* the multiplicity of orientations
available to the audience and the difficulty that a given set of communicators will tend to experience in trying to address them simultaneously.
Nevertheless, integration can be regarded as a matter of degree, measured
by high or low inter-correlations between orientations across levels. Neither
does the specification of this dimension entail a particular judgement
about its value or an assumption that communication works 'better' when
these roles are complementary. For example, the Kennedy-Nixon debates
might be described as a communication form in which the politicians acted
as gladiators, the media professionals performed as moderators and many
members of the audience expected to enjoy the contest as spectators. This
kind of expectation on the part of some audience members might, indeed,
be revealing since it highlights the similarity, perhaps even the inter-
changeability of the gladiatorial and the actor/performer roles. However,
if system integration can be measured in this way, then some of its further
consequences should also be traceable — in terms, say, of the prevalence
of alienation in the audience or of the efficacy of information transfer.

2 *Inter-level distancing.* The relative distance between the audience
and the media system, on the one hand, and between the electorate and
the political system, on the other, might be measured by the degree to
which audience roles correspond more closely with media personnel roles
or with party spokesmen roles. Closeness of correspondence might
indicate the relative credibility of the media, and the trustworthiness of
politicians, for the audience, while lack of correspondence might reflect a
failure of one or the other set of communicators to address themselves
relevantly to the needs of the audience.

3 *Cross-level influences.* The principles that normatively relate media
organizations to political institutions in a particular society may help to
shape the role definitions regarded as appropriate by those occupying

different positions in the communication system. Various specific hypotheses may be derived from this possibility:

a) Media systems with a high degree of political autonomy are likely to give professional communicators considerable freedom to adopt a variety of role orientations. This will leave audience role options wide open as well and tend to oblige political spokesmen to perform in multi-functional fashion. This might not be equally palatable to all politicians (some of whom might have a distaste for the actor/performer role, for example). In such systems, then, we might find more evidence of 'role distancing' among politicians and 'type-casting' forms of division of labour among newsmen in the media.

b) Where public-service type goals prevail in media organizations, watchdog functions will be favoured by media professionals and audience members will be encouraged to assume the monitor role; this will exert pressure on politicians to give primacy to the information-provider role. On the other hand, more commercially-oriented media might give greater prominence to entertainer roles because of assumptions about audience preferences for the spectator role. Conformity on the part of political spokesmen would lead them to adopt actor/performer roles.

c) Where political parties control the media, the gladiatorial role will be adopted more often by political spokesmen while the role of editorial guide will be adopted by media personnel; this will exert pressure on audience members to assume the partisan role.

d) Systems governed by more authoritative and paternalistic goals might have either of two consequences for audience members: audience roles could tend to follow those assumed by party and media communicators, involving a greater emphasis, then, on partisan and monitor roles; or audience expectations would be in conflict with the equivalent orientations of message senders, with resulting tendencies to avoid political information, distrust the media and feel alienated from politics.

Political Institutions vs. Media Institutions: norms and structures

A second point of entry to the analysis of political communication systems springs initially from the necessary involvement of two kinds of actors — political spokesmen and media personnel — in recurrent patterns of interaction with each other. These can be seen as operating on two planes: of boundary maintenance between organizations; and of message production. In the first case, members of the top echelons of both organizations might maintain contacts aimed at regulating the relationships between the two; resolving conflicts where they arise and generally defining the boundaries between them and maintaining the smooth functioning of the system. But of course, second, the bulk of interaction between professional communicators and politicians is concerned (commonly at somewhat lower levels) more directly with political output as such. This takes place in both formal contexts — such as press conferences, briefings, interviews and so on — and informal ones — such as a confidential exchange of views over a drink. The products of these interactions include not only streams of specific messages — on problems of the day, policies evolved to deal with them, arguments for and against alternative positions, the personalities involved in controversy, etc. — but also (and more importantly) those more abiding ground rules that prescribe the standardized formats through which information is regularly presented to the public (Dearlove, 1974). The interacting parties on both planes are perpetually caught up in a tension between needs of mutual accommodation and various sources of conflict. Without minimal accommodation, little or no communication would take place, and nobody's purposes would be realized. Yet the conflicting functions (and independent power bases of the two sides) ensure that the terms of accommodation will continually be open to renewal and revision.

The conduct of the main participants in this relationship is often assessed from essentially one-sided standpoints: for example, that of the political activist who treats media output as a trivialized version of his own more lofty concerns (Crossman, 1968); or that of the journalist who regards politicians as inveterate corrupters of the independence of the press. A more analytical approach might aim instead to identify the sources of certain more or less constant influences on the behaviour of both interacting parties insofar as they subscribe to different codes of conduct and belong to different kinds of organization. Such constant factors may be found in two critical structural dimensions that influence the relationship between the parties concerned: the degree of *professionalization* characteristic of the personnel of media and political institutions; and the degree of *bureaucratization* characteristic of the two organizations.

Recent studies of mass media institutions have paid much attention to issues centring on the professionalization of staff communicators (Elliott, 1972; McLeod and Hawley, 1964; Nayman, 1973; Tunstall, 1971; Kumar, 1975). Although the degree to which media personnel exhibit all the characteristics usually ascribed to established professions might be debated, the influence of professional norms on their outlook is greater than in the case of politicians, (Lattimore and Nayman, 1974). Some dimensions of this distinction may include the following:

1 *Bases of legitimacy.* These differ for the two sets of actors. Thus, whereas politicians derive their legitimacy from the authority of the causes they espouse, the degree of consensus among the interests they articulate and public acceptance of the procedures by which they have been chosen to represent such interests, media personnel are legitimated chiefly through their fidelity to professional codes.

2 *The service function.* The centrality of the service function in the

behaviour of media professionals is reflected in the claim commonly made
by them to be concerned primarily to *serve* the audience members' 'right
to know', as distinct from the primary concern of the politician to
persuade them in the cause of political and partisan goals.

3. *Autonomy*. The work rewards that media men enjoy also derive
partly from their professional autonomy. Such an emphasis might clash
with the politician's often-held view of media personnel as essentially
middlemen in the political communication process. This potential conflict
becomes yet more acute when politicians, who commonly are disposed
toward more ideological criteria of political truth, are confronted with
the tendency of media professionals to adhere to more empirical, sceptical
(perhaps cynical) and many-sided description of political reality.
All this suggests an essential discrepancy between the codes of conduct
accepted by political spokesmen and those that regulate the behaviour of
professional communicators, irrespective of any higher-order principles
that might be shared by both.

Another set of tensions stems from structural differences that obtain
not between media professionals and politicians as members of different
occupations but between the organizations to which they belong. Many
mass media enterprises are formal institutions governed at some level of
their organization by bureaucratic norms and procedures. Political parties,
on the other hand, exist for long periods of time as relatively skeletal
organizations, which are fully mobilized only periodically or in crisis
situations, and which have only a rather loose hold over those of their
members who are not fully remunerated for their political activity. They
are not designed, therefore, to exert full bureaucratic control over
politicians and cannot base their modes of operation on purely bureaucratic standards. One consequence of this is that, once appointed, media
personnel enjoy relative security and need not be legitimated by the
consent of others outside their own employing organization. The position
of the politician, on the other hand, is essentially less secure, more
bedevilled by uncertainty and more dependent on a continual renewal
of the consent of his supporters. The vulnerability of the politician, in
contrast to the bureaucratic security of the professional communicator,
is illustrated by the highly visible and readily identified position of
individual responsibility that the politician holds, as against the greater
diffusion of responsibility that obtains in media organizations. To the
politician, then, the protective bureaucratic shells of the media must seem
intrinsically difficult to penetrate, provoking frustrations that may be
less comprehensible and more irritating to individuals who do not usually
operate in a bureaucratic environment and who could also resent
bureaucratic challenges to the supremacy of their societal functions.

As has been noted before, the potential tension inherent in these
structural differences must be managed and contained, if the interests of

both sides are to be accommodated. This suggests that one task in the
analysis of political communication systems would involve an examination
of the formal and informal mechanisms that span the boundaries between
the two kinds of organizations. Apart from the evolution of basic ground
rules that regulate the production and dissemination of political communication contents, these range from the establishment of specialized
agencies (such as publicity and public relations departments) for coping
with the demands of the other side, the development of formal and
informal procedures for airing complaints, the setting up of various
regulatory bodies, such as press councils, broadcasting councils, regulatory
commissions and enquiry commissions that exist to relate the workings of
the mass media to certain criteria of the public interest, or appointments
that place individuals familiar with the values of one sphere in key positions
in the organization of the other, to the ostensibly informal mixing of
politicians and media personnel in social circles outside work.

Political Culture as a Source of Regulating Mechanisms

A final point of analytical departure arises from the fact that, apart from
the procedures and mechanisms that are evolved by political and media
institutions to govern the relationships between them, all political systems
generate principles derived from the tenets of their political cultures, for
regulating the political role of the mass media. Such organizing principles
are vital, since the contributions of the mass media to the political process
are too important to be left to chance. Thus, communication processes
are involved in the legitimation of authority and serve functions of political
articulation, mobilization and conflict-management. They set much of the
agenda of political debate. They are partly responsible for determining
which political demands in society will be aired, and which will be
relatively muted. They affect the chances of governments and other
political actors to secure essential supports. In short, they are so closely
intertwined with political processes that they must be regulated in some
appropriate and accepted way.

The manner of such attempted regulation is ultimately traceable to
the influence of various tenets of political culture. The most basic one is,
of course, the degree to which freedom of expression is cherished as a
basic political value or, conversely the degree to which restrictions on it
are regarded as necessary and permissible for the sake of other political
goals. Closely related is the value placed on ensuring the existence of outlets for voicing a variety of opinions and securing their ability to operate
in a fashion unhampered by potential attempts of political actors to
influence or dominate them. Political-cultural factors bearing on the
structure of prevailing opinions may also play a part — for example, how
far are the predominant positions polarized, to what extent do they tend

to be expressed in ideological or pragmatic forms and what is the manner of their relationship to underlying bases of social differentiation and cleavage. On another level one might identify the influence of assumptions about the suitability of market mechanisms for advancing society's communication goals: societies that share the basic tenets of freedom of political expression might differ in their conception of the desirability of subjecting communication outlets to economic constraints and to the pressures of a free market. Finally, political cultures may differ in the degree to which they value the political sphere itself as a dignified and important realm of activity, informed involvement in which deserves to be promoted.

Although all such tenets are relevant, no one-to-one relationship can be traced between any single strand of political culture and any specific principle designed to govern the role of the mass media in politics. In the end, the central issue in the relationship between media and political institutions revolves around the *media's relative degree of autonomy* and to what extent and by what means this is allowed to be constrained. Thus, it is the overall cultural 'mix' in a given society that will tend to fix the position of the media on the subordination-autonomy continuum and determine which constraints are permitted some degree of control over them. At least three main sources of constraints *directly* subordinating the media to political institutions may be identified: legal, normative and structural, respectively.

Legal constraints include all those rules and regulations defining the rights and obligations of media institutions that are ultimately enforceable by the executive and judicial arms of the state. They primarily define the area within which the media may exercise freedom of expression, circumscribed as the case may be by libel laws, legally protected rights of privacy, restrictions on national security grounds, the imposition of censorship on political comment, etc.

Normative constraints refer to expectations of political and public service by media organizations, for which they may be held socially accountable without falling under the direct control of either state or party machinery. They often arise from a conviction that the normal operation of the market mechanism is either insufficient to promote accepted communication goals or may work against them, and they typically invite attempts to ensure that the existing media disperse not merely entertaining fare but also a full and varied supply of political information and analysis suited to the needs of a conscientious citizenry. Some, by now classic, expressions of such 'social responsibility' doctrines, especially as they apply to the press, are to be found in the recommendations of the Commission on Freedom of the Press (1947) and in Siebert *et al.* (1956) and Rivers and Schramm (1969).

Structural constraints concern the degree to which formal or semiformal linkages may be forged between media institutions and political bodies. Thus, political parties, for example, may be involved in the organization of media enterprises through ownership, financial contributions or representation on policy-making bodies, or linkages may be established instead via a tradition of editorial support for the party's goals and policies. The phenomenon of press-party parallelism, comprehensively analysed by Seymour-Ure (1974), obviously belongs to this area of constraint.

Apart from these *direct* sources of political constraints media organizations labour under a host of other constraints, some of which may be employed by political institutions in order to gain some measure of *indirect* control and influence over the media.[5] Prominent among these are the economic constraints. These apply not only to commercial media organizations (where advertising revenue might be regulated or taxed directly by the political authorities) but also to non-commercial media institutions whose cash inflows (be they licence fees, governmental or non-governmental subsidies) may be subjected to government approval or influence. Thus, the business and administrative personnel of media organizations, who are charged with their economic and financial viability and well-being, might be especially sensitive to external pressures affecting their organizations' finances, and consequently act as a potential channel for the introduction of political influence on their message outputs. Similarly, political control or regulation focused ostensibly on the technologies of mass communication (such as licensing the use of the airwaves, or control of the import or price of newsprint) may be used as a form of leverage to exert influence over media policies. More generally, we may, following Gerbner (1969) identify a variety of 'power roles' both inside and outside of media institutions, that are capable of affecting mass communicators' decisions, consequently inducing them to act as (willing or unwilling) channels of political influence on the media.

The two main media of political communication, broadcasting and the press, tend, for historical, economic and technological reasons, to be differently placed with respect to these constraints, and to exhibit different degrees of vulnerability to them. However, these differences are relative rather than absolute and some important similarities between them may, moreover, be identified. For example, although 'public service broadcasting' immediately comes to mind as an instance of normative

---

5 The distinction between 'direct' and 'indirect' sources of political control over the media constitutes yet another boundary problem. Clearly, some forms of control, such as economic ones, are so inextricably interwoven with political relationships that they may be regarded also as 'direct' controls. Our distinction, however, is based on whether a given constraint can be traced to *direct political relationships* between the media and political institutions, or whether it operates via other potential *mechanisms* of control.

constraint on broadcasting, it has a close analogue in the previously mentioned 'social responsibility theory of the press', with its attendant codes of journalistic practice and press councils set up to pronounce on instances of their infraction. Similarly, although 'parallelism' to political parties may seem more common to the press because of the relative multiplicity of outlets characteristic of that medium, in some countries at least separate broadcasting organizations have been instituted to follow political or other socio-cultural divisions (such as the Dutch system or the system that prevailed in Chile until the 1973 military coup). In other countries representatives of political parties are admitted to membership of the governing bodies of broadcasting organizations on a pluralistic basis (e.g. Austria).

Nevertheless, some crucial differences between these media still obtain. First, in many democratic countries newspapers have traditionally belonged in the private sector, whereas the dependence of broadcast transmission on scarce wave-lengths immediately placed first radio and then television in the public domain. Many consequences have flowed from this distinction. Perhaps the most important one is the development of a regulatory licensing system for broadcasting, which was either totally absent or far looser in the case of the press. A related difference concerns the number of outlets, typically numerous in the case of the press in contrast to the relative paucity of broadcasting outlets, often resulting in the monopolistic or duopolistic position of many broadcasting institutions. Yet another difference might be identified in the relatively greater vulnerability of the press to market forces, from which broadcasting organizations have often been more sheltered (with the obvious exception of commercial broadcasting organizations). As a result of all of these factors, the presumed power of broadcasting has been enhanced, and consequently means of controlling or neutralizing its potential rivalry to political institutions have had to be found. These have emerged in the form of norms requiring impartiality in the handling of controversial issues, non-editorializing, and the maintenance of a balance between the major political tendencies of the day.

Perhaps these inter-media contrasts are reflected in two main differences so far as the imposition of constraining principles of organization is concerned. First, it is far easier for newspapers to become involved in political controversy as participants rather than as mere referees; from this point of view, variations in media-party parallelism across countries and time periods, with possibly major consequences for audience behaviour and response, are more likely to be found in the press field than in broadcasting. Second, simply because broadcasting organizations are located in the public sector, they will tend, other factors being equal, to be situated nearer the subordination pole of the autonomy-subordination continuum than the press system of the same society is likely to be.

The foregoing discussion has focused on the differential degree to which the two kinds of media institutions — broadcasting and the press — may be *subjected* to these constraints. The capacity to *apply* these constraints to the mass media raises another important institutional distinction — this time focusing on the two main types of political organizations: state institutions and political parties. State institutions are endowed with supreme political authority in society, and the machinery through which they exercise this is the legal code. Consequently, their constraints over media institutions are usually clearly definable and highly visible. The manner in which they impose them is very closely observed and monitored by other political actors, and, in competitive democracies at least, they walk a narrow tight-rope in their relations with media organizations, which are prepared to mobilize defences against prescriptions deemed excessive as measured against the norms of the political culture. Party organizations, on the other hand, are regarded as legitimate competitors in the political arena and are consequently allowed to mobilize all the resources available to them, including communication resources, in the pursuit of their political aims. This does not imply a free-for-all situation, since this competition is regulated by certain rules of the political game that are also prescribed by the political culture. Nevertheless, they are in a sense less confined in their relationships with media organizations. A concomitant of this greater degree of operational manoeuverability is, of course, the absence of any legal power over the mass media system.

In addition to state institutions and political parties a further institutional element with some constraining influence over the media should be mentioned. Pluralistic societies are dotted with a variety of pressure groups, some of them striving to promote more or less overtly political aims. Although the degree to which they can exert an influence over the mass media is, on the face of it, relatively slight, certain media organizations sometimes behave in ways suggestive of a degree of sensitivity to such sources of pressure. Again, an inter-medium difference may apply here. Those sections of the press that are directly dependent only on the patronage of their own readers and advertisers might feel partially insulated from such pressures. Party-linked newspapers may, furthermore, function as if completely free of any pressure group influence that does not stem from sources affiliated with their own parties. On the other hand, broadcasting organizations, whose clientele is co-terminous with society as a whole, may be more vulnerable and exposed in this respect. Hence the conclusion reached by some observers that broadcasting organizations tend to behave as if afraid of their own shadows (Smith, 1973).

Since we conceive of communication processes as forming a system, variations in the regulatory connections between political and media institutions should have definite consequences for other components of the system, including content outputs and audience orientations thereto. Some examples of possible linkages of this kind are presented in the following hypotheses:

1 Party-tied media systems will produce a higher proportion of 'one-sided' political content, tending as a result to activate partisan role orientations among members of the audience as well as selective exposure mechanisms. They will also tend to produce dissensus rather than consensus issue agendas, giving rise in turn to a higher degree of conflict over issue priorities among electors dependent on the different media outlets.

2 The more subordinate the media system, the greater will be the degree of free access to communication outlets allowed for the statements and manifestoes of party spokesmen as originally conceived. This may increase the frequency of partisan and monitor roles.

3 The greater the autonomy of the media system, the greater will be its tendency to generate 'balanced' political information contents (in ways which both *reflect* and *protect* its autonomous status). It will consequently perform primarily 'moderator' and 'watchdog' functions, which will tend to activate 'liberal citizen' and 'monitor' role orientations among its audience. Autonomous media systems are likely in turn to be found in two main variants.

a) Commercially supported autonomous media systems might favour the presentation of political materials in terms of the conflicts and the strategies of political manoeuvering, focusing on personalities at the expense of issue coverage of the political scene. This will tend especially to precipitate and cater to a greater frequency of 'spectator' roles.

b) Non-commercial and semi-commercial media systems that are normatively disposed to public service goals will produce higher proportions of issue-oriented political outputs and will tend especially to generate a higher incidence of 'monitor' role orientations among audience members.

Conclusion

The view of political communication presented in this paper draws upon the concept of a system as a set of input-output relationships that bind its constituent elements in a network of mutual dependencies. Such a model has both theoretical and empirical utilities. It should facilitate a comparative analysis of the political communication systems of different societies, and it has generated hypotheses on the basis of which a series of cross-national investigations could be launched.

Utilization of the main components of the system as analytical entry points provides, moreover, a set of complementary perspectives on the political communication process. From the standpoint of 'audience roles', this is seen in terms of *mutual orientations* to communication content that link (or fail to link) audience members with media personnel and political spokesmen. The structural/institutional perspective provides a view of the system in terms of *conflicting goals and interests*, ascribing these conflicts to structural differences between media and political institutions. Finally, the regulatory perspective focuses on the processes by which these conflicts are *institutionalized and managed* through the application of normative criteria, to which all participants subscribe to the extent that they share in and recognize the legitimacy of the political culture from which they derive.

The model thus aims to take account of both consensus and conflict relationships in political communication transactions. At this stage, however, it still awaits validation through a sustained programme of empirical research.

References

Blumler, Jay G., 1973: 'Audience Roles in Political Communication: Some Reflections on Their Structure, Antecedents and Consequences'. Paper presented to the International Political Science Association Congress, Montreal.

Blumler, Jay G. and McLeod, Jack M., 1974: 'Communication and Voter Turnout in Britain'. In Morris Janowitz (Ed.), *Sociological Theory and Survey Research*, Beverly Hills, California: Sage.

Blumler, Jay G. and McQuail, Denis, 1968: *Television in Politics.* London Faber & Faber.

Cohen, Stanley and Young, Jock (Eds.), 1973: *The Manufacture of News.* London: Constable.

Commission on Freedom of the Press, 1947: *A Free and Responsible Press.* Chicago: University of Chicago Press.

Crossman, Richard, 1968: 'The Politics of Viewing'. *New Statesman* 76 (July-December) pp. 525–30.

Dearlove, John, 1974: 'The BBC and the Politicians'. *Index* 3 (1), 23–33.

Deutsch, Karl, 1963: *The Nerves of Government.* New York: The Free Press.

Elliott, Philip, 1972: *The Making of a Television Series.* London: Constable.

Fagen, Richard, 1966: *Politics and Communication.* Boston: Little Brown.

Galnoor, Itzhak, 1973: 'The Politics of Public Information'. Paper presented to the International Political Science Association Congress, Montreal.

Gerbner, George, 1969: 'Institutional Pressures upon Mass Communicators'. In Paul Halmos (Ed.), *The Sociology of Mass Communicators* Sociological Review Monographs, 13. Keele: University of Keele.

Hadenius, Stig, Hoyer, Svennik and Weibull, Lennart, 1973: 'Towards a Comparative Perspective on Political Communication'. Paper presented to the International Political Science Association Congress, Montreal.

Halloran, James D., Elliott, Philip and Murdock, Graham, 1970: *Demonstrations and Communication: A Case Study*. Harmondsworth: Penguin.

Halmos, Paul (Ed.), 1969: *The Sociology of Mass Media Communicators*. Sociological Review Monographs 13. Keele: University of Keele.

Kumar, Krishan, 1975: 'Holding the Middle Ground: The BBC, the Public and the Professional Broadcaster', *Sociology* 9(3), reproduced in this volume.

Lattimore, Dan L. and Nayman, Oguz B., 1974: 'Professionalism of Colorado's Daily Newsmen: A Communicator Analysis'. *Gazette* 20 (1), pp. 1–10.

McCombs, Maxwell E. and Shaw, Donald L., 1972: 'The Agenda-Setting Function of the Mass Media'. *Public Opinion Quarterly* 36 (2), pp. 176–87.

McLeod, Jack M., Becker, Lee B. and Byrnes, James E., 1973: 'Another Look at the Agenda-Setting Function of the Press'. *Communication Research* 1(2).

Mendelsohn, Harold and Crespi, Irving, 1970: *Polls, Television and the New Look in Politics*. Scranton: Chandler.

Nayman, Oguz B., 1973: 'Professional Orientations of Journalists: An Introduction to Communicator Analysis Studies'. *Gazette* 19 (4), pp. 195–212.

Rivers, William L. and Nyhan, Michael J., (Eds.), 1973: *Aspen Notebook on Government and the Media*. New York: Praeger.

Rivers, William L. and Schramm, Wilbur, 1969: *Responsibility in Mass Communication*. New York: Harper and Row.

Sears, David O. and Freedman, Jonathan L., 1967: 'Selective Exposure to Communication: A Critical Review'. *Public Opinion Quarterly* 31 (2), pp. 194–213.

Seymour-Ure, Colin, 1974: *The Political Impact of Mass Media*. London: Constable.

Siebert, Fred, Peterson, T. and Schramm, Wilbur, 1956: *Four Theories of the Press*. Urbana: University of Illinois Press.

Smith, Anthony, 1973: *The Shadow in the Cave*. London: Allen & Unwin.

Tan, Alexis, 1973: 'A Role Theory: A Dissonance Analysis of Message Content Preferences'. *Journalism Quarterly* 50 (2), pp. 278–84.

Tichenor, Philip J., Donohue, George A. and Olien, Clarice N., 1973: 'Mass Communication Research: Evolution of a Structural Model'. *Journalism Quarterly* 50 (3), pp. 419–25.

Tunstall, Jeremy, 1971: *Journalists at Work*. London: Constable.

Verba, Sidney, Nie, Norman H. and Kim, Jae-On, 1971: *The Modes of Democratic Participation: A Cross-National Comparison*. Beverley Hills, California: Sage.

Wade, Serena E., 1973: 'Media Effects on Changes in Attitude towards

the Rights of Young People'. *Journalism Quarterly* 50 (2), pp. 229—36 and 347.
Wamsley, Gary L. and Pride, Richard A., 1972: 'Television Network News'. *Western Political Quarterly* 25 pp. 434—50.

12

Media Professionalism in the Third World: the transfer of an ideology

Peter Golding

Introduction

Mass media in Africa, Latin America and Asia have developed, almost invariably, as derivatives of those in the advanced industrialized countries. They do not appear spontaneously at an appropriate moment in social evolution, but have been transplanted from metropolitan centres. This simple fact of colonial history has enormous implications for analysis of the structure and role of media in the Third World, most importantly it means that accounts of the media in a single country which make no reference to an international context of dependence are empirically and theoretically barren.

This observation can be placed in two theoretical contexts. The first is the notion of the transfer of technology, which turns attention to the implications for development of exporting industrial technology from the richer nations to the Third World, particularly the frequent conflict between the need for appropriate technology and the exporting ambitions of technology manufacturers. The second context is the problem of cultural imperialism, implying a normative component to the structural relations of dependence between advanced and under-developed societies. Cultural imperialism includes the results of international media, educational and cultural systems and is a more inclusive term than media imperialism.

Thus in looking at one particular aspect of media in the Third World, professionalism among 'communicators', two correctives to much of the usual debate need to be introduced. First, it is impossible to consider the media or practices within them separately, with the implication that communicators and communications are an independent variable whose injection into a society in a modern, 'professional' form will trigger development. Rooted in the theory which sees development simply as a process of occupational differentiation this leads to conclusions, such as Pye's, that 'In a fundamental sense modernization involves the emergence of a professional class of communicators' (Pye, 1963 p. 78). This begs a good many questions about 'modernization' which cannot be looked at here, and some about professional communicators which can.[1] Second, it is inadequate to condemn the circumstantial indications of cultural dependence without demonstration of the concrete practices by which it is sustained.[2]

This chapter is concerned with the thesis that Third World countries are exactly like industrialized nations, only a bit behind — when they catch up with appropriate help they will be modernized, i.e. westernized. Criticisms of this idea, though now widespread, even commonplace, at least in academic discussions, have largely passed by mass communications analysis. In this chapter the particular concept of professionalism is examined. It is suggested that far from being a set of practices which media occupations in the Third World should acquire to 'catch up', media professionalism is an ideology that has been transferred in parallel to the transfer of technology and as part of the general stream of cultural dependence. As Stokke puts it unequivocally, 'Extreme neo-imperialist relations at the cultural level mean briefly that the dominant power (for instance the former colonial power) provides the teaching, the training, and the creative work (and even the language) . . . ' (Stokke, 1971 p. 94). I shall concentrate on broadcasting in Africa and draw on research on broadcast journalism in Nigeria for data.[3]

The catching-up thesis implies two tasks for the laggardly. First, they must acquire modern technology; the media apparatus must be tried, tested and marketed in advanced nations. Second, they must acquire the attitudes and skills necessary to operate these media in a professional way. This latter concern has prompted much research on the 'professionalization' of communicators in the Third World, particularly by American or American-trained researchers seeking confirmation and replication of their own journalism education conventions. McLeod and Rush, for example, were gratified to find Latin American seminar participants 'had sufficient media experience to justify their treatment as experienced news-men comparable to those US newsmen previously studied . . . ' (McLeod and Rush, 1969a). In Chile Mernanteau-Horta found his respondents showing a 'clear professional identification' (Mernanteau-Horta, 1967).[4] The significance of these studies and the thinking they represent is that we should examine 'professionalization' as the acquisition not merely of competence, but also of values and attitudes thought appropriate to the

1 I have suggested some of the theoretical problems in an earlier article (Golding, 1974b).
2 This exactly parallels the argument in Murdock and Golding, Chapter 3 in this volume.
3 This research was part of a comparative study of news broadcasting carried out in collaboration with Philip Elliott, James D. Halloran and Adrian Wells. (Golding *et al.*, forthcoming)
4 See also, *inter alia* McLeod and Rush (1969b), Nayman *et al.* (1973), McLeod and Hawley (1964), Head (1963).

implementation of media skills. It is this transfer of an ideology which this chapter examines.

Media Professionalism — the Mechanisms of Transfer

It is generally the case that professions in colonial nations have developed in ways quite different from those in industrialized societies. In particular their ties to the apparatus of colonial administration place them at the behest of a powerful regulating agency which removes the self-controlling autonomy normally a defining characteristic of a profession. Thus it is the ideology, but not the practice of professionalism, at least in its ideal form, which is transferred.[5] In a sense the concept of professionalism is in any case misused in the context of the mass media. Those traits normally isolated as peculiar to the professions: personalized client relationships, skill based on theoretical knowledge, an ethic of altruistic service, organization, and control over entry to the occupation, are very largely absent from media occupations. Indeed, the notion of direct individual client service is quite contrary to the very defining nature of mass communication. Following Johnson's (1973) analysis it is interesting to note that the usual civil service character of broadcasting bureaucracies in many Third World countries has ironically succeeded in implanting 'professionalism' whereas it is less apparent in the media of richer countries.

However, in general it is more valuable to examine those 'professional' traits which do appear, and whose diffusion is taken to signify 'professionalization', notably increased training and professional education, association into professional organizations, and an ethos of public service and disinterestedness. Professionalization has been, in effect, integration into a dominant global culture of media practices and objectives as developed in the media of the advanced industrialized societies. This integration has been achieved through three mechanisms: institutional transfer, training and education, and the diffusion of occupational ideologies.

Institutional transfer
Essentially three models of broadcasting organization have been transferred to the Third World; that of the BBC, largely though not exclusively to British colonial territories; the French model, to French colonial territories; and the less centralized, more commercial organization developed in North America. Effectively this means a split between the 'public service' and commercial forms of organization, between government and advertising financial support, and between varying degrees of state control.

5 For this argument in detail see T. Johnson (1973).

Broadcasting came to colonial territories initially as a service to settler communities, to provide them with news from home, to reaffirm their authority, and to sustain cultural links with the imperial centre. Broadcasting was to become a major strut in the very apparatus of colonialism, as clearly foreseen by the Plymouth Committee in 1937. 'We envisage the development of Colonial broadcasting — and its justification — not only as an instrument of entertainment for Europeans . . . but also as an instrument of advanced administration, an instrument not only, and perhaps not even primarily for the entertainment but rather for the enlightenment and education of the more backward sections of the population . . . ' (Plymouth Committee, 1937 pp. 5—6).

Entertainment was not proscribed, indeed it was hoped it might divert possibly dissident tendencies. The patrician tone of an investigation in 1949 into broadcasting in British West Africa captures exactly the mix of imperial anthropology and cultural ethnocentrism which lay behind broadcasting plans of the time: 'It is necessary for all talks to be of short duration and framed in simple language. The average African's powers of concentration over long periods are limited . . . . The African's taste in entertainment is varied . . . European light music, dance music of the strict tempo style (not hot swing), brass bands, African choirs and singing bands, hymn singing. The African likes short plays of the thriller type but not the long drawn-out serial play. . . . The more educated African likes a quiz in English and similar types of programme.' (Turner and Byron, 1949 p. 25.)

As Ainslie puts it, 'in the early sixties, the BBC could look with some satisfaction on a whole brood of more or less dutiful offspring in East and West Africa, all fashioned in the maternal image . . . ' (Ainslie, 1968 p. 158). From bureaucratic job titles to programme styles the BBC was reproduced all over the developing world of broadcasting. Objectives, form, organization, assumptions and contents were all transplanted from the citadel of Broadcasting House, London to the furthest outposts of Empire. In French territories *la mission civilisatrice* was served by a much more centralized colonial broadcasting network, based on powerful regional stations using a lot of French domestically-produced material. Thus local stations were relatively undeveloped until the formation of SORAFOM (Société de Radiodiffusion de la France d'Outre-Mer) in 1956, and retained, indeed increased, their integration into the French colonial broadcasting system (Gibbons, 1974). American commercial broadcasting systems, based on a multiplicity of stations producing cheap programming for the purpose of renting local audiences to advertisers, appeared mostly in Latin America and in other spheres of US influence like the Philippines.

Thus media institutional forms developed in the Third World grew as extensions and imitations of those in industrialized societies. The implications of this for programming and institutional growth have been explored elsewhere.[6] Katz, for example, has argued that an 'uncritical transplantation' of radio norms to television in developing nations has left a residue of inappropriate and unnecessary objectives; specifically 'the goal of non-stop broadcasting, the orientation toward an everybody audience, and the striving for up-to-the-minute news' (Katz, 1973 p. 382). Institutional transfer involved far more than organizational replication; it meant the wholesale acquisition of modes of practice, standards and assumptions which came to displace discussion of possible preferences or alternatives.

Education, training and qualifications

In industrialized countries, though most notably in Britain, media occupations very often eschew formal training and education. The creative skills associated with journalism and production are deemed innate, though the technical skills are recognized as requiring tuition, not necessarily of a formal kind. This craft-consciousness, emphasizing experience, talent and creativity, is antagonistic to the formally monitored training system associated with professionalism, though both approaches seek individual personal qualities for vocational success. Because of the speed with which broadcasting in the Third World has developed, and the urgency with which ex-colonial nations wished to indigenize and expand broadcasting, they have relied on training schemes to fill the gap left by repatriated colonial experts. Up to this point, however, these experts had been in charge, and consequently indigenous broadcasters had low status and little executive experience. So training schemes became totally dependent on the same expatriate experts whose presence the training was intended to render unnecessary.

Such a logic, of course, belongs to the general problem of what some writers call 'the intellectual pillage of the Third World'.[7] Large numbers of students from the Third World come to study in industrialized nations.[8] Those that return take with them not only skills, but values and attitudes, and not least a receptivity to the men and machines they have learned to work with. As Gollin notes, such training schemes are frequently 'adjuncts of economic and military assistance'. He points out that 'implicit in the idea of foreign study is the view that through an exposure to the values, norms and practices of economically advanced societies the trainees may come in time to change their perspectives on their society, their work roles, or themselves in ways which will strengthen their later effectiveness as change agents' (Gollin, 1967 p. 362). Many will prefer to stay and

6 In particular by Katz, Wedell, Pilsworth and Shinar (forthcoming). I am grateful to Mick Pilsworth for a preview of and discussions about this research.

7 See, for example, Buchanan (1972) pp. 19–39, Rodney (1972) pp. 261–87.

8 In 1973 there were 10,000 undergraduates and nearly 15,000 graduates from overseas in UK universities (UGC, 1975 p. 2). The number of foreign students in American higher education institutions increased from 29,813 in 1950/51 to 134,959 in 1969/70 (USDHEW).

enjoy the rewards their skills will attract in the richer country — the familiar problem of the 'brain drain'.[9]

Training of media professionals has taken three forms; the attachment of experts from the industrialized countries to media in the Third World, courses and attachments in industrialized countries, and courses and training centres in the Third World. The BBC sent experts to broadcasting units throughout the Empire, reaching a peak during the 1950s (see Wilkinson, 1972). These experts carried with them not only the considerable and often unique skills of BBC trained staff, but executive styles and programme philosophies of inescapable stamp. Nearly 60 BBC staff were seconded to the Nigerian Broadcasting Corporation alone between 1950 and 1960. Naturally their work was more than advisory, it was executive, exemplary and authoritative.

Courses and attachments in industrialized countries developed very often as part of the cold war contest for allegiances in the Third World, 'assisting the foreign policy of the host nation in maintaining and extending its prestige, influence and favourable image in the world, perhaps particularly in the uncommitted nations' (Benne, in Sanders, 1963 pp. 81—2). Very often these courses served symbolic functions for the host as great as their direct utility for participants. Head remarks that 'the innumerable overseas scholarship, training, attachment, and orientation programmes which siphon off African broadcasting personnel and keep their organizations in a state of disruption constitute an unconscionable abuse of foreign technical aid programmes. Embassies appear to compete on a "body count" basis — the more host country personnel they ship home for training programmes the higher their efficiency ratings, irrespective of the qualifications of the trainees or the quality and relevance of their overseas experience. Some embassy officials are not above a little arm twisting — "After all we've done for your broadcasting system the least you can do is give us one or two trainees".' (Head, 1974 p. 359).

Courses are popular, the attraction of overseas travel and the prestige of association with a major media organization lure large numbers of much needed staff away from their own media. The BBC began radio courses for overseas broadcasters in 1951. In the next twenty years over 500 broadcasters attended the courses, over half from Africa. Television courses have been run since 1966, and in the first five years 165 broadcasters attended courses (Seymour, 1974 p. 272—3). The more centralized French broadcasting system laid even greater emphasis on training in the metropolitan capital. SORAFOM trained 300 African broadcasters in the first year of its training centre, the Studio-Ecole de Maisons Lafitte near Paris. In 1962 SORAFOM became l'Office de Cooperation Radiophonique

9 For a discussion see Godfrey (1970).

(OCORA), which took on the role of developing television in French African territories, while still having central control over staffing, equipment, and planning (see Gibbons, 1974 pp. 107—112). The final cumulative centralization came with the amalgamation of OCORA into ORTF in 1969.

Formal training schemes are supplemented by attachments, which are offered by many larger broadcasting organizations. A UNESCO report by two African broadcasters summed up growing unease about both overseas training and attachments, though the report was never published. The authors point out that 'Most senior personnel of African broadcasting organizations today are products of overseas training.' They condemn such training as largely inconsequential, but go on to sound a more sceptical note. 'In recent years the offering of . . . attachments has been viewed as a prestige item by many countries. It is a rather simple and inexpensive way in which advanced countries can give aid to developing countries. It certainly looks good on the credit side of the aid ledger but in most cases the benefits derived by the recipient country do not justify the time spent on the attachment . . . . Usually African broadcasters going on attachments . . . either have to spend long periods learning a foreign language or return home after a tour of near mute observation. . . . In their present form, most attachments, especially those arranged for junior staff, tend to give officers a holiday and return them home confused while their organizations suffer by losing their services during the period of attachment.' (Quarmyne and Bebey, 1967 pp. 43—4.)

Such criticisms have led to demands for the establishment of training courses or permanent centres actually in the countries where the trainees will work. Set up by expatriates within broadcasting organizations, or at universities, or independently under the auspices of such bodies as UNESCO, or the International Press Institute, they have till recently emphasized the print media.[10] Such courses ostensibly emphasize the practical skills of professional media production, steering delicately clear of political sensitivities. But the very avoidance of discussing objectives leaves a vacuum in which imported assumptions and conventions becomes the standards by which achievement or professional competence are measured. Aspinall, a UNESCO expert attached to the Mass Communications Institute at Lagos University, remarked after a conference there that 'for many participants it was the first time consideration had been given to the use of broadcasting toward specific developmental ends' (Aspinall, 1971 p. 6). The myth of value-free technology imbibed in western-run production training had emphasized the non-purposive, non-

10 For descriptive accounts see Scotton (1974), UNESCO (1965), Hachten (1968), and for a more recent UNESCO statement, UNESCO (1975). By 1968, when its third Ford Foundation grant expired, the IPI training scheme in Nairobi had produced over 300 African journalists.

ideological role of broadcasting. Syllabuses were transplanted wholesale, as at the American-instigated Jackson College of Journalism, established at the University of Nigeria, Nsukka in 1961 with virtually a complete North American style school of journalism curriculum, including heavy doses of advertising, public relations, and so on. The 'expat expert' was used wherever possible, whatever the obstacles. At the American-financed university in Kabul, one of the two full-time instructors (both American) in the journalism faculty wrote that 'the primary problem is the feeling of helplessness which comes from not knowing enough about the country and the people to truly understand the people and their culture and from teaching through an interpreter' (Snider, 1968 p. 317). Teaching in English is more usually the norm.

The status of alien education and training is secured by the prize of qualifications. Education systems which have grown as extensions of the colonial system offer both entry qualifications into elite occupations, and certification of competence within those occupations. Based on the assumption of universally applicable standards, skills and practices, the global quest for British City and Guilds or GCE 'O' levels or French *'Brevet'*, later becomes a competition for certificates, degrees and diplomas in journalism or broadcasting. The assumption is neatly expressed by Demarath, writing of what he terms the 'instrumental professions': 'Although professionalization is no cure for all present deficiencies it could play an invaluable pedagogical role by educating technicians to the trans-national, trans-cultural and trans-ideological dimensions of development' (Demerath, 1973 p. 332). Ironically the very universality of qualifications makes media 'professionals' less vocationally than career orientated in many countries, a view encouraged by the civil service status and procedures of their employing organizations. Thus their careers become 'spiralist' and qualifications are competitively preferred for entry into any sector in the higher levels of very rapidly growing post-independence civil services.

These ambitions are often exploited by correspondence schools of journalism or broadcasting, trading on the hopes of hundreds of young African media aspirants. One promises free booklets on enrolment like 'Make Yourself a Master of Public Relations' and 'Make Yourself a Master of Magic Phrases'. The carrot of 'Top-Level Jobs' is dangled before students promised 'expert tuition to give that wonderful WORD POWER everyone seeks'. The ultimate in international professionalization.

Occupational ideologies

Less tangible or explicit than either organization or training are the contextual values and assumptions built into the very ethos of media professionalism as it is transferred to developing countries. These values

generate both general 'philosophies' of broadcasting and specific understandings about correct and laudable practice in the production of mass
communications. One general model is that of 'public service' media, a
liberal BBC vision expressing the professional ideal in a mass society.
Hachten links this with the assumption of universalism: 'The African
newsman, underpaid and lacking in social status, must be made to understand that he belongs to a worldwide fraternity based on an ethic of public
service' (Hachten, 1968 p. 125). The public service conception of broadcasting as an inoffensive utility serving an undifferentiated mass audience
formulated particularly in the elitist, stridently anti-commercial, formative
years of the BBC, stresses the apolitical nature of broadcasting. A second
general model, more often found in American spheres of influence, is the
commercial form of broadcasting with its accompanying ideology of
pragmatic audience maximization via entertainment. A third model, that
of the media as didactic or socially impelling, has many variants of course,
depending on the direction envisaged by its operators as socially desirable.
Partly because of the sheer scale of capital required, broadcasting is controlled by government in all African countries, though the pressure this
places on the professional autonomy of broadcasters can be over-stated.
Professionalism is often an elastic enough concept to accept relatively
large intrusions from the 'corporate patron', in Johnson's terminology.
Like the other ideologies the didactic model is based on assumptions
about the role of the media in industrial societies, particularly their
direct and immediate influence, transferred to the rural societies into
which the media have been transplanted.

More specific ideologies appear as models of good practice and implicit
statements of acceptable and unacceptable standards. The greatest
influence is in the programme material imported from overseas media.
This is a phenomenon most often discussed in the context of television.
But in 1972, 26 African services were still relaying or retransmitting BBC
news bulletins. Large quantities of tapes of topical discussions flow out
from the BBC to African radio stations (Wilkinson, 1974 p. 224). Between
1960 and 1970 ORTF provided roughly eighteen thousand hours of radio
programmes a year to French African radio stations (Stokke, 1971 p. 113).
The greater experience and resources of American, British and French
stations, among others, give these programmes a technical sophistication
which audiences come to demand for all material, including domestic
production. Thus African producers, already aware of the professional
superiority of these products, become bound to emulate them in style,
philosophy and format. Professionalism becomes imitation.

This has been even more true of television programmes. The assumed
need for continuous broadcasting, the demands of a largely elite audience,
cosmopolitan in tastes and interests, and the high costs of production,
have forced most Third World television stations to rely heavily on

imported material[11] (a fate shared by many smaller industrial countries). These imports can be purchased at a fraction of the minimum cost of producing equal amounts of domestic programming. The effect of this is, first, that broadcasting has acquired a global uniformity of style and content, creating that very universality of standards preached by the 'professionalizers', and in turn the audience expectations which reinforce demands for more of the same and thus the security of the market. Second, local broadcasters, when making their own programmes, adopt styles and models so competently used in the imported material. There is great variation in this, and it is far from universal,[12] but local discussions, quiz shows, sports magazines, variety packages often derive almost directly from foreign originals. As for formats, so for practice; performers, producers, announcers, writers, technicians, directors all have ready examples of correct practice in deciding appropriate procedures and attitudes.

One particular professional ideology is the devotion to broadcasting's impartiality, and the objectivity of its news provision. Before looking more closely at a case study, one or two points should be made. The impartiality of broadcasting and of broadcasters is built into the notion of the institutional separation of broadcasting from the state, derived first from nineteenth-century theories of the press and second from precedents established by British broadcasting in its embryonic years.[13] Most Third World broadcasting organizations are not separate from the state. Yet professional detachment survives as a goal at a second level, that of daily production and occupational practice. Thus journalists employed in broadcasting organizations which are simply an arm of an information ministry, nonetheless retain, at some level, a commitment to professional disinterestedness, impartiality and objectivity. For Pye it is this that characterizes the evolution from traditional to modern communication systems. 'There may be much confusion and lack of precision in this concept of profession, but there is one central assumption upon which the entire modern communications industry is built. This is the assumption that objective and unbiased reporting of events is possible and desirable and that the sphere of politics in any society can be best observed from a neutral or non-partisan perspective. Traditional communications processes on the other hand tended in general to be so closely wedded to social and political processes

11 This market is examined in detail in Varis (1973), and more accessibly in Nordenstreng and Varis (1974). For discussion of the implications see, *inter alia*, Schiller (1969), Katz *et al.* (*op. cit.*), Tunstall (forthcoming).
12 This touches on the complex wider issues in 'media imperialism' which are beyond the brief of this chapter, though very relevant to it. Katz *et al.*(*op. cit.*), Chapter 5, provides many examples. Tunstall (*op. cit.*) a useful historical context.
13 This bald statement conceals a much broader argument examined in Golding *et al.* (*op. cit.*) Chapters 3 & 4. See also Smith (1973).

that the very act of receiving and transmitting messages called for some display of agreement and acceptance . . . . The emergence of professionalized communicators is thus related to the development of an objective, analytical and non-partisan view of politics' (Pye, 1963 pp. 78—9). In fact this transition has not and could not occur. To reduce a large debate to an over-simplified proposition: however 'professionalized' the communicators, their market and work situations compromise any possible institutional neutrality, so that modern and traditional communications remain 'wedded to social and political processes'. Thus the injunction on the very first page of a major training manual for African journalists: 'A Reporter is just that — a reporter. He is not a writer. . . . And most important of all, he is not a politician' (IPI (n.d.) p. 3), remains the professional ideal, but is in practice impossible.

This particular professional ideology is transferred also at an intermediate level, that of the organizational separation of news and current affairs in most broadcasting organizations. Where it is absent it is assumed to be a goal in the evolutionary differentiation of the institution. The separation reaffirms the strict neutrality and objectivity of news by contrast with the licenced discursiveness, even tendentiousness of 'current affairs'. The problems of sustaining this aspect of professional ideology in a dependent situation can be illustrated very briefly by a case study from Nigeria.

The Limits of Professional Autonomy — A Case Study

The West African press remained a politicized institution until very late in its history, partly because of the very recent establishment of a commercially based press, partly because of its role in pre-independence nationalist movements. In Nigeria leading journalists were often primarily political figures even after the spread of American popular press approaches and methods in the 1930s and 1940s. Nigerian journalism was born of anti-colonial protest, baptized in the flood of nationalist propaganda and matured in party politics. The pre-independence political activism of the press is a living memory for most contemporary journalists, its success a tribute to the potential power of their craft. This is true as much for broadcasting journalists as for those in the press, though the particular configurations of broadcasting place extra strains on the difficult resolution of professional and political goals. The following data are drawn from a study of all journalists working in the main broadcasting stations in Nigeria (see note 3).

Many had arrived in broadcast journalism indirectly, through a variety of civil service jobs, or teaching. Although committed to such professional goals as training and formal qualifications (47% had completed some form of course), many saw their future elsewhere, in public relations, the civil service or commerce. Thus the qualifications are an entry into a stratum rather than a profession.

Of those who had a professional qualification, over half (25% of all journalists) had a foreign degree or diploma, and many of the remainder planned to seek one. Nigerian journalists share the universal belief that many journalistic skills are unteachable. Yet they concede that training is required to master the broadcasting technology which otherwise frustrates the craft of journalism. Desperately aware of the low status of their job,[14] most expressed satisfaction at the appearance of qualifications which would both upgrade the occupation and facilitate easier moves into other spheres of activity.

Nigerian journalists tend to enter professional training programmes after initial experience. For one thing this means employers will second them and foot the bill. It also means they are most likely to enter specifically vocational courses even though they intend to use the qualification as a general entry to elite occupations. Thus they tend to value the courses for 'broadening horizons' or providing a general educational veneer, in other words for supplying an outlook and values rather than specific skills. Those unable to find or pay for full-time courses resorted to the kinds of correspondence courses referred to earlier, or to general courses. Younger journalists can often be seen in their breaks huddled over an antiquated teach-yourself text on 'British Constitution' or 'A-Level Commerce' as they painfully seek approbation from remote supervisors and the eventual, dearly-bought but vital certificate. Courses abroad are often arranged through the unions, and east European sponsors in particular, often them-selves journalists' unions, channel their scholarships this way.

Professional models are drawn not only from training and qualifications, but also from foreign media. *Time* and *Newsweek* were each read, and admired, by roughly three-quarters of the journalists, twice the proportion regularly reading any Nigerian current affairs magazine. Nearly half claimed to read a British quality daily, almost certainly an exaggeration given the cost and availability of such papers, but indicative of their symbolic status. African newspapers, with the rare exception of one of the Ghanaian dailies, are seldom seen, and in fact hardly any African-based publications find their way into Nigerian newsrooms. The high regard for American and European media is strengthened by the lack of credibility of domestic media. (A study in Korea stressed the sense of futility many journalists there felt; only 18% thought the public found the media reliable and accurate (Chong Lim Kim and Jin Hwan Oh, 1974).)

Despite all their trained observation of impartiality, Nigerian journalists often spoke of commitment to 'development news'. The tensions between the idea of news as information deliberately selected and shaped to serve

14 For an interesting account of this see Enaharo (1973).

defined social purposes, and news as an objective and randomly selected capture of reality, disinterestedly distributed, often proved difficult for African journalists caught between two currents of thought. For outside experts this is a problem to be solved by education and experience until adequate professionalism is acquired. Barton, for some years director of the IPI Africa Programme, has written of 'the clash of loyalties between journalism and what might be called the African idea' (Barton, 1969 p. 42), which tormented his trainees.

Of course, the 'African idea', despite its local flavour and idiosyncrasies, has a wider pedigree and indeed touches on wider current debates in world journalism, about the relative possibilities or merits of committed or detached objective journalism.[15] In Nigeria notions of development journalism did not derive from considered immersion in the writings of the Prague-based International Organization of Journalists, Lenin, or even Nkrumah. Rather it was a natural view of journalism on which the non-purposive, neutral, professional ideology of the Western fourth estate had been imposed. Thus a natural inclination to see journalism as socially purposive is given a guilt complex by training in the creed and practice of objective reporting as preached and conducted in European and American media.

Development journalism was produced in four ways. First, by stressing the generally educative function of news, either about specific pieces of information or by the arousal of general awareness of events and their implications. Second, by producing stories which displayed particular social needs or problems it was hoped that government would be provoked into action. Third, by giving prominence to local self-help projects news could encourage emulation of such activities in other communities. Finally, the news could tackle specific problems, such as elite corruption, often with prudent obliqueness. For this reason both the Agnew resignation and the Watergate saga were followed with avid interest by Nigerian journalists and given great prominence. Both a gleeful, almost mischievous delight in the embarrassment and humbling of a super-power, as well as the subtle moral parallels for their own country, made these stories unfailingly fascinating. Watergate carried with it, of course, the additional attraction of being a running tribute to the social importance and professional power of the journalist.

Central to professionalism is the concept of autonomy. Yet in concentrating on autonomy from the state or overt political interference, the limits to professional autonomy in the work situation of African journalists are often ignored. There is no room here greatly to elaborate this, but one or two observations can illustrate the point. The raw materials available to,

15 Re-emerging in the American fuss over the 'New Journalism' (see, e.g. Weber, 1974), and a variety of conflicts over committed versus objective journalism (see, e.g. Merrill 1974, Johnstone 1972/3, Janowitz 1975).

say, Nigerian newsrooms, are severely constrained. The difficulties of domestic news collection, due both to tight control and problems of resources and physical communications create an unusually heavy diet of foreign news. Yet foreign news is expensive to obtain directly, and thus is totally dependent on the services of the major (European and American) news and news film agencies (see Elliott and Golding, 1974). The news values and social values assumed by the agencies (see Harris, 1975) become models for the aspiring Nigerian journalist, admiration for competence rapidly broadening into acquisition of a shared view of journalism and the world it surveys (not least of African affairs). The most striking feature of comparative analyses of news is the similarity of products available around the world.[16]

In other words, the development of professionalism among Nigerian journalists is nothing more than their increasing integration into a community sharing values and standards developed by major Western news media. Via formal training or eduction, through exposure to the authoritative products of Western media, or from routine dependence on the primary production of world news by European and American media, professionalism is induced in the form of an ideological convergence, a necessary emulation of the objectives and definitions of those foreign media.

Professionalism in Context

Professionalism then is a particular set of practices whose appropriateness needs to be questioned in the situation of Third World media. The transfer of the ideology of professionalism runs parallel to the transfer of technology, which can be alternatively understood as the problem of technological dependence (Cooper, 1972). The media in the large-scale capital intensive form in which they have developed in urbanized industrialized societies, are classic instances of this problem. Import-substituting industrialization is designed to serve the market dominated by elite consumers, who require the goods used and demanded by elites in industrialized countries. The technology for their manufacture is only available from these countries whose quasi-monopoly control of unique technologies is reinforced by the international patent system (Patel, 1974; Vaitsos, 1972).

It is often easy for outside analysts to condemn as inappropriate for others, sophisticated technologies whose benefits they continue to enjoy. But the question of appropriateness can be raised, and with it the question of whether what is good professionalism in one context is necessarily beneficial in another, or whether professionalism is merely the ideological

16 A conclusion demonstrated and elaborated in Golding *et al.* (*op. cit.*), and briefly in Golding (1974a).

Trojan horse for the commercial expansion of technological enterprise in the developed world.

Rather then consider new forms of broadcasting technology Western countries have often provided 'aid' in the form of dumping. Mackay describes the acquisition of a transmitter for the Nigerian Broadcasting Corporation in 1951: 'The famous Normandy Beachhead mobile transmitter of the BBC . . . was available for purchase . . . . Seven years had elapsed since the transmitter had been assembled but apparently it was in a reasonable state of repair . . . . It worked on test in London . . . . Years later Director Chalmers ruefully wrote that the people concerned must have had a good lunch beforehand' (Mackay, 1964 p. 17). The very development of expensive television, available only to urban elites, has been questioned. Prestige projects abound; in March 1976 Nigeria announced the setting up of a national colour television network in a country where, as elsewhere in the developing world, even a black and white set costs as much as a farmer's annual income. Emphasis is often on production or transmission rather than on reception facilities. Yet cheap alternatives have been demonstrated, though at the cost of falling short of international professional standards (see Papenek, 1974 pp. 70–6, 156). Advocates of intermediate or alternative technology have stressed the possibilities available in labour-intensive techniques, using local resources.[17] With different assumptions about appropriate media technology go different assumptions about the best ways of using media, or in other words of professional practice.[18] Gurevitch and Elliott (1973) have argued that professionalism in industrialized media will be eroded by new, more accessible technologies. If this is at all true it would seem fruitful to consider the possibility that developing countries might avoid the problems requiring such erosion.

All consideration of alternatives or appropriateness must be aware of the context of cultural dependence, of the ways in which professionalism ensures the reproduction of institutions and practices from the advanced industrial societies. Professionalism is a stabilizing philosophy, a prop for the status quo, for pragmatism against utopianism, proficiency against ideology. The argument is best known in the writings of Shils, who sees the creation of a foreign-educated modern class, 'bound together by their high evaluation of the possession of some segment of modern culture' as a buffer against the over-zealous and impatient demands of those having 'hostilities which are irrelevent to the tasks of modernisation (Shils, 1963

17 Intermediate technologists are not without their critics, see Dickson (1974), Chapter 6. Cowlan (1973) gives some interesting examples of irrelevant attempts to use media for development and argues for less sophisticated more relevant methods.
18 For a parallel argument in some respects on health care see Frankenberg and Leeson, (1974).

pp. 67, 71). Such a view serves to reemphasize the political dimension of an ideology like professionalism. In turn this serves as a reminder that 'media imperialism' is but part of a broader cultural dependence, itself only intelligible as part of a general economic and historical process of imperialism, however defined.

It remains for the full effects of professional ideologies on media in the Third World to be investigated.[19] Considering that the media are intended for primarily rural audiences, are technically simple and cheap, are orientated to the outdoor (rather than studio-bound) cultures, accept the socially purposive as legitimate and continue to question spurious commitments to objectivity, and take into account the relationship between traditional and innovatory media (see Ugboajah, 1972), all these must have consequences for that set of practices and standards considered media professionalism. It has been the aim of this chapter to suggest that such reconsiderations must begin from the position that media professionalism is an ideology imposed on countries in a situation of dependence, and concealing more than merely prescriptions for technical proficiency.

References

Ainslie, R., 1968: *The Press in Africa.* New York: Walker & Co.

Aspinall, R., 1971: *The Training of Broadcasters in Africa.* mimeo.

Barton, F., 1969: *African Assignment.* Zurich: IPI.

Buchanan, K., 1972: *The Geography of Empire.* Nottingham: Spokesman Books.

Chong Lim Kim and Jin Hwan Oh, 1974: 'Perceptions of Professional Efficacy Among Journalists in a Developing Country. *Journalism Quarterly*, 51 (1), pp. 73—8.

Cooper, C., 1972: 'Science, Technology, & Production in the Under-developed Countries: an Introduction'. *Journal of Development Studies* 9 (1), pp. 1—18.

Cowlan, B., 1973. 'Thinking small: some comments on the role of mass media for economic and social development. *Educational Broadcasting International* 6 (2), pp. 79—83.

Cruise O'Brien, R., 1975: 'Domination and Dependence in Mass Communication'. *Institute of Development Studies, Bulletin* 6 (4), pp. 85—99.

Demerath, N. J., 1973: 'Foreign Aid and the Instrumental Professions'. *Sociological Review Monograph* 20 pp. 281—309.

Dickson, D., 1974: *Alternative Technology and the Politics of Technical Change.* Glasgow: Fontana.

Elliott, P. and Golding, P., 1974: 'Mass Communication and Social Change'. In E. de Kadt and G. Williams (1974), pp. 229—54.

19 For some interesting thoughts in the context of a research design in this area see Cruise O'Brien (1975).

Enaharo, P., 1973: 'Africa's Besieged Press'. *Africa* 21, pp. 28—32.

Frankenberg, R. and Leeson, J., 1974: 'The Sociology of Health Dilemmas in the Post-Coloured World'. In E. de Kadt and G. Williams (1974), pp. 255—78.

Gerbner, G. *et al.* (Eds.), 1974: *Communications Technology and Social Policy*. New York: J. Wiley & Sons, Inc.

Gibbons, R. Arnold, 1974: 'Francophone West and Equatorial Africa'. In S. W. Head (1974), pp. 107—124.

Godfrey, E. M., 1970: 'The Brian Drain from Low Income Countries'. *Journal of Development Studies* 6 (3), pp. 235—47.

Golding, P., 1974a: Electronic News, *Intermedia* 2 (2), pp. 1—3.
    1974b; Media Role in National Development'. *Journal of Communication*, 24 (3), pp. 39—53.

Golding, P. and Elliott, P. (forthcoming) *Making the News*.

Gollin, A. E., 1967: 'Foreign Study and Modernisation; the transfer of technology through education.' *International Social Science Journal* 19 (3), pp. 359—77.

Gurevitch, M. and Elliott, P., 1973: 'Communication Technologies and the Future of the Broadcasting Professions.' In Gerbner, G. *et al.* (Eds.) pp. 505—20.

Hachten, W. A., 1968: 'The Training of African Journalists.' *Gazette* 14 (2), pp. 101—110.
    1971: *Muffled Drums; The News Media in Africa*. Ames, Iowa: Iowa State University Press.

Harris, P., 1975: *International News Media and Underdevelopment*. M.Phil thesis, University of Leicester.

Head, S. W., 1963: 'Can a Journalist be a Professional in a Developing Country?' *Journalism Quarterly* 40 (4), pp. 594—98.
    (Ed.), 1974: *Broadcasting in Africa*. Philadelphia: Temple University Press.

International Press Institute, (n.d.): *The African Newsroom*. Zurich: IPI.

Janowitz, M., 1975: 'Professional Models in Journalism.' *Journalism Quarterly* 52 (4).

Johnson, T., 1973: 'Imperialism and the Professions.' *Sociological Review Monograph* 20, pp. 281—309

Johnstone, J. *et al.* 1972/3: 'The professional values of American newsmen.' *Public Opinion Quarterly* XXVI (1) pp. 522—40.

de Kadt, E. and Williams, G. (Eds.), 1974: *Sociology and Development*. London: Tavistock.

Katz, E., 1973: 'Television as a Horseless Carriage.' In Gerbner *et al.* (Eds.), 1974 pp. 381—92.

Katz, E., Wedell, G., Pilsworth, M., Shinar, D. forthcoming, *Broadcasting and National Development*.

Mackay, I. K., 1964: *Broadcasting in Nigeria*. Ibadan University Press.

McLeod, J. and Hawley, S., 1964: 'Professionalisation Among Newsmen.' *Journalism Quarterly* 41 pp. 529—39.

McLeod, J. and Rush, R., 1969a: 'Professionalization of Latin American and US Journalists, I, *Journalism Quarterly* 46 (3) pp. 583—90.

1969b: 'Professionalization of Latin American and US Journalists, II' *Journalism Quarterly* 46 (4) pp. 784—9.

Mernanteau-Horta, D., 1967: 'Professionalization of Journalists in Santiago de Chile'. *Journalism Quarterly* 44 (4) pp. 715—24.

Merrill, J. C., 1974: *The Imperative of Freedom*. New York: Hastings House.

Nayman, O. *et al.*, 1973: 'Journalism as a Profession in a Developing Society.' *Journalism Quarterly* 50 (1) pp. 68—76.

Nordenstreng, K. and Varis, T., 1974: *Television Traffic — a one-way street?* Paris: UNESCO.

Papenek, V., 1974: *Design for the Real World*. Paladin.

Patel, S. J., 1974: 'The Technological Dependence of Developing Countries.' *Journal of Modern African Studies* 12 (1) pp. 1—18.

Plymouth Committee, 1937: *Interim Report of a Committee on Broad-Casting Services in the Colonies*. Colonial No. 139. HMSO.

Pye, L. W. (Ed.), 1963: *Communications and Political Development*. Princeton University Press.

Quarmyne, A. T. and Bebey, F., 1967: *Training for Radio and Television in Africa*. UNESCO.

Rodney, W., 1972: *How Europe Underdeveloped Africa*. London: Bogle-L'ouverture Publications.

Sanders, I. T. (Ed.), 1963: *The Professional Education of Students from Other Lands*. New York: Council on Social Work Education.

Schiller, H., 1968: *Mass Communication and American Empire*. New York: Augustus M. Kelley.

Scotton, J. F., 1974: 'Training in Africa.' In S. Head (Ed.), 1974, pp. 281—90.

Seymour, 1974: 'British Broadcasting Corporation.' In S. Head (Ed.), 1974, pp. 271—6.

Shils, E., 1963: 'Demagogues and Cadres in the Political Development of the New States.' In Pye (Ed.), 1963, pp. 64—77.

Smith, A., 1973: *The Shadow in the Cave*. London: Allen and Unwin.

Snider, P. B., 1968: 'Experiences of a Journalism Teacher in Afghanistan.' *Journalism Quarterly* 45 (2) pp. 316—18.

Stokke, O., 1971: *Reporting Africa*. Uppsala: Scandinavian Institute of African Studies.

Tunstall, J., (forthcoming): *The Media are American*. London: Constable

Turner, L. W. and Byron, F. A. W., 1949: *Broadcasting Survey of the British West African Colonies*. London: Crown Agents.

Ugboajah, F. O., 1972: 'Traditional-urban media model; stocktaking for African development.' *Gazette* 18 (2) pp. 76—95.

UGC, 1975: *Statistics of Education 6*.

UNESCO, 1965: *Professional Training for Mass Communications*. Paris. 1975: *Training for Mass Communications*. Paris.

US Dept. Health, Education and Welfare, annual: *Digest of Educational Statistics*. Washington.

Vaitsos, C. V., 1972: 'Patents Revisited: Their Function in Developing countries.' *Journal of Development Studies* October.

Section III

The Mediation of Cultural Meanings

Introduction

The ideas of the ruling class are in every epoch the ruling ideas, i.e., the class which is the ruling *material* force of society, is at the same time its ruling *intellectual* force. The class which has the means of material production at its disposal, has control at the same time over the means of mental production, so that thereby generally speaking, the ideas of those who lack the means of mental production are subject to it. The ruling ideas are nothing more than the ideal expression of the dominant material relationships grasped as ideas; hence of the relationship which make the one class the ruling class, therefore the ideas of its dominance. (Marx and Engels, 1970 p. 64.)

The discussion of the meaning of media messages and their place in the culture of capitalist and other societies has rather curious and contradictory theoretical antecedents. Early American research focused on the effects of the media on individuals rather than the area of 'meaning' or the relationship between the media and more general social and economic organization and this social psychological impulsion tended to obscure the analysis of media messages which was in any case dependent on the impoverished methodology of content analysis. On the other hand, orthodox Marxist thinking on the subject stressed a form of economic determinism and took for granted the ideological content of the media, in seeing culture as simply the reflection of the base, the economic infrastructure of society. To a large extent, the articles in this section of the Reader revolve around issues which emerged from these traditions.

The first article by Stuart Hall offers an authoritative account of recent developments in Marxist theory, which lie behind much contemporary research on the state, mass culture and mass communications. Hall indicates the way in which a re-examination of the dialectical relationship between sub-structure and super-structure in the Marxist model has led to a more complexly articulated and relevant theoretical basis for the understanding of ideology, and hence of the media's role in maintaining and reproducing the dominant ideology of a society. Moreover, Hall's discussion of the encoding and decoding process in mass communications in terms of the dominant or hegemonic code, the professional code, the negotiated and the oppositional code, considerably develops the links between semiological analysis and a Marxist theory of ideology in an area which should yield some interesting research results. Hall's article also raises important questions about the place of the concept of culture in the Marxist tradition.

The work of the Frankfurt School represents an earlier development of a critical philosophical variant of Marxism, 'critical theory', which rejected both the economic determinism of Soviet Marxism and the empirical positivism of the American tradition of mass communications research. An understanding of the Frankfurt School's extensive analysis of cultural subjects can be impeded both by the anti-systematic nature of 'critical theory' and the contradictions embedded in their work. It has been said that reading a piece by Adorno or Benjamin brings to mind a comment the film maker Jean-Luc Goddard once made when asked if his films had a beginning, a middle and an end, 'Yes', he replied, 'but not necessarily in that order'. (Jay, 1973 p. 176) The movement of the Frankfurt School to America, with the advent of Fascism, led the group to focus their attention on an advanced monopoly capitalist state with a non-fascist but nonetheless manipulative popular culture. From a dominant concern with the family and socialization, the Frankfurt School turned to the analysis of the 'culture industry'. The article included here, 'Culture industry: enlightenment as mass deception', illustrates the main features of Adorno and Horkheimer's critique of mass culture. Adorno's work was largely concerned with cultural criticism in which the conditioning force of concrete social and economic relationships were dealt with only schematically.

The impetus of Adorno's work was culturally elitist and pessimistic about mass culture and the implication was that the only real and authentic culture rests on a specific kind of art. Adorno once wrote admiringly of Schoenberg's music that 'It requires the listener spontaneously to compose its inner movements and demands of him not mere contemplation but *praxis*' (Adorno, 1967 pp. 149–50). Bourgeois culture, in the eyes of the Frankfurt School, was 'affirmative' in that it suggested a better and more valuable world, '*une promesse de bonheur*', different from the everyday world of earning a living, but realizable by every individual from within. Nevertheless this realization is an illusion which serves the *status quo*. The culture of a monopoly capitalist society, mass culture, does not have even these illusionary advantages. The *inner* freedom of *laisser faire* capitalism gives way to a more totalitarian state and to a repressive form of mass culture. Adorno points to the technique of 'pseudo individualism' in popular music.

By pseudo-individualism we mean endowing cultural mass production with the halo of free choice or open market on the basis of standardization itself. Standardization of song hits keeps the customers in line by doing their listening for them, as it were. Pseudo-individualism for its part, keeps them in line by making them forget that what they listen to . . . [has been] pre-digested. (Adorno, 1941 p. 25.)

Adorno does not suggest that this kind of manipulation is part of a conscious 'fascist conspiracy' but that it is guided by the same blind economic determinism as that of capitalist societies as a whole. (Slater, 1976)

The article indicates the extent of Horkheimer's and Adorno's cultural pessimism and their idealistic but somewhat passive attitude towards art. Walter Benjamin's article, however, although he was a figure associated with the Frankfurt School, develops rather different themes. Adorno and Benjamin had extensive disagreements over the analysis of mass culture. Benjamin, much influenced by Brecht, argued that the new media should not be dismissed as 'manipulative' but should be 'functionally transformed' in the interests of the working class. Benjamin points out in the Reader article that the technical reproducibility of the work of art could have positive implications in that loss of 'aura' meant the final emancipation of art from its 'parasitical dependence on ritual'. (Benjamin, 1973 p. 10) Brecht's influence on Benjamin meant that he was much more concerned with the material basis of culture and its place in concrete class struggles. Hence Benjamin sees film as a new dynamic and politicized medium.

James Carey's article attempts to illuminate the differences and common problems of American mass communications research and a European based study of contemporary culture. He indicates their different theoretical assumptions, and attempts to analyse from an American viewpoint the difficulties and potential of cultural studies. It is interesting in relation to this to compare the way in which Carey dismisses theories of ideology on the grounds of their non-predictive nature for individuals with Hall's very different and more sophisticated discussion of ideological hegemony. The article is in fact fascinating in its revelation of the schism which still exists between American and European research and which it purports to span.

The work of the Frankfurt School raised a great many problems in terms of conceptualizing the relationship between cultural objects and the material basis of society, in terms of the introduction of aesthetics into an apparently sociological theory and in terms of analysis of media content. Chaney takes up one set of these problems in his discussion of the role of fiction in mass entertainment. Chaney argues from a specifically 'cultural' position on mass communications. In his perspective, society is a humanly constructed and meaningful reality created and sustained through communication. Reality is seen as a 'coherent view of experience which is held by individuals or groups . . . our version of what goes on around us' (Kreiling, 1976 p. 79). The issues centre, then, not on the effects of the media nor the uses made of the media by audiences, but on the way in which mass communication produces definitions of situations and socially constructed realities. In this article Chaney treats fiction as performance and experience which is altered by the emergence of the mass media through a loss of distance, in terms of the removal of narrative boundaries. Chaney argues that 'fictional experience has become reduced to consuming commodities provided by others', an argument not dissimilar to that of Adorno on popular music and Chaney also argues, like Adorno and Benjamin, that it is the *experience* of fiction through text and performance which must be understood first rather than the economic relationships involved.

Hebdige's article explores the relationship between the social structure of West Indian society and its music and proceeds to examine the development of reggae in immigrant areas in English cities and its appropriation by the skinhead group. Hebdige stresses the expressive and political functions of Jamaican sub-cultures and in so doing points to the underlying material forces.

References

Adorno, T. W., 1941: (with the assistance of George Simpson) 'On popular music' *Studies in Philosophy and Social Science* IX (1).
1967: *Prisms.* London: Neville Spearman.
Benjamin, W., 1973: *Understanding Brecht.* London: New Left Books.
Kreiling, A., 1976: 'Recent British Communication Research'. *Communication Research* January 1976.
Marx, K. and Engels, F., 1970: *The German Ideology.* London: Lawrence and Wishart.
Jay, M., 1973: *The Dialectical Imagination.* London: Heinemann.
Slater, P., 1977: *The Origins and Significance of the Frankfurt School: A Marxist Perspective.* London: Routledge and Kegan Paul.

13

Culture, the Media and the 'Ideological Effect'

Stuart Hall

Culture has its roots in what Marx, in *The German Ideology*, called man's 'double relation': to nature and to other men. Men, Marx argued, intervene in nature and, with the help of certain instruments and tools, use nature to reproduce the material conditions of their existence. But, from a very early point in the history of human development, this intervention in nature through labour is *socially* organized. Men collaborate with one another — at first, through the collective use of simple tools, the rudimentary division of labour and the exchange of goods — for the more effective reproduction of their material conditions. This is the beginning of social organization, and of human history. From this point forward, man's relation to nature becomes socially mediated. The reproduction of human society, in increasingly complex and extended forms, and the reproduction of material existence are fundamentally linked: in effect, the adaptation of nature to man's material needs is effected only through the forms which his social collaboration with other men assume. Men, then, reproduce themselves as 'social individuals' through the social forms which their material production assumes. No matter how infinitely complex and extended are the social forms which men then successively develop, the relations surrounding the material reproduction of their existence forms the determining instance of all these other structures. From this given matrix — the forces and relations of production, and the manner in which they are socially organized, in different historical epochs — arise all the more elaborate forms of social structure, the division of labour, the development of the distinction between different types of society, new ways of applying human skill and knowledge to the modification of material circumstances, the forms of civil and political association, the different types of family and the state, men's beliefs, ideas and theoretical constructions, and the types of social consciousness appropriate to or 'corresponding to' them. This is the basis for a *materialist* understanding of social development and human history; it must also be the basis of any materialist or non-idealist definition of culture. Marx, in fact, argued that there is no 'labour' or production *in general* (Marx,

1973). Production always assumes specific historical forms, under determinate conditions. The types of society, social relationship and human culture which arise under these specific historical conditions will also assume a determinate form. One type of production differs fundamentally from another: and since each stage in the development of material production will give rise to different forms of social cooperation, a distinct type of technical and material production, and different kinds of political and civil organization, human history is divided, through the developing modes of production, into distinctive and historically specific *stages* or *epochs*. Once material production and its corresponding forms of social organization reach a complex stage of development, it will require considerable analysis to establish precisely how the relationship between these levels can be conceptualized. Precisely *how* to think this relationship between material and social production and the rest of a developed social formation, constitutes perhaps *the* most difficult aspect of a materialist theory. We shall return to this question in a moment. But a materialist account must, by definition, encompass some concrete way of thinking this relationship — normally referred to, within Marxist analyses, by way of the metaphor of 'base' and 'the superstructures' — if it is not to desert the ground of its originating premise the foundation of human culture in labour and material production. Marx's 'materialism' adds to this premise at least one other requirement: that the relationship must be thought within determinate historical conditions — it must be made *historically specific*. It is this second requirement which distinguishes a historical materialist theory of human society and culture from, say, a materialism grounded in the simple fact of man's physical nature (a 'vulgar' or as Marx calls it, an undialectical materialism) or one which gives the determining instance to technological development alone. What Korsch, among others, has called 'the principle of historical specificity' in Marx's materialism is clearly enunciated in *The German Ideology* (where Marx's theory becomes, for the first time, fully 'historical') and afterwards in his mature work. 'The fact is . . . that *definite* individuals who are productively active in a *definite* way enter into these *definite* social and political relations. Empirical observation must in each separate instance bring out empirically and without any mystification and speculation, the connection of the social and political structure with production'. (Marx 1965) (our emphasis.) To this basis or 'anatomy' Marx also relates 'the production of ideas, of conceptions, of consciousness' — the sphere of 'mental production'. For Marx, the relations which govern the social organization of material production are specific — 'definite' — for each phase or stage: each constitutes its own 'mode'. The social and cultural superstructures which 'correspond' to each mode of production will, likewise, be historically specific. For Marx, each of the major modes of production in human history to date have been based fundamentally on one type of the exploitation of the labour of some by others. Modes of production — however complex, developed and productive they become — are therefore founded on a root antagonistic contradiction. But this contradiction, the social forms in which it is institutionalized, the theoretical laws which 'explain' it, and the forms of 'consciousness' in which the antagonism is lived and experienced, work out in, again, definite and historically specific ways. Most of Marx and Engles's work was devoted to analysing the historically determinate 'laws and tendencies' governing the *capitalist* mode of production: and in analysing the different superstructural and ideological forms appropriate to this stage in society's material development. It was consonant with their theory that this mode, and the corresponding social forms, exhibited its own specific laws and tendencies; that these were founded on a specific type of contradiction, between how labour was expended and goods produced, and the way the value of labour was expropriated; and that this dynamic, expansive phase of material development was historically *finite* — destined to evolve and expand through a series of transformations, reach the outer limits of its potential development, and be superseded by another stage in human history — impelled, not by external force but by 'inner connection' (Marx, 1961.) Indeed, Marx saw each mode of production as driven to develop, through its higher stages, precisely by the 'overcoming' of the contradictions intrinsic to its lower stages; reproducing these antagonisms on a more advanced level; and hence destined to disappear through this development of contradictions. This analysis, worked out at the level of economic forms and processes, constituted the subject matter of *Capital*.

Now, since each mode of material and social organization was historically specific, so the forms of social life corresponding to it was bound to assume a 'definite' and historically distinct shape and form. 'This mode of production must not be considered simply as being the reproduction of the physical existence of the individuals. Rather, it is a definite form of activity of these individuals, a definite form of expressing their life, a definite *mode of life* on their part. As individuals express their life, so they are. What they are, therefore, coincides with their production, both with *what* they produce and with *how* they produce it.' (Marx, 1965.) The social and material forms of production, the way labour was organized and combined with tools to produce, the level of technical development, the institutions through which goods circulated and value was realized, the types of civil association, of family life and of the state appropriate to it — this ensemble of relations and structures exhibited an identifiable configuration, a pattern, a 'mode of living' for the social individuals and groups within it. This patterning, was, so to speak, the result of the interconnections between the different levels of social practice. The pattern also expressed how the combined result of these interconnecting levels was 'lived', as a totality, by its 'bearers'. This seems to be the best way of grasping, within a materialist theory (in which the term itself plays no significant part), where precisely *culture* arises. To put it metaphorically, 'culture' refers us to the arrangement — the *forms* — assumed by social existence under determinate historical conditions. Provided the metaphor is understood as of heuristic value only, we might say that if the term 'social' refers to the *content* of the relationships into which men involuntarily enter in any social formation, then 'culture' refers to the forms which those relationships assume. (The form/content distinction is not, however, one which we can push very far. It should also be borne in mind that Marx, who gives considerable attention to the *forms* which value assumes in the capitalist mode of production, uses the term differently from the way it has been employed above.) At the risk of conflating two divergent theoretical discourses, we might bear in mind here a point which Roger Poole makes of Lévi-Strauss in the Introduction to the latter's work on *Totemism* (1969). 'Instead of asking for the hundredth time "*What* is totemism", he asks us for the first time . . . "How are totemic phenomena arranged?" The move from "what" to "how", from the substantive to the adjectival attitude, is the first radically different thing, the first "structural" thing, to notice about the work before us.' 'Culture', in this sense, does not refer to something substantively different from 'social': it refers to a different *aspect* of essentially the same phenomena.

Culture, in this meaning of the term, is the objectivated design to human existence when 'definite men under definite conditions' 'appropriate nature's productions in a form adapted to his own wants' and 'stamps that labour as exclusively human' (*Capital* I). This is very close to what we might call the 'anthropological' definition of culture. (In their different ways, the theoretical work of Raymond Williams (1960), the modification of Williams by Thompson (1960), and, in the very different context provided by its basic functionalism, the studies of 'material culture and social structure' of primitive or colonial peoples by social anthropologists, belong to this tradition.)

However, Marx and, more especially, Engels rarely use 'culture' or its cognates in this simply descriptive sense. They use it more dynamically and more developmentally — as a decisive material or *productive force*. Human culture is the result and the record of man's developing mastery over nature, his capacity to modify nature to his use. This is a form of human knowledge, perfected through social labour, which forms the basis for every new stage in man's productive and historical life. This is not a 'knowledge' which is abstractly stored in the head. It is materialized in production, embodied in social organization, advanced through the development of practical as well as theoretical technique, above all, preserved in and transmitted through *language*. In *The German Ideology* Marx speaks of 'a material result, a sum of productive forces, a historically created relation of individuals to nature and to one another, which is handed down to each generation from its predecessor . . . is, indeed, modified by the new generation, but also . . . prescribes for it its conditions of life and gives it a definite development, a specific character.' It is this which distinguishes men from the animal kingdom. Engels accords the dynamic elements in this process 'first' to 'labour, after it and then with it, speech . . .. The reaction on labour and speech of the development of the brain and its attendant senses, of the increasing clarity of consciousness, power of abstraction and of judgement, gave both labour and speech an ever-renewed impulse to further development . . .' ('Labour In The Transition From Ape To Man', Engels, 1950a.) Marx in a famous passage in *Capital*, compares favourably 'the worst of architects' with the 'best of bees' in this: 'that the architect raises his structure in imagination before he erects it in reality . . . . He not only effects a change of form . . . but he also realizes a purpose of his own that gives the law to his *modus operandi* . . . ' (*Capital* I, p. 178.) Earlier, he had identified language, the principal medium through which this knowledge of man's appropriation and adaptation of nature is elaborated, stored, transmitted and applied, as a form of 'practical consciousness' arising 'from the need, the necessity of intercourse with other men' (Marx, 1965). Later, he describes how this accumulated knowledge can be expropriated from the practical labour and skill of the worker, applied as a distinct productive force to modern industry for its further development and thus pressed 'into the service of capital' (*Capital* I, p. 361). Here, *culture* is the accumulated growth of man's power over nature, materialized in the instruments and practice of labour and in the medium of signs, thought, knowledge and language through which it is passed on from generation to generation as man's 'second nature' (Cf Woolfson, 1976).

Now *The German Ideology* — on which many of these seminal formulations depend — is the text in which Marx insists that history cannot be read as the sum of the consciousness of mankind. Ideas, conceptions, etc. arise 'in thought' but must be explained in terms of material practice, not the other way around. This is perfectly consistent with the general proposition that culture, knowledge and language have their basis in social and material life and are not independent or autonomous of it. Generally speaking, however, Marx in this text saw material needs fairly straight-forwardly and transparently reflected in the sphere of thought, ideas, and language; the latter changing when, and in keeping with how, their 'basis' changes. A social formation is not thought of as consisting of a set of 'relatively autonomous' practices, but as an expressive totality; in which the 'needs' or tendencies of the determining base are mediated in a homologous way at the other levels; and where everything stems from 'real, active men' and their 'active life process', their historical *praxis* 'under definite material limits, presupposes and conditions independent of their will'. In a related but slightly different formulation, we would then expect each of the practices concerned to reveal 'surprising correspondences', each being understood as so many forms of 'human energy'. (AS in Williams, 1961.)

The problem is how to account for the fact that, in the realm of ideas, meaning, value, conceptions and consciousness, men can 'experience' themselves in ways which do not fully correspond with their real situation. How can men be said to have a 'false' consciousness of how they stand or relate to the real conditions of their life and production? Can language, the medium through which human culture in the 'anthropological sense' is transmitted, *also* become the instrument through which it is 'distorted'? (Cf. Thompson, 1960); the instrument by which men elaborate accounts and explanations, make sense of and become conscious of their 'world', which *also* binds and fetters, rather than frees them? How can thought conceal aspects of their real conditions rather than clarify them? In short, how can we account for the fact that 'in all ideology', men (who are the 'producers of their consciousness, ideas, etc.') and their circumstances are mystified, 'appear upside down as in a *camera obscura*'? The reason, fundamentally, is offered in the second half of the same sentence from *The German Ideology*: it is essentially because these men are 'conditioned by a definite development of their productive forces and of the intercourse corresponding to these'. It is because men are, so to speak, *de-centered* by the determinate conditions under which they live and produce, and depend on circumstances and conditions which are not of their making and which they enter involuntarily, that they cannot, in any full and uncontradictory sense, be the collective *authors* of their actions. Their practice cannot unmediatedly realize their goals and intentions. Hence the terms through which men 'make sense' of their world, experience their objective situation as a subjective experience, and 'come to consciousness' of who and what they are, are not in their own keeping and will not, consequently, transparently reflect their situation. Hence the fundamental *determinacy* of what Marx called 'the superstructures' — the fact that practices in these domains are conditioned elsewhere, experienced and realized only in *ideology*.

The radically limiting concept of *ideology* has a de-centering and si displacing effect on the freely developing processes of 'human culture'. It opens up the need to 'think' the radical and systematic disjunctures between the different levels of any social formation: between the material relations of production, the social practices in which class and other social relations are constituted (here Marx locates 'the superstructures' — civil society, the family, the juridico-political forms, the state), and the level of 'ideological forms' — ideas, meanings, conceptions, theories, beliefs, etc. and the forms of consciousness which are appropriate to them. (Cf. the formulation in the famous *Preface*, 1859 (Bottomore and Rubel 1963).) In *The German Ideology* — specifically devoted to the third 'level' which, in

German thought, had achieved a positively stratospheric autonomy from material life and, at the same time, in the form of Hegel's Absolute Spirit, had been installed as the very motor of the whole system — Marx offers a more detailed account of how these disjunctures arise. With the advancing division of labour (on which expanding material production depends) the distinction between mental and manual labour appears: each is installed in distinct spheres, in different practices and institutions, indeed in different social strata (e.g. the rise of the intelligentsia, the professional ideologues): mental labour appears as wholly autonomous from its material and social base and is projected into an absolute realm, 'emancipating itself from the real'. But also, under the conditions of capitalist production, the means of mental labour are expropriated by the ruling classes. Hence we come, not simply to 'ideology' as a necessary level of any capitalist social formation, but to the concept of *dominant* ideology — of 'ruling ideas'. 'The class which is the ruling material force is at the same time its ruling intellectual force . . . has control over the means of mental production so that, generally speaking, the ideas of those who lack the means of mental production are subject to it . . . . The ruling ideas are nothing more than the ideal expression of the dominant material relationships . . . grasped as ideas; hence of the relationships which make the one class the ruling one, therefore the ideas of its dominance . . . . Insofar as they rule as a class and determine the extent and compass of an epoch . . . they rule also as thinkers, as producers of ideas, and regulate the production and distribution of the ideas of their age . . . . ' (Marx, 1965 p. 60.)

In what follows I shall be concentrating specifically on this ideological dimension. But it should be said at once that the term *culture* continues to have an ambiguous and unspecified relation to the model outlined here. There appears to be a theoretical discontinuity between the problematic in which the term 'culture' has been developed and the terms of classical Marxist theory. The ambiguity arises because, if we transpose it into a Marxist framework, 'culture' now appears to refer to at least *two* levels, which are closely related but which, considered under the single rubric, 'culture', tend to be uneasily collapsed. The capitalist mode of production depends upon the 'combination' of those who own the means of production and those who have only their labour to sell, together with the tools and instruments of production. In this relation ('relations of/forces of production') labour is *the* commodity which has the capacity to produce a value greater than the materials on which it works; and that surplus which is left over when the labourer is paid his upkeep (wages) is expropriated by those who own the means of production, and realized through commodity exchange on the market. This relation, at the level of the mode of production, then produces the constituted classes of capitalism in the field of class practices and relations ('the superstructures'); and, through its own peculiar mechanisms and effects, in the field of ideologies and consciousness.

Now the conditions under which the working class lives its social practice will exhibit a distinctive shape; and that practice will, to some extent, be shaped by that class (in practice and struggle with other classes) — and these shapes can be said to constitute the ways they organize themselves socially: the forms of working class *culture*. (Works like Hoggart's *Uses of Literacy* and of Roberts's *Classic Slum* point to some of the ways in which the 'culture' of that class, in particular periods, registers its peculiar modes of material and social existence.) These social class practices and relations will embody certain characteristic values and meanings of the class, so that its 'culture' is *lived*. But there is also the distinct area in which classes 'experience' their own practice, make a certain kind of sense of it, give accounts of it and use ideas to bring to it a certain imaginary coherence — the level of what we might call *ideology proper*. Its principal medium of elaboration is the practice of language and consciousness, for it is through language that meaning is given. These 'meanings' which we attribute to our relations and by means of which we grasp, in consciousness, how we live and what we practice, are not simply the theoretical and ideological projections of individuals. To 'give sense' in this way, is fundamentally, to locate oneself and one's experience, one's conditions, in the already objectivated ideological *discourses*, the sets of ready-made and preconstituted 'experiencings' displayed and arranged through language which fill out the ideological sphere. And this domain of ideology and consciousness is frequently, and confusingly, *also* called 'culture': though, as we have already seen, we may find either an accurate or a distorted reflection of practice in ideology, and there is no necessary correspondence of transparency between them. Marx himself has partly contributed to this conflation by calling both the spheres of social class practices and the field of ideologies by single terms — 'the superstructures', and, even more confusingly, 'the ideological forms'. But how can both the lived practices of class relations *and* the mental representations, images and themes which render them intelligible, ideologically, be both 'ideological forms'? This question is made even more obscure because we now commonly, and mistakenly, interpret the term ideology to mean *false* — imaginary conceits, phantom beliefs about things which appear to exist but are not real. The ideas we have about our conditions *may* be 'unreal': but how can social practices be 'unreal'? To clarify the question, let us rephrase it on the basis of a different aspect of Marx's theory: one which contains the germ, the outline, of that more developed theory of ideology which succeeds the one we have been outlining. (Cf. Mepham, 1974; Geras, 1972.) For Marx, capitalism is the most dynamic and rapidly expanding mode of production so far to be seen in human history. One consequence of its dynamic but antagonistic movement is that, within its logic, production comes progressively to depend on the increasing 'socialization' or interdependence of labour. At this level, capitalism contributes to the further development and transformation of man's productive powers. But this continuing all-sided interdependence of labour in the sphere of production is, at every moment under capitalism, realized in and organized through *the market*. And in the market, men's all-sided interdependence, the basis of their 'sociality', is experienced as 'something alien and objective, confronting the individual, not as their relation to one another, but as their subordination to relations which subsist independently of them, and which arise out of collisions between mutually indifferent individuals'. (Marx, 1973 p. 157.) So the progressively social character of production appears as a condition of mutual unconnectedness and indifference. Thus *both* the 'socialization' of labour, and its opposite — the sale of labour as an individual commodity, the private appropriation of its products, its fragmentation through the market and commodity exchange, etc. — are true: that is, the contradictory nature, and the structurally antagonistic character of its production under the determinate conditions of capitalism. We must begin to grasp the fundamentally antagonistic nature of culture under capitalist conditions in an analogous way.

We can discover a number of critical points about how this might be done by following for a moment, the way Marx handles this contradiction between the social character of labour and the individual nature of its realization under capitalism. What accomplishes this dislocation, from social production to individual realization is commodity exchange in the market. The market of course, *really exists*. It is not the figment of anyone's imagination. It is a *mediation* which enables one kind of relation (social) to appear (i.e. *really* to appear) as another kind of relation (individual. (Marx, 1973 p. 255.) This second relation is not 'false' in the sense that it does not exist: but it is 'false' in the sense that, within its limits, it cannot express and embody the full social relation on which the system ultimately rests. The market re-presents a system which requires both production and exchange, as if it consisted of exchange only. That of course was the key premise of much of political economy. It therefore has the function, at one and the same time, of: (a) transforming one relation into its opposite; (*camera obscura*) (b) making the latter, which is *part of* the relations of production and exchange under capitalism, appear as, or *stand for* the whole (this is the theory of *fetishism*, developed in Chapter I of *Capital* I); (c) making the latter — the real foundations of capitalist society, in production, — *disappear from view* (the effect of *concealment*). Hence, we can only 'see' that labour and production are realized through the market: we can no longer 'see' that it is in production that labour is exploited and the surplus value extracted. These three 'functions' make market relationships under capitalism, simultaneously, 'real' and *ideological*. They are ideological, not because they are a fantasy, but because there is a structural dislocation between what Marx calls the levels of 'real relations', where capitalism conducts its business, and the form of appearance, the ideological structures and relations — what he calls the 'phenomenal forms' — through which that business is accomplished. This distinction between 'real relations' and *how they appear* is the absolute pivot of the 'theory of ideology' which is contained — but in an implicit and untheorized manner — in Marx's later and more mature work. It can be seen that, far from there being a *homologous* relationship between the material basis of practice, in capitalism, and how it *appears*, these now have to be thought, rigorously, as two related but systematically dislocated articulations of a capitalist social formation. They relate, but through their systematic differences — through a necessary series of *transformations*. The level of ideology, of consciousness and of experiencing must be thought in terms of this de-centering of material practice *through* ideological forms and relations. There must be distinct levels of practice corresponding to these two sites of the social formation. To understand the role of ideology, we must also be able to account for the mechanisms which consistently sustain, in reality, a set of representations which are not so much false to, as a *false inflection* of, the 'real relations' on which, in fact, they depend. (Let us remember that, since the market does exist and people buy and sell things, market *ideologies* are materialized in market practices.)

We can take this one step further. For not only does socially inter-dependent labour *appear*, in the sphere of the market, as a set of mutually independent and indifferent relations: but this second level of ideological relations gives rise to a whole set of theories, images, representations and discourses which *fill it out*. The various discourses of wages, and prices, of the 'individual buyer and seller', of the 'consumer', of 'the labour contract'; or the elaborate contract theories of property enshrined in the legal system; or the theories of possessive individualism, of individual 'rights and duties', of 'free agents', of the 'rights of man' and of 'representative democracy' — in short, the whole enormously complex sphere of legal, political, economic and philosophical discourses which compose the dense ideological complex of a modern capitalist society, all stem from or are rooted in the same premises upon which the market and the ideas of a 'market society' and of 'market rationality' are founded. Marx makes this connection clear in a telling passage, where he takes leave of 'this noisy sphere where everything takes place on the surface and in view of all men', and follows the capitalist process into 'the hidden abode of production'. The latter sphere — the sphere of exchange — he remarks, 'is in fact a very Eden of the innate rights of man. There alone rule Freedom, Equality, Property and Bentham. Freedom because both buyer and seller of a commodity . . . are [i.e. appear to be] constrained by their own free will . . . . Equality because each enters [appears to enter] into relation with the other as with a simple owner of commodities . . . . Property because each disposes [appears to dispose] only of what is his own . . . . And Bentham because each looks [appears to look] only to himself . . . . Each looks to himself only, and no one troubles himself about the rest, and just because they do so, do they all, in accordance with the pre-established harmony of things, or under the auspicies of an all-shrewd providence, work together to their mutual advantage, for the common weal and in the interest of all.' (*Capital* I, p. 176) (Cf. *Grundrisse*, p. 245, our clarifications.) It is crucial to the whole force of this ironic passage that the discourses both of everyday life and of high political, economic or legal theory arise from, not the ideological relation of the market exchange only, but (to put it clumsily but necessarily) from the way the real relations of production are *made to appear* in the form of the ideological or 'imaginary' relations of market exchange. It is also crucial that 'ideology' is now understood not as what is hidden and concealed, but precisely as what is most open, apparent, manifest — what 'takes place on the surface and in view of all men'. What is hidden, repressed, or inflected out of sight, are its real foundations. This is the source or site of its *unconsciousness.*

This point is of the utmost importance: but it is not easy to grasp. For how can the realm in which we think, talk, reason, explain and experience ourselves — the activities of consciousness — be unconscious? We may think here of the most obvious and 'transparent' forms of consciousness which operate in our everyday experience and ordinary language: common sense. What passes for 'common sense' in our society — the residue of absolutely basic and commonly-agreed, consensual wisdoms — helps us to classify out the world in simple but meaningful terms. Precisely, common sense does not require reasoning, argument, logic, thought: it is spontaneously available, thoroughly recognizable, widely shared. It *feels*, indeed, as if it has always been there, the sedimented, bedrock wisdom of 'the race', a form of 'natural' wisdom, the content of which has changed hardly at all with time. However, common sense does have *a content*, and a history. As Nowell-Smith reminds us (1974), when Robinson Crusoe was left entirely on his own in his natural state on a desert island, what he 'spontaneously' developed was not universally common ideas but a distinctly 'primitive capitalist' mentality. In the same way, contemporary forms of common sense are shot through with the debris and traces of previous, more developed ideological systems; and their reference point is to what passes, without exception, as the wisdom of *our* particular age and society, overcast with the glow of traditionalism. It is precisely its 'spontaneous' quality, its transparency, its 'naturalness', its refusal to be made to examine the premises on which it is founded, its resistance to change or to correction, its effect of instant recognition, and the closed circle in which it moves which makes common sense, at one and the same time, 'spontaneous', ideological *and unconscious.* You cannot learn, through common sense, *how things are*: you can only discover *where they fit* into the existing scheme of things. In this way, its very taken-for-grantedness is what establishes it as a medium in which its own premises and presuppositions are being rendered *invisible* by its apparent transparency. (Cf. Gramsci, 1968.) It was in this general sense that Marx talked about the ideological forms in which men 'become conscious' — treating the process of *becoming conscious* (in either an active, revolutionary or a passive, common-sense way) as a distinct process, with its own logic, mechanisms and 'effects'; not to be condensed or collapsed into other social practices. It is also in this general sense that Althusser speaks of ideology as 'that new form of specific unconsciousness called "consciousness". (1965.) Althusser argues that, though ideologies usually consist of systems of representations, images and concepts, 'it is above all as structures that they impose on the vast majority of men. They are perceived-accepted-suffered cultural objects and they act functionally on men via a process that escapes them'. Ideologies are, therefore, the sphere of the *lived* — the sphere of *experiencing*, rather than of 'thinking'. 'In ideology men do indeed express, not the relation between them and their conditions of existence [e.g. the socialization of labour under capitalism] but *the way* they "live" the relation between them and their conditions of existence [i.e. the way we live, through market relationships, the real conditions of capitalist production] . . . the expression of the relation between men and their "world" . . . the (overdetermined) unity of the real relation and the imaginary relation between them and the real conditions of existence.' (Althusser, 1965.) This is a crucial reformulation.

We can see that this way of conceptualizing culture and ideology implies a very different way of 'thinking' the relationship between the material basis and the complex superstructures than that which seems to lie at the heart of *The German Ideology*. Althusser and his 'school' have been principally responsible for criticising the 'humanist-historicist' manner in which the different levels of social practice are conceptualized and related in that text, and in subsequent theorists which follow on from it. He calls it 'Hegelian', because, though society is seen as full of contradictions, mediations and dialectical movement, the social formation is nevertheless, in the end, reducible to a *simple* structure, with 'one principle of internal unity', which 'unrolls' evenly throughout all the different levels. This is the conception of a social formation as an 'expressive totality'. When this manner of thinking a society is brought within the scope of Marx's 'determination in the last instance by the economic', then every other level of the social formation — civil life, the forms of the state, political, ideological and theoretical practices — are all, ultimately, 'expressive of', and therefore reducible to, a single contradiction — 'moved by the simple play of a principle of *simple* contradiction' (Althusser, 1965 p. 103). From this 'base', cultural and ideological forms appear simply as so many reflexive objectivations of a single, undifferentiated, *human praxis* — which, under conditions of capitalist production, becomes reified and alienated: its 'one principle of

internal unity is itself only possible on the absolute condition of taking
the whole concrete life of a people for the externalization-alienation of
an internal spiritual principle'. As against this, Althusser proposes that we
must understand a social formation as 'an ever pre-given structured complex whole'. There is no simple essence, underlying or pre-dating this
structured complexity, to which any single practice — e.g. the production
of ideology — can be effectively reduced. As Marx himself argued at
length, 'The simplest economic category . . . can only ever exist as the
unilateral and abstract relation of a pre-given, living concrete whole'.
(Marx, 1973, Introduction.) We must therefore 'think' a society or social
formation as ever and always constituted by a set of complex practices;
each with its own specificity, its own modes of articulation; standing in
an 'uneven development' to other, related practices. Any relation within
this structured complexity will have its registration, its 'effects', at *all* the
other levels of the totality — economic, social, political, ideological; none
can be reduced to or collapsed into the other. If, nevertheless, this social
formation — now conceptualized not as an 'economic basis' and its
'reflexive superstructures' but rather as a structure-superstructure *complex*
— is not to be conceptualized as a series of totally independent, autonomous and unrelated practices, then this relatedness must be 'thought'
through the different mechanisms and articulations which connect one
with another within the 'whole' — articulations which do not proceed in
an inevitable tandem, but which are linked through their *differences*,
through the dislocations between them, rather than through their similarity,
correspondence or identity. (Cf. Hall, 1974.) The principle of determinacy —
which, as we saw, is fundamental to any materialist theory — must
therefore be thought, not as the simple determination of one level (e.g. the
economic) over all the others, but as the structured sum of the different
determinations, the structure of their overall effects. Althusser gives to
this double way of conceiving the 'relative autonomy' of practices *and*
their 'determination in the last instance', the term, *over-determination*.
When there is a fusion or 'ruptural conjuncture' between all the different
levels, this is not because the 'economic' ('His Majesty, The Economy')
has detached itself and 'appeared' on its own as a naked principle of
determination, but because the contradictions at the different levels have
all *accumulated* within a single conjuncture. That conjuncture is then
over-determined by all the other instances and effects: it is 'structured in
dominance'. (Althusser, 1965.)

   We can now attempt to 'cash' this distinctive way of thinking the interplay of practices and relations within a social formation by considering
the level of 'ideological practice' and its principal mediator — language.
The production of various kinds of social knowledge takes place through
the instrumentality of thinking, conceptualization and symbolization. It
operates primarily and principally through language — that set of objective

signs and discourses which materially embody the processes of thought
and mediate the communication of thought in society. Language is, as
Saussure insisted, fundamentally *social*. The individual can only think
and speak by first situating himself within the language system. That
system is socially constructed and sustained: it cannot be elaborated from
the individual speaker alone. Hence speech and the other discourses —
including what Voloshinov calls 'inner speech' — constitute systems of
signs which objectivate and intermediate 'thinking': they *speak us* as much
as we speak in and through them. To express ourselves within this
objectivated system of signs we must have access to the rules and conventions which govern speech and articulation; to the various *codes* — the
precise number and disposition of the codes will vary from one linguistic
and cultural community to another — through which social life is *classified
out* in our culture.

Now in so far as all social life, every facet of social practice, is
mediated by language (conceived as a system of signs and representations,
arranged by codes and articulated through various discourses), it enters fully
into material and social practice. Its distribution and usages will be fundamentally structured by all the other relations of the social formation which
employ it. Volosinov (1973) observes that 'the forms of signs are conditioned
above all by the social organization of the participants involved and also
by the immediate condition of their interaction'. Vygotsky therefore
insists that language, like all other social phenomena, is 'subject to all
the premises of historical materialism'. Its usage will therefore reflect
the class structuring of capitalist social relations. It will be dependent on
the nature of the social relations in which it is embedded, the manner in
which its users are socially organized together, the social and material
contexts in which it is employed. At the same time, this 'world of signs'
and discourses has its own, internal laws, rules, codes and conventions, its
own modes and mechanisms. The principal element in the articulation of
language is the *sign*. Signs are the material registration of meaning. Signs
communicate, not simply because they are social phenomena and are part
of material reality, but because of the specific function which they have
of *refracting* that reality of which they are a part. As the structural
linguists have shown, a sign does not carry meaning by unilaterally
standing for an object or event in the 'real world'. There is no such transparent, one-to-one relationship between sign, the thing to which it refers,
and what that thing 'means'. Signs communicate meaning because the way
they are *internally* organized together within a specific language system or
set of codes, articulates the way things are related together in the objective
social world. 'Signs', Barthes (1967) argues, 'cut at one and the same time
into two floating kingdoms'. Thus, events and relations in the 'real' world
do not have a single natural, necessary and unambiguous meaning which
is simply projected, through signs, into language. The same set of social

relations can be differently organized to *have a meaning* within different linguistic and cultural systems. (Even at the simplest level, we know that the Eskimos have several different terms for what we call 'snow'.) And this disjuncture between the different ways of classifying out a domain of social life in different cultures is even more striking when we move from the denotation of natural objects to the signification of complex social relations. Certain ideological domains will be fully inscribed ideologically in one social formation, thoroughly articulated in a complex field of ideological signs, while others will remain relatively 'empty' and undeveloped. Rather than speaking of such relations as 'having a meaning' we must think of language as *enabling things to mean*. This is the social practice of *signification*: the practice through which the 'labour' of cultural and ideological representation is accomplished. It follows that the ways in which men come to understand their relation to their real conditions of existence, under capitalism, are subject to the *relay of language*: and it is this which makes possible that ideological displacement or inflection, whereby the 'real' relations can be culturally signified and ideologically inflected as a set of 'imaginary lived relations'. As Volosinov puts it, 'A sign does not simply exist as a part of reality — it reflects and refracts another reality. Therefore it may distort that reality or be true to it, or may perceive it from a special point of view, and so forth. Every sign is subject to the criteria of ideological evaluation . . . . The domain of ideology coincides with the domain of signs. They equate with one another. Wherever a sign is present, ideology is present too. Everything ideological possesses a semiotic value'. (1973.) Volosinov recognizes that this sphere will, in any social formation, be organized into a complex *ideological field of discourses*, whose purpose is to endow the social relations which are grasped as 'intelligible' within that particular field as having a certain, a 'definite' *kind* of intelligibility: 'the domain of the artistic image, the religious symbol, the scientific formula and the judicial ruling, etc. Each field of ideological creativity has its own kind of orientation towards reality and each refracts reality in its own way. Each field commands its own special function within the unity of social life. But it is their semiotic character that places all ideological phenomena under the same general condition'. (Volosinov, 1973 pp. 10—11.) Poulantzas has recently attempted to lay out the various *regions* into which the dominant ideologies under capitalism are organized. He argues that, under capitalism, the *juridico-political* region of ideology will play a dominant role; its function being, in part, to hide or 'mask' the determinant role which the level of the economic plays in this mode of production — so that 'everything takes place as if the centre of the dominant ideology is never in the place where real knowledge is to be sought'; and that other ideological regions — philosophic, religious and moral ideologies — will tend to 'borrow notions' from that instance (the juridico-political) which plays the dominant role. (Poulantzas, 1965 pp. 211—12.) Whether we accept this particular resumé or not, it is of critical importance to understand that ideologies are not simply the 'false understandings' of individuals; nor can the individual subject be conceptualized as the source or author of ideology. (We insist on this point, since one of the recent developments in materialist theory, which seeks to combine Marxism with Freudian psychoanalysis, sees the fundamental moment at which the individual subject 'positions' himself or herself in ideology as occurring as an unconscious, individual and trans-cultural process, at the moment when, via the Oedipus complex, men 'enter culture'). Important as this line of theorizing is in accounting for the subjective moment of the entry into ideology, it is of critical importance to stress that ideology as a *social practice* consists of the 'subject' positioning himself in the specific complex, the objectivated field of discourses and codes which are available to him in language and culture at a particular historical conjuncture — what C. Wright Mills calls 'situated actions' and 'vocabularies of motives'. (Mills, 1963.)

As Eco has observed, 'Semiology shows us the universe of ideologies arranged in codes and sub-codes within the universe of signs'. (Eco, 'Articulations Of The Cinematic Code'.) It is principally the nature of signs and the arrangement of signs into their various codes and sub-codes, ensembles and sub-ensembles, and what has been called the 'inter-textuality' of codes, which enable this 'work' of cultural signification to be ceaselessly accomplished in societies. Connotative codes, above all, which enable a sign to 'reference' a wide domain of social meanings, relations and associations, are the means by which the widely distributed forms of social knowledge, social practices, the taken-for-granted knowledge which society's members possess of its institutions, beliefs, ideas and legitimations are 'brought within the horizon' of language and culture. These codes constitute the criss-crossing frames of reference, the sedimentations of meaning and connotation, which cover the face of social life and render it classifiable, intelligible, meaningful. (Hall, 1972; 1974.) They constitute the 'maps of meaning' of a culture. Barthes calls them 'fragments of ideology'. . . . 'These signifieds have a very close communication with culture, knowledge and history and it is through them, so to speak, that the environmental world invades the system [of language] (Barthes, 1967). To each of these cultural lexicons 'there corresponds . . . a corpus of practices and techniques; these collections imply on the part of system consumers . . . different degrees of knowledge (according to differences in their 'culture') which explains how the same lexis . . . can be decyphered differently according to the individual concerned without ceasing to belong to a given "language" . . . ' (*op. cit.*). The different areas of social life, the different levels and kinds of relation and practice, appear to be 'held together' in social intelligibility by this web of preferred meanings. These networks are clustered into *domains*, which appear to *link*, naturally, certain things to certain other things, within a context, and to exclude others. These domains of meaning, then, have the whole social order and social practice refracted within their classifying schemes.

Marx however insisted, not merely that men live their relations to their real conditions of existence 'in ideology', but that, in the capitalist mode of production, they will 'think' those conditions, in general, within the limits of a *dominant* ideology; and that, generally, this will tend to be the ideology of the *dominant classes*. The fact that the proletariat 'lives' the collective socialization of labour, under capitalism, through the fragmenting form of *the market*, and thinks this condition of its material life within the discourses which organize market practices ideologically (or that, under capitalism the proletariat 'lives' the expropriation of surplus value in the 'ideological form' of *wages* — a form giving rise to its own ideological discourses: wage bargaining, economism, what Lenin called 'trade union consciousness', 'a fair days wage for a fair day's work', etc.) is not, for Marx, simply a *descriptive* feature of capitalism. These ideological inflexions perform a pivotal role in the maintenance of capitalist relations and in their continuing domination within the social formation. Before, then, considering what role the mass media play in relation to these processes, we must briefly examine *how* this notion of dominant ideology is to be understood. What relation does a dominant ideology have to the 'dominant', and to the 'dominated' classes? What functions does it perform for Capital and for the continuation of capitalist relations? What are the mechanisms by which this 'work' is accomplished?

Three Related Concepts of 'Domination'

In a recent article, which represents a considerable modification of his earlier position, Raymond Williams argues that 'in any particular period there is a central system of practices, meanings and values which we can properly call dominant and effective . . . which are organized and lived'. This is understood, not as a static structure — 'the dry husks of ideology' (Williams, 1973) but as a *process* — the process of incorporation. Williams cites the educational institutions as one of the principal agencies of this process. By means of it, certain of the available meanings and values through which the different classes of men live their conditions of life are 'chosen for emphasis', others discarded. More crucially, the many meanings and values which lie outside of the selective and selecting emphases of this central core are continually 'reinterpreted, diluted, or put into forms which support or at least do not contradict other elements within the effective dominant culture'. The dominant system must therefore continually make and remake itself so as to 'contain' those meanings, practices and values which are oppositional to it. Williams therefore understands any society to contain many more systems of meaning and value than those incorporated in its 'central system of practices, meanings and values' — 'no mode of production and therefore no dominant society or order . . . and therefore no dominant culture in reality exhausts human practice, human energy, human intention'. What then constitutes the 'dominance' of these dominant meanings and practices are the mechanisms which allow it to select, incorporate and therefore also exclude elements in 'the full range of human practice' (the selectivity of *tradition* plays a key role here). Williams identifies two classes of alternative meaning and practice. There are 'residual' forms of alternative or oppositional culture, which consist of meanings and values which cannot find expression within the dominant structure, 'but which are principally drawn from the past and from a previous stage in the social formation'. Ideas associated with the rural past and with 'organic society' are examples of *residual* elements in our culture. They have often formed the basis (the English 'culture-and-society' tradition is the best example) of a critique of existing cultural forms and tendencies: but they 'threaten it', so to speak, from the past. *Emergent* forms are the area of new practices, new meanings and values. Both residual and emergent forms of culture may, of course, be partially 'incorporated' into the dominant structure: or they may be left as a deviation or enclave which varies from, without threatening, the central emphases.

Despite his continuing stress on experience and intention, this definition of 'dominant culture' in Williams clearly owes a great deal to Gramsci's pivotal and commanding notion of *hegemony*. (Gramsci, 1968.) Gramsci argued that 'hegemony' exists when a ruling class (or, rather, an alliance of ruling class fractions, a 'historical bloc') is able not only to coerce a subordinate class to conform to its interests, but exerts a 'total social authority' over those classes and the social formation as a whole. 'Hegemony' is in operation when the dominant class fractions not only dominate but *direct* — lead: when they not only possess the power to coerce but actively organize so as to command and win the consent of the subordinated classes to their continuing sway. 'Hegemony' thus depends on a combination of force and consent. But — Gramsci argues — in the liberal-capitalist state, consent is normally in the lead, operating behind 'the armour of coercion'. Hegemony, then, cannot be won in the productive and economic sphere alone: it must be organized at the level of the state, politics and the superstructures — indeed the latter is the *terrain* on which 'hegemony' is accomplished. In part, 'hegemony' is achieved by the *containment* of the subordinate classes within the 'superstructures': but crucially, these structures of 'hegemony' work *by ideology*. This means that the 'definitions of reality', favourable to the dominant class fractions, and institutionalized in the spheres of civil life and the

state, come to constitute the primary 'lived reality' as such for the subordinate classes. In this way ideology provides the 'cement' in a social
formation, 'preserving the ideological unity of the entire social bloc'. This
operates, not because the dominant classes can prescribe and proscribe, in
detail, the mental content of the lives of subordinate classes (they too,
'live' in their own ideologies), but because they strive and to a degree
succeed in *framing* all competing definitions of reality *within their range*,
bringing all alternatives within their horizon of thought. They set the
limits — mental and structural — within which subordinate classes 'live'
and make sense of their subordination in such a way as to sustain the
dominance of those ruling over them. Gramsci makes it plain that ideological hegemony must be won and sustained through the existing
ideologies, and that at any time this will represent a complex *field* (not a
single, univocal structure), bearing 'traces' of previous ideological systems
and sedimentations, and complex ideological notations referring to the
present. 'Hegemony' cannot be sustained by a single, unified 'ruling class'
but only by a particular conjunctural alliance of class fractions; thus the
content of dominant ideology will reflect this complex interior formation
of the dominant classes. Hegemony is accomplished through the agencies
of the superstructures — the family, education system, the church, the
media and cultural institutions, as well as the coercive side of the state —
the law, police, the army, which *also*, in part, 'work through ideology'. It
is crucial to the concept that hegemony is not a 'given' and permanent
state of affairs, but has to be actively won and *secured*: it can also be lost.
Gramsci was preoccupied with Italian society, in which, for long periods,
various alliances of the ruling classes had ruled through 'force' without
taking over an authoritative and legitimate *leadership* in the state. There
is no *permanent* hegemony: it can only be established, and analysed, in
concrete historical conjunctures. The reverse side of this is that, even under
hegemonic conditions, there can be no total incorporation or absorption
of the subordinate classes (such as, for example, is foreseen in Marcuse's
One Dimensional Man). The dominated classes, which have their own
objective basis in the system of productive relations, their own distinctive
forms of social life and class practice remain — often as a separate, distinct,
dense and cohesive structure — a *corporate* class culture which is nevertheless *contained*. When these subordinated classes are not strong or sufficiently
organized to represent a 'counter-hegemonic' force to the existing order,
their own corporate structures and institutions can be used, by the dominant
structure (hegemonized), as a means of enforcing their continued subordination. The trade unions, which arise as a defensive set of institutions
in the working class, can nevertheless be used to provide a structure which
perpetuates the *corporateness* of that class, confining its opposition within
limits which the system can contain (e.g. 'economism'). However, for
Gramsci, this does not represent the total disappearance of a subordinate

class into the culture of a hegemonic bloc, but the *achieved complementarity* between hegemonic and subordinate classes and their cultures. This complementarity — Gramsci calls it an unstable equilibrium — is the one moment of the class struggle which never disappears; but it can be more or less open, more or less contained, more or less oppositional. In general, then, 'hegemony' achieves the establishment of a certain *equilibrium* in the class struggle so that, whatever are the concessions the ruling 'bloc' is required to make to win consent and legitimacy, its fundamental basis will not be overturned. 'In other words, the dominant group is coordinated concretely with the general interests of the subordinate groups, and the life of the state is conceived as a continuous process of formation and superceding of unstable equilibria . . . between the interests of the fundamental group and those subordinate groups — equilibria in which the interests of the dominant group prevail, but only up to a certain point, i.e. stopping short of narrowly corporate economic interests'. (Gramsci, 1968 p. 182.) For Gramsci, this often has a great deal to do with the manner in which, at the level of the superstructures and the state, particular interests can be represented as 'general interests' in which all classes have an equal stake.

The immense theoretical revolution which Gramsci's concept of 'hegemony' represents (over, for example, the much simpler and more mechanical formulations of many parts of *The German Ideology*) cannot be overstressed. Through this concept, Gramsci considerably enlarges the whole notion of domination. He places it fundamentally in 'the relations between structure and superstructure which must be accurately posed and resolved if the forces which are active in a particular period are to be correctly analysed . . . '. (p. 177.) In doing so, he sets the concept at a critical distance from all types of economic or mechanical reductionism, from both 'economism' and conspiracy theory. He redefines the whole notion of *power* so as to give full weight to its non-coercive aspects. He also sets the notion of domination at a distance from the direct expression of narrow class interests. He understands that ideology is not 'psychological or moralistic but structural and epistemological'. Above all he allows us to begin to grasp the central role which the superstructures, the state and civil associations, politics and ideology, play in securing and cementing societies 'structured in dominance', and in actively conforming the whole of social, ethical, mental and moral life in their overall tendencies to the requirements of the productive system. This *enlarged* concept of class power and of ideology has provided one of the most advanced theoretical bases for elaborating a 'regional' theory of the much-neglected and often reduced spheres of the superstructural and ideological complexes of capitalist societies.

The third concept of domination is also closely inspired by and elaborated from Gramsci, though it is critical of the traces of 'historicism' in Gramsci's philosophical approach to materialism. This is the thesis, signalled in an exploratory manner in Althusser's important and influential essay, 'Ideology and Ideological State Apparatuses'. (1971.) This introduces the key notion of *reproduction* which has played an extremely important role in recent theorizing on these issues. Briefly, Althusser argues that capitalism as a productive system reproduces the conditions of production 'on an expanded scale', and this must include *social reproduction* — the reproduction of labour power and of the relations of production. This includes wages, without which labour power cannot reproduce itself; skills, without which labour power cannot reproduce itself as a developing 'productive force'; and 'appropriate ideas' — 'a reproduction of its submission to the rules of the established order, i.e. a reproduction of submission to the ruling ideology for the workers, and a reproduction of the ability to manipulate the ruling ideology correctly for the agents of exploitation and repression . . . it is the forms and under the forms of ideological subjection that provision is made for the reproduction of the skills of labour power' (Althusser, 1971 p. 128). But this expanded notion of 'social reproduction' precisely requires the agency of all those apparatuses which are apparently not directly linked in with production as such. The reproduction of labour power through the wage requires *the family*: the reproduction of advanced skills and techniques requires the *education system*; the 'reproduction of the submission to the ruling ideology' requires the *cultural institutions*, the *church* and the *mass media*, the *political apparatuses* and the overall management of the state, which, in advanced capitalism, increasingly takes all these other, 'nonproductive' apparatuses into its terrain. Since the state is the structure which ensures that this 'social reproduction' is carried through (a) with the consent of the whole society, since the state is understood as 'neutral', above class interests, and (b) in the long-term interests of the continued hegemony of capital and of the ruling class bloc, Althusser calls all the apparatuses involved in this process (whether or not they are strictly organized by the state) 'ideological state apparatuses'. (In fact, both Althusser and Poulantzas — who follows Althusser closely in this — exaggerate the role of the state and undervalue the role of other elements in the reproduction of capitalist social relations.) Unlike the coercive institutions of the state, these ISAs rule principally *through ideology.* Althusser recognizes that the ruling classes do not 'rule' *directly* or in their own name and overt interests, but via the necessary displacements, examined earlier, through the 'class neutral' structures of the state, and the complexly constructed field of ideologies. But the 'diversity and contradictions' of these different spheres in which the different apparatuses function are nevertheless unified 'beneath the ruling ideology'. In this arena Althusser gives pride of place to what he calls 'the School-Family' couple. He understands 'ruling ideology' here in terms of his exposition (summarized earlier) — as the 'system of ideas and representations' by means of which men understand and 'live' an imaginary relation to their real conditions of existence: 'What is represented in ideology is therefore not the system of the real relations which governs the existence of men, but the imaginary relation of those individuals to the real relations in which they live'.

Althusser is, here, despite important differences in terminology and in theoretical perspective, moving very close to the terrain of Gramsci's work (far closer than in the now acknowledgedly 'over-theoreticist' formulations of some parts of *Reading Capital*): but with at least two significant differences of stress. First, Althusser insists that, since the terrain of ideologies is not simple but complex, and consists not simply of 'ruling ideas' but of a field of ideological thematics constituted by *the relation* 'in ideas' between dominant and subordinate classes, what the ISAs reproduce must be the ruling ideology 'precisely in its contradictions'. Ideological reproduction thus becomes 'not only the stake but also the site of class struggle . . . '. Second, he insists that the form of the 'unity' which the ISAs accomplish is closer to that of a 'teeth-gritting harmony' than a functional 'fit'. But both these aspects of his Notes — the idea of continuing struggle and of a *contradictory* reproduction in the sphere of ideology — though actively insisted upon, appear, in fact, more marginal to the theoretical heart of his argument, which centres upon the concept of continuing reproduction of the social relations of a system. This has the effect (as compared with Gramsci) of making Althusser's outline more functionalist that he would clearly like.

What Does Ideology 'Do' For The Dominant Capitalist Order?

Gramsci, following Marx, suggested that there were 'two, great floors' to the superstructures — civil society and the state. (Marx, we recall, had called them both 'ideological' or 'phenomenal forms'. Gramsci, it should be noted, is particularly confusing as to the distinction between the two — a matter made more complex because, in the conditions of advanced monopoly capitalism, the boundaries between these two 'floors' are, in any case, shifting. Cf. Gramsci, 1968 p. 206ff.) One way of thinking the general function of ideology, in relation to these two spheres, is in terms of what Poulantzas (1968) calls *separation* and *uniting*! In the sphere of market relations and of 'egoistic private interest' (the sphere, pre-eminently, of 'civil society') the productive classes *appear* or are represented as (a) individual economic units driven by private and egoistic interests alone, which are (b) bound by the multitude of invisible contracts — the 'hidden hand' of capitalist exchange relations. As we have remarked, this re-presentation has the effect, first, of *shifting* emphasis and visibility from production to exchange, second of *fragmenting* classes into individuals, third of *binding* individuals into that 'passive community' of consumers. Likewise, in the sphere of the state and of juridico-political ideology, the political classes and class relations are represented as individual subjects (citizens, the voter, the sovereign individual in the eyes of the law and the representative system, etc.); and these individual political legal subjects are then 'bound together' as members of a *nation*, united by the 'social contract', and by their common and mutual 'general interest'. (Marx calls the general interest 'precisely the generality of self-seeking interests'.) Once again, the class nature of the state is masked: classes are redistributed into individual subjects: and these individuals are united within the imaginary coherence of the state, the nation and the 'national interest'. It is surprising how many of the dominant ideological regions accomplish their characteristic inflexions by way of this mechanism.

Poulantzas brings together a number of critical functions of ideology within this paradigmatic ideological *figure*. The first general ideological effect under capitalism appears to be that of *masking and displacing*. Class domination, the class-exploitative nature of the system, the source of this fundamental expropriation in the sphere of production, the determinacy in this mode of production of the economic — time and again the general manner in which the ideologies of the dominant culture function is to mask, conceal or repress these antagonistic foundations of the system. The second general effect, then, is that of *fragmentation* or separation. The unity of the different spheres of the State are dispersed into the theory of the 'separation of powers'. (Althusser, 1971.) The collective interests of the working classes are fragmented into the internal oppositions between different strata of the class. The value which is collectively created is individually and privately appropriated. The 'needs' of producers are represented as the 'wants' of consumers — the two so separate that they can, in fact, be set against one another. In most of the dominant regions of this ideological field, the constituting category is what Poulantzas calls 'individuals-persons'. The moral, juridical, representational and psychological lexicons of the dominant system of practices, values and meanings could literally not be constituted at all without this thoroughly bourgeois category of 'possessive individuals'. (Hence Althusser's stress on ideology 'interpellating the subject'). The third ideological 'effect' is that of imposing an *imaginary unity or coherence* on the units so re-presented; and thus of replacing the real unity of the first level with the 'imaginary lived relations' of the third. This consists of the reconstituting of individual person-subjects into the various ideological totalities — the 'community', the 'nation', 'public opinion', 'the consensus', the 'general interest', the 'popular will', 'society', 'ordinary consumers', (even Mr Heath's great conglomerate, the 'trade union of the nation'!) At this level, unities are once again produced; but now in forms which mask and displace the level of class relations and economic contradictions and *represents* them as non-antagonistic totalities. This is Gramsci's hegemonic function of *consent* and *cohesion*.

One of the critical sites of this masking-fragmenting-uniting process is the state, especially under modern advanced capitalist conditions. We cannot elaborate on a Marxist theory of the state at this point. But the important fact about the state, for our purposes, is that it is the sphere, *par excellence*, where the *generalization* and *universalizing* of class interests into 'the general interest' takes place. Hegemony is founded not only on force but on consent and leadership precisely because, within it, class interests are generalized in their passage through the mediation of the state: Gramsci refers to this process as 'the decisive passage from the structure to the sphere of the complex superstructures'. (Gramsci, 1968 p. 181.) The state is necessary to ensure the conditions for the continued expansion of Capital. But it also functions on behalf of Capital — as what Engels called the 'ideal total capitalist', often securing the long-term interests of Capital against the narrow and immediate class interests of particular sections of the capitalist classes. In this lies its relative independence of any alliance of ruling classes. (Rather than *ruling* the state, like Lenin's 'executive committee', these classes must *rule through the mediation of* the state, where, precisely (through its different ideological discourses) class interests can assume the form of 'the general interest' and (as Marx remarked in *The German Ideology*) are given 'the form of universality and represent[ed] . . . as the only rational, universally valid ones'. It is in this function, above all — secured not only by the dominant ideologies of the state but by its relations and structures — that the state imposes an 'order which legalizes and perpetuates this [class] oppression by moderating the collision between the classes'. (Lenin, 1933.) It was Engels who remarked that 'once the state has become an independent power *vis-à-vis* society, it produces forthwith a further ideology. It is indeed amongst professional politicians, theorists of public law and jurists of private law that the connection with economic facts gets lost for fair . . . the interconnections between conceptions and their material conditions of existence become more and more complicated, more and more obscured by intermediary links . . . '. (Engels, 1950b.)

The third arena of ideological effects which we must mention has to do, not with the process of ideological re-presentation, but with securing legitimacy and winning consent for these representations. The questions of legitimacy and consent are crucial for Gramsci's concept of 'hegemony', since it is through them that the dominant classes can use the field of ideologies positively to *construct* hegemony (what Gramsci calls the educative and ethical functions); but, also, because it is through them that the dominant system comes to win a certain *acceptance* from the dominated classes. The same processes of masking-fragmenting-uniting, commented on before are to be found in this process of securing the legitimacy and assent of the subordinated to their subordination. Here, in the structures of political representation and of 'separate powers' and of liberties and freedoms, which lie at the core of bourgeois-liberal formal democracy, both as superstructures and as lived ideologies, the operation of one class upon another in *shaping and producing consent* (through the selective forms of social knowledge made available) is rendered invisible: this exercise of ideological class domination is dispersed through the fragmentary agencies of a myriad individual wills and opinions, separate powers; this fragmentation of opinion is then *reorganized* into an imaginary coherence in the mystical unity of 'the consensus', into which free and sovereign individuals and their wills 'spontaneously' flow. In this process, that consent-to-hegemony whose premises and preconditions are con-stantly structuring the sum of what individuals in society think, believe and want, is represented, in appearance, as a freely given and 'natural' coming-together into a *consensus* which legitimates the exercise of power. This structuring and reshaping of consent and consensus — the reverse side of 'hegemony' — is one of the principal kinds of work which the dominant ideologies perform.

Only at this point is it possible to attempt to situate, in the most general terms, the ideological role and effects sustained by the mass media in contemporary capitalist societies. The ideological role of the media is by no means their only or exclusive function. The modern forms of the media first appear decisively, though on a comparatively minor scale as compared with their present density — in the eighteenth century, with and alongside the transformation of England into an agrarian capitalist society. Here, for the first time, the artistic product becomes a commodity; artistic and literary work achieves its full realization as an exchange value in the literary market; and the institutions of a culture rooted in market relation-ships begin to appear: books, newspapers and periodicals; booksellers and circulating libraries; reviews and reviewing; journalists and hacks; best-sellers and pot-boilers. The first new 'medium' — the novel, intimately connected with the rise of the emergent bourgeois classes (Cf. Watt, 1957) — appears in this period. This transformation of the relations of culture and of the means of cultural production and consumption also provokes the first major rupture in the problematic of 'culture' — the first appearance of the modern 'cultural debate'. (Cf. Lowenthal, 1961.) (It is one of those great ironies that the very historical moment when this is happening is the one which, retrospectively, was represented by the con-servative parts of the culture-and-society tradition and its hiers, as the last gasp of the 'organic community'.) The evolution of the media, historically, cannot be traced here. But it is closely connected with the next profound transformation — that through which an agrarian capitalist society and culture becomes an industrial-urban capitalist one. This sets the scene, and provides the material basis and the social organization for the second great phase of change and expansion in the media of cultural production and distribution. The third phase coincides with the transformation from first-stage to second-stage industrial capitalism, or from *laissez-faire* to what is rather ambiguously called advanced 'monopoly' capitalism. This 'long', uneven and in many ways uncompleted transition, lasting from about the 1880s — through popular imperialism (in which the new popular press took deep root); the 'remaking' of English working-class culture (Steadman-Jones, 1975) and the rise of suburbia; the concentration and incorporation of capital; the reorganization of the capitalist division of labour; enormous productive and technological expansion; the organization of mass markets and of mass domestic consumption, etc. — to the present. This is the phase in which the modern mass media come into their own, massively expand and multiply, install themselves as the principal means and channels for the production and distribution of culture, and absorb more and more of the spheres of public communication into their orbit. It coincides with and is decisively connected with everything that we now understand as characterizing 'monopoly' capitalism (and which was, for a very long period, ideologically mis-appropriated in the theory of 'mass society'). In the later stages of this development, the media have penetrated right into the heart of the modern labour and productive process itself, grounded in the reorganization of Capital and the state and marshalled within the same scale of mass organizations as other economic and technical parts of the system. These aspects of the growth and expansion of the media, historically, have to be left to one side by the exclusive attention given here to media as 'ideological apparatuses'.

Quantitatively and qualitatively, in twentieth-century advanced capitalism, the media have established a decisive and fundamental leadership in the cultural sphere. Simply in terms of economic, technical, social and cultural resources, the mass media command a qualitatively greater slice than all the older, more traditional cultural channels which survive. Far more important is the manner in which the whole gigantic complex sphere of public information, intercommunication and exchange — the production and consumption of 'social knowledge' in societies of this type — depends upon the mediation of the modern means of communication. They have progressively *colonized* the cultural and ideological sphere. As social groups and classes live, if not in their productive then in their 'social' relations, increasingly fragmented and sectionally differentiated lives, the mass media are more and more responsible (a) for providing the basis on which groups and classes construct an 'image' of the lives, meanings, practices and values of *other* groups and classes; (b) for providing the images, representations and ideas around which the social totality, composed of all these separate and fragmented pieces, can be coherently grasped as a *'whole'*. This is the first of the great cultural functions of the modern media: the provision and the selective construction of *social knowledge*, of social imagery, through which we perceive the 'worlds', the 'lived realities' of others, and imaginarily reconstruct their lives and ours into some intelligible 'world-of-the-whole', some 'lived totality'.

As society under the conditions of modern Capital and production grows more complex and multi-faceted, so it is experienced as more 'pluralistic' in form. In regions, classes and sub-classes, in cultures and subcultures, neighbourhoods and communities, interest-groups and associative minorities, *varieties* of life-patterns are composed and recomposed in bewildering complexity. So an apparent plurality, an infinite variety of ways of classifying and ordering social life offer themselves as 'collective representations' in place of the great unitary ideological universe, the master 'canopies of legitimation', of previous epochs. The second function of the modern media is to reflect and *reflect on* this *plurality*; to provide a constant *inventory* of the lexicons, life-styles and ideologies which are objectivated there. Here the different types of 'social knowledge' are classified and ranked and ordered, assigned to their referential contexts within the preferred 'maps of problematic social reality'. (Geertz, 1964.) The media's function here, as Halloran has remarked, is 'the provision of social realities where they did not exist before or the giving of new directions to tendencies already present, in such a way that the adoption of the new attitude or form of behaviour is made a socially acceptable mode of conduct, whilst failure to adopt is represented as socially disapproved deviance'. (Halloran, ed., 1970.) Here the social knowledge which the media selectively circulate is ranked and arranged within the great normative and evaluative classifications, within the *preferred* meanings and interpretations. Since, as we argued earlier, there is no unitary ideological discourse into which all of this selective social knowledge can be programmed, and since many more 'worlds' than that of a unitary 'ruling class' must be selectively represented and classified in the medias apparently open and diverse manner, this assignment of social relations to their classifying schemes and contexts is, indeed, the site of an enormous *ideological labour*, of ideological *work*: establishing the 'rules' of each domain, actively ruling in and ruling out certain realities, offering the maps and codes which mark out territories and assign problematic events and relations to explanatory contexts, helping us not simply to *know more* about 'the world' but to *make sense of it*. Here the line, amidst all its contradictions, in conditions of struggle and contradiction, between *preferred* and *excluded* explanations and rationales, between permitted and deviant behaviours, between the 'meaningless' and the 'meaningful', between the incorporated practices, meanings and values and the oppositional ones, is ceaselessly drawn and redrawn, defended and negotiated: indeed, the 'site and stake' of struggle. 'Class', Volosinov observed, 'does not coincide with the sign community, i.e. with the community which is the totality of users of the same set of signs for ideological communication. Thus various different classes will use one and the same language. As a result, differently oriented accents intersect in every ideological sign. Sign becomes the arena of the class struggle. This social *multi-accentuality* of the ideological sign is a very crucial aspect. By and large, it is thanks to this intersecting of accents that a sign maintains its vitality and dynamism. . . A sign that has been withdrawn from the pressures of the social struggle — which, so to speak, crosses beyond the pale of the class struggle — inevitably loses force, degenerating into allegory and becoming the object not of a live social intelligibility but of philological comprehension'. (*op cit.*, p. 23.)

The third function of the media, from this point of view, is to organize, orchestrate and *bring together* that which it has selectively represented and selectively classified. Here, however fragmentarily and 'plurally', some degree of integration and cohesion, some imaginary coherence and unities must begin to be constructed. What has been made visible and classified begins to shake into an *acknowledged order*: a complex order, to be sure, in which the direct and naked intervention of the *real* unities (of class, power, exploitation and interest) are forever held somewhat at bay through the more neutral and integrative coherence of public opinion. From this difficult and delicate negotiatory work, the problematic areas of *consensus and consent* begin to emerge. In the interplay of opinions, freely given and exchanged, to which the idea of consensus always makes its ritual bow, *some* voices and opinions exhibit greater weight, resonance, defining and limiting power — for the pure consensus of classical liberal-democratic theory has long since given way to the reality of the more shaped and structured consensus, constructed in the unequal exchange between the unorganized masses and the great organizing centres of power and opinion — the consensus of the 'big battalions', so to speak. Nevertheless, in its own way and time, room must be found for other voices, for 'minority' opinions, for 'contrary' views, so that a shape, to which all reasonable men can begin to attach themselves, emerges. This forms the great unifying and consolidating level of the media's ideological work: the generative structure beneath the media's massive investment in the surface immediacy, the phenomenal multiplicity, of the social worlds in which it traffics. The production of consensus, the construction of legitimacy — not so much the finished article itself, but the whole process of argument, exchange, debate, consultation and speculation by which it emerges — is the third key aspect of the media's ideological effect.

Finally, what are the actual *mechanisms* which enable the mass media to perform this 'ideological work'? In the class democracies, the media are not, on the whole, directly commanded and organized by the state (though, as in the case of British broadcasting, the links may be very close): they are not directly subverted by a section of the 'ruling class' speaking in its own voice: they cannot be directly colonized by one of the ruling-class parties: no major interest of Capital can exercise its access to the channels of communication without some 'counter-vailing' voice: in their day-to-day administration and practices, the media are set to work within the framework of an impartial professional-technical set of working ideologies (e.g. the 'neutral' structure of news values, applied, like the rule of law, 'equally' to all sides) though the configurations which they offer are strikingly selective, drawn from an extremely limited *repertoire*, the open operation of 'bias' is the exception rather than the rule. How, then, do the discourses of the media become systematically penetrated and inflected by dominant ideologies?

We can only refer here to some of the mechanisms, taking television here as the paradigm instance, by which the media achieve their ideological effects. The media, as we have suggested, are socially, economically and technically organized apparatuses, for the production of messages, signs arranged in complex discourses: symbolic 'goods'. The production of symbolic messages cannot be accomplished without passing through the relay of language, broadly understood as the systems of signs which signify meaning. Events on their own cannot, as we have tried to show, signify: they must be *made intelligible*; and the process of social intelligibility consists precisely in those practices which translate 'real' events (whether drawn from actuality or fictionally constructed) into symbolic form. This is the process we have called *encoding*. But encoding (Hall, 1974) means precisely that — selecting the codes which assign meanings to events, placing events in a referential context which attribute meaning to them (fictional codes perform this work too; it is not limited to the codes of 'actuality' and naturalism). There are significantly different ways in which events — especially problematic or troubling events, which breach our normal, common-sense expectations, or run counter to the given tendency of things or threaten the status quo in some way — can be encoded. The selection of codes, those which are the *preferred* codes in the different domains, and which appear to embody the 'natural' explanations which most members of the society would accept (that is, which appear naturally to incarnate the 'rationality' of our particular society), casts these problematic events, consensually, somewhere within the *repertorie* of the dominant ideologies. We must remember that this is not a single, unitary, but a plurality of dominant discourses: that they are not deliberately selected by encoders to 'reproduce events within the horizon of the dominant ideology', but constitute the *field* of meanings within which they must choose. Precisely because they have become 'universalized and naturalized', they appear to be the only forms of intelligibility available; they have become sedimented as 'the only rational, universally valid ones'. (Marx, 1965.) The premises and preconditions which sustain their rationalities have been rendered invisible by the process of ideological masking and taking-for-granted we earlier described. They seem to be, even to those who employ and manipulate them for the purposes of encoding, simply the 'sum of what we already know'. That they contain premises, that these premises embody the dominant definitions of the situation, and represent or refract the existing structures of power, wealth and domination, hence that they *structure* every event they signify, and *accent* them in a manner which reproduces the given ideological structures — this process has become unconscious, even for the encoders. It is masked, frequently, by the intervention of the professional ideologies — those practical-technical routinizations of practice (news values, news sense, lively presentation, 'exciting pictures', good stories, hot news, etc.) which, at the phenomenal level, structure the everyday practices of encoding, and set the encoder within the bracket of a professional-technical neutrality which, in any case, distances him effectively from the ideological content of the material he is handling and the ideological inflexions of the codes he is employing. Hence, though events will not be systematically encoded in a single way, they will tend, systematically, to draw on a very limited ideological or explanatory repertoire; and that repertoire (though in each case it requires ideological 'work' to bring new events within its horizon) will have the overall tendency of making things 'mean' within the sphere of the dominant ideology. Further, since the encoder wants to enforce the explanatory reach, the credibility and the effectiveness of the 'sense' which he is making of events, he will employ the whole repertoire of encodings (visual, verbal, presentations, performance) to 'win consent' in the audience; not for his own 'biased' way of interpreting events, but for the legitimacy of the *range or limits* within which his encodings are operating. These 'points of identification' make the preferred reading of events credible and forceful: they sustain its preferences through the *accenting* of the ideological field (Volosinov would say that they exploit the sign's ideological flux); they aim to 'win the consent' of the audience, and hence structure the manner in which the receiver of these signs will *decode* the message. We have tried to show, elsewhere (Hall, 1974; Morley, 1974) that audiences, whose decodings will inevitably reflect their own material and social conditions, will not necessarily *decode* events within the same ideological structures as those in which they have been encoded. But the overall intention of 'effective communication' must, certainly, be to 'win the consent' of the audience to the *preferred reading*, and hence to get him to decode within the hegemonic framework. Even when decodings are not made, through a 'perfect transmission', within the hegemonic framework, the great range of decodings will tend to be 'negotiations' *within* the dominant codes — giving them a more situational inflexion — rather than systematically decoding them in a *counter*-hegemonic way. 'Negotiated' decodings, which allow wide 'exceptions' to be made in terms of the way the audience situates itself within the hegemonic field of ideologies, but which also legitimate the wider reach, the inclusive reference, the greater overall coherence of the dominant encodings, reflect and are based upon what we called, earlier, the structured complementarity of the classes. That is, the areas for negotiation within the hegemonic codes provide precisely those necessary *spaces* in the discourse where corporate and subordinate classes insert themselves. Since the media not only are widely and diffusely distributed thoughout the classes, but bring them within the grid of social communication, and must continually reproduce their own popular legitimacy for commanding that ideological territory, these negotiated spaces and inflexions, which permit the subordinate readings to be contained within the larger ideological syntagms of the dominant codes, are absolutely pivotal to media legitimacy, and give that legitimacy a popular basis. The construction of a 'consensus' basis for media work is how, in part, this work of legitimation is realized.

The legitimation for this process of ideological construction and deconstruction which structures the processes of encoding and decoding is underpinned by the position of the media apparatuses. These are not, as we have suggested, by and large in our kinds of society, directly owned and organized by the state. But there is a crucial sense (it may be this which enabled Althusser to call them, nevertheless, 'Ideological *State* Apparatuses) in which it must be said that the media relate to the ruling class alliances, not directly but indirectly; and hence they have some of the characteristics – the 'relative autonomy' – of the State Apparatuses themselves. Broadcasting, for example, functions, like the Law, and the governmental bureaucracies, under the rubric of the 'separation of powers'. Not only can it not be commandeered by any single class or class party directly; but this direct and explicit command (like its reverse, a deliberate inclination towards them, or 'bias', on the part of the communicators) would immediately destroy the basis of their legitimacy – since it would reveal an open complicity with ruling-class power. The media, then, like other state complexes in the modern stage of capitalist development, absolutely depend on their 'relative autonomy' from ruling-class power in the narrow sense. These are enshrined in the operational principles of broadcasting – 'objectivity', 'neutrality', 'impartiality' and 'balance': or, rather, these are the practices through which broadcasting's 'relative neutrality' is realized. (Hall, 1972.) Balance, for example, ensures that there will always be a two-sided dialogue, and thus always more than one definition of the situation available to the audience. In the political sphere, broadcasting here reproduces with remarkable exactness the forms of parliamentary democracy, and of 'democratic debate', on which other parts of the system – the political apparatuses, for example, – are constituted. The ideological 'work' of the media, in these conditions, does *not*, then, regularly and routinely, depend on *subverting* the discourse for the direct support of one or another of the major *positions* within the dominant ideologies: it depends on the underwiring and underpinning of that *structured ideological field* in which the positions play, and over which, so to speak, they 'contend'. For though the major political parties sharply disagree about this or that aspect of policy, there are fundamental agreements which bind the opposing positions into a complex unity: all the presuppositions, the limits to the argument, the terms of reference, etc., which those elements within the system must *share* in order to 'disagree'. It is this underlying 'unity' which the media underwrite and reproduce: and it is in this sense that the ideological inflexion of media discourses are best understood, not as 'partisan' but as fundamentally oriented 'within the mode of reality of the state'. The role of shaping and organizing *consensus*, which is necessarily a complex not a simple entity, is critical here. What constitutes this, not simply as a field, but as a field which is 'structured in dominance', is the way its limits operate — to rule certain kinds of interpretation 'in' or 'out', to effect its systematic *inclusions* (for example, those 'definitions of the situation' which regularly, of necessity and legitimately 'have access' to the structuring of any controversial topic) and *exclusions* (for example, those groups, interpretations, positions, aspects of the reality of the system which are regularly 'ruled out of court' as 'extremist', 'irrational', 'meaningless', 'utopian', 'impractical', etc.). (Cf: Hall on the structuring of topics, 1975. Cf. also Connell, Curti and Hall, 1976.)

Inevitably we have had to confine ourselves here to very broad mechanisms and processes, in order to give some substance to the general proposition advanced. This proposition can now be stated in a simple way, against the background of the theoretical and analytic framework established in the essay. The media serve, in societies like ours, ceaselessly to perform the critical ideological work of 'classifying out the world' within the discourses of the dominant ideologies. This is neither simply, nor conscious, 'work': it is *contradictory work* — in part because of the internal contradictions between those different ideologies which constitute the dominant terrain, but even more because these ideologies which constitute the dominant terrain, but even more because these ideologies struggle and contend for dominance in the field of class practices and class struggle. Hence there is no way in which the 'work' can be carried through without, to a considerable degree, also reproducing the contradictions which structure its field. Thus we must say that the work of 'ideological reproduction' which they perform is by definition work in which counter-acting tendencies — Gramsci's 'unstable equilibria' — will constantly be manifested. We can speak, then, only of the *tendency* of the media — but it is a systematic tendency, not an incidental feature — to reproduce the ideological field of a society in such a way as to reproduce, also, its structure of domination.

References

Althusser, L., 1965: *For Marx*. New Left Books.
  1971: 'Ideology and the State'. In *Lenin & Philosophy And Other Essays*. New Left Books.
Barthes, R., 1967: *Elements Of Seminology*. Cape.
Bottomore, T. and Rubel, M., 1963: *Karl Marx: Selected writings in sociology and social philosophy*, Penguin.
Connell, I., Curti, L. and Hall, S., 1976: 'The "Unity" of Current Affairs TV', *WPCS* 9, Centre for Contemporary Cultural Studies, Birmingham.
Eco, U. (undated): 'Articulations Of The Cinematic Code', *Cinematics* I.
Engels, F., 1950a: 'Labour In The Transition From Ape To Man'. In Marx and Engels, *Selected Works* vols. 2. Lawrence & Wishart.
  1950b: 'Feuerbach And The End Of Classical German Philosophy'. In Marx and Engels, *Selected Works*, vol. 2. Lawrence & Wishart.
Geertz, C., 1964: 'Ideology As A Cultural System'. In Apter (Ed.), *Ideology and Discontent*. New York: Free Press.
Geras, N., 1972: 'Marx and The Critique of Political Economy'. In R. Blackburn (Ed.), *Ideology In Social Science*. Fontana.
Gramsci, A., 1968: *Prison Notebooks*. Lawrence and Wishart.
Hall, S., 1972: 'External/Internal Dialectic In Broadcasting'. In *Fourth Symposium On Broadcasting*, Dept. of Extra-Mural Studies, University of Manchester.
  1972: 'Determinations Of the News Photograph'. *WPCS* 3. CCCS, Birmingham.
  1974a: 'Deviancy, Politics And the Media'. In Rock, P. and McIntosh, M. (Eds.), *Deviance & Social Control*. Tavistock.
  1974b: 'Encoding And Decoding In The TV Discourse'. *Culture And Education*, Council Of Europe, Strassburg.
  1974c: 'Marx's Notes On Method'. *WPCS* 6, CCCS, Birmingham.
  1975: 'The Structured Communication Of Events'. In *Getting The Message Across*. UNESCO, Paris.
Halloran, J., 1970: 'The Social Effects Of Television', in Halloran, J. (Ed.), *The Effects Of Television*, Panther.
Hoggart, R., 1957: *The Uses Of Literacy*. Harmondsworth: Penguin.
Lenin, V. I., 1933: *The State and Revolution*. Little Lenin Library, Lawrence & Wishart.
Lévi-Strauss, C., 1969: *Totemism*. Penguin.
Lowenthal, L., 1961: *Literature, Popular Culture & Society*, Englewood Cliffe; Prentice Hall.
Marx, K., 1961: *Capital* I, Foreign Languages Publishing House, Moscow.
  1965: *The German Ideology*. Lawrence and Wishart.
  1973: *The Grundrisse*, transl. Nicolaus, M. Penguin.
  1971: *Critique of Political Economy*, ed. Dobb, M. Lawrence and Wishart.
Mepham, J., 1974: 'The Theory Of Ideology In *Capital*'. *WPCS* 6, CCCS, Birmingham.
Mills, C. Wright, 1963: *Power, Politics & People*. Oxford University Press.
Morley, D., 1974: 'Reconceptualizing The Media Audience: towards an

348   STUART HALL

ethnography of audiences. CCCS, Occasional paper, Birmingham.

Nowell-Smith, G., 1974: 'Common Sense'. *Radical Philosophy* 7.

Poulantzas, N., 1965: *Political Power and Social Classes*. New Left Books and Sheed & Ward.

Steadman-Jones, G., 'Working Class Culture And Working Class Politics, 1870–1900'. *Journal of Social History*.

Thompson, E. P., 1960: Review of *The Long Revolution. New Left Review* 9, (10).

Volosinov, V. N., 1973: *Marxism and The Philosophy of Language*. New York: Seminar Press.

Watt, I., 1957: *The Rise of The Novel*. Pelican.

Williams, R., 1961: *The Long Revolution*. Pelican.

1973: 'Base And Superstructure'. *New Left Review* 85.

14

The Culture Industry: Enlightenment as mass deception

T. W. Adorno and M. Horkheimer

The sociological theory that the loss of the support of objectively established religion, the dissolution of the last remnants of precapitalism, together with technological and social differentiation or specialization, have
led to cultural chaos is disproved every day; for culture now impresses the
same stamp on everything. Films, radio and magazines make up a system
which is uniform as a whole and in every part. Even the aesthetic activities
of political opposites are one in their enthusiastic obedience to the rhythm
of the iron system. The decorative industrial management buildings and
exhibition centers in authoritarian countries are much the same as anywhere
else. The huge gleaming towers that shoot up everywhere are outward signs
of the ingenious planning of international concerns, toward which the un-
leashed entrepreneurial system (whose monuments are a mass of gloomy
houses and business premises in grimy, spiritless cities) was already hasten-
ing. Even now the older houses just outside the concrete city centers look
like slums, and the new bungalows on the outskirts are at one with the
flimsy structures of world fairs in their praise of technical progress and
their built-in demand to be discarded after a short while like empty food
cans. Yet the city housing projects designed to perpetuate the individual
as a supposedly independent unit in a small hygienic dwelling make him all
the more subservient to his adversary — the absolute power of capitalism.
Because the inhabitants, as producers and as consumers, are drawn into the
center in search of work and pleasure, all the living units crystallize into
well-organized complexes. The striking unity of microcosm and macrocosm
presents men with a model of their culture: the false identity of the general
and the particular. Under monopoly all mass culture is identical, and the
lines of its artificial framework begin to show through. The people at the
top are no longer so interested in concealing monopoly: as its violence becomes more open, so its power grows. Movies and radio need no longer pre-
tend to be art. The truth that they are just business is made into an ideology
in order to justify the rubbish they deliberately produce. They call themselves industries; and when their directors' incomes are published, any
doubt about the social utility of the finished products is removed.

Interested parties explain the culture industry in technological terms. It is alleged that because millions participate in it, certain reproduction processes are necessary that inevitably require identical needs in innumerable places to be satisfied with identical goods. The technical contrast between the few production centers and the large number of widely dispersed consumption points is said to demand organization and planning by management. Furthermore, it is claimed that standards were based in the first place on consumers' needs, and for that reason were accepted with so little resistance. The result is the circle of manipulation and retroactive need in which the unity of the system grows ever stronger. No mention is made of the fact that the basis on which technology acquires power over society is the power of those whose economic hold over society is greatest. A technological rationale is the rationale of domination itself. It is the coercive nature of society alienated from itself. Automobiles, bombs, and movies keep the whole thing together until their leveling element shows its strength in the very wrong which it furthered. It has made the technology of the culture industry no more than the achievement of standardization and mass production, sacrificing whatever involved a distinction between the logic of the work and that of the social system. This is the result not of a law of movement in technology as such but of its function in today's economy. The need which might resist central control has already been suppressed by the control of the individual consciousness. The step from the telephone to the radio has clearly distinguished the roles. The former still allowed the subscriber to play the role of subject, and was liberal. The latter is democratic: it turns all participants into listeners and authoritatively subjects them to broadcast programs which are all exactly the same. No machinery of rejoinder has been devised, and private broadcasters are denied any freedom. They are confined to the apocryphal field of the 'amateur', and also have to accept organization from above. But any trace of spontaneity from the public in official broadcasting is controlled and absorbed by talent scouts, studio competitions and official programs of every kind selected by professionals. Talented performers belong to the industry long before it displays them; otherwise they would not be so eager to fit in. The attitude of the public, which ostensibly and actually favours the system of the culture industry, is a part of the system and not an excuse for it. If one branch of art follows the same formula as one with a very different medium and content; if the dramatic intrigue of broadcast soap operas becomes no more than useful material for showing how to master technical problems at both ends of the scale of musical experience — real jazz or a cheap imitation; or if a movement from a Beethoven symphony is crudely 'adapted' for a film sound-track in the same way as a Tolstoy novel is garbled in a film script: then the claim that this is done to satisfy the spontaneous wishes of the public is no more than hot air. We are closer to the facts if we explain these phenomena as inherent in the technical and personnel apparatus which, down to its last cog, itself forms part of the economic mechanism of selection. In addition there is the agreement — or at least the determination — of all executive authorities not to produce or sanction anything that in any way differs from their own rules, their own ideas about consumers, or above all themselves.

In our age the objective social tendency is incarnate in the hidden subjective purposes of company directors, the foremost among whom are in the most powerful sectors of industry — steel, petroleum, electricity, and chemicals. Culture monopolies are weak and dependent in comparison. They cannot afford to neglect their appeasement of the real holders of power if their sphere of activity in mass society (a sphere producing a specific type of commodity which anyhow is still too closely bound up with easy-going liberalism and Jewish intellectuals) is not to undergo a series of purges. The dependence of the most powerful broadcasting company on the electrical industry, or of the motion picture industry on the banks, is characteristic of the whole sphere, whose individual branches are themselves economically interwoven. All are in such close contact that the extreme concentration of mental forces allows demarcation lines between different firms and technical branches to be ignored. The ruthless unity in the culture industry is evidence of what will happen in politics. Marked differentiations such as those of A and B films, or of stories in magazines in different price ranges, depend not so much on subject matter as on classifying, organizing, and labeling consumers. Something is provided for all so that none may escape; the distinctions are emphasized and extended. The public is catered for with a hierarchical range of mass-produced products of varying quality, thus advancing the rule of complete quantification. Everybody must behave (as if spontaneously) in accordance with his previously determined and indexed level, and choose the category of mass product turned out for his type. Consumers appear as statistics on research organization charts, and are divided by income groups into red, green, and blue areas; the technique is that used for any type of propaganda.

How formalized the procedure is can be seen when the mechanically differentiated products prove to be all alike in the end. That the difference between the Chrysler range and General Motors products is basically illusory strikes every child with a keen interest in varieties. What connoisseurs discuss as good or bad points serve only to perpetuate the semblance of competition and range of choice. The same applies to the Warner Brothers and Metro Goldwyn Mayer productions. But even the differences between the more expensive and cheaper models put out by the same firm steadily diminish: for automobiles, there are such differences as the number of cylinders, cubic capacity, details of patented gadgets; and for films there are the number of stars, the extravagant use of technology, labor, and equipment, and the introduction of the latest psychological formulas. The universal criterion of merit is the amount of 'conspicuous production', of blatant cash investment. The varying budgets in the culture industry do not bear the slightest relation to factual values, to the meaning of the products themselves. Even the technical media are relentlessly forced into uniformity. Television aims at a synthesis of radio and film, and is held up only because the interested parties have not yet reached agreement, but its consequences will be quite enormous and promise to intensify the impoverishment of aesthetic matter so drastically, that by tomorrow the thinly veiled identity of all industrial culture products can come triumphantly out into the open, derisively fulfilling the Wagnerian dream of the *Gesamtkunstwerk* — the fusion of all the arts in one work. The alliance of word, image, and music is all the more perfect than in *Tristan* because the sensuous elements which all approvingly reflect the surface of social reality are in principle embodied in the same technical process, the unity of which becomes its distinctive content. This process integrates all the elements of the production, from the novel (shaped with an eye to the film) to the last sound effect. It is the triumph of invested capital, whose title as absolute master is etched deep into the hearts of the dispossessed in the employment line; it is the meaningful content of every film, whatever plot the production team may have selected.

The man with leisure has to accept what the culture manufacturers offer him. Kant's formalism still expected a contribution from the individual, who was thought to relate the varied experiences of the senses to fundamental concepts; but industry robs the individual of his function. Its prime service to the customer is to do his schematizing for him. Kant said that there was a secret mechanism in the soul which prepared direct intuitions in such a way that they could be fitted into the system of pure reason. But today that secret has been deciphered. While the mechanism is to all appearances planned by those who serve up the data of experience, that is, by the culture industry, it is in fact forced upon the latter by the power of society, which remains irrational, however we may try to rationalize it; and this inescapable force is processed by commercial agencies so that they give an artificial impression of being in command. There is nothing left for the consumer to classify. Producers have done it for him. Art for the masses has destroyed the dream but still conforms to the tenets of that dreaming idealism which critical idealism balked at. Everything derives from consciousness: for Malebranche and Berkeley, from the consciousness of God; in mass art, from the consciousness of the production team. Not only are the hit songs, stars, and soap operas cyclically recurrent and rigidly invariable types, but the specific content of the entertainment itself is derived from them and only appears to change. The details are interchangeable. The short interval sequence which was effective in a hit song, the hero's momentary fall from grace (which he accepts as good sport), the rough treatment which the beloved gets from the male star, the latter's rugged defiance of the spoilt heiress, are, like all the other details, ready-made clichés to be slotted in anywhere; they never do anything more than fulfill the purpose allotted them in the overall plan. Their whole *raison d'être* is to confirm it by being its constituent parts. As soon as the film begins, it is quite clear how it will end, and who will be rewarded, punished, or forgotten. In light music, once the trained ear has heard the first notes of the hit song, it can guess what is coming and feel flattered when it does come. The average length of the short story has to be rigidly adhered to. Even gags, effects, and jokes are calculated like the setting in which they are placed. They are the responsibility of special experts and their narrow range makes it easy for them to be apportioned in the office. The development of the culture industry has led to the predominance of the effect, the obvious touch, and the technical detail over the work itself — which once expressed an idea, but was liquidated together with the idea. When the detail won its freedom, it became rebellious and, in the period from Romanticism to Expressionism, asserted itself as free expression, as a vehicle of protest against the organization. In music the single harmonic effect obliterated the awareness of form as a whole; in painting the individual colour was stressed at the expense of pictorial composition; and in the novel psychology became more important than structure. The totality of the culture industry has put an end to this. Though concerned exclusively with effects, it crushes their insubordination and makes them subserve the formula, which replaces the work. The same fate is inflicted on whole and parts alike. The whole inevitably bears no relation to the details — just like the career of a successful man into which everything is made to fit as an illustration or a proof, whereas it is nothing more than the sum of all those idiotic events. The so-called dominant idea is like a file which ensures order but not coherence. The whole and the parts alike; there is no antithesis and no connection. Their prearranged harmony is a mockery of what had to be striven after in the great bourgeois works of art. In Germany the graveyard stillness of the dictatorship already hung over the gayest films of the democratic era.

The whole world is made to pass through the filter of the culture industry. The old experience of the movie-goer, who sees the world outside as an extension of the film he has just left (because the latter is intent upon reproducing the world of everyday perceptions), is now the producer's guideline. The more intensely and flawlessly his techniques duplicate empirical objects, the easier it is today for the illusion to prevail that the outside world is the straightforward continuation of that presented on the screen. This purpose has been furthered by mechanical reproduction since the lightning takeover by the sound film. Real life is becoming indistinguishable from the movies. The sound film, far surpassing the theatre of illusion, leaves no room for imagination or reflection on the part of the audience, who is unable to respond within the structure of the film, yet deviate from its precise detail without losing the thread of the story; hence the film forces its victims to equate it directly with reality. The stunting of the mass-media consumer's powers of imagination and spontaneity does not have to be traced back to any psychological mechanisms; he must ascribe the loss of those attributes to the objective nature of the products themselves, especially to the most characteristic of them, the sound film. They are so designed that quickness, powers of observation, and experience are undeniably needed to apprehend them at all; yet sustained thought is out of the question if the spectator is not to miss the relentless rush of facts. Even though the effort required for his response is semi-automatic, no scope is left for the imagination. Those who are so absorbed by the world of the movie — by its images, gestures, and words — that they are unable to supply what really makes it a world, do not have to dwell on particular points of its mechanics during a screening. All the other films and products of the entertainment industry which they have seen have taught them what to expect; they react automatically. The might of industrial society is lodged in men's minds. The entertainments manufacturers know that their products will be consumed with alertness even when the customer is distraught, for each of them is a model of the huge economic machinery which has always sustained the masses, whether at work or at leisure — which is akin to work. From every sound film and every broadcast program the social effect can be inferred which is exclusive to none but is shared by all alike. The culture industry as a whole has moulded men as a type unfailingly reproduced in every product. All the agents of this process, from the producer to the women's clubs, take good care that the simple reproduction of this mental state is not nuanced or extended in any way.

The art historians and guardians of culture who complain of the extinction in the West of a basic style-determining power are wrong. The stereotyped appropriation of everything, even the inchoate, for the purposes of mechanical reproduction surpasses the rigor and general currency of any 'real style', in the sense in which cultural *cognoscenti* celebrate the organic precapitalist past. No Palestrina could be more of a purist in eliminating every unprepared and unresolved discord than the jazz arranger in suppressing any development which does not conform to the jargon. When jazzing up Mozart he changes him not only when he is too serious or too difficult but when he harmonizes the melody in a different way, perhaps more simply, than is customary now. No medieval builder can have scrutinized the subjects for church windows and sculptures more suspiciously than the studio hierarchy scrutinizes a work by Balzac or Hugo before finally approving it. No medieval theologian could have determined the degree of the torment to be suffered by the damned in accordance with the *ordo* of divine love more meticulously than the producers of shoddy epics calculate the torture to be undergone by the hero or the exact point to which the leading lady's hemline shall be raised. The explicit and implicit, exoteric and esoteric catalogue of the forbidden and tolerated is so extensive that it not only defines the area of freedom but is all-powerful inside it. Everything down to the last detail is shaped accordingly. Like its counterpart, avant-garde art, the entertainment industry determines its own language, down to its very syntax and vocabulary, by the use of anathema. The constant pressure to produce new effects (which must conform to the old pattern) serves merely as another rule to increase the power of the conventions when any single effect threatens to slip through the net. Every detail is so firmly stamped with sameness that nothing can appear which is not marked at birth, or does not meet with approval at first sight. And the star performers, whether they produce or reproduce, use this jargon as freely and fluently and with as much gusto as if it were the very language which it silenced long ago. Such is the ideal of what is natural in this field of activity, and its influence becomes all the more powerful, the more technique is perfected and diminishes the tension between the finished product and everyday life. The paradox of this routine, which is essentially travesty, can be detected and is often predominant in everything that the culture industry turns out. A jazz musician who is playing a piece of serious music, one of Beethoven's simplest minuets, syncopates it involuntarily and will smile superciliously when asked to follow the normal divisions of the beat. This is the 'nature' which, complicated by the ever-present and extravagant demands of the specific medium, constitutes the new style and is a 'system of non-culture, to which one might even concede a certain "unity of style" if it really made any sense to speak of stylized barbarity'[1].

The universal imposition of this stylized mode can even go beyond what is quasi-officially sanctioned or forbidden; today a hit song is more readily forgiven for not observing the 32 beats or the compass of the ninth than for containing even the most clandestine melodic or harmonic detail which does not conform to the idiom. Whenever Orson Welles offends against the tricks of the trade, he is forgiven because his departures from the norm are regarded as calculated mutations which serve all the more strongly to confirm the validity of the system. The constraint of the technically-conditioned idiom which stars and directors have to produce as 'nature' so that the people can appropriate it, extends to such fine nuances that they almost attain the subtlety of the devices of an avant-garde work as against those of truth. The rare capacity minutely to fulfill the obligations of the natural idiom in all branches of the culture industry becomes the criterion of efficiency. What and how they say it must be measurable by everyday language, as in logical positivism. The producers are experts. The idiom demands an astounding productive power, which it absorbs and squanders. In a diabolical way it has overreached the culturally conservative distinction between genuine and artificial style. A style might be called artificial which is im-

1   Nietzsche, *Unzeitgemässe Betrachtungen, Werke*, Vol. I (Leipzig, 1917), p. 187.

posed from without on the refractory impulses of a form. But in the culture industry every element of the subject matter has its origin in the same apparatus as that jargon whose stamp it bears. The quarrels in which the artistic experts become involved with sponsor and censor about a lie going beyond the bounds of credibility are evidence not so much of an inner aesthetic tension as of a divergence of interests. The reputation of the specialist, in which a last remnant of objective independence sometimes finds refuge, conflicts with the business politics of the Church, or the concern which is manufacturing the cultural commodity. But the thing itself has been essentially objectified and made viable before the established authorities began to argue about it. Even before Zanuck acquired her, Saint Bernadette was regarded by her latter-day hagiographer as brilliant propaganda for all interested parties. That is what became of the emotions of the character. Hence the style of the culture industry, which no longer has to test itself against any refractory material, is also the negation of style. The reconciliation of the general and particular, of the rule and the specific demands of the subject matter, the achievement of which alone gives essential, meaningful content to style, is futile because there has ceased to be the slightest tension between opposite poles: these concordant extremes are dismally identical; the general can replace the particular, and vice versa.

Nevertheless, this caricature of style does not amount to something beyond the genuine style of the past. In the culture industry the notion of genuine style is seen to be the aesthetic equivalent of domination. Style considered as mere aesthetic regularity is a romantic dream of the past. The unity of style not only of the Christian Middle Ages but of the Renaissance expresses in each case the different structure of social power, and not the obscure experience of the oppressed in which the general was enclosed. The great artists were never those who embodied a wholly flawless and perfect style, but those who used style as a way of hardening themselves against the chaotic expression of suffering, as a negative truth. The style of their works gave what was expressed that force without which life flows away unheard. Those very art forms which are known as classical, such as Mozart's music, contain objective trends which represent something different to the style which they incarnate. As late as Schönberg and Picasso, the great artists have retained a mistrust of style, and at crucial points have subordinated it to the logic of the matter. What Dadaists and Expressionists called the untruth of style as such triumphs today in the sung jargon of a crooner, in the carefully contrived elegance of a film star, and even in the admirable expertise of a photograph of a peasant's squalid hut. Style represents a promise in every work of art. That which is expressed is subsumed through style into the dominant forms of generality, into the language of music, painting, or words, in the hope that it will be reconciled thus with the idea of true generality. This promise held out by the work of art that it will create truth by lending new shape to the conventional social forms is as necessary as it is hypocritical. It unconditionally posits the real forms of life as it is by suggesting that fulfillment lies in their aesthetic derivatives. To this extent the claim of art is always ideology too. However, only in this confrontation with tradition of which style is the record can art express suffering. That factor in a work of art which enables it to transcend reality certainly cannot be detached from style; but it does not consist of the harmony actually realized, of any doubtful unity of form and content, within and without, of individual and society; it is to be found in those features in which discrepancy appears: in the necessary failure of the passionate striving for identity. Instead of exposing itself to this failure in which the style of the great work of art has always achieved self-negation, the inferior work has always relied on its similarity with others — on a surrogate identity.

In the culture industry this imitation finally becomes absolute. Having ceased to be anything but style, it reveals the latter's secret: obedience to the social hierarchy. Today aesthetic barbarity completes what has threatened the creations of the spirit since they were gathered together as culture and neutralized. To speak of culture was always contrary to culture. Culture as a common denominator already contains in embryo that schematization and process of cataloging and classification which bring culture within the sphere of administration. And it is precisely the industrialized, the consequent, subsumption which entirely accords with this notion of culture. By subordinating in the same way and to the same end all areas of intellectual creation, by occupying men's senses from the time they leave the factory in the evening to the time they clock in again the next morning with matter that bears the impress of the labor process they themselves have to sustain throughout the day, this subsumption mockingly satisfies the concept of a unified culture which the philosophers of personality contrasted with mass culture.

And so the culture industry, the most rigid of all styles, proves to be the goal of liberalism, which is reproached for its lack of style. Not only do its categories and contents derive from liberalism — domesticated naturalism as well as operetta and revue — but the modern culture monopolies form the economic area in which, together with the corresponding entrepreneurial types, for the time being some part of its sphere of operation survives, despite the process of disintegration elsewhere. It is still possible to make one's way in entertainment, if one is not too obstinate about one's own concerns, and proves appropriately pliable. Anyone who resists can only survive by fitting in. Once his particular brand of deviation from the norm has been noted by the industry, he belongs to it as does the land-reformer to capitalism. Realistic dissidence is the trademark of anyone who has a new idea in business. In the public voice of modern society accusations are seldom audible; if they are, the perceptive can already detect signs that the dissident will soon be reconciled. The more immeasurable the gap between chorus and leaders, the more certainly there is room at the top for everybody who demonstrates his superiority by well-planned originality. Hence, in the culture industry, too, the liberal tendency to give full scope to its able men survives. To do this for the efficient today is still the function of the market, which is otherwise proficiently controlled; as for the market's freedom, in the high period of art as elsewhere, it was freedom for the stupid to starve. Significantly, the system of the culture industry comes from the more liberal industrial nations, and all its characteristic media, such as movies, radio, jazz, and magazines, flourish there. Its progress, to be sure, had its origin in the general laws of capital. Gaumont and Pathé, Ullstein and Hugenberg followed the international trend with some success; Europe's economic dependence on the United States after war and inflation was a contributory factor. The belief that the barbarity of the culture industry is a result of 'cultural lag', of the fact that the American consciousness did not keep up with the growth of technology, is quite wrong. It was pre-Fascist Europe which did not keep up with the trend toward the culture monopoly. But it was this very lag which left intellect and creativity some degree of independence and enabled its last representatives to exist — however dismally. In Germany the failure of democratic control to permeate life had led to a paradoxical situation. Many things were exempt from the market mechanism which had invaded the Western countries. The German educational system, universities, theaters with artistic standards, great orchestras, and museums enjoyed protection. The political powers, state and municipalities, which had inherited such institutions from absolutism, had left them with a measure of the freedom from the forces of power which dominates the market, just as princes and feudal lords had done up to the nineteenth century. This strengthened art in this late phase against the verdict of supply and demand, and increased its resistance far beyond the actual degree of protection. In the market itself the tribute of a quality for which no use had been found was turned into purchasing power; in this way, respectable literary and music publishers could help authors who yielded little more in the way of profit than the respect of the connoisseur. But what completely fettered the artist was the pressure (and the accompanying drastic threats), always to fit into business life as an aesthetic expert. Formerly, like Kant and Hume, they signed their letters 'Your most humble and obedient servant', and undermined the foundations of throne and altar. Today they address heads of government by their first names, yet in every artistic activity they are subject to their illiterate masters. The analysis Tocqueville offered a century ago has in the meantime proved wholly accurate. Under the private culture monopoly it is a fact that 'tyranny leaves the body free and directs its attack at the soul. The ruler no longer says: You must think as I do or die. He says: You are free not to think as I do; your life, your property, everything shall remain yours, but from this day on you are a stranger among us'.[2] Not to conform means to be rendered powerless, economically and therefore spiritually — to be 'self-employed'. When the outsider is excluded from the concern, he can only too easily be accused of incompetence. Whereas today in material production the mechanism of supply and demand is disintegrating, in the superstructure it still operates as a check in the rulers' favor. The consumers are the workers and employees, the farmers and lower middle class. Capitalist production so confines them, body and soul, that they fall helpless victims to what is offered them. As naturally as the ruled always took the morality imposed upon them more seriously than did the rulers themselves, the deceived masses are today captivated by the myth of success even more than the successful are. Immovably, they insist on the very ideology which enslaves them. The misplaced love of the common people for the wrong which is done them is a greater force than the cunning of the authorities. It is stronger even than the rigorism of the Hays Office, just as in certain great times in history it has inflamed greater forces that were turned against it, namely, the terror of the tribunals. It calls for Mickey Rooney in preference to the tragic Garbo, for Donald Duck instead of Betty Boop. The industry submits to the vote which it has itself inspired. What is a loss for the firm which cannot fully exploit a contract with a declining star is a legitimate expense for the system as a whole. By craftily sanctioning the demand for rubbish it inaugurates total harmony. The connoisseur and the expert are despised for their pretentious claim to know better than the others, even though culture is democratic and distributes its privileges to all. In view of the ideological truce, the conformism of the buyers and the effrontery of the producers who supply them prevail. The result is a constant reproduction of the same thing.

A constant sameness governs the relationship to the past as well. What is new about the phase of mass culture compared with the late liberal stage is the exclusion of the new. The machine rotates on the same spot. While determining consumption it excludes the untried as a risk. The moviemakers distrust any manuscript which is not reassuringly backed by a best-seller. Yet for this very reason there is never-ending talk of ideas, novelty, and surprise, of what is taken for granted but has never existed. Tempo and dynamics serve this trend. Nothing remains as of old; everything has to run incessantly, to keep moving. For only the universal triumph of the rhythm of mechanical production and reproduction promises that nothing changes, and nothing unsuitable will appear. Any additions to the well-proven culture inventory are too much of a speculation. The ossified forms — such as the sketch, short story, problem film, or hit song — are the standardized average of late liberal taste, dictated with threats from above. The people at the top in the culture agencies, who work in harmony as only one

2   Alexis de Tocqueville, *De la Démocratie en Amérique*, Vol. II (Paris, 1864), p. 151.

manager can with another, whether he comes from the rag trade or from college, have long since reorganized and rationalized the objective spirit. One might think that an omnipresent authority had sifted the material and drawn up an official catalogue of cultural commodities to provide a smooth supply of available mass-produced lines. The ideas are written in the cultural firmament where they had already been numbered by Plato — and were indeed numbers, incapable of increase and immutable.

Amusement and all the elements of the culture industry existed long before the latter came into existence. Now they are taken over from above and brought up to date. The culture industry can pride itself on having energetically executed the previously clumsy transposition of art into the sphere of consumption, on making this a principle, on divesting amusement of its obtrusive naïvetés and improving the type of commodities. The more absolute it became, the more ruthless it was in forcing every outsider either into bankruptcy or into a syndicate, and became more refined and elevated — until it ended up as a synthesis of Beethoven and the Casino de Paris. It enjoys a double victory: the truth it extinguishes without it can reproduce at will as a lie within. 'Light' art as such, distraction, is not a decadent form. Anyone who complains that it is a betrayal of the ideal of pure expression is under an illusion about society. The purity of bourgeois art, which hypostasized itself as a world of freedom in contrast to what was happening in the material world, was from the beginning bought with the exclusion of the lower classes with whose cause, the real universality, art keeps faith precisely by its freedom from the ends of the false universality. Serious art has been withheld from those for whom the hardship and oppression of life make a mockery of seriousness, and who must be glad if they can use time not spent at the production line just to keep going. Light art has been the shadow of autonomous art. It is the social bad conscience of serious art. The truth which the latter necessarily lacked because of its social premises gives the other the semblance of legitimacy. The division itself is the truth: it does at least express the negativity of the culture which the different spheres constitute. Least of all can the antithesis be reconciled by absorbing light into serious art, or vice versa. But that is what the culture industry attempts. The eccentricity of the circus, peepshow, and brothel is as embarrassing to it as that of Schönberg and Karl Kraus. And so the jazz musician Benny Goodman appears with the Budapest string quartet, more pedantic rhythmically than any philharmonic clarinettist, while the style of the Budapest players is as uniform and sugary as that of Guy Lombardo. But what is significant is not vulgarity, stupidity, and lack of polish. The culture industry did away with yesterday's rubbish by its own perfection, and by forbidding and domesticating the amateurish, although it constantly allows gross blunders without which the standard of the exalted style cannot be perceived. But what is new is that the irreconcilable elements of culture, art and distraction, are subordinated to one end and subsumed under one false formula: the totality of the culture industry. It consists of repetition. That its characteristic innovations are never anything more than improvements of mass reproduction is not external to the system. It is with good reason that the interest of innumerable consumers is directed to the technique, and not to the contents — which are stubbornly repeated, outworn, and by now half-discredited. The social power which the spectators worship shows itself more effectively in the omnipresence of the stereotype imposed by technical skill than in the stale ideologies for which the ephemeral contents stand in.

Nevertheless the culture industry remains the entertainment business. Its influence over the consumers is established by entertainment; that will ultimately be broken not by an outright decree, but by the hostility inherent in the principle of entertainment to what is greater than itself. Since all the trends of the culture industry are profoundly embedded in the public by the whole social process, they are encouraged by the survival of the market in this area. Demand has not yet been replaced by simple obedience. As is well known, the major reorganization of the film industry shortly before World War I, the material prerequisite of its expansion, was precisely its deliberate acceptance of the public's needs as recorded at the box-office — a procedure which was hardly thought necessary in the pioneering days of the screen. The same opinion is held today by the captains of the film industry, who take as their criterion the more or less phenomenal song hits but wisely never have recourse to the judgment of truth, the opposite criterion. Business is their ideology. It is quite correct that the power of the culture industry resides in its identification with a manufactured need, and not in simple contrast to it, even if this contrast were one of complete power and complete powerlessness. Amusement under late capitalism is the prolongation of work. It is sought after as an escape from the mechanized work process, and to recruit strength in order to be able to cope with it again. But at the same time mechanization has such power over a man's leisure and happiness, and so profoundly determines the manufacture of amusement goods, that his experiences are inevitably after-images of the work process itself. The ostensible content is merely a faded foreground; what sinks in is the automatic succession of standardized operations. What happens at work, in the factory, or in the office can only be escaped from by approximation to it in one's leisure time. All amusement suffers from this incurable malady. Pleasure hardens into boredom because, if it is to remain pleasure, it must not demand any effort and therefore moves rigorously in the worn grooves of association. No independent thinking must be expected from the audience: the product prescribes every reaction: not by its natural structure (which collapses under reflection), but by signals. Any logical connection calling for mental effort is painstakingly avoided. As far as possible, developments must follow from the immediately preceding situation and never from the idea of the whole. For the attentive movie-goer any individual scene will give him the whole thing. Even the set pattern itself still seems dangerous, offering some meaning — wretched as it might be — where only meaninglessness is acceptable. Often the plot is maliciously deprived of the development demanded by characters and matter according to the old pattern. Instead, the next step is what the script writer takes to be the most striking effect in the particular situation. Banal though elaborate surprise interrupts the story-line. The tendency mischievously to fall back on pure nonsense, which was a legitimate part of popular art, farce and clowning, right up to Chaplin and the Marx Brothers, is most obvious in the unpretentious kinds. This tendency has completely asserted itself in the text of the novelty song, in the thriller movie, and in cartoons, although in films starring Greer Garson and Bette Davis the unity of the sociopsychological case study provides something approximating a claim to a consistent plot. The idea itself, together with the objects of comedy and terror, is massacred and fragmented. Novelty songs have always existed on a contempt for meaning which, as predecessors and successors of psychoanalysis, they reduce to the monotony of sexual symbolism. Today detective and adventure films no longer give the audience the opportunity to experience the resolution. In the non-ironic varieties of the genre, it has also to rest content with the simple horror of situations which have almost ceased to be linked in any way.

Cartoons were once exponents of fantasy as opposed to rationalism. They ensured that justice was done to the creatures and objects they electrified, by giving the maimed specimens a second life. All they do today is to confirm the victory of technological reason over truth. A few years ago they had a consistent plot which only broke up in the final moments in a crazy chase, and thus resembled the old slapstick comedy. Now, however, time relations have shifted. In the very first sequence a motive is stated so that in the course of the action destruction can get to work on it: with the audience in pursuit, the protagonist becomes the worthless object of general violence. The quantity of organized amusement changes into the quality of organized cruelty. The self-elected censors of the film industry (with whom it enjoys a close relationship) watch over the unfolding of the crime, which is as drawn-out as a hunt. Fun replaces the pleasure which the sight of an embrace would allegedly afford, and postpones satisfaction till the day of the pogrom. In so far as cartoons do any more than accustom the senses to the new tempo, they hammer into every brain the old lesson that continuous friction, the breaking down of all individual resistance, is the condition of life in this society. Donald Duck in the cartoons and the unfortunate in real life get their thrashing so that the audience can learn to take their own punishment.

The enjoyment of the violence suffered by the movie character turns into violence against the spectator, and distraction into exertion. Nothing that the experts have devised as a stimulant must escape the weary eye; no stupidity is allowed in the face of all the trickery; one has to follow everything and even display the smart responses shown and recommended in the film. This raises the question whether the culture industry fulfills the function of diverting minds which it boasts about so loudly. If most of the radio stations and movie theaters were closed down, the consumers would probably not lose so very much. To walk from the street into the movie theater is no longer to enter a world of dream; as soon as the very existence of these institutions no longer made it obligatory to use them, there would be no great urge to do so. Such closures would not be reactionary machine wrecking. The disappointment would be felt not so much by the enthusiasts as by the slow-witted, who are the ones who suffer for everything anyhow. In spite of the films which are intended to complete her integration, the housewife finds in the darkness of the movie theater a place of refuge where she can sit for a few hours with nobody watching, just as she used to look out of the window when there were still homes and rest in the evening. The unemployed in the great cities find coolness in summer and warmth in winter in these temperature-controlled locations. Otherwise, despite its size, this bloated pleasure apparatus adds no dignity to man's lives. The idea of 'fully exploiting' available technical resources and the facilities for aesthetic mass consumption is part of the economic system which refuses to exploit resources to abolish hunger.

The culture industry perpetually cheats its consumers of what it perpetually promises. The promissory note which, with its plots and staging, it draws on pleasure is endlessly prolonged; the promise, which is actually all the spectacle consists of, is illusory: all it actually confirms is that the real point will never be reached, that the diner must be satisfied with the menu. In front of the appetite stimulated by all those brilliant names and images there is finally set no more than a commendation of the depressing everyday world it sought to escape. Of course works of art were not sexual exhibitions either. However, by representing deprivation as negative, they retracted, as it were, the prostitution of the impulse and rescued by mediation what was denied. The secret of aesthetic sublimation is its representation of fulfillment as a broken promise. The culture industry does not sublimate; it represses. By repeatedly exposing the objects of desire, breasts in a clinging sweater or the naked torso of the athletic hero, it only stimulates the unsublimated forepleasure which habitual deprivation has long since reduced to a masochistic semblance. There is no erotic situation which, while insinuating and exciting, does not fail to indicate unmistakably that things can never go that far. The Hays Office merely confirms the ritual of Tantalus that the culture industry has established anyway. Works of art are ascetic and unashamed; the culture industry is pornographic and prudish. Love is downgraded to romance. And, after the descent, much is permitted; even license as a marketable speciality has its quota bearing the trade description 'daring'. The mass production of the sexual automatically achieves its repression. Because of his ubiquity, the film star with whom one is meant to fall in love is from the outset a copy of himself. Every tenor voice comes to sound like a Caruso record, and the 'natural' faces of Texas girls are like the successful models by whom Hollywood has typecast them. The mechanical reproduction of beauty, which reactionary cultural fanaticism wholeheartedly serves in its methodical idolization of individuality, leaves no room for that unconscious idolatry which was once essential to beauty. The triumph over beauty is celebrated by humor — the *Schadenfreude* that every successful deprivation calls forth. There is laughter because there is nothing to laugh at. Laughter, whether conciliatory or terrible, always occurs when some fear passes. It indicates liberation either from physical danger or from the grip of logic. Conciliatory laughter is heard as the echo of an escape from power; the wrong kind overcomes fear by capitulating to the forces which are to be feared. It is the echo of power as something inescapable. Fun is a medicinal bath. The pleasure industry never fails to prescribe it. It makes laughter the instrument of the fraud practised on happiness. Moments of happiness are without laughter; only operettas and films portray sex to the accompaniment of resounding laughter. But Baudelaire is as devoid of humor as Hölderlin. In the false society laughter is a disease which has attacked happiness and is drawing it into its worthless totality. To laugh at something is always to deride it, and the life which, according to Bergson, in laughter breaks through the barrier, is actually an invading barbaric life, self-assertion prepared to parade its liberation from any scruple when the social occasion arises. Such a laughing audience is a parody of humanity. Its members are monads, all dedicated to the pleasure of being ready for anything at the expense of everyone else. Their harmony is a caricature of solidarity. What is fiendish about this false laughter is that it is a compelling parody of the best, which is conciliatory. Delight is austere: *res severa verum gaudium.* The monastic theory that not asceticism but the sexual act denotes the renunciation of attainable bliss receives negative confirmation in the gravity of the lover who with foreboding commits his life to the fleeting moment. In the culture industry, jovial denial takes the place of the pain found in ecstasy and in asceticism. The supreme law is that they shall not satisfy their desires at any price; they must laugh and be content with laughter. In every product of the culture industry, the permanent denial imposed by civilization is once again unmistakably demonstrated and inflicted on its victims. To offer and to deprive them of something is one and the same. This is what happens in erotic films. Precisely because it must never take place, everything centers upon copulation. In films it is more strictly forbidden for an illegitimate relationship to be admitted without the parties being punished than for a millionaire's future son-in-law to be active in the labor movement. In contrast to the liberal era, industrialized as well as popular culture may wax indignant at capitalism, but it cannot renounce the threat of castration. This is fundamental. It outlasts the organized acceptance of the uniformed seen in the films which are produced to that end, and in reality. What is decisive today is no longer puritanism, although it still asserts itself in the form of women's organizations, but the necessity inherent in the system not to leave the customer alone, not for a moment to allow him any suspicion that resistance is possible. The principle dictates that he should be shown all his needs as capable of fulfillment, but that those needs should be so pre-determined that he feels himself to be the eternal consumer, the object of the culture industry. Not only does it make him believe that the deception it practices is satisfaction, but it goes further and implies that, whatever the state of affairs, he must put up with what is offered. The escape from everyday drudgery which the whole culture industry promises may be compared to the daughter's abduction in the cartoon: the father is holding the ladder in the dark. The paradise offered by the culture industry is the same old drudgery. Both escape and elopement are predesigned to lead back to the starting point. Pleasure promotes the resignation which it ought to help to forget.

Amusement, if released from every restraint, would not only be the antithesis of art but its extreme role. The Mark Twain absurdity with which the American culture industry flirts at times might be a corrective of art. The more seriously the latter regards the incompatibility with life, the more it resembles the seriousness of life, its antithesis; the more effort it devotes to developing wholly from its own formal law, the more effort it demands from the intelligence to neutralize its burden. In some revue films, and especially in the grotesque and the funnies, the possibility of this negation does glimmer for a few moments. But of course it cannot happen. Pure amusement in its consequence, relaxed self-surrender to all kinds of associations and happy nonsense, is cut short by the amusement on the market: instead, it is interrupted by a surrogate overall meaning which the culture industry insists on giving to its products, and yet misuses as a mere pretext for bringing in the stars. Biographies and other simple stories patch the fragments of nonsense into an idiotic plot. We do not have the cap and bells of the jester but the bunch of keys of capitalist reason, which even screens the pleasure of achieving success. Every kiss in the revue film has to contribute to the career of the boxer, or some hit song expert or other whose rise to fame is being glorified. The deception is not that the culture industry supplies amusement but that it ruins the fun by allowing business considerations to involve it in the ideological clichés of a culture in the process of self-liquidation. Ethics and taste cut short unrestrained amusement as 'naive' — naïveté is thought to be as bad as intellectualism — and even restrict technical possibilities. The culture industry is corrupt; not because it is a sinful Babylon but because it is a cathedral dedicated to elevated pleasure. On all levels, from Hemingway to Emil Ludwig, from Mrs Miniver to the Lone Ranger, from Toscanini to Guy Lombardo, there is untruth in the intellectual content taken ready-made from art and science. The culture

industry does retain a trace of something better in those features which
bring it close to the circus, in the self-justifying and nonsensical skill of
riders, acrobats and clowns, in the 'defense and justification of physical as
against intellectual art'.[3] But the refuges of a mindless artistry which represents what is human as opposed to the social mechanism are being relentlessly hunted down by a schematic reason which compels everything to
prove its significance and effect. The consequence is that the nonsensical
at the bottom disappears as utterly as the sense in works of art at the top.

The fusion of culture and entertainment that is taking place today leads
not only to a depravation of culture, but inevitably to an intellectualization
of amusement. This is evident from the fact that only the copy appears: in
the movie theater, the photograph; on the radio, the recording. In the age
of liberal expansion, amusement lived on the unshaken belief in the future:
things would remain as they were and even improve. Today this belief is
once more intellectualized; it becomes so faint that it loses sight of any
goal and is little more than a magic-lantern show for those with their backs
to reality. It consists of the meaningful emphases which, parallel to life itself, the screen play puts on the smart fellow, the engineer, the capable girl,
ruthlessness disguised as character, interest in sport, and finally automobiles
and cigarettes, even where the entertainment is not put down to the advertising account of the immediate producers but to that of the system as a
whole. Amusement itself becomes an ideal, taking the place of the higher
things of which it completely deprives the masses by repeating them in a
manner even more stereotyped than the slogans paid for by advertising
interests. Inwardness, the subjectively restricted form of truth, was always
more at the mercy of the outwardly powerful than they imagined. The
culture industry turns it into an open lie. It has now become mere twaddle
which is acceptable in religious bestsellers, psychological films, and women's
serials as an embarassingly agreeable garnish, so that genuine personal
emotion in real life can be all the more reliably controlled. In this sense
amusement carries out that purgation of the emotions which Aristotle once
attributed to tragedy and Mortimer Adler now allows to movies. The
culture industry reveals the truth about catharsis as it did about style.

The stronger the positions of the culture industry become, the more
summarily it can deal with consumers' needs, producing them, controlling
them, disciplining them, and even withdrawing amusement: no limits are
set to cultural progress of this kind. But the tendency is immanent in the
principle of amusement itself, which is enlightened in a bourgeois sense. If
the need for amusement was in large measure the creation of industry,
which used the subject as a means of recommending the work to the masses
— the oleograph by the dainty morsel it depicted, or the cake mix by a

3   Frank Wedekind, *Gesammelte Werke*, Vol. IX (Munich, 1921), p. 426.

picture of a cake — amusement always reveals the influence of business, the sales talk, the quack's spiel. But the original affinity of business and amusement is shown in the latter's specific significance: to defend society. To be pleased means to say Yes. It is possible only by insulation from the totality of the social process, by desensitization and, from the first, by senselessly sacrificing the inescapable claim of every work, however inane, within its limits to reflect the whole. Pleasure always means not to think about anything, to forget suffering even where it is shown. Basically it is helplessness. It is flight; not, as is asserted, flight from a wretched reality, but from the last remaining thought of resistance. The liberation which amusement promises is freedom from thought and from negation. The effrontery of the rhetorical question, 'What do people want?' lies in the fact that it is addressed — as if to reflective individuals — to those very people who are deliberately to be deprived of this individuality. Even when the public does — exceptionally — rebel against the pleasure industry, all it can muster is that feeble resistance which that very industry has inculcated in it. Nevertheless, it has become increasingly difficult to keep people in this condition. The rate at which they are reduced to stupidity must not fall behind the rate at which their intelligence is increasing. In this age of statistics the masses are too sharp to identify themselves with the millionaire on the screen, and too slow-witted to ignore the law of the largest number. Ideology conceals itself in the calculation of probabilities. Not everyone will be lucky one day — but the person who draws the winning ticket, or rather the one who is marked out to do so by a higher power — usually by the pleasure industry itself, which is represented as unceasingly in search of talent. Those discovered by talent scouts and then publicized on a vast scale by the studio are ideal types of the new dependent average. Of course, the starlet is meant to symbolize the typist in such a way that the splendid evening dress seems meant for the actress as distinct from the real girl. The girls in the audience not only feel that they could be on the screen, but realize the great gulf separating them from it. Only one girl can draw the lucky ticket, only one man can win the prize, and if, mathematically, all have the same chance, yet this is so infinitesimal for each one that he or she will do best to write it off and rejoice in the other's success, which might just as well have been his or hers, and somehow never is. Whenever the culture industry still issues an invitation naïvely to identify, it is immediately withdrawn. No one can escape from himself any more. Once a member of the audience could see his own wedding in the one shown in the film. Now the lucky actors on the screen are copies of the same category as every member of the public, but such equality only demonstrates the insurmountable separation of the human elements. The perfect similarity is the absolute difference. The identity of the category forbids that of the individual cases. Ironically, man as a member of a species has been made a reality by the culture industry. Now any person signifies only those attributes by which he can replace everybody else: he is interchangeable, a copy. As an individual he is completely expendable and utterly insignificant, and this is just what he finds out when time deprives him of this similarity. This changes the inner structure of the religion of success — otherwise strictly maintained. Increasing emphasis is laid not on the path *per aspera ad astra* (which presupposes hardship and effort), but on winning a prize. The element of blind chance in the routine decision about which song deserves to be a hit and which extra a heroine is stressed by the ideology. Movies emphasize chance. By stopping at nothing to ensure that all the characters are essentially alike, with the exception of the villain, and by excluding non-conforming faces (for example, those which, like Garbo's, do not look as if you could say 'Hello sister!' to them), life is made easier for movie-goers at first. They are assured that they are all right as they are, that they could do just as well and that nothing beyond their powers will be asked of them. But at the same time they are given a hint that any effort would be useless because even bourgeois luck no longer has any connection with the calculable effect of their own work. They take the hint. Fundamentally they all recognize chance (by which one occasionally makes his fortune) as the other side of planning. Precisely because the forces of society are so deployed in the direction of rationality that anyone might become an engineer or manager, it has ceased entirely to be a rational matter who the one will be in whom society will invest training or confidence for such functions. Chance and planning become one and the same thing, because, given men's equality, individual success and failure — right up to the top — lose any economic meaning. Chance itself is planned, not because it affects any particular individual but precisely because it is believed to play a vital part. It serves the planners as an alibi, and makes it seem that the complex of transactions and measures into which life has been transformed leaves scope for spontaneous and direct relations between man. This freedom is symbolized in the various media of the culture industry by the arbitrary selection of average individuals. In a magazine's detailed accounts of the modestly magnificent pleasure-trips it has arranged for the lucky person, preferably a stenotypist (who has probably won the competition because of her contacts with local bigwigs), the powerlessness of all is reflected. They are mere matter — so much so that those in control can take someone up into their heaven and throw him out again: his rights and his work count for nothing. Industry is interested in people merely as customers and employees and has in fact reduced mankind as a whole and each of its elements to this all-embracing formula. According to the ruling aspect at the time, ideology emphasizes plan or chance, technology or life, civilization or nature. As employees, men are reminded of the rational organization and urged to fit in like sensible people. As customers, the freedom of choice, the charm of novelty, is demonstrated to them on the screen or in the press by means of the human and personal anecdote. In either case they remain objects.

The less the culture industry has to promise, the less it can offer a meaningful explanation of life, and the emptier is the ideology it disseminates. Even the abstract ideals of the harmony and beneficence of society are too concrete in this age of universal publicity. We have even learned how to identify abstract concepts as sales propaganda. Language based entirely on truth simply arouses impatience to get on with the business deal it is probably advancing. The words that are not means appear senseless; the others seem to be fiction, untrue. Value judgments are taken either as advertising or as empty talk. Accordingly ideology has been made vague and noncommittal, and thus neither clearer nor weaker. Its very vagueness, its almost scientific aversion from committing itself to anything which cannot be verified, acts as an instrument of domination. It becomes a vigorous and prearranged promulgation of the status quo. The culture industry tends to make itself the embodiment of authoritative pronouncements, and thus the irrefutable prophet of the prevailing order. It skilfully steers a winding course between the cliffs of demonstrable misinformation and manifest truth, faithfully reproducing the phenomenon whose opaqueness blocks any insight and installs the ubiquitous and intact phenomenon as ideal. Ideology is split into the photograph of stubborn life and the naked lie about its meaning — which is not expressed but suggested and yet drummed in. To demonstrate its divine nature, reality is always repeated in a purely cynical way. Such a photological proof is of course not stringent, but it is overpowering. Anyone who doubts the power of monotony is a fool. The culture industry refutes the objection made against it just as well as that against the world which it impartially duplicates. The only choice is either to join in or to be left behind: those provincials who have recourse to eternal beauty and the amateur stage in preference to the cinema and the radio are already — politically — at the point to which mass culture drives its supporters. It is sufficiently hardened to deride as ideology, if need be, the old wish-fulfillments, the father-ideal and absolute feeling. The new ideology has as its objects the world as such. It makes use of the worship of facts by no more than elevating a disagreeable existence into the world of facts in representing it meticulously. This transference makes existence itself a substitute for meaning and right. Whatever the camera reproduces is beautiful. The disappointment of the prospect that one might be the typist who wins the world trip is matched by the disappointing appearance of the accurately photographed areas which the voyage might include. Not Italy is offered, but evidence that it exists. A film can even go so far as to show the Paris in which the American girl thinks she will still her desire as a hopelessly desolate place, thus driving her the more inexorably into the arms of the smart American boy she could have met at home anyhow. That this goes on, that, in its most recent phase, the system itself reproduces the life of those of whom it consists instead of immediately doing away with them, is even put down to its credit as giving it meaning and worth. Continuing and continuing to join in are given as justification for the blind persistence of the system and even for its immutability. What repeats itself is healthy, like the natural or industrial cycle. The same babies grin eternally out of the magazines; the jazz machine will pound away for ever. In spite of all the progress in reproduction techniques, in controls and the specialities, and in spite of all the restless industry, the bread which the culture industry offers man is the stone of the stereotype. It draws on the life cycle, on the well-founded amazement that mothers, in spite of everything, still go on bearing children and that the wheels still do not grind to a halt. This serves to confirm the immutability of circumstances. The ears of corn blowing in the wind at the end of Chaplin's *The Great Dictator* give the lie to the anti-Fascist plea for freedom. They are like the blond hair of the German girl whose camp life is photographed by the Nazi film company in the summer breeze. Nature is viewed by the mechanism of social domination as a healthy contrast to society, and is therefore denatured. Pictures showing green trees, a blue sky, and moving clouds make these aspects of nature into so many cryptograms for factory chimneys and service stations. On the other hand, wheels and machine components must seem expressive, having been degraded to the status of agents of the spirit of trees and clouds. Nature and technology are mobilized against all oppositon; and we have a falsified memento of liberal society, in which people supposedly wallowed in erotic plush-lined bedrooms instead of taking open-air baths as in the case today, or experiencing breakdowns in prehistoric Benz models instead of shooting off with the speed of a rocket from A (where one is anyhow) to B (where everything is just the same). The triumph of the gigantic concern over the initiative of the entrepreneur is praised by the culture industry as the persistence of entrepreneurial initiative. The enemy who is already defeated, the thinking individual, is the enemy fought. The resurrection in Germany of the antibourgeois 'Haus Sonnenstösser', and the pleasure felt when watching *Life with Father*, have one and the same meaning.

In one respect, admittedly, this hollow ideology is in deadly earnest: everyone is provided for. 'No one must go hungry or thirsty; if anyone does, he's for the concentration camp!' This joke from Hitler's Germany might shine forth as a maxim from above all the portals of the culture industry. With sly naïveté, it presupposes the most recent characteristic of society: that it can easily find out who its supporters are. Everybody is guaranteed formal freedom. No one is officially responsible for what he thinks. Instead everyone is enclosed at an early age in a system of churches, clubs, professional associations, and other such concerns, which constitute the most sensitive instrument of social control. Anyone who wants to avoid ruin must see that he is not found wanting when weighed in the scales of this apparatus. Otherwise he will lag behind in life, and finally perish. In every career, and especially in the liberal professions, expert knowledge is linked with prescribed standards of conduct; this can easily lead to the illusion that expert knowledge is the only thing that counts. In fact, it is part of the irrational planning of this society that it reproduces to a certain degree only the lives of its faithful members. The standard of life enjoyed corresponds very closely to the degree to which classes and individuals are essentially bound up with the system. The manager can be relied upon, as can the lesser employee Dagwood — as he is in the comic pages or in real life. Anyone who goes cold and hungry, even if his prospects were once good, is branded. He is an outsider; and, apart from certain capital crimes, the most mortal of sins is to be an outsider. In films he sometimes, and as an exception, becomes an original, the object of maliciously indulgent humor; but usually he is the villain, and is identified as such at first appearance, long before the action really gets going: hence avoiding any suspicion that society would turn on those of good will. Higher up the scale, in fact, a kind of welfare state is coming into being today. In order to keep their own positions, men in top posts maintain the economy in which a highly-developed technology has in principle made the masses redundant as producers. The workers, the real bread-winners, are fed (if we are to believe the ideology) by the managers of the economy, the fed. Hence the individual's position becomes precarious. Under liberalism the poor were thought to be lazy; now they are automatically objects of suspicion. Anybody who is not provided for outside should be in a concentration camp or at any rate in the hell of the most degrading work and the slums. The culture industry, however, reflects positive and negative welfare for those under the administrators' control as direct human solidarity of men in a world of the efficient. No one is forgotten; everywhere there are neighbors and welfare workers, Dr Gillespies and parlor philosophers whose hearts are in the right place and who, by their kind intervention as of man to man, cure individual cases of socially-perpetuated distress — always provided that there is no obstacle in the personal depravity of the unfortunate. The promotion of a friendly atmosphere as advised by management experts and adopted by every factory to increase output, brings even the last private impulse under social control precisely because it seems to relate men's circumstances directly to production, and to reprivatize them. Such spiritual charity casts a conciliatory shadow onto the products of the culture industry long before it emerges from the factory to invade society as a whole. Yet the great benefactors of mankind, whose scientific achievements have to be written up as acts of sympathy to give them an artificial human interest, are substitutes for the national leaders, who finally decree the abolition of sympathy and think they can prevent any recurrence when the last invalid has been exterminated.

By emphasizing the 'heart of gold', society admits the suffering it has created: everyone knows that he is now helpless in the system, and ideology has to take this into account. Far from concealing suffering under the cloak of improvised fellowship, the culture industry takes pride in looking it in the face like a man, however great the strain on self-control. The pathos of composure justifies the world which makes it necessary. That is life — very hard, but just because of that so wonderful and so healthy. This lie does not shrink from tragedy. Mass culture deals with it, in the same way as centralized society does not abolish the suffering of its members but records and plans it. That is why it borrows so persistently from art. This provides the tragic substance which pure amusement cannot itself supply, but which it needs if it is somehow to remain faithful to the principle of the exact reproduction of phenomena. Tragedy made into a carefully calculated and accepted aspect of the world is a blessing. It is a safeguard against the reproach that truth is not respected, whereas it is really being adopted with cynical regret. To the consumer who — culturally — has seen better days it offers a substitute for long-discarded profundities. It provides the regular movie-goer with the scraps of culture he must have for prestige. It comforts all with the thought that a tough, genuine human fate is still possible, and that it must at all costs be represented uncompromisingly. Life in all the aspects which ideology today sets out to duplicate shows up all the more gloriously, powerfully and magnificently, the more it is redolent of necessary suffering. It begins to resemble fate. Tragedy is reduced to the threat to destroy anyone who does not cooperate, whereas its paradoxical significance once lay in a hopeless resistance to mythic destiny. Tragic fate becomes just punishment, which is what bourgeois aesthetics always tried to turn it into. The morality of mass culture is the cheap form of yesterday's children's books. In a first-class production, for example, the villainous character appears as a hysterical woman who (with presumed clinical accuracy) tries to ruin the happiness of her opposite number, who is truer to reality, and herself suffers a quite untheatrical death. So much learning is of course found only at the top. Lower down less trouble is taken. Tragedy is made harmless without recourse to social psychology. Just as every Viennese operetta worthy of the name had to have its tragic finale in the second act, which left nothing for the third except to clear up misunderstandings, the culture industry assigns tragedy a fixed place in the routine. The well-known existence of the recipe is enough to allay any fear that there is no restraint on tragedy. The description of the dramatic formula by the housewife as 'getting into trouble and out again' embraces the whole of mass culture from the idiotic women's serial to the top production. Even the worst ending which began with good intentions confirms the order of things and corrupts the tragic force, either because the woman whose love runs counter to the laws of the game plays with her death for a brief spell of happiness, or because the sad ending in the film all the more clearly stresses the indestructibility of actual life. The tragic film becomes an institution for moral improvement. The masses,

demoralized by their life under the pressure of the system, and who show
signs of civilization only in modes of behavior which have been forced on
them and through which fury and recalcitrance show everywhere, are to
be kept in order by the sight of an inexorable life and exemplary behavior.
Culture has always played its part in taming revolutionary and barbaric
instincts. Industrial culture adds its contribution. It shows the condition
under which this merciless life can be lived at all. The individual who is
thoroughly weary must use his weariness as energy for his surrender to the
collective power which wears him out. In films, those permanently desperate situations which crush the spectator in ordinary life somehow become
a promise that one can go on living. One has only to become aware of one's
own nothingness, only to recognize defeat and one is one with it all. Society
is full of desperate people and therefore a prey to rackets. In some of the
most significant German novels of the pre-Fascist era such as Döblin's
Berlin Alexanderplatz and Fallada's *Kleiner Mann, Was Nun*, this trend was
as obvious as in the average film and in the devices of jazz. What all these
things have in common is the self-derision of man. The possibility of becoming a subject in the economy, an entrepreneur or a proprietor, has been
completely liquidated. Right down to the humblest shop, the independent
enterprise, on the management and inheritance of which the bourgeois
family and the position of its head had rested, became hopelessly dependent. Everybody became an employee; and in this civilization of employees
the dignity of the father (questionable anyhow) vanishes. The attitude of
the individual to the racket, business, profession or party, before or after
admission, the Führer's gesticulations before the masses, or the suitor's before his sweetheart, assume specifically masochistic traits. The attitude into
which everybody is forced in order to give repeated proof of his moral
suitability for this society reminds one of the boys who, during tribal initiation, go round in a circle with a stereotyped smile on their faces while the
priest strikes them. Life in the late capitalist era is a constant initiation rite.
Everyone must show that he wholly identifies himself with the power
which is belaboring him. This occurs in the principle of jazz syncopation,
which simultaneously derides stumbling and makes it a rule. The eunuch-
like voice of the crooner on the radio, the heiress's smooth suitor, who falls
into the swimming pool in his dinner jacket, are models for those who
must become whatever the system wants. Everyone can be like this omnipotent society; everyone can be happy, if only he will capitulate fully and
sacrifice his claim to happiness. In his weakness society recognizes its
strength, and gives him some of it. His defenselessness makes him reliable.
Hence tragedy is discarded. Once the opposition of the individual to society
was its substance. It glorified 'the bravery and freedom of emotion before
a powerful enemy, an exalted affliction, a dreadful problem'.[4] Today

4   Nietzsche, *Götzendämmerung, Werke*, Vol. VIII, p. 136.

tragedy has melted away into the nothingness of that false identity of society and individual, whose terror still shows for a moment in the empty semblance of the tragic. But the miracle of integration, the permanent act of grace by the authority who receives the defenseless person — once he has swallowed his rebelliousness — signifies Fascism. This can be seen in the humanitarianism which Döblin uses to let his Biberkopf find refuge, and again in socially-slanted films. The capacity to find refuge, to survive one's own ruin, by which tragedy is defeated, is found in the new generation; they can do any work because the work process does not let them become attached to any. This is reminiscent of the sad lack of conviction of the homecoming soldier with no interest in the war, or of the casual laborer who ends up by joining a paramilitary organization. This liquidation of tragedy confirms the abolition of the individual.

In the culture industry the individual is an illusion not merely because of the standardization of the means of production. He is tolerated only so long as his complete identification with the generality is unquestioned. Pseudo individuality is rife: from the standardized jazz improvization to the exceptional film star whose hair curls over her eye to demonstrate her originality. What is individual is no more than the generality's power to stamp the accidental detail so firmly that it is accepted as such. The defiant reserve or elegant appearance of the individual on show is mass-produced like Yale locks, whose only difference can be measured in fractions of millimeters. The peculiarity of the self is a monopoly commodity determined by society; it is falsely represented as natural. It is no more than the moustache, the French accent, the deep voice of the woman of the world, the Lubitsch touch: finger prints on identity cards which are otherwise exactly the same, and into which the lives and faces of every single person are transformed by the power of the generality. Pseudo individuality is the prerequisite for comprehending tragedy and removing its poison: only because individuals have ceased to be themselves and are now merely centers where the general tendencies meet, is it possible to receive them again, whole and entire, into the generality. In this way mass culture discloses the fictitious character of the 'individual' in the bourgeois era, and is merely unjust in boasting on account of this dreary harmony of general and particular. The principle of individuality was always full of contradiction. Individuation has never really been achieved. Self-preservation in the shape of class has kept everyone at the stage of a mere species being. Every bourgeois characteristic, in spite of its deviation and indeed because of it, expressed the same thing: the harshness of the competitive society. The individual who supported society bore its disfiguring mark; seemingly free, he was actually the product of its economic and social apparatus. Power based itself on the prevailing conditions of power when it sought the approval of persons affected by it. As it progressed, bourgeois society did also develop the individual. Against the will of its leaders, technology has changed human beings from children into persons. However, every advance in individuation of this kind took place at the expense of the individuality in whose name it occurred, so that nothing was left but the resolve to pursue one's own particular purpose. The bourgeois whose existence is split into a business and a private life, whose private life is split into keeping up his public image and intimacy, whose intimacy is split into the surly partnership of marriage and the bitter comfort of being quite alone, at odds with himself and everybody else, is already virtually a Nazi, replete both with enthusiasm and abuse; or a modern city-dweller who can now only imagine friendship as a 'social contact': that is, as being in social contact with others with whom he has no inward contact. The only reason why the culture industry can deal so successfully with individuality is that the latter has always reproduced the fragility of society. On the faces of private individuals and movie heroes put together according to the patterns on magazine covers vanishes a pretense in which no one now believes; the popularity of the hero models comes partly from a secret satisfaction that the effort to achieve individuation has at last been replaced by the effort to imitate, which is admittedly more breathless. It is idle to hope that this self-contradictory, disintegrating 'person' will not last for generations, that the system must collapse because of such a psychological split, or that the deceitful substitution of the stereotype for the individual will of itself become unbearable for mankind. Since Shakespeare's *Hamlet*, the unity of the personality has been seen through as a pretense. Synthetically produced physiognomies show that the people of today have already forgotten that there was ever a notion of what human life was. For centuries society has been preparing for Victor Mature and Mickey Rooney. By destroying they come to fulfill.

The idolization of the cheap involves making the average the heroic. The highest-paid stars resemble pictures advertising unspecified proprietary articles. Not without good purpose are they often selected from the host of commercial models. The prevailing taste takes its ideal from advertising, the beauty in consumption. Hence the Socratic saying that the beautiful is the useful has now been fulfilled — ironically. The cinema makes propaganda for the culture combine as a whole; on radio, goods for whose sake the cultural commodity exists are also recommended individually. For a few coins one can see the film which cost millions, for even less one can buy the chewing gum whose manufacture involved immense riches — a hoard increased still further by sales. *In absentia*, but by universal suffrage, the treasure of armies is revealed, but prostitution is not allowed inside the country. The best orchestras in the world — clearly not so — are brought into your living room free of charge. It is all a parody of the never-never land, just as the national society is a parody of the human society. You name it, we supply it. A man up from the country remarked at the old

Berlin Metropol theatre that it was astonishing what they could do for the money; his comment has long since been adopted by the culture industry and made the very substance of production. This is always coupled with the triumph that it is possible; but this, in large measure, is the very triumph. Putting on a show means showing everybody what there is, and what can be achieved. Even today it is still a fair, but incurably sick with culture. Just as the people who had been attracted by the fairground barkers overcame their disappointment in the booths with a brave smile, because they really knew in advance what would happen, so the movie-goer sticks knowingly to the institution. With the cheapness of mass-produced luxury goods and its complement, the universal swindle, a change in the character of the art commodity itself is coming about. What is new is not that it is a commodity, but that today it deliberately admits it is one; that art renounces its own autonomy and proudly takes its place among consumption goods constitutes the charm of novelty. Art as a separate sphere was always possible only in a bourgeois society. Even as a negation of that social purposiveness which is spreading through the market, its freedom remains essentially bound up with the premise of a commodity economy. Pure works of art which deny the commodity society by the very fact that they obey their own law were always wares all the same. In so far as, until the eighteenth century, the buyer's patronage shielded the artist from the market, they were dependent on the buyer and his objectives. The purpose-lessness of the great modern work of art depends on the anonymity of the market. Its demands pass through so many intermediaries that the artist is exempt from any definite requirements — though admittedly only to a certain degree, for throughout the whole history of the bourgeoisie his autonomy was only tolerated, and thus contained an element of untruth which ultimately led to the social liquidation of art. When mortally sick, Beethoven hurled away a novel by Sir Walter Scott with the cry: 'Why, the fellow writes for money', and yet proved a most experienced and stubborn businessman in disposing of the last quartets, which were a most extreme renunciation of the market; he is the most outstanding example of the unity of those opposites, market and independence, in bourgeois art. Those who succumb to the ideology are precisely those who cover up the contradiction instead of taking it into the consciousness of their own production as Beethoven did: he went on to express in music his anger at losing a few pence, and derived the metaphysical *Es Muss Sein* (which attempts an aesthetic banishment of the pressure of the world by taking it into itself) from the housekeeper's demand for her monthly wages. The principle of idealistic aesthetics — purposefulness without a purpose — reverses the scheme of things to which bourgeois art conforms socially: purposelessness for the purposes declared by the market. At last, in the demand for entertainment and relaxation, purpose has absorbed the realm of purposelessness. But as the insistence that art should be disposable in terms of money becomes absolute, a shift in the internal structure of cultural commodities begins to show itself. The use which men in this antagonistic society promise themselves from the work of art is itself, to a great extent, that very existence of the useless which is abolished by complete inclusion under use. The work of art, by completely assimilating itself to need, deceitfully deprives men of precisely that liberation from the principle of utility which it should inaugurate. What might be called use value in the reception of cultural commodities is replaced by exchange value; in place of enjoyment there are gallery-visiting and factual knowledge: the prestige seeker replaces the connoisseur. The consumer becomes the ideology of the pleasure industry, whose institutions he cannot escape. One simply 'has to' have seen *Mrs Miniver*, just as one 'has to' subscribe to *Life* and *Time*. Everything is looked at from only one aspect: that it can be used for something else, however vague the notion of this use may be. No object has an inherent value; it is valuable only to the extent that it can be exchanged. The use value of art, its mode of being, is treated as a fetish; and the fetish, the work's social rating (misinterpreted as its artistic status) becomes its use value — the only quality which is enjoyed. The commodity function of art disappears only to be wholly realized when art becomes a species of commodity instead, marketable and interchangeable like an industrial product. But art as a type of product which existed to be sold and yet to be unsaleable is wholly and hypocritically converted into 'unsaleability' as soon as the transaction ceases to be the mere intention and becomes its sole principle. No tickets could be bought when Toscanini conducted over the radio; he was heard without charge, and every sound of the symphony was accompanied, as it were, by the sublime puff that the symphony was not interrupted by any advertising: 'This concert is brought to you as a public service'. The illusion was made possible by the profits of the united automobile and soap manufacturers, whose payments keep the radio stations going — and, of course, by the increased sales of the electrical industry, which manufactures the radio sets. Radio, the progressive latecomer of mass culture, draws all the consequences at present denied the film by its pseudo-market. The technical structure of the commercial radio system makes it immune from liberal deviations such as those the movie industrialists can still permit themselves in their own sphere. It is a private enterprise which really does represent the sovereign whole and is therefore some distance ahead of the other individual combines. Chesterfield is merely the nation's cigarette, but the radio is the voice of the nation. In bringing cultural products wholly into the sphere of commodities, radio does not try to dispose of its culture goods themselves as commodities straight to the consumer. In America it collects no fees from the public, and so has acquired the illusory form of disinterested, unbiased authority which suits Fascism admirably. The radio becomes the universal mouthpiece of the Führer; his voice rises from street loud-speakers to resemble the howling of sirens announcing panic — from which modern propaganda can scarcely be distinguished anyway. The National Socialists knew that the wireless gave shape to their cause just as the printing press did to the Reformation. The metaphysical charisma of the Führer invented by the sociology of religion has finally turned out to be no more than the omnipresence of his speeches on the radio, which are a demoniacal parody of the omnipresence of the divine spirit. The gigantic fact that the speech penetrates everywhere replaces its content, just as the benefaction of the Toscanini broadcast takes the place of the symphony. No listener can grasp its true meaning any longer, while the Führer's speech is lies anyway. The inherent tendency of radio is to make the speaker's word, the false commandment, absolute. A recommendation becomes an order. The recommendation of the same commodities under different proprietary names, the scientifically based praise of the laxative in the announcer's smooth voice between the overture from *La Traviata* and that from *Rienzi* is the only thing that no longer works, because of its silliness. One day the edict of production, the actual advertisement (whose actuality is at present concealed by the pretense of a choice) can turn into the open command of the Führer. In a society of huge Fascist rackets which agree among themselves what part of the social product should be allotted to the nation's needs, it would eventually seem anachronistic to recommend the use of a particular soap powder. The Führer is more up-to-date in unceremoniously giving direct orders for both the holocaust and the supply of rubbish.

Even today the culture industry dresses works of art like political slogans and forces them upon a resistant public at reduced prices; they are as accessible for public enjoyment as a park. But the disappearance of their genuine commodity character does not mean that they have been abolished in the life of a free society, but that the last defense against their reduction to culture goods has fallen. The abolition of educational privilege by the device of clearance sales does not open for the masses the spheres from which they were formerly excluded, but, given existing social conditions, contributes directly to the decay of education and the progress of barbaric meaninglessness. Those who spent their money in the nineteenth or the early twentieth century to see a play or to go to a concert respected the performance as much as the money they spent. The bourgeois who wanted to get something out of it tried occasionally to establish some rapport with the work. Evidence for this is to be found in the literary 'introductions' to works, or in the commentaries on *Faust*. These were the first steps toward the biographical coating and other practices to which a work of art is subjected today. Even in the early, prosperous days of business, exchange-value did carry use value as a mere appendix but had developed it as a prerequisite for its own existence; this was socially helpful for works of art. Art exercised some restraint on the bourgeois as long as it cost money. That is now a thing of the past. Now that it has lost every restraint and there is no need to pay any money, the proximity of art to those who are exposed to it completes the alienation and assimilates one to the other under the banner of triumphant objectivity. Criticism and respect disappear in the culture industry; the former becomes a mechanical expertise, the latter is succeeded by a shallow cult of leading personalities. Consumers now find nothing expensive. Nevertheless, they suspect that the less anything costs, the less it is being given them. The double mistrust of traditional culture as ideology is combined with mistrust of industrialized culture as a swindle. When thrown in free, the now debased works of art, together with the rubbish to which the medium assimilates them, are secretly rejected by the fortunate recipients, who are supposed to be satisfied by the mere fact that there is so much to be seen and heard. Everything can be obtained. The screenos and vaudevilles in the movie theater, the competitions for guessing music, the free books, rewards and gifts offered on certain radio programs, are not mere accidents but a continuation of the practice obtaining with culture products. The symphony becomes a reward for listening to the radio, and — if technology had its way — the film would be delivered to people's homes as happens with the radio. It is moving toward the commercial system. Television points the way to a development which might easily enough force the Warner Brothers into what would certainly be the unwelcome position of serious musicians and cultural conservatives. But the gift system has already taken hold among consumers. As culture is represented as a bonus with undoubted private and social advantages, they have to seize the chance. They rush in lest they miss something. Exactly what, is not clear, but in any case the only ones with a chance are the participants. Fascism, however, hopes to use the training the culture industry has given these recipients of gifts, in order to organize them into its own forced battalions.

Culture is a paradoxical commodity. So completely is it subject to the law of exchange that it is no longer exchanged; it is so blindly consumed in use that it can no longer be used. Therefore it amalgamates with advertising. The more meaningless the latter seems to be under a monopoly, the more omnipotent it becomes. The motives are markedly economic. One could certainly live without the culture industry, therefore it necessarily creates too much satiation and apathy. In itself, it has few resources itself to correct this. Advertising is its elixir of life. But as its product never fails to reduce to a mere promise the enjoyment which it promises as a commodity, it eventually coincides with publicity, which it needs because it cannot be enjoyed. In a competitive society, advertising performed the social service of informing the buyer about the market; it made choice easier and helped the unknown but more efficient supplier to dispose of his goods. Far from costing time, it saved it. Today, when the free market is coming to an end, those who control the system are entrenching themselves in it.

It strengthens the firm bond between the consumers and the big combines. Only those who can pay the exorbitant rates charged by the advertising agencies, chief of which are the radio networks themselves; that is, only those who are already in a position to do so, or are co-opted by the decision of the banks and industrial capital, can enter the pseudo-market as sellers. The costs of advertising, which finally flow back into the pockets of the combines, make it unnecessary to defeat unwelcome outsiders by laborious competition. They guarantee that power will remain in the same hands — not unlike those economic decisions by which the establishment and running of undertakings is controlled in a totalitarian state. Advertising today is a negative principle, a blocking device: everything that does not bear its stamp is economically suspect. Universal publicity is in no way necessary for people to get to know the kinds of goods — whose supply is restricted anyway. It helps sales only indirectly. For a particular firm, to phase out a current advertising practice constitutes a loss of prestige, and a breach of the discipline imposed by the influential clique on its members. In wartime, goods which are unobtainable are still advertised, merely to keep industrial power in view. Subsidizing ideological media is more important than the repetition of the name. Because the system obliges every product to use advertising, it has permeated the idiom — the 'style' — of the culture industry. Its victory is so complete that it is no longer evident in the key positions: the huge buildings of the top men, floodlit stone advertisements, are free of advertising; at most they exhibit on the rooftops, in monumental brilliance and without any self-glorification, the firm's initials. But, in contrast, the nineteenth-century houses, whose architecture still shamefully indicates that they can be used as a consumption commodity and are intended to be lived in, are covered with posters and inscriptions from the ground right up to and beyond the roof; until they become no more than backgrounds for bills and sign-boards. Advertising becomes art and nothing else, just as Goebbels — with foresight — combines them: *l'art pour l'art*, advertising for its own sake, a pure representation of social power. In the most influential American magazines, *Life* and *Fortune*, a quick glance can now scarcely distinguish advertising from editorial picture and text. The latter features an enthusiastic and gratuitous account of the great man (with illustrations of his life and grooming habits) which will bring him new fans, while the advertisement pages use so many factual photographs and details that they represent the ideal of information which the editorial part has only begun to try to achieve. The assembly-line character of the culture industry, the synthetic, planned method of turning out its products (factory-like not only in the studio but, more or less, in the compilation of cheap biographies, pseudodocumentary novels, and hit songs) is very suited to advertising: the important individual points, by becoming detachable, interchangeable, and even technically alienated from any connected meaning, lend themselves to ends external to the work. The effect, the trick, the isolated repeatable device, have always been used to exhibit goods for advertising purposes, and today every monster close-up of a star is an advertisement for her name, and every hit song a plug for its tune. Advertising and the culture industry merge technically as well as economically. In both cases the same thing can be seen in innumerable places, and the mechanical repetition of the same culture product has come to be the same as that of the propaganda slogan. In both cases the insistent demand for effectiveness makes technology into psycho-technology, into a procedure for manipulating men. In both cases the standards are the striking yet familiar, the easy yet catchy, the skilful yet simple; the object is to overpower the customer, who is conceived as absent-minded or resistant.

By the language he speaks, he makes his own contribution to culture as publicity. The more completely language is lost in the announcement, the more words are debased as substantial vehicles of meaning and become signs devoid of quality; the more purely and transparently words communicate what is intended, the more impenetrable they become. The demythologization of language, taken as an element of the whole process of enlightenment, is a relapse into magic. Word and essential content were distinct yet inseparable from one another. Concepts like melancholy and history, even life, were recognized in the word, which separated them out and preserved them. Its form simultaneously constituted and reflected them. The absolute separation, which makes the moving accidental and its relation to the object arbitrary, puts an end to the superstitious fusion of word and thing. Anything in a determined literal sequence which goes beyond the correlation to the event is rejected as unclear and as verbal metaphysics. But the result is that the word, which can now be only a sign without any meaning, becomes so fixed to the thing that it is just a petrified formula. This affects language and object alike. Instead of making the object experiential, the purified word treats it as an abstract instance, and everything else (now excluded by the demand for ruthless clarity from expression — itself now banished) fades away in reality. A left-half at football, a blackshirt, a member of the Hitler Youth, and so on, are no more than names. If before its rationalization the word had given rise to lies as well as to longing, now, after its rationalization, it is a straitjacket for longing more even than for lies. The blindness and dumbness of the data to which positivism reduces the world pass over into language itself, which restricts itself to recording those data. Terms themselves become impenetrable; they obtain a striking force, a power of adhesion and repulsion which makes them like their extreme opposite, incantations. They come to be a kind of trick, because the name of the prima donna is cooked up in the studio on a statistical basis, or because a welfare state is anathematized by using taboo terms such as 'bureaucrats' or 'intellectuals', or because base practice uses the name of the country as a charm. In general, the name — to which magic most easily attaches — is undergoing a chemical change: a metamorphosis into capricious, manipulable designations, whose effect is admittedly now calculable, but which for that very reason is just as despotic as that of the archaic name. First names, those archaic remnants, have been brought up to date either by stylization as advertising trade-marks (film stars' surnames have become first names), or by collective standardization. In comparison, the bourgeois family name which, instead of being a trade-mark, once individualized its bearer by relating him to his own past history, seems antiquated. It arouses a strange embarassment in Americans. In order to hide the awkward distance between individuals, they call one another 'Bob' and 'Harry', as interchangeable team members. This practice reduces relations between human beings to the good fellowship of the sporting community and is a defense against the true kind of relationship. Signification, which is the only function of a word admitted by semantics, reaches perfection in the sign. Whether folksongs were rightly or wrongly called upper-class culture in decay, their elements have only acquired their popular form through a long process of repeated transmission. The spread of popular songs, on the other hand, takes place at lightning speed. The American expression 'fad', used for fashions which appear like epidemics — that is, inflamed by highly-concentrated economic forces — designated this phenomenon long before totalitarian advertising bosses enforced the general lines of culture. When the German Fascists decide one day to launch a word — say, 'intolerable' — over the loudspeakers the next day the whole nation is saying 'intolerable'. By the same pattern, the nations against whom the weight of the German 'blitzkrieg' was thrown took the word into their own jargon. The general repetition of names for measures to be taken by the authorities makes them, so to speak, familiar, just as the brand name on everybody's lips increased sales in the era of the free market. The blind and rapidly spreading repetition of words with special designations links advertising with the totalitarian watchword. The layer of experience which created the words for their speakers has been removed; in this swift appropriation language acquires the coldness which until now it had only on billboards and in the advertisement columns of newspapers. Innumerable people use words and expressions which they have either ceased to understand or employ only because they trigger off conditioned reflexes; in this sense, words are trade-marks which are finally all the more firmly linked to the things they denote, the less their linguistic sense is grasped. The minister for mass education talks incomprehendingly of 'dynamic forces', and the hit songs unceasingly celebrate 'reverie' and 'rhapsody', yet base their popularity precisely on the magic of the unintelligible as creating the thrill of a more exalted life. Other stereotypes, such as memory, are still partly comprehended, but escape from the experience which might allow them content. They appear like enclaves in the spoken language. On the radio of Flesch and Hitler they may be recognized from the affected pronunciation of the announcer when he says to the nation, 'Good night, everybody!' or

'This is the Hitler Youth', and even intones 'The Führer' in a way imitated by millions. In such clichés the last bond between sedimentary experience and language is severed which still had a reconciling effect in dialect in the nineteenth century. But in the prose of the journalist whose adaptable attitude led to his appointment as an all-German editor, the German words become petrified, alien terms. Every word shows how far it has been debased by the Fascist pseudo-folk community. By now, of course, this kind of language is already universal, totalitarian. All the violence done to words is so vile that one can hardly bear to hear them any longer. The announcer does not need to speak pompously; he would indeed be impossible if his inflection were different from that of his particular audience. But, as against that, the language and gestures of the audience and spectators are coloured more strongly than ever before by the culture industry, even in fine nuances which cannot yet be explained experimentally. Today the culture industry has taken over the civilizing inheritance of the entrepreneurial and frontier democracy — whose appreciation of intellectual deviations was never very finely attuned. All are free to dance and enjoy themselves, just as they have been free, since the historical neutralizaton of religion, to join any of the innumerable sects. But freedom to choose an ideology — since ideology always reflects economic coercion — everywhere proves to be freedom to choose what is always the same. The way in which a girl accepts and keeps the obligatory date, the inflection on the telephone or in the most intimate situation, the choice of words in conversation, and the whole inner life as classified by the now somewhat devalued depth psychology, bear witness to man's attempt to make himself a proficient apparatus, similar (even in emotions) to the model served up by the culture industry. The most intimate reactions of human beings have been so thoroughly reified that the idea of anything specific to themselves now persists only as an utterly abstract notion: personality scarcely signifies anything more than shining white teeth and freedom from body odor and emotions. The triumph of advertising in the culture industry is that consumers feel compelled to buy and use its products even though they see through them.

15

The Work of Art in the Age of Mechanical Reproduction

Walter Benjamin

> *Our fine arts were developed, their types and uses were established,*
> *in times very different from the present, by men whose power of action*
> *upon things was insignificant in comparison with ours. But the amazing*
> *growth of our techniques, the adaptability and precision they have*
> *attained, the ideas and habits they are creating, make it a certainty that*
> *profound changes are impending in the ancient craft of the Beautiful. In*
> *all the arts there is a physical component which can no longer be*
> *considered or treated as it used to be, which cannot remain unaffected by*
> *our modern knowledge and power. For the last twenty years neither*
> *matter nor space nor time has been what it was from time immemorial.*
> *We must expect great innovations to transform the entire technique of*
> *the arts, thereby affecting artistic invention itself and perhaps even*
> *bringing about an amazing change in our very notion of art (Valéry,*
> *1964).*

Preface

When Marx undertook his critique of the capitalistic mode of production, this mode was in its infancy. Marx directed his efforts in such a way as to give them prognostic value. He went back to the basic conditions underlying capitalistic production and through his presentation showed what could be expected of capitalism in the future. The result was that one could expect it not only to exploit the proletariat with increasing intensity, but ultimately to create conditions which would make it possible to abolish capitalism itself.

The transformation of the superstructure, which takes place far more slowly than that of the substructure, has taken more than half a century to manifest in all areas of culture the change in the conditions of production. Only today can it be indicated what form this has taken. Certain prognostic requirements should be met by these statements. However, theses about the art of the proletariat after its assumption of power or about the art of a classless society would have less bearing on these demands than theses about the developmental tendencies of art under present conditions of production. Their dialectic is no less noticeable in the superstructure than in the economy. It would therefore be wrong to underestimate the value of such theses as a weapon. They brush aside a number of outmoded concepts, such as creativity and genius, eternal value and mystery — concepts whose uncontrolled (and at present almost uncontrollable) application would lead to a processing of data in the Fascist sense. The concepts which are introduced into the theory of art in what follows differ from the more familiar terms in that they are completely useless for the purposes of Fascism. They are, on the other hand, useful for the formulation of revolutionary demands in the politics of art.

I

In principle a work of art has always been reproducible. Man-made artifacts could always be imitated by men. Replicas were made by pupils in practice of their craft, by masters for diffusing their works, and, finally, by third parties in the pursuit of gain. Mechanical reproduction of a work of art, however, represents something new. Historically, it advanced intermittently and in leaps at long intervals, but with accelerated intensity. The Greeks knew only two procedures of technically reproducing works of art: founding and stamping. Bronzes, terra cottas, and coins were the only art works which they could produce in quantity. All others were unique and could not be mechanically reproduced. With the woodcut graphic art became mechanically reproducible for the first time, long before script became reproducible by print. The enormous changes which printing, the mechanical reproduction of writing, has brought about in literature are a familiar story. However, within the phenomenon which we are here examining from the perspective of world history, print is merely a special, though particularly important, case. During the Middle Ages engraving and etching were added to the woodcut; at the beginning of the nineteenth century lithography made its appearance.

With lithography the technique of reproduction reached an essentially new stage. This much more direct process was distinguished by the tracing of the design on a stone rather than its incision on a block of wood or its etching on a copperplate and permitted graphic art for the first time to put its products on the market, not only in large numbers as hitherto, but also in daily changing forms. Lithography enabled graphic art to illustrate everyday life, and it began to keep pace with printing. But only a few decades after its invention, lithography was surpassed by photography. For the first time in the process of pictorial reproduction, photography freed the hand of the most important artistic functions which henceforth devolved only upon the eye looking into a lens. Since the eye perceives more swiftly than the hand can draw, the process of pictorial reproduction was accelerated so enormously that it could keep pace with speech. A film operator shooting a scene in the studio captures the images at the speed of an actor's speech. Just as lithography virtually implied the illustrated newspaper, so did photography foreshadow the sound film. The technical reproduction of sound was tackled at the end of the last century. These convergent endeavors made predictable a situation which Paul Valéry pointed up in this sentence: 'Just as water, gas, and electricity are brought into our houses from far off to satisfy our needs in response to a minimal effort, so we shall be supplied with visual or auditory images, which will appear and disappear at a simple movement of the hand, hardly more than a sign' (Valéry. 1964). Around 1900 technical reproduction had reached a standard that not only permitted it to reproduce all transmitted works of art and thus to cause the most profound change in their impact upon the public; it also had captured a place of its own among the artistic processes. For the study of this standard nothing is more revealing than the nature of the repercussions that these two different manifestations — the reproduction of works of art and the art of the film — have had on art in its traditional form.

II

Even the most perfect reproduction of a work of art is lacking in one element: its presence in time and space, its unique existence at the place where it happens to be. This unique existence of the work of art determined the history to which it was subject throughout the time of its existence. This includes the changes which it may have suffered in physical condition over the years as well as the various changes in its ownership.[1] The traces of the first can be revealed only by chemical or physical analyses which it is impossible to perform on a reproduction; changes of ownership are subject to a tradition which must be traced from the situation of the original.

The presence of the original is the prerequisite to the concept of authenticity. Chemical analyses of the patina of a bronze can help to establish this, as does the proof that a given manuscript of the Middle Ages stems from an archive of the fifteenth century. The whole sphere of authenticity is outside technical — and, of course, not only technical — reproducibility.[2]

1   Of course, the history of a work of art encompasses more than this. The history of the 'Mona Lisa', for instance, encompasses the kind and number of its copies made in the 17th, 18th, and 19th centuries.
2   Precisely because authenticity is not reproducible, the intensive penetration of certain (mechanical) processes of reproduction was instrumental in differentiating and grading authenticity. To develop such differentiations was an important func-

Confronted with its manual reproduction, which was usually branded as a forgery, the original preserved all its authority; not so *vis à vis* technical reproduction. The reason is twofold. First, process reproduction is more independent of the original than manual reproduction. For example, in photography, process reproduction can bring out those aspects of the original that are unattainable to the naked eye yet accessible to the lens, which is adjustable and choses its angle at will. And photographic reproduction, with the aid of certain processes, such as enlargement or slow motion, can capture images which escape natural vision. Second, technical reproduction can put the copy of the original into situations which would be out of reach for the original itself. Above all, it enables the original to meet the beholder halfway, be it in the form of a photograph or a phonograph record. The cathedral leaves its locale to be received in the studio of a lover of art; the choral production, performed in an auditorium or in the open air, resounds in the drawing room.

The situations into which the product of mechanical reproduction can be brought may not touch the actual work of art, yet the quality of its presence is always depreciated. This holds not only for the art work but also, for instance, for a landscape which passes in review before the spectator in a movie. In the case of the art object, a most sensitive nucleus — namely, its authenticity — is interfered with whereas no natural object is vulnerable on that score. The authenticity of a thing is the essence of all that is transmissible from its beginning, ranging from its substantive duration to its testimony to the history which it has experienced. Since the historical testimony rests on the authenticity, the former, too, is jeopardized by reproduction when substantive duration ceases to matter. And what is really jeopardized when the historical testimony is affected is the authority of the object.[3]

One might subsume the eliminated element in the term 'aura' and go on to say: that which withers in the age of mechanical reproduction is the aura of the work of art. This is a symptomatic process whose significance points beyond the realm of art. One might generalize by saying: the technique of reproduction detaches the reproduced object from the domain of tradition. By making many reproductions it substitutes a plurality of copies for a unique existence. And in permitting the reproduction to

tion of the trade in works of art. The invention of the woodcut may be said to have struck at the root of the quality of authenticity even before its late flowering. To be sure, at the time of its origin a medieval picture of the Madonna could not yet be said to be 'authentic'. It became 'authentic' only during the succeeding centuries and perhaps most strikingly so during the last one.

3   The poorest provincial staging of *Faust* is superior to a Faust film in that, ideally, it competes with the first performance at Weimar. Before the screen it is unprofitable to remember traditional contents which might come to mind before the stage — for instance, that Goethe's friend Johann Heinrich Merck is hidden in Mephisto, and the like.

meet the beholder or listener in his own particular situation, it reactivates the object reproduced. These two processes lead to a tremendous shattering of tradition which is the obverse of the contemporary crisis and renewal of mankind. Both processes are intimately connected with the contemporary mass movements. Their most powerful agent is the film. Its social significance, particularly in its most positive form, is inconceivable without its destructive, cathartic aspect, that is, the liquidation of the traditional value of the cultural heritage. This phenomenon is most palpable in the great historical films. It extends to ever new positions. In 1927 Abel Gance exclaimed enthusiastically: 'Shakespeare, Rembrandt, Beethoven will make films . . . all legends, all mythologies and all myths, all founders of religion, and the very religions . . . await their exposed resurrection, and the heroes crowd each other at the gate' (Gance, 1927). Presumably without intending it, he issued an invitation to a far-reaching liquidation.

III

During long periods of history, the mode of human sense perception changes with humanity's entire mode of existence. The manner in which human sense perception is organized, the medium in which it is accomplished, is determined not only by nature but by historical circumstances as well. The fifth century, with its great shifts of population, saw the birth of the late Roman art industry and the Vienna Genesis, and there developed not only an art different from that of antiquity but also a new kind of perception. The scholars of the Viennese school, Riegl and Wickhoff, who resisted the weight of classical tradition under which these later art forms had been buried, were the first to draw conclusions from them concerning the organization of perception at the time. However far-reaching their insight, these scholars limited themselves to showing the significant, formal hallmark which characterized perception in late Roman times. They did not attempt — and, perhaps, saw no way — to show the social transformations expressed by these changes of perception. The conditions for an analogous insight are more favorable in the present. And if changes in the medium of contemporary perception can be comprehended as decay of the aura, it is possible to show its social causes.

The concept of aura which was proposed above with reference to historical objects may usefully be illustrated with reference to the aura of natural ones. We define the aura of the latter as the unique phenomenon of a distance, however close it may be. If, while resting on a summer afternoon, you follow with your eyes a mountain range on the horizon or a branch which casts its shadow over you, you experience the aura of those mountains, of that branch. This image makes it easy to comprehend the social bases of the contemporary decay of the aura. It rests on two circumstances, both of which are related to the increasing significance of the masses in contemporary life. Namely, the desire of contemporary masses to bring things 'closer' spatially and humanly, which is just as ardent as their bent toward overcoming the uniqueness of every reality by accepting its reproduction.[4] Every day the urge grows stronger to get hold of an object at very close range by way of its likeness, its reproduction. Unmistakably, reproduction as offered by picture magazines and newsreels differs from the image seen by the unarmed eye. Uniqueness and permanence are as closely linked in the latter as are transitoriness and reproducibility in the former. To pry an object from its shell, to destroy its aura, is the mark of a perception whose 'sense of the universal equality of things' has increased to such a degree that it extracts it even from a unique object by means of reproduction. Thus is manifested in the field of perception what in the theoretical sphere is noticeable in the increasing importance of statistics. The adjustment of reality to the masses and of the masses to reality is a process of unlimited scope, as much for thinking as for perception.

IV

The uniqueness of a work of art is inseparable from its being imbedded in the fabric of tradition. This tradition itself is thoroughly alive and extremely changeable. An ancient statue of Venus, for example, stood in a different traditional context with the Greeks, who made it an object of veneration, than with the clerics of the Middle Ages, who viewed it as an ominous idol. Both of them, however, were equally confronted with its uniqueness, that is, its aura. Originally the contextual integration of art in tradition found its expression in the cult. We know that the earliest art works originated in the service of a ritual — first the magical, then the religious kind. It is significant that the existence of the work of art with reference to its aura is never entirely separated from its ritual function.[5] In other words, the unique value of the 'authentic' work of art has its basis in ritual, the location of its original use value. This ritualistic basis, however remote, is still recog-

---

4 To satisfy the human interest of the masses may mean to have one's social function removed from the field of vision. Nothing guarantees that a portraitist of today, when painting a famous surgeon at the breakfast table in the midst of his family, depicts his social function more precisely than a painter of the 17th century who portrayed his medical doctors as representing this profession, like Rembrandt in his 'Anatomy Lesson'.

5 The definition of the aura as a 'unique phenomenon of a distance however close it may be' represents nothing but the formulation of the cult value of the work of art in categories of space and time perception. Distance is the opposite of closeness. The essentially distant object is the unapproachable one. Unapproachability is indeed a major quality of the cult image. True to its nature, it remains 'distant, however close it may be'. The closeness which one may gain from its subject matter does not impair the distance which it retains in its appearance.

nizable as secularized ritual even in the most profane forms of the cult of beauty.[6] The secular cult of beauty, developed during the Renaissance and prevailing for three centuries, clearly showed that ritualistic basis in its decline and the first deep crisis which befell it. With the advent of the first truly revolutionary means of reproduction, photography, simultaneously with the rise of socialism, art sensed the approaching crisis which has become evident a century later. At the time, art reacted with the doctrine of *'l'art pour l'art'*, that is, with a theology of art. This gave rise to what might be called a negative theology in the form of the idea of 'pure' art, which not only denied any social function of art but also any categorizing by subject matter. (In poetry, Mallarmé was the first to take this position.)

An analysis of art in the age of mechanical reproduction must do justice to these relationships, for they lead us to an all-important insight: for the first time in world history, mechanical reproduction emancipates the work of art from its parasitical dependence on ritual. To an ever greater degree the work of art reproduced becomes the work of art designed for reproducibility.[7] From a photographic negative, for example, one can make any number of prints; to ask for the 'authentic' print makes no sense. But

6   To the extent to which the cult value of the painting is secularized the ideas of its fundamental uniqueness lose distinctness. In the imagination of the beholder the the uniqueness of the phenomena which hold sway in the cult image is more and more displaced by the empirical uniqueness of the creator or of his creative achievement. To be sure, never completely so; the concept of authenticity always transcends mere genuineness. (This is particularly apparent in the collector who always retains some traces of the fetishist and who, by owning the work of art, shares in its ritual power.) Nevertheless, the function of the concept of authenticity remains determinate in the evaluation of art; with the secularization of art, authenticity displaces the cult value of the work.

7   In the case of films, mechanical reproduction is not, as with literature and painting, an external condition for mass distribution. Mechanical reproduction is inherent in the very technique of film production. This technique not only permits in the most direct way but virtually causes mass distribution. It enforces distribution because the production of a film is so expensive that an individual who, for instance, might afford to buy a painting no longer can afford to buy a film. In 1927 it was calculated that a major film, in order to pay its way, had to reach an audience of nine million. With the sound film, to be sure, a setback in its international distribution occurred at first: audiences became limited by language barriers. This coincided with the Fascist emphasis on national interests. It is more important to focus on this connection with Fascism than on this setback, which was soon minimized by synchronization. The simultaneity of both phenomena is attributable to the depression. The same disturbances which, on a larger scale, led to an attempt to maintain the existing property structure by sheer force led the endangered film capital to speed up the development of the sound film. The introduction of the sound film brought about a temporary relief, not only because it again brought the masses into the theaters but also because it merged new capital from the electrical industry with that of the film industry. Thus, viewed from the outside, the sound film promoted national interests, but seen from the inside it helped to internationalize film production even more than previously.

the instant the criterion of authenticity ceases to be applicable to artistic production, the total function of art is reversed. Instead of being based on ritual, it begins to be based on another practice — politics.

V

Works of art are received and valued on different planes. Two polar types stand out: with one, the accent is on the cult value; with the other, on the exhibition value of the work.[8] Artistic production begins with ceremonial objects destined to serve in a cult. One may assume that what mattered was their existence, not their being on view. The elk portrayed by the man of the Stone Age on the walls of his cave was an instrument of magic. He did expose it to his fellow men, but in the main it was meant for the spirits. Today the cult value would seem to demand that the work of art remain hidden. Certain statues of gods are accessible only to the priest in the cella; certain Madonnas remain covered nearly all year round; certain sculptures on medieval cathedrals are invisible to the spectator on ground level. With the emancipation of the various art practices from ritual go increasing opportunities for the exhibition of their products. It is easier to exhibit a portrait bust that can be sent here and there than to exhibit the statue of a divinity that has its fixed place in the interior of a temple. The same holds for the painting as against the mosaic or fresco that preceded it. And even though the public presentability of a mass originally may have been just as great as that of a symphony, the latter originated at the moment when its public presentability promised to surpass that of the mass.

With the different methods of technical reproduction of work of art, its fitness for exhibition increased to such an extent that the quantitative shift between its two poles turned into a qualitative transformation of its nature. This is comparable to the situation of the work of art in prehistoric times when, by the absolute emphasis on its cult value, it was, first and foremost, an instrument of magic. Only later did it come to be recognized as a work of art. In the same way today, by the absolute emphasis on its exhibition value the work of art becomes a creation with entirely new

8   This polarity cannot come into its own in the aesthetics of Idealism. Its idea of beauty comprises these polar opposites without differentiating between them and consequently excludes their polarity. Yet in Hegel this polarity announces itself as clearly as possible within the limits of Idealism. We quote from his *Philosophy of History*:
   Images were known of old. Piety at an early time required them for worship, but it could do without *beautiful* images. These might even be disturbing, In every beautiful painting there is also something nonspiritual, merely external, but its spirit speaks to man through its beauty. Worshipping, conversely, is concerned with the work as an object, for it is but a spiritless stupor of the soul. . . . Fine art has arisen . . . in the church . . . , although it has already gone beyond its principle as art.

functions, among which the one we are conscious of, the artistic function, later may be recognized as incidental.[9] This much is certain: today photography and the film are the most serviceable exemplifications of this new function.

VI

In photography, exhibition value begins to displace cult value all along the line. But cult value does not give way without resistance. It retires into an ultimate retrenchment: the human countenance. It is no accident that the portrait was the focal point of early photography. The cult of remembrance of loved ones, absent or dead, offers a last refuge for the cult value of the picture. For the last time the aura emanates from the early photographs in

---

Likewise, the following passage from *The Philosophy of Fine Art* indicates that Hegel sensed a problem here.

> We are beyond the stage of reverence for works of art as divine and objects deserving our worship. The impression they produce is one of a more reflective kind, and the emotions they arouse require a higher test. . . . G. W. F. Hegel, *The Philosophy of Fine Art*, trans., with notes, by F. P. B. Osmaston, Vol. 1, p. 12, London, 1920.

The transition from the first kind of artistic reception to the second characterizes the history of artistic reception in general. Apart from that, a certain oscillation between these two polar modes of reception can be demonstrated for each work of art. Take the Sistine Madonna. Since Hubert Grimme's research it has been known that the Madonna originally was painted for the purpose of exhibition. Grimme's research was inspired by the question: What is the purpose of the molding in the foreground of the painting which the two cupids lean upon? How, Grimme asked further, did Raphael come to furnish the sky with two draperies? Research proved that the Madonna had been commissioned for the public lying-in-state of Pope Sixtus. The Popes lay in state in a certain side chapel of St. Peter's. On that occasion Raphael's picture had been fastened in a niche-like background of the chapel, supported by the coffin. In this picture Raphael portrays the Madonna approaching the papal coffin in clouds from the background of the niche, which was demarcated by green drapes. At the obséquies of Sixtus a pre-eminent exhibition value of Raphael's picture was taken advantage of. Some time later it was placed on the high altar in the church of the Black Friars of Piacenza. The reason for this exile is to be found in the Roman rites which forbid the use of paintings exhibited at obsequies as cult objects on the high altar. This regulation devalued Raphael's picture to some degree. In order to obtain an adequate price nevertheless, the Papal See resolved to add to the bargain the tacit toleration of the picture above the high altar. To avoid attention the picture was given to the monks of the far-off provincial town.

9 Bertolt Brecht, on a different level, engaged in analogous reflections: 'If the concept of "work of art" can no longer be applied to the thing that emerges once the work is transformed into a commodity, we have to eliminate this concept of the very thing as well. For it has to go through this phase without mental reservation, and not as noncommittal deviation from the straight path; rather, what happens here with the work of art will change it fundamentally and erase its past to such an extent that should the old concept be taken up again — and it will, why not?— it will no longer stir any memory of the thing it once designated'.

the fleeting expression of a human face. This is what constitutes their melancholy, incomparable beauty. But as man withdraws from the photographic image, the exhibition value for the first time shows its superiority to the ritual value. To have pinpointed this new stage constitutes the incomparable significance of Atget, who, around 1900, took photographs of deserted Paris streets. It has quite justly been said of him that he photographed them like scenes of crime. The scene of a crime, too, is deserted; it is photographed for the purpose of establishing evidence. With Atget, photographs become standard evidence for historical occurrences, and acquire a hidden political significance. They demand a specific kind of approach; free-floating contemplation is not appropriate to them. They stir the viewer; he feels challenged by them in a new way. At the same time picture magazines begin to put up signposts for him, right ones or wrong ones, no matter. For the first time, captions have become obligatory. And it is clear that they have an altogether different character than the title of a painting. The directives which the captions give to those looking at pictures in illustrated magazines soon become even more explicit and more imperative in the film where the meaning of each single picture appears to be prescribed by the sequence of all preceding ones.

VII

The nineteenth-century dispute as to the artistic value of painting versus photography today seems devious and confused. This does not diminish its importance, however, if anything, it underlines it. The dispute was in fact the symptom of a historical transformation the universal impact of which was not realized by either of the rivals. When the age of mechanical reproduction separated art from its basis in cult, the semblance of its autonomy disappeared forever. The resulting change in the function of art transcended the perspective of the century; for a long time it even escaped that of the twentieth century, which experienced the development of the film.

Earlier much futile thought had been devoted to the question of whether photography is an art. The primary, question — whether the very invention of photography had not transformed the entire nature of art — was not raised. Soon the film theoreticians asked the same ill-considered question with regard to the film. But the difficulties which photography caused traditional aesthetics were mere child's play as compared to those raised by the film. Whence the insensitive and forced character of early theories of the film. Abel Gance, for instance, compares the film with hieroglyphs: 'Here, by a remarkable regression, we have come back to the level of expression of the Egyptians . . . . Pictorial language has not yet matured because our eyes have not yet adjusted to it. There is as yet insufficient respect for, insufficient cult of, what it expresses' (Gance, 1927). Or, in the words of Séverin-

Mars: 'What art has been granted a dream more poetical and more real at the same time! Approached in this fashion the film might represent an incomparable means of expression. Only the most high-minded persons, in the most perfect and mysterious moments of their lives, should be allowed to enter its ambience' (Séverin-Mars, quoted by Gance). Alexandre Arnoux concludes his fantasy about the silent film with the question: 'Do not all the bold descriptions we have given amount to the definition of prayer?' (Arnoux, 1929). It is instructive to note how their desire to class the film among the 'arts' forces these theoreticians to read ritual elements into it — with a striking lack of discretion. Yet when these speculations were published, films like *L'Opinion Publique* and *The Gold Rush* had already appeared. This, however, did not keep Abel Gance from adducing hieroglyphs for the purposes of comparison nor Séverin-Mars from speaking of the film as one might speak of paintings by Fra Angelico. Characteristically, even today ultrareactionary authors give the film a similar contextual significance — if not an outright scared one, then at least a supernatural one. Commenting on Max Reinhardt's film version of *A Midsummer Night's Dream,* Werfel states that undoubtedly it was the sterile copying of the exterior world with its streets, interiors, railroad stations, restaurants, motocars, and beaches which until now had obstructed the elevation of the film to the realm of art. 'The film has not yet realized its true meaning, its real possibilities . . . these consist in its unique faculty to express by natural means and with incomparable persuasiveness all that is fairylike, marvelous, supernatural'. (Werfel, 1935.)

VIII

The artistic performance of a stage actor is definitely presented to the public by the actor in person; that of the screen actor, however, is presented by a camera, with a twofold consequence. The camera that presents the performance of the film actor to the public need not respect the performance as an integral whole. Guided by the cameraman, the camera continually changes its position with respect to the performance. The sequence of positional views which the editor composes from the material supplied him constitutes the completed film. It comprises certain factors of movement which are in reality those of the camera, not to mention special camera angles, close-ups, etc. Hence, the performance of the actor is subjected to a series of optical tests. This is the first consequence of the fact that the actor's performance is presented by means of a camera. Also, the film actor lacks the opportunity of the stage actor to adjust to the audience during his performance, since he does not present his performance to the audience in person. This permits the audience to take the position of a critic, without experiencing any personal contact with the actor. The audience's identification with the actor is really an identification with the camera. Consequently the audience takes the position of the camera, its approach is that of testing.[10] This is not the approach to which cult values may be exposed.

IX

For the film, what matters primarily is that the actor represents himself to the public before the camera, rather than representing someone else. One of the first to sense the actor's metamorphosis by this form of testing was Pirandello. Though his remarks on the subject in his novel *Si Gira* were limited to the negative aspects of the question and to the silent film only, this hardly impairs their validity. For in this respect, the sound film did not change anything essential. What matters is that the part is acted not for an audience but for a mechanical contrivance — in the case of the sound film, for two of them. 'The film actor', wrote Pirandello, 'feels as if in exile — not only from the stage but also from himself. With a vague sense of discomfort he feels inexplicable emptiness: his body loses its corporeality, it evaporates, it is deprived of reality, life, voice, and the noises caused by his moving about, in order to be changed into a mute image, flickering an instant on the screen, then vanishing into silence . . . . The projector will play with his shadow before the public, and he himself must be content to play before the camera'. This situation might be characterized as follows: for the first time — and this is the effect of the film — man has to operate with his whole living person, yet forgoing its aura. For aura is tied to his presence; there can be no replica of it. The aura which, on the stage, emanates from Macbeth, cannot be separated for the spectators from that of the actor. However, the singularity of the shot in the studio is that the camera is substituted for the public. Consequently, the aura that envelops the actor vanishes, and with it the aura of the figure he portrays.

It is not surprising that is should be a dramatist such as Pirandello who, in characterizing the film, inadvertently touches on the very crisis in which we see the theater. Any thorough study proves that there is indeed no

10 'The film . . . provides — or could provide — useful insight into the details of human actions . . . . Character is never used as a source of motivation; the inner life of the persons never supplies the principal cause of the plot and seldom is its main result'. (Bertolt Brecht, *Versuche*, 'Der Dreigroschenprozess', p. 268.) The expansion of the field of the testable which mechanical equipment brings about for the actor corresponds to the extraordinary expansion of the field of the testable brought about for the individual through economic conditions. Thus, vocational aptitude tests become constantly more important. What matters in these tests are segmental performances of the individual. The film shot and the vocational aptitude test are taken before a committee of experts. The camera director in the studio occupies a place identical with that of the examiner during aptitude tests.

greater contrast than that of the stage play to a work of art that is completely subject to or, like the film, founded in, mechanical reproduction. Experts have long recognized that in the film 'the greatest effects are almost always obtained by "acting" as little as possible . . .'. In 1932 Rudolf Arnheim saw 'the latest trend . . . in treating the actor as a stage prop chosen for its characteristics and . . . inserted as the proper place'.[11] With this idea something else is closely connected. The stage actor identifies himself with the character of his role. The film actor very often is denied this opportunity. His creation is by no means all of a piece; it is composed of many separate performances. Besides certain fortuitous considerations, such as cost of studio, availability of fellow players, décor, etc., there are elementary necessities of equipment that split the actor's work into a series of mountable episodes. In particular, lighting and its installation require the presentation of an event that, on the screen, unfolds as a rapid and unified scene, in a sequence of separate shootings which may take hours at the studio; not to mention more obvious montage. Thus a jump from the window can be shot in the studio as a jump from a scaffold, and the ensuing flight, if need be, can be shot weeks later when outdoor scenes are taken. Far more paradoxical cases can easily be construed. Let us assume that an actor is supposed to be startled by a knock at the door. If his reaction is not satisfactory, the director can resort to an expedient: when the actor happens to be at the studio again he has a shot fired behind him without his being forewarned of it. The frightened reaction can be shot now and be cut into the screen version.

11 Rudolf Arnheim, *Film als Kunst*, Berlin, 1932, pp. 176 f. In this context certain seemingly unimportant details in which the film director deviates from stage practices gain in interest. Such is the attempt to let the actor play without make-up, as made among others by Dreyer in his *Jeanne d'Arc*. Dreyer spent months seeking the forty actors who constitute the Inquisitors' tribunal. The search for these actors resembled that for stage properties that are hard to come by. Dreyer made every effort to avoid resemblances of age, build, and physiognomy. If the actor becomes a stage property, this latter, on the other hand, frequently functions as actor. At least it is not unusual for the film to assign a role to the stage property. Instead of choosing at random from a great wealth of examples, let us concentrate on a particularly convincing one. A clock that is working will always be a disturbance on the stage. There it cannot be permitted its function of measuring time. Even in a naturalistic play, astronomical time would clash with theatrical time. Under these circumstances it is highly revealing that the film can, whenever appropriate, use time as measured by a clock. From this more than from many other touches it may clearly be recognized that under certain circumstances each and every prop in a film may assume important functions. From here it is but one step to Pudovkin's statement that 'the playing of an actor which is connected with an object and is built around it . . . is always one of the strongest methods of cinematic construction' (W. Pudovkin, *Filmregie und Filmmanuskript*, Berlin, 1928, p. 126)'. The film is the first art form capable of demonstrating how matter plays tricks on man. Hence, films can be an excellent means of materialistic representation.

Nothing more strikingly shows that art has left the realm of the 'beautiful semblance' which, so far, had been taken to be the only sphere where are could thrive.

X

The feeling of strangeness that overcomes the actor before the camera, as Pirandello describes it, is basically of the same kind as the estrangement felt before one's own image in the mirror. But now the reflected image has become separable, transportable. And where is it transported? Before the public.[12] Never for a moment does the screen actor cease to be conscious of this fact. While facing the camera he knows that ultimately he will face the public, the consumers who constitute the market. This market, where he offers not only his labor but also his whole self, his heart and soul, is beyond his reach. During the shooting he has as little contact with it as any article made in a factory. This may contribute to that oppression, that new anxiety which, according to Pirandello, grips the actor before the camera. The film responds to the shriveling of the aura with an artificial build-up of the 'personality' outside the studio. The cult of the movie star, fostered by the money of the film industry, preserves not the unique aura of the person but the spell of the personality, the phony spell of a commodity. So long as the movie-makers' capital sets the fashion, as a rule no other revolutionary merit can be acredited to today's film than the promotion of a revolutionary criticism of traditional concepts of art. We do not deny that in some cases today's films can also promote revolutionary criticism of social conditions, even of the distribution of property. However, our present study is no more specifically concerned with this than is the film production of Western Europe.

It is inherent in the technique of the film as well as that of sports that everybody who witnesses its accomplishments is somewhat of an expert. This is obvious to anyone listening to a group of newspaper boys leaning on their bicycles and discussing the outcome of a bicycle race. It is not

12 The change noted here in the method of exhibition caused by mechanical reproduction applies to politics as well. The present crisis of the bourgeois democracies comprises a crisis of the conditions which determine the public presentation of the rulers. Democracies exhibit a member of government directly and personally before the nation's representatives. Parliament is his public. Since the innovations of camera and recording equipment make it possible for the orator to become audible and visible to an unlimited number of persons, the presentation of the man of politics before camera and recording equipment becomes paramount. Parliaments, as much as theaters, are deserted. Radio and film not only affect the function of the professional actor but likewise the function of those who also exhibit themselves before this mechanical equipment, those who govern. Though their tasks may be different, the change affects equally the actor and the ruler. The trend is toward establishing controllable and transferrable skills under certain social conditions. This results in a new selection, a selection before the equipment from which the star and the dictator emerge victorious.

for nothing that newspaper publishers arrange races for their delivery boys. These arouse great interest among the participants, for the victor has an opportunity to rise from delivery boy to professional racer. Similarly, the newsreel offers everyone the opportunity to rise from passer-by to movie extra. In this way any man might even find himself part of a work of art, as witness Vertoff's *Three Songs About Lenin* or Ivens' *Borinage*. Any man today can lay claim to being filmed. This claim can best be elucidated by a comparative look at the historical situation of contemporary literature.

For centuries a small number of writers were confronted by many thousands of readers. This changed toward the end of the last century. With the increasing extension of the press, which kept placing new political, religious, scientific, professional, and local organs before the readers, an increasing number of readers became writers — at first, occasional ones. It began with the daily press opening to its readers space for 'letters to the editor'. And today there is hardly a gainfully employed European who could not, in principle, find an opportunity to publish somewhere or other comments on his work, grievances, documentary reports, or that sort of thing. Thus, the distinction between author and public is about to lose its basic character. The difference becomes merely functional; it may vary from case to case. At any moment the reader is ready to turn into a writer. As expert, which he had to become willy-nilly in an extremely specialized work process, even if only in some minor respect, the reader gains access to authorship. In the Soviet Union work itself is given a voice. To present it verbally is part of a man's ability to perform the work. Literary license is now founded on polytechnic rather than specialized training and thus becomes common property.[13]

13 The privileged character of the respective techniques is lost. Aldous Huxley writes:
Advances in technology have led . . . to vulgarity. . . . Process reproduction and the rotary press have made possible the indefinite multiplication of writing and pictures. Universal education and relatively high wages have created an enormous public who know how to read and can afford to buy reading and pictorial matter. A great industry has been called into existence in order to supply these commodities. Now, artistic talent is a very rare phenomenon; whence it follows . . . that, at every epoch and in all countries, most art has been bad. But the proportion of trash in the total artistic output is greater now than at any other period. That it must be so is a matter of simple arithmetic. The population of Western Europe has a little more than doubled during the last century. But the amount of reading — and seeing — matter has increased, I should imagine, at least twenty and possibly fifty or even a hundred times. If there were n men of talent in a population of x millions, there will presumably be 2n men of talent among 2x millions. The situation may be summed up thus. For every page of print and pictures published a century ago, twenty or perhaps even a hundred pages are published today. But for every man of talent then living, there are now only two men of talent. It may be of course that, thanks to universal education, many potential talents which in the past would have been stillborn are now enabled to realize themselves. Let us assume, then, that there are now three or even four men of talent to every one of earlier times.

All this can easily be applied to the film, where transitions that in literature took centuries have come about in a decade. In cinematic practice, particularly in Russia, this change-over has partially become established reality. Some of the players whom we meet in Russian films are not actors in our sense but people who portray *themselves* — and primarily in their own work process. In Western Europe the capitalistic exploitation of the film denies consideration to modern man's legitimate claim to being reproduced. Under these circumstances the film industry is trying hard to spur the interest of the masses through illusion-promoting spectacles and dubious speculations.

XI

The shooting of a film, especially of a sound film, affords a spectacle unimaginable anywhere at any time before this. It presents a process in which it is impossible to assign to a spectator a viewpoint which would exclude from the actual scene such extraneous accessories as camera equipment, lighting machinery, staff assistants, etc. — unless his eye were on a line parallel with the lens. This circumstance, more than any other, renders superficial and insignificant any possible similarity between a scene in the studio and one on the stage. In the theater one is well aware of the place from which the play cannot immediately be detected as illusionary. There is no such place for the movie scene that is being shot. Its illusionary nature is that of the second degree, the result of cutting. That is to say, in the studio the mechanical equipment has penetrated so deeply into reality that its pure aspect freed from the foreign substance of equipment is the result of a special procedure, namely, the shooting by the specially adjusted camera and the mounting of the shot together with similar ones. The equipment-free aspect of reality here has become the height of artifice; the sight of immediate reality has become an orchid in the land of technology.

Even more revealing is the comparison of these circumstances, which differ so much from those of the theater, with the situation in painting. Here the question is: How does the cameraman compare with the painter?

It still remains true to say that the consumption of reading — and seeing — matter has far outstripped the natural production of gifted writers and draughtsmen. It is the same with hearing-matter. Prosperity, the gramophone and the matter that has increased out of all proportion to the increase of population and the consequent natural increase of talented musicians. It follows from all this that in all the arts the output of trash is both absolutely and relatively greater than it was in the past; and that it must remain greater for just so long as the world continues to consume the present inordinate quantities of reading-matter, seeing-matter, and hearing-matter. (Aldous Huxley, *Beyond the Mexique Bay. A Traveller's Journal*, London, 1949, pp. 274 ff. First published in 1934.) This mode of observation is obviously not progressive.

To answer this we take recourse to an analogy with a surgical operation. The surgeon represents the polar opposite of the magician. The magician heals a sick person by the laying on of hands; the surgeon cuts into the patient's body. The magician maintains the natural distance between the patient and himself; though he reduces it very slightly by the laying on of hands, he greatly increases it by virtue of his authority. The surgeon does exactly the reverse; he greatly diminishes the distance between himself and the patient by penetrating into the patient's body, and increases it but little by the caution with which his hand moves among the organs. In short, in contrast to the magician — who is still hidden in the medical practitioner — the surgeon at the decisive moment abstains from facing the patient man to man; rather, it is through the operation that he penetrates into him.

Magician and surgeon compare to painter and cameraman. The painter maintains in his work a natural distance from reality, the cameraman penetrates deeply into its web.[14] There is a tremendous difference between the pictures they obtain. That of the painter is a total one, that of the cameraman consists of multiple fragments which are assembled under a new law. Thus, for contemporary man the representation of reality by the film is incomparably more significant than that of the painter, since it offers, precisely because of the thoroughgoing permeation of reality with mechanical equipment, an aspect of reality which is free of all equipment. And that is what one is entitled to ask from a work of art.

XII

Mechanical reproduction of art changes the reaction of the masses toward art. The reactionary attitude toward a Picasso painting changes into the progressive reaction toward a Chaplin movie. The progressive reaction is characterized by the direct, intimate fusion of visual and emotional enjoyment with the orientation of the expert. Such fusion is of great social significance. The greater the decrease in the social significance of an art form, the sharper the distinction between criticism and enjoyment by the public. The conventional is uncritically enjoyed, and the truly new is

14 The boldness of the cameraman is indeed comparable to that of the surgeon. Luc Durtain lists among specific technical sleights of hand those 'which are required in surgery in the case of certain difficult operations. I choose as an example a case from oto-rhinolaryngology; . . . the so-called endonasal perspective procedure; or I refer to the acrobatic tricks of larynx surgery which have to be performed following the reversed picture in the laryngoscope. I might also speak of ear surgery which suggests the precision work of watchmakers. What range of the most subtle muscular acrobatics is required from the man who wants to repair or save the human body! We have only to think of the couching of a cataract where there is virtually a debate of steel with nearly fluid tissue, or of the major abdominal operations (laparotomy)'. — Luc Durtain, *op. cit.*

criticized with aversion. With regard to the screen, the critical and the receptive attitudes of the public coincide. The decisive reason for this is that individual reactions are predetermined by the mass audience response they are about to produce, and this is nowhere more pronounced than in the film. The moment these responses become manifest they control each other. Again, the comparison with painting is fruitful. A painting has always had an excellent chance to be viewed by one person or by a few. The simultaneous contemplation of paintings by a large public, such as developed in the nineteenth century, is an early symptom of the crisis of painting, a crisis which was by no means occasioned exclusively by photography but rather in a relatively independent manner by the appeal of art works to the masses.

Painting simply is in no position to present an object for simultaneous collective experience, as it was possible for architecture at all times, for the epic poem in the past, and for the movie today. Although this circumstance in itself should not lead one to conclusions about the social role of painting, it does constitute a serious threat as soon as painting, under special conditions and, as it were, against its nature, is confronted directly by the masses. In the churches and monasteries of the Middle Ages and at the princely courts up to the end of the eighteenth century, a collective reception of paintings did not occur simultaneously, but by graduated and hierarchized mediation. The change that has come about is an expression of the particular conflict in which painting was implicated by the mechanical reproducibility of paintings. Although paintings began to be publicly exhibited in galleries and salons, there was no way for the masses to organize and control themselves in their reception.[15] Thus the same public which responds in a progressive manner toward a grotesque film is bound to respond in a reactionary manner to surrealism.

XIII

The characteristics of the film lie not only in the manner in which man presents himself to mechanical equipment but also in the manner in which, by means of this apparatus, man can represent his environment. A glance at occupational psychology illustrates it in a different perspective. The film has enriched our field of perception with methods which can be illustrated by those of Freudian theory. Fifty years ago, a slip of the tongue passed more or less unnoticed. Only exceptionally may such a slip have re-

15 This mode of observation may seem crude, but as the great theoretician Leonardo has shown, crude modes of observation may at times be usefully adduced. Leonardo compares painting and music as follows: 'Painting is superior to music because, unlike unfortunate music, it does not have to die as soon as it is born. . . . Music which is consumed in the very act of its birth is inferior to painting which the use of varnish has rendered eternal'. (Trattato I, 29.)

vealed dimensions of depth in a conversation which had seemed to be taking its course on the surface. Since the *Psychopathology of Everyday Life* things have changed. This book isolated and made analysable things which had heretofore floated along unnoticed in the broad stream of perception. For the entire spectrum of optical, and now also acoustical, perception the film has brought about a similar deepening of apperception. It is only an obverse of this fact that behavior items shown in a movie can be analysed much more precisely and from more points of view than those presented on paintings or on the stage. As compared with painting, filmed behavior lends itself more readily to analysis because of its incomparably more precise statements of the situation. In comparison with the stage scene, the filmed behavior item lends itself more readily to analysis because it can be isolated more easily. This circumstance derives its chief importance from its tendency to promote the mutual penetration of art and science. Actually, of a screened behavior item which is neatly brought out in a certain situation, like a muscle of a body, it is difficult to say which is more fascinating, its artistic value or its value for science. To demonstrate the identity of the artistic and scientific uses of photography which heretofore usually were separated will be one of the revolutionary functions of the film.[16]

By close-ups of the things around us, by focusing on hidden details of familiar objects, by exploring commonplace milieux under the ingenious guidance of the camera, the film, on the one hand, extends our comprehension of the necessities which rule our lives; on the other hand, it manages to assure us of an immense and unexpected field of action. Our taverns and our metropolitan streets, our offices and furnished rooms, our railroad stations and our factories appeared to have us locked up hopelessly. Then came the film and burst this prison-world asunder by the dynamite of the tenth of a second, so that now, in the midst of its far-flung ruins and debris, we calmly and adventurously go traveling. With the close-up, space expands; with slow motion, movement is extended. The enlargement of a snapshot does not simply render more precise what in any case was visible, though unclear: it reveals entirely new structual formations of the subject. So, too, slow motion not only presents familiar qualities of movement but reveals in them entirely unknown ones 'which, far from looking like retarded rapid

16 Renaissance painting offers a revealing analogy to this situation. The incomparable development of this art and its significance rested not least on the integration of a number of new sciences, or at least of new scientific data. Renaissance painting made use of anatomy and perspective, of mathematics, meterology, and chromatology. Valéry writes: 'What could be further from us than the strange claim of a Leonardo to whom painting was a supreme goal and the ultimate demonstration of knowledge? Leonardo was convinced that painting demanded universal knowledge, and he did not even shrink from a theoretical analysis which to us is stunning because of its very depth and precision. . . .'—Paul Valéry, *Pièces sur l'art*, 'Autour de Corot', Paris, p.191.

movements, give the effect of singularly gliding, floating, supernatural motions'. (Arnheim, 1932.) Evidently a different nature opens itself to the camera than opens to the naked eye — if only because an unconsciously penetrated space is substituted for a space consciously explored by man. Even if one has a general knowledge of the way people walk, one knows nothing of a person's posture during the fractional second of a stride. The act of reaching for a lighter or a spoon is familiar routine, yet we hardly know what really goes on between hand and metal, not to mention how this fluctuates with our moods. Here the camera intervenes with the resources of its lowerings and liftings, its interruptions and isolations, its extensions and accelerations, its enlargements and reductions. The camera introduces us to unconscious optics as does psychoanalysis to unconscious impulses.

XIV

One of the foremost tasks of art has always been the creation of a demand which could be fully satisfied only later.[17] The history of every art form shows critical epochs in which a certain art form aspires to effects which could be fully obtained only with a changed technical standard, that is to say, in a new art form. The extravagances and crudities of art which thus appear, particularly in the so-called decadent epochs, actually arise from

17 'The work of art', says André Breton, 'is valuable only in so far as it is vibrated by the reflexes of the future.' Indeed, every developed art form intersects three lines of development. Technology works toward a certain form of art. Before the advent of the film there were photo booklets with pictures which flitted by the onlooker upon pressure of the thumb, thus portraying a boxing bout or a tennis match. Then there were the slot machines in bazaars; their picture sequences were produced by the turning of a crank.

   Secondly, the traditional art forms in certain phases of their development strenuously work toward effects which later are effortlessly attained by the new ones. Before the rise of the movie the Dadaists' performances tried to create an audience reaction which Chaplin later evoked in a more natural way.

   Thirdly, unspectacular social changes often promote a change in receptivity which will benefit the new art form. Before the movie had begun to create its public, pictures that were no longer immobile captivated an assembled audience in the so-called *Kaiserpanorama*. Here the public assembled before a screen into which steroscopes were mounted, one to each beholder. By a mechanical process individual pictures appeared briefly before the stereoscopes, then made way for others. Edison still had to use similar devices in presenting the first movie strip before the film screen and projection were known. This strip was presented to a small public which stared into the apparatus in which the succession of pictures was reeling off. Incidentally, the institution of the *Kaiserpanorama* shows very clearly a dialectic of the development. Shortly before the movie turned the reception of pictures into a collective one, the individual viewing of pictures in these swiftly outmoded establishments came into play once more with an intensity comparable to that of the ancient priest beholding the statute of a divinity in the cella.

the nucleus of its richest historical energies. In recent years, such barbarisms were abundant in Dadaism. It is only now that its impulse becomes discernible: Dadaism attempted to create by pictorial — and literary — means the effects which the public today seeks in the film.

Every fundamentally new, pioneering creation of demands will carry beyond its goal. Dadaism did so to the extent that it sacrificed the market values which are so characteristic of the film in favor of higher ambitions — though of course it was not conscious of such intentions as here described. The Dadaists attached much less importance to the sales value of their work than to its uselessness for contemplative immersion. The studied degradation of their material was not the least of their means to achieve this uselessness. Their poems are 'word salad' containing obscenities and every imaginable waste product of language. The same is true of their paintings, on which they mounted buttons and tickets. What they intended and achieved was a relentless destruction of the aura of their creations, which they branded as reproductions with the very means of production. Before a painting of Arp's or a poem by August Stramm it is impossible to take time for contemplation and evaluation as one would before a canvas of Derain's or a poem by Rilke. In the decline of middle-class society, contemplation became a school for asocial behavior; it was countered by distraction as a variant of social conduct.[18] Dadaistic activities actually assured a rather vehement distraction by making works of art the center of scandal. One requirement was foremost: to outrage the public.

From an alluring appearance or persuasive structure of sound the work of art of the Dadaists became an instrument of ballistics. It hit the spectator like a bullet, it happened to him, thus acquiring a tactile quality. It promoted a demand for the film, the distracting element of which is also primarily tactile, being based on changes of place and focus which periodically assail the spectator. Let us compare the screen on which a film unfolds with the canvas of a painting. The painting invites the spectator to contemplation; before it the spectator can abandon himself to his associations. Before the movie frame he cannot do so. No sooner has his eye grasped a scene than it is already changed. It cannot be arrested. Duhamel, who detests the film and knows nothing of its significance, though something of its structure, notes this circumstance as follows: 'I can no longer think what I want to think. My thoughts have been replaced by moving images' (Duhamel, 1930). The spectator's process of association in view

18 The theological archetype of this contemplation is the awareness of being alone with one's God. Such awareness, in the heyday of the bourgeoisie, went to strengthen the freedom to shake off clerical tutelage. During the decline of the bourgeoisie this awareness had to take into account the hidden tendency to withdraw from public affairs those forces which the individual draws upon in his communion with God.

of these images is indeed interrupted by their constant, sudden change. This constitutes the shock effect of the film, which, like all shocks, should be cushioned by heightened presence of mind.[19] By means of its technical structure, the film has taken the physical shock effect out of the wrappers in which Dadaism had, as it were, kept it inside the moral shock effect.[20]

XV

The mass is a matrix from which all traditional behavior toward works of art issues today in a new form. Quantity has been transmuted into quality. The greatly increased mass of participants has produced a change in the mode of participation. The fact that the new mode of participation first appeared in a disreputable form must not confuse the spectator. Yet some people have launched spirited attacks against precisely this superficial aspect. Among these, Duhamel has expressed himself in the most radical manner. What he objects to most is the kind of participation which the movie elicits from the masses. Duhamel calls the movie 'a pastime for helots, a diversion for uneducated, wretched, worn-out creatures who are consumed by their worries . . . , a spectacle which requires no concentration and presupposes no intelligence . . . , which kindles no light in the heart and awakens no hope other than the ridiculous one of someday becoming a "star" in Los Angeles' (Duhamel, 1930). Clearly, this is at bottom the same ancient lament that the masses seek distraction whereas art demands concentration from the spectator. That is a commonplace. The question remains whether it provides a platform for the analysis of the film. A closer look is needed here. Distraction and concentration form polar opposites which may be stated as follows: A man who concentrates before a work of art is absorbed by it. He enters into this work of art the way legend tells of the Chinese painter when he viewed his finished painting. In contrast, the distracted mass absorbs the work of art. This is most obvious with regard to buildings. Architecture has always represented the prototype of a work of art the reception of which is consummated by a collec-

19 The film is the art form that is in keeping with the increased threat to his life which modern man has to face. Man's need to expose himself to shock effects is his adjustment to the dangers threatening him. The film corresponds to profound changes in the apperceptive apparatus — changes that are experienced on an individual scale by the man in the street in big-city traffic, on a historical scale by every present-day citizen.

20 As for Dadaism, insights important for Cubism and Futurism are to be gained from the movie. Both appear as deficient attempts of art to accommodate the pervasion of reality by the apparatus. In contrast to the film, these schools did not try to use the apparatus as such for the artistic presentation of reality, but aimed at some sort of alloy in the joint presentation of reality and apparatus. In Cubism, the premonition that this apparatus will be structurally based on optics plays a dominant part; in Futurism it is the premonition of the effects of this apparatus which are brought out by the rapid sequence of the film strip.

tivity in a state of distraction. The laws of its reception are most instructive.

Buildings have been man's companions since primeval times. Many art forms have developed and perished. Tragedy begins with the Greeks, is extinguished with them, and after centuries its 'rules' only are revived. The epic poem, which had its origin in the youth of nations, expires in Europe at the end of the Renaissance. Panel painting is a creation of the Middle Ages, and nothing guarantees its uninterrupted existence. But the human need for shelter is lasting. Architecture has never been idle. Its history is more ancient than that of any other art, and its claim to being a living force has significance in every attempt to comprehend the relationship of the masses to art. Buildings are appropriated in a twofold manner: by use and by perception — or rather, by touch and sight. Such appropriation cannot be understood in terms of the attentive concentration of a tourist before a famous building. On the tactile side there is no counterpart to contemplation on the optical side. Tactile appropriation is accomplished not so much by attention as by habit. As regards architecture, habit determines to a large extent even optical reception. The latter, too, occurs much less through rapt attention than by noticing the object in incidental fashion. This mode of appropriation, developed with reference to architecture, in certain circumstances acquires canonical value. For the tasks which face the human apparatus of perception at the turning points of history cannot be solved by optical means, that is, by contemplation, alone. They are mastered gradually by habit, under the guidance of tactile appropriation.

The distracted person, too, can form habits. More, the ability to master certain tasks in a state of distraction proves that their solution has become a matter of habit. Distraction as provided by art presents a convert control of the extent to which new tasks have become soluble by apperception. Since, moreover, individuals are tempted to avoid such tasks, art will tackle the most difficult and most important ones where it is able to mobilize the masses. Today it does so in the film. Reception in a state of distraction, which is increasing noticeably in all fields of art and is symptomatic of profound changes in apperception, finds in the film its true means of exercise. The film with its shock effect meets this mode of reception halfway. The film makes the cult value recede into the background not only by putting the public in the position of the critic, but also by the fact that at the movies this position requires no attention. The public is an examiner, but an absent-minded one.

Epilogue

The growing proletarianization of modern man and the increasing formation of masses are two aspects of the same process. Fascism attempts to organize the newly created proletarian masses without affecting the property structure which the masses strive to eliminate. Fascism sees its salvation in giving these masses not their right, but instead a chance to express themselves.[21] The masses have a right to change property relations; Fascism seeks to give them an expression while preserving property. The logical result of Fascism is the introduction of aesthetics into political life. The violation of the masses, whom Fascism, with its *Führer* cult, forces to their knees, has its counterpart in the violation of an apparatus which is pressed into the production of ritual values.

All efforts to render politics aesthetic culminate in one thing: war. War and war only can set a goal for mass movements on the largest scale while respecting the traditional property system. This is the political formula for the situation. The technological formula may be stated as follows: Only war makes it possible to mobilize all of today's technical resources while maintaining the property system. It goes without saying that the Fascist apotheosis of war does not employ such arguments. Still, Marinetti says in his manifesto on the Ethiopian colonial war: 'For twenty-seven years we Futurists have rebelled against the branding of war as antiaesthetic . . . . Accordingly we state: . . . War is beautiful because it establishes man's dominion over the subjugated machinery by means of gas masks, terrifying megaphones, flame throwers, and small tanks. War is beautiful because it initiates the dreamt-of metalization of the human body. War is beautiful because it enriches a flowering meadow with the fiery orchids of machine guns. War is beautiful because it combines the gunfire, the cannonades, the cease-fire, the scents, and the stench of putrefaction into a symphony. War is beautiful because it creates new architecture, like that of the big tanks, the geometrical formation flights, the smoke spirals from burning villages, and many others . . . . Poets and artists of Futurism ! . . . remember these principles of an aesthetics of war so that your struggle for a new literature and a new graphic art . . . may be illumined by them!'

This manifesto has the virtue of clarity. Its formulations deserve to be accepted by dialecticians. To the latter, the aesthetics of today's war appears as follows: If the natural utilization of productive forces is impeded by the property system, the increase in technical devices, in speed, and in the sources of energy will press for an unnatural utilization, and

21 One technical feature is significant here, especially with regard to newsreels, the propagandist importance of which can hardly be overestimated. Mass reproduction is aided especially by the reproduction of masses. In big parades and monster rallies, in sports events, and in war, all of which nowadays are captured by camera and sound recording, the masses are brought face to face with themselves. This process, whose significance need not be stressed, is intimately connected with the development of the techniques of reproduction and photography. Mass movements are usually discerned more clearly by a camera than by the naked eye. A bird's-eye view best captures gatherings of hundreds of thousands. And even though such a view may be as accessible to the human eye as it is to the camera, the image received by the eye cannot be enlarged the way a negative is enlarged. This means that mass movements, including war, constitute a form of human behavior which particularly favors mechanical equipment.

this is found in war. The destructiveness of war furnishes proof that society has not been mature enough to incorporate technology as its organ, that technology has not been sufficiently developed to cope with the elemental forces of society. The horrible features of imperialistic warfare are attributable to the discrepancy between the tremendous means of production and their inadequate utilization in the process of production — in other words, to unemployment and the lack of markets. Imperialistic war is a rebellion of technology which collects, in the form of 'human material', the claims to which society has denied its natural material. Instead of draining rivers, society directs a human stream into a bed of trenches; instead of dropping seeds from airplanes, it drops incendiary bombs over cities; and through gas warfare the aura is abolished in a new way.

'*Fiat ars — pereat mundus*', says Fascism, and, as Marinetti admits, expects war to supply the artistic gratification of a sense perception that has been changed by technology. This is evidently the consummation of '*l'art pour l'art*'. Mankind, which in Homer's time was an object of contemplation for the Olympian gods, now is one for itself. Its self-alienation has reached such a degree that it can experience its own destruction as an aesthetic pleasure of the first order. This is the situation of politics which Fascism is rendering aesthetic. Communism responds by politicizing art.

References

Arnheim, R., 1932: *Film als Kunst*. Berlin, p. 176 f.

Arnoux, A., 1929: *Cinema Pris*, p. 28.

Duhamel, G., 1930: *Scenes de la vie future*. Paris, p. 52.

Gance, A., 1927: 'Le temps de l'image est venu'. *L'Art cinématographique* vol. 2, pp. 94f.

Pirandello, L., 1927: *Si Gira*. Quoted by Pierre-Quint, L., 'Signification du Cinéma', *L'Art cinématographique* vol. 2 p. 14—15.

Valéry, P., 1964: *Aesthetics*, 'The conquest of ubiquity' p. 225 Trans. Manheim, R., New York: Pantheon Books, Bollingen Series.

Werfel, F., 1935: ' "Ein Sommernachtstraum", Ein film von Shakespeare und Reinhardt'. *Neues Wiener Journal*, cited in *Lu*, November.

16

Mass Communication Research and Cultural Studies: an American view

James W. Carey

I

In the years following World War II American social science made an unprecedented incursion into European intellectual life. The phrase 'American
social science' covers rather too much territory, of course, and I principally
refer to the dominant strain of that work, a strain that can be labelled with
catch phrases such as behaviorist, positivist, empiricist, to a lesser extent,
pragmatist: behavioral psychology and functional sociology if a more
specific designation is needed. This reverse Atlantic crossing did not reflect
any necessary superiority of American social science; rather it reflected
the general economic and cultural situation of post World War II. A kind
of intellectual Marshall Plan grew up because of the disruption the war
visited on European scholarship: a good part of a generation of scholars
lost in battle, traditions disrupted, universities in disarray, and a modern
Diaspora which drove great scholars to work in unfamiliar and often
unreceptive settings.

Like the Marshall Plan the outward flow of American scholarship was
not matched by a flow of European thought back into North America. In
the years immediately following the war Americans experienced little loss
from this one-way flow of intellectual trade but in more recent years
European scholarship has reasserted itself through the resurgence of such
pre-war traditions as Marxism and phenomenology and new bodies of
thought such as structuralism reflecting a distinctively European mileu.
Unfortunately, this work as yet has had little influence on American
social science which remains rather blissfully unaware of European work
except that representing modifications Europeans make on essentially
American ideas and research.

The situation in communication research mirrors the general pattern
in the social sciences. When communication research developed in Europe,
the tide of American intellectual exporting was at its crest and there was
little communication research literature that was not stamped 'made in
America'. In the early 1950s American communication research made
deep inroads into Europe and words like 'mass', 'effects', and 'functions',

words which signalled American preoccupations, organized the relevant research on both sides of the Atlantic. In more recent years European communication research has turned for inspiration to classical figures in European social thought, to Marxism and phenomenology, to structuralism and to native traditions of literary criticism which derived from and have influenced these larger intellectual movements. Unfortunately, news of these developments in European communication research has filtered only indirectly back to the United States. What is called cultural science on the continent and, less pretentiously, cultural studies in Britain has been generally misunderstood, ignored, or misinterpreted in the United States.

In this essay I would like to redress this imbalance somewhat by relating the principal traditions of American communication research to cultural studies and by emphasizing certain dilemmas common to both. I wish as well to acknowledge the important corrective European communication research provides to the biases of American scholarship. My object in doing this is to widen the dialogue over the most effective paths communication research might take in the future, though I must admit there is something distinctively American about the tones in which I cast the argument. Finally, in presenting this argument I am drawing heavily upon the work of an American anthropologist, Clifford Geertz, who has been peculiarly receptive to contemporary European scholarship. (Geertz, 1973.)

II

In the fall of 1973 a conference was held in London on 'The Future of Communications Studies', To the ears of an American auditor two remarks at the conference initially were confusing and then revealing. Raymond Williams, the distinguished fellow of Jesus College, Cambridge, commented that 'the study of communications was deeply and almost disastrously deformed by being confidently named the study of "mass-communications" * In a subsequent discussion session, Stuart Hall, the Director of the Centre for Contemporary Culture at the University of Birmingham, commented that when his centre originally was named, they considered a number of titles including that of communications to describe their work. In his opinion the wisest decision they had made was to call the centre one for contemporary culture rather than communications. Williams and Hall were broaching a concern that never crosses an American's mind: the use of the terms communications and mass communications as useful descriptors in this area of scholarship. What, pray tell, could they have in mind?

Williams argued that it was now time to bury the term 'mass-communications' as a label for departments, research programs, and con-ferences. The term is disastrous, he thought, for three reasons. First, it limits studies to a few specialized areas such as broadcasting and film and what is miscalled 'popular literature' when there is 'the whole common area of discourse in speech and writing that always needs to be considered'. Second, the term mass has become lodged in our language in its weakest sense, the large ultimate mass audience, and prevents the analysis of 'specific modern communication situations and of most specific modern communications conventions and forms'. Third, because the audience was conceived of as a mass, the only question worth asking was how, and when then whether film, television, or books corrupted people. Consequently, it was always much easier to get funding for these kinds of impact studies than any other kind of research.

Much of what Williams says, with appropriate modifications in vocabulary, is so understandable, even congenial, to American students of communications, that it is easy to overlook his distinctive emphasis. Williams is suggesting that studies of mass communications create unacceptable limitations on study and certain blindness as well. The blindness is that the term generally overlooks the fact that communication is first of all a set of practices, conventions, and forms, and in studying 'mass situations', these phenomena are assumed to exist, but never are investigated. Second, the term limits and isolates study by excluding attention to the forms, conventions, and practices of speech and writing as well as to the mass media and, therefore, necessarily distorts understanding. His highlighting of conventions, forms, and practices reflects a distinctively European emphasis on praxis and the influence of literary criticism which attends to the forms and conventions of particular works. Finally, Americans have never been able to escape, despite their emphasis on small groups, the bias which the word 'mass' brings to their studies.

Stuart Hall's objection to the word communication is somewhat more opaque, though I think it has a similar intention. Hall believes that the word communication narrows study and isolates it substantively and methodologically. Substantively, it narrows the scope of study to products explicitly produced by and delivered over the mass media. The study of communication is, therefore, generally isolated from the study of literature and art, on the one hand, and from the expressive and ritual forms of everyday life — religion, conversation, sport — on the other. The word culture, which in its anthropological sense directs us toward the study of an entire way of life, is replaced by the word communication which directs us to the study of one isolated segment of existence. Methodologically, the word communication isolates us from an entire body of critical, interpretive, and comparative methodology that has been at the heart of anthropology and the study of literature.

Now Americans can easily dismiss these criticisms as a misunderstanding. They might claim that they have not divorced the study of mass communication from speech, writing, and other forms. Too much is being read into the organization of departments and journals. Or they might argue that they have placed limitations on the range and scope of their studies, but only to achieve a subject matter amenable to treatment with scientific methods and scientific theories. The dismissals jump too easily to the lips, however, and it would be well to suspend judgment until a fuller understanding can be gained of the difference between British, Continental, and American work in this field.

European and American work derives from quite different kinds of intellectual puzzles and is grounded in two different metaphors for communication. Now I realize that the generalization is too large and that plenty of exceptions can be found on both sides of the Atlantic, but I wish simply to express preponderant tendencies in thought. American studies are grounded in a transmission or transportation view of communication. They see communication, therefore, as a process of transmitting messages at a distance for the purpose of control. The archetypal case of communication then is persuasion, attitude change, behavior modification, socialization through the transmission of information, influence, or conditioning. I call this a transmission or transportation view because its central, defining terms have much in common with the usage of communication in the nineteenth century as another term for transportation. It is also related strongly to the nineteenth-century desire to use communication and transportation to extend influence, control, and power over wider distances and over greater populations.

By contrast, the preponderant view of communication in European studies is a ritual one: communication is viewed as a process through which a shared culture is created, modified, and transformed. The archetypal case of communication is ritual and mythology, for those who come at the problem from anthropology; art and literature, for those who come at the problem from literary criticism and history. A ritual view of communication is not directed toward the extension of messages in space, but the maintenance of society in time; not the act of imparting information or influence, but the creation, representation, and celebration of shared beliefs. If a transmission view of communication centers on the extension of messages across geography for purposes of control, a ritual view centers on the sacred ceremony which draws persons together in fellowship and commonality.

Now the differences between these views can be seen as mere transpositions of one another. However they have quite distinct consequences, substantively and methodologically. They obviously derive from differing problematics; that is, the basic question that puzzles American students is quite different from the basic question that puzzles European students.

The problematic of British studies, or so I think, can be stated as a question: what is the relationship between culture and society, or more generally, between expressive forms, particularly art, and social order? By American scholars this problem is not even seen as a problem. There is art, of course, and there is society, but to chart the relationship between them is taken to be, for a student in communication, an exercise in redundancy. However, in British cultural studies as well as in many European streams of thought one of the principal, though not exclusive tasks of scholarship, is to work through the relationship of expressive form to social order.

The British sociologist Tom Burns put this nicely once when he observed that the task of art is to make sense out of life. The task of social science is to make sense out of the senses we make out of life. By such reasoning the social scientist stands toward his material — cultural forms such as religion, ideology, journalism, everyday speech — as the literary critic stands toward the novel, play, or poem. He has to figure out what it means, what interpretations it presents of life, and how it relates to the senses of life historically found among a people.

Note what Burns simply takes for granted. There is, on the one hand, life existence, experience, behavior, and, on the other hand, attempts to find the meaning and significance in this experience and behavior. British culture is on this reading the meaning and significance British people find through art, religion, and so forth in their experience. To study British culture is to seek order within these forms, to bring out in starker relief the claims and meanings of British culture, and to state systematically the relations between the multiple forms directed to the same end: to render experience comprehensible and charged with affect. But what is called the study of British culture can also be called the study of communications, for what we are studying in this context are the ways in which experience is worked into understanding and then disseminated and celebrated (the distinctions, like those relating to dialogue, are not sharp).

Communication studies in the United States have exhibited quite a different intention. They have found most problematic in communication the conditions under which persuasion occurs. Now to reduce the rich variety of American studies to this problematic is, I will admit, a simplification verging on burlesque, yet it does capture a significant part of the truth. American studies of communication, mass and interpersonal, have aimed at stating the precise psychological and sociological conditions under which attitudes are changed, formed, or reinforced, behavior stabilized or redirected. Specific forms of culture — art, ritual, journalism — enter the analysis only indirectly, if at all; they enter only insofar as they contribute to such sociological conditions or constitute such psychological forces. They enter, albeit indirectly, in discussions of dissonance reduction, rational versus irrational motives and persuasive tactics, differing styles of family organization, or in sharp distinctions rendered between reality and fantasy-oriented communication. But expressive forms are exhausted as intellectual objects suitable for attention by students of communications once relevance to matters of behavior change have been demonstrated. The relation of these forms to social order, the historical transformation of these forms, their entrance into a subjective world of meaning and significance, the interrelations among them, and their role in creating a general culture — a way of life and a pattern of significance — is never entertained seriously.

This difference of substance and intent is related also to a difference in strategy in dealing with a persistent methodological dilemma of the social sciences and of different meanings of that crucial word, empirical. Let me try to elucidate these differences in a somewhat circuitous way and to set the stage for a more systematic analysis of the contribution of cultural studies to the analysis of these problems.

II

In a remarkable essay, 'On the Teaching of Modern Literature', Lionel Trilling attempted to define the notion 'modern' and to use it to present a series of dilemmas inherent in our scholarship. Modern, in phrases such as 'modern literature,' has had a rather vagrant career. As used, for example, by Matthew Arnold in his essay 'On the Modern Element in Literature' (1857) it had a wholly honorific meaning: it referred to certain timeless intellectual virtues. Modern literature in Arnold's view exhibited virtues such as repose, serenity, free activity of the mind, reason, and tolerance. By such standards nineteenth-century literature was not 'modern' and the great modern age was Periclean Athens. Modern, then, is one of those words — original is another — that suffered an inversion of meaning: as Arnold used it, it referred to qualities existing timelessly from the beginning demanding our respect. It came to mean contemporary — the most recent — and, in phrases such as literary modernism, to possess qualities just the opposite of what Arnold intended: not repose and serenity, but frenetic and violent activity; not reason, but the demonic; not free activity, but control by the unconscious; and not tolerance, but aggression. Modern came to be identified, in other words, with certain aspects of the romantic movement. That movement held aloft two ideas in rather sharp conflict. First, it emphasized the creativity of the artist: his ability to build literally a world of meaning and significance out of his own intellectural resources. The same movement also painted human nature as far from identified with reason and repose, but as controlled by archaic forces, irrational passions, and demonic and convulsive dreams. These notions later re-entered art via the social studies — one need only mention Freud, Nietzsche, and Fraser — and left for the social sciences the same dilemma they created in modern art: man is the creator of reality through the agency of his own mind (a proposition, in one form or other, at the heart of cultural studies) and yet he is in the decisive grip of historical, environmental and unconscious forces over which he has little control (a basic postulate of American communication research).

Consciously or not, this dilemma grips the social sciences; it was even given precise formulation in a famous essay of Reinhard Bendix, 'Social Science and the Distrust of Reason'. Let me try to state the problem. Social scientists, with few exceptions, attempt to explain human behavior by references to certain laws or functions which control behavior. These laws and functions have little reference to the operation of reason, consciousness, or individually determined choice. Often, of course, behavior is seen to be controlled by the same demonic and historical forces which surface in modern literature. Behavior obeys laws of conditioning and reinforcement, of satisfying pre-logical functions such as dissonance reduction or sublimation, or expresses buried urges and scars such as an inferiority complex or will to power. Now the question that immediately arises is: where, exactly do these laws and functions come from? We have no choice other than to respond: from the mind of the scientist or, more generally, from communities of scientists. But then must we conclude that the behavior of the scientist also is under the control of these same laws and functions? Is not the activity of the scientist qua scientist determined by conditioning and reinforcement, by the functional necessities of personality and social systems, by the eruption of the demonic and of unconsciousness? Scientific thought perhaps has no relation to truth because it cannot be explained by truth; it too is a prejudice and a passion, however sophisticated. If the laws of human behavior control the behavior of the scientist, his work his nonsense; if not, just what kind of sense can be made of if?

This dilemma was at the heart of Karl Mannheim's *Ideology and Utopia*. Ideology originated as a philosophical term but was appropriated and converted by social science into a weapon. As intellectuals generally do not like to be in the grip of an ideology or to be called ideologists, one must make a sharp distinction between political science, which theoretically and empirically captures the truth, and ideology, which is a tissue of error, distortion, and self-interest, as in 'fascist ideology'. Consequently, we proclaim the 'end of ideology', because we now have a scientific theory of politics. But how does one make the distinction between these forms? The political theory of scientists might be just one more ideology: distortion and fantasy in the service of self-interest, passion and prejudice.

There is no easy answer to the question. Clifford Geertz calls this dilemma 'Mannheim's Paradox': 'Where, if anywhere, ideology leaves off and science begins has been the Sphinx's Riddle of much of modern sociological thought and the rustless weapon of its enemies'. (Geertz, 1973 p. 194.) But the dilemma is general: where does conditioning leave off and science begin? Where does class interest leave off and science begin? Where does the unconscious leave off and science begin? The significance of the dilemma for this essay is twofold: first, the study of communication in Europe can be traced to the initial confrontation of this dilemma in that literature dealing with the sociology of knowledge.

Second, the principal strategies employed by communication researchers can be seen as devices for escaping Mannheim's Paradox.

Social scientists do not necessarily reflect on the significance of what they are doing when adopting particular research strategies, and certainly they do not think of themselves as dealing with Mannheim's Paradox. But one important way of looking at the major traditions of social science work is to examine these traditions as varying strategies for dealing with 'social science and the distrust of reason'. In the study of communication there have been three strategies for attacking the problem, though naturally they parallel the strategies adopted in the other social sciences. The first is to conceive of the study of communication as a behavioral science whose objective is the elucidation of laws. The second is to conceive of it as a formal science whose objective is the elucidation of structures. The third is to conceive of it as a cultural science whose objective is the elucidation of meaning.

Let us look first at the behavioral science strategy and also stay with the example of ideology. There are two principal explanations of ideology that have emerged from the behavioral sciences. Geertz calls them an interest theory and a strain theory, though for us it would be perhaps more felicitious to label them a causal and functional explanation. A causal explanation attempts to root ideology in the solid ground of social structure. It explains ideological positions by deriving them from the interests of various groups, particularly social classes. It attempts to predict the adoption of ideological positions on the basis of class membership thereby deriving ideology from antecedent causation. Eventually such an argument starts to creak because it is difficult to predict ideology on the basis of class or, indeed, on any other set of variables. Though ideology is more predictable than many other social phenomena, the net result of causal explanations is relatively low correlations between class position and ideological position. When this form of analysis breaks down, a shift of explanatory apparatus is made. In functional explanations ideology is seen less as caused by structural forces than as satisfying certain needs or functions of the personality or society. Geertz calls this latter view a strain theory because it starts from the assumption of the chronic malintegration of the personality and society. It describes life as inevitably riddled by contradictions, antinomies, and inconsistencies. These contradictions give rise to strains for which ideology provides an answer. If in causal explanations ideology is derived from antecedent factors, in functional explanations ideology is explained as a mechanism for restoring equilibrium to a system put out of joint by the contrariness of modern life. In one model men pursue power; in the other they feel anxiety. In one model ideology is a weapon for goring someone else's ox; in a functional model it is a device for releasing tension. In the causal model the *petit-bourgeois* shopkeeper's anti-Semitism is explained by class position; in the functional model the same anti-Semitism is explained as catharsis — the displacement of tension on to symbolic enemies.

These same patterns of explanation are found throughout the behavioral sciences. They attempt to explain phenomena by assimilating them to either a functional or causal law. Both have their weaknesses: causal laws are usually weak at prediction; functional laws are usually obscure in elucidating comprehensible and powerful functions. Moreover, while both explanations are presented as based on empirical data, the data are connected to operative concepts — like catharsis or interest — by rather questionable and arbitrary operational definitions.

However, the principal concern is not to question the power of the explanations, but to see how they deal with Mannheim's Paradox. The behavioral sciences attempt to deal with the paradox in two ways. First, it can be claimed that the behavioral laws elucidated are only statistically true and, therefore, while they apply, like the laws of mechanics, to everyone in general, they apply to no one in particular. Because such laws only explain a portion of the variance in the data, it can be asserted that the behavior of the scientist is not governed necessarily by it. A second way to escape the dilemma is simply to claim that the laws do not apply to the scientist qua scientist because in the act of comprehending the law he escapes its force. This species of scientific elitism is the strategy most frequently adopted, though usually implicitly. The scientist's knowledge gives him a special ability to criticise the assertions of others, particularly ideological assertions, in terms of their truthfulness.

Now neither of these strategies is particularly effective, but perhaps the greatest disservice they perform for ideology, or for that matter for any other symbolic form to which they are applied, is that they dispose of the phenomenon in the very act of naming it. They assume that the flattened scientific forms of speech and prose, that peculiar quality of presumed disinterest and objectivity, are the only mode in which truth can be formulated. What they object to in ideology is hyperbole.

The study of communication in the United States has been dominated by attempts to create a behavioral science and to elucidate laws or functions of behavior. These attempts include most of the work on attitude change and dissonance theory, influence and diffusion theory, and uses and gratifications analysis. It includes, naturally, that rather overplowed terrain of audience effects. And the same dilemmas have been encountered in communications that appear in the study of ideology.

There have been no formal theories of communication active in American scholarship. In allied fields, however, there have been formal theories of some scope and power and they have had at the least an imaginative effect on the study of communications. Modern linguistics, systems theory, and cybernetics are differing attempts to build formal theories of social phenomena. Moreover, under the influence of Noam

Chomsky's success in linguistics, movements such as cognitive psychology, cognitive anthropology, and ethnoscience have attempted to displace behavioral modes of explanation with formal theories. In Europe a number of varieties of structuralism, particularly that identified with Claude Lévi-Strauss, are presented as formal theories, and such theories have now begun to surface as the explicit background of studies in communication. (Leymore, 1975.) It is worth noting that much of this work is derivative from modern linguistics, though it is rarely as precise or systematic in form as cybernetics or transformational linguistics.

Formal theories deal with Mannheim's Paradox by turning away from the study of behavior. Therefore, formal theorists avoid postulating or demonstrating lawlike principles governing the behavior of subjects or scientists. This can be seen most clearly in the distinction between competence and performance at the center of linguistic theory. Modern linguists are not attempting to explain linguistic behavior or performance — the actual deployment of actual sentences by actual subjects — but linguistic competence: the abstract ability of a native speaker in principle to utter the grammatical sentences of a language. Formal theorists begin then from an irrefragable, empirical universal — the ability of humans to produce novel utterances (sentences neither heard nor spoken before) or, as with Lévi-Strauss, the presence in all cultures of systems of symbolic opposition (up-down, stop-go, red-green) — and then build theoretical machines, mechanisms, or structures capable of producing these phenomena. The trick is to build the deep structure of mind or culture out of the fugitive materials of cultural universals.

The difference between behavioral and formal solutions to Mannheim's Paradox is much the same as the difference between induction and deduction and therefore represents the continuing struggle of empiricism and rationalism as scientific programs.

I wish neither to belabor nor to gainsay these two traditions of work. I merely suggest that they do not exhaust the tasks of trained intelligence. We can discern a third goal of intellectual work in communications, a goal more congenial to the problems communications researchers are called upon daily to address. Cultural studies or cultural science does not, however, escape Mannheim's Paradox; in fact it embraces it and in doing so it runs the risk of falling into a vicious relativism. Cultural studies also has far more modest objectives than other traditions. It does not seek to explain human behavior, but to understand it. It does not seek to reduce human action to underlying causes or structures but to interpret its significance. It does not attempt to predict human behavior, but to diagnose human meanings. It is, more positively, an attempt to bypass the rather discrete empiricism of behavioral studies and the esoteric apparatus of formal theories and to descend deeper into the empirical world. The goals of communications-studies as a cultural science are therefore more modest, but also more human at least in the sense of attempting to be truer to human nature and experience as it ordinarily is encountered. For many students of cultural studies the starting point, as with Clifford Geertz, is Max Weber:

> Believing with Max Weber, that man is an animal suspended in webs of significance he himself has spun, I take culture to be those webs, and the analysis of it to be therefore not an experimental science in search of law but an interpretive one in search of meaning. It is explication I am after construeing social expressions on their surface enigmatical (sic). (Geertz, 1973 p. 5.)

Now that is altogether too arch so let me explicate it with an unpretentious and transparent example of the type of scene communication researchers should be able to examine. Let us imagine a conversation on the meaning of death. One party to the conversation, a contemporary physician, argues that death occurs with the cessation of brain waves. The test he declares is observable empirically, and so much the better, it makes the organs of the deceased available for quick transplant into waiting patients. A second party to the conversation, a typical middle-American, declares that death occurs on the cessation of the heartbeat. Evidence for this, too, is empirically available, although it occurs before the cessation of brain waves. Life is perhaps slightly shortened, but because the heart has long been a symbol of human emotions, the test allows for the recognition of the affective aspect of death, the relation of death to the ongoing life of a community. A third party to the conversation, let us say, an Irish peasant, finding these first two definitions rather abhorrent, argues that death occurs three days after the cessation of the heartbeat. This too is empirically verifiable; days can be counted as well as anything else. In the interim the person, as at an Irish wake, is treated as if he is alive. The 'as if' gives away too much: he is alive for three days after the cessation of heartbeats. Death among such peasants occurs with social death, the final separation of the person from a human community. Prior to that he is, for all intents and purposes, alive for he is responded to as a particularly functionless living being. A fourth party to the conversation argues that death occurs seven days prior to the cessation of the heartbeat. He is, let us say, a member of the tribe Colin Turnbull described so vividly in *The Mountain People*. Among this starving people life ceases when food can no longer be gathered or scrambled for. The person is treated as if he were dead during a phase in which we would declare he was alive. Again, ignore the 'as if': the definition is as cognitively precise and affectively satisfying as anything put forth by a neuro-surgeon. The definition is simply: the particular meaning that a group of people assign to death.

What are we to do with this scene? We certainly cannot choose among these definitions on the basis of the scientific truth of one and the whimsy of the others. Death is not given unequivocally in experience by inflexible biological and social markers, and this has been true since long before the existence of artificial life-support systems. We can, however, show how differing definitions of death point toward differing values and social purposes: fixations on prolonging life by 'artificial means', on preserving the continuity of community existence, to reduce the sharpness of the break between life and death. But as to choosing among them on any presumed scientific grounds, we must, at least at this point, remain agnostics.

What more can be done with the scene? Do we want to ask what caused these individuals to hold to these strange definitions? We might naturally inquire after that, but one cannot imagine producing a 'law-like' statement concerning it other than a tautology like 'all people have definitions of death, however varied, because death is something that must be dealt with'. The only causal statement that one might imagine is a historical one: a genetic account of how these views grew over time among various people and were changed, displaced, and transformed. But such an analysis is not likely to produce any law-like statements because it seems intuitively obvious that every people demands a separate history: there are as many reasons for holding differing definitions of death as there are definitions of death.

Could we inquire into the functions these various definitions serve? One supposes so, but that does not seem promising. There is certainly not a priori reason to assume that such definitions serve any function at all. One can imagine elaborate speculations on the role of death in strengthening social solidarity. But this sort of thing runs into the anomaly of all functional analyses: a tribesman starts to figure out if death occurred and ends up strengthening the solidarity of society. There is no necessary relationship between these two activities. 'The concept of a latent function', as Geertz argues, 'is usually invoked to paper over this anomalous state of affairs, but it rather names the phenomenon (whose reality is not in question) than explains it; and the net result is that functional analyses . . . remain hopelessly equivocal'. (Geertz, 1973 p. 206.)

Might one in such a situation go looking for the deep structure of mind underlying these diverse surface definitions? Again, one might do so, but it is hard to see how such an exercise would help us understand this particular scene. We might, à la Lévi-Strauss, go looking for the commonality of semantic structure underlying these definitions of death and therefore out of the variety of definitions produce an elegant vision of a universal meaning of death. But this sort of thing ends up verging on a charade and in any event there are enough particular individuals and particular scenes such as I have described to 'make any doctrine of man which sees him as the bearer of changeless truths of reason — an "original logic" proceeding from "the structure of the mind" — seem merely quaint, an academic curiosity'.

No, our inability to deal with the artificial situation I have created and the innumerable ones we are daily called to comment on and study is not the result of failing to understand the laws of behavior or the functions of social practices, though insofar as these things can be discovered it would not hurt us to understand them. Nor does our speechlessness in the face of empirical events result from failure to understand the universal structure of the mind or the nature of cognition, though, again, we could know more of that too. The inability to deal with events such as the death scene derives from our failure, to put it disingenuously, to understand them: to be able to grasp the imaginative universe in which the acts of our actors are signs. What we face in our studies of communication is the consistent challenge to untangle, again from Geertz, 'a multiplicity of complex conceptual structures, many of them superimposed upon or knotted into one another, which are at once strange, irregular, and inexplicit and which he [the student] must contrive somehow first to grasp and then to render'. (Geertz, 1973 p. 10.) To repeat, we are challenged to grasp hold of the meanings people build into their words and behavior and to make these meanings, these claims about life and experience, explicit and articulate. We have to untangle, as I have attempted to do, albeit briefly, the meanings placed on death and innumerable other phenomena.

Of course, social scientists do place meanings on their subject's experience. Behaviorists through experiments and others through formal structures are trying to tell us what thought or action means. But the meanings such scientists produce have no necessary relation to the subjective intentions or sensed apprehensions of the people they study. As one observer acidly put it: 'social scientists go around telling people what it is they (people) think'. However, the first task of social science is to understand the meaningful structure of symbols in terms of which people bury their dead. This has usually been called, as method, *verstehen*. However, it is no long-distance mind reading, but an attempt to decipher the interpretations people cast on their experience, interpretations available out in the public world.

A cultural science of communication, then, views human behavior, or more accurately human action, as a text. Our task is to construct a 'reading' of the text. The text itself is a sequence of symbols — speech, writing, gesture — that contain interpretations. Our task, like that of a literary critic, is to interpret the interpretations. As Geertz elegantly summarized the position in an essay on the 'Balinese Cockfight':

The culture of a people is an ensemble of texts, themselves ensembles which the anthropologist strains to read over the shoulders of those to whom they properly belong . . . . In the cockfight, then, the Balinese forms and discovers his temperament and his society's temper at the same time. Or more exactly, he forms and discovers a particular face of them. Not only are there a great many other cultural texts providing commentaries on status hierarchy and self regard in Bali; but there are a great many other critical sectors of Balinese life besides the stratificatory . . . that receives such attention . . . . What it says about life is not unqualified nor even unchallenged by what other equally eloquent cultural statements say about it. But there is nothing more surprising in this than in the fact that Racine and Moliere were contemporaries, or that the same people who arrange chrysanthemums cast swords. (Geertz, 1973 pp. 452–3.)

To speak of human action through the metaphor of a text is perhaps unusual, though it should not sound so to students of communication. The metaphor emphasizes that the task of the cultural scientist is closer to that of a literary critic or a scriptural scholar than it is to a behavioral scientist. Hence, the connection of this reading of the discipline with the work of critics like Kenneth Burke, Raymond Williams, Richard Hoggart, and the classical discipline of hermeneutics. Our 'texts' are not always printed on pages or chiselled in stone — though sometimes they are. Usually, they are texts of public utterance or shaped behavior. But we are faced just like the literary critic with figuring out what the text says, of constructing a reading of it. Doing communication research (or cultural studies) 'is like trying to read (in the sense of "construct a reading of") a manuscript — foreign, faded, full of ellipses, incoherencies, suspicious emendations, and tendentious commentaries but written not in conventionalized graphs of sound but in transient examples of shaped behavior'. (Geertz, 1973 p. 10.)

To pursue this just a step further, suppose we undress the death scene; that is, deverbalize it, strip it of words. What we observe now is not a conversation, but a set of actions. We are interested in the actions because they have meaning — they are an orchestration of gestural symbols. We need to decipher — though it is not so mechanical as cracking a code — what is being said through behavior. What we observe are people silently holding a wake, measuring brain waves, rolling relatives into ravines, and, of course, a good deal more. From such fugitive and fragmentary data we have to construct a reading of the situation: to interpret the meanings in these symbols as gestures. No one will contend this is particularly easy. There are enough methodological dilemmas here to keep us occupied for a few generations. But to look at communications as, if you will forgive me, communication — as an interpretation, a meaning construed from and placed upon experience, that is addressed to and interpreted by someone — allows us to concentrate on the subject matter of the enterprise and not some extrinsic and arbitrary formula which accounts for it.

Why do we wish to construct a reading? The answer to this question shows both the modesty and importance of communication studied as a cultural science. The objective of the cultural sciences is not so much to answer our questions, but as Geertz puts it, 'to make available to us answers that others guarding other sheep in other valleys have given and thus to include them in the consultable record of what man has said'. (Geertz, 1973 p. 30.) This is a modest goal: to understand the meanings that others have placed on experience, to build up a veridical record of what has been said at other times, in other places, and in other ways; to enlarge the human conversation by comprehending what others are saying. Modest though this goal is, the inability to engage in such conversation must condemn the modern social sciences to failure. Not understanding their subjects — that unfortunate word — they do not converse with them so much as impose meanings on them. Social scientists have political theories and subjects have political ideologies; the behavior of social scientists is free and rationally informed while their subjects are conditioned and ruled by habit and superstition — not good intellectual soil for a working democracy.

The great achievement of the human mind and its extension in culture — though it is as much a naked necessity as an achievement — is the creation of a wide variety of cultural forms through which reality can be created. Science, with its claim to being the only cultural achievement that was a veridical map of reality, held us back as much as it advanced our understanding of how this miracle was accomplished. The greatest advance that has been made in recent social theory is the erosion of that field of concepts on which many of the great mock wars of late-nineteenth- and early-twentieth-century social science were fought. Of particular significance is the abandonment of the struggle to find the irreducible difference between the 'primitive' and modern mind. The distinction between the unbridled superstition of the native and the untrammelled rationalism of the citizen, between the affectively charged life-space of the primitive magician and the coolly geometrical world of the modern scientist, to state the case rather too baldly, appears now to have taught us more about the political purposes and personal conceits of social scientists than about the nature of human thought. Once the intellectual membrane separating the primitive from the modern mind was pierced, influence ran in both directions. The mind of the savage slowly yielded its logical structure, and patterns of primitive, though not therefore erroneous, forms of intellection among modern man, stood out in bolder relief.

The significance of the discovery of the commonalities in human thought is not that men are both primitive and modern, creatures of both reason and superstition, which seems to be the easily achieved construction placed on this discovery. Rather its significance lies in the realization that human thought does not consist in the production of irrefrageable maps of the objective world (science) and error-filled sketches of a mystic reality. Human thought, on the new model, is seen more as interpretations men apply to experience, constructions of widely varying systems of meanings, which cannot be exhaustively verified by the methods of science. What men create is not just one reality, but multiple realities. Reality cannot be exhausted by any one symbolic form be it scientific, religious, or aesthetic. Consequently, the true human genius and necessity is to build up models of reality by the agency of differing types of symbols — verbal, written, mathematical, gestural, kinesthetic — and by differing symbolic forms — art, science, journalism, ideology, ordinary speech, religion, mythology — to state but part of the catalogue. In trying to understand the meanings persons place on experience, then, it is necessary to work through a theory of fictions: a theory explaining how these forms operate, the semantic devices they employ, the meanings they sustain, the particular glow they cast over experience.

Understanding a culture is a complex matter and as Geertz says, thinking particularly of ritual:

One can start anywhere in a culture's repertoire of forms and end up anywhere else. One can stay . . . within a single, more or less bounded form and circle steadily within it. One can move between forms in search of broader unities or informing contrasts. One can even compare forms from different cultures to define their character in reciprocal relief. But whatever the level at which one operates, and however intricately, the guiding principle is the same: societies like lives contain their own interpretations. One only has to learn how to gain access to them. (Geertz, 1973 p. 453.)

At each point in this circling the task remains the same: to seize upon the interpretations people place on existence and to systematize them so they are more readily available to us. This is a process of making large claims from small matters: studying particular rituals, poems, plays, conversations, songs, dances, theories, and myths and gingerly reaching out to the full relations within a culture or a total way of life. For the student of communications other matters press in: how do changes in forms of communications technology affect the constructions placed on experience? How does such technology change the forms of community in which experience is apprehended and expressed? What, under the force of history, technology, and society, is thought about, thought with, and to whom is it expressed?

III

It is unfortunate that to mention cultural studies to most communications researchers resurrects the image of the sterile arguments concerning mass and popular culture that littered the field a few decades back. That was part of the disaster Raymond Williams referred to earlier. Yet many who worked in popular culture were on the right track. The question they were raising, which they and others promptly obscured, was a simple but profound one: what is the significance of living in the world of meanings conveyed by popular art? What is the relationship between the meanings found in popular art and in forms such as science, religion, and ordinary speech? How, in modern times, is experience cast up, interpreted, and congealed into knowledge and understanding? The task now for students of communications or mass communications or, as the British prefer, contemporary culture is to turn recent advances in the science of culture toward the characteristic products of contemporary life: news stories, bureaucratic language, love songs, political rhetoric, daytime serials, television drama, talk shows, and the wider world of contemporary leisure, ritual and information. It is not to the study of the masses or the mass media but to the study of contemporary culture we must turn: to relate the industrial production of culture and the conventions through which it is produced to the wider world of meaning, significance and interpretation — to an entire way of life. To come full circle, those were some of the forms and practices Raymond Williams felt had slipped by us when Americans confidently named our field the study of mass communications.

References

Geertz, Clifford, 1973: *The Interpretation of Cultures*. New York: Basic Books.

Leymore, Varda Langhold, 1975: *Hidden Myth: Structure and Symbolism in Advertising*. London: Heinemann.

17

Reggae, Rastas and Rudies

Dick Hebdige

Babylon on Beeston Street

The bars they could not hold me,
Walls could not control me.

From the Wailer's *Duppy Conqueror.*

I was born with the English language and it
proved to be my enemy.

James Baldwin (in interview).

Revolution soon — come.

Bulldog quoted in Thomas (1973).

The experience of slavery recapitulates itself perpetually in the every-day interactions of the Jamaican black. It is principally responsible for the unstable, familial structure (disrupting the traditionally strong kinship networks which survive among the peoples of West Africa) and obviously goes on determining patterns of work and relations with authority. It remains an invisible shaping presence which haunts the slums of Ghost Town and even now defies exorcism. It is interpolated into every verbal exchange which takes place in every Jamaican slum. As Hiro (1973) points out: 'the evolution of the creole language was related directly to the mechanics of slavery'. Communication was systematically blocked by the white overseer who banded slaves of different tribes together on the plantations so that cultural links with Africa were effectively severed. The laws which forbade the teaching of English to slaves meant that the new language was secretly appropriated (by rough approximation, by lip reading, etc.) and transmitted orally. The seventeenth-century English spoken by the master class was refracted through the illicit channels of

communication available to the black and used to embody the subterranean semantics of a nascent culture which developed in direct defiance
of the master's wishes. Distortion was inevitable, perhaps even deliberate.

Subsequently, the language developed its own vocabulary, syntax and
grammar; but it remains essentially a shadow-language fulfilling in a more
exaggerated and dramatic way those requirements, which under normal
circumstances, are satisfied by regional working-class accents and group
argot. Form implicitly dictates content, and poles of meaning, fixed
immutably in a bitter and irreversible experience, silently reconstruct that
experience in everyday exchange. This fact is intuitively grasped by the
members of certain West Indian subcultures, and language is used as a
particularly effective means of resisting assimilation and preventing
infiltration by members of the dominant groups. As a screening device
it has proved to be invaluable; and the 'Bongo talk' and patois of the Rude
Boy deliberately emphasize its subversive rhythms so that it becomes an
aggressive assertion of racial and class identities. As a living index to the
extent of the black's alienation from the cultural norms and goals of those
who occupy higher positions in the social structure, the creole language
is unique.

The expulsion of the black from the wider linguistic community meant
that a whole culture evolved by a secret and forbidden osmosis. Deprived
of any legitimate cultural exchange, the slave developed an excessive
individualism and a set of cultural artefacts which together represent the
vital symbolic transactions which had to be made between slavery and
freedom, between his material condition and his spiritual life, between his
experience of Jamaica and his memories of Africa. In a sense, the transition
was never satisfactorily accomplished, and the black Jamaican remains
suspended uneasily between two worlds neither of which commands a
total commitment. Unable to repair this cultural and psychological breach,
he tends to oscillate violently from one world to the other and ultimately
he idealizes both. Ultimately, indeed, he is exiled from Jamaica, from
Africa, from Britain and from Brixton, and sacrifices his place in the real
world to occupy an exalted position in some imaginative inner dimension
where action dissolves into being, where movement is invalidated and
difficult at the best of times, where solutions are religious rather than
revolutionary.

In fact, the initial rationalizations of slavery took an explicitly
religious form. Barred from the white man's churches, the slave learnt the
Christian doctrine obliquely and grafted it, with varying degrees of success,
on to the body of pagan beliefs which he had carried over from Africa. The
residual superstitions (voodoo, witchcraft, etc.) persist even now beneath
the surface of the Christian faith and periodically reassert themselves in
their original forms in the hills and rural areas of Jamaica. The schools of
Christian worship native to Jamaica still retain the ancient practices of the

trance, spirit-possession, and 'speaking in tongues'. As a means of articulating a group response to slavery, these nonconformist churches were to prove very valuable indeed. By appealing at once to the individual (through the doctrine of personal 'grace') and to the group (by promising collective redemption), they provided an irresistible solution — a means not of closing the gulf but of transcending it completely. The Bible offered limitless scope for improvization and interpretation. The story of Moses leading the suffering Israelites out of captivity was immediately applicable and won a permanent place in the mythology of the Jamaican black. The various cults pursued the ambiguous apocalypse, proclaiming at different times divine revolutions, *post mortem* revelations. Whenever God seemed to be procrastinating, there were always the chiliastic cults of the rural areas ready to hurry things up. Even now, on occasion 'Pocomania' (literally 'a little madness') spreads with brief but devastating effect through the townships of the hills, and the Revival is, of course, always there to be revived. Judgement Day, the Day of Turnabout is never remote: it is always the day after tomorrow. And Judgement Day is dear to the heart of every Rasta and every Rudie; and for these it means the redistribution of an exclusively secular power.

Christianity still permeates the West Indian imagination, and a Biblical mythology continues to dominate, but among the unemployed young and the deviant adult population this mythology has been turned back upon itself so that the declared ascendancy of Judaeo-Christian culture (with its emphasis on work and repression) can be scrutinized and ultimately rejected. Instrumental in this symbolic reversal were the Rastafarians.

The Rastafarians believe that the (now deceased) Emperor Haile Selassie of Ethiopia is God and that his accession to the Ethiopian throne fulfils the prophecy made by Marcus Garvey, 'Look to Africa, when a black king shall be crowned, for the day of deliverance is near'. But the religious milieu in which Rastafarianism evolved demanded a specifically Biblical mythology and this had to be re-appropriated to serve a different set of cultural needs, just as the 'Protestant Ethic' in Western Europe had performed its own re-appropriation of the original Judaic form. By a dialectical process of redefinition, the Scriptures, which had constantly absorbed and deflected the revolutionary potential of the Jamaican black, were used to locate that potential, to negate the Judaeo-Christian culture. In the more concise idiom of the Jamaican street-boys, the Bible was taken, read and 'flung back rude'.

Thus, Haile Selassie is not only the Ras Tafari, the Negus, the King of Kings, and the Living God, but also specifically the Conquering Lion of the Tribe of Judah. (Recently, the simple appellation 'Jah' has been used.) In these formulations the racial and religious problems which had preoccupied the Jamaican black for centuries converged and found immediate and simultaneous resolution. Predictably, the cult drew its support chiefly from the slums of Kingston. The UCWI research paper of 1960, *The Ras Tafari Movement in Kingston, Jamaica*, reporting a first-hand study of the movement, managed to set out a broad base of beliefs common to all Rastafarians. (M. G. Smith *et al.*, 1960.) Thus:

1 Ras Tafari is the Living God.
2 Ethiopia is the black man's home.
3 Repatriation is the way of redemption for black men. It has been foretold and will occur shortly.
4 The ways of the white man are evil, especially for the black.

The most striking feature is how the Biblical metaphors have been elaborated into a total system — a code of seeing — at once supple and holistic, universal in application, and lateral in direction. The black races are interpreted as the true Israelites and Solomon and Sheba are the black ancestors of Haile Selassie, the black god. Babylon really covers the western world. The police, the Church, and the Government are the agents of imperialism and will share the terrible fate of the white oppressors. Ethiopia is the true name for all Africa. Since 1655, the white man and his brown ally have held the black man in slavery; and although physical slavery was abolished in 1838, it continues in a disguised form. All black men are Ethiopians and the Jamaican Government is not their government. The only true government is the theocracy of the Emperor Haile Selassie. Capitalism is the system of Babylon. Marriage in church is sinful; the true Ethiopian should merely live with a black 'Queen' whom he should treat with the utmost respect. (She, for her part, must never straighten her hair.) Alcohol is forbidden, as is gambling. Jamaican beliefs in obeah, magic and witchcraft are seen as superstitious nonsense. Revivalism compounds mental slavery. Ganja is sacred. Worldly possessions are not necessary and the individual ownership of property is frowned upon. Work is good but alienated labour is quite simply a perpetuation of slavery. All brethren are reincarnations of ancestral slaves; reincarnation is the reaffirmation of a lost culture and tradition. All brethren who regard Ras Tafari as God, regard man as God. 'Men' are mortal, sinners and oppressors. 'Men' are those who know the Living God, the brethren and are immortal and One. (One locksman will address another as 'bra' (brother) and double up the first person singular 'I and I' — instead of using the 'you and I' construction.)

Beyond these 'certainties' which remain relatively static, the locksman habitually resorts to the rhetorical modes of the Bible — the riddle, the paradox, the parable — to demonstrate that he is in possession of the 'true word'. Michael Thomas (1973) quotes a hermetic locksman called Cunchyman who tells how he has conquered the tyranny of work by 'capturing' an axe (which can kill thirteen men who use it for chopping wood all their lives) and hanging it on the wall.

Such syncretic and associative patterns of thought make all knowledge immediately (i.e., magically) accessible. Thus, when sufficiently stoned, the locksman will, as Michael Thomas (1973) asserts, discuss literally anything (e.g., which is more powerful — lightning or electricity) with all the casuistry and conviction of a Jesuit priest. Ultimately, technology capitulates to belief; belief succumbs to knowledge; and thought is really felt. At this point, a harmonious relationship between the inner and outer dimensions is made possible and the 'bra' is said to 'head rest with Jah'. This explicit identification with the Godhead automatically demands a denial of linear systems; an end to all distinctions, and invites an extreme subjectivism. Of course, the conversion of science into poetry did not lead to the expected redistribution of real power. But the crucial act of faith constitutes an archetypal technique of appropriation which escaped the traditional religious displacement by grounding God; it entailed a radical reappraisal of the black Jamaican's potential. We need only turn to the Rude Boy to assess the revolutionary significance of the Rasta perspective. For the secularization of the Rasta Godhead coincided with the politicization of the dispossessed Rude Boy, and the new aesthetic which directed and organized the locksman's perceptions, found a perfect form in reggae.

Music and the Overthrow of Form

Reggae itself is polymorphous — and to concentrate upon one component at the expense of all others involves a reduction of complex cultural processes. Thus, reggae is transmogrified American 'soul' music, with an overlay of salvaged African rhythms, and an undercurrent of pure Jamaican rebellion. Reggae is transplanted Pentecostal. Reggae is the Rasta hymnal, the heart cry of the Kingston Rude Boy, as well as the nativized national anthem of the new Jamaican government. The music is a mosaic which incorporates all the strands that make up black Jamaican culture; the call and response patterns of the Pentecostal Church, the devious scansion of Jamaican street talk, the sex and the cool of United States R and B, the insistent percussion of the locksmen's jam-sessions, are all represented.

Even the etymology of the word 'reggae' invites controversy. In Michael Thomas (1973), Bulldog, A Rude Boy who has made the grade in West Kingston, claims that it was derived from 'ragga' which was an 'uptown' way of saying 'raggamuffin' and that the implied disapproval was welcomed by those who had liked the music. Alternatively, there have been readings which stress the similarity with the word *raga* (the Indian form) and still others which claim that reggae is simply a distortion of Reco (who, with Don Drummond, was one of the original 'ska' musicians). The emergence of the music itself has provoked even fiercer debate, and one's response to the music depends upon whether one believes the music evolved spontaneously out of a group experience or as part of a conscious policy of nativization dictated from above.

Broadly speaking, though, the commercial interests of the entrepreneurs who controlled the new record industry militated against any large-scale intervention by the central government. Moreover, the impetus toward Africanization was already showing itself in the development of the Ras Tafari movement and in the disillusioned withdrawal of the unemployed youth. The locksmen were not only the militant core of the Rasta movement; they also provided a nucleus around which less coherent forms of protest could gather, and the dialogue which ensued found operatic expression in reggae.

Before 'ska', Jamaica had little distinctive music of its own. Jamaican 'mento' was a rather emasculated musical form, combining local dialect 'folk songs' with a watery version of African rhythm — but in the 1950s, American R and B began to attract attention. Men like Duke Reid were quick to recognize the potential for profit and launched themselves as disc-jockeys forming the flamboyant aristocracy of the shantytown slums; the era of the sound system began. Survival in the highly competitive world of the backyard discos, where rival disc-jockeys vied for the title of the 'boss-sound', demanded ingenuity and enterprise; and, as R and B began to lose its original impetus in the late fifties, the more ambitious d-j's branched out into record production themselves. Usually, an instrumental recording was all that was necessary, and the d-j would improvise the lyrics. The 'ska' beat made its debut on these early unlabelled discs. Ska is a kind of jerky shuffle played on an electric guitar with the treble turned right up. The emphasis falls on the upbeat rather than on the offbeat as in R and B and is accentuated by the bass, drums and brass sections. Ska is structurally a back-to-front version of R and B.

Once again, as with language and religion, distortion of the original form appears to be deliberate, as well as inevitable; and inversion seems to denote appropriation, signifying that a cultural transaction has taken place. However, the alchemy which turned soul into ska was by no means simple. The imported music interacted with established subterranean forms carried across from Africa and these forms left an indelible mark on the semantic of ska.

The burra dance was particularly significant; played on the bass, funde and repeateer drums, it constituted an open celebration of criminality. Since the early 30s, it had been the custom for the inhabitants of the West Kingston slums to welcome discharged prisoners back into the communities with the 'burra'. As the locksmen began to clash regularly with the police in the late 40s, a liaison developed between locksmen and hardened criminals. The dreadlocks of the Rastamen were absorbed into the arcane iconography of the outcast and many Rastas openly embraced the outlaw status which the authorities seemed determined to thrust upon them. Still more made permanent contacts in the Jamaican underworld whilst serving prison terms for ganja offences. In time, the locksmen took over the burra dance completely, calling the burra drums 'akete drums'. Inevitably, the criminal ambience which surrounded the music survived the transference and the Niyabingi dance which replaced the burra translated the original identification with criminal values into an open commitment to terrorist violence. The crime and music of West Kingston were thus linked in a subtle and enduring symbiosis; and they remained yoked together even after the infiltration of soul. Moreover, the locksmen continued to direct the new music, and to involve themselves creatively in its production. Meanwhile, a survey in 1957 had revealed that 18% of the labour force was without work. It had now become conceivable that: 'many young persons will pass through the greater part of their lives having never been regularly employed'. (Doxey, 1969.) The embittered youth of West Kingston, abandoned by the society which claimed to serve them, were ready to look to the locksman, to listen to his music, and to emulate his posture of withdrawal. Behind the swagger and the sex, the violence and the cool of the Rude Boy music of the sixties stands the visionary Rastaman with his commodious rhetoric, his all embracing metaphors.

And so, ska was resilient, armoured music; 'rough and tough' in more ways than one. Its inception guaranteed it against serious interference from above. The stigma which was originally attached to ska by the official arbiters of good taste in Jamaica relates to the criminal connotations of the 'burra' dance, and the early attempts on the part of the government at manufacturing a national sound were frankly unsuccessful. Eddie Seaga, one-time member of the Jamaican Labour Government tried to impose a nationalist bias on the new music, and recruited Bryon Lee to promote Jamaica abroad. The music suffered somewhat in the translation. Bryon Lee was too polished to play ska properly, and raw ska was too 'rude' to interest a world market at that time.

So, ska was left, more or less to its own devices. In the early sixties, the record industry developed under the auspices of Seaga at *West Indian Records*, Ken Khouri at Federal Studies and Chris Blackwell, a white man and son of a plantation owner at *Island* records. But Blackwell did not confine himself to the West Indies; he soon went on to exploit the market in England, where more records were being sold to the homesick rudies than to the native Jamaicans. Blackwell bought premises in the Kilburn Road and began to challenge the monopoly which the *Bluebeat* label had managed to acquire over the West Indian record market in Britain.

His triumph over Bluebeat was publicly acknowledged in 1964, when he launched the first nationally popular ska record, *My Boy Lollipop*, sung with an endearing nasal urgency by the sixteen year old Millie Small. Sometime in the summer of 1966, the music altered recognizably and ska modulated into 'rocksteady'. The horns were given less emphasis or were dropped altogether, and the sound became somewhat slower, more somnambulant and erotic. The bass began to dominate and, as rocksteady, in its turn, became heavier, it became known as reggae. Over the years, reggae attracted such a huge following that Michael Manley used a reggae song *Better Must Come* in his 1972 election campaign. His *People's National Party* won by an overwhelming majority.

But this does not mean that the music was defused; for simultaneously, during this period, the Rude Boys were evolving a visual style which did justice to the tesselated structure of ska. The American soul-element was reflected in the self-assured demeanour; the sharp flashy clothes, the 'jive-ass' walk which the street boys effected. The politics of ghetto pimpery found their way into the street-talk of shanty-town Jamaica, and every Rude Boy, fresh from some poor rural outback, soon began to wheel and deal with the best of them in the ubiquitous bars of Ghost Town and Back O'Wall. The Rude Boy lived for the luminous moment, playing dominoes as though his life depended on the outcome — a big-city hustler with nothing to do, and, all the time rocksteady, ska and reggae gave him the means with which to move effortlessly — without even thinking. Cool, that distant and indefinable quality, became almost abstract, almost metaphysical, intimating a stylish kind of stoicism — survival and something more.

And, of course, there were the clashes with the police. The ganja, and the guns, and the 'pressure' produced a steady stream of Rude Boys desperate to test their strength against the law, and the judges replied with longer and longer sentences. As Michael Thomas (1973) puts it: every Rudie was 'dancing in the dark' with ambitions to be 'the coolest Johnny-Too-Bad on Beeston Street'. Prince Buster lampooned the Bench and sang of 'Judge Dread', who on side one, sentences weeping Rude Boys to 500 years and 10,000 lashes, on side two, grants them a pardon, and throws a party to celebrate their release. The dreary mechanics of crime and punishment, of stigmatization and incorporation, are reproduced endlessly in tragi-comic form on these early records, and the ska classics, like the music of the 'burra' which preceded them, were often a simple celebration of deviant and violent behaviour. Sound system rivalries, street fights, sexual encounters, boxing matches, horse races, and experiences in prison, were immediately converted into folk-song and stamped with the ska beat. The disinherited Dukes and Earls, the Popes and Princes of early ska came across as music-hall gangsters and Prince Buster warned in deadly earnest, with a half-smile that 'Al Capone's guns don't argue'.

But in the world of '007' where the Rude Boys 'loot' and 'shoot' and 'wail' while 'out on probation', 'the policemen get taller', and 'the soldiers get longer' by the hour; and in the final confrontation, the authorities must always triumph. So there is always one more confrontation on the cards, and there is always a higher authority still, and that is where Judgement Day works itself back into Reggae, and the Rastas sing of an end to 'sufferation' on the day when Judge Dread will be consumed in his own fire. The Rastafarian influence on reggae had been strong since the earliest days — ever since Don Drummond and Reco Rodrigues had played tunes like *Father East*, *Addis Ababa*, *Tribute to Marcus Garvey* and *Re-incarnation*. And even Prince Buster, the 'Boss', the Main Man, the individualist par excellence, at the height of the anarchic Rude Boy period, could exhort his followers in *Free Love* to 'act true', to 'speak true', to 'learn to love each other', advising the dissident Rudies that 'truth is our best weapon' and that 'our unity will conquer'.

As the music matured, it made certain crucial breaks with the R and B which had provided the original catalyst. It became more 'ethnic', less frenzied, more thoughtful, and the political metaphors and dense mythology of the locksmen began to insinuate themselves more obtrusively into the lyrics. Groups like the Wailers, the Upsetters, the Melodians and the Lionaires emerged with new material which was often revolutionary, and always intrinsically Jamaican. Some Rude Boys began to grow the dreadlocks, and many took to wearing woolen stocking caps, often in the green, gold and red of the Ethiopian flag to proclaim their alienation from the West. This transformation went beyond style to modify and channel the Rude Boys' consciousness of class and colour. Without overstressing the point there was a trend away from the undirected violence, bravado and competitive individualism of the early sixties, towards a more articulate and informed anger; and if crime continued to offer the only solution ·available, then there were new distinctions to be made. A Rude Boy quoted in Nettleford (1970) exhibits a 'higher consciousness' in his comments on violence:

It's not the suffering brother you should really stick up it is these big merchants that have all these places . . .

As the Rastas themselves began to turn away from violent solutions to direct the new aesthetic, the Rude Boys, steeped in ska, soon acquired the locksmen's term of reference, and became the militant arm of the Rasta movement. Thus, as the music evolved and passed into the hands of the locksmen there was an accompanying expansion of class and colour consciousness through the West Indian community. Of course, I would not isolate the emergence of a 'higher consciousness' from larger developments in the ghettos and on the campuses of the United States. But I would stress the unique way in which these external developments were mediated to the Rude Boy (in Brixton as well as Back O'Wall), how they were digested, interpreted and reassembled by the omniscient Rasta Logos situated at the heart of reggae music. In spite of Manley and Seaga, reggae remained intact. It was never dirigible, protected, as it was, by language, by colour, and by a culture which had been forced to cultivate secrecy against the intrusions of the Master Class.

Moreover, the form of reggae itself militated against outside inter-

ference and guaranteed a certain amount of autonomy. Reggae reversed
the established pattern of pop music by dictating a strong repetitive
bassline which communicated directly to the body and allowed the singer
to 'scat' across the undulating surface of the rhythm. The music and the
words are synchronized in good reggae and co-ordinated at a level which
eludes a fixed interpretation. Linguistic patterns become musical patterns;
both merge with the metabolism until sound becomes abstract, meaning
non-specific. Language abdicates to body-talk, belief and intuition; in
form and by definition, reggae resists definition. The form, then, is
inherently subversive; and it was in the area of form that the Jamaican
street boys made their most important innovations.

The Skinhead Interlude — when the Stomping had to Stop

At the moment we're hero-worshipping the Spades
We're going back to dancing close — because the Spades do it.
                19 year old mod quoted in Hamblett and Deverson, Eds. (1964) p. 22.

There is no need to reiterate the early history of reggae in this country.
Gradually ska took over from bluebeat as the steady pulse which set the
pace of the black Britons' nightlife. The era of the African 'waterfront
boys' which Colin MacInnes (1957) describes was definitely on the wane
and the Jamaican hustler, pimp and dealer began to come into his own.
The music was transmitted through an underground network of shebeens
(house parties), black clubs, and the record shops in Brixton and Peckham,
and Ladbroke Grove, which catered almost exclusively to a West Indian
clientele. Almost but not quite. The early music mobilized an undefined
aggressiveness and generated a cult of extreme individualism, its appeal
was not confined to the members of the black community only. It soon
became also the theme music of the 'hard mods', who often lived in the
same depressed areas of South London where the immigrants congregated,
and who soon started emulating the style of the Rude Boy contingent.
Thus, they wore the 'stingy-brim' (pork pie) hats and the shades of the
Jamaican hustler and even went out of their way to embrace the emblems
of poverty which the immigrant often found unavoidable.* In 1964, at
Margate and Brighton, mods were seen in boots and braces, sporting the
close crop which artificially reproduces the appearance of the short negro
hair styles, favoured at the time by the West Indian blacks. In 1965,
Prince Buster's *Madness* became something of a craze in some mod circles.
That liaison between black and white Rude Boy cultures which was to
last until the end of the decade and was to provoke such a puzzled
reaction from the commentators of youth culture had begun in earnest.

* Thus, the 'hard mods' short levis were a white translation of the West Indian's
ankle-swinger trousers.

Ska obviously fulfilled the needs which mainstream pop music could no longer supply. It was a subterranean sound which had escaped commercial exploitation at a national level and was still 'owned' by the subcultures which had originally championed it. It also hit below the belt in the pleasantest way possible and spoke of the simplicities of sex and violence in a language which was immediately intelligible to the quasi-delinquent adolescent fringe of working-class culture. White 'progressive' music was becoming far too cerebral and drug-orientated to have any relevance for the 'hard mods' whose lives remained totally insulated from the articulate and educated milieu in which the new hippy culture was germinating. And of course, the BBC was hardly the ideal medium — ska became scratchy and lost all its punch when played on a transistor — there was simply not enough bass. Thus, the music remained secret and was disseminated in the Masonic atmosphere of close communal and subcultural interactions. The *Ram Jam* in Brixton was one of the first clubs in London where white and black youths mixed in numbers; but already the disreputable and violent associations began to accumulate round the new music. There were tales of knives, and ganja at the *Ram Jam*, and there were more than enough risks for any white Rudie prepared to take his life into his hands to step into Brixton, and prove his pilled-up manhood.

By 1967, the skinhead had emerged from this larval stage and was immediately consigned by the press to the 'violent menace' category which the mainstream pop culture of the time appeared increasingly reluctant to occupy. As the startling flora and fauna of San Francisco were making their spectacular debut along the Kings Road in the summer, Dandy Livingstone, the first British reggae star to gain national recognition, sang *Rudy a Message to You* to audiences in the less opulent boroughs of South London, and rallied his followers around a different standard altogether. The links which bound the hard mod to the Rude Boy subculture were drawn even tighter in the case of the skinhead. The long open coats worn by some West Indians were translated by the skinheads into the 'crombie' which became a popular article of dress amongst the more reggae-oriented groups (i.e., amongst those who defined themselves more as midnight ramblers than as afternoon Arsenal supporters). Even the erect carriage and the loose limbed walk which characterize the West Indian street-boy were (imperfectly) simulated by the aspiring 'white negroes'. In clubs like the *A-Train*, *Sloopy's* and *Mr B's* the skinheads mingled with young West Indians, called each other 'rass' and 'pussy clot' cracked their fingers like thoroughbred Jamaicans with as much panache and as little wincing as possible, talked 'orses' and 'pum-pum' and moved with as much studied cool as they could muster.

This spontaneous movement towards cultural integration was unprecedented but it was not to have any permanent salutary effect on race relations within South London's working-class communities. For, despite the fact that the skinhead might dance the 'shuffle' or the 'reggay' with a certain amount of style, despite the fact that he might speak a few random phrases of patois with the necessary disregard for English syntax, it was all a little artificial — just a bit too contrived to be convincing. Despite everything, he could never quite make that cultural transition. And when he found himself unable to follow the thick dialect and densely packed Biblical allusions which mark the later reggae he must have felt even more hopelessly alienated. Excluded even from the ranks of the excluded, he was left out in the cold, condemned to spend his life in Babylon because the concept of Zion just didn't make sense. And even if he could make that sympathetic passage from Notting Hill to Addis Ababa, from a whiteness which wasn't worth much anyway, to a blackness which just might mean something more, he only found himself trapped further in an irresolvable contradiction. For the Rude Boys had come of age and the skins were sentenced to perpetual adolescence, and although Desmond Dekker topped the British charts in 1969 with *Israelite* (a cry to Ethiopia) the brief miscegenation of the sixties was at an end.

The 'Africanization' (or 'Rastification') of reggae which I have already emphasised in the sections on Jamaica, militated against any permanently close contact between black and white youth cultures.

By the early 70s, the growing stress upon purely black themes was proving insupportable to even skinhead ears and tended to prohibit white involvement. This parting of the ways had been preparing for years outside the dance-halls, in the daytime world of school and work. Firstly, as Dilip Hiro points out, the close proximity into which black and white children were thrown at school tended to break down the cruder racial myths. The illusion of white superiority could hardly be supported by children who were growing up next to their supposed superiors without noticing any appreciable difference either in performance or potential. On leaving school, nonetheless, the black and white school leavers were thrown into fierce competition for what unskilled work was available, and the white youth, more often than not, was given preference. If the black school leaver sought skilled work he was likely to be even more bitterly disappointed. According to the *Observer* (14 July 1968) white youths in 'deprived' areas of black settlement like Paddington and Notting Hill were almost five times more likely to get skilled jobs than coloured youngsters. To the first generation of immigrants from the West Indies, England had promised a golden future, and if that promise had not been fulfilled, there seemed little point in looking elsewhere. In fact, to do so would be to admit defeat and failure. Whereas the older West Indian might go on working on the buses or queueing up for the dole, concealing his bitterness behind an insouciant smile, the young black Briton was less inclined to shrug and forbear.

The reassessment of the African heritage currently underway in

Jamaica and the USA was bound to provide channels through which his anger could be directed and his dignity retrieved. Thus the cry of the Rastas for African redemption was welcomed by the disappointed diaspora of South London. Exiled first from Africa, and then from the West Indies to the cold and inhospitable British Isles, the longing for the Healing of the Breach was felt with an even greater poignancy by the dispossessed Rude Boys of Shepherds Bush and Brixton.

The cult of Ras Tafari appealed at least as strongly to the black youth of Great Britain as it did to their cousins in Jamaica. If anything it proved even more irresistible, giving the stranded Community at once a name and a future, promising the Lost Tribes of Israel just retribution for the centuries of slavery, cultivating the art of withdrawal so that rejection could be met by rejection. All this was reflected in and communicated through the music which had found in Britain an even larger and more avid audience than in its country of origin. Of course, the skinheads turned away in disbelief as they heard the Rastas sing of the 'have-nots' seeking 'harmony' and exhorting their black brothers to 'be good in (their) neighbourhood'. More odious still to the skinheads was the Rasta greeting of 'Peace and Love' which many young Rudies adopted (along with the Rasta handclasp). The wheel had come full circle and the skinhead, who had sought refuge from the posturing beatitudes of the pot-smoking hippie in the introverted coterie of the black delinquent young, was confronted with what appeared to be the very attitudes which had originally dictated his withdrawal. It must have seemed, as the Rudies closed their ranks, that they had also changed their sides, and the doors were doubly locked against the bewildered skinhead.

Such an outcome had been inevitable sooner or later. The transposed religion, the language, the rhythm, and the style of the West Indian immigrant guaranteed his culture against any deep penetration by equivalent white groups. Simultaneously, the apotheosis of alienation into exile enabled him to maintain his position on the fringes of society without feeling any sense of cultural loss. For the rest, the Biblical terms, the fire, the locks, and Haile Selassie *et al.* served to resurrect politics, providing the mythical wrappings in which the bones of the economic structure could be clothed so that exploitation could be revealed and countered in the ways traditionally recommended by the Rastafarian. The metasystem thus created was constructed around precise and yet ambiguous terms of reference and whilst remaining rooted in the material world of suffering and oppression, it could escape, literally at a 'moment's' notice, into an ideal dimension which transcended the time-scale of the dominant ideology. If a more straightforward language of rebellion had been chosen, it would have been more easily dealt with and assimilated by the dominant class against which it was directed. Paradoxically, 'dread' only communicates so long as it remains incomprehensible to its intended victims, suggesting the unspeakable rites of an insatiable vengeance. And the exotica of Rastafarianism provided distractive screens behind which the Rude Boy culture could pursue its own devices unhindered and unseen.

References

Doxey, G. V., 1969: *Survey of the Jamaican Economy*. Govt. Report.
Hamblett, C. and Deverson, J., 1964: *Generation X*. Tandem Books.
Hiro, D., 1973: *Black British, White British*. Pelican.
MacInnes, C., 1957: *City of Spades*. Weidenfeld and Nicolson.
Nettleford, R., 1970: *Mirror, Mirror*. William Collins and Sangster (Jamaica), Ltd.
Smith, M. G., Angier, R. and Nettleford, R., 1960: *The Ras Tafarian Movement in Kingston, Jamaica*. Institute for Social and Economic Research, UCWI, Kingston, Jamaica.
Thomas, M., 1973: 'The Wild Side of Paradise'. *Rolling Stone*, 9 July.

18

Fictions in Mass Entertainment

David Chaney

The adjustment of reality to the masses and of the masses to reality is a process of unlimited scope, as much for thinking as for perception.
(Benjamin, 1970 p. 225.)

In this paper I want to talk about some issues related to different types of fictional experience. By fictional experience I mean participation, however passively, in performances whose central rationale is not functional. Examples of such performances might take the form of dramatic stagings, recorded narratives or ritual acts. Such performances may incidentally assist the achievement of individual or collective aspirations, but their prime significance for the community does not rest on any such heuristic qualities. Although fictional experience is often articulated through stories which have not 'actually' happened, it is not an illusory experience, it is a distinct kind of social participation which we engage in for its own sake. It is a 'story we tell ourselves about ourselves' — a form of communal self-reflection. Thus fiction is not seen as the opposite of factual but as cultural phenomena in which men symbolically express some limited understanding of their life in a particular socio-cultural milieu. As our concern is with interpretation rather than evaluation, the characterization of fiction presented here does not provide for intrinsic differences between cultural traditions, for example between the pure as opposed to the applied arts.

In the first part of the paper I shall discuss the distinctiveness of fictional experience. I will not point to a number of examples and hope to deduce what it is about them that enables us to agree that they are fictions, but will explore the distinction between doing something for whatever reason and doing something self-consciously so that the 'doing' rather than the 'something' is emphasized. There are a multiplicity of occasions, for example when we play or when we narrate a story, in which we are forced to reflect how we normally go about everyday experience. I shall therefore introduce some material from the academic literature on play and narrative to elucidate features of fictional reflection. This will provide a basis for an insight into how we can most usefully understand the changes in fictional experience which have taken place as popular culture in urban-industrial societies has become a culture of mass entertainment. To take an absurdly extreme example, I take it for granted that to participate in the production and appreciation of a medieval festival (cf. Southern, 1975) is a very different type of fictional experience to becoming a regular member of the audience for 'Coronation Street'. I also take it for granted that we cannot hope to begin to appreciate the differences unless we base our analysis on the contrasts in communal, technical and productive relationships through which each performance is 'staged'. To conceptualize these relationships as a conglomerate base through which a common 'fictional entity' is mediated, and thus changed, is to miss the illuminating senses in which fictional experience is articulated in those relationships (and vice versa). I hope to clarify this point in the course of the paper, for now it is sufficient to claim that the majority of sociological studies of mass culture have treated the performance as a thing or commodity which is consumed with better or worse 'effects' according to some version of the process of mediation through such relationships.

It may be that to approach the study of mass entertainment through a vocabulary of 'fiction', 'performance' and 'the constitution of reality' will seem puzzling. We take the distinction between art and life pretty much for granted, conventionally using some sense of more-or-less real to distinguish between them; and assume that the distributive facilities of mass communication merely enlarge the scale on which 'art-like' occasions are available to the general public. The consequence of these presuppositions, as can be seen in a summary perusal of the history of mass-communications research, is to pose a number of questions about who produces what for whom and whether it is 'good' for them — in ways that are always recognized to be difficult to specify. I do not share an approach which tries to answer descriptive questions about who and whom, although I think the answers to such questions are always interesting, but instead believe that how the members of any particular society make the distinction between art and everyday life will have crucial implications for what they expect the real world to include and be like. I therefore recommend that we try to take apart our presuppositions about how we recognize different sorts of experience, in order that we can more fully appreciate the significance of changes in the way we order our expectations. Fictional experience is therefore an extremely loose reference to that class of occasions which have in common certain cultural expectations rather than any shared phenomenal features. An important aspect of how our society takes itself, as well as its art, for granted, may be elucidated by inquiring into the significance of why some of us take the fictional depiction of the routine slaughter of human beings as seriously (Gerbner, 1970) as we, and others, take the fictional elaboration of Hamlet's ambivalence about the necessity of morality.

The making of fictional experience is therefore a mode of social participation analogous to all other modes of human work. It is distinctive in that it is inherently self-conscious, the result of participants' work; the performance is generally meaningful as a mode of discourse independent of the intentions of the author(s). There is therefore a level of meaning to a performance in which human experience is displayed as if it were real experience. Fiction here does not refer to the sort of social participation but to the topic (subject) of that participation, to the narrative which comprises the distinctive character of the performance. This approach throws into relief an implicit feature of the social organization of the making of fictions — the participants must be sensitive to the conventional boundaries which mark off the narrative discourse of the performance from the discourse of staging that performance. I will use a characterization of these boundaries in the fictions of mass entertainment as a way of illuminating the articulation of fictional experience in human work. The significance of this approach is that it is the beginning of an alternative to the sociological consumerism mentioned in the previous paragraph, an alternative in which we take seriously the idea that popular art interprets its context: '. . . what is the significance of conceiving the world on the terms laid down by popular art, and what is the relationship between this form of consciousness and other forms — scientific, ethnic, religious, mythological — which popular art variously displaces, penetrates or merely co-exists with'? (Carey & Kreiling, 1974 p. 226.)

To elucidate the idea of conventional boundaries we can refer to the work of Erving Goffman.[1] Once we put on one side the question of whether or not there is a bed-rock reality to which doubts about illusion can be compared, we realize that it is more useful to compare 'basic frameworks for understanding' than assume that each individual's understanding is private to himself. One of these frameworks is theatrical presentation in which the actors hope they share some common understanding with the audience, thereby implying that: ' . . . a corpus of transcription practices must be involved for transforming a strip of offstage, real activity into a strip of staged being'. (Goffman, 1975 p. 138.) The process of transformation can of course involve potentially infinite layers of embedding in which the theatrical frame is used to depict actors staging a theatrical frame: 'The rehearsal of a play is a re-keying, just as is a rehearsal staged within a play a part of its scripted content; but in the two cases, the rim of the activity is quite different, the first being a rehearsal and the second a play. Obviously, the two rehearsals have radically different statuses as parts of the real world'. (*ibid* p. 82). Our concern is not really with the sophistry of the dramaturgic metaphor but with the use of rules for distinguishing between the 'rim' of different activities. The term 'rules' in this context is not

1 The reference to a 'Goffman-type' approach is misleading, I am specifically taking up the idea of frame as developed in his most recent book; I am not writing as somebody particularly influenced by his work.

meant to imply that normal, competent members of a society carry a mental dictionary around with them so that they can look up potentially puzzling features of others' behaviour, dress or speech, but that styles of interaction are collusive — participants have more or less willingly and/or consciously to observe and recognize constitutive conventions to get that 'strip of activity' accomplished.

It is precisely because the negotiation of comprehensible experience is a routine feature of social interaction that analyses of mundane accomplishments by ethnomethodologists frequently appear leaden in their exhaustiveness. When our concern is with styles of fictional experience we have an opportunity to incorporate studies of the specificity of interactional exchanges in a comparative context there ostensibly similar behaviour has a different frame. Besides fictional depiction, traditional examples of such shifts in context are benign or malignant deceptions and engagement in play: 'Play is behaviour of which the central mode of operation is to puzzle, to tease, to doubt at reality. The "as-if" of the metaphor, the contradiction of the paradox, and the specificity of rule are the realities of its substance . . . the unknown is *homo ludens*'s adventure'. (Reilly, 1974 p. 141.) When we play we create a sense of order which is intentionally limited, not in terms of our involvement but in terms of the significance of our actions. Play therefore frames its content in such a way that the adherence to rules and particularly the rule that the frame is self-conscious is central: to be totally absorbed in the world of play is to become a fantasist, it is to lose the distance which gives us some sense of control. Our participation in play is a deliberate exploration of the salience of framing, it turns analogy from a tool into a justification: 'Play is thus defined by a double reference, on the one hand to our normal world (the real things that are to be transformed to bracketed) and on the other to the unreality given to them'. (Omvedt, 1966 p. 6.)[2]

The crucial shift in our analysis turns on the idea of distance, a self-consciousness of the possible import of our participation. The actions, the behaviour undertaken when playing have a different significance to the same actions when not playing. Therefore play is not marked off by distinct behaviour, or by a distinct attitude when participating, but by the relationship between 'playing' and the behaviour of play which normally constitutes routine experience. Play lacks consequences because it encapsulates itself, we can usually choose to end the play and resume conventional responsibilities. And thus play's connotations of a lack of seriousness — it involves a suspension of conventional constraints. I do not wish to become involved in a digression about the extent to which fiction is a mode of play, or whether they are completely distinct modes

2 The relationships between play and fiction, as are all the points made in this paper, are more fully discussed in Chaney (forthcoming).

of sensibility. The salience of play to the subject of this essay derives from the way in which any analysis of play is forced into a concern with meta-phoric representation — participation in a phraseology of action in which the crucial concern is with the manner of phrasing rather than the action. Clifford Geertz's paper on the cockfight in Balinese culture offers a very illuminating discussion of the interaction between drama and theme. Although each playing of the cocks is a particular situation, the exemplary aura of that which is played is such that crucially significant tones of a style of life are re-enacted: 'Quartets, still lifes and cockfights are not merely reflections of a pre-existing sensibility analogically represented: they are positive agents in the creation and maintenance of such a sensibility'. (Geertz, 1972 p. 28.) A metaphor is a form of persuasive imagery and inasmuch as it depends upon an unlikely combination of phenomena (George is lion-like) it works through an implicit fracturing of frames. A painting, or play or novel, etc., is similarly persuasive — the ostensible representation only becomes sensible when its status as a painted representation becomes clear. The painting needs our prior sense of the ability reflexively to reflect on the structure of perception.

When we shift from participating in a particular instance of the social construction of reality — the use of a relevant frame — to framing that participation so that there is a double-frame, then this external frame provides a *story* which makes sense of the embedded activities. It has been argued that if the proper concern of the human studies is with understand-ing rather than explaining social experience (the import of this distinction has been fairly exhaustively discussed recently; for those unfamiliar with the topic two introductory books are Outhwaite, 1975 and Rickman, 1967), then the analyst is necessarily as involved in formulating stories as are the participants in reflecting on their experience. (To put it baldly, how could the sociologist have a privileged position available to him when he was being a sociologist that allowed him to formulate frames for experience that were 'better than' the frames employed in the course of that experience?) Mink has discussed the work of several theorists of the historian's profession who have been led to related conclusions: 'The features which enable a story to flow and us to follow, then, are the clues to the nature of historical understanding. An historical narrative . . . makes them intelligible by unfolding the story which connects their significance'. (Mink, 1970 p. 545.) At this point in his discussion Mink makes another point which has been stressed in our preceeding paragraphs: 'But to under-stand what a story is, is to know what it is to *follow* a story, that is . . . what in general are the features of a story which makes it followable. And this in turn is not significantly different from following a game in progress'. (Mink, pp. 544—5, emphasis in original.) The danger of using game rather than play in this analogy is that games might suggest an unknown out-come; one might follow a game to discover the winner. Although for the naive student history might be like this, the professional accomplishment of history has not such surprises; and indeed for most narrative dramas such as those by Shakespeare or Hollywood films it would seem inappropriate to dismiss them because you know how they ended, and for many arts — like painting — the 'ending' is inextricably available from the beginning. It therefore seems more appropriate to suggest that narratives, like play, are a mode of persuasive framing which offer an interpretive stance through the relationship between the 'events' and the synoptic vision framing those events.

The use of 'persuasive' in this context does not mean that the orderliness of our stories is misleading through being selective. We need a way of making order out of chaos, so that we have a frame for a story which is both selective and convincing because its implicit order 'makes sense': in writing our history we find it obvious to begin with temporal succession, but this is not a cultural universal; it depends upon a prior sense of time (and the relationships between events) which is divisible into years. We do not play because we are searching for order or because we like following rules, but we use our criteria of order to provide rules to 'make sense' of social situations. When we play we use the rules of social interaction arbitrarily as in the games and routines partners in sexual play make up for themselves. In such erotic encounters participants may enact a characterization of themselves as masterful or coquettish, etc., although recognizing that the strategies which inform such identities are fragile constructs. But if we do not play because we like following rules, we nonetheless constitute rule-governed occasions so that we can enjoy the power of flirting with identity and knowing that the order which underlies identity is conditional upon our consent. (It is perhaps in this sense that the attempt to create a revolutionary political order sometimes seems 'playful', cf. Willener, 1970.) As the pleasure comes from 'playing' with order the culmination of that order in unexpected victory (or conversion) is not central, although a dramatic resolution (and thus celebration) of that order might be essential: '. . . in the configurational comprehension of a story which one *has followed*, the end is connected with the promise of the beginning as well as the beginning with the promise of the end, . . . To comprehend temporal succession means to think of it in both directions at once'. (Willener, 1970 p. 554 emphasis in original.)

The thesis that part of the persuasive force of fiction derives from the 'story-ness' of the narrative frame, is illuminated by an emphasis on the reflexive character of interpretive frames. A good illustration is provided by Weider's discussion of 'the convict code' in penal settings. (Weider, 1974.) (The convict code is traditionally understood to be those norms and rules which preclude any great intimacy between warder and convict, that is, they inform a persistent 'them' and 'us' attitude.) This code is interpretive in the sense that it provides an orderly structure within which the relationships of staff and inmates can seem plausible to both. This is not to say that the code is an integrative device but that it serves to impede integration and at the same time 'explain' the obstacles to integration. One way of conceptualizing explanatory accounts is to think of them as a theory which explains something 'out there'. Weider illustrates that approach by the example of a travelogue in which there are a set of pictures and an accompanying sound-track; sound and picture are distinct and the former is employed to make sense of the latter. The convict code is not such an interpretive sound-track, it is through its use by the participants that the code is more than a neutral commentary, it has interpretive force: 'The code, then, is much more a *method* of moral persuasion and justification than it is a substantive account of an organized way of life. It is a way, or set of ways, of causing activities to be seen as morally, repetitively, and constrainedly organized'. (Weider, 1974 p. 158 emphasis in original.) The narrative in this example is therefore not a frame which is artifically devised to explain a set of events and actions independently known: '. . . the code differs from a "scientific" explanation of actual patterns of resident conduct in several important respects. Its employment *simultaneously identifies and 'explains'* the particular events it renders observable' (Weider, 1974 p. 170 emphasis added); the frame is only analytically separable from the process of knowing.

I hope that a feature of this paper that some may have found puzzling, will now be clearer. I have several times claimed that we need identifying characteristics of fictional experience, and yet I have not examined a particular performance or a fictional tradition for clues to such characteristics. My reasons for not doing so may be apparent, in that such examples are only recognizable through a prior knowledge of the characteristics I am trying to elucidate. I have adopted an alternative strategy and cited comparable discussions of reflexive framing, occasions on which participants re-create experience for its own sake rather than for what it can accomplish. This approach has been used to make three points about narratives: (1) they are cognitive, they involve deliberately changing the relationship between experience and its routine accomplishment; (2) they are configurational, in that they offer a synoptic vision; and therefore (3) they are reflexive, in that a narrative provides for its own possibility. To the extent that these points are valid, fictional experience, or more specifically popular art, is a form of consciousness offering a distinct style of understanding.

It is important to emphasize at this point that forms of consciousness are not abstract entities which hang unsupported in some mysterious social space. They are articulated through social relationships which in the European tradition have usually taken the form of an individual or group producing an object which can be sold, although the process of selling may not involve ownership but instead access as in the case of a theatrical performance. In the course of the last two hundred years it has become possible for all types of fictional performance to be infinitely reproduced so that the performance is potentially available to an anonymous and massive audience. The process of reproduction may be implicit in the type of performance as in the example of a radio broadcast or a photographic print, in which case it does not make sense to look for an original which is copied. For other types of performance, the obvious example being an oil painting or a sculpture, there is an original, but very high-quality reproductions can easily be mass-produced. It should be stressed that to describe these possibilities does not mean that all contemporary fictional performances are made for or available to a mass audience — as in the case of fashionable clothes the very existence of mass production has provided very lucrative opportunities for a small group of individual producers who can guarantee originality. Infinite reproducibility has meant, however, that popular art, where audience members by definition cannot afford the costs of unique performances, has been characterized by a process of standardization, centralization and concentration of ownership of distributive facilities. I do not think I need to provide a precise definition of popular art here; I am referring to those fictional performances produced for the general population (such a vague generalization does not mean that I am ignoring the enormous differences between different groups within the general population).

Standardization, by which I mean the gradual replacement of regional differences, has been an uneven process and has been to some extent disguised by the growth of communities of style such as generational differences. In the case of television, for example, the attempt to mark regional differences by insisting on a number of commercial companies has only been an insult to the inhabitants of those areas with supposedly distinctive regional interests. The developments of local broadcasting both public and commercial, are a contrasting case in which to some extent there does seem to have been slight recovery of local initiative and diversity. Centralization is an obviously related process which refers to the accumulation of reproductive facilities and professional skills in metropolitan centres. One reason for this will be the cost of capital resources, another will be the fashionable character of mass culture industries. Dealing as they do with ephemera, the producers tend to develop life-styles characterized by the traditional features of an urban leisured class — ostentatious display, numerous but rather stylized relationships and a nervous concern with novelty. (It is this style which underlies media producers' use of a counterpoint between authenticity and artificiality when they reflect on their work in fictional reports.) The salience of capital resources is particularly relevant to the third process of concentration of ownership. It is again difficult to generalize about all forms of mass culture but in the main the aspiration to reach a mass audience requires investment in technical facilities which are increasingly owned by corporate resources (for some relevant documentation and discussion see Murdock and Golding, 1974).

I have presented this very brief sketch of major characteristics of the productive relationships of contemporary popular art, because they underlie what I take to be a central feature of our fictional experience: that it is made by a small elite for an anonymous audience. (The use of elite may be queried here but I think it is justified in that the group is obviously influential in the dissemination of information, although it may not be directly connected to the power elite as in societies where the state controls most of the productive resources.) The significance of the distinction between elite and audience is that the narratives of mass culture become leisure rather than play. The latter — play — is an analytic concept in that it refers to a particular sense of following a rule; it is therefore understood structurally while leisure is understood substantively. Leisure is a descriptive term which refers to a way of characterizing time; it became meaningful in the context of industrialization in which time at work was something owned by another and so leisure was a private resource. Paradoxically, the use of such a possession is demonstrated through patronage of a wide range of pursuits and activities provided by a very diffuse 'leisure industry'. The consequent circulation of resources is functional for the economy as a whole, while the very buying of individual leisure tastes encourages the feeling that the articulation of such tastes is the expression of a property right: 'The point to be made is that these pursuits are wholly secular, organized for a commercial market, or at least for a user public, and, by and large, limited to what can be so organized'. (Burns, 1973 p. 46.) Fictional experience in a culture of mass entertainment is the democracy of a cultural supermarket.

It is not my intention to argue that a trend towards leisure is a necessary consequence of the industrialization of popular art. I have tried to argue that when the possibilities of serial reproduction for fictional experience are articulated through structures of productive relationships oriented towards profitability, then performances will tend to become commodities, with consequences for the form of consciousness possible to which I shall return. In order to indicate the complexity of the changes initiated by mechanization of culture, we have to go back to the distinctiveness of fictional experience. I have argued that fictional experience is not less 'real' than other types of social experience; it is the way we participate. This necessarily means that the distinctiveness of fictional experience will change in different social milieux. Another way of putting this is to say that the identity of a performance is not necessarily inherent in the performance — it is mediated through a fabric of constitutive practices. Traditionally the unique work of art is identified through its aura: 'What is aura? A peculiar web of space and time: the unique manifestation of a distance, however near it may be'.

(Benjamin, 1972 p. 20.)[3] When there is no sensible distinction between original and copy, when, that is, the performance is simultaneously available to infinite audiences, identity can no longer depend on the constitution of distance. Thus the decay of aura is part of a process of democratization of objects and experience. A sense of the 'universal equality of things' means that the maker of performances is forced to immerse himself in the world he is commenting upon. His distinctive techniques justify themselves because they presume a neutrality in their use, they are designed to provide the best possible use of themselves rather than the best possible expression of the producer's 'vision'; 'What distinguishes the novel from the story . . . is its essential dependence on the book'. (Benjamin, 1970 p. 87.)

One aspect of our fictional experience has shifted from the social relationships of story-telling to the social relationships of making and distributing books, and in this sense the character of the experience has been crucially re-structured. The conventions of particularistic media, for example story-telling or easel painting, have meant that the story-teller or painter is continually 'present' when we listen to or look at their work. We are continually reminded that this is a personal account, it is an expression of a private sense of experience through shared forms of representation. In contrast, the anonymity of reproducible performances means that representational conventions change from being a device to presuppositions, they presume collective norms of understanding in order for experience to become private: 'Magician and surgeon compare to painter and cameraman. The painter maintains in his work a natural distance from reality, the cameraman penetrates deeply into its web. There is a tremendous difference between the pictures they obtain. That of the painter is a total one, that of the cameraman consists of multiple fragments *which are assembled under a new law.* (Benjamin, 1970 pp. 235−6 emphasis added.)

The idea that communicative technology can operate like a surgeon's knife and needle only makes sense if it is borne in mind that the technology provides for changing conventions of staging. Williams, in a comparatively rare discussion of the relationships between technology and cultural form, has pointed to the 'fit' between seemingly unrelated innovations: 'Indeed it is one of the most striking instances of the complicated relations between new forms of experience and new kinds of technology that Strindberg

3 This is a suitable point to acknowledge the influence that the work of Walter Benjamin has had on the ideas behind this paper, in addition to the material cited in the text see also (1973); I should also acknowledge at this point my interest in the discussions of mass culture by theorists of the 'Frankfurt School', although I do not explore here the debate between, for example, Benjamin and Adorno over the possibilities of mass entertainment − for an introduction to the literature see Slater (1974).

was experimenting with moving dramatic images in the same decade in which, in quite another environment, the pioneers of motion pictures were discovering some of the technical means that would eventually make this kind of dramatic imagery possible and in the end even commonplace'. (Williams, 1974 pp. 56–7.) More specifically he notes that television has been able to develop the potential inherent in the 'natural-ness' of the camera. Because of its mobility and ubiquity the status of the camera in framing news and information is rarely questioned, so that it is easy to stage naturalistic dramas within the conventions of documentary (the Loach/Garnett team has acquired some notoriety in this respect) and even film routine events — families, boardrooms, etc. — as unscripted dramas.[4] Williams argues that the breadth of televisual entertainment, despite its relative technical deficiencies *vis-a-vis* the cinema, ubiquitously available has meant that the ambiguities of television reality are an inherent feature of domestic experience. Thus the technical innovations have facilitated a new stance for narrative presentation, but this stance has had to be articulated within the structure of realism predicated by the dominant framework of productive relationships.

I think it necessary to expand this last point which has been put a little cryptically. I have argued that the presentation of the narratives of mass entertainment as leisure has meant that these narratives have become commodities to be owned. I have further argued that the character of these narratives as fictional experience involves a re-constitution of the 'real' context of fiction. It might be argued that art, because of its marginal position in the corpus of legitimate knowledge of our society, could be seen as a model of revolutionary change. Thus one might expect fictional utopias to inform both the goals and the styles of counter-cultural accounts of alternative realities. Intermittently this has happened in different societies at different times, for example one might instance Russian Futurism in the first decade of the Revolution and certain aspects of 'freak' culture, particularly in America, in the 1960s. More commonly, however, the reconstitution of the boundaries between real and fictional in popular art has been done in such a way that fictional experience has echoed the presuppositions of the dominant norms of reality. What may be called an hypothesis of 'reflection' might be interpreted as a version of economic determinism — that there is a clear correspondence between systemic 'needs' and the ideological messages broadcast through the media. Such 'left-functionalism' is not only subject to the same criticisms as any other functionalist thesis, it also fails to take account of the experience and intentions of participants in the production and enjoyment of popular art, as well as being forced to distort the heterogeneous character of that

4 Unfortunately I do not have space here to take up the implications of documentary narrative in any medium, but a book that has stimulated a lot of ideas is Stott (1973).

art, and finally it cannot specify the mechanisms through which any such correspondence is directed. (An example of functional prescription which, although they are not specifically concerned with popular art, illustrate the specificity of causal theories are Craig's laws of literary development, for example, 'The rise of a genre is likely to occur along with the rise of a class [e.g., in average wealth, in the proportion of the population belonging to it]'. Craig, 1975 p. 160.)

The alternative is to investigate the extent to which the predominant forms of life available in the everyday world are taken as unproblematic in fictional experience, and thereby given an implicit sensibility: 'My purpose here, then, is to study the ways in which television maintains hegemony and legitimates the status quo'. (Tuchman, 1974 p. 5.) The stance of fictional experience towards its topic, in terms of a continuum from criticism to endorsement, is articulated through social structures which are continually emergent. (In Williams's (1973) valuable discussion of hegemony in Marxist cultural theory he distinguishes between residual and emergent forms of both alternative and oppositional culture.) The typifications employed in formulating entertainment, such as the sexist characterization of women, are not personally spiteful — they are institutional practices which 'make sense of' an inherent elision of the complexity of fictions as performances: 'We think that mass media should similarly be viewed as one big, bad clinical record'. (Molotch and Lester, [in Tuchman, 1974 p. 54] refer here to Garfinkel's paper on 'good' organizational reasons for 'bad' clinical records, in which Garfinkel addresses the difficulties for researchers in deriving appropriate information from clinical files; the central point of the analogy is that the 'world' the media report or reflect is assembled, as are clinical records, in terms of 'organizationally relevant purposes and routines' rather than in terms of abstract universally recognizable features of the way the subjects of these reports [the world] 'really are'.)

It is interesting, and consistent with points made earlier in this paper, that the area of mass entertainment that has been most thoroughly investigated in relation to conventions of staging is the world of 'fact' supposedly reported in the news.[5] The distinction between fact and fiction may be said to be consistent with a thesis of ideological hegemony, in that the presentation of news 'as it happens' fleshes out ideological versions of 'objectivity' and 'freedom' so that a mode of construction of reality is reified as the world as it is rather than realizing that: 'We can summarize: News is a constructed reality; newsmaking is political work'. (Tuchman, 1974 p. 64.) Perhaps more relevantly to the general character of this paper, the distinction between fact and fiction through the unproblematic objectivity of 'facts' can be seen to serve the 'fiction-ality'

5 The best introduction to this field is the papers and bibliographic references in Tuchman, 1974; another useful source is Cohen and Young (1973).

of fictional experience. Entertainment is something to be consumed for its own sake, it is vicarious experience which would not accept itself as a way of knowing but implies a contextual world which can be taken for granted. The use of 'it' here imputes an active identity to entertainment which is obviously impossible. The grammatical form is an abbreviated reference to participants' constitutive practices — the emergent form through which the fiction is narrated.

The salience of the implied contrast between fact and fiction to a culture of mass entertainment is brought out by pointing to the accumulation of trivial knowledge. It can be argued that the most alienating cultural style comes in that middlebrow genre exemplified by *The Guinness Book of Records.* In this type of book the insignificant and uninteresting, and often humanly degrading, are thrown together, the only spurious coherence being their status as 'facts'. The absence of order not only gives each of the constituent nuggets of information an equivalent weight, but necessarily implies a range of experience which is atomized and potentially bizarre. The sur-reality is not spectacular, there is no dramatic largesse to offer an alternative phrasing of order — rather the audience is assumed to be decontextualized so that the narrative becomes the technology's omniscient ability to report; the sense that knowledge is related to purpose is inherently fractured. The contrast being drawn here is between the comprehensive stance of narrative which frames understanding and the minutiae of that which is newsworthy:

But comprehension is an individual act of seeing-things-together, . . . As the human activity by which elements of knowledge are converted into *understanding*, it is the synoptic vision without which . . . we might forever pass . . . in some nightmare quiz show where nothing relates 'fact' to 'fact' except the fragmented identities of the participants and the mounting total of the score. (Mink, 1970 p. 553 emphasis in original.)

I hope that a number of strands in the paper are by now coming together. I have emphasized the necessity of shared representational conventions, a frame, in staging fictional performances; but the use of these conventions is not sufficient to define the occasion as one in which a fictional performance is taking place (we occasionally act out characteristics of identities without thinking that we are acting in the sense of participating in a play). Representational conventions are utilized in fictional experience when they are structured by a 'script', that is there is an authorial control over the use and adaptation of conventions. (Although for convenience I use mainly theatrical terms here, the argument is not specific to the theatre or related media; we know that a painting is a painting rather than a drawing, illustration, map, doodle, etc., because we recognize a version of some kind of narrative authority.) Acceptance of the authority of a script is a socially negotiated consensus which will shift

through time and between cultures — the obvious example is the re-
negotiation of form in most media in contemporary art — but in an era of
unique works of art any recognition of author-ity will involve a self-
consciousness of the difference (distance) between the work of the author
and our response to it. When performances become anonymous, in the
sense that they primarily gain identity through exemplification of media
potential, then fictional distance, both as intentional structure and as
stance to contextual 'reality', becomes inherently problematic. Distance
is problematic in mass entertainment because it is not 'given' in the
narrative structure of the performance — the conventions of the
performance are not self-consciously arbitrary. To go back to an earlier
example, partners in sexual play may enact identities for mutual gratification. There is obviously no firm dividing line between this and fetishism,
but part of the frisson of play is a refusal to take the occasion seriously on
its own terms. When we fail to make this refusal the fantasy ceases to be
a game, the presuppositions of play become obsessive. (It is perhaps in
this way that professional sportsmen are such ambiguous figures in public
mythology; they are fetishists not in the sense that they neurotically
observe rituals and routines — although they very frequently do — but in
the sense that they are reifying a diversion into a life.)

The paradox arises that the ubiquity of public recognition ceases to
copy a world 'out there' but becomes the sole means by which we know a
world to be 'there'; mass entertainment does not lay down a new set of
terms for apprehending reality, that which we know to be real is incorporated in and indistinguishable from mass entertainment. To put this
argument in another way: the technology of mass communication has
meant that knowledge is made public (democratization) but is at the same
time negated through being forced to be phrased in the categories used by
the owners of technology (i.e., the relevant elite and their servant intellectuals). The imagery of events happens in a collage of associations which
transcend the frames of fictional experience. It is perhaps not surprising
that so much contemporary art appears dissonant in rupturing conventional
orders of narrative structure: in seeking to retrieve some autonomy the artist
is forced to query either his own narrative stance or the politics of everyday experience. In either case art becomes reflexive rather than romantic,
fetishism robs culture of one of its most important features — the sensual
elaboration of experience. In a culture of entertainment hedonism is
restricted to consumption and erotica necessarily become pornographic.
The *promesse du bonheur* intrinsic to a work of art is stunted and distorted. Instead the time spent in consumption is ritualized and empty. The
unity of contemporary style is not a form of life with inherent dialectical
contradictions, thus it lacks the vitality of speech; instead it is a potential
for use which is so universal that it precludes use; the ubiquity of form
swamps all dialectical contrasts: 'Culture is a paradoxical commodity. So

completely is subject to the law of exchange that it is no longer exchanged; it is so blindly consumed in use that it can no longer be used.
Therefore it amalgamates with advertising'. (Horkheimer and Adorno,
1972 p. 161.)

I have referred above to the problematic character of fictional distance
in mass entertainment. I have tried to show that certain features of the way
the performances of mass entertainment are made has changed their status
as narrative fictions; the distinction between art and everyday life has
become blurred. And yet this shift in narrative stance does not allow only
one consequence. The implicit ambiguity of 'reality', when fictional
experience is part of the collective norms of understanding, facilitates the
exploitation of ambiguity to re-structure what can be taken for granted.
The contrast here is between reification and democratization, in which
the former has the guise of the latter. That is, the cultural supermarket
offers equality of access while leaving the filling of the shelves (the constitution of the performance) an unexplicated given. Democratizing
fictional experience involves more than creating options for audiences. To
fulfil its potential, democratization involves a continual querying of the
conventions authors use to distinguish their work as fictions. It would be
incorrect to imply that this potential has never been explored in mass
entertainment. Perhaps significantly, televisual drama often proves one of
the most stimulating areas of innovation in this respect, but the problems
of the options for fictional dissonance rather than consensus have not
been thought through. The mechanism of culture, inasmuch as it was
part of that total transformation of social relationships referred to as
industrialization, involved an inherent re-casting of authority relationships;
the structure of reality was patently being assembled through human
action. Therefore fictional experience became political in that criteria of
assembly were always debateable. It is not surprising that the articulation
of power conventionally takes the form of masking such a politics, so
that knowledge remains descriptive not analytic.[6] It is for these reasons
that shifts in fictional distance both imply the democratization of
experience and denote reification of commodities.

There is a further layer of complexity in that, as I noted earlier, the
sociologist in formulating his account does not have a privileged position —
an independent narrative stance somehow 'above' the constitutive practices
of other authors. The concept of distance is as salient to his work as it is
to any other narrative. If fictional experience has become reduced to consuming commodities provided by others, we need in our discussion to avoid
echoing that reduction. The argument is therefore that if our analysis rests

6 I was introduced to the idea that power relationships preclude certain possibilities
   becoming 'issues' as much as directing a resolution of any particular issue by Lukes
   (1974); an approach to communication that has been greatly developed in
   Pateman (1975).

at the level of who buys what sort of performance, then we can only offer a description of entertainment as it is done. In order to get at the character of contemporary entertainment we will have to recover a distance so that the presumed context can be clarified. We do not go about this by empirical studies of what is watched because such a study presumes to 'know' the differences between the observed fiction and the audience's everyday world. Instead we must focus on the sense of experience as it is formulated in popular art, precisely how the distinctiveness of fiction is recognized and sustained in a performance. This injunction demands that we do not dissolve the performance into its social background but treat seriously its own claims to distinctiveness. The analytic stance adopted in this paper therefore has methodological implications, in that it queries the framework within which the merits of procedures are conventionally assessed, most importantly the theoretical significance of the word 'mass' as a characterization of communicative relationships. Williams makes the same point through the use of the analogy of socialization; he argues that in conventional social science the concept has been constructed to facilitate questions of procedure rather than questions of consciousness and experience: 'What the process (socialization) has in common, in many different societies, is given a theoretical priority over just the radical differences of "ways" and "functioning", and over the highly differential character of being a "member" of the society'. (Williams, 1974 p. 120, see also 1973.)

It would obviously be inappropriate to hope to locate an evaluative scale against which performances could be measured to assess their worth. And yet this paper has clearly involved contrasts between forms of fictional potential implying a strongly critical stance. The contradiction is resolved if it is realized that the judgements introduced here are not grounded in textual features alone, as they would be in a conventional critical vocabulary, but focus on the text as it is performed, the social constitution of the text. Reflexivity is, like narrative, a word that is rapidly acquiring too many diverse usages to be employed without qualification, but the relationship between self-consciousness and distance which I have used to explore the idea of narrative frame is essentially reflexive. If we presume an alternative to the alienating cultural styles discussed earlier, it may be that we have to begin by a deliberate consideration and use of reflexivity to 'bracket' cultural experience which we take for granted. Thus alienation would become our method rather than our fate: 'The old [alienation] effects quite remove the object represented from the spectator's grasp, turning it into something that cannot be altered; the new are not odd in themselves, though the unscientific eye stamps anything strange as odd. The new alienations are only designed to free socially-conditioned phenomena from the stamp of familiarity which protects them against our grasp today'. (Brecht, in Willett (Ed.), 1964 p. 192.)

References

Benjamin, W., 1970: *Illuminations*. London: Cape.
    1972: 'A Short History of Photography'. *Screen*.
    1973: *Understanding Brecht*. London: New Left Books.

Burns, T., 1973: 'Leisure in Industrial Society'. In M. Smith *et al.* (Eds.), *Leisure and Society in Britain*. London: Allen Lane.

Carey, J. W. and Kreiling, A. L., 1974: 'Popular Culture and Uses and Gratifications'. In J. G. Blumler and E. Katz (Eds.), *The Uses of Mass Communications*. London: Sage.

Chaney, D. (forthcoming): *Taking Popular Art Seriously*. London: E. Arnold.

Cohen, S. and Young, J., 1973: *The Manufacture of News*. London: Constable.

Craig, D., 1975: 'Towards Laws of Literary Development'. In *Marxists on Literature*. London: Penguin.

Geertz, C., 1972: 'Deep Play'. *Daedalus* 101.

Gerbner, G., 1970: 'Cultural Indicators: The Case of Violence in TV Drama'. *Annals of American Academy of Politics and Social Science* Vol. 388.

Goffman, E., 1975: *Frame Analysis*. London: Penguin.

Horkheimer, M. and Adorno, T. W., 1972: 'The Culture Industry'. In *Dialectic of Enlightenment*. New York: Herder and Herder.

Lukes, S., 1974: *Power*. London: Macmillan.

Mink, L. O., 1970: 'History and Fiction as Modes of Comprehension'. *New Literary History* Vol. 1 (3).

Murdock, G. and Golding, P., 1974: 'For a Political Economy of Mass Communications'. In R. Miliband and J. Saville (Eds.), *Socialist Register 1973*. London: Merlin.

Molotch, H. and Lester, M., 1974: 'Accidents, Scandals and Routines'. In G. Tuchman, *op. cit.*

Omvedt, G., 1966: 'Play as an Element in Social Life', *Berkeley Journal of Sociology* Vol. 11.

Outhwaite, W., 1975: *Understanding Social Life*. London: Allen and Unwin.

Pateman, T., 1975: *Language, Truth and Politics*. Devon: Stroud and Pateman.

Reilly, M., 1974: *Play as Exploratory Learning*. London: Sage.

Rickman, H. P., 1967: *Understanding and the Human Studies*. London: Heinemann.

Slater, P., 1974: 'The Aesthetic Theory of the Frankfurt School'. *Cultural Studies* 6.

Southern, R., 1975: *The Medieval Theatre in the Round*. London: Faber and Faber.

Stott, W., 1973: *Documentary Expression and Thirties America*. New York: Oxford University Press.

Tuchman, G. (Ed.), 1974: *The TV Establishment*. New Jersey: Prentice Hall.

Weider, D. L., 1974: 'Telling the Code'. In R. Turner (Ed.), *Ethnomethodology*. London: Penguin.

Willener, A., 1970: *The Action-Image of Society*. London: Tavistock.

Willett, J., (Ed.), 1964: *Brecht on Theatre*. London: Eyre Methuen.

Williams, R., 1973: 'Base and Superstructure in Marxist Cultural Theory'. *New Left Review* 82.

1974: *Television: Technology and Cultural Form*. London: Fontana.

Index